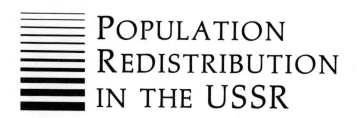

POPULATION REDISTRIBUTION IN THE USSR

POPULATION REDISTRIBUTION IN THE USSR

It's Impact on Society, 1897-1977

Robert A. Lewis
Richard H. Rowland

PRAEGER

PRAEGER SPECIAL STUDIES • PRAEGER SCIENTIFIC

Library of Congress Cataloging in Publication Data

Lewis, Robert A
    Population redistribution in the USSR.

    Bibliography: p.
    Includes index.
    1. Migration, Internal--Russia--History.
2. Russia--Population--History. I. Roland, Richard H.,
joint author. II. Title.
HB2067.L48   301.32'6'0947   79-18076
ISBN 0-03-050641-7

Published in 1979 by Praeger Publishers
A Division of Holt, Rinehart and Winston/CBS, Inc.
383 Madison Avenue, New York, New York 10017 U.S.A.

© 1979 by Praeger Publishers

9 038 987654321

Printed in the United States of America

ACKNOWLEDGEMENTS

This is the second volume of a three-volume series on population change in Russia and the USSR since 1897, which has been supported by Grant HD 05585 of the Center for Population Research of the National Institute of Child Health and Human Development. Additional support was provided by the Kennan Institute for Advanced Russian Studies of the Woodrow Wilson International Center for Scholars, where Robert Lewis spent the 1976 academic year and Richard Rowland spent part of the summer of 1977. The support of these two institutions is acknowledged gratefully. The beginnings of our study of population change in Russia and the USSR go back more than a decade to San Diego State College, where Robert Lewis and J. William Leasure received support from the National Science Foundation to develop the data-processing procedures and to investigate migration in Russia and the USSR. This support also is acknowledged gratefully, as is the contribution of Professor J. William Leasure of the Department of Economics, San Diego State University.

Professor Ralph S. Clem of the Department of International Relations, Florida International University, worked with us for many years and co-authored the first volume of this series. We thank him for the appreciable contribution that he has made to the overall project. We have learned much about ethnicity in multinational states from Professor Walker Connor of the State University of New York, Brockport, who consulted with us on parts of Chapter 9, which covers the implications of this study. For his contribution, we are greatly appreciative. Above all, we would like to express our deepest appreciation to Jane Rowland for flawlessly and cheerfully typing draft after draft of the manuscript. Her efforts immeasurably facilitated the completion of this study. Richard Rowland, along with the excellent assistance of Pamela Gray of the Office of Community Development, San Bernadino County, also drafted the maps. We thank the editors of the Slavic Review, Demography, and the International Migration Review for permitting us to reproduce parts of previously published articles.

CONTENTS

LIST OF TABLES

ix

xi

xiii

LIST OF MAPS

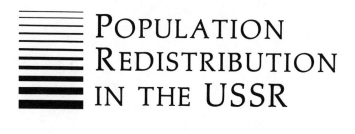

POPULATION REDISTRIBUTION IN THE USSR

1

INTRODUCTION

Population redistribution in Russia and the USSR since 1897 and its impact on society are the themes of this study. The chief subjects to be investigated are patterns of redistribution, migration, urbanization, rural population change, differential natural increase, and the socioeconomic problems related to these processes. Our intent, of course, is to explain the redistributional patterns that have occurred in this century, but in order to do this we must first describe these patterns in as much detail as possible. Although we cannot document all of the migration that has occurred in this turbulent century, our chief concern is to describe the major migratory streams, their continuity over time, and any major changes in these streams. There will be less emphasis on natural increase than on migration, largely because data on natural increase are much more limited, but the contribution of natural increase to population redistribution will be investigated insofar as it is possible. In order to explain population redistribution, a universal approach has been adopted, and general formulations are tested in the Soviet context; where general concepts prove inadequate, however, conditions specific to the USSR will be investigated. If demographic processes in the USSR are universal, we can, at the very least, make guarded forecasts as to the societal consequences of population redistribution, based on the universal experience.

As might be expected in a population study, we have extensively utilized the national censuses that have been taken in Russia and the USSR since 1897. However, formidable problems in their use were encountered, because there was almost a complete lack of territorial and definitional comparability among the first three censuses, which necessitated more than a decade of data processing. Basic demographic data for the total, urban, and rural populations from the 1897, 1926, 1939, 1959, and 1970 censuses and appropriate censuses of surrounding countries have been reordered into a set of comparable internal units for the present-day territory of the USSR, based upon consistent definitions of the demographic variables. Although the period covered by the censuses and the intervals between them are not entirely satisfactory, these censuses provide a large volume of basic population data for a major portion of the world for a significant period of time and constitute the chief source of data for this study. Where appropriate, of course, other sources of data were used, particularly in the analysis of the redistributional patterns and in the assessment of post-1970 trends.

This volume is a part of a larger study entitled Population Change in Russia and the USSR: 1897-1970, which is primarily based on our comparable series of data. The first volume has been completed and dealt with nationality and population change.[1] The series began with a volume focusing on nationalities and their relationship to population change, because ethnicity is perhaps the fundamental characteristic in terms of classifying the population in a multinational state such as the USSR, and because nationalities in a multinational state generally stratify along socioeconomic lines and population change relates primarily to differences in socioeconomic levels. The third volume will be devoted primarily to an investigation of population growth and its societal consequences on an aggregate as well as a regional basis with emphasis on fertility, mortality, age and sex composition, and work force.

The first part of the first volume was devoted to background information for the series, in order to avoid needless repetition in the following volumes. In this background to the series, we outlined in some detail our methodology, the interrelationship between population change and modernization, the procedures that were used to reorder the census data, and the necessary geographic background. In this introduction to the present volume, we will summarize or extract parts of these more detailed discussions to the degree that we think necessary, and for a more detailed discussion of these subjects we refer the reader to our earlier volume.

GENERAL APPROACH

The chief working hypothesis of this study is that people throughout the world tend to react in the same manner to the socioeconomic forces that influence their demographic behavior—whether they live under "capitalist" or "communist" regimes or anything in between. Thus, we take a universal, or general, approach to the analysis of population change in Russia and the USSR, because we contend that population change relates primarily to modernization, and not directly to political or ideological systems or to cultural or historical factors unique to any one country. We do, however, acknowledge that governments can affect demographic processes by means of population, economic, social, and other policies. Essentially what has been done is to test empirically in the Soviet context relevant generalizations that, because of historical scholarly circumstances, have been formulated mainly in the West. There appear to be few demographic surprises to be found in the USSR. Uniqueness of phenomena is a conclusion that must be tested and verified. As a matter of scientific policy, one should only concede some peculiarity or uniqueness to a given nation or ideology if the data force it upon him. Since there are gross signs that modernization and population change are occurring independent of political boundaries and that their connection with other demographic variables are also independent, the most scientific attitude would be to hypothesize that the causal determinism is not "culture-bound." In the broadest sense, the following questions have been posed: (1) What are the expected population trends and their correlates? (2) What patterns actually occurred and to what were they related? (3) How did the Soviet government affect these patterns? (4) What impact have these trends had upon Soviet society? All of these questions cannot be answered definitively, largely because of the lack of data and resources, which, to a greater or lesser extent, is the chief problem in all social research. We have attempted to restrict ourselves to asking questions that are appropriate to the accuracy and coverage of the data, and at times, as might be expected, we have had to use variables that are not precisely representative of the phenomena or characteristics in question because of the nature of the information. Where general formulations did not explain the processes being studied, conditions specific to the USSR were investigated.

Universal formulations cannot completely or always explain population change in the USSR. Theory may be inadequately formulated, as it often is, and frequently data are insufficient. Moreover, there are conditions specific to the USSR that explain certain aspects of population change. For example, migration theory cannot explain certain aspects of population change, such as the forced resettlement of the Crimean Tatars; and wars, famines, and collectivization have resulted in substantial losses of population and have affected population trends, although primarily in the short term. Long-term trends have been largely affected by the processes of modernization. The most reasonable approach is first to test general demographic concepts in the USSR to determine if, or to what extent, they explain the processes under investigation and then, where necessary, to examine conditions specific to the USSR in order to explain further these processes.

MODERNIZATION AND POPULATION CHANGE

Population change may be defined as changes in the numbers, geographic distribution, and characteristics of a population, including, for our purposes, the demographic trends of mortality, fertility, and migration and such socioeconomic aspects as urbanization, work force, education, and the status of women. The description and documentation of demographic and socioeconomic trends may provide new and useful information, particularly if, as is the case in this study, such changes have not been well understood before. To explain these changes, however, one requires a schema that will systematize the various elements of population change, link population change to social change in general, and incorporate concepts that provide a significant degree of explanation for the phenomena involved. The schema that best satisfies these requirements is the process of social change known as "modernization."

Because modernization encompasses changes in virtually all aspects of society, there is a very real problem of defining this process of social change without being trivial, on the one hand, or tautological, on the other. Various scholars have viewed modernization from different perspectives, often from within the confines of academic disciplines or topical interests. Yet, it appears there is a consensus that modernization is best defined broadly to include a number of more limited aspects of social change that can, in turn, be examined in greater detail. Thus, for our purposes, modernization is defined as that form of societal change encompassing the changes in the economic, technological, demographic, political, social, and psychological aspects of human society that began in Western Europe around 1800. Briefly, these changes included significant increases in economic production (the Industrial Revolution), advances in technology and science (especially the use of inanimate sources of power), consolidation of so-called nation-states as forms of political organization, a realignment of family structures and a diminution of the importance of kinship, a sharp rise in ethnicity, a change from ascriptive to achievement status, and increased motivation and achievement orientation. Economic development, through the creation of job opportunities in nonagricultural sectors, is the major agent of population change; in particular it affects population redistribution. The shift from ascriptive to merit or achievement systems also influences population change, notably fertility. Demographic changes also have been integral to the modernization process. Furthermore, the recognition of the mutually reinforcing relationships among these aspects of modernization is included in the definition. Although not all aspects of population change can be directly attributed to modernization, this dramatic form of social change has had a profound impact upon the population of any society that has modernized.

The elements of population change with which we are concerned are fertility, mortality, urbanization, migration, education, work force, and the status of women. With modernization and economic development, dramatic changes occur among all elements of population change. Mortality declines with improved agricultural technology, food distribution, and public health. Fertility declines as family size is controlled to facilitate the attainment of social and economic aspirations, the economic utility of children decreases, family structures realign, and women enter the modern work force. Urbanization takes place as people leave rural areas for job opportunities in the cities. Substantial migration occurs from rural to urban places and from one region to another, because economic development normally takes place in a few areas and cities. Modernization and economic development are also associated with higher levels of education, a shift from agricultural to nonagricultural employment, and the gradual integration of women into modern sectors. The elements of population change interact with other aspects of modernization and with one another. Thus, significant relationships exist between urbanization and fertility, fertility and the status of women, the status of women and education, and so on. Finally, the demographic changes associated with modernization appear to have been virtually universal, occurring in all countries that have modernized.

Migration

Our concern in this volume is population redistribution, which is defined as regional changes in the proportion of a country's population and results from either migration or differential natural increase. With economic development, migration tends to be more important than natural increase in the redistribution of a population. The migration of population to cities and regions of industrial growth is another aspect of population change that historically has been associated with modernization and economic development. Migration, when defined as permanent or semipermanent changes in residence (in contrast to nomadic wanderings or seasonal migrations), is a useful indicator of population change and modernization; modernized societies have been characterized by significant geographic mobility. The volume of migration directly related to modernization and economic development has been substantial, considering the totality of rural-to-urban, intraregional, interregional, and international movements. It would be an oversight to omit rural-to-rural migration as an important element in population change, because such movements have been significant in the past. In many respects, however, these movements have little in common with modernization, although the declines in mortality associated with modernization may have prompted out-migration. Our focus is modernization and population change; therefore, rural-to-rural movements will be considered in this study only briefly, mainly as a necessary background and in order to cover all types of migration.

This study of migration, as well as the use of migration as an indicator of modernization, centers primarily around the economic motivations behind the movement of population. We recognize, of course, that countless folk through the ages, refugees or displaced persons, have migrated in response to noneconomic forces, such as religious, racial, or political persecutions. To realize the importance of these types of migration, one only has to recall the history of Europe in the twentieth century. We can take little account of them here beyond the recognition and assessment of those movements of a forced or idiosyncratic nature that fall within the scope of this study; any explanation of these movements will be of an individual nature and largely beyond the framework of our analysis. Other forms of migration, such as the premodern movements of peoples responding to population pressures or natural calamities, or the modern movement of retired persons and others to regions that offer environmental or cultural amenities, are likewise not the major concern here. The migration with which we are concerned—that which is economically motivated—has been and very probably will continue to be the most important in modernized societies.

It is not necessary for our purposes, even if it were possible, to establish in great detail the links between economic development and migration or to review migration theory in great detail, because as a result of a general lack of data for the USSR we cannot definitively establish all of the interrelationships between these two sets of processes, although we can test the major links. What essentially occurs with economic development is a massive redistribution of a country's population, largely as a result of migration. This is empirically obvious in any country that has achieved a high level of economic development. Migration largely represents a continuous adjustment by a population to changing economic conditions, in particular, to job opportunities. As a result of the changes in the structure of production and consumption, which occur with economic development, the locus of production changes. These changes require a considerable redistribution of the population through migration, because geographic patterns of natural increase do not conform to the emerging areas of economic development. The mechanization of agriculture also intensifies the need for migration.

Simon Kuznets has described the processes involved very succinctly:

We conceive of economic growth and population redistribution as linked by a continuous chain of interdependent variables. On the one hand, the growth in population that tends to accompany economic growth may in itself stimulate migration from the more densely to the more thinly settled areas, and to the extent that this movement results in discovery and opening up of natural resources valuable to the settled area, it will provide an attraction to further migration. More important in recent times is the differential effect of technological progress upon the distribution of economic opportunities through structural changes involved in industrialization and urbanization: the revolutionizing of agriculture, with sharply increasing labor productivity and concomitant narrowing of economic opportunities for residents of the countryside in general; the expansion of capital and the movement of labor into newly growing sectors—manufacturing, construction, transportation, communications, trade and other service branches—which, unlike agriculture, are not tied to the land but tend to concentrate their operations in what have become the urban agglomerates of modern society. Thus, to the extent that economic growth is induced by technological change, population redistribution is likely to result, for the distribution of a country's population at any given time may be viewed as a rough adjustment to the distribution of economic opportunities. Moreover, technological change is usually specific, with differential impact upon sectors of the economy and upon economic opportunities in different parts of the country; and, once started, it tends to proceed at a rapid pace. The rapidity and magnitude of the differential impacts that accompany modern economic growth are such that the vital processes of birth and death can play but a minor role in adjusting the distribution of population to economic opportunities in different parts of the country.[2]

Thus, people move primarily in response to job opportunities, although not all movement is economically motivated and not all economic development requires migration to be realized, and the chief economic function of migration is to equalize the supply of and demand for labor on a regional basis. If migration does not function adequately in this respect, economic development can be impeded. Migration is particularly important in economic development, because labor supply is generally outweighed by other locational factors, such as resources, transportation, and markets.[3]

The spatial patterns of natural increase that are associated with economic development also necessitate and stimulate migration. With economic development and, more recently, modern medicine, mortality decline in both urban and rural areas is generally accomplished rather easily and quickly, because relatively little socioeconomic change is required. A significant fertility differential persists between urban and rural areas, however, even though fertility levels eventually converge, because fertility is related more closely to the socioeconomic environment and thus requires more social change. What essentially occurs is that fertility, and thus natural increase and the growth of the native work force, declines first in the more modernized urban-industrial areas and ultimately reaches very low levels or even natural decrease. Even in the premodern period, migration was necessary for urban growth, because urban mortality frequently was higher than urban fertility and rural mortality. Because of the often significant rural-urban fertility differential, natural increase remains high in rural areas, particularly in early and intermediate stages of economic development, although with out-migration, which is usually concentrated in the younger, more fertile age groups, natural increase can decline considerably even though fertility remains relatively high. In short, the pattern that prevails is one of relatively low natural increase and growth of the native work force in the more modernized areas, where job opportunities are usually expanding, and relatively high natural increase and growth of the native work force in the rural areas, where employment is generally declining because of mechanization of agriculture. This imbalance of labor supply and demand is equalized by migration. This situation can best be exemplified by comparing work force growth in developing and developed areas. Developing countries are generating substantial labor surpluses, while many developed countries have experienced labor shortages in recent years. This, of course, is the basis for the considerable immigration that has occurred in northern Europe, from other parts of Europe as well as other world regions. Just as the world has developed and developing areas, any country that experiences economic development has developed and developing regions, and the demographic transition that occurs regionally necessitates considerable migration in order not to impede economic growth.

Thus, regional differences in migration can be viewed in terms of regional economic growth and the growth of the native work force. Where the native work force is growing rapidly and there is little or no economic development, one can expect out-migration, or at the very least no in-migration, at least in the short term. However, economic development, which produces jobs, can be conditioned by rises in labor productivity, and the growth of the native work force, which is related to the labor supply, can be conditioned by the skill levels of the work force. Conversely, where the native work force is not growing and there is much economic development, one can usually expect substantial in-migration.[4] Because of variations in past natural increase that governs the growth of the work force, the general cyclical or erratic nature of economic development, and changing requirements in skill levels of labor, it is difficult for any region to balance perfectly for any extended period of time economic growth and the growth of the native work force so as to produce no migration, even though in-migration and out-migration can be minimized. Using similar reasoning, Eugene M. Kulischer has pointed out that historically populations have striven to improve their standard of life and in doing so had three options: (1) economic development, (2) birth control, and (3) out-migration.[5] Because economic development in early times was arduous due to slow technological progress and birth control was difficult in traditional rural settings, the most common human response was out-migration in order to equalize economic density, which largely accounts for the perpetual and universal movements of peoples, particularly with a growing population and a fixed area.

Economic development results in the increased geographic mobility of a population and is selective regionally and frequently by ethnic group.[6] Migration can be viewed as an indicator of modernization, and generally the more modernized areas and the more modernized ethnic groups are more mobile, as well as having lower fertility, higher rates of urbanization, higher educational levels, and so forth. Thus, for example, rural out-migration generally occurs first in the more modernized areas and among the more modernized groups and later spreads to other areas and groups. Ultimately, the total population is integrated into the modern sectors of the economy. In addition to factors related to modernization, one reason for the regional differential in mobility is simply that more people move short distances than long distances, and the first areas of out-migration are generally closer to the growing urban-industrial areas. Long-distance moves probably require a higher level of motivation, particularly in earlier periods when transportation was difficult or expensive, and information about other areas was relatively scant. Yet, the most important factor appears to be differences in wages or standard of living, although exact levels cannot be specified, aside from stating that generally the greater the differential the greater the migration. Simon Kuznets has stated this concept as follows:

> Spread of information, the greater perception of costs of staying put than of the positive returns from migration, the threshold concept which suggests that some minimum imbalance between costs and returns or some minimum change in this imbalance is necessary to induce migration, and the relative roles of differential natural increase and migration in the redistribution of population, are all important facets of the process by which population adjusts to growth-induced changes in differential economic opportunity.[7]

Migration related to modernization and economic development can also be considered as a function of push-pull forces, or those conditions, largely economic, existing at the points of origin (push) and destination (pull). Between the origin and potential destination are other considerations, termed "intervening obstacles," that impede movement to varying degrees and at different times for diverse classes of migrants.[8] Migration streams develop and are followed by counterstreams, resulting in directional biases in migration. Younger persons, especially those in their late teens, twenties, and early thirties, the more educated, and those with professional and managerial occupations are more prone to migrate. Migration is related to certain stages

of life, such as marriage and completion of education, but career variables
are more influential. The unemployed migrate more than the employed. Migration is not particularly selective with respect to sex. As economic development progresses to high levels, the importance of economic factors appear
to diminish. Pull factors appear to be more important than push factors in
the explanation of migration.[9] There are other influences upon the decision
to migrate, such as the availability of information concerning conditions at
both the origin and destination and the inertia that militates against any move.
Yet, the basic conceptualization of migration as a balancing of conditions,
notably those relating to economic opportunities, provides the framework for
discussing the majority of moves connected with modernization.

In historical perspective, the high rates of population growth in rural
agricultural areas, brought about by declines in mortality during the initial
stages of modernization, created a strong push factor that resulted in out-migration. In many instances, poor conditions in agriculture exacerbated the
pressure on the land, and eventually the mechanization of agriculture contributed to a labor surplus in rural areas. Combined with these push forces in
rural areas were the pull forces of opportunity engendered by economic development and industrialization. The location of economic development was,
for the most part, confined to urban areas, specific regions, and certain
countries; thus, streams of migrants were directed along the economic gra-
dient to cities and to developing regions and countries. The function of migration has been, therefore, to balance the supply of and demand for labor
between rural and urban areas and among regions and countries, thereby facilitating economic development. The well-documented experiences of the
United States and Japan are illustrative of the redistribution of population to
areas of economic development.

Although this discussion has centered on economic aspects of migration,
which are the dominant ones, noneconomic factors should not be totally neglected. Young people in rural areas the world over who have finished high
school have a high propensity to migrate and, in addition to economic factors,
cultural factors (bright lights, if you will), and conditions of work and life in
general, have been influential, particularly when considered in conjunction
with wage differentials. Migration can also be induced by consumption, including such activities as education and retirement.

Migration is a demographic phenomenon fraught with consequences for
both the sending and receiving communities. Because migration tends to be
selective of certain groups within society (young adults and persons with certain skills or qualifications), the age and sex structure of the population, as
well as other aspects such as employment and growth of the work force, at
both origin and destination of the migration stream are affected. Furthermore, the movement of people from rural areas into cities, as well as from
one region of a country to another (particularly if different ethnic groups or
races are involved), is a potentially disjunctive process, as individuals are
shifted into unfamiliar or even hostile social and economic environments.
The historical migration of individuals from areas of lesser to greater opportunities, across natural and political boundaries, often in the face of uncer-

tainty and physical danger, testifies to the attraction of areas of economic development.

Urbanization

Of all the facets of population associated with modernization, perhaps no other has been as dramatic and visible as the urbanization of human society. Although there is some disagreement among scholars regarding the nature of urban-modern as opposed to rural-traditional life styles, nevertheless, it is clear that urbanization has had a momentous impact upon society and particularly upon other demographic trends. Although cities have existed for millennia, the trend toward rapid urbanization began in Western Europe around 1800; the rate at which the urban population has increased since that time has far outstripped total population growth, and the high growth rate of the urban population has accelerated consistently in relation to total population growth. Thus, the percentage of the world's population living in urban areas has steadily increased since 1800: in 1800, 2.4 percent of the total population lived in cities over 20,000; in 1850, 4.3 percent; in 1900, 9.2 percent; in 1950, 20.9 percent; and by 1970 the urban population had grown to 28.2 percent of the world's population.[10] Urbanization has reached its highest levels in those countries that have modernized: in Western Europe, the United States, Canada, Japan, Australia, and New Zealand. Although international comparisons are difficult because of different definitions of "urban," it is safe to say that as of 1970 all of these modernized countries had over 65 percent of their populations in urban areas.[11] Urban populations in contemporary developing countries range generally between 10 and 40 percent of the population, with levels inclined to be lower in Africa and Asia and higher in Eastern Europe and Latin America.[12] This section describes the relationships between urbanization and its correlates (principally economic development and industrialization), details the linkages between urbanization and other elements of population change, and, finally, examines the concepts concerning the impact of urban life upon society.

Initially, however, the distinction between urbanization and urban growth should be considered briefly because the two terms are often confused and they represent somewhat different processes. Urbanization can be defined as the process of population concentration involving an increase in the percentage of the total population residing in urban areas (that is, the level of urbanization) by whatever criteria these urban areas are defined. Urban growth refers simply to an increase in the urban population itself; urbanization takes this one step further by comparing urban growth with the change in the total or the rural population. It is, therefore, possible to have significant urban growth without urbanization, if rural population growth equals or exceeds urban growth.[13] Urbanization entails a structural change in the total population, with an increasing share in urban areas. The social and economic impact of such a transformation upon society has been profound, as will be discussed.

The increasing levels of urbanization associated with modernization have been coincident with, and to a large degree brought about by, economic development and industrialization. At the outset we must note that this relationship, like virtually all social and economic relationships, is not a perfect one, and there are deviations from the positive correlation between increased urbanization and economic development-industrialization, both in a temporal sense and in regard to individual cities. In the initial stages of economic development, for instance, labor availability in the cities may satisfy demand, delaying rural-to-urban migration. Labor intensity in the industrialization process is also an important factor in determining labor requirements and thus the rate of urbanization. Moreover, changes in the structure of employment that occur with economic development result in a relative decline in industrial employment and an increase in tertiary employment. Since urbanization is a finite process (100 percent is the limit) and economic development presumably is not, the relationship between the two processes diverges in later stages of modernization.[14] Yet, the two processes of urbanization and economic development-industrialization have generally been complementary. Economic development, particularly industrialization, provided the impetus for urbanization by creating job opportunities that attracted migrants from rural areas.[15] The application of increasingly more advanced technologies and a higher degree of labor specialization supported higher levels of urbanization.[16] The concentration of population in the cities aided economic development by providing adequate labor, both in numbers and with requisite skills, facilitating economies of scale, promoting interindustry transportation and linkages, and providing large markets.[17] Thus, economic development-industrialization and urbanization have been mutually reinforcing trends, with each providing conditions that sustain the other.

Urbanization as an element of population change is linked with other demographic trends associated with modernization. Investigators have noted that fertility is lower in urban than in rural areas,[18] and we have noted already that urbanization was caused largely by the migration of people from rural to urban areas. Both of these demographic phenomena are, in turn, related to the existence of socioeconomic opportunity in urban areas. Urban areas are the most modern areas, areas of maximum upward social mobility and opportunities for economic advancement, and, as people aspire to achieve these higher levels, large families may stand in the way. Lower urban fertility is therefore an indicator of modernization in that lower fertility entails an appraisal of the role of children, which takes into account the aspirations of parents for socioeconomic achievement. Not to be overlooked, of course, is the fact that children may have become economic liabilities in cities (particularly with the enactment of social welfare legislation that reduced their labor value), whereas in rural areas their labor had been an asset.[19]

Migration as an element of population change associated with modernization has two facets: rural-to-urban migration, on the one hand, and intraregional, interregional, and/or international migration, on the other. The two are not mutually exclusive, because a large share of intraregional, interregional, and international migration is also rural to urban. It is logical here to dichotomize the migration component and to discuss rural-to-urban migration together with urbanization. Just as the existence of socioeconomic opportunities in the cities influenced fertility, so did it attract migrants from rural areas. As is the case with most migration, the pull of job opportunities in urban areas was usually combined with a push from rural areas, resulting from poor agricultural conditions, excessive population growth, mechanization of agriculture, and consequent decline in the demand for rural labor—in short, a lack of opportunities in rural areas. In addition to job opportunities, the cities are also cultural, political, and educational centers and have an attraction beyond the purely economic. Rural-to-urban migration provided substantial shares of the growth of cities associated with urbanization, supplementing to varying degrees the natural increase of the cities themselves. Indeed, in-migration to cities was especially important in the past as many cities were characterized by natural decrease due to high urban mortality.[20]

In addition to fertility and migration, urbanization has been linked to other elements of population change, such as education and the structure of the labor force. Educational levels attained by the population are almost universally higher in urban than in rural areas. The urban labor force is naturally concentrated in nonagricultural occupations; with advanced economic development and urbanization, the service (tertiary) sector assumes increasing importance.

The impact of urbanization upon society has been profound, but recent experience, particularly that stemming from the developing countries, suggests that qualifications are required in the general concepts concerning the nature of societal transformations associated with urbanization. The dichotomy of so-called folk-urban ideal types suggested by Robert Redfield and Louis Wirth,[21] among others, which counterposed urban and rural societies in terms of values, goals, and societal relations, has been called into question by others who point to the maintenance of "traditional" practices and values in urban areas and the existence of "nontraditional" traits in rural areas.[22] Research in some urban areas has shown that rural in-migrants ease their transition to urban life through various social institutions and by residential segregation.[23] At this point it seems unclear as to the exact means by which rural dwellers adapt to demographic behavior that is more rational in an urban setting, although the availability of education and socioeconomic opportunity is clearly a necessary factor.[24] Urban residence is not always a sufficient condition to influence demographic behavior, but rather it must be combined with socioeconomic opportunity, which, in the past (but not necessarily in contemporary developing countries), was located mainly in the cities. Also, it appears that at least two generations are required to complete the transition from rural to urban life. Thus, our view of cities as the centers of modernization may accord well with a retrospective analysis of modern societies but may need some modification for understanding those countries that are only now modernizing. Nevertheless, urbanization is still a strong indicator of modernization.

POPULATION POLICY

Population practice is what people do in terms of demographic behavior, population policy is the attempt by governments to change practice for whatever reason, and population theory represents an attempt to explain practice. If the Soviet government were able to control demographic behavior by means of successfully implemented population policies, general theory could not be effectively applied to the USSR to explain population processes, because the government would control demographic behavior and, thus, policy would explain practice. However, the control of demographic behavior is generally very difficult, because in most instances it is complexly interrelated with a variety of other very stable socioeconomic trends. Some aspects of demographic behavior are relatively easy to control, because they are not intimately related to the socioeconomic environment. Mortality can be controlled relatively easily, at least in the short run, because relatively little personal initiative, expense, or social change are required, and everyone favors the idea of living longer. International migration is also rather easy to control with border controls and domestic employment and welfare legislation.

Population variables that are closely interrelated with the socioeconomic environment are very difficult to control, because a change in the socioeconomic environment is usually required to influence such variables as fertility, internal migration, urbanization, suburbanization, rural depopulation, and ethnic assimilation. Most governments have policies concerning, at least, some of these aspects of population, but it would seem that in general these policies have not been very successful, although it is difficult to determine what would have occurred in the absence of a policy or to differentiate long-term from short-term effects. The chief reason for a lack of success in implementing population policy is that governments generally have not been willing to exert the necessary effort or expense to change sufficiently the socioeconomic environment or certain key trends and thus population trends. A lack of understanding of how socioeconomic processes affect demographic behavior has probably contributed to the failure of population policies. Major exceptions are policies that are backed by considerable force, such as programs of genocide, forced labor, and forced settlement. Coercion, to be successful, of course, requires great effort and is highly undesirable; it is also questionable whether it could be successful for an extended period of time for a large population. D. V. Glass has documented the failure of the population policies designed to increase fertility in Western Europe in the 1930s.[25] The general failure of governments in the developing world to lower fertility without the necessary modernization is probably the most outstanding example of the failure of population policies to effect a change in a demographic trend, at least in the short run.[26] However, some countries in Western Europe have achieved notable success in combating excessive population concentration.[27]

Propaganda usually does not affect demographic behavior. The assumption that a statement of policy or opinion of a political, ethnic, or religious leader will affect to a significant degree demographic behavior should be seriously questioned. An effort must be made in this regard to ascertain what a government or a leader can control by edict without making major changes in a society or using force and how people respond to authority, whether it be from fear or loyalty, when it is in their best interest to act otherwise. The Catholic church has considerable religious authority and a well-developed information network; yet, in developed countries Catholic fertility is generally low, despite papal edicts encouraging the contrary.

Migration Policies in the USSR

The Soviet government has not put forth a comprehensive, systematic set of policies concerning the various aspects of population distribution or redistribution in the USSR. This is somewhat surprising in that the USSR has a centrally planned economy and a totalitarian government, which has often been credited with affecting, to a considerable degree, most aspects of its citizens' lives, including their freedom to move. Thus, to facilitate economic development and the building of socialism, a high-priority goal, one might expect the Soviet government to have considerable control over the movement of its population. Furthermore, as we will demonstrate in the empirical section of this study, the policies that it does have to affect the redistribution of its population have not been very effectively implemented, probably even less so than the "democratic" countries of Western Europe.[28] In most instances, economic planning has taken precedence over population planning with population being viewed primarily as a means of production rather than as an end in itself as Soviet theory implies.[29] Although not officially stated, it can be inferred that the chief policy of the Soviet government with regard to population redistribution is that migration should equalize the supply of and demand for labor on a regional basis, that is, people should move to jobs. This is, of course, what most governments expect in order to maximize economic development, although some governments have made attempts to avoid excessive concentration of population.

There are, however, officially stated policies as to the desired distribution of population under socialism and communism. Once again, Marxist ideology does not provide detailed guidelines for the future, but only a few rather fragmentary and cursory statements. The basic tenets are concerned with an elimination of the distinctions between town and country, a more equal distribution of industry and population, and limitation of the size of large cities. In the Communist Manifesto, Marx and Engels declared that the bourgeoisie had greatly increased the urban population and created enormous cities, which ruled the countryside but had rescued "a considerable part of the population from the idiocy of rural life."[30] They returned to this subject in point nine of their general program that calls for "Combination of agriculture with manufacturing industries; gradual abolition of the distinctions between town and country, by a more equable distribution of the population over the country."[31] Later, Engels elaborated on this theme by stressing that the abolition of the distinctions between town and country was necessary for both industry and agriculture, because of the pollution and waste that were created by large cities. The end result would be a safeguarding of public health and the use of industrial wastes in agriculture. This was to be achieved by the greatest possible uniformity in the distribution of industry, which was possible because the new order would produce conditions that outweighed "the labor of transporting raw materials or fuel from more distant places." He goes on to predict the eventual disappearance of big cities.[32]

As might be expected, these tenets provided the basis for Lenin's thinking on the subject, and he envisaged a new distribution of mankind as a result of unifying agricultural and industrial production and an elimination of the concentration of huge numbers of people in large cities.[33] He also called for a "free distribution of the population over the territory of Russia and a rational economic utilization of the masses of peripheral land in Russia."[34]

These rather fragmentary statements have been incorporated into a set of official industrial-locational principles, two of which call for the even distribution of industrial production throughout the country and the elimination of the contradiction between cities and rural areas. Although primarily related to Lenin's theorizing on imperialism, another locational principle that might have some relevance to the more even distribution of population is the equalization of industrial production in non-Russian developing areas.[35] It would appear, however, that the locational principles relating to the more even distribution of industry to date have received scant, if any, attention in Soviet planning.[36]

Because population redistribution in the USSR primarily has involved migration to urban centers, policies affecting urbanization are of the utmost importance for the purposes of this study. There is no Soviet urbanization policy, if one defines urbanization, as we do, as the percentage of the total population residing in urban centers and, thus, makes a distinction between urban growth and urbanization. That is, there is no Soviet policy that states that the level of urbanization will be raised a certain number of percentage points in a given year or period.

There are, however, policies concerning urban growth by size groups. In accord with Marxist doctrine, Soviet planners have been attempting to limit growth of large cities since the early 1930s, largely by restricting urban construction and administrative measures. The June Plenum of the Communist party in 1931 issued a decree prohibiting the construction of new industrial enterprises in Moscow and Leningrad. Because this restriction had little immediate effect, in 1932 with the introduction of the internal passport system, they attempted administratively to limit the growth of the largest cities and Moscow, in particular, by instituting the propiska system, which, in short, required official permission for work and residence in these cities. This measure was intended to be temporary, but is still in existence.[37] The propiska system will be discussed in greater detail below. In 1935 it was decreed that Moscow's population was not to exceed 5 million.[38] Khar'kov, Kiev, Rostov-na-Donu, Gor'kiy, and Sverdlovsk were added in 1939 to the list of cities in which industrial construction was to be limited. In 1956 it was decreed by the Soviet government that further industrial construction or expansion of existing industrial enterprises was to be prohibited in the following cities: Moscow, Leningrad, Kiev, Gor'kiy, Baku, Tashkent, Khar'kov, Novosibirsk, Kuybyshev, Sverdlovsk, Chelyabinsk, Kazan', Perm', Rostov-na-Donu, Volgograd, Saratov, Ufa, Voronezh, Donetsk, Dnepropetrovsk, Odessa, Zaporozh'ye, Minsk, Sumgait, Riga, Erevan, Yaroslavl', Tula, L'vov, Irkutsk, Khabarovsk, Ivanovo, Vladivostok, Penza, Kalinin, Groznyy, Arkhangel'sk, Ryazan', Murmansk, Nikolayev, Voroshilovgrad, Tallin, Taganrog, Kramatorsk, Komsomol'sk-na-Amure, Sevastopol', Magnitogorsk, and the cities of Moscow Oblast. Construction or expansion of industrial enterprises was to be limited in the following cities: Omsk, Krasnoyarsk, Alma-Ata, Novokuznetsk, Krivoy Rog, Karaganda, Nizhniy Tagil, Krasnodar, Barnaul, Izhevsk, Kemerovo, Astrakhan', Kirov, Tomsk, Makeyevka, Zhdanov, Vil'nyus, Kaunas, Frunze, Dushanbe, Dneprodzerzhinsk, Saransk, and Angarsk. More recently, this list was expanded to include Bryansk, Kursk, Tol'yatti, Ul'yanovsk, Orenburg, and Kishinev. In 1963 the construction of scientific and planning institutes, construction bureaus, experimental facilities, higher-education establishments, and tekhnikums was prohibited in Moscow and the cities of Moscow Oblast.[39]

This list of cities whose growth is to be regulated includes all cities over 200,000 in 1959, except Tbilisi, Gorlovka, Kaliningrad, and Prokop'-yevsk. It also includes seven cities below 200,000, of which Saransk (91,034), Sumgait (52,186), and Tol'yatti (72,411) had fewer than 100,000 inhabitants. Therefore, aside from a few exceptions, Soviet policy in terms of limiting the growth of large cities is directed to cities larger than 200,000. More specifically, according to planning guidelines published in 1958, cities in the 100,000 to 250,000 class were to be limited to a population of 250,000 or less. In the past, this was the size class that was most often considered optimum, at least in terms of providing services to a population.[40] Recently, in the determination of optimum size more attention has been given to the cost of production and viewing, at least theoretically, optimum size in terms of urban systems (unified system of settlement) rather than isolated individual cities. It is with the achievement of such a system of settlement that the distinctions between town and country are to be eliminated in the future.[41]

The corollary of the policy to limit the growth of large cities was that small cities (below 50,000), medium cities (50,000-100,000), and new cities, by implication, were to receive the bulk of the industrial investment. According to Robert J. Osborn, the 1958 Directive specified that "most new industrial construction (new plants or expansion of existing plants) was to be directed to cities classified as medium-size (50,000-100,000) and small (under 50,000)."[42] This policy began to be particularly emphasized in the late 1960s, and was included in the directives of the Twenty-Second, Twenty-Third, Twenty-Fourth, and Twenty-Fifth Party Congresses.[43] According to D. G. Khodzhayev, 70 percent of all projects cleared for planning and design in 1965 for construction in subsequent years (the list includes projects of R 2.5 million or more to be built in 1967-70) were to be located in small or medium-size cities.[44] In conjunction with the directives of the Twenty-Third Party Congress (the Five-Year Plan for 1966-70) Gosplan compiled a list of large cities, mainly with a population of 250,000 or more, where new large-scale enterprises were to be limited or prohibited, and a recommended list of 529 small- and medium-size cities, which were regarded as favorable for the location of new industrial enterprises. However, B. S. Khorev maintains that this plan does not solve the problems of small cities, because only about 25 percent of the cities on the list were small (less than 20,000), while over 70 percent were semimedium- or medium-size (20,000-50,000 or 50,000-100,000) cities. Furthermore, he points out that over 50 percent of all the semimedium- and medium-size cities were on the recommended list, but only 13 percent of all small cities were on the list.[45]

In short, it appears that the policies aimed at the stimulation of small- and medium-size cities are directed more at the medium-size cities and relatively neglect the small cities. The limitation of the growth of large cities and increased investment in smaller cities was reiterated in the Twenty-Fourth Party Congress (the Five-Year Plan for 1971-75) and the Twenty-Fifth Party Congress (the Five-Year Plan for 1976-80). The purpose of these policies is to limit the growth of large cities, to tap unutilized labor (in particular female labor) in smaller cities, and to alleviate labor shortages in larger cities, although the existence of labor surpluses in smaller cities is somewhat questionable, as will be discussed later (see Chapter 5).

Aside from the ideologically motivated statements of policy, which to a significant degree have not been implemented (as will be demonstrated in the following sections of this study), there is no systematic migration policy in the USSR. Although recent party congresses have called for limiting the growth of large cities and the development of small and medium cities and the east, existing Soviet studies of migration and urbanization devote relatively little attention to policy and even less attention to the evaluation of policy. Migration problems related to eastern development constitute the chief exception to this lack of emphasis on policy. This is a surprising situation for a country with a centrally planned economy. It is frequently assumed, without evidence, that since the economy is planned, so is migration.[46] This apparently was the reasoning behind not including migration questions in the 1939 and 1959 censuses. P. G. Pod'yachikh, the director of the Soviet census, maintained in 1957 that since migration in the USSR was predominantly planned, there was no theoretical or practical need for its study.[47] B. S. Khorev and O. V. Larmin, who have discussed migration policy in some detail, recommend the formulation of a migration policy, largely because, to a significant degree, people are not moving where the government wants them to move.[48] Existing policies generally do not address the major migration problems in the USSR, which include migration out of labor deficit areas into labor surplus areas and a lack of geographic mobility in many agricultural areas where there is a labor surplus. In fact, attempts to limit the growth of large cities, most of which are experiencing labor shortages, at least in the Russian Soviet Federative Socialist Republic (RSFSR), have very probably aggravated these labor shortages.

The chief migration policy in the USSR is that people should move to jobs and thus equalize the supply of and demand for labor on a regional basis, the economic function of migration. This policy must be largely inferred, although at times it is mentioned in passing.[49] Empirically, this can be demonstrated by the relative concentration of industry in the USSR. With their emphasis on heavy industry, which has led to considerable population concentration, areas with resources for heavy industry have been emphasized in their developmental plans. The Donetsk-Dnepr, Urals, Kazakhstan, and Siberia are notable examples. Other areas, such as the Center and the Northwest, have experienced considerable concentration of industry, because of economics of agglomeration, skilled labor, transportation, and other aspects of their infrastructure. Labor has generally been considered the most mobile factor of production. There are no long-standing policies specifically directed toward providing employment in local areas, although the development of small and medium cities was motivated by the existence of surplus labor, in addition to its effect on limiting the growth of large cities. Current plans call for the location of labor-intensive industries in areas where surplus labor is available, but there appears to have been no radical change in regional investment priorities.[50] Therefore, testing the degree to which migration is fulfilling its chief economic function will be one of the purposes of this study.

Migration Controls

It is commonly thought that migration is strictly controlled by the government in the USSR;[51] and if indeed this were true, general formulations would have limited utility in the explanation of geographic mobility in the Soviet Union. Although there has been variation over time in the effectiveness of migration controls and incentives, the Soviet government has not controlled the movement of its population to a significant degree, and most migration has been the result of individual volition. That the chief migration problems in the USSR, by their own admission, have been a perennially high rate of labor turnover and a large number of people moving out of areas where the government wants them to remain into areas where their labor is not needed can be viewed as empirical confirmation of this lack of control over migration. Although the subject had not been discussed in the literature until fairly recently, the consensus among those writing on migration in the USSR in the past few years is that the bulk of the migration is unorganized.[52]

The general misconception concerning freedom of movement in the USSR is probably related to (1) the existence of legislation that would appear to control migration, (2) the prevalence of forced labor, particularly in the 1930s, (3) the labor freeze during World War II, and (4) the resettlement of certain nationalities during World War II. The two chief types of compulsory migration in the USSR are political and criminal prisoners and army draftees. Although there were millions of political prisoners in the 1930s, they currently probably number in the hundreds of thousands and on an annual basis constitute a small percentage of the total migrants. Even though in the past political prisoners and deported nationalities together numbered in the millions, they still comprised a relatively small percentage of the total migration during the Soviet period, when the population of the USSR underwent a drastic redistribution as will be documented in the remainder of this study.

Upward of 2 million youths are annually drafted,[53] but, of course, most of this migration is temporary. Furthermore, for the purposes of this study, neither of these categories are important, because we are primarily studying the migration related to modernization, and in the 1959 and 1970 censuses, the military and prisoners were enumerated at their former residences. There was, however, a de facto enumeration in the 1897 and 1926 censuses when there were many fewer military personnel and prisoners. The migration data from the registration system, however, do include the military. Thus, that the number of prisoners and soldiers is difficult to estimate does not affect the results of our study, because they generally are not included in our statistics.

Organized Migration

Organized migration is directed by the government, generally by means of granting subsidies or certain privileges to migrants, and primarily includes labor recruiting, agricultural resettlement, public appeals, service after completion of education, and work transfers. With the exception of the compulsory service after completion of certain types of education, which has not been vigorously enforced and might be considered as semicompulsory, organized migration in the USSR is not compulsory, and, at least currently, does not comprise a large percentage of the total migrants. A. V. Topilin estimated that in recent years organized migration accounted for not more than 10 or 12 percent of the total migration and has been declining in importance since the 1930s and 1940s when it comprised 30 to 40 percent of the total migrants.[54]

The chief agency for the planned redistribution of labor has been the Organized Labor Recruiting Service (Organabor), which was established in 1930 but replaced by the State Committee for the Utilization of Labor Resources in 1967. Between 1930 and 1970, Organabor resettled 28 million workers, but only 20 percent of these placements occurred in the 1951-70 period.[55] In this latter period, there was a sharp decline in the number of recruited workers. Between 1951 and 1955, recruitment totaled 2,833,400 workers but declined sharply in the 1966-70 period, when only 573,100 workers were recruited, or only about 4 percent of the total migrants.[56] In the past, Organabor recruited unskilled labor primarily in rural areas, although more recently rural recruits have declined sharply and urban workers predominate. Between 1948 and 1955, financial grants-in-aid were generally from R 30 to R 60,[57] but recently they have been increased to a maximum of R 200, except in northern areas where the recruit may receive the equivalent of two months pay.[58] Recruitment by Organabor is based on one- to three-year contracts and is voluntary, although apparently at times it has been used to rid Moscow and other cities of petty criminals, alcoholics, and other undesirables.[59]

Agricultural resettlement has also declined in importance in the past two decades. Between 1918 and 1950, more than 3 million rural inhabitants, or about 850,000 families, were resettled primarily from densely inhabited rural areas in the west to the eastern area of the USSR. No data are available for the entire Soviet Union after 1950, but within the RSFSR almost 1.5 million persons, or 337,000 families, were resettled between 1951 and 1970, of which more than 900,000 were resettled in Siberia and the Far East. During this period agricultural resettlement in the RSFSR declined from 111,000 families between 1951 and 1955 to 56,000 families between 1966 and 1970, or by almost half.[60] Since 1959 grants of from R 130 to R 300 have been given to each head of a family, depending upon the area of settlement, and from R 27.5 to R 60 for each family member. Various loans and credits are given to the settlers to build a home and buy livestock.[61] A. Z. Maykov states that this program is strictly voluntary.[62]

Another form of organized migration is public appeals (obshchestvennyy prizyv) to young people to work in remote areas on construction projects or programs like the New Lands of Kazakhstan, generally for short periods of time, for example, a summer. In some instances, however, it involves permanent settlement. Travel and other expenses are frequently paid by the Komsomol, even though there is little control over the migrant.[63] This is also a voluntary program, although at times pressure has been exerted on the Komsomol members in terms of career and educational advancement.[64] This is not an important type of migration, largely because it is mainly temporary and sporadic, although millions of youths have participated in the program.

In terms of sheer numbers, the potentially most effective type of organized migration is the obligation of day-school graduates of higher education, specialized middle education (technikumy), and vocational schools (professional'no-technichiskiye uchilishcha) to work for three years at a job and a place assigned by the government, which frequently is in a remote, labor-deficit area such as Siberia. In 1974 day-school divisions of higher education graduated 416,700 persons, which was almost twice as many as in 1965. Day-time graduates of specialized middle schools in 1974 totaled 737,900, more than twice as many as in 1965.[65] However, there are many ways to avoid this "obligatory" service; therefore, it is impossible to estimate with any precision the actual number of graduates who are assigned or who fulfill their assignments. Robert J. Osborn has summarized the situation:

> As for the obligation of graduates of higher education and the technikums, who after graduation are assigned to a given employer for three years, enforcement has been nearly impossible. . . . not even the device of withholding of university and institute diplomas until the graduates complete their assignments has been effective in inducing everyone to complete the required service. Enterprises are forbidden by regulation to hire graduates who have not finished their job assignments. . . . But according to numerous Soviet young people whom the writer has met who have seen the job assignment routine in action, enterprises in need of skilled labor usually ignore this. The formal requirement that such job leavers reimburse the state for the cost of their education (on the order of 4,000 rubles for a complete higher education) likewise remains a dead letter. Graduating students have a certain choice in their assignments too. Those with top grades or a veteran's status get first choice of the jobs which are offered.

Those whose families live in the city where they are studying are generally offered jobs there.[66]

Many vocational school graduates also avoid service with impunity, because enterprises do not report violations.[67] In 1974 daytime vocational schools graduated 1,618,000 students, a sizable number of migrants if they were controlled.[68] However, it is widely reported that many of the graduates never appear at their job assignments, and many of those that do appear leave before fulfilling their obligation. A 1968 survey of 12 sovkhozy in Kuybyshev Oblast indicated that 55 percent of the 275 assigned graduates left before completing their assignment, and in Smolensk Oblast, 92 percent of 53 graduates that were assigned to six farms left.[69] Therefore, it would appear that even though the Soviet government has the legal mechanisms to control the migration of its graduates, at least for three years, they do not effectively exercise this control. Moreover, in the strictest sense, the migration of graduates that is controlled is not compulsory, in that students can freely choose whether to continue their education at the expense of the state or not.

It is difficult to specify how many workers are transferred by the administration of their place of work to another locality. The number is probably not significant, and to judge from the labor legislation, these transfers are voluntary. If workers do not choose to go, they can terminate their work contracts.[70] Thus, this would not seem to be a significant type of organized migration.

Administrative Regulations

The widespread impression that the Soviet government has exercised significant control over the movement of its population probably stems largely from the existence of an internal passport system and legal and administrative regulations, as well as from the reports of the resettlement of certain nationalities and forced labor. Clearly, the existing administrative measures would be adequate to control population movement to a great degree, if they were rigorously enforced. There is much evidence, however, that they have not been vigorously enforced (a subject that will be discussed in subsequent chapters). Indeed, the direct control of population movement requires much effort and great repression. Even if the existing measures have not been implemented effectively, a central question is: What would have happened if there were no policy?

Administrative attempts to control migration have been primarily related to the internal passport system. The original intent of the passport system was to control the movement of the Soviet population, despite the fact that the article in the 1939 edition of the <u>Bol'shaya Sovtskaya Entsiklopediya</u> begins with such a statement but ends with a statement claiming that the intent was not to limit the freedom of movement of the population within the USSR.[71] Movement within Tsarist Russia was restricted by an internal passport system and the requirement to register one's arrivals, departures, and changes of residence. [72] Additional attempts were made after the Emancipation to restrict the movement of the rural population, particularly to the east, but since the various measures were ineffective, in 1904 migration was legalized for everyone in rural areas. [73] Shortly after the Revolution, the passport system was used to control special classes, and during the Civil War workbooks were issued as a means of identification. After the Civil War a system of identity cards (legitimatsiya) was adopted, and in 1932 the internal passport system was reinstated for persons over age 16, except for kolkhozniki and members of the armed forces. [74] However, in certain border zones, the Baltic republics, Moscow Oblast and parts of Leningrad Oblast, all permanent residents are issued a passport. Sovkhoz workers usually are issued passports and work on the basis of labor contracts. The passport contains such information as name, date and place of birth, nationality, marital status, dependents, criminal record, and draft status.

Passports are issued by the militia at the place of permanent residence and must be obtained before changing residence. According to the new passport decree of August 28, 1974, all citizens of the USSR over age 16 will be issued a new type of passport between January 1, 1976, and December 31, 1981. This legislation includes kolkhozniki but excludes members of the armed forces and Soviet citizens whose permanent residence is abroad and are temporarily in the USSR. [75]

The chief means employed by the government to control population movement has been the registration procedures that have been implemented in conjunction with the passport system. Within 24 hours of arrival, passports or appropriate travel papers must be registered with the militia, and a valid exit visa from the former residence is required. Permission for permanent residence (propiska) is required and is stamped in the passport. Permission for residence can be permanent or temporary (more than 45 days residence in cities); the latter is intended for those working or visiting temporarily or those who have temporary passports. [76] For example, in the 1966-70 period, there were about 200,000 workers in Moscow with a temporary propiska. [77] Temporary residents generally live with friends or relatives or in housing provided by their employer, and this status can eventually become permanent. Those holding a permanent propiska usually have permanent living quarters or are put on a waiting list for housing. It would seem that this is a measure related to available housing and is designed to regulate the movement of the population and to limit the growth of certain cities, because currently, and probably in the past as well, there are more people who want to live in cities than there are places for them to live. [78] In practice, however, it is related to employment, in that people rarely receive a propiska without employment, [79] which, of course, is to be expected given the labor and housing shortages that exist in the USSR.

In certain cities (rezhimnyye), special regulations have been imposed with regard to receiving a propiska in order to limit their population. In 1932 with the establishment of the passport system, Moscow and some of the largest cities were placed in this category. [80] It is very probable that the cities that were previously listed whose population was to be limited also would fall into this category. We will attempt to test empirically the effectiveness of these regulations in Chapter 5. It would appear, however, that these regulations have not been very effective in terms of the intent of the government, although cities such as Moscow, Leningrad, Kiev, and many of the other capitals clearly would be much larger if there were no residence restrictions. In short, these restrictions have impeded the growth of certain cities but not stopped or controlled it. Many cities have exceeded their planned size; the general plan for Moscow, for example, calls for a population of no more than 7.5 million by the period 1985-90, which is less than its current population. [81] V. I. Perevedentsev points out that the propiska system is not effective or desirable, because if there are jobs available, workers will be needed and probably inconvenienced by commuting long distances, and if there are no jobs, there is no need for restrictions. [82] These restrictions have resulted in much commuting to work from outside the major cities; for example, in 1970 some 380,000 workers commuted daily into Moscow. [83] Around Leningrad, and probably around other cities as well, it is common practice for migrants to join a sovkhoz near the city for housing, so that most of the family members can work in the city, even though housing and labor shortages are experienced by the sovkhozy. [84] Other ways to circumvent propiska restrictions are to marry a resident of a rezhimnyy city (who are often in great demand), accept a job such as in the service occupations (which is not desirable but in great demand), or simply live there illegally with friends or relatives. Employers greatly in need of labor may overlook the failure of job applicants to obtain a propiska and may even provide them with housing. [85] Another problem related to the propiska system is that it discourages movement out of certain large cities by pensioners (20 percent of Moscow's population was of pension age in 1970) and others that might move if they thought they could return if they so desired. [86]

Attempts to control the movement of the kolkhoz population were also related to the internal passport system, in that kilkhozniki were not issued passports; there appears to be no legal provision for them to receive one as long as they retain the status of a kolkhoznik. Kolkhozniki, however, can be recruited for employment in other sectors of the economy and receive passports. They can also receive documents (spravki) permitting them to work temporarily in a city or construction project and this status can become permanent. From the existing legislation, it is somewhat difficult to define the restrictions on movement of the kolkhoz population, because the enforcement of the decrees probably varied in time and some of the decrees probably were not published or available outside the USSR or were applied only locally. There appears to be no law preventing a person from leaving a kolkhoz. The 1928 legislation on agricultural collectives stated that termination of membership in collectives with few exceptions required only a personal request, which could not be denied and need not be justified. [87]

Subsequent legislation appears to be designed to regulate, rather than prevent, kolkhoz migration and to specify the obligations to the kolkhoz of the kolkhoz members that migrate temporarily or permanently. As might be expected, the legislation reflects the problems that arose in regulating migration.

In December 1930, Organabor was established as the legally sanctioned method
of recruiting labor, particularly in rural areas. [88] According to a 1931 decree, seasonal and permanent migrants were to be recruited from kolkhozy
only on a planned basis by means of agreements concluded with the kolkhoz. [89]
This was a period of considerable mobility of the rural population as a result
of collectivization, and this legislation probably was an attempt to regulate
this migration in the interests of the economy. There was much seasonal
migration (otkhodnichestvo) during this period to work in industry and construction. The March 17, 1933, decree stipulated that seasonal work contracts must be approved by the kolkhoz management and that anyone who vio-
lated this regulation would be expelled from the kolkhoz. The decree, in particular, specified those who left before sowing and returned at harvest time
to collect their share of the harvest. [90] This reflected the problem that many
seasonal and permanent migrants left their families on the kolkhoz and thereby
attempted to retain their position in the kolkhoz and receive a part of the proceeds and use of the private plot allocated to them by the kolkhoz. Others
apparently did not settle their accounts before permanently leaving the kolkhoz.
The famine of 1932-33 probably greatly stimulated such migration.

The decree of July 21, 1938, began with a statement to the effect that in
the recruitment of kolkhoz labor there was some disorganization, because
labor was recruited from kolkhozy with labor shortages and insufficient recruitment occurred in kolkhozy with labor surpluses. There was also needless competition among organizations, and some workers were accepting advances from more than one organization. The remainder of the decree sought
to regularize the procedures for recruiting labor from kolkhozy, especially
in certain areas having a large number of normal workers, by specifying the
organization that could recruit labor. [91] In 1942 kolkhoz labor was included
in the wartime job freeze, but enforcement was relaxed after the war and the
decree was abrogated in 1956. [92] A 1961 publication reiterated that seasonal
or permanent work outside the kolkhoz by a kolkhoz member required the
permission of the kolkhoz and that enterprises were not to employ kolkhozniki
without the proper documentation from the kolkhoz. [93]

A 1973 publication on kolkhoz law restated that joining or leaving a kolkhoz is voluntary and that migration from a kolkhoz for industrial employment
was planned. It also stipulated the conditions for terminating kolkhoz membership: (1) permanent employment in industry or other sectors of the economy, (2) a move to another kolkhoz, (3) the transformation of a kolkhoz to a
sovkhoz, (4) the expulsion of a member from a kolkhoz, and (5) the death of
a kolkhoz member. The application of a kolkhoz member to terminate membership in the kolkhoz is reviewed by the management of the kolkhoz and the
kolkhoz assembly within three months of its submission. No conditions for
denying the request are stated, but permission to leave is required. Any dis-
agreements in the final accounting are to be settled by a peoples court. Transfer to another kolkhoz requires the agreement of both kolkhoz assemblies,
except that in the case of marriage to a member of another kolkhoz, the permission of the kolkhoz assembly is not required for terminating membership.
Passports are issued by the local militia after presentation of the necessary

documents.[94] There is no indication that young people in the kolkhoz are forced to join the kolkhoz upon reaching maturity. However, because passports are normally issued by the local militia, those leaving presumably must satisfy the local regulations and have made arrangements for employment or schooling and housing where they plan to move.

These regulations must be interpreted in terms of the prevailing economic conditions. On the one hand, the collectivization, famine, and deteriorating economic conditions in rural areas during the 1930s were followed by a major war, with catastrophic population losses, a crop failure, and rehabilitation, all of which resulted in mass migration. On the other hand, forced industrialization resulted in a great demand for labor in urban areas and on construction sites and an extremely rapid rate of urbanization. Employers, therefore, probably frequently overlooked the proper documentation, and there were many ways, legal and illegal, of acquiring a passport and a propiska. A seasonal worker at a plant could gradually achieve a change in status from kolkhoznik to worker with the aid of the management, and a rural student who continued his education in a city could receive a passport.

It is generally thought in the West that Soviet government strictly controls the movement of the rural population and rural migration to urban areas. This view seems to exaggerate the control of the government and overemphasize the importance of the rural population not having a passport. That permission from the kolkhoz assembly is required before a kolkhoznik can leave the kolkhoz suggests there is some control over rural population movement, although the extent or the conditions of the control are not known. Clearly, it must be acknowledged that practice probably was not always in conformity with the law and that enforcement of the existing regulations probably varied in time. Nevertheless, there is no provision in the law that specifically prevents a kolkhoznik from leaving a kolkhoz. Soviet demographers have assumed that kolkhoz members can easily leave a kolkhoz and move to a city. More important, however, is that empirical evidence indicates that the volume of rural out-migration was so great that it would seem to preclude extensive control, particularly considering that organized rural out-migration has declined greatly in importance.

According to Soviet estimates, between 1926 and 1939, urban in-migrants from rural areas totaled 18.7 million or almost two-thirds of the urban growth and another 5.8 million was accounted for by the change of status of rural settlements to urban settlements, which was partly the result of migration. Thus, the average annual growth of in-migrants from rural areas during this period was about 2 million, and this was a net figure. There clearly was also considerable urban-to-rural movement and rural-to-rural migration, as there is at present. Between 1939 and 1959, based on the above two categories, the average annual number of urban in-migrants from rural areas was about 1.5 million and between 1959 and 1970, about 2 million. Between 1926 and 1970 net migration to urban areas from rural areas totaled some 60 million people, and change of status of settlements added another 18 million.[95] If data were available on the total number of rural out-migrants since 1926 (rather than net rural-to-urban migration, the number of rural-to-rural migrants since 1926, and the number of rural out-migrants since 1970), they would very probably indicate that about 100 million had left rural areas since 1926, and most of this out-migration was from kolkhozy. Moreover, much of the recent rural out-migration has been from rural areas experiencing severe labor shortages, such as the Non-Chernozem Zone and West Siberia, to the detriment of the rural economy and in opposition to the desires of the government. In an effort to solve this problem, the Soviet government has exclusively stressed incentives rather than coercion. Thus, the existing regulations undoubtedly have impeded migration and kept undesirable elements out of the cities but have not controlled it. Therefore, statements such as "migration from village to city is not the object of direct government regulation"[96] seem valid, at least currently, and very probably in the past as well. Recall that the USSR has experienced virtually an unprecedented rate of urbanization, which would have been impossible without mass migration from rural areas.

Another administrative measure that affected migration was the job freeze and youth labor draft, which was in effect from 1940 to 1956 and was designed to prohibit the movement of workers of government and cooperative and social enterprises without permission of the director of the establishment.[97] In 1942 kolkhozy were included in the job freeze. Once again the effectiveness of such a measure is open to question. Robert J. Osborn maintains that "much evidence suggests that in the postwar years it was being enforced only sporadically, if at all."[98] It appears that even during the war control over the movement of population was far from effective. About 25 million people were evacuated during World War II from occupied territories and areas near the front primarily to eastern regions, and eventually almost all of them returned to the western areas.[99] U.S. correspondents reported that by July 1944, about a year before the end of the war, half of the refugees had returned to the liberated areas, despite the fact that the government urged them to remain in the east.[100] Some of the return migration was planned, but most of it was spontaneous. There was also a significant migration to the newly annexed western regions that had experienced sizable population losses.[101] Yet this was the period of maximum control over the population, at least in terms of legislation. This is not to say, however, that the job freeze did not affect the majority of the population in the unoccupied areas. It does indicate the difficulty in controlling population movement when conditions or the desires of the people dictate otherwise. Also worthy of mention, although not related to the job freeze, is that during and shortly after World War II, the Volgo-Germans, Crimean Tatars, Kalmyks, Chechen, Ingush, Karachay, and Balkars were forcibly resettled in the east, but these movements constituted only a relatively small percentage of the total migration during this period, even though it was clearly an example of a successful migration policy.

Our interest in the effectiveness of policies designed to control population movement in the USSR is related to our intent, where feasible, to test universal formulations in the Soviet Union in an attempt to explain these movements. It is difficult to state with precision at this juncture how effective these policies were, although in subsequent chapters a further analysis of these policies will be undertaken. However, the common impression that population movement in the USSR has to a great degree been controlled by the government appears to be erroneous. Events such as wars, famines, and collectivization have resulted in mass migration not envisaged by government plans. In addition, rapid industrialization has resulted in a fundamental redistribution of the Soviet population, apparently largely as a result of free migration. Until about 1930, the Soviet government did not control the country sufficiently to make a serious attempt at controlling the movement of its population. In the 1930s, in addition to collectivization, a famine, and deteriorating economic conditions in rural areas, the USSR experienced an unprecedented rate of urbanization. There is no evidence to indicate that migration was substantially controlled by the government during this period. Despite restrictive legislation, World War II and its aftermath resulted in mass migrations. A high rate of urbanization and attendant migration has been characteristic of the postwar period, and it would appear that governmental influence on migration has diminished during this period. Most existing legislation appears to have been designed to solve problems related to migration rather than systematically to control population movement. Very probably, restrictions on the movement of the kolkhoz population impeded out-migration, and the propiska system certainly impeded in-migration to certain cities, preventing their excessive growth. Migration programs organized by the government were largely voluntary and probably facilitated migration rather than controlling or directing it, and some programs resulted only in temporary migration. Their impact has also diminished with time. The picture that emerges is that the Soviet government has had some influence on migration, but that population movement in the USSR during the Soviet period has been predominantly free.

IMPACT ON SOCIETY

To understand Soviet society, or any society, adequately, one must understand the political, economic, geographic, social, and demographic forces that are shaping that society and to which the government will react. Such an understanding would help us to anticipate and interpret the course of events in the USSR in the next decade or so—a task that has been relatively neglected, despite the considerable academic and governmental emphasis on Soviet studies over the past few decades.

Modernization activates demographic forces through population growth, redistribution, and changes in the composition of the population that play a major role in the processes of social change. The effect of a given population change on a society depends on how the population variables are interrelated to other variables related to modernization. These interrelationships result in major differences in the effects of population change between developed and developing societies and affect, to a limited extent, how the changes are perceived. The dramatic decline in fertility and mortality and the rise in life expectancy that have occurred in developed countries clearly have had an immense impact on these societies and in particular on the lives of individuals. The rapid population growth that has been caused by declining mortality and high fertility in developing countries is generating intensive pressures in these societies.

Depending on socioeconomic conditions, population growth can result in obstacles to economic growth by affecting savings, investment, and dependency ratios; differential growth of various subpopulations has ethnic and political consequences in that tensions can result when all groups do not share equally in the advantages and disadvantages of population growth; increased demand for housing, education, employment, and health facilities can occur; growth in the size of bureaucracies in general and of such nongovernmental organizations as business firms, labor unions, political parties, and universities influences society; the need for more government services and more government regulations with the growth of population shapes a society; and changes in life-style and demand for services as a population becomes older or younger have an economic and social impact. The massive redistribution of population involving rapid urbanization and rural depopulation that occurs with economic development obviously results in radical and fundamental social and cultural change encompassing all aspects of life. In short, the decline in fertility and mortality and the rapid urbanization that has been associated with modernization have had a momentous impact on peoples' lives.

In the Soviet context, a number of demographic and geographic forces will have a discernible impact on Soviet society. These forces include a low and generally declining rate of population growth, sharp regional differentials in rates of population growth related to low Slavic and generally moderate to high non-Slavic fertility, an aging "European" population, severe regional labor shortages resulting in part from the fact that migration is not meeting the needs of the economy, widespread rural depopulation in "European" areas, rapidly growing rural populations in many "non-European" areas, rapid urbanization, the maldistribution of population relative to industrial resources, the multinational character of the USSR and the differential mixing and integration of the nationalities into the modern society, and very high and increasing female work force participation rates.

Obviously, many of these forces relate to migration or will induce migration. Many of the contemporary and future domestic problems of the Soviet Union, in fact, relate to migration and the urbanization that has accompanied it. The USSR has experienced and is experiencing a rapid rate of economic and social change, which also results in considerable cultural change. Because demographic processes are intimately interrelated and are closely interrelated to the socioeconomic environment, demographic variables, in general, and migration and urbanization, in particular, are good measures of the socioeconomic change that occurs with modernization. With respect to migration and urbanization as indicators of social change, modernization and its driving force, economic development, eventually result in a massive redistribution of a country's population, because of the necessity on the part of the population to adjust continually to changing economic conditions. This

ultimately results in almost a complete change of residence from rural to urban areas. In essence, the conclusion that can be drawn from surveying the
world literature on migration is that people move primarily for jobs and economic improvement, and the young and the more educated have the highest
propensity to migrate. The chief economic function of migration is to equalize
the supply of and demand for labor on a regional basis, and if migration does
not fulfill this function, economic problems, in the form of areas with surplus
labor or areas deficient in labor, ensue. For example, in the USSR in the
1980s without migration, the Slavic areas, where most of the economic development is expected to occur, will experience little or no change in the size of
their work force, whereas most of the "non-European areas" will have moderate to rapid rates of population growth and increase in their work force.
Unless there are fundamental changes in regional investment policy or significant migration, areas of labor surplus and deficit will develop, and economic development will be impeded.

Even if there is substantial migration and economic problems are
avoided, these processes very probably will result in ethnic problems. In
multinational societies, migration and urbanization result in much geographic
mixing of ethnic groups, and the world over, under a variety of conditions,
this results in ethnic tensions and the rise of ethnic consciousness for a variety of reasons.[102] In the USSR, most ethnic groups have officially designated homelands, in contrast to the United States and other immigrant countries, and the combination of ethnicity, which is highly irrational and emotional, with a homeland further intensifies ethnicity and ethnic conflict. Most
homelands in the USSR are still largely homogeneous in terms of ethnic composition, which includes the traditional areas of Russian settlement, and
much of the expected redistribution of the Soviet population will be from ethnic
homeland to ethnic homeland with in-migrants being considered intruders into
a homeland; in addition are the usual tensions that occur when ethnic groups
come together. Thus, if the "non-Europeans" do not move to the Slavic areas
of economic development in sufficient numbers there will be economic problems, but if they do, there will very probably be increased ethnic problems.
The Soviet government also has yet to face the ethnic problems associated
with the drastic population redistribution that ultimately results from economic development. We will have more to say on these subjects in subsequent
chapters.

In short, our message is that with a knowledge of migratory and other
demographic processes and how they interrelate with the socioeconomic environment, one can make guarded forecasts as to certain basic demographic
and socioeconomic changes that will occur in the next decade or two. Recall
that the workers and the parents for the next 20 years have already been
born, which greatly facilitates our forecasts. In addition, migration and urbanization are crucial variables in the analysis of demographic and socioeconomic change, because they are intimately interrelated with such factors as
fertility, mortality, work force, education, ethnicity, family life, marriage,
divorce, crime, and, above all, economic development. The migration and
urbanization that have accompanied modernization have fundamentally altered

millions upon millions of lives. Although we will not investigate all of the above subjects in detail, our primary purpose is to study migration and urbanization in the USSR, a country that comprises one-sixth of the earth's surface since the turn of the century, and to attempt to appraise the chief consequences of migration and urbanization on Soviet society and thereby contribute to a better understanding of Soviet society.

DATA AND METHODS

Since the end of the nineteenth century, a relatively large volume of census data has been published for the Russian Empire and the USSR. National censuses were conducted in 1897, 1926, 1939, 1959, and 1970, and they are the chief sources of socioeconomic data for Russia and the USSR, even though the periods that they cover, the intervals between the various censuses, and the range of data collected are not entirely satisfactory. Nevertheless, data from these censuses have been used relatively little in the study of Russian and Soviet society, both inside and outside the USSR. Where they have been used, moreover, their use has been limited chiefly to aggregate data, that is, data for the country as a whole. This situation is also true in the study of population change, although there are a few exceptions.[103]

Aside from the general reluctance of many scholars to delve into numerous volumes of purely statistical data, the primary reason that these censuses have been used relatively little is very probably owing to the many data problems that one encounters in their use. The chief data problem is the lack of territorial and definitional comparability of data among the various censuses, which makes valid comparisons over time difficult. With respect to population change, population trends and their interrelationships cannot be measured over time. The authors have attempted to solve this problem, and the results of the work are 19 data matrices that comprise the basic data for the study and make possible the application of various demographic and statistical methods. Eighteen of the data matrices are for the 1897-1959 period and consist of roughly 50 to 100 variables each. The remaining matrix is for the 1959-70 period and consists of nearly 150 variables. In all of the matrixes, the data are based upon 19 regions.

The chief sources of data for this study are the Russian and Soviet censuses of 1897, 1926, 1939, 1959, and 1970; all population data used in this study are de facto.[104] Data from the 1939 census will be used to a lesser extent, because relatively little information was published for administrative units below the republic level. Because the national territory of the USSR has changed several times since the latter part of the nineteenth century, the contemporary national territory differs from the national territory in 1897 and 1926. Consequently, in order to provide even aggregate data for the present-day national territory of the USSR, it was necessary to gather data from East European censuses and other sources for the border areas, that is, areas formerly outside but currently within the USSR.[105] Because the Soviet Union has a large, diverse population, aggregate population data for

MAP 1.1

Economic Regions: 1961

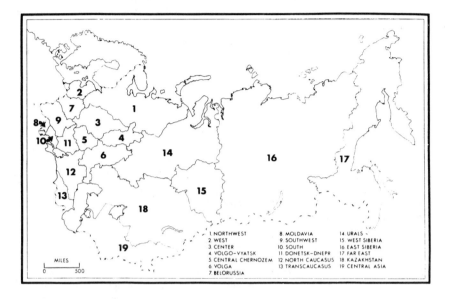

1. NORTHWEST
2. WEST
3. CENTER
4. VOLGO-VYATSK
5. CENTRAL CHERNOZEM
6. VOLGA
7. BELORUSSIA
8. MOLDAVIA
9. SOUTHWEST
10. SOUTH
11. DONETSK-DNEPR
12. NORTH CAUCASUS
13. TRANSCAUCASUS
14. URALS
15. WEST SIBERIA
16. EAST SIBERIA
17. FAR EAST
18. KAZAKHSTAN
19. CENTRAL ASIA

the USSR are often too gross to be meaningful. Moreover, frequent and drastic changes in the internal administrative divisions into which census and
other data are ordered over the past century have made it very difficult to
compare regional demographic and other data from one point in time to another. For example, the number of major enumeration units in 1897 was
about 90; in 1926, about 190; and in 1959 and 1970, about 140 each. To solve
this problem it was necessary to reorder the data for each census into a common set of territorial units. For this purpose the "major" (krupnyye) Soviet
economic regions of 1961 were chosen (Map 1.1). These regions were selected because 1959 and 1970 census units conform to them without major adjustment and because certain other socioeconomic data pertinent to the analysis were presented in these regions.

In order to allocate population data into comparable territorial units
(the economic regions), the authors have assumed that, except for urban con-
centrations, population is evenly distributed within each administrative unit;
therefore, a variation in area would result in a proportionate variation in
population. The "rural" population and rural population characteristics of
the political divisions in 1897 and 1926 were allocated to the various economic
regions on the basis of the area of each administrative division that fits into
the appropriate economic region. All centers with a population of 15,000
and over were individually allocated to the appropriate economic region. By

combining rural and urban components, it was possible to allocate the total population and total population characteristics into the economic regions for the various census years.

Available tests indicate that the error involved in these procedures was not great. For example, recently the Soviet government published population estimates of the 1926 population in 1970 political units (oblasts or equivalent units), without indicating the procedures used to derive the estimates.[106] No data were provided for areas that were outside the USSR in 1926, so the western border regions and the Far East cannot be compared with our data that include estimates for the entire present-day territory of the USSR for the various census years. However, these data can be aggregated into most of the 1961 economic regions and compared with our estimates. There was a very close correspondence between the two sets of estimates; in most cases they were within 1 percent of one another and never above 5 percent. Moreover, using the same techniques as we did, Ralph S. Clem has developed estimates of the 1926 population in 1959 political units (oblasts or equivalent units), which can also be aggregated and compared with our estimates. These two sets of estimates were also very close; almost always within 2 percent and in most cases within 0.5 percent of each other.[107] Elsewhere we have evaluated other aspects of our estimates.[108]

In order to provide a larger scale of analysis, the 19 economic regions have been aggregated into two types of larger regions: the Western and Eastern USSR and 4 quadrants. The Eastern USSR consists of the Urals, West Siberia, East Siberia, the Far East, Kazakhstan, and Central Asia, while the Western USSR consists of the remaining 13 economic regions. The 4 quadrants are Northern European USSR (Northwest, West, Center, Volgo-Vyatsk, Central Chernozem, Volga, Belorussia, and Southwest), the European Steppe (Moldavia, South, Donetsk-Dnepr, and North Caucasus), the Russian East (Urals, West Siberia, East Siberia, and the Far East), and the Non-Slavic South (Transcaucasus, Kazakhstan, and Central Asia). These two types of larger regions will be referred to as "gross regions."

Still another problem was the lack of comparable definitions of demographic and socioeconomic characteristics. With the exception of sex and age, definitions among the various Soviet censuses were not comparable. Therefore, it was necessary to make major statistical adjustments in order to obtain comparable data. The very best definition of a particular population characteristic was not always obtained, but the definitions utilized in this study are as nearly comparable as possible.

Thus, for the first time, comparisons over time, based on comparable territorial units and definitions, can be made for the present-day territory of the USSR, employing a wide variety of census variables, which pertain primarily to nationality, urbanization, labor force, sex, age, fertility, and literacy. Specifically, 19 matrices have been generated, each containing roughly 50 to 150 demographic and socioeconomic variables for 19 regions for the census years of 1897, 1926, 1959, and 1970 (see Appendix A and the first book of this series for a listing and discussion of the variables).

Because the basic procedures used to allocate the census data have already been described in detail, we have summarized them only briefly here.[109]

The total, urban, and rural populations by economic region for the various census years provide the basis for establishing the general patterns of population redistribution. Migration to urban centers, in particular, has been the chief source of the significant population redistribution that has occurred since 1897, and the latter part of this study is largely based on the urban data derived by the procedures that we have developed. Because the urban definitions in the various censuses varied considerably, it was necessary to select a comparable definition, so that valid comparisons over time could be made. Centers of 15,000 or more were chosen as the standard definition, because centers with a population of 15,000 were the smallest centers for which data were available for all census years (as will be discussed in greater detail in Chapter 3).

Data are not available to document in detail the massive migrations that resulted from the tumultuous events that have occurred in the USSR in this century. Place-of-birth data are, however, available in the 1897 and 1926 censuses, and place-of-residence data for the two years prior to the census were tabulated in the 1970 census. No migration questions were included in the 1939 and 1959 censuses. Since 1950 migration data are available from the passport registration system.

Migration can be measured for a rather indefinite period prior to the 1897 and 1926 censuses from place-of-birth data referring to the number of persons who, at the time of the census, lived in an uyezd or guberniya other than the one in which they were born. The data are tabulated for total, urban, and rural categories. From place-of-birth data the relative magnitude and direction of migration—the most important attributes in the analysis of migration—can be derived, but these data have certain limitations. They provide only the net result of migration between the time of birth and the time of enumeration. The chief limitations are that the number of migrants in any given year cannot be determined and migrants who have died or returned to their place of birth are not counted. Moreover, intermediate moves are not recorded. Place-of-birth data cannot be allocated into our comparable territorial units. There are also problems unrelated to the nature of place-of-birth data. The national territory for which the 1897 and 1926 migration data are available does not conform to the contemporary territory of the USSR. Another problem is that gubernii and uyezdy vary in area and configuration, and thus a move from the center of one unit might result in the crossing of a political boundary, whereas in another unit a move of an equal distance might not. Yet another problem is that the urban definitions used in the 1897 and 1926 censuses are not comparable with one another and do not conform to our urban definition.[110] The differing urban definitions, however, are not crucial to our analysis, because it can be reasonably assumed that the data in both censuses are representative of predominantly urban and rural areas. Despite these problems, the availability of place-of-birth data permits an extensive analysis of migration, and since internationally this has been a standard measure of migration, comparisons with other countries can be made.

Migration can also be measured by the data in the 1970 census referring to the previous residence of those who changed their residence in the two years preceding the census. These data are based on a 25-percent sample and have been tabulated for the total, urban, and rural categories. They also represent the net result of migration, in that those who move and die are not recorded and all moves are not taken into account. Furthermore, those in the military service, overseas, or away from their permanent residence for less than six months are not counted. A major problem is that no other country has used the migration definition of the 1970 Soviet census, so comparisons with other countries are impossible. Nevertheless, this census provides useful data for the study of recent migration.

Migration data are also collected in conjunction with the internal passport system and the requirement to register arrivals and departures, that is, propiska and vypiska. Upon registration for departure or arrival, migrants fill out a questionnaire (otryvnyy talon adresnykh listkov), which includes data on sex, age, nationality, and other characteristics, even though data on migrant characteristics are rarely published. Unfortunately, such questions as social class, education, and occupation, which are important in the analysis of migration, are not included in the questionnaire. The following migrants are included in the statistics: (1) those who moved to take up a permanent residence, (2) those who moved to work regardless of the time period, (3) those who moved to study for more than 45 days in areas with passports and more than 30 days in areas without passports, (4) those on official business (komandirovka) for more than 45 days in areas with passports and more than 30 days in areas without passports, and (5) members of the families of the above migrants.[111] Arriving and departing migrants fill out the form regardless of whether they hold a permanent or a temporary propiska.

These data have been gathered since 1939, but published data are available only since 1950. Data are based on a 20-to-50 percent sample of the questionnaires, depending upon the number of migrants. Although data have been gathered in rural areas since 1953, they are unreliable, because many of those without passports do not register and data about them have not been published. Although urban-to-urban movements appear to be reliably recorded, urban-to-rural and rural-to-urban movements are 10 percent or more underregistered. The major reasons for the underregistration are: (1) some who leave do not register; (2) in some cities people build their own homes and are not subject to propiska regulations; (3) members of the armed services are not subject to the registration regulations; (4) some housing authorities do not keep accurately the household book (domovaya kniga) that lists all occupants, and some passport agencies do not accurately register arrivals and departures; and (5) internal passports are absent in many rural areas.[112] Although the data are collected for administrative units down to the oblast level and are used for annual population estimates, they have been published only for republics, economic regions, cities over 500,000, and republic capitals.

In order to enhance our analysis, we have applied various demographic and statistical methods to these matrices. In doing so, we have attempted to utilize the simplest methods possible given the particular task at hand. Of the methods, perhaps the most important are rank correlation and factor analysis. The 5 percent confidence level for a rank correlation coefficient based on an N of 19 is 0.461. Factor analysis, although complex, is necessary to our analysis. This method distinguishes clusters of highly interrelated variables (factors). From the application of this method to each of the 19 matrices, major demographic relationships in Russia and the USSR emerged. In addition, we utilize various locational indexes, such as the dissimilarity index and the coefficient of redistribution. In this volume, use will be made only of select rank correlation coefficients. An extensive discussion of the factor analysis results will be deferred to the third volume of the series, because of the summary nature of this technique and the fact that many variables in the factor analysis (age, sex, and so on) will be emphasized in that volume.

Although this study is primarily based on census data for the 1897-1970 period, we are also interested in an assessment of post-1970 trends whenever possible. Thus, we will employ to a certain extent the most recent population data available at the time this research was being conducted. For example, considerable use will be made of population estimates for 1974 and 1977.[113]

At the outset, we should emphasize that we have attempted to guard against any analytical interpretations that cannot be supported reasonably by our data. All social and economic data are, of course, approximations of reality, approximations that vary in accuracy according to the complexity of the phenomena to be observed and to the rigor with which information is collected. In this regard, census data are probably more accurate than most other social and economic data, because considerable efforts are taken to ensure the completeness and accuracy of the enumeration, fairly uniform procedures and methods exist that can be employed, and much of the information sought is rather straightforward. Nevertheless, we recognize the limitations of our data, particularly inasmuch as the original information required considerable modification. We are convinced, however, that the major questions posed in this study can be answered to a significant degree through an analysis of these data. After working with these data on these questions for a long time and obtaining either expected or reasonable relationships, we are confident that the error in the data is within tolerable limits. Indeed, we have checked all of our calculations and every effort has been made to be as accurate as possible. To avoid rounding errors in our calculations, we have not rounded the absolute data presented in the tables, but this does not mean that we consider the data accurate to that degree. The compilation of a set of data matrices enables us to describe and explain population change in Russia and the USSR to an extent that previously was not possible.

The previous volume of this series included a chapter on the geographic background of the USSR as it relates to population change. In particular, the relationship between the natural environment and population distribution was investigated in that chapter, as well as historical trends in regional economic development. Because these subjects are a necessary background to the present study, we refer the reader to our previous work.

NOTES

1. Robert A. Lewis, Richard H. Rowland, and Ralph S. Clem, Nationality and Population Change in Russia and the USSR (New York: Praeger, 1976), p. 456.

2. Simon Kuznets and Dorothy Swaine Thomas, eds., Population Redistribution and Economic Growth: United States, 1870-1950, vol. 1 (Philadelphia: American Philosophical Society, 1957), p. 2. Simon Kuznets has expanded and elaborated this summary statement in the introduction to Volume 3 of this series.

3. Ibid., vol. 3, p. xxvi.

4. A. J. Jaffe, "Amount and Structure of International Migration: The Organizer's Report for Section 9.1," General Conference of the International Union for the Scientific Study of Population, London, September 1969, p. 9.17; and A. J. Jaffe and Seymour L. Wolfbein, "Internal Migration and Full Employment in the U.S.," Journal of the American Statistical Association 40 (September 1945): 351-63.

5. Eugene M. Kulischer, Europe on the Move (New York: Columbia University Press, 1948), p. 319.

6. For a fuller discussion of ethnicity and modernization, see Lewis, Rowland, and Clem, Nationality and Population Change, pp. 83-122.

7. Kuznets and Thomas, Population Redistribution and Economic Growth, xxiv-xxv.

8. Everett S. Lee, "A Theory of Migration," Demography 3, no. 1 (1966): 47-57.

9. R. Paul Shaw, Migration Theory and Fact (Philadelphia: Regional Science Research Institute, 1975), pp. 133-34.

10. United Nations, Bureau of Social Affairs, Report on the World Social Situation including Studies of Urbanization in Underdeveloped Areas (ST/SOA/33), 1957, p. 114; and United Nations, Department of Economic and Social Affairs, Growth of the World's Urban and Rural Population, 1920-2000 (ST/SOA/Series A/44), 1969, p. 58.

11. United Nations, Department of Economic and Social Affairs, Demographic Yearbook—1971, pp. 139-51.

12. Ibid.

13. Kingsley Davis, "The Urbanization of the Human Population," Cities (New York: Knopf, 1970), pp. 4-5; and Robert A. Lewis and Richard H. Rowland, "Urbanization in Russia and the USSR: 1897-1966," Annals of the Association of American Geographers 59 (December 1969): 779.

14. Davis, "Urbanization of the Human Population," pp. 13-15.

15. Ibid., p. 13; and Adna Ferrin Weber, The Growth of Cities in the Nineteenth Century (Ithaca, N.Y.: Cornell University Press, 1963), chap. 3.

16. Jack P. Gibbs and Walter T. Martin, "Urbanization, Technology, and the Division of Labor: International Patterns," American Sociological Review 27 (October 1962): 667-77; and William Fielding Ogburn, "Technology and Cities: The Dilemma of the Modern Metropolis," Sociological Quarterly 1 (July 1960): 139-53.

17. Bert F. Hoselitz, "The Role of Cities in the Economic Growth of Underdeveloped Countries," Journal of Political Economy 61 (June 1953): 195-208; and Weber, Growth of Cities.

18. A. J. Jaffe, "Urbanization and Fertility," American Journal of Sociology 48 (July 1942): 48-60.

19. Ibid., pp. 58-60; and Calvin Goldscheider, Population, Modernization, and Social Structure (Boston: Little, Brown, 1971), p. 150.

20. Weber, Growth of Cities, chap. 4.

21. Robert Redfield, "The Folk Society," American Journal of Sociology 52 (January 1947): 293-308; and Louis Wirth, "Urbanism as a Way of Life," American Journal of Sociology 44 (July 1938): 1-24.

22. Oscar Lewis, "Further Observations on the Folk-Urban Continuum and Urbanization with Special Reference to Mexico City," in The Study of Urbanization, ed. Philip M. Hauser and Leo F. Schnore (New York: Wiley, 1967), pp. 491-503; and Philip M. Hauser, "Observations on the Urban-Folk and Urban-Rural Dichotomies as Forms of Western Ethnocentrism," in The Study of Urbanization, ed. Philip M. Hauser and Leo F. Schnore (New York: Wiley, 1967), pp. 503-17.

23. Janet Abu-Lughod, "Migrant Adjustment to City Life: The Egyptian Case," American Journal of Sociology 67 (July 1961): 22-32.

24. Allan Schnaiberg, "The Modernizing Impact of Urbanization: A Causal Analysis," Economic Development and Cultural Change 20 (October 1971): 80-104.

25. D. V. Glass, Population Policies and Movements in Europe (London: Frank Cass, 1967).

26. Kingsley Davis, "Population Policy: Will Current Programs Succeed?" Science 158 (November 10, 1967): 730-39.

27. James L. Sundquist, Dispersing Population (Washington, D.C.: Brookings Institution, 1975).

28. Ibid.

29. For a discussion of this subject, see George J. Demko and Roland J. Fuchs, "Demography and Urban and Regional Planning in Northeastern Europe" (Paper presented at the Conference on Demography and Urbanization in Eastern Europe, UCLA, Los Angeles, California, February 5-9, 1976), pp. 3-4.

30. Karl Marx and Friedrich Engels, Collected Works (New York: International, 1975), 6: 488.

31. Ibid., p. 505.

32. Friedrich Engels, Herr Eugen Duhring's Revolution in Science (Chicago: Charles H. Kerr, 1935), pp. 309-12.

33. V. I. Lenin, Polnoye Sobraniye Sochineniy, vol. 26 (Moscow: Gosudarstvennoye Izdatel'stvo Politicheskoy Literatury, 1961), p. 74. (The transliteration system used in this study is that of the Board on Geographical Names.)

34. Ibid., vol. 16, p. 227, as cited in B. S. Khorev, Problemy Gorodov, 2d ed. (Moscow: Izdatel'stvo "Mysl'," 1975). For a discussion of Marxist views of population distribution and urban planning see Robert J. Osborn,

Soviet Social Policies: Welfare, Equality and Community (Homewood, Ill.: Dorsey Press, 1970), pp. 187-231.

35. I. S. Koropeckyj, Locational Problems in Soviet Industry before World War II (Chapel Hill: University of North Carolina Press, 1971), p. 55.

36. Lewis, Rowland, and Clem, Nationality and Population Change, pp. 116-22.

37. Khorev, Problemy Gorodov, pp. 78-79.

38. Osborn, Soviet Social Policies, p. 202.

39. Khorev, Problemy Gorodov, p. 86.

40. Osborn, Soviet Social Policies, pp. 202-3.

41. Khorev, Problemy Gorodov, pp. 3-140.

42. Osborn, Soviet Social Policies, p. 203.

43. D. G. Khodzhayev, ed., Puti Razvitiya Malykh i Srednikh Gorodov (Moscow: Izdatel'stvo "Nauka," 1967), pp. 3-7; XXIV S'ezd Kommunisticheskoy Partii Sovetskogo Soyuza, vol. 2 (Moscow: Izdatel'stvo Politicheskoy Literatury, 1971), p. 290; Osnovnyye Napravleniya Razvitiya Narodnogo Khozyaystva SSSR na 1976-1980 Gody (Moscow: Izdatel'stvo Politicheskoy Literatury, 1975), p. 78; and Chauncy D. Harris, Cities of the Soviet Union (Chicago: Rand McNally, 1970), p. 47.

44. D. G. Khodzhayev, "The Planning of the Distribution of Production in Population Centers and Some Problems in Population Geography," Soviet Geography: Review and Translation 8 (October 1967): 627.

45. B. S. Khorev, ed., Malyy Gorod (Moscow: Izdatel'stvo Moskovskogo Universiteta, 1972), pp. 196-97.

46. D. I. Valentey, ed., Marksistsko-Leninskaya Teoriya Narodonaseleniya (Moscow: Izdatel'stvo "Mysl'," 1971), pp. 92-104.

47. V. I. Perevedentsev, Metody Izucheniya Migratsii Naseleniya (Moscow: Izdatel'stvo "Nauka," 1975), p. 48.

48. Khorev, Problemy Gorodov, pp. 354-422; and O. V. Larmin, Metodologicheskiye Problemy Izucheniya Narodonaseleniya (Moscow: Izdatel'stvo "Statistika," 1974), pp. 198-239.

49. Valentey, Marksistsko-Leninskaya Teoriya Narodonaseleniya, p. 101.

50. Osnovnyye Napravleniya Razvitiya Narodnogo Khozyaystva SSSR na 1976-1980 Gody, p. 78.

51. For example, see Merle Fainsod, How Russia is Ruled (Cambridge, Mass.: Harvard University Press, 1965), p. 376.

52. See Perevedentsev, Metody Izucheniya Migratsii Naseleniya, p. 5; V. M. Moiseyenko, "Nekotoryye Voprosy Upravleniya Migratsionnymi Protsessami Naseleniya," in Voprosy Teorii i Politiki Narodonaseleniya, ed. D. I. Valentey and E. Yu. Burnashev (Moscow: Izdatel'stvo Moskovskogo Universiteta, 1970), p. 130; V. V. Pokshishevskiy, "Migratisya Naseleniya kak Obshchestvennoye Yavleniye i Zadachi Statisticheskogo i Izucheniya," in Statistika Migratsii Naseleniya, ed. A. G. Volkov (Moscow: "Statistika," 1973), pp. 18-19; R. V. Tatevosov, "Issledovaniye Prostranstvennykh Zakonomernostey Migratsii Naseleniya," in ibid., p. 35; Zh. A. Zayonchkovskaya, Novosely v Gorodakh (Moscow: "Statistika," 1972), p. 12; V. I. Perevedentsev,

Migratsiya Naseleniya i Trudovyye Problemy Sibiri (Novosibirsk: Izdatel'stvo "Nauka," Sibirskoye Otdeleniye, 1966), pp. 116-18; and B. S. Khorev and V. M. Moiseyenko, eds., Migratsionnaya Podvizhnost' Naseleniya v SSSR (Moscow: "Statistika," 1974), pp. 10-15.

53. Murray Feshbach and Stephen Rapawy, "Soviet Population and Manpower Trends and Policies," in Soviet Economy in a New Perspective, U.S. Congress, Joint Economic Committee Print (Washington, D.C.: Government Printing Office, 1976), p. 147.

54. A. V. Topilin, Territorial'noye Pereraspredeleniye Trudovykh Resursov v SSSR (Moscow: Izdatel'stvo "Ekonomika," 1975), pp. 13-14.

55. Yu. A. Matveyev, "Organizovannyy Nabor kak Odna iz Osnovnykh Form Planovogo Pereraspredeleniya Rabochey Sily," in Migratsiya Naseleniya RSFSR, ed. A. Z. Maykov (Moscow: Izdatel'stvo "Statistika," 1973), pp. 65-66.

56. Ibid., pp. 65-75.

57. Ibid., p. 75.

58. For a detailed description of the subsidies by region and industry, see Sbornik Zakonodatel'nykh Aktov o Trude (Moscow: "Yuridicheskaya Literatura," 1974), pp. 650-53.

59. Osborn, Soviet Social Policies, pp. 157-58.

60. A. Z. Maykov, "Effektivnost' Sel'skokhozyaystvennogo Pereseleniya," in Migratsiya Naseleniya RSFSR, pp. 80-81.

61. L. L. Rybakovskiy, Regional'nyy Analiz Migratsii (Moscow: Izdatel'stvo "Statistika," 1973), p. 135.

62. Maykov, "Effektivnost' Sel'skokhozyaystvennogo Pereseleniya," p. 79.

63. Topilin, Territorial'noye Pereraspredeleniye Trudovykh Resursov v SSSR, pp. 127-28.

64. Osborn, Soviet Social Policies, p. 157.

65. USSR, Narodnoye Khozyaystvo SSSR v 1974 G. (Moscow: "Statistika," 1975), p. 694.

66. Osborn, Soviet Social Policies, pp. 144-45.

67. Ibid., p. 120.

68. Narodnoye Khozyaystvo SSSR v 1974 G., p. 567.

69. Khorev and Moiseyenko, Migratsionnaya Podvizhnost' Naseleniya v SSSR, p. 68.

70. A. S. Pashkov, ed., Sovetskoye Trudovoye Pravo (Moscow: "Yuridicheskaya Literatura," 1976), p. 231.

71. "Pasport," Bol'shaya Sovetskaya Entsiklopediya, 1939 44: 322-23.

72. "Pasport," Entsiklopedicheskiy Slovar' 22 (St. Petersburg: Type-Lithografiya I. A. Efrom, 1897): 923-25; and F. J. M. Feldbrugge, ed., Encyclopedia of Soviet Law (Dobbs Ferry, N.Y.: Oceana, 1973), pp. 489-91.

73. J. William Leasure and Robert A. Lewis, "Internal Migration in Russia in the Late Nineteenth Century," Slavic Review 27 (September 1968): 382.

74. "Pasport," Bol'shaya Sovetskaya Entsiklopediya, pp. 322-23.

75. Byulleten' Minvuza SSSR, no. 12 (1974), pp. 11-12. The passport decree of 1974 is published in this source in its entirety.

76. Feldbrugge, Encyclopedia of Soviet Law, p. 490.

77. Khorev and Moiseyenko, Migratsionnaya Podvizhnost' Naseleniya SSSR, p. 153.

78. Perevedentsev, Metody Izucheniya Migratsii Naseleniya, p. 103.

79. Ibid., p. 104.

80. Khorev, Problemy Gorodov, p. 79.

81. M. Ya. Vydro, Naseleniye Moskvy (Moscow: Izdatel'stvo "Statistika," 1976), p. 15.

82. V. I. Perevedentsev, "Goroda i Gody," Literaturnaya Gazeta, February 26, 1969, p. 2.

83. USSR, Narodonaseleniye (Moscow: Izdatel'stvo "Statistika," 1973), p. 21.

84. Maykov, "Effektivnost' Sel'skokhozyaystvennogo Pereseleniya," p. 129.

85. Osborn, Soviet Social Policies, p. 205.

86. Khorev, Problemy Gorodov, pp. 391-92.

87. N. Ozertskovskiy, ed., Polozheniye o Sel'skokhozyaystvennoy Kooperatsii (Moscow: Knigosoyuz, 1928), p. 198.

88. N. G. Aleksandrov, Soviet Labour Law (Delhi, India: University Book House, 1962), p. 93.

89. F. Belolutskiy, ed., Kolkhozno-Kooperativnoye Zakonodatel'stvo: Sbornik (Moscow: "Sovetskoye Zakonodatel'stvo," 1931), p. 144.

90. Trudovoye Zakonodatel'stvo SSSR: Sbornik Zakonov, Ukazov, i Postanovleniy (Moscow: Yuridicheskoye Izdatel'stvo N. K. Yu. SSSR, 1941), pp. 39, 83.

91. Ibid., pp. 36-37.

92. Aleksandrov, Soviet Labour Law, p. 102.

93. Spravochnik po Zakonodatel'stvu dlya Kolkhoznika (Moscow: Gosudarstvennoye Izdatel'stvo Yuridicheskoy Literatury, 1961), p. 96.

94. Kolkhoznoye Pravo (Moscow: Yuridicheskaya Literatura, 1973), pp. 67-71.

95. V. M. Moiseyenko, "Rol' Migratsii v Formirovanii Gorodskogo Naseleniya SSSR v Sovremennykh Usloviyakh," Problemy Narodonaseleniya (Moscow: "Statistika," 1973), p. 50.

96. Khorev and Moiseyenko, Migratsionnaya Podvizhnost' Naseleniya v SSSR, p. 66.

97. Vedomosti Verkhovnogo Soveta SSSR, no. 20 (1940), p. 1.

98. Osborn, Soviet Social Policies, p. 143.

99. Sh. M. Munchayev, "Evakuatsiya Naseleniya v Gody Velikoy Otechestvennoy Voyny," Istoriya SSSR, no. 3 (1975), p. 138.

100. Kulischer, Europe on the Move, pp. 294-96.

101. Ibid., pp. 299-300.

102. Walker Connor, "Nation-Building or Nation-Destroying?" World Politics 24 (April 1972): 319-55.

103. For example, see Frank Lorimer, The Population of the Soviet Union: History and Prospects (Geneva: League of Nations, 1946); and Harris, Cities of the Soviet Union.

104. Russian Empire, Tsentral'nyy Statisticheskiy Komitet Ministerstva Vnutrennikh Del, Pervaya Vseobshchaya Perepis' Naseleniya Rossiyskoy Imperii, 1897 G., 89 vols.; USSR, Tsentral'noye Statisticheskoye Upravleniye SSSR, Vsesoyuznaya Perepis' Naseleniya 1926 Goda, 66 vols.; USSR, Tsentral'noye Statisticheskoye Upravleniye pri Sovete Ministrov SSSR, Itogi Vsesoyuznoy Perepisi Naseleniya 1959 Goda, 16 vols.; and USSR, Tsentral'noye Statisticheskoye Upraveleniye pri Sovete Ministrov SSSR, Itogi Vsesoyuznoy Perepisi Naseleniya 1970 Goda, 7 vols.

The 1897 census was conducted on February 9 (January 28 according to the Julian calendar), the 1926 census on December 17, the 1939 census on January 17, and the 1959 and 1970 censuses on January 15. In the computation of average annual rates a period of 29.9 years is used for the 1897-1926 period; 12.1 years for 1926-39; 20.0 years for 1939-59; 11.0 years for 1959-70; 43.1 years for 1926-70; and 73.0 years for 1897-70.

105. For a list of these censuses and other sources, see Robert A. Lewis and Richard H. Rowland, "Urbanization in Russia and the USSR: 1897-1966," Annals of the Association of American Geographers 59 (December 1969): 777, n. 3.

106. USSR, Naseleniye SSSR, 1973 (Moscow: Izdatel'stvo "Statistika," 1975), pp. 14-25.

107. Ralph S. Clem, "Estimating Regional Populations from the 1926 Soviet Census," Soviet Studies, forthcoming. In this article, Clem compares his estimates with the Soviet estimates.

108. J. William Leasure and Robert A. Lewis, Population Changes in Russia and the USSR: A Set of Comparable Territorial Units (San Diego, Calif.: San Diego State College Press, 1966), pp. xi-xii.

109. Lewis, Rowland, and Clem, Nationality and Population Change, pp. 29-60; and Leasure and Lewis, Population Changes.

110. For a discussion of the urban definitions used in these censuses, see Leasure and Lewis, "Internal Migration in Russia in the Late Nineteenth Century," p. 376; and J. William Leasure and Robert A. Lewis, "Internal Migration in the USSR: 1897-1926," Demography 4, no. 2 (1966): 482.

111. Perevedentsev, Metody Izucheniya Migratsii Naseleniya, pp. 43-47.

112. P. G. Pod'yachikh, "Sostoyaniye Statistiki Migratsii Naseleniya v SSSR i Mery po Eye Uluchsheniyu," Problemy Migratsii Naseleniya i Trudovykh Resursov (Moscow: Izdatel'stvo "Statistika," 1970), pp. 122-28.

113. USSR, Prezidium Verkhovnogo Soveta Soyuza Sovetskikh Sotsialisticheskikh Respublik, SSSR: Administrativno-Territorial'noye Deleniye Soyuznykh Respublik na 1 Yanvarya 1977 Goda (Moscow, 1977), pp. 13-522, 651-56; and USSR, Prezidium Verkhovnogo Soveta Soyuza Sovetskikh Sotsialisticheskikh Respublik, SSSR: Administrativno-Territorial'noye Deleniye Soyuznykh Respublik na 1 Yanvarya 1974 Goda (Moscow, 1974), pp. 5, 636-50.

2

REGIONAL POPULATION
DISTRIBUTION AND REDISTRIBUTION

A fundamental redistribution of the Soviet population has occurred in this century. If current trends persist, and there is no reason to think they will not, by the end of the century the USSR will attain patterns of population distribution similar to other highly urbanized countries. The massive redistribution of the population that has occurred has been related largely to modernization and its driving force, economic development, processes that have basically changed Soviet life and undoubtedly will continue to do so in the future. However, conditions specific to the USSR, such as wars, famines, and collectivization, also have had a major impact on the redistribution of the Soviet population. These events, in fact, have generated waves of migrants numbering in the millions. One only has to think of the armies, both foreign and domestic, that have rampaged across the heavily populated western part of the USSR in this century to appreciate the magnitude of these migrations, even though much of it was temporary in nature. Clearly, the USSR in this century has been a country on the move, as a result of economic development and catastrophic events.

The purpose of this chapter is to establish the basic patterns of population redistribution that have occurred in this century and, where possible, to relate them to migration and natural increase, although not all of the migration, as well as changes in natural increase, can be documented because of a lack of statistics. As the USSR is a multinational state, the redistribution of specific nationalities also merits attention, but because these patterns were discussed in considerable detail in the first book of the series, they will not be focused upon here. Much of the population redistribution that has occurred has been related to urbanization; the analysis of urbanization, however, will be discussed in a subsequent chapter. Urban growth and rural population change will be considered in this chapter only in a summary manner as they relate to total population redistribution. These subjects also will be analyzed in greater detail in subsequent chapters. For the sake of historical continuity, we will begin our discussion with a brief outline of early migration and settlement.

SUMMARY DISCUSSION

A remarkable stability has been characteristic of the trends in population redistribution in the USSR over the past 400 years. The Mongols drove the Russian population into the forests of Northern European USSR, where conditions were not especially favorable for agriculture, and population growth, the attraction of superior agricultural resources, and the development of the Russian state resulted in an intense impetus for out-migration. The Russian population spread to the south and then to the east; first to agricultural frontiers and later to areas of urban-industrial development. This movement out of Northern European USSR to the south and the east is essentially the migration history of the Russians for the past 400 years.

Since 1897, Northern European USSR has experienced a steady and substantial decline in its share of the total population, and all economic regions within Northern European USSR have registered a relative decline. In the aggregate all other quadrants have had a substantial increase in their share, as a result of migration and differential natural increase. Recently, there have been two major changes in the long-term patterns of population redistribution. Since 1959, the Russian East has experienced a declining share of the total population, and between 1970 and 1977 the European Steppe for the first time since 1897 registered no relative gain. Thus, since 1970 the Non-Slavic South is the only quadrant that has had a relative gain. Since 1897, the Eastern USSR has significantly increased its relative share of the total population, from less than a fifth to more than a third, and the Non-Slavic South has been the chief contributor to this relative gain, largely as a result of its higher natural increase.

The decline in the share of the urban and rural population of Northern European USSR since 1897 was close to that of its total population. Most of the relative shift in the urban population was to the Russian East, but after 1959 this trend was reversed. The Eastern USSR increased its share of the urban population more rapidly than its share of either the total or rural population. The general trend in the redistribution of the rural population has been a shift to the southern areas of the USSR, as a result of rural depopulation in the Slavic areas and more rapid rural natural increase in the Non-Slavic South.

Generally, there was a close correspondence between the average annual percentage change in the total, urban, and rural populations and their redistribution, but this relationship was not invariant, because rates of increase or decrease are influenced by the base population. Since 1897, the Eastern USSR has grown at about twice the rate of the Western USSR, and Northern European USSR has had the slowest rate of growth and the Russian East and the Non-Slavic South have had the fastest rates. Rates of growth in all quadrants have declined since 1970, but the Non-Slavic South still has by far the fastest rate of growth. The Central Chernozem and the Volgo-Vyatsk are the only economic regions that have had a declining total population since 1970.

Since 1897, the urban population has grown at about three times the rate of the total population, which reflects the very rapid industrialization and urbanization that has occurred since 1926. The period of the greatest growth was 1926-39, when the urban population grew 6.5 percent per year; that of the Eastern USSR, 9.5 percent; and that of the Russian East, 10.7 percent. The rural population of the USSR increased at a very slow rate between 1897 and 1970, and since 1926 it has declined absolutely. Between 1897 and 1970, all economic regions of Northern European USSR had declining rural populations, whereas the remaining economic regions generally had increasing rural populations. Since 1959, the only economic regions to have had an appreciable increase in their rural population are Central Asia, Kazakhstan, Transcaucasus, Moldavia, the South, and the North Caucasus.

Wars, famines, and epidemics were characteristic of much of the 1897-1926 period, and these catastrophic events resulted in mass migrations, major population losses, and a sharp decline in natural increase. There was a major shift in the distribution of the total, urban, and rural population out of Northern European USSR and most economic regions within it to the European Steppe and the Russian East. The share of the total population of the Non-Slavic South declined slightly because of population losses. There was a shift in the total, urban, and rural population to the Eastern USSR. Migration patterns based on the 1897 and 1926 censuses support these patterns of redistribution. There was a striking similarity between the periods before the 1897 and 1926 censuses in the patterns of in-migration, out-migration, and net migration, which demonstrates the strength and persistence of major migratory streams and indicates that the underlying conditions that promoted migration were still in effect. There was a tendency for people to move to areas of higher income as measured by surrogate variables, which supports the contention that there was some degree of universality with respect to migratory processes.

During the 1927-39 period, the shift of the total, urban, and rural population out of Northern European USSR continued at the expense of all other quadrants. The Russian East had the greatest relative gain in its share of the total population and was the only quadrant to register an increase in its share of the urban population. The 1926-39 period had the greatest urban growth of any period, and this was the dominant trend in population redistribution during this period and accounted for much of the shift to the Russian East. In addition to Northern European USSR, the European Steppe had a relative decline in its rural population, and the Non-Slavic South had the greatest relative gain, although the Russian East also registered a gain. The shift in the total, urban, and rural population to the Eastern USSR continued. Thus, the 1926-39 period was characterized by a major redistribution of the population from rural to urban areas and the continued relative shift of the total, urban, and rural population to the east. Migration and natural increase data for this period are scant, so little can be said about the sources of population redistribution, aside from acknowledging the large volume of rural-to-urban migration.

The outstanding characteristic of population redistribution during the 1939-59 period was a dramatic shift of the total, urban, and rural populations out of Northern European USSR and all of its economic regions. In fact, the population of Northern European USSR declined absolutely during this period, largely because of war losses. In terms of the distribution of the total population, all quadrants except Northern European USSR and virtually all other economic regions had increases in their share of the total population. The major shift of the urban population was to the Russian East, whereas the major pattern in the redistribution of the rural population was to the Non-Slavic South. The shift of the total, urban, and rural population to the Eastern USSR continued and was appreciable. It would appear that, even during the wartime job freeze, the Soviet government's control over migration was far from absolute or effective. Truly horrendous war losses and a lack of data on migration and natural increase make it very difficult to analyze the population redistribution that occurred during this period.

The 1959-70 period was characterized by a continuation of the shift in the total population out of Northern European USSR, but for the first time since 1897 the Russian East experienced a decline in its share of the total and urban populations. The Non-Slavic South had the greatest relative increase in its total, urban, and rural population, reflecting the fact that since 1959 the dominant trend in population redistribution was the shift to the Non-Slavic South. Most of the shift in the rural population was to the Non-Slavic South. Although the shift of the total and rural population to the east continued, for the first time the Eastern USSR had a decline in its share of urban population. Migratory trends in general support these patterns of population redistribution, although patterns of regional natural increase are more influential in population redistribution. With respect to net in-migration rates between 1959 and 1970, the South, North Caucasus, Kazakhstan, Central Asia, and the West were the leading regions, whereas the Volgo-Vyatsk, West Siberia, and the Central Chernozem were the outstanding regions of net out-migration. As to the analysis of total migration, the expected patterns largely emerged, with respect to mobility, distance, age, ethnicity, education, and links to economic variables, although the relationships with economic variables were not always as strong as might be expected.

Since 1970, the major patterns of population redistribution are the continued shift out of Northern European USSR and the Russian East and the continued dominance of the Non-Slavic South in the shift of the total population. For the first time, the European Steppe registered no relative gain. Thus, all of the redistribution of the total Soviet population was to the Non-Slavic South. Migration patterns are fundamentally a continuation of the previous period, and it would appear that the labor problems in Siberia have not been solved, which accounts for the continued shift out of the Russian East despite government drives to the contrary.

DETAILED DISCUSSION

Early Migration and Settlement

Migration, colonization, and territorial expansion have been characteristic features of Russian history since the earliest times. But Russian history is not unique in this respect, for human history is largely the story of the migration of peoples and the colonization of the world. [1] A change in a major trend of population redistribution is highly significant, because it indicates a change in the underlying conditions affecting population redistribution. Early migration and settlement will be briefly surveyed in order to outline the major trends in redistribution prior to 1897, so that they can be compared with post-1897 trends.

By the first century A.D., Slavs first appeared in the historical record and occupied a broad area of the mixed forest zone roughly between the middle Dnieper and the Vistula rivers. [2] Between the sixth and eleventh centuries, they spread over a vast area. Migratory streams went south to the lower Danube and the Balkans and westward toward the Elbe River, where they became known as the Southern and Western Slavs, respectively. From the middle Dnieper, the Eastern Slavs spread to the north, northeast, and east as far as Lake Onega, the basins of the Oka and upper Don rivers, and toward the Volga in the mixed forest zone. They also spread to the south into the steppe, particularly the western steppe, at times as far as the shores of the Black Sea, but the steppe was the domain of a succession of nomadic groups, who made agricultural settlement very hazardous.

Between the tenth and thirteenth centuries, the Kievan Russian state consolidated all of the East Slav tribes, and its territory extended from Lake Ladoga to the Black Sea and from the Carpathian Mountains to the middle Volga. In the northeast, settlement extended beyond the Volga along the Vyatka River. As in previous periods, the density of settlement was sparse; most of the population was concentrated in widely dispersed nodes, where conditions were favorable for agriculture. A significant redistribution of population occurred from the south to the west and north, largely because of internal dissention and nomadic invasions. The forest steppe and steppe areas around Kiev were largely depopulated, and migratory streams flowed to the west and the north. Thus, Eastern Slav settlement was confined primarily to the forest areas, and the steppe was to remain the domain of the nomads.

The Mongol conquest that occurred in the middle of the thirteenth century resulted in virtually the complete depopulation of the steppe and forest steppe except for a few nomads, a significant redistribution of the Eastern Slav population, the destruction of most of the major cities, and a decline in population. For over a century, migratory streams flowed to the north, where the Russian population sought protection in the forest from the frequent Mongol incursions. Thus, Russian agricultural settlement was confined to the mixed forest and taiga where in the north and northeast it displaced Finno-Ugric tribes.

In the fourteenth century, the Moscow Principality began the consolidation of the Russian state by gradually annexing other principalities and adjoining lands. First it expanded to the east and north, and then further to the north and northwest to the Arctic Ocean. During the sixteenth century, its expansion was predominantly to the west and southwest. By the end of the century, after conquering the Tatar Khanates, the Russian state controlled a large area in the east from the mouth of the Volga to the Ural Mountains and beyond. By the middle of the seventeenth century, Russians controlled the forest area all the way to the Pacific Ocean. During the seventeenth century, they also continued to expand to the west, incorporating the territories on the left bank of the Dnieper. It was with the acquisition of these territories, especially those east of the Volga, that the multinational character of the population of the Russian state began to develop.

The southward advance of the Russian population, however, was impeded by the Crimean Tatars who were supported by Turkey. It was not until the end of the eighteenth century with the subjugation of the Crimean Tatars that the steppe was completely secure for colonization. Significant migration to the forest steppe began in about the middle of the sixteenth century, however, when the population of the Russian state numbered about 6 to 7 million people. During the seventeenth century, the flow of Russian migrants to the south and southeast to the forest steppe, the northern part of the steppe, and the Volga Basin continued at an intensified rate, and this migratory stream converged with that of the Ukrainians from the right bank of the Dnieper River.

During the eighteenth and first half of the nineteenth century, the boundaries of the Russian state were greatly expanded. In the northwest, they acquired the Baltic area; in the west, they acquired the areas of Ukrainian and Belorussian settlement, as well as Bessarabia and a large part of Poland; and in the south they occupied the littoral of the Black Sea, the North Caucasus, and the Transcaucasus. In the middle of the nineteenth century, they incorporated Kazakhstan and Central Asia and the southern part of the Far East.

The former pattern of migration from the densely settled central Russian areas to sparsely settled frontier areas with relatively superior agricultural resources persisted during the eighteenth and first half of the nineteenth centuries. In fact, to the present the central Russian areas with their relatively inferior agricultural resources and their former substantial rate of natural increase have remained the chief areas of out-migration in Russia and the USSR. At the beginning of the eighteenth century, about 50 percent of the population of European Russia was still concentrated in the forest zone, and the middle Volga and the left-bank Ukraine accounted for another 25 percent. The southern steppe was still very sparsely settled by Russians and Ukrainians. Thus, the Russian population was still largely confined to the forest areas, a legacy of the Mongol invasion. During the eighteenth century, the chief areas of colonization were the southern steppe, the southeast, and the area adjoining the Urals on the west. V. V. Pokshishevskiy has estimated net migration to the forest steppe and the steppe during the seventeenth and eighteenth centuries at roughly 3.3 million, 1 million of which was Ukrainian migration from the right bank of the Dnieper River.[3] This migration resulted in a major redistribution of the Russian population, considering that at the end of the seventeenth century the population of the Russian state was roughly between 15 and 16 million.

In the first half of the nineteenth century, migration to agricultural frontier areas continued; the southern steppe and the southeast, in particular the North Caucasus, were the major areas of in-migration. Industrial development around Moscow and St. Petersburg resulted in migration to these centers. During the eighteenth century, the forest steppe and the northern fringes of the steppe had become densely settled, and during the nineteenth century, these regions were a major area of out-migration. Between 1800 and 1863, net out-migration from the forest steppe totaled about 1 million, and the chief area of net in-migration was the southern steppe, where net in-migration reached about 2.6 million.[4] Thus, by the first part of the nineteenth century the forest steppe and steppe of European Russia had been basically settled. Up to the middle of the nineteenth century there was relatively little migration to Siberia. Slavic migration to the Transcaucasus and Kazakhstan was insignificant during this period.

In the latter half of the nineteenth and early twentieth centuries, migration to the south declined, and migration to the east increased greatly. Significant migratory streams also flowed to urban-industrial areas, most notably the northwest, the central industrial, and the Baltic areas. Migration to the east in the latter half of the nineteenth and early twentieth centuries has been estimated at about 6.5 million, approximately a third of which migrated to Kazakhstan.[5] The major areas of out-migration to the east were the densely settled areas of the mixed forest, forest steppe, and northern part of the steppe. The southern steppe remained a major area of in-migration in the latter part of the nineteenth and early part of the twentieth centuries.

Thus, the general pattern of migration in the territory of the present-day USSR has remained essentially the same for about the past 400 years. After being driven into the forests of Russia by nomadic invasions, with an increasing population, limited agricultural resources, and the expansion of the Russian state, the Russian population began to spread to the south and then to the east—first to agricultural frontiers and later to areas of urban-industrial development.

General Patterns of Population
Distribution and Redistribution

Only the gross redistributional patterns can be derived from the following tables and maps that present percentage point change by region in the total, urban, and rural populations, because this measure only indicates the net result of migration and regional differences in natural increase, including, of course, regional differentials in population losses due to famine, epidemics, and war. They do show, however, regional shifts in the share of the population and are therefore a reasonable starting point for the investigation of population redistribution. Nevertheless, our comparable data make it possible for the first time to measure the regional shifts in the total, urban, and rural populations that have occurred since 1897.

Our purpose is to describe in a summary fashion the general trends in the redistribution of the population of the present-day territory of the USSR since 1897. In subsequent sections and chapters, an attempt will be made to

TABLE 2.1

Regional Distribution and Redistribution of the Total Population
by Gross Region: 1897-1977

Region	Percentage Distribution					
	1897	1926	1939	1959	1970	1977
Western USSR	80.8	77.9	75.5	69.8	68.1	66.9
Eastern USSR	19.2	22.1	24.5	30.2	31.9	33.1
Northern European USSR	61.7	57.9	54.5	48.1	45.1	43.7
European Steppe	15.5	16.5	16.8	17.3	17.9	17.9
Russian East	10.9	13.9	15.8	19.2	18.3	18.1
Non-Slavic South	12.0	11.7	12.9	15.6	18.7	20.3

	Percentage Point Change						
	1897– 1926	1926– 39	1939– 59	1959– 70	1926– 70	1897– 1970	1970– 77
Western USSR	-2.9	-2.4	-5.7	-1.7	-9.8	-12.7	-1.2
Eastern USSR	2.9	2.4	5.7	1.7	9.8	12.7	1.2
Northern European USSR	-3.8	-3.4	-6.4	-3.0	-12.8	-16.6	-1.4
European Steppe	1.0	0.3	0.5	0.6	1.4	2.4	0.0
Russian East	3.0	1.8	3.4	-0.9	4.4	7.4	-0.2
Non-Slavic South	-0.3	1.2	2.7	3.1	7.0	6.7	1.6

Note: The regions in this and subsequent tables are a com-
bination of the following economic regions: Eastern USSR—Urals,
West Siberia, East Siberia, Far East, Kazakhstan, Central Asia;
Western USSR—the 13 regions not in the Eastern USSR; Northern
European USSR—Northwest, West, Center, Volgo-Vyatsk, Central
Chernozem, Volga, Belorussia, Southwest; European Steppe—Moldavia,
South, Donetsk-Dnepr, North Caucasus; Russian East—Urals, West Si-
beria, East Siberia, Far East; Non-Slavic South—Transcaucasus,
Kazakhstan, Central Asia.

Sources: See Chapter 1, nn. 104, 105, and 113.

isolate the migration and natural increase components for the intercensal periods (although this is not always possible) and to analyze population redistribution in greater detail. It should be noted that in these and subsequent tables, unless otherwise indicated, centers with a population of 15,000 or more comprise the urban population, and centers below this limit constitute the rural population. In analyzing the measures of redistribution, it should be kept in mind that the intercensal periods vary in duration; the 1897-1926 period is 29.9 years, the 1926-39 period is 12.1 years, the 1939-59 period is 20 years, the 1959-70 period is 11 years, the 1926-70 period is 43.1 years, and the 1897-1970 period is 73 years.

Measures of population distribution and redistribution indicate that historical trends have to a great degree continued to the present (Table 2.1). Since 1897, the Eastern USSR has experienced an increasing share of the total population, and Northern European USSR, which has traditionally contained by far the largest percentage of the population, has had a continuous and substantial decline in its share of the total population. The other major regions increased their share. In fact, if there had been no redistribution of the population and Northern European USSR had maintained its 1897 share of the population, there would have been some 40 million more people in this region in 1970. The economic regions of traditional Russian settlement, which are the Northwest, Center, Volgo-Vyatsk, Central Chernozem, and Volga, declined in their share of the total population from 37.9 percent in 1897 to 29.5 percent in 1970 or 8.4 percentage points. Although the patterns of redistribution outlined in this section will be analyzed subsequently, suffice it to say at this juncture, not all of the relative decline in the share of Northern European USSR was the result of out-migration—war losses and differential natural increases were also important.

The European Steppe increased its share of the population, but not as much as might be expected, largely because of major population losses as a result of war and famine and, more recently, relatively low natural increase. Even more important, however, was the fact that by the 1926-39 period the European Steppe no longer attracted large numbers of rural migrants. In fact, during this period the rural population decreased, which was related primarily to rapid industrialization and urbanization and deteriorating economic conditions in rural areas, as the result of collectivization. The Russian East increased its share of the population up until about 1959, mainly as the result of in-migration; subsequently, out-migration and declining natural increase have reversed the long-term trend in the redistribution of the population to the Russian East. The Non-Slavic South has increased its share of the population, particularly since 1939, primarily because of relatively high natural increase, in-migration, and relatively modest war losses. The net result of the population redistribution in the USSR between 1897 and 1970 has been a significant shift of population from the Western USSR to the Eastern USSR. Despite the significant redistribution of the population, Northern European USSR still accounts for almost 50 percent of the total population. Data for the 1926-70 period roughly indicate the redistribution that has occurred during the planning and forced industrialization period.

TABLE 2.2

Regional Distribution and Redistribution of the Total Population by Economic Region: 1897-1977

Region	Percentage Distribution						Percentage Point Redistribution						
	1897	1926	1939	1959	1970	1977	1897-1926	1926-39	1939-59	1959-70	1926-70	1897-1970	1970-77
Northwest	6.4	6.2	6.4	5.5	5.3	5.4	-0.2	0.2	-0.9	-0.2	-0.9	-1.1	0.1
West	4.6	3.4	3.0	2.9	2.8	2.8	-1.2	-0.4	-0.1	-0.1	-0.6	-1.8	0.0
Center	12.2	12.6	13.1	11.9	11.1	10.7	0.4	0.5	-1.2	-0.8	-1.5	-1.1	-0.4
Volgo-Vyatsk	4.9	4.3	4.5	4.0	3.5	3.2	-0.6	0.2	-0.5	-0.5	-0.8	-1.4	-0.3
Central Chernozem	6.6	6.6	5.4	4.2	3.7	3.3	0.0	-1.2	-1.2	-0.5	-2.9	-2.9	-0.4
Volga	7.8	7.4	6.3	6.0	5.9	5.8	-0.4	-1.1	-0.3	-0.1	-1.5	-1.9	-0.1
Belorussia	5.2	4.6	4.6	3.9	3.7	3.7	-0.6	0.0	-0.7	-0.2	-0.9	-1.5	0.0
Moldavia	1.2	1.2	1.3	1.4	1.5	1.5	0.0	0.1	0.1	0.1	0.3	0.3	0.0
Southwest	14.0	12.8	11.2	9.7	9.1	8.8	-1.2	-1.6	-1.5	-0.6	-3.7	-4.9	-0.3
South	3.0	2.7	2.5	2.4	2.6	2.7	-0.3	-0.2	-0.1	0.2	-0.1	-0.4	0.1
Donetsk-Dnepr	6.3	7.1	7.6	7.9	7.8	7.6	0.8	0.5	0.3	-0.1	0.7	1.5	-0.2
North Caucasus	5.0	5.5	5.4	5.6	6.0	6.0	0.5	-0.1	0.2	0.4	0.5	1.0	0.0
Transcaucasus	3.7	3.5	4.2	4.6	5.1	5.3	-0.2	0.7	0.4	0.5	1.6	1.4	0.2
Urals	7.3	7.1	7.5	8.9	8.4	8.1	-0.2	0.4	1.4	-0.5	1.3	1.1	-0.3
West Siberia	1.6	3.7	4.1	4.9	4.4	4.2	2.1	0.4	0.8	-0.5	0.7	2.8	-0.2
East Siberia	1.7	2.2	2.7	3.3	3.4	3.4	0.5	0.5	0.6	0.1	1.2	1.7	0.0
Far East	0.3	0.9	1.5	2.1	2.1	2.3	0.6	0.6	0.6	0.0	1.2	1.8	0.2
Kazakhstan	3.9	3.7	3.2	4.5	5.4	5.6	-0.2	-0.5	1.3	0.9	1.7	1.5	0.2
Central Asia	4.4	4.5	5.5	6.5	8.2	9.4	0.1	1.0	1.0	1.7	3.7	3.8	1.2

Sources: See Chapter 1, nn. 104, 105, and 113.

MAP 2.1

Regional Distribution of Total Population: 1897

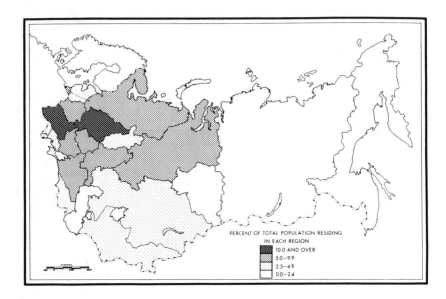

MAP 2.2

Regional Distribution of Total Population: 1926

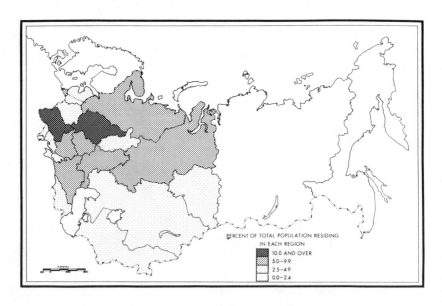

MAP 2.3

Regional Distribution of Total Population: 1939

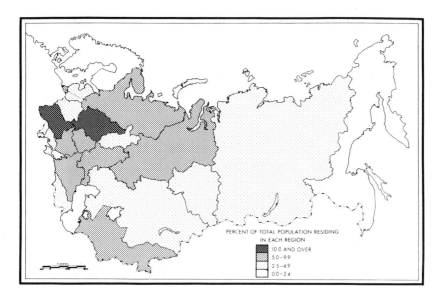

MAP 2.4

Regional Distribution of Total Population: 1959

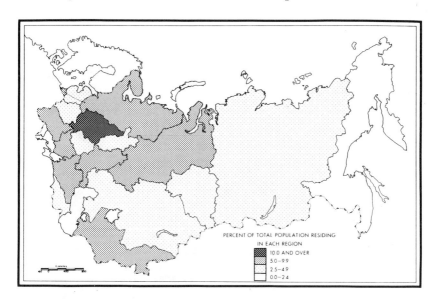

MAP 2.5

Regional Distribution of Total Population: 1970 and 1977

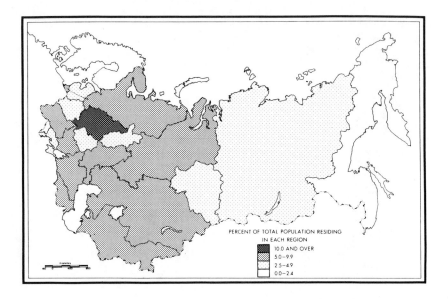

MAP 2.6

Regional Redistribution of Total Population: 1897-1926

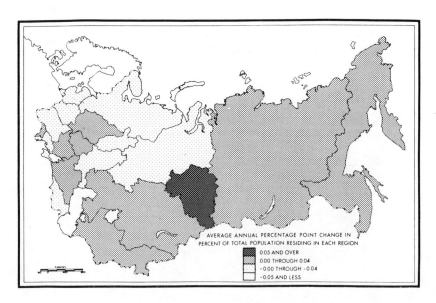

MAP 2.7

Regional Redistribution of Total Population: 1926-39

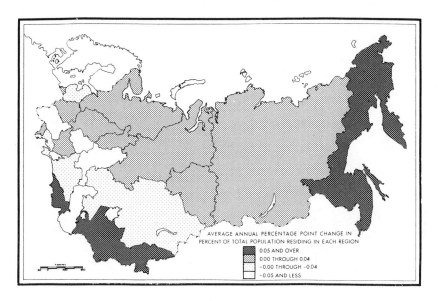

MAP 2.8

Regional Redistribution of Total Population: 1939-59

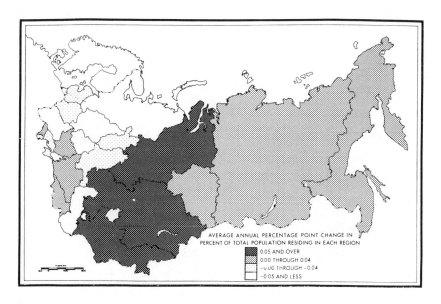

MAP 2.9

Regional Redistribution of Total Population: 1959-70

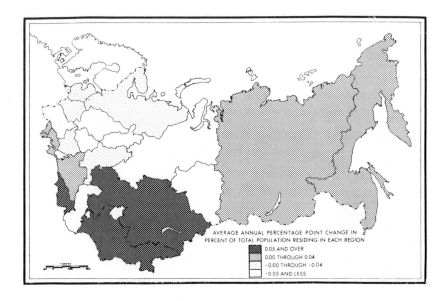

MAP 2.10

Regional Redistribution of Total Population: 1926-70

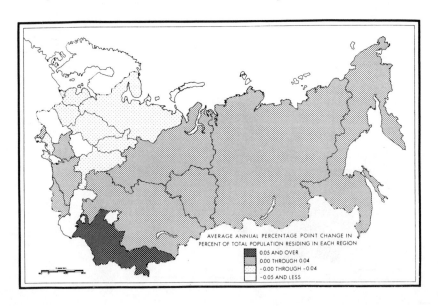

MAP 2.11

Regional Redistribution of Total Population: 1897-1970

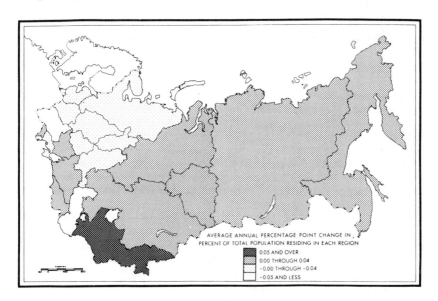

MAP 2.12

Regional Redistribution of Total Population: 1970-77

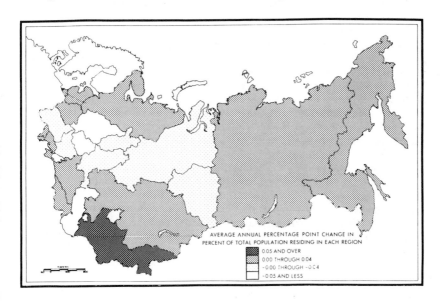

The 1977 data presented in Table 2.1 are official Soviet estimates and therefore may not be as accurate as the census data. Because urban and rural data are available only according to the official definitions, they have not been included in the following tables pertaining to urban and rural redistribution. Urban and rural population trends since 1970, however, will be analyzed in subsequent chapters. Nevertheless, 1977 data for the total population indicate a continuation of the 1959-70 trends. Between 1970 and 1977, Northern European USSR and the Russian East continued to lose relatively, although at a slower rate. The European Steppe registered no gain for the first time since 1897. Thus, the Non-Slavic South is the only quadrant to register a relative gain. The shift to the Eastern USSR has intensified on the basis of average annual percentage point change. In the analysis of the shifts in population, one should bear in mind that these are shifts relative to the growth of the total USSR population and do not necessarily indicate that a region registering a declining share is experiencing an absolute decline in population.

The distribution and redistribution of the total population by economic regions permit a more refined investigation of patterns of redistribution (Table 2.2 and Maps 2.1-2.12). The general shift of the total population to the east can be seen in Maps 2.1-2.5, which depict the regional distribution of the total population from 1897 to 1970. Despite the significant redistribution of the population to the east, the Western USSR still contains over two-thirds of the population. By 1970, the Center had the largest share of the total population and Moldavia had the smallest. No separate map for 1977 was included, because the map patterns are identical to those of 1970, although the percentages were generally not identical. Between 1897 and 1970 and 1926 and 1970, all regions in Northern European USSR had a decline in their shares of the total population, and before 1939 values were either negative or showed only modest increases (Table 2.2). The greatest relative decline occurred during the 1939-59 period, reflecting the effect of World War II and the proportionately greater war losses in western parts of European USSR. With a few exceptions, the values for the remaining regions are positive, showing a general redistribution away from Northern European USSR. In the European Steppe, the Donetsk-Dnepr and North Caucasus registered sizable relative gains since 1897, and the South declined slightly, although more recently it has an increasing share. The Urals and West Siberia had an increasing share of total population until 1959 but then registered relative declines. East Siberia and the Far East barely increased their shares after 1959. The economic regions comprising the Non-Slavic South have substantially increased their relative shares, particularly since 1959, largely as a result of higher natural increase. Between 1897 and 1970 Central Asia had the greatest relative gain of any region and the Southwest had the greatest loss.

Maps 2.6-2.12 show the redistribution of the total population for the various intercensal periods and have been compiled on the basis of average annual percentage point change to eliminate the influence of the varying intercensal periods, so that comparisons can be made from period to period. To facilitate further comparisons among the maps, comparable intervals have been used for each series of maps. It was not necessary to present maps

TABLE 2.3

Average Annual Percentage Point Redistribution of the Total Population
by Economic Region: 1897-1977

Region	1897–1926	1926–39	1939–59	1959–70	1926–70	1897–1970	1970–77
Northwest	-0.01	0.02	-0.05	-0.02	-0.02	-0.02	0.01
West	-0.04	-0.03	-0.01	-0.01	-0.01	-0.02	0.00
Center	0.01	0.04	-0.06	-0.07	-0.03	-0.02	-0.06
Volgo-Vyatsk	-0.02	0.02	-0.03	-0.05	-0.02	-0.02	-0.04
Central Chernozem	0.00	-0.10	-0.06	-0.05	-0.07	-0.04	-0.06
Volga	-0.01	-0.09	-0.02	-0.01	-0.03	-0.03	-0.01
Belorussia	-0.02	0.00	-0.04	-0.02	-0.02	-0.02	0.00
Moldavia	0.00	0.01	0.01	0.01	0.01	0.00	0.00
Southwest	-0.04	-0.13	-0.08	-0.05	-0.09	-0.07	-0.04
South	-0.01	-0.02	-0.01	0.02	-0.00	-0.01	0.01
Donetsk-Dnepr	0.03	0.04	0.02	-0.01	0.02	0.02	-0.03
North Caucasus	0.02	-0.01	0.01	0.04	0.01	0.01	0.00
Transcaucasus	-0.01	0.06	0.02	0.05	0.04	0.02	0.03
Urals	-0.01	0.03	0.07	-0.05	0.03	0.02	-0.04
West Siberia	0.07	0.03	0.04	-0.05	0.02	0.04	-0.03
East Siberia	0.02	0.04	0.03	0.01	0.03	0.02	0.00
Far East	0.02	0.05	0.03	0.00	0.03	0.02	0.03
Kazakhstan	-0.01	-0.04	0.07	0.08	0.04	0.02	0.03
Central Asia	0.00	0.08	0.05	0.15	0.09	0.05	0.17

Sources: See Chapter 1, nn. 104, 105, and 113.

TABLE 2.4

Regional Distribution and Redistribution of the Urban
Population by Gross Region: 1897-1970

Region	Percentage Distribution				
	1897	1926	1939	1959	1970
Western USSR	87.7	83.5	76.3	68.5	68.9
Eastern USSR	12.3	16.5	23.7	31.5	31.1
Northern European USSR	63.0	56.8	51.1	45.2	45.3
European Steppe	20.4	22.0	21.1	18.9	19.0
Russian East	6.3	10.4	17.3	22.9	21.0
Non-Slavic South	10.3	10.8	10.6	13.0	14.7

	Percentage Point Change					
	1897-1926	1926-39	1939-59	1959-70	1926-70	1897-1970
Western USSR	-4.2	-7.2	-7.8	0.4	-14.6	-18.8
Eastern USSR	4.2	7.2	7.8	-0.4	14.6	18.8
Northern European USSR	-6.2	-5.7	-5.9	0.1	-11.5	-17.7
European Steppe	1.6	-0.9	-2.2	0.1	-3.0	-1.4
Russian East	4.1	6.9	5.6	-1.9	10.6	14.7
Non-Slavic South	0.5	-0.2	2.4	1.7	3.9	4.4

Sources: See Chapter 1, nn. 104 and 105.

TABLE 2.5

Regional Distribution and Redistribution of the Rural
Population by Gross Region: 1897–1970

Region	Percentage Distribution				
	1897	1926	1939	1959	1970
Western USSR	80.1	77.0	75.4	70.6	67.4
Eastern USSR	19.9	23.0	24.6	29.4	32.6
Northern European USSR	61.6	57.9	55.7	49.5	44.9
European Steppe	15.0	15.8	15.5	16.4	17.0
Russian East	11.4	14.4	15.3	16.9	16.1
Non-Slavic South	12.1	11.9	13.5	17.2	22.1

	Percentage Point Change					
	1897–1926	1926–39	1939–59	1959–70	1926–70	1897–1970
Western USSR	−3.1	−1.6	−4.8	−3.2	−9.6	−12.7
Eastern USSR	3.1	1.6	4.8	3.2	9.6	12.7
Northern European USSR	−3.7	−2.2	−6.2	−4.6	−13.0	−16.7
European Steppe	0.8	−0.3	0.9	0.6	1.2	2.0
Russian East	3.0	0.9	1.6	−0.8	1.7	4.7
Non-Slavic South	−0.2	1.6	3.7	4.9	10.2	10.0

Sources: See Chapter 1, nn. 104 and 105.

based on percentage point change for the various periods, in that the patterns would be the same as those for the average annual rates, which are presented in Table 2.3. Maps 2.6-2.12 also substantiate the trend in population redistribution to the east; in particular the shift to the east between 1939 and 1959 stands out. The recent continuation of this trend and the shift to the Non-Slavic South can be seen in the maps depicting redistribution since 1959. The 1897-1970 and 1926-70 maps show the cumulative effect of these shifts. Compared with the 1959-70 period, there have been no abrupt changes since 1970, although a few rather small changes in redistribution have resulted in changes in the map patterns. Kazakhstan, however, experienced a rather sizable decline in its redistribution index. The Center, Volgo-Vyatsk, Central Chernozem, Southwest, Donetsk-Dnepr, the Urals, and West Siberia continue to experience the greatest relative losses, and Central Asia continues to register the greatest relative gains.

Tables 2.4 and 2.5 show the distribution and redistribution of the urban and rural population by gross region and also indicate a decline in the share of these populations in Northern European USSR that was close to that of the total population. In terms of the distribution of the urban population, the urban share of Northern European USSR since 1897 has been close to that of the total population, whereas the urban share of the European Steppe has been above its share of the total population. The opposite situation prevailed in the Non-Slavic South since 1897 and in the Russian East until 1959. The European Steppe, however, experienced a decline in its share of the urban population since 1926. Most of the relative regional shift in the urban population was to the Russian East, but after 1959 there was a reversal of this trend. The Non-Slavic South made significant gains in its proportion of the urban population since 1939, even though its level of urbanization is relatively low. Since 1897, the Eastern USSR increased its share of the urban population more rapidly than its share of either the total or rural populations, but in the Non-Slavic South the situation was reversed, which reflects the increasing rural depopulation in the RSFSR and the moderate to rapid growth of the rural population in the Non-Slavic South.

As to the distribution of the rural population, the rural share of the quadrants was close to its share of the total population, except that the rural share of the Russian East declined appreciably after 1959 and that of the Non-Slavic South increased significantly. The general trend in the redistribution of the rural population has been a shift out of Northern European USSR to the southern areas of the USSR, in particular to the Non-Slavic South. A significant shift also occurred from the Western USSR to the Eastern USSR in both the urban and rural populations.

The regional distribution and the redistribution of the urban and rural population are shown in Tables 2.6-2.9 and Maps 2.13-2.22. The most obvious pattern of the redistribution of the urban population during the period of rapid industrialization, 1926-70, is the outward shift from the traditional Russian areas of settlement primarily to the Russian East, Kazakhstan, and the Donetsk-Dnepr, although the Center has maintained its relative position. The sharpest relative declines were in the Northwest, Southwest, South, and

TABLE 2.6

Regional Distribution and Redistribution of the Urban Population
by Economic Region: 1897-1970

| Region | Percentage Distribution | | | | | Percentage Point Redistribution | | | | | |
	1897	1926	1939	1959	1970	1897-1926	1926-39	1939-59	1959-70	1926-70	1897-1970
Northwest	14.1	11.0	10.5	7.5	7.1	-3.1	-0.5	-3.0	-0.4	-3.9	-7.0
West	6.8	4.7	2.5	2.4	2.7	-2.1	-2.2	-0.1	0.3	-2.0	-4.1
Center	15.0	16.5	18.6	16.5	15.2	1.5	2.1	-2.1	-1.3	-1.3	0.2
Volgo-Vyatsk	0.9	1.7	2.8	3.0	3.1	0.8	1.1	0.2	0.1	1.4	2.2
Central Chernozem	4.9	3.6	2.3	2.3	2.7	-1.3	-1.3	0.0	0.4	-0.9	-2.2
Volga	6.8	6.3	5.9	6.5	6.7	-0.5	-0.4	0.6	0.2	0.4	-0.1
Belorussia	3.6	3.0	2.5	2.1	2.7	-0.6	-0.5	-0.4	0.6	-0.3	-0.9
Moldavia	1.7	1.0	0.4	0.6	0.7	-0.7	-0.6	0.2	0.1	-0.3	-1.0
Southwest	10.9	9.9	6.0	4.8	5.3	-1.0	-3.9	-1.2	0.5	-4.6	-5.6
South	6.9	4.7	3.2	2.5	2.6	-2.2	-1.5	-0.7	0.1	-2.1	-4.3
Donetsk-Dnepr	6.7	8.0	11.7	10.3	10.0	1.3	3.7	-1.4	-0.3	2.0	3.3
North Caucasus	5.1	8.2	5.8	5.6	5.7	3.1	-2.4	-0.2	0.1	-2.5	0.6
Transcaucasus	4.3	4.7	4.1	4.4	4.6	0.4	-0.6	0.3	0.2	-0.1	0.3
Urals	4.1	5.1	8.1	11.1	9.9	1.0	3.0	3.0	-1.2	4.8	5.8
West Siberia	1.0	2.7	4.3	6.0	5.3	1.7	1.6	1.7	-0.7	2.6	4.3
East Siberia	0.6	1.4	2.5	3.3	3.2	0.8	1.1	0.8	-0.1	1.8	2.6
Far East	0.5	1.1	2.3	2.6	2.4	0.6	1.2	0.3	-0.2	1.3	1.9
Kazakhstan	1.0	1.5	2.7	4.0	4.7	0.5	1.2	1.3	0.7	3.2	3.7
Central Asia	5.0	4.6	3.7	4.6	5.4	-0.4	-0.9	0.9	0.8	0.8	0.4

Sources: See Chapter 1, nn. 104 and 105.

TABLE 2.7

Average Annual Percentage Point Redistribution of the Urban Population
by Economic Region: 1897–1970

Region	1897–1926	1926–39	1939–59	1959–70	1926–70	1897–1970
Northwest	-0.10	-0.04	-0.15	-0.04	-0.09	-0.10
West	-0.07	-0.18	-0.01	0.03	-0.05	-0.06
Center	0.05	0.17	-0.11	-0.12	-0.03	0.00
Volgo-Vyatsk	0.03	0.09	0.01	0.01	0.03	0.03
Central Chernozem	-0.04	0.11	0.00	0.04	-0.02	-0.03
Volga	-0.02	-0.03	0.03	0.02	0.01	-0.00
Belorussia	-0.02	-0.04	-0.02	0.05	-0.01	-0.01
Moldavia	-0.02	-0.05	0.01	0.01	-0.01	-0.01
Southwest	-0.03	-0.32	-0.06	0.05	-0.11	-0.08
South	-0.07	-0.12	-0.04	0.01	-0.05	-0.06
Donetsk-Dnepr	0.04	0.31	-0.07	-0.03	0.05	0.05
North Caucasus	0.10	-0.20	-0.01	0.01	-0.06	0.01
Transcaucasus	0.01	-0.05	0.02	0.02	-0.00	0.00
Urals	0.03	0.25	0.15	-0.11	0.11	0.08
West Siberia	0.06	0.13	0.09	-0.06	0.06	0.06
East Siberia	0.03	0.09	0.04	-0.01	0.04	0.04
Far East	0.02	0.10	0.02	-0.02	0.03	0.03
Kazakhstan	0.02	0.10	0.07	0.06	0.07	0.05
Central Asia	-0.01	-0.07	0.05	0.07	0.02	0.01

Sources: See Chapter 1, nn. 104 and 105.

TABLE 2.8

Regional Distribution and Redistribution of the Rural Population
by Economic Region: 1897-1970

| Region | Percentage Distribution | | | | | Percentage Point Redistribution | | | | | |
	1897	1926	1939	1959	1970	1897–1926	1926–39	1939–59	1959–70	1926–70	1897–1970
Northwest	5.6	5.4	5.0	4.2	3.8	-0.2	-0.4	-0.8	-0.4	-1.6	-1.8
West	4.3	3.2	3.2	3.2	3.0	-1.1	0.0	0.0	-0.2	-0.2	-1.3
Center	11.9	11.9	11.2	9.0	7.5	0.0	-0.7	-2.2	-1.5	-4.4	-4.4
Volgo-Vyatsk	5.4	4.7	5.1	4.5	3.8	-0.7	0.4	-0.6	-0.7	-0.9	-1.6
Central Chernozem	6.8	7.0	6.5	5.3	4.6	0.2	-0.5	-1.2	-0.7	-2.4	-2.2
Volga	7.9	7.6	6.4	5.6	5.3	-0.3	-1.2	-0.8	-0.3	-2.3	-2.6
Belorussia	5.3	4.8	5.3	4.9	4.6	-0.5	0.5	-0.4	-0.3	-0.2	-0.7
Moldavia	1.2	1.2	1.6	1.9	2.1	0.0	0.4	0.3	0.2	0.9	0.9
Southwest	14.4	13.2	13.0	12.7	12.4	-1.2	-0.2	-0.3	-0.3	-0.8	-2.0
South	2.6	2.4	2.3	2.4	2.7	-0.2	-0.1	0.1	0.3	0.3	0.1
Donetsk-Dnepr	6.2	7.0	6.3	6.4	5.9	0.8	-0.7	0.1	-0.5	-1.1	-0.3
North Caucasus	5.0	5.1	5.3	5.7	6.3	0.1	0.2	0.4	0.6	1.2	1.3
Transcaucasus	3.6	3.3	4.2	4.7	5.6	-0.3	0.9	0.5	0.9	2.3	2.0
Urals	7.6	7.4	7.3	7.6	7.1	-0.2	-0.1	0.3	-0.5	-0.3	-0.5
West Siberia	1.6	3.9	4.0	4.2	3.6	2.3	0.1	0.2	-0.6	-0.3	2.0
East Siberia	1.8	2.3	2.8	3.4	3.5	0.5	0.5	0.6	0.1	1.2	1.7
Far East	0.3	0.9	1.2	1.8	1.8	0.6	0.3	0.6	0.0	0.9	1.5
Kazakhstan	4.2	4.0	3.3	4.7	5.9	-0.2	-0.7	1.4	1.2	1.9	1.7
Central Asia	4.3	4.5	6.0	7.7	10.6	0.2	1.5	1.7	2.9	6.1	6.3

Sources: See Chapter 1, nn. 104 and 105.

TABLE 2.9

Average Annual Percentage Point Redistribution of the Rural
Population by Economic Region: 1897-1970

Region	1897-1926	1926-39	1939-59	1959-70	1926-70	1897-1970
Northwest	-0.01	-0.03	-0.04	-0.04	-0.04	-0.02
West	-0.04	0.00	0.00	-0.02	-0.00	-0.02
Center	0.00	-0.06	-0.11	-0.14	-0.10	-0.06
Volgo-Vyatsk	-0.02	0.03	-0.03	-0.06	-0.02	-0.02
Central Chernozem	0.01	-0.04	-0.06	-0.06	-0.06	-0.03
Volga	-0.01	-0.10	-0.04	-0.03	-0.05	-0.04
Belorussia	-0.02	0.04	-0.02	-0.03	-0.00	-0.01
Moldavia	0.00	0.03	0.02	0.02	0.02	0.01
Southwest	-0.04	-0.02	-0.02	-0.03	-0.02	-0.03
South	-0.01	-0.01	0.01	0.03	0.01	0.00
Donetsk-Dnepr	0.03	-0.06	0.01	-0.05	-0.03	-0.00
North Caucasus	0.00	0.02	0.02	0.05	0.03	0.02
Transcaucasus	-0.01	0.07	0.03	0.08	0.05	0.03
Urals	-0.01	-0.01	0.02	-0.05	-0.01	-0.01
West Siberia	0.08	0.01	0.01	-0.05	-0.01	0.03
East Siberia	0.02	0.04	0.03	0.01	0.03	0.02
Far East	0.02	0.02	0.03	0.00	0.02	0.02
Kazakhstan	-0.01	-0.06	0.07	0.11	0.04	0.02
Central Asia	0.01	0.12	0.09	0.26	0.14	0.09

Sources: See Chapter 1, nn. 104 and 105.

MAP 2.13

Regional Distribution of Urban Population: 1897

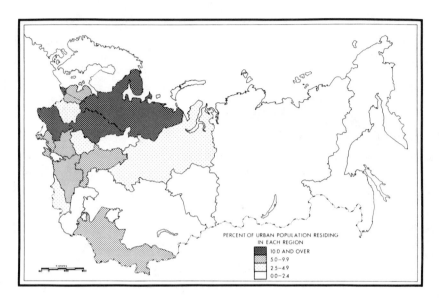

MAP 2.14

Regional Distribution of Urban Population: 1926

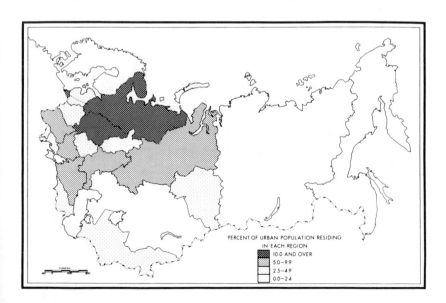

MAP 2.15

Regional Distribution of Urban Population: 1939

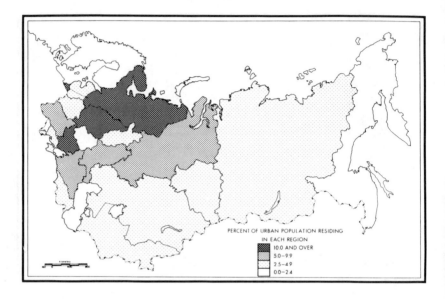

MAP 2.16

Regional Distribution of Urban Population: 1959

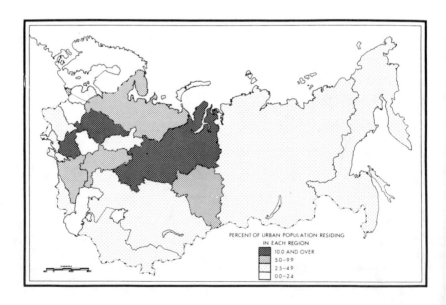

MAP 2.17

Regional Distribution of Urban Population: 1970

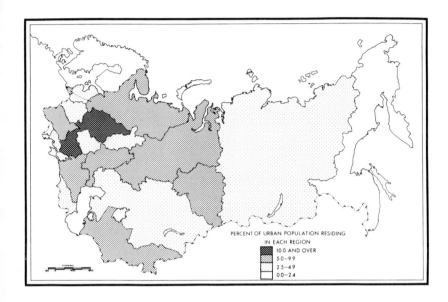

PERCENT OF URBAN POPULATION RESIDING
IN EACH REGION

▓	10.0 AND OVER
▒	5.0 – 9.9
░	2.5 – 4.9
☐	0.0 – 2.4

MAP 2.18

Regional Distribution of Rural Population: 1897

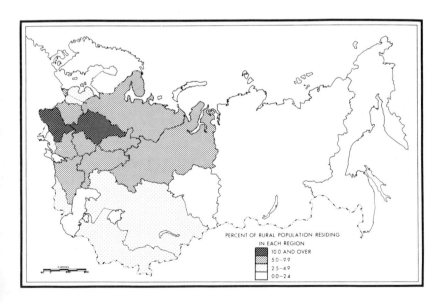

PERCENT OF RURAL POPULATION RESIDING
IN EACH REGION

▓	10.0 AND OVER
▒	5.0 – 9.9
░	2.5 – 4.9
☐	0.0 – 2.4

MAP 2.19

Regional Distribution of Rural Population: 1926

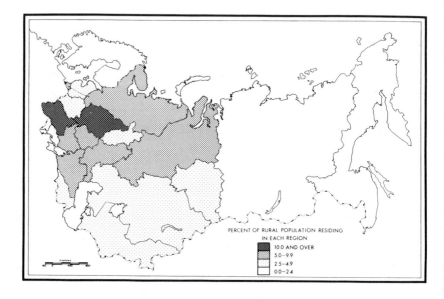

PERCENT OF RURAL POPULATION RESIDING
IN EACH REGION

- 10.0 AND OVER
- 5.0—9.9
- 2.5—4.9
- 0.0—2.4

MAP 2.20

Regional Distribution of Rural Population: 1939

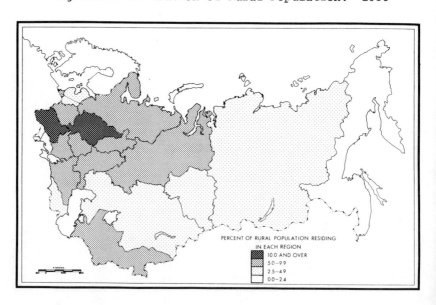

PERCENT OF RURAL POPULATION RESIDING
IN EACH REGION

- 10.0 AND OVER
- 5.0—9.9
- 2.5—4.9
- 0.0—2.4

MAP 2.21

Regional Distribution of Rural Population: 1959

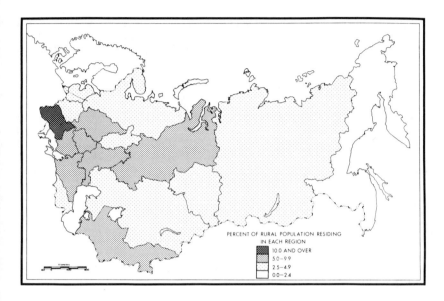

MAP 2.22

Regional Distribution of Rural Population: 1970

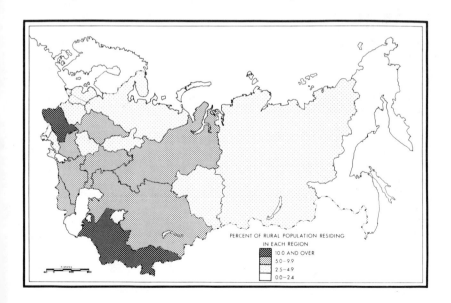

West. Until 1959, the Russian East and the Donetsk-Dnepr were areas of rapid urban growth and industrialization; between 1959 and 1970, however, there was a shift to the western areas of the USSR, particularly to the lesser developed regions, although Kazakhstan and Central Asia registered appreciable gains. There was also a shift in the urban population within Northern European USSR eastward to the Volgo-Vyatsk and the Volga regions. The maps portraying the distribution of the urban population (Maps 2.13-2.17) confirm these patterns; they first show a concentration of the urban population in the Western USSR, then a spreading eastward, and after 1959 a reversal of the eastward trend back to the Western USSR, in particular to such regions as the Central Chernozem, Belorussia, West, and Southwest.

As to the general patterns of the regional redistribution of the rural population, a general shift out of all regions comprising Northern European USSR to the south is discernible, largely as a result of the more rapid rural natural increase in the Non-Slavic South and considerable rural depopulation, particularly in recent years, in such northern areas as the RSFSR, Belorussia, and the West. Central Asia, Kazakhstan, Transcaucasus, North Caucasus, and Moldavia, all largely non-Slavic areas, have had relative increases in their proportion of the rural population and have yet to experience appreciable rural out-migration. These patterns are particularly evident in the 1959-70 period. Despite some decline, the Southwest continues to have the largest share of the rural population. Maps 2.18-2.22 graphically depict these patterns. From the distribution maps, one can see the relative shift in the location of the rural population from a concentration in Western USSR to the east, in particular the southeast.

General Patterns of Population Growth

Generally, there is a close correspondence between the average annual percentage change in a population and the redistribution of a population, but this relationship is not invariant, because rates of increase or decrease depend upon the base population, and thus a high rate of growth in a region with a very small population can result in very little redistribution of a population. It should be noted that obviously the average annual growth of the population is related to two factors: migration and natural increase.

Table 2.10 presents average annual growth or decline in the total population for gross regions. As was the case with the patterns of redistribution, there was a wide variation in rates of change, but in general they conform to the patterns of redistribution, at least in terms of comparing rankings. In particular, between 1897 and 1970 the Eastern USSR grew at more than twice the rate of the Western USSR, and Northern European USSR experienced the least growth and even a decline in the 1939-59 period.

The magnitude of the regional variations can be seen by comparing them with the growth of the total USSR population. Between 1897 and 1970, the population of the contemporary territory of the USSR did not quite double, increasing from about 125 million to almost 242 million or by 0.9 percent per

TABLE 2.10

Average Annual Percentage Change of the Total Population by Gross Region: 1897-1977

Region	1897–1926	1926–39	1939–59	1959–70	1926–70	1897–1970	1970–77
Western USSR	0.9	0.9	-0.0	1.1	0.5	0.7	0.7
Eastern USSR	1.5	2.0	1.5	1.8	1.7	1.6	1.5
Northern European USSR	0.7	0.7	-0.3	0.8	0.3	0.5	0.4
European Steppe	1.2	1.3	0.5	1.6	1.0	1.1	0.8
Russian East	1.8	2.2	1.4	0.9	1.5	1.6	0.7
Non-Slavic South	0.9	1.9	1.4	3.0	1.9	1.5	2.1
USSR total	1.0	1.2	0.4	1.3	0.8	0.9	1.0

Sources: See Chapter 1, nn. 104, 105, and 113.

TABLE 2.11

Crude Birth, Death, and Natural Increase Rates of Russia
and the USSR: 1896-1974

Year	Crude Birth Rate	Crude Death Rate	Crude Rate of Natural Increase
1896-1900	49.5	32.1	17.4
1901-1905	47.7	31.0	16.7
1926	44.0	20.3	23.7
1937-39	37.6	17.9	19.7
1953-55	25.8	8.7	17.1
1963-65	19.7	7.1	12.6
1966-68	17.6	7.5	10.1
1969-71	17.4	8.2	9.2
1972-74	17.8	8.6	9.2

Note: Data for the prerevolutionary period are for
European Russia; the 1926 data were not available for the
entire Soviet territory as of that date.

Sources: A. G. Rashin, Naseleniye Rossii za 100 Let
(Moscow: Gosstatizdat, 1956), pp. 168, 188, 218; USSR,
Narodnoye Khozyaystvo SSSR v 1974 G. (Moscow: "Statis-
tika," 1975), p. 44; and David M. Heer, "The Demographic
Transition in the Russian Empire and the Soviet Union,"
Journal of Social History 1 (Spring 1968): 207-12.

year. In the 1959-70 period, the average annual percentage increase of the
total USSR population was 1.3 percent (15.8 percent for the 11 years) and was
the highest for any intercensal period since 1897. The modest growth of the
Soviet population in this century is the result of huge population losses largely
because of war and the decline in natural increase. Direct and indirect
losses of population as a result of wars, famines, and economic disorganization approach 90 million people.[6] The higher rates of population growth between 1926 and 1939 and 1959 and 1970 can be explained largely by the absence of war. Furthermore, birth rates and rates of natural increase were
also relatively high during much of the 1926 to 1939 period, thus contributing
to relatively rapid growth and offsetting losses from famine and collectivization.

TABLE 2.12

Average Annual Percentage Change of the Total Population
by Economic Region: 1897-1977

Region	1897-1926	1926-39	1939-59	1959-70	1926-1970	1897-1970	1970-77
Northwest	0.9	1.5	-0.4	1.0	0.5	0.7	1.0
West	-0.0	0.3	0.2	1.2	0.4	0.2	1.0
Center	1.1	1.5	-0.1	0.7	0.6	0.8	0.4
Volgo-Vyatsk	0.5	1.5	-0.3	0.1	0.3	0.4	-0.1
Central Chernozem	1.0	-0.5	-0.9	0.3	-0.5	0.1	-0.4
Volga	0.8	-0.2	0.1	1.3	0.3	0.5	0.7
Belorussia	0.6	1.3	-0.5	1.0	0.4	0.5	0.7
Moldavia	1.0	1.5	0.8	2.0	1.3	1.2	1.2
Southwest	0.7	0.1	-0.4	0.7	0.0	0.3	0.4
South	0.7	0.4	0.2	2.1	0.8	0.7	1.4
Donetsk-Dnepr	1.4	1.7	0.6	1.2	1.0	1.2	0.7
North Caucasus	1.3	1.0	0.6	1.9	1.0	1.2	1.0
Transcaucasus	0.8	2.6	0.9	2.3	1.7	1.4	1.5
Urals	0.9	1.6	1.3	0.9	1.3	1.1	0.4
West Siberia	3.9	2.0	1.2	0.4	1.2	2.3	0.3
East Siberia	1.8	3.1	1.4	1.4	1.9	1.9	1.2
Far East	4.4	4.9	2.2	1.5	2.8	3.4	2.1
Kazakhstan	0.8	-0.1	2.1	3.1	1.7	1.4	1.5
Central Asia	1.1	2.7	1.3	3.4	2.2	1.8	2.8
USSR total	1.0	1.2	0.4	1.3	0.8	0.9	1.0

Sources: See Chapter 1, nn. 104, 105, and 113.

According to available data, during this century crude birth rates have declined more than crude death rates and thus crude natural increase has declined (Table 2.11). The most rapid decreases in rates of births, deaths, and natural increase occurred after World War II. By the 1960s and 1970s, regional variations in reported crude death rates were relatively slight, although there had been significant variations in the past. There was, however, considerable variation in reported crude birth rates. Most of the "European" population (Slavs, Latvians, Estonians, Jews, and so forth) were characterized by low fertility, and the Turkic and/or Muslim population, hereafter referred to as the Turkic-Muslims, generally have moderate to high fertility. There has been an increase in the regional variation in fertility in this century.

Since 1970, there has been a continuation of the 1959-70 trends in the regional growth of the total population, but the rates of growth have diminished, particularly in the Northern European USSR and the European Steppe (Table 2.10). The Non-Slavic South remained dominant with respect to growth.

Table 2.12 depicts the average annual increase or decrease in the total population by economic region. Between 1926 and 1970, variations in the rates of change for the economic regions comprising Northern European USSR were not great, and all were low relative to the USSR average. However, there was considerable variation in the rates over time; the 1939-59 period was generally characterized by a decrease in population in most economic regions of Northern European USSR. Relatively high rates of population growth were characteristic of economic regions comprising the Non-Slavic South and the Russian East, although there were significant regional and temporal variations. The regions comprising the European Steppe generally had rates above the USSR average. Since 1970, all regions, except the Far East, experienced a decline in their rates of growth as compared with the 1959-70 period. The most notable declines occurred in Kazakhstan, the North Caucasus, and the Transcaucasus, but Moldavia, the Central Chernozem, the South, the Volga, and Central Asia also registered appreciable declines. Since 1970, the Central Chernozem and the Volgo-Vyatsk are the only regions to experience a decline in their populations. Maps 2.23-2.29 show the patterns of differential regional growth, in particular the more rapid growth in the east.

The urban population (Tables 4.7 and 7.1) grew much more rapidly than the total or rural populations, which, of course, reflects the rapid industrialization and urbanization that has occurred especially since the late 1920s. Thus, the urban population grew more rapidly between 1926 and 1970 than between 1897 and 1970. The period of the greatest urban growth was 1926 to 1939, especially in the Russian East, which experienced the greatest overall growth of any region in this century, 10.7 percent, even though there has been a decline in this growth rate in recent years. Once again, as might be expected, a close relationship between average annual change and redistribution of the urban population can be observed.

An examination of the average annual growth rates of the urban population by economic region (Table 4.8 and Maps 4.12-4.17) highlights the very rapid urban growth that occurred particularly in some economic regions between 1926 and 1939. All of the regions of the Russian East, Kazakhstan, and

MAP 2.23

Change in Total Population: 1897-1926

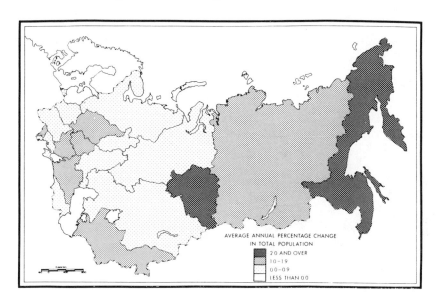

MAP 2.24

Change in Total Population: 1926-39

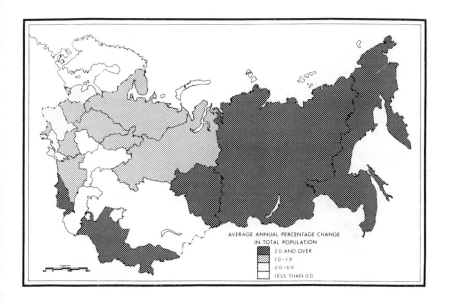

MAP 2.25

Change in Total Population: 1939-59

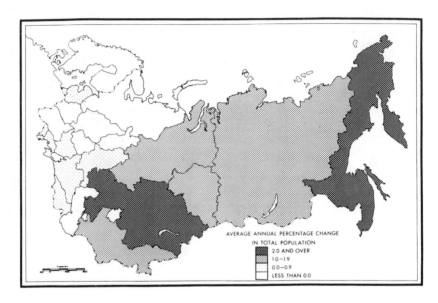

MAP 2.26

Change in Total Population: 1959-70

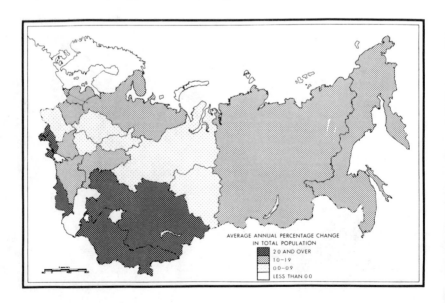

MAP 2.27

Change in Total Population: 1926-70

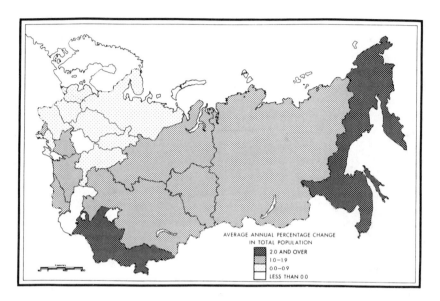

MAP 2.28

Change in Total Population: 1897-1970

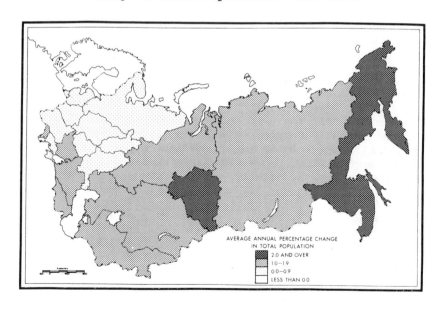

MAP 2.29

Change in Total Population: 1970-77

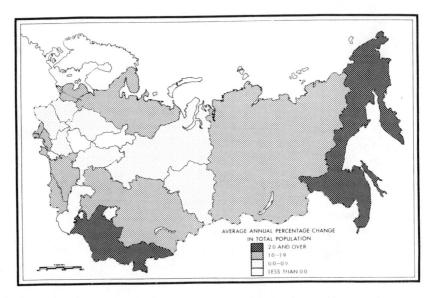

AVERAGE ANNUAL PERCENTAGE CHANGE
IN TOTAL POPULATION
2 0 AND OVER
1 0 - 1 9
0 0 - 0 9
LESS THAN 0 0

Volgo-Vyatsk increased at an average annual rate of over 10 percent per year, and the Donetsk-Dnepr grew almost 10 percent annually. Urban growth in the Center was also great, especially in absolute terms. Although the urban population of the USSR more than doubled during this period (increasing from about 22 million to almost 49 million), these rapidly growing regions grew considerably faster than the USSR urban population. The exceptionally rapid urban growth in some of the lesser developed regions can partially be explained by a low base urban population, but nevertheless their urban growth resulted in a considerable redistribution of the urban population. During the 1926-39 period, the slowest growth was in the western border regions that were partially or wholly outside the USSR during this period (Map 4.13). Urban growth during the 1939-59 period reflects the influence of the war (Map 4.14). Since 1959, the rate of growth in these regions has generally diminished and some western regions have increased, as the growth rate of the total urban population of the USSR has declined. Considerable temporal and regional variation can be observed, although it is less than that of the total population.

The rural population of the USSR increased at a very slow rate between 1897 and 1970, and since 1926 has declined (Table 7.2). This is not unexpected considering the economic and social change that has occurred in the USSR. In fact, it is surprising that there was not a greater decline in the rural population, considering the rapid rates of economic growth. More than 50 percent of the population of the USSR in 1970 still lived in centers with a population of fewer than 15,000. Clearly, there still remains a large reservoir of potential rural migrants. The main reason for this relatively large rural population is that the rural population of the Non-Slavic South is still growing fairly rapidly. Table 7.2, which depicts the average annual rates of increase or decrease by economic regions, indicates that most of the Slavic areas have experienced a considerable decline in the rural population largely as a result of rural out-migration, which is currently intensifying. The economic regions of Northern European Russia and the Russian East are notable examples. Much of the increase in the rural population of the European Steppe can be attributed to the growth of the rural population in Moldavia, the South, and the North Caucasus. In the South a large portion of the rural growth is related to nonagricultural pursuits, in particular, tourism. The growth rates for Central Asia and Kazakhstan between 1959 and 1970 are particularly notable. There is, once again, a correspondence between the regional average annual rates of change and the redistribution of the rural population, and whereas the Western USSR has had a declining rural population, the Eastern USSR has been characterized by a substantial growth in its rural population.

Aggregate Measures of Population Redistribution

The degree to which the Soviet population has redistributed since 1897 and whether it is becoming regionally more concentrated or dispersed are relevant considerations in the investigation of population distribution and redistribution in the USSR. Coefficients of redistribution and the dissimilarity index measure these characteristics of a population. The coefficient of redistribution measures changes in the distribution of a population or a population characteristic and is calculated by comparing the percentage distribution at one point in time with that of another point in time. The absolute value of the sum of either the positive or negative differences represents the coefficient of redistribution and can vary from 0 to 100, with 0 indicating no redistribution and 100 indicating complete redistribution.

Table 2.13 presents coefficients of redistribution for the total, urban, and rural populations, calculated on the basis of the economic regions. Once again, it should be recalled that the periods vary in duration, and thus the longer the period, the more redistribution might be expected. Since 1897 and 1926 there has been a considerable redistribution of the total, urban, and rural populations. The 16.9 coefficient for the total population since 1897 means that 16.9 percent of the 1970 population, or over 40 million people, would have to be shifted in order to reach the 1897 level. The urban population has had the greatest redistribution, which was especially high in the 1926-39 period. The rural population also experienced greater redistribution than the total population and its 1959-70 value was particularly notable. In terms of the average annual percentage point rate of redistribution of the total population, the 1897-1926 period had the slowest annual rate of redistribution, having less than half the rate of the other three intercensal periods. The 1926-39 period had the highest annual rate, 0.42, compared to 0.34 and 0.35

TABLE 2.13

Coefficients of Redistribution of the Total, Urban, and
Rural Populations of Russia and the USSR: 1897–1970

	Total	Urban	Rural
1897–1926	5.0	11.7	4.7
1926–39	5.1	15.0	4.8
1939–59	6.7	9.3	6.2
1959–70	3.9	4.1	6.2
1926–70	12.9	18.3	14.8
1897–1970	16.9	25.3	17.5
1970–77	2.0	—	—

Sources: See Chapter 1, nn. 104, 105, and 113.

for the 1939-59 and 1959-70 periods, respectively. The annual rate for the
1970-77 period (0.29) was somewhat lower than those for the 1926-70 period.
The highest rate for the urban population was 1.24 and occurred in the 1926-
39 period; the other intercensal periods ranged between 0.37 and 0.47. The
highest average annual rate, 0.56, for the rural population occurred in the
1959-70 period and the lowest, 0.16, was in the 1897-1926 period.

The dissimilarity index measures the degree of concentration or dispersal of a population, by comparing the percentage distribution of a population by region with the value that would represent an even regional distribution of the population—that is, an identical percentage of the population residing in each region. The dissimilarity index is the sum of either the positive or negative differences. A value of 0 indicates a uniform regional distribution of the population, and a value of 100, or almost 100, represents a
complete concentration of a population in one region. However, in the case
of a dissimilarity index based on the 19 economic regions, an additional refinement was necessary. Because an equal distribution here means 5.3 percent in each region (100.0 percent divided by 19), the sum of the percentages
is 100.7 (5.3 percent times 19), and there was a substantial difference between the positive and negative differences. Therefore, the dissimilarity
index here was calculated by summing the absolute values of the positive and
negative differences and dividing the sum by two. The Soviet economic regions vary considerably in area, so even if the index were 0, this does not
mean there is an even distribution by area. This index also does not take
into account variations in the distribution of a population within an economic
region, which, of course, can be and are considerable.

TABLE 2.14

Dissimilarity Indexes of the Total, Urban, and Rural
Populations of Russia and the USSR: 1897-1977

	1897	1926	1939	1959	1970	1977
Total	23.8	23.3	21.1	19.9	19.9	20.2
Urban	30.5	28.6	29.9	26.7	23.3	—
Rural	23.8	22.9	20.0	18.0	19.2	—

Sources: See Chapter 1, nn. 104, 105, and 113.

Nevertheless, Table 2.14 indicates that the trend in the USSR since
1897 has been a more nearly even distribution of the total, urban, and rural
populations in terms of the economic regions and that the population is closer
to being uniformly distributed regionally than it is to being highly concentrated.
This trend is in conformity with the Soviet policy of a more even distribution
of the Soviet population, even though this consideration has not received high
priority in their planning. Urbanization, of course, is a concentration of a
population; the urbanized areas of the USSR currently cover only about 0.3
percent of the USSR. [7] Regionally, however, there was a stronger trend
toward a uniformly distributed urban population than toward that of the total
or rural population, although the urban level was higher than that of the total
and rural population. The increase in the index of the urban population between 1926 and 1939 can probably be accounted for by the fact that much of
the urban growth occurred in established centers during this period. The increase in the index of the rural population between 1959 and 1970 reflects the
growth of the rural population in many southern areas and its decline elsewhere.

Population Redistribution: 1897-1926

The 1897-1926 period was an extremely chaotic one in Russian and Soviet history. World War I, the Revolution, the Civil War, foreign military
invasions, a drastic deterioration of the economy, food shortages, famine,
and epidemics resulted in mass migrations, major population losses, and a
sharp decline in natural increase. Data are insufficient to measure with any
reasonable precision the demographic effects of these catastrophic occurrences, particularly on a regional basis. Our major concern is migration
during this turbulent period when large segments of the population were displaced, because reliable data on regional natural increase are not available.

Migration

Elsewhere we have described and analyzed in detail migration from place-of-birth data presented in the 1897 and 1926 censuses.[8] To avoid unnecessary duplication, the results of these studies will be summarized briefly here. Patterns derived from the 1897 census are included, for comparative purposes, even though they apply to the period prior to 1897 and because migration patterns prior to 1897 were probably fairly similar to those in the decade or so after 1897. By 1926, prewar levels of production had been achieved again, largely as a result of the New Economic Policy, and economic and political conditions had become relatively stable. Therefore, this census provides a basis for evaluating the net effect of the chaotic conditions on internal migration. It should be pointed out also that neither the 1926 territory of the USSR nor the 1897 territory of Russia conform to the present-day territory of the USSR. Nevertheless, the relative magnitude and direction of migration for the periods prior to these censuses can be derived for an area only slightly different from the present-day territory of the USSR. It also should be mentioned that the data from these two censuses are not entirely comparable for four reasons: (1) by 1926 the political administrative structure of the USSR had been drastically altered, and in 1926 there were about twice as many political units as in 1897; (2) because of the territorial losses primarily along the western border, the area of the USSR in 1926 is not comparable to that of the Russian Empire in 1897; (3) the definition of intra-guberniya migration was somewhat different in the 1897 census from that of the 1926 census; and (4) the urban definition used in these censuses is not the same and is not based on a standard criterion, although the data are representative of predominantly urban areas.

Total In-Migration. According to the 1897 census, out of a population of 125,600,000 (which excluded the Finnish gubernii), 85.4 percent, or some 107,200,000 people, were classified as natives; that is, they lived in the same uyezd or city in which they were born. Although the area of the political units varies considerably, making it impossible to derive precisely comparable distances for the various types of migration, a reasonably good approximation of the distance of migration can be obtained from available census data. Local or intra-guberniya migration can be measured from data on the number of people who in 1897 were living in the same guberniya in which they had been born but who had moved across an uyezd or city boundary; 5.2 percent of the population of the Russian Empire, or some 6.5 million people, are included in this category. Inter-guberniya migration, or the number of people in 1897 living in a guberniya other than the one in which they were born (subsequently referred to as in-migration), exceeded intra-guberniya migration and totaled 9 percent of the population, or some 11.3 million people. The remaining 0.5 percent of the Russian population consisted of immigrants from foreign countries.

On a world basis, more migration usually occurs locally than over long distances; but according to the above data, migration in Russia prior to 1897 did not conform to this pattern. There was, however, considerably more

MAP 2.30

Total In-Migration: 1897

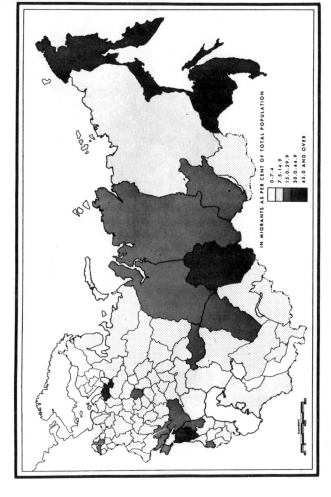

IN MIGRANTS AS PER CENT OF TOTAL POPULATION

0.7.4
7.5-14.9
15.0-29.9
30.0-44.9
45.0 AND OVER

MAP 2.31

Total In-Migration: 1926

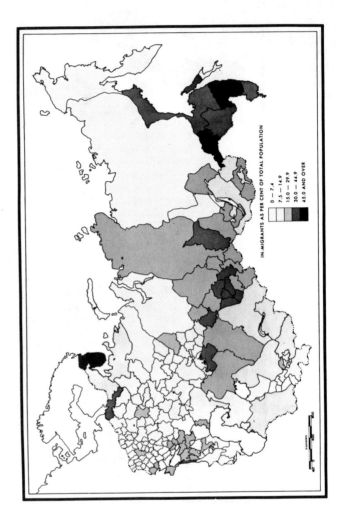

IN-MIGRANTS AS PER CENT OF TOTAL POPULATION

0 — 7.4
7.5 — 14.9
15.0 — 29.9
30.0 — 44.9
45.0 AND OVER

86

local migration in the Russian Empire than the data indicate, because a migrant who moved a short distance, but across a guberniya boundary, was included in the same category as one who moved across the entire country. However, on the basis of indexes of contiguous and linked gubernii, it was determined that 75 percent or more of the total, urban, and rural immigrants were from contiguous or linked gubernii.

There probably was relatively more migration in the period before 1926 than in the period before 1897. In 1926, out of a de facto population of 147,027,915, natives (those born in the same place or settlement in which they were enumerated) comprised 76 percent and migrants, 23.6 percent. According to data for the permanent population, 51.9 percent of the migrants were intra-guberniya migrants and 48.1 percent were in-migrants. The permanent population in the 1926 census refers to that population living permanently at the place of enumeration and born within the 1926 borders of the USSR, but it is not the de jure population because temporary residents were not allocated to their places of permanent residence. There was also considerable migration to contiguous and linked units in the period prior to the 1926 census, although slightly less than in 1897. More than 50 percent of the migrant-survivors migrated between 1917 and 1926 and 22.7 percent in the previous three years.

A regional investigation of total in-migration in 1897 reveals that the gubernii in European Russia, roughly north of the steppe, had few in-migrants in proportion to their total population; generally less than 7 percent of the population of each of these gubernii was born in other gubernii (Map 2.30). The steppe and southern Siberia were the areas of greatest in-migration, and here the proportion of the in-migrants to the total population of most political units generally ranged from 12 to 33 percent. In the Far East very high relative gains, from 39 to 72 percent, were characteristic, primarily because of their small populations rather than because of a large number of in-migrants. Migration to the political divisions of the Transcaucasus and Central Asia was not great, generally less than 10 percent.

Regional patterns of total in-migration derived from place-of-birth data in the 1926 census are strikingly similar to those derived from place-of-birth data in the 1897 census. With few exceptions, the European USSR roughly north of the steppe was an area with few in-migrants—generally fewer than 7.5 percent of its total population (Map 2.31). Political units in the steppe from the western border to the Altay Mountains and southern Siberia had proportionately many more migrants. The North Caucasus and southern West Siberia were areas of particularly intense in-migration. In the northern areas, Soviet Central Asia, and the Transcaucasus, there were relatively few in-migrants. The patterns of total in-migration from the 1926 census conform closely to the trends in the redistribution and growth of the total population between 1897 and 1926.

Urban In-Migration. According to the 1897 census, migration to urban areas was less than to rural areas but constituted a relatively large share of the total migration. Of the intra-guberniya migrants, 40 percent went to urban

MAP 2.32

Urban In-Migration: 1897

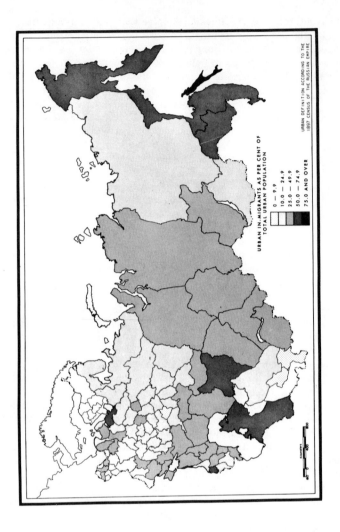

URBAN IN-MIGRANTS AS PER CENT OF
TOTAL URBAN POPULATION

0 — 9.9
10.0 — 24.9
25.0 — 49.9
50.0 — 74.9
75.0 AND OVER

URBAN DEFINITION ACCORDING TO THE
1897 CENSUS OF THE RUSSIAN EMPIRE

MAP 2.33

Urban In-Migration: 1926

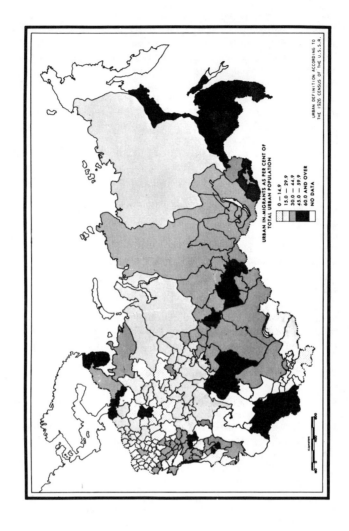

URBAN IN-MIGRANTS AS PER CENT OF
TOTAL URBAN POPULATION

0 — 14.9
15.0 — 29.9
30.0 — 44.9
45.0 — 59.9
60.0 AND OVER
NO DATA

URBAN DEFINITION ACCORDING TO
THE 1926 CENSUS OF THE U.S.S.R.

areas; of the inter-guberniya migrants, 44.4 percent; and of the foreign migrants, 36.8 percent. The gubernii in the area north of the steppe in European Russia, excluding the more urbanized gubernii, had few in-migrants relative to their total population, but in the aggregate, 59 percent of the total urban in-migrants moved into the urban centers of this area (Map 2.32). In relative terms the greatest urban in-migration occurred in the European Steppe, Stepnoy Kray, Siberia, and the Far East, but these areas had only about 23 percent of the urban in-migrants.

Although only somewhat more than 33 percent of the migrants went to urban areas in the period prior to 1926, migrants constituted 49 percent of the urban population, and this was 2.4 percentage points or over 5 million migrants more than in 1897. About 66 percent of the urban migrants in both 1897 and 1926 were from other gubernii. Relatively low urban in-migration rates were characteristic of the Northern European USSR prior to the 1926 census, where migrants comprised less than 15 percent of the urban population of most political units (Map 2.33). In absolute terms, however, this was where the bulk of the urban in-migration occurred. Urban in-migration proportions were the highest in the steppe and southern Siberia, but these areas had relatively small urban populations. As might be expected, patterns of urban in-migration generally conform to the trends in the redistribution and growth of the urban population between 1897 and 1926.

Rural In-Migration. Prior to 1897, there was more rural migration than urban migration with respect to both intra-guberniya and inter-guberniya migration, constituting 60 percent of the former and 55.6 percent of the latter. Relative to the rural population there was little rural in-migration to gubernii north of the steppe in European Russia, the chief area of out-migration. It was normally less than 5 percent of the rural population of each guberniya (Map 2.34). In the European Steppe, Stepnoy Kray, Siberia, and the Far East, rural in-migration was relatively much greater, but in absolute terms these gubernii had many fewer migrants than those in the chief area of out-migration. In Central Asia and the Transcaucasus rural in-migration was slight.

Prior to 1926, the majority of the migrants, 62.9 percent, went to rural areas, and according to the migrant data for the permanent population, almost 66 percent of these were intra-guberniya migrants. Nevertheless, only 18.1 percent of the rural population were migrants. Prior to 1897, a smaller percentage, 57.4, of the total migrants went to rural areas, and they comprised only 9.7 percent of the rural population.

Rural in-migration percentages prior to 1926 were normally low in the European USSR but were higher in a few units of the southern Ukraine and in the North Caucasus (Map 2.35). The greatest rural in-migration occurred in the eastern steppe and southern Siberia, where up to 40 percent of the rural population were migrants. Elsewhere in the USSR, there was little rural in-migration. These patterns support the trends in redistribution and growth of the rural population.

MAP 2.34

Rural In-Migration: 1897

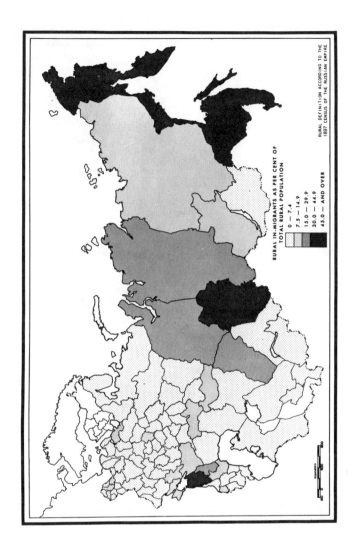

RURAL IN-MIGRANTS AS PER CENT OF
TOTAL RURAL POPULATION

0 — 7.4
7.5 — 14.9
15.0 — 29.9
30.0 — 44.9
45.0 — AND OVER

RURAL DEFINITION ACCORDING TO THE
1897 CENSUS OF THE RUSSIAN EMPIRE

MAP 2.35

Rural In—Migration: 1926

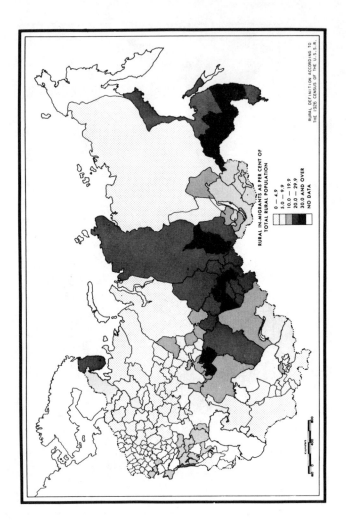

RURAL IN-MIGRANTS AS PER CENT OF
TOTAL RURAL POPULATION

0 — 4.9
5.0 — 9.9
10.0 — 19.9
20.0 — 29.9
30.0 AND OVER
NO DATA

RURAL DEFINITION ACCORDING TO
THE 1926 CENSUS OF THE U.S.S.R.

MAP 2.36

Total Out-Migration: 1897

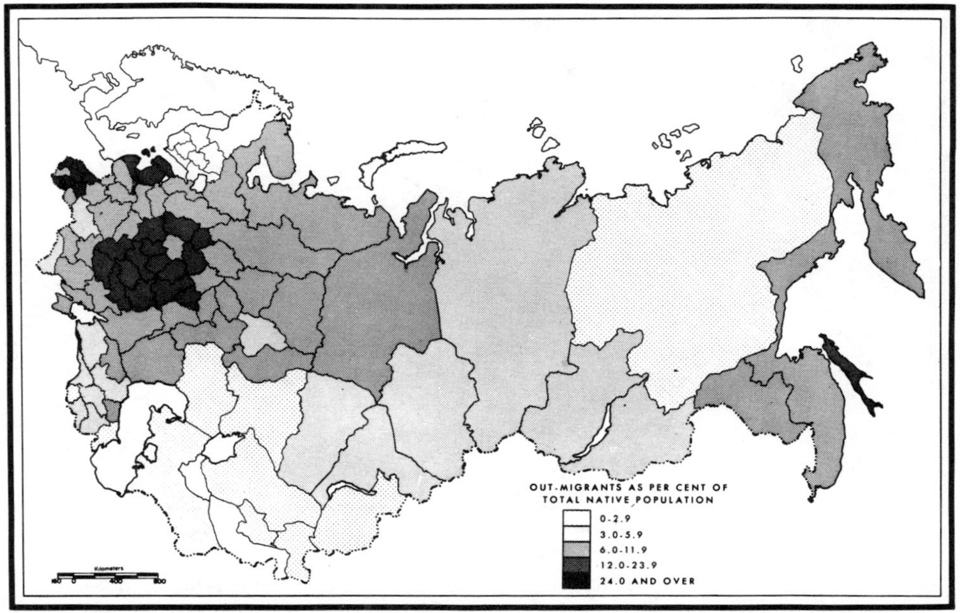

OUT-MIGRANTS AS PER CENT OF
TOTAL NATIVE POPULATION

0 - 2.9
3.0 - 5.9
6.0 - 11.9
12.0 - 23.9
24.0 AND OVER

MAP 2.37

Total Out—Migration: 1926

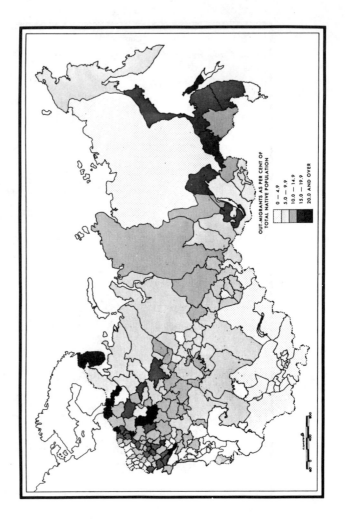

OUT-MIGRANTS AS PER CENT OF
TOTAL NATIVE POPULATION

0 — 4.9
5.0 — 9.9
10.0 — 14.9
15.0 — 19.9
20.0 AND OVER

Total Out-Migration. Prior to the 1897 census, total out-migration comprised 9.8 percent of the total native guberniya population. There were no data in the 1897 census as to out-migration from urban and rural areas. The gubernii roughly north of the steppe in European Russia that had relatively few in-migrants comprised the chief area of out-migration (Map 2.36). Elsewhere in the empire out-migration was generally much less than in central European Russia.

There were relatively and absolutely more total out-migrants prior to 1926 than prior to 1897. The European USSR, excluding the North Caucasus and a few gubernii along the western border, was the chief area of out-migration (Map 2.37). Because the area north of the steppe in the European USSR had relatively few in-migrants compared to out-migrants, most gubernii in this area experienced a net loss in population through migration. In the southern Ukraine, however, high in-migration rates canceled out the effect of the high out-migration rates. Elsewhere out-migration rates were generally low, except in the eastern part of Siberia, which, too, had particularly high in-migration rates. Both of these rates were affected by the small populations of most of the political units in Siberia. No data are available in the 1926 census on urban and rural out-migration by guberniya.

Frank Lorimer has attempted to establish the major migration streams based upon 29 census districts as presented in the 1926 census and net flows derived from place-of-birth data. The most important stream was from European USSR to the Urals, Siberia, and the Far East and totaled 2.7 million persons. Another important stream to the east was from European USSR to Kazakhstan and Central Asia, which accounted for some 900,000 persons. Net migration according to place-of-birth data from northern European USSR and the western Ukraine to the Donetsk and Caucasus areas, in particular the North Caucasus, totaled 1.2 million "net" migrants. Another major stream, 540,000 net migrants, occurred primarily from northern European USSR southwest to the western Ukraine. Migration from European USSR to the Central Industrial and Leningrad-Karelia regions formed two streams with a total of 662,000 migrants.[9]

Analysis of Migration Patterns

In the studies cited, an attempt was made to test the hypothesis that migrants moved to areas of higher income. Because income data were scant, income differences were approximated from such substitute variables as work force, literacy, urbanization, and several agricultural variables, which were correlated by guberniya with measures of migration. In general, in the periods prior to both the 1897 and 1926 censuses, it can be inferred from the correlations and other data that there was a tendency for people to move to areas with a higher standard of living, although it must be acknowledged that many of the correlation coefficients were relatively low. In short, people were generally moving out of agriculture into relatively urban, industrial, and literate areas, or to rural areas with a higher sown acreage per person and per household and with greater net agricultural production per person.

One might expect that prior to 1926 the patterns of migration would be substantially different than patterns prior to 1897, because millions of people were displaced by the tumultuous events that occurred after 1914. Yet, there was a remarkable similarity in the migration patterns of the two periods, the chief areas of out-migration and in-migration were roughly the same, and the dominant migratory streams from Northern European USSR to the European Steppe and to the east persisted, despite the chaotic conditions. This, of course, demonstrates the strength of major migratory flows and indicates that the underlying conditions that promoted this migration were still in effect. This was further demonstrated by the fact that in both periods there was a tendency for people to move to areas of higher income as measured by surrogate variables. Of course, that the economy had been rehabilitated by 1926 and a large percentage of the migrants moved in the period immediately prior to 1926 were important factors in the explanation of the persistence of these migratory trends. Given the chaotic conditions, it is reasonable to assume that there was little governmental control over migration during this period.

Sources of Population Redistribution: 1897-1926

It is impossible to isolate the relative contribution of migration and natural increase to the regional population redistribution that occurred between 1897 and 1926, because of a lack of data on both migration and natural increase. Before the Revolution, data were inadequate for this purpose. Vital statistics were collected largely for European Russia, and official regional population estimates were derived without taking migration into consideration. During the war and Revolution, data collection was seriously disrupted. The catastrophic population losses and decline in natural increase that resulted from wars, famines, and epidemics cannot be accurately estimated or apportioned regionally and drastically affected the redistribution of the Russian and Soviet populations. There was also emigration from the Russian Empire. Between 1897 and 1914, net emigration from European Russia, including the North Caucasus, has been estimated at 1.3 million persons.[10] Most of this emigration was from the western border areas, and Jews predominated in this migration. A rather broad zone along the western border of Russia from the Gulf of Finland to the Black Sea formed a migratory watershed. To the west of this zone migrants went westward, usually to the United States; to the east they went eastward, mainly beyond the Urals; and in the zone along the border they tended to go both directions.[11] Net migration from European Russia to Asiatic Russia between 1897 and 1914 has been estimated at 3.6 million.[12] Between 1897 and 1926, the population of the present-day territory of the USSR increased by 34.2 percent from 125 to 167.7 million people.

There have been a number of estimates of population losses on the post-World War I territory of the USSR, which exclude the western territories acquired after World War II. These estimates are rather gross approximations and vary depending upon the 1914 population and expected rate of natural increase accepted by the investigators. Using different criteria for both of these factors, E. Z. Volkov and Frank Lorimer estimate a population deficient for the total USSR in 1926 boundaries of 28 million between 1914 and

1927.[13] Lorimer allocates this loss according to the following: emigration, 2 million; civilian deaths, 14 million; military deaths, 2 million; and birth deficit, 10 million. Eugene Kulischer estimates the excess mortality of this period at 12 million rather than 16 million and apportions the losses as follows: military losses during World War I, 2 million; military and civilians killed during the Civil War, 1.5 million; epidemics during the Civil War, 2 million; the famine of 1922-23, 3 million; and the remainder are attributed to a general increase in mortality. His estimate of the total loss is between 20 and 23 million, with emigration accounting for about 1.5 million and a birth deficit of from 9 to 10 million.[14] B. Ts. Urlanis has estimated the birth deficit for the World War I period of the present-day territory of the USSR at 7 million, whereas other Soviet scholars have estimated it as high as 9 to 10 million.[15] E. Z. Volkov estimates epidemic losses between 1914 and 1923 in European Russia at 3.3 million.[16]

In addition to these losses, many people were displaced by war and famine. Registered refugees from the war zones to other parts of Russia at the end of May 1916 were enumerated at 3.3 million, and officially sanctioned refugees from the famine of 1922-23, who had permission to travel on the railroad from July 1921 to July 1922, totaled over 850,000.[17] These figures, of course, are only a part of the migration resulting from war and famine. At the beginning of the war, Russia had a standing army of 1.4 million and during the war another 14.4 million were mobilized, which led to a further redistribution of the population.[18]

Most of these estimates as to population losses and redistribution are gross and do not include the western areas of present-day USSR. Nevertheless, population losses were truly mind-boggling and waves of humanity were put into motion. Although these losses cannot be apportioned regionally with any precision, it can be assumed that the European USSR suffered the greatest losses. The total population in 1926 boundaries increased slightly between 1914 and 1918 and thereafter decreased rather sharply. Based on crude procedures, Volkov estimates that between 1914 and 1918 only the North Caucasus and Turkestan suffered population losses, but between 1918 and 1923 the population of European USSR declined by almost 7 million and the population of the total USSR declined by more than 7 million persons.[19] The famine of 1922-23 affected some 33 gubernii with a population of over 40 million. Although the Volga-Ural area suffered the worst, the Ukraine, Crimea, North Caucasus, and Kirgizia also suffered greatly.[20] Some 3 million starved, about an additional million died of epidemics, and there was mass out-migration.[21] Civil War campaigns also were conducted largely in European USSR and the North Caucasus, and the German and Austrian armies occupied the Ukraine for a short period after 1918. Millions left the border areas that were lost after the war.

These general trends can be roughly observed in Tables 2.10 and 2.12 and Map 2.23. However, these patterns are affected by the rather rapid population increase between 1897-1914 (regionally the population grew by a third or more) and by the significant migration that occurred immediately prior to 1926, when conditions had more or less normalized. The western border area stands out as an area of particularly slow population growth, largely as a result of out-migration during and after occupation. From the West Region, Jews and others were evacuated during the war, refugees fled, Germans were repatriated, and Russians emigrated when the Baltic states became independent.[22] Siberia and the Far East grew fairly rapidly because they were not affected seriously by war and famine and they were a major area of in-migration. The North Caucasus grew relatively rapidly even though it was a major battle area during the Civil War and suffered famine losses. There was major migration to this region before 1914 and probably after the famine, in that it has a much higher than expected growth. The slow growth in the Volga and Volgo-Vyatsk, as well as in the South, probably reflects famine losses. Kazakhstan and Central Asia also suffered major population losses. Turkestan had a particularly sharp decrease in population between 1914 and 1918, over a million according to Volkov.[23] There was a draft rebellion in 1916, which was caused by efforts to mobilize the native population for labor at the front and was severely suppressed. Many emigrated and many died as a result of the hostilities. In 1917 there was a severe famine in Turkestan. The population in many areas declined sharply, 25 percent or more, as a result of famine and rebellion.[24] For both the urban and rural populations, growth was the slowest in Northern European USSR, and the fastest in the Russian East. The Donetsk-Dnepr and the North Caucasus had rather high rates (Tables 4.7, 4.8, 7.1, 7.2 and Maps 4.12 and 7.1). Some redistribution occurred between urban and rural areas in that the urban population grew at about twice the rate of the rural population.

In Tables 2.1 and 2.2 and Maps 2.1, 2.2, and 2.6 the net redistributional patterns substantiate the gross regional trends in population growth between 1897 and 1926. There was a major shift in the distribution of the total population away from Northern European USSR and almost all regions within it to the European Steppe and the Russian East. The share of the Non-Slavic South declined slightly because of population losses. Even though there are insufficient data to document the assertion, migration may have been the chief source of population redistribution. The Revolution and the Civil War led to the disruption of the economy and, especially, to the importation of grain from the steppe to the northern areas of European USSR, and major food shortages resulted. Millions of people left the cities of the north for rural areas, in particular to the south and east, although the German occupation of the Ukraine temporarily interrupted this migration. Many rural inhabitants of the north also went south and east. In addition, millions of people were displaced by foreign occupation of the western border areas and the Civil War. After 1920, there was a mass migration out of famine areas to cities, particularly in Northern European USSR, and to areas where food was available. This was followed by reflux from the eastern regions back to the West, partially because the Russian population was driven out by the indigenous population.[25] In short, much of the population of the USSR was on the move during this period, and gross indicators of redistribution can show only rather crudely the net results of the mass migrations and population losses that occurred during this period.

Nevertheless, Tables 2.4 and 2.5 indicate a significant shift of both the urban and rural populations out of Northern European USSR primarily to the Russian East but also to the European Steppe. Rank correlation coefficients based on the economic regions indicate that total population redistribution and growth were highly associated (0.952), but rural population redistribution (0.964) was related more closely to total population redistribution than was urban redistribution (0.635). Total population growth also was related more closely to rural growth (0.963) than urban growth (0.511). This reflects the numerical dominance of the rural population.

The effect of natural increase on population redistribution during this period, however, should not be discounted. There are official vital statistics for the 1926-27 period for the boundaries of that period, but they are of very dubious reliability and cover mainly the Slavic areas.[26] It would appear from these data that by 1926 crude birth rates tended to be uniformly rather high, generally over 40 per thousand, although there had been some decline, at least in the western areas, since the turn of the century. Fertility in Latvia and Estonia, which were outside the USSR, was at relatively low levels. Crude death rates were generally in the moderate range, although it would appear that there was considerable underreporting. One might hypothesize, however, that mortality declined first in the Slavic areas and probably remained at traditional levels in most of the non-Slavic areas. Nevertheless, regional variations in natural increase during this period were probably not great, discounting losses due to war, mobilization, epidemic, and famine. Because losses due to these events were greater in the Western USSR than the Eastern USSR, regional patterns of natural increase probably contributed to the redistribution of the population to the east. The net emigration from the western areas also supported this trend.

Population Redistribution: 1926-39

There are also insufficient data to measure migration and regional natural increase in the 1926-39 period. However, because there was no major war and accompanying population losses during this period and the period is of shorter duration, measures of regional population redistribution and change are more useful in portraying the patterns of population redistribution in this period than in the previous one. A major famine did occur in 1932-33 in the Ukraine, the lower Volga, the North Caucasus, and Western Siberia, and collectivization and the settling of the nomads undoubtedly caused an appreciable loss of life. Using available fertility and mortality data and the 1926 and 1939 census populations, Frank Lorimer estimated a population deficit of some 5 million lives with respect to expected natural increase.[27] He acknowledges that this estimate is crude, given the data limitations. Famine losses were probably in the millions, although there are no firm estimates.[28] As a result of the settling of the nomads and the agricultural colonization of Kazakhstan, the Kazakh population of the USSR declined from almost 4 million in 1926 to barely more than 3 million in 1939. Considering natural increase, the total loss was perhaps 1.5 million. Several tens of thousands of Kazakhs emigrated to China.[29] Even though these losses are appreciable, they do not compare with the losses in the 1897-1926 period, and patterns of population redistribution between 1926-39 were affected much less by catastrophic events. Between 1926 and 1939, the population of the present-day territory increased by 15.1 percent from 167.7 million to 193 million.

Even though data are insufficient to measure migration and regional natural increase for this period, it can be stated that urban in-migration was probably the predominant source of population redistribution between 1926 and 1939. The urban population grew very rapidly at an average annual rate of 6.5 percent, whereas the rural population declined slightly. Thus, there was an appreciable redistribution of population between urban and rural areas. In absolute terms, the urban population in centers of 15,000 or more increased from slightly more than 22 million in 1926 to almost 49 million in 1939, or by 26.5 million, which was more than 2 million per year. The percentage of the population living in urban centers almost doubled, increasing from about 13 percent to 25 percent. According to the official definitions of urban almost 66 percent of the urban growth was the result of rural-to-urban migration.[30]

Conditions in the USSR during this period were highly conducive to rural out-migration and are generally well known, at least in their broad outline. This was the period of extremely rapid forced industrialization, which produced high rates of industrial growth and provided urban employment opportunities on a massive scale. At the beginning of the period, there was, as in the past, a large surplus agricultural population, variously estimated at from 9 to 20 million people, and conditions of life in rural areas were very poor, even though there had been a redistribution of land.[31] The rapid forced collectivization of agriculture resulted in a complete breakdown of the rural economy, which was related very probably to the famine of 1932-33 that further stimulated out-migration. Hundreds of thousands of kulaks were deported and perhaps millions fled.[32] Livestock herds, including draft animals, were reduced drastically, falling to below 50 percent of their former level. Agricultural mechanization, particularly in the latter part of the period, greatly reduced labor requirements, contributing to the excess rural population. The government took much of the agricultural production at low prices to feed the growing urban population and to provide raw materials for industry. In short, economic conditions worsened considerably in rural areas and at times were very chaotic, whereas ample employment opportunities were being created in the cities. The response was massive out-migration from the impoverished rural areas to the cities.[33]

Government-sponsored migration to the rural areas of the east to lessen the density of the rural population of European USSR was limited during this period, even though agricultural colonization had been resumed during the late 1920s. Between 1925 and 1929 some 900,000 migrants were transplanted to the east, but this does not include those that went without official sanction. They mainly left areas where agricultural income was the lowest and industrialization was insufficient to absorb the surplus rural population, such as the Ukraine (probably the western part), the Central Chernozem, the Middle

Volga, and Belorussia. After 1930, this type of migration declined sharply but rose somewhat in the late 1930s. Between 1938 and 1940, about 170,000 families participated in officially sponsored rural colonization.[34] Once again, many more very probably migrated on their own initiative.

Vital statistics are available for 1940 by economic region and oblasts or equivalent units, but they are also of dubious reliability. For example, in 1970 it was reported that until the 1950s, underregistration of births in Central Asia was between 10 and 25 percent and both births and deaths were still being underreported.[35] Since the 1958-59 period, the reported net reproduction rate has increased considerably in Central Asia; in Tadzhikistan it rose from 1.7 percent in the 1958-59 period to 2.7 percent in the 1972-73 period.[36] Since 1940, the crude birth rate has risen unexpectedly in a number of other areas. In 1940, the reported crude death rate in Central Asia (14.5 per thousand) and the Transcaucasus (12.0) was significantly below that of the RSFSR (20.6), the Central Region (18.9), or the national average (18.0). The reported crude birth rate of the RSFSR (33.0 per thousand) was above the national average (31.2), about the same as Central Asia, and above that of the Transcaucasus (30.4).[37] During this period, one might have expected crude death and birth rates to be significantly lower in the more developed and urbanized parts of the USSR, even if differences in the age structure are taken into account.

Nevertheless, according to the 1940 data, the crude natural increase rate for the USSR was 13.2 per thousand. The Baltic, Northwest, Center, Volgo-Vyatsk, and Central Chernozem regions were below the national average, and the Ukraine, Belorussia, and the other regions of Western USSR were generally close to it. The Eastern USSR was growing through natural increase at a rate of about five points per thousand faster than the national average. Thus, it would appear that by 1940 regional differentials in reported natural increase supported the patterns of population redistribution, although available data should be viewed with considerable skepticism.

From data on average annual rates of growth or decline (Tables 2.10, 2.12, 4.7, 4.8, 7.1, and 7.2 and Maps 2.24, 4.13, and 7.2), the general pattern of regional population growth can be derived and reasonable inferences can be made. Between 1926 and 1939, the total population of Northern European USSR grew well below the national average, although it accounted for about a third of the total growth, and all other major regions grew well above it (Table 2.10). With respect to the urban population, Northern European USSR also grew the slowest, even though its urban population almost doubled and accounted for over 45 percent of the urban growth of the USSR during this period. There was considerable rural depopulation in Northern European USSR, because the rural population declined at an average annual rate of 0.3 percent, or by some 4 million, and although the total population increased by about 8.5 million, the urban population increased by over 12 million. The urban population of the European Steppe also grew faster than the total population, and there was also a decline in the rural population. The Russian East experienced phenomenal urban growth, even though in absolute terms it was only 50 percent that of Northern European USSR. The growth of the rural population of the Russian East was very modest, 0.4 percent per year, which was well below its natural increase; thus, most migrants to the east went to urban areas, and there was considerable out-migration from the rural areas of the east. According to Soviet estimates, about 4.7 million migrants moved east, including Kazakhstan and Central Asia, between 1926 and 1939, of which about 3 million moved to the Russian East.[38] Even though the Non-Slavic South experienced a rate of urban growth that was close to the national average, this was the outstanding area in terms of rural population growth, and its rural population grew by more than 2 million or about 1 percent per year. Considerable urbanization, however, did occur because the urban rate of growth was much higher than that of the rural.

In terms of the economic regions, the most notable occurrences are the declines in the total population of the Central Chernozem, the Volga, and Kazakhstan. The decline in Kazakhstan can be explained by the tremendous losses of life that resulted from the settling of the nomads and agricultural colonization. The Central Chernozem and the Volga have been traditional areas of excess rural population. Their proximity to major areas of urban growth, both to the north and south, probably accounts for their losses of population (Map 2.24), although famine losses also could have been influential. All of the losses were in their rural populations. The economic regions in European USSR that had the greatest growth in population were generally those that experienced the greatest urban growth, because the rural population generally declined in European USSR. In fact, the regions with the greatest declines in rural population were the regions of outstanding urban growth. Notable examples are the Northwest, the Center, and the Donetsk-Dnepr, which were major regions of urban growth. During this period, Moscow grew by some 2 million and Leningrad by 1.5 million. The decline in the urban population of Moldavia can be explained by the fact that Moldavia was largely outside the USSR during this period and did not benefit from the rapid industrialization that occurred in the USSR. Moreover, the Romanian government deemphasized the industrialization of Bessarabia, the province that comprises most of the present-day Moldavian SSR.[39] The West was also outside the USSR during this period and, thus, was not influenced by developments in the USSR. The rapid rate of urban growth of the Volgo-Vyatsk can be explained largely by its low urban population and not by the fact that it was a major region of urban growth. The urban growth patterns will be further analyzed in subsequent chapters.

Patterns of redistribution between 1926 and 1939 are not as pronounced as the rates of change, although there is a correspondence between the two measures, because they are measured by percentage point change, which is not influenced by differences in the base population. With respect to the total population, there was a shift out of Northern European USSR, particularly to the Russian East, which experienced the greatest increase in the share of the total population (Table 2.1). The Non-Slavic South also had an appreciable relative gain. With respect to the urban population, all major regions, except the Russian East, registered a decline in their share of the total urban population (Table 2.4). The Russian East, however, had only a modest increase in its share of the rural population, indicating that most of its population growth was in the urban sector, and the major redistribution of the rural population was to the Non-Slavic South (Table 2.5).

Redistribution according to economic regions conforms to the average annual rates of change by economic region (Tables 2.2, 2.6, and 2.8 and Maps 2.2, 2.3, and 2.7). As might be expected, total population redistribution and total population growth were highly related (a rank correlation coefficient of 0.952), but the rural population redistribution (0.521) and the urban redistribution (0.487) show considerably less correlation. With respect to total population, redistribution diminished as compared to the 1897-1926 period. The relationship between total population growth and rural (0.670) and urban (0.483) growth also diminished. The relatively low correlation between the total and urban populations occurred chiefly because Kazakhstan had rapid urban growth but total and rural population decline, due to the substantial population losses experienced by the nomadic Kazakhs. The regions of rural loss with little urban growth had the greatest relative losses in terms of total population redistribution. Particularly notable is Kazakhstan, which experienced a sharp loss in its rural population, but a significant gain in its urban population. However, the rural loss outweighed the urban gain, and its share of the total USSR population declined. With respect to their share of the total, urban, and rural populations, most western regions declined and most eastern regions increased.

In general, the 1926-39 period was a period characterized by a major redistribution of the population from rural areas to urban areas and the continued relative shift of the population to the east, particularly with respect to the urban population. The patterns of rural population change (with declines or slow increases in most western regions and the greatest growth in the Non-Slavic South) that were established in this period have continued and intensified to the present. It would appear that the traditional shift of the population, especially the rural population, from Northern European USSR to the European Steppe gradually ceased, as rural areas in the steppe were filled and as an industrial-urban economy replaced the traditional agrarian economy. This period marks the beginning of the rapid modernization of Soviet society, and population redistribution in this period (and for that matter from this point on) was related to a predominant degree to the modernization and industrialization of the USSR. The rapid industrialization and unprecedented rate of urbanization that occurred during this period greatly reduced the excess rural population, which had been a perennial societal problem in Russia and the USSR, and resulted in a massive shift to more productive pursuits. Yet in 1940, surplus labor on kolkhozy was still estimated at about 5 million workers.[40]

Population Redistribution: 1939-59

Truly horrendous war losses and a lack of data on migration and regional natural increase make it very difficult to analyze the population redistribution that occurred during this period. The war losses cannot be estimated with any reasonable accuracy or apportioned regionally, because data on regional natural increase are available only for 1940 and 1959, and they are of dubious reliability.[41] Deaths directly attributed to World War II have been estimated at 20 to 22 million, and, including indirect losses, decline in natural increase below expected levels at not less than 50 million.[42] If one accepts the official natural increase rates of 1940 and 1950 for the USSR, and assumes that in the absence of a war the population would have grown during this period at the median rate, there is a deficit of about 53 million people. In the present-day territory of the USSR, the population increased by 8.2 percent from 193.0 to 208.8 million between 1939 and 1959.[43] Sometime in 1941 the population in the present-day territory of the USSR reached 200 million, but it was not until sometime in 1956 that the Soviet population once again reached 200 million (it should be mentioned that the official Soviet estimate of the 1939 population of the USSR is more than 2 million below our estimate, largely because they do not include any population figures in 1939 for Kaliningradskaya Oblast, Zakarpatskaya Oblast, Tuvinskaya ASSR, or southern Sakhalin). Part of the war losses was due to net emigration. Emigrants mainly comprised Germans from the USSR and East Prussia, Poles, Jews, and Japanese, and immigrants mainly included Ukrainians, although about 100,000 Armenians immigrated into the Soviet Union during this period.[44] The net loss through international migration was upwards of 3 million people, including about 2 million during the war and about 1 million shortly after the war.[45]

During the war, the major population movement was out of areas that were threatened by the German invasion, which was a large area, considering that the territory ever occupied by the Germans had an estimated population of some 85 million people, or about 44 percent of the 1939 population of the present-day territory of the USSR.[46] Over 1,300 major industrial enterprises, together with their workers, were relocated, primarily to the Urals, Siberia, Kazakhstan, and Central Asia, and many kolkhozy and machine tractor stations with their equipment were evacuated to the east. In addition, large numbers of people fled from the front as the Germans advanced. The total number of people that went east between June 1941 and October 1942, the period of the deepest German penetration, has been estimated at upwards of 20 million, and by some estimates, upwards of 25 million persons. Virtually all of these migrants eventually returned to the West.[47] In fact, millions returned to their former homes as soon as the Germans were driven out, well before the war was over, despite the job freeze and the disapproval of the Soviet government. U.S. correspondents reported that, by July 1944, 50 percent of the migrants had returned to the liberated areas.[48] During the war, these migrants went primarily to the urban areas of the east, where they provided the labor for the evacuated and newly developed industries.

During and shortly after the war, several nationalities were deported to the east, mainly to Central Asia and Kazakhstan, and they numbered over a million people. About 400,000 Volga Germans were deported shortly after the war began as a security measure. In 1944, about 225,000 Crimean Tatars were deported, and shortly thereafter the Kalmyks, Chechen, Ingush, Karachay, and Balkars were resettled from the North Caucasus to the east, allegedly as a result of their collaboration with the Germans. In the late 1950s, except for the Volga Germans and the Crimean Tatars, all of the deported nationalities were allowed to return to their homelands.[49]

Shortly after the war there was a major influx into the newly acquired western territories and southern Sakhalin that had suffered considerable population losses as a result of emigration and excess mortality during the war. Most of the 400,000 Japanese in northern Sakhalin and the Kuril Islands fled or were repatriated after the war; the population loss in the western territories has been estimated at 20 percent of their total population.[50] The total influx is not known, but 400,000 people moved to Kaliningradskaya Oblast, and another 400,000 moved to southern Sakhalin.[51] Migration into the West, Southwest, and Belorussia to secure these areas and to take advantage of the economic opportunities afforded by the population losses must have been considerable. Another important short-term migratory stream was to Kazakhstan between 1954 and 1962, when about 800,000 people moved to Kazakhstan in conjunction with the New Lands Program.[52]

Aside from the above migrations, which were caused by the war and other relatively short-term events, much migration occurred after the war and was related to the rehabilitation of the economy and the continued rapid industrialization and urbanization. This migration, in addition to the regional differentials in war losses, probably accounts for the considerable population redistribution that occurred during this period. Limited data are available for urban migration, according to the official definitions of urban, and they appear to substantiate this contention. The definition of the urban population used in the census varied by republic, and generally the lower limit was settlements of between 1,000 and 3,000 inhabitants with from 60 to 85 percent of their work force in nonagricultural pursuits.[53] Between 1939 and 1959, the urban population according to this definition increased from 60.4 to 100.0 million. Most of this increase, however, occurred after 1950; between 1939 and 1950 the increase was 9 million, but between 1950 and 1959 the urban population increased 30.6 million.[54]

Total net migration to urban centers, which in effect is net migration from rural areas, totaled over 14 million between 1950 and 1959 (Table 2.15), or about 47 percent of the urban increase during this period, according to data from the passport registration system. For the 1939-59 period, net migration to urban areas is estimated officially at 24.6 million or 62 percent of the total urban increase, so presumably rural migration to urban areas was relatively greater before 1950. Change in the status of settlements during this period accounted for 7 million persons and natural increase, 8 million.[55] Net urban migration as a percent of the urban population (Table 2.15) is a reasonable approximation of the growth of the urban population as a result of migration. Table 2.16 shows urban migration by republic and compares it with the percentage of the 1959 urban population. It would appear that the RSFSR's share of the total net urban migration was significantly below its share of the 1959 urban population, and for the Ukraine and Kazakhstan the reverse occurred. These republics account for most of the redistribution of the urban population that occurred as a result of migration.

TABLE 2.15

Urban Migration in the USSR: 1950-59

Year	Urban Arrivals (thousands)	Urban Departures (thousands)	Net Urban Migration (thousands)	Net Urban Migration as a Percent of Urban Population
1950	7,683.8	5,809.8	1,874.0	2.7
1951	8,150.5	6,287.2	1,863.3	2.6
1952	8,183.7	6,515.6	1,668.1	2.2
1953	9,551.1	6,957.1	2,594.0	3.2
1954	8,987.9	7,655.0	1,332.9	1.6
1955	8,719.3	7,696.3	1,023.0	1.2
1956	8,865.2	7,535.3	1,329.9	1.5
1957	8,626.3	7,330.2	1,296.1	1.4
1958	8,811.3	7,511.9	1,299.4	1.4
USSR total	77,579.1	63,298.4	14,280.7	

Note: Based on official urban definitions.

Source: USSR, Naseleniye SSSR, 1973 (Moscow: Izdatel'stvo "Statistika," 1975), p. 178.

TABLE 2.16

Net Urban Migration by Republic: 1950-59

Republic	Net Urban Migration (thousands)	Percent of Total Net Urban Migration	Percent of 1959 USSR Urban Population
RSFSR	8,486.4	59.4	61.6
Ukraine	3,037.0	21.3	19.2
Belorussia	398.6	2.8	2.5
Uzbekistan	278.6	2.0	2.7
Kazakhstan	791.1	5.5	4.1
Georgia	235.4	1.7	1.7
Azerbaydzhan	142.5	1.0	1.8
Lithuania	110.3	0.8	1.1
Moldavia	123.4	0.9	0.6
Latvia	151.2	1.1	1.2
Kirgizia	84.0	0.6	0.7
Tadzhikistan	113.7	0.8	0.7
Armenia	119.5	0.8	0.9
Turkmeniya	110.0	0.8	0.7
Estonia	99.0	0.7	0.7
USSR total	14,280.7	100.2	100.2

Note: Based on official urban definitions.

Source: USSR, Naseleniye SSSR, 1973 (Moscow: Izdatel'stvo "Statistika," 1975), pp. 178-85.

With respect to policy, the job freeze was discontinued in 1956, but it would appear that this had little effect on urban migration; in fact, there was a decline in urban migration in 1957 (Table 2.15). This would seem to substantiate Robert J. Osborn's claim that "much evidence suggests that in the postwar years it was being enforced only sporadically, if at all."[56] There was a significant rise in urban arrivals in 1953, which was due to net urban in-migration from rural areas, in that there was no significant change in the number of urban departures. That this was not a particularly good year in agriculture may explain partially this rise in migration to urban areas. Between 1950 and 1959, there were some 140 million movers out of and into urban areas. The control of such a large volume of migration obviously would entail considerable effort and would not be very productive. In addition, these data do not include all the migration that occurred during this period, because rural-to-rural migration is not included. One has only to think of the total migration that had occurred during the Soviet period to realize what a truly monumental task would have been required to control it. Clearly, the control of such a volume of migration would be unprecedented in human history.

Vital statistics are also available for 1950, but they, too, are not above suspicion. There are unexpected movements in the rates, and crude death rates are among the lowest in the Transcaucasus and Central Asia regions, where the crude birth rates remain unexpectedly low. The crude natural increase rate for the USSR was 17.0 per thousand with a crude birth rate of 26.7 and a crude death rate of 9.7. The Western USSR had natural increase rates generally two or three points per thousand below the USSR average, whereas the Eastern USSR had rates that exceeded the USSR average, generally in the range of four to six points per thousand.[57] Therefore, once again, the rate of natural increase would appear to support the redistribution of the population to the east, at least by 1950.

Northern European USSR was the only quadrant that had a decline in its population between 1939 and 1959 (Table 2.10), and all the economic regions within it registered a decline or very slow growth (Table 2.12 and Map 2.25). All of the growth during this period occurred in the Eastern USSR. The urban population of the Eastern USSR grew at more than twice the rate of the Western USSR, and the Russian East had the highest average annual rate of growth (Table 4.7). All gross regions experienced a decline in their rural populations except the Non-Slavic South (Table 7.1), and the Northern European USSR had a rapid rate of rural depopulation, with all economic regions experiencing a rapid rate of decline (Table 7.2). The high depopulation rate of the Far East was influenced by a small rural base population, and the high rate for Kazakhstan can be explained partially by the New Lands Program.

The net result of the regional growth or decline in population during the 1939-59 period was a dramatic shift in the share of the population out of Northern European USSR to the Eastern USSR (Table 2.1). All economic regions in Northern European USSR had negative values with respect to population redistribution (Table 2.2), and all other economic regions, except the South, had positive values (Map 2.8). There was also a major redistribution of the urban population to the Eastern USSR, in particular to the Russian East

(Table 2.4). Both Northern European USSR and the European Steppe declined in their share of the urban population. Economic regions in the Western USSR generally declined in their share of the urban population or increased only slightly, and the major urbanized regions (the Northwest, Center, and Donetsk-Dnepr) registered particularly sharp declines (Table 2.6). The Urals, West Siberia, and Kazakhstan had the greatest gains. The chief shift of the rural population was out of Northern European USSR especially to the Non-Slavic South but also to the Russian East and the European Steppe (Table 2.5). No economic region in the Northern European USSR increased its share of the rural population, and all economic regions outside Northern European USSR increased their share. The high rate for Central Asia reflects a sizable rural population with a relatively high natural increase rate and relatively little rural out-migration. The New Lands Program in conjunction with relatively high natural increase largely accounts for the shift to Kazakhstan.

Total population redistribution and growth continue to be correlated highly (0.928) during this period, but there was an appreciable strengthening of the relationship with both rural (0.861) and urban (0.780) redistribution, as compared with the previous period. Rank correlation coefficients between total population growth and rural (0.871) and urban (0.732) growth also increased substantially. One might, therefore, infer that these changes were related to the diminishing numerical dominance of the rural population and that there was some correspondence between regions of rural and urban growth.

Thus, the 1939-59 period witnessed a continued appreciable redistribution of the Soviet population away from Northern European USSR to the Eastern USSR, in particular, although the average annual percentage point change was only slightly above the previous and subsequent periods. This shift was pronounced in both the urban and rural populations, which is the continuation of a long-term trend. Population redistribution toward the European Steppe was modest, as in the previous period. The major shift of the urban population was to the Russian East, whereas the major pattern in the redistribution of the rural population was to the Non-Slavic South. Although war losses clearly affected the redistribution of the population, most of the population redistribution, especially urban growth, was related to the high rates of economic development and industrialization that occurred after 1950.

Population Redistribution: 1959-70

Because of the absence of war and the greater availability of data on migration and natural increase during this period, population redistribution can be analyzed in the 1959-70 period in greater detail than in previous periods. Between January 15, 1959 and January 15, 1970, the Soviet population increased by 33 million people, from 208.8 to 241.7 million, or 15.8 percent. The major shift in the total population during this period was to the south, in particular to the most southern regions (Tables 2.1 and 2.2 and Maps 2.4, 2.5, and 2.9). By far the greatest gain was in the Non-Slavic South, although

the European Steppe also increased its share of the total population. Central
Asia, Kazakhstan, and the Transcaucasus all registered appreciable relative
increases. In the European Steppe, however, only the North Caucasus, the
South, and Moldavia had relative gains. The greatest outward shifts occurred
in a belt of regions extending from the western Ukraine to West Siberia, with
the Center, Central Chernozem, and the Southwest experiencing the greatest
relative losses. The long-term shift of the population out of Northern European USSR continued at a high average annual rate. The traditional Russian
areas of settlement in the west continued to register relative losses in population as they have for the past century. The Center, Central Chernozem,
Volgo-Vyatsk, and Northwest had 30.1 percent of the total population in 1897
but only 23.6 percent in 1970. The reversal of the long-term trend of population redistribution to the Russian East was the most notable occurrence
during this period. For the first time during an intercensal period, the Russian East's share of the total population declined, although only the Urals and
West Siberia registered relative losses.

The most immediate factor in the regional population shifts was regional
variations in rates of population growth (Tables 2.10 and 2.12 and Map 2.26).
Unlike the preceding periods, all regions increased their population in this
intercensal period. This, of course, reflects the fact that the 1959-70 period
was free of any major social disturbances, such as wars and collectivization,
which marked earlier intercensal periods. In fact, in the 1959-70 period,
the average annual percentage increase of the total population was the highest
of any intercensal period, 1.3 percent. The Non-Slavic South was the leading
gross region with respect to the growth of population, and Northern European
USSR and the Russian East had rates well below the USSR average. As might
be expected, there was a close correspondence between average annual growth
by economic region and redistribution. A rank correlation of 0.952 confirms
this relationship. Outstanding regions of population growth were Central
Asia, Kazakhstan, and the Transcaucasus, whereas the Volgo-Vyatsk, Central Chernozem, and West Siberia had the lowest rates of increase and very
slight population growth.

The redistribution of the rural population is related more closely than
the urban population to that of the total population. Rank correlation coefficients of 0.926 and 0.398 support this contention. However, there is a moderate relationship (0.516) between the urban and rural patterns of redistribution. With respect to the redistribution of the urban population, Northern
European USSR and the European Steppe barely increased their share, the
Russian East experienced an appreciable relative decline, and the Non-Slavic
South had the only significant gain. The Center, Urals, and West Siberia had
the greatest relative losses, whereas Central Asia and Kazakhstan had the
greatest relative gains (Tables 2.4 and 2.6 and Maps 2.16, 2.17, and 4.15).
For the first time since 1897, there was a decline in the urban share of the
Eastern USSR.

The redistribution of the rural population exemplifies to an even greater
degree the shift to the south (Tables 2.5 and 2.8 and Maps 2.21, 2.22, and
7.5). There was a major shift out of Northern European USSR, and to a lesser

degree, the Russian East—both regions of rural depopulation. The bulk of the shift was to the Non-Slavic South, although the European Steppe registered a slight relative gain. The shift to the Non-Slavic South was due to high rural natural increase. All economic regions in the Northern European USSR experienced a relative decline, and the decline of the Center was particularly sharp. The regions comprising the Russian East had relative losses or only slight gains. The situation was somewhat similar in the European Steppe, with the exception of the North Caucasus, which experienced an appreciable relative gain in the share of the rural population. The regions of the Non-Slavic South had the greatest relative gains, reflecting a significant shift of the rural population to these non-Slavic areas.

As might be expected, average annual percentage changes of the urban and rural population correspond to the trends in their redistribution (Tables 4.7, 4.8, 7.1, and 7.2 and Maps 4.15 and 7.5). Respective rank correlations were 0.879 and 0.965. Only the urban population of the Russian East grew at a rate that was below the USSR average of 3.1 percent, and the Non-Slavic South grew the fastest. With respect to the urban growth of economic regions, the relatively rapid growth of such economically backward regions as Moldavia, Belorussia, the Central Chernozem, the Southwest, and the Volgo-Vyatsk is particularly notable, as well as that of Kazakhstan, Central Asia, and the West (Map 4.15).

The rural population declined in Northern European USSR and the Russian East, where all economic regions registered a decline except East Siberia and the Far East, which had modest increases despite their small base populations. The Non-Slavic South had the greatest increase by far, and all economic regions within it grew well above the average for the USSR, which was essentially no growth. In the European Steppe, the South, and North Caucasus, the rural populations grew at intermediate rates, and the Southwest and Donetsk-Dnepr declined. In general, all regions outside the Non-Slavic South experienced rural population losses or only slight gains, except for Moldavia, the South, and the North Caucasus. Rural growth was associated more closely with total growth (the rank correlation coefficient was 0.910) and total redistribution (0.865) than was urban growth (0.414 and 0.421). This indicates that where the rural population grew the fastest so did the total population and reflects the role of the higher rural natural increase in the growth of the total population, despite the high rates of urbanization and urban growth that prevailed during this period.

Migration

Definitions. Although data on migration for the 1959-70 period are more abundant than in previous intercensal periods, the available data suffer from a lack of comparability, and there are significant differences in the patterns of migration that are derived from these data. In addition, they do not measure migration adequately; for example, there are no data as to the total number of persons moving in a given year.

Net migration can be estimated as a residual from vital statistics and total population data from the censuses. However, natural increase data for all years between the censuses are available only by republic. [58] Therefore, natural increase must be estimated for economic regions and lower-order political units on the basis of data for only some of the intercensal years. In the censuses, total population data are de facto, except for the military who are enumerated at their place of induction. [59] Dependents of the military are enumerated also on a de facto basis, and vital statistics of the military are recorded at their place of residence, although there are no data to confirm these assumptions. Total population estimates are made regionally for the years between censuses on the basis of vital statistics and migration data from the registration system. Because of errors in these data, there frequently are significant differences between the census data and the population estimates, and therefore the estimates for the intervening years are revised after a census. The chief problems appear to be that there are no reliable data on rural-to-rural migration and migration data from the registration system includes the military and the censuses do not. If or how they reconcile this difference is unknown. Births between 1959 and 1970 appear to be slightly underregistered, 1 to 3 percent; deaths appear to be somewhat underregistered also, particularly in rural areas and among the older age groups. [60] That the errors are the same direction minimizes the effect on natural increase, and it can probably be assumed that the natural increase data are reasonably reliable. In some parts of the country, however, there appears to be significant underregistration of births and deaths. Thus, net migration estimates based on the residual method are rather crude, in that they contain errors in enumeration and vital registration and they give no indication of the magnitudes of in-migration and out-migration. Because the Soviet censuses are de facto, they include temporary residents, those away from their permanent residence for less than six months. These estimates indicate the direction and, to a certain degree, the magnitude of population shifts as a result of migration.

As was previously noted, the registration system provides data primarily on urban in-migration and includes those that change their permanent residence, those that move for work, either permanent or seasonal (regardless of the amount of time), and those that move to study or to perform government business for more than 30 days in rural areas without a passport system and for more than 45 days in areas with the passport system. [61] Family members also are included. The military are included, as well as those who move to foreign countries, although it appears that the military register as moving to the armed forces when they leave and do not specify their location; when they return they register, apparently, as having returned from the armed forces. The chief deficiencies of these data are that they do not include rural-to-rural migration, because much of the rural population did not have passports, and rural-to-urban migration is measured on a net basis. Although P. G. Pod'-yachikh maintains that the data are satisfactory and the divergence between urban arrivals and urban departures are slight, [62] others maintain that the data on arrivals are more accurate than those on departures, because departures are not registered as fully and people often do not go where they say they are going. [63] The register data do not include moves within cities.

Migration data from the 1970 census are based upon two points that were covered during the census: (1) How long have you continuously resided in this population point? and (2) For those living here less than two years, indicate the place of your previous permanent residence. The data were collected on the basis of a 25 percent sample and did not include movements within urban areas or rural settlements. The military, those moving to foreign countries, and those away from their permanent residence for less than six months were not included as migrants. In the United States and other countries collecting place-of-residence data, the question is generally asked, Where did you live one year ago or five years ago? Thus, the Soviet data are not comparable either in terms of time or place of former residence. It should be pointed out, however, that with respect to asking place of previous residence, the Soviets have conformed to recommendations of the United Nations. The U.S. data do not include those that moved and returned, intermediary moves, or those that move and die. The Soviet data only register the last move and include return migrants, but they exclude the place of origin of the migrants. The 1970 Soviet census data differ from the register data, largely because the census data measure changes in residence rather than movers and exclude the military and temporary movers.

Thus, there are significant differences in definition among the measures of migration. V. I. Perevedentsev points out that because, in contrast to the register data, the census data enumerate those that have changed their residence in the previous two years and not those that have moved and exclude temporary migrants, the military, and those moving to foreign countries one would expect the number of migrants enumerated in the census to be fewer than those included in the register system.[64] Data from the census and estimates of the total number of movers support this contention. As we will discuss later, estimates of the total number of movers in 1970 based on the register data range between 14 and 16 million, whereas according to the 1970 census the number of persons changing their residence in the previous two years was only 13.9 million persons, or roughly half as many migrants. In addition, according to the census, roughly as many women migrated to urban areas as men, whereas register data for 1969 and 1970 indicate that about 55 percent of the migrants to urban centers were men.[65] That the census data does not include the military could account for this difference.

There are also significant differences in the migratory patterns derived from the various sources of data. Peter J. Grandstaff has investigated these divergences, primarily statistically rather than in terms of definition. He has compared interrepublic migration balances from the census with estimates of net migration derived from the residual method, using natural increase data and estimates of total population by republic for 1968 and 1969. He acknowledges the definitional problems in the census and points out that the census data are very approximate in that "persons who moved more than once, let us say from republic A to republic B to republic C, would have been recorded as going from B to C when in fact the A to B to C sequence means that on balance A lost population, B neither gained nor lost and C gained." The chief differences between these two measures of migration was that, according to the census, the RSFSR had a net in-migration of 176,000, whereas according to the residual estimates there was a net out-migration of 156,000; Central Asia experienced net out-migration according to the census and net in-migration according to the residual estimates. He suggests that the census data are erroneous, because migration from the RSFSR to Central Asia was discouraged by the government and thus some respondents did not report their previous residence. He also points out the problem of collecting retrospective information. [66] Elsewhere, in conjunction with a statistical analysis of the divergences in the interregional migratory patterns derived from the three sources of data, he compared estimates of urban arrivals from the census with urban arrivals from the register system and found the former to be 41 percent below the latter. [67]

There probably was some underreporting in the census; most socioeconomic data contain errors. Surely retrospective responses are a problem, although in the USSR most respondents can refer to their passport. There was also an important definitional difference between the census data and the residual estimates. Although neither source of data included the military, the residual estimates include temporary residents, those away from their permanent residence for less than six months, but the census data excluded them. According to the 1959 census, there were about 580,000 temporary residents in the USSR, and according to the 1970 census, about 284,000 temporary residents. The chief categories of temporary residents were probably seasonal workers, visitors, and tourists. Since the census was taken in January, very probably residual estimates for tourist areas, such as the Crimea, were inflated by the presence of tourists.

Moreover, estimates derived from the residual method tend to be rather crude, because they incorporate the errors in the vital statistics and the estimates of the total population. For example, according to the residual estimates of net migration by republic that Grandstaff presented for 1968 and 1969, there were 316,000 net in-migrants to all units of the USSR and 225,000 net out-migrants, or some 40 percent fewer net out-migrants. If one assumes that there was no international migration, net out-migrants and net in-migrants should balance, but the net figures are relatively small and a small absolute difference results in an appreciable relative difference. It is expected also that there should be fewer urban in-migrants reported in the census than derived from the register system, because the register includes the military and most temporary migrants and the census does not. With respect to Central Asia, it is also likely that a part of the net in-migration based on residual estimates is the result of underreporting. Between the 1958/59 and 1969/70 periods, there was an unexpected rise in fertility as measured by net reproduction rates in Tadzhikistan (from 1.7 to 2.7), Uzbekistan (from 2.1 to 2.6), and Turkmeniya (from 2.1 to 2.7). B. A. Borisov claims that there was underreporting of births in Central Asia during this period. [68]

Nevertheless, Grandstaff is correct in pointing out that according to available data net in-migration to the RSFSR and net out-migration from Central Asia are not expected patterns. That the census data on migration did not record all moves, the military, and temporary residents could have affected these patterns, but, of course, there is no way to determine whether these divergences were the result of census errors or definitional differences or both. Most other migration patterns derived from the census data appear to be reasonable and expected. The central point is that there are major differences in definition among the various measures of migration in the USSR, and these differences should be taken into consideration in evaluating the migration patterns that will be discussed subsequently.

Migration Patterns. Regional variations in population growth are the result of regional variations in net migration and natural increase. Because vital statistics are available for all years only by republic, estimates for economic regions of the RSFSR and the Ukraine and for oblasts or equivalent units were made based on the rates of the midpoint year, which were inflated by 3 percent to take into account the divergence between our estimate for the total USSR by economic region and the 1959-70 absolute population increase (Table 2.17 and Maps 2.38 and 2.39). Data by oblast or equivalent unit were not available for Belorussia, Kazakhstan, and the Central Asian republics. Comparison of net migration and natural increase rates with total population increase suggests high positive relationships. Rank correlation confirms this observation, because both variables are related, significantly and positively, to rates of population increase; the correlation with net migration is 0.78 and with natural increase, 0.70.

With respect to migration rates, the South, the North Caucasus, Kazakhstan, Central Asia, and the West were the leading regions of net in-migration, but in absolute terms the North Caucasus, Central Asia, Kazakhstan, and the South were dominant. That there were more than 800,000 net in-migrants than net out-migrants testifies to the approximate nature of estimates based on vital statistics and census data, because there was no appreciable net immigration into the USSR during this period. As has already been mentioned, a major portion of this discrepancy probably can be accounted for by underreporting of vital statistics, particularly in Central Asia. The discrepancy between total natural increase and total population growth was only about 2.5 percent, so a small amount of underreporting would result in the observed net in-migration. The South's leading position reflects the fact that the census was taken in the middle of winter and was de facto, and the Crimea is a major winter resort area. The Crimea had the highest net in-migration rate for any oblast or equivalent unit, 29.3 percent. Thus, it is probable that some "migrants" to this region were winter vacationers, who were enumerated here rather than in their usual place of residence. However, that the South ranked fifth with respect to increase in per capita capital investment between 1960 and 1967 would seem to indicate that its high rate of net in-migration is related also to economic factors and not solely to climatic amenities and census technicalities.[69]

Two other regions of net in-migration that merit attention are the Northwest and Center. Their rates are somewhat misleading, because they are influenced greatly by high rates of net in-migration to Moscow and Leningrad. With the exception of these two cities and their respective oblasts plus Mur-

TABLE 2.17

Net Migration and Natural Increase by Economic Region: 1959-70

Region	Population Growth	Natural Increase	Net Migration	Net Migration as Percent of July 1964 Population	Net Migration as Percent of Population Growth	Natural Increase as Percent of July 1964 Population	Percent of Total Natural Increase
Northwest	1,414,842	1,152,635	262,207	2.1	18.5	9.4	3.6
West	846,748	558,100	288,648	4.5	34.1	9.2	1.7
Center	1,931,196	1,706,536	224,660	0.9	11.6	6.7	5.3
Volgo-Vyatsk	94,779	892,838	-798,059	-9.6	-842.0	10.8	2.8
Central Chernozem	231,333	738,093	-506,760	-5.7	-219.1	8.3	2.3
Volga	1,833,004	1,576,490	256,514	1.9	14.0	11.7	4.9
Belorussia	947,690	1,214,300	-266,610	-3.1	-28.1	14.3	3.8
Moldavia	684,396	609,000	75,396	2.3	11.0	18.6	1.9
Southwest	1,694,120	2,388,205	-694,085	-3.3	-41.0	11.2	7.5
South	1,314,482	634,639	679,843	12.0	51.7	11.2	2.0
Donetsk-Dnepr	2,248,869	1,786,548	462,321	2.6	20.6	10.0	5.6
North Caucasus	2,763,031	1,815,814	947,217	7.1	34.3	13.6	5.7
Transcaucasus	2,790,502	2,777,100	13,402	0.1	0.4	25.3	8.7
Urals	1,796,142	2,724,978	-928,836	-4.6	-51.7	13.6	8.5
West Siberia	543,963	1,337,778	-793,815	-7.3	-145.9	12.3	4.2
East Siberia	1,167,022	1,227,957	-60,935	-0.8	-5.2	15.9	3.8
Far East	769,583	683,199	86,384	1.8	11.2	14.4	2.1
Kazakhstan	3,698,879	2,918,600	780,279	6.6	19.6	25.0	9.1
Central Asia	6,122,903	5,325,900	797,003	4.8	9.9	33.3	16.6
USSR total	32,893,484	32,068,710	824,744	3.6	2.5	14.1	100.0

Sources: 1970 Soviet census (see Chapter 1, n. 104); USSR, Narodnoye Khozyaystvo SSSR v 1964 G. (Moscow: "Statistika," 1965), pp. 38-39; and Naseleniye SSSR, 1973 (Moscow: Izdatel'stvo "Statistika," 1975), pp. 70-83.

MAP 2.38

Total Net Migration: 1959-70

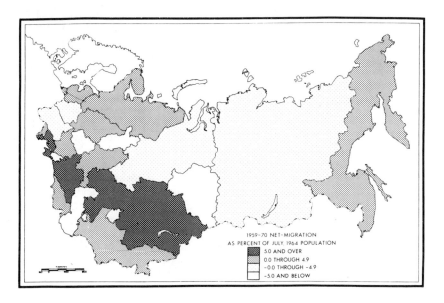

1959-70 NET-MIGRATION
AS PERCENT OF JULY, 1964 POPULATION
5.0 AND OVER
0.0 THROUGH 4.9
-0.0 THROUGH -4.9
-5.0 AND BELOW

MAP 2.39

Total Natural Increase: 1959-70

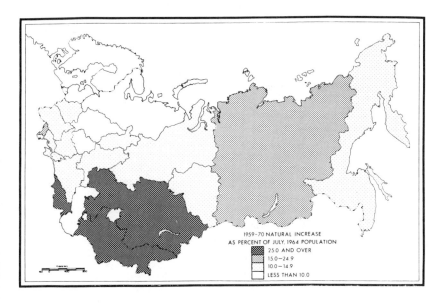

1959-70 NATURAL INCREASE
AS PERCENT OF JULY, 1964 POPULATION
25.0 AND OVER
15.0 — 24.9
10.0 — 14.9
LESS THAN 10.0

manskaya Oblast, all other component units in these two regions had net out-migration.

With respect to net out-migration rates, the Volgo-Vyatsk, West Siberia, and the Central Chernozem were the outstanding regions, but if absolute net out-migration is considered, the Urals, Volgo-Vyatsk, West Siberia, and the Southwest were the leading regions. The Volgo-Vyatsk and Central Cherno-zem have been major regions of net out-migration for some time, but the presence of West Siberia, the Urals, and East Siberia in this category is a relatively recent occurrence, because until fairly recently, they have been major regions of net in-migration. In the Russian East only the Far East has maintained its traditional role as a major region of net in-migration. However, it too has pockets of net out-migration; in fact, one of its compo-nent units, Sakhalinskaya Oblast, had the highest net out-migration rate (19.3 percent) of any oblast or equivalent unit. Such out-migration is unexpected, because the Russian East has and has had a chronic labor shortage.

With respect to net migration by oblast or equivalent unit, in general the rates of the component units correspond to those of the region. However, the pattern is somewhat mixed for units of the Donetsk-Dnepr and the Volga, and in East Siberia only the ethnic units experienced net in-migration. In the Center, all units outside Moskovskaya Oblast (including the city of Moscow) actually had net out-migration; and in the Southwest, only Kievskaya Oblast (including the city of Kiev) experienced net in-migration. In the Urals, all units except Tyumenskaya Oblast registered net out-migration. In the Trans-caucasus, only Armenia had net in-migration; and in Central Asia, only Turk-meniya had net out-migration.

The contribution of net migration to regional total population growth is shown in Table 2.17. The values are only meaningful with respect to net in-migration, because where there was net out-migration all of the growth was the result of natural increase. The only region where the contribution of net in-migration to total population growth was greater than natural increase was the South. About a third of the population growth of the North Caucasus and the West was due to net in-migration, whereas in the remaining regions of net in-migration, it was less.

Natural increase rates, the 1959-70 absolute natural increase divided by the July 1964 population, in the Slavic and Baltic areas were low, the Cen-ter and Central Chernozem having the lowest values (Table 2.17 and Map 2.39). Highest rates were registered in such predominantly non-Slavic areas as Central Asia and the Transcaucasus. Although in Kazakhstan Slavs are a plurality, the relatively large proportion of non-Slavs results in moderate levels of fertility and natural increase. The variation in the natural increase rates largely reflects differences in fertility rather than mortality. Regional variations in the crude death rate rarely exceed the mean by more than one or two points per thousand, averaging about seven per thousand in 1964. There was, however, considerable regional variation in crude birth rates. In the mid-1960s, crude birth rates in Slavic areas generally ranged between 15 and 20 per thousand, but in such non-Slavic areas as the Transcaucasus and Central Asia they exceeded 30 per thousand.

TABLE 2.18

Interregional Migration Rates by Economic Region: 1968-70

Region	Percent of 1970 Total, Urban, or Rural Populations Comprised of:									
	In-Migrants			Out-Migrants			Net Migrants			Migration Turnover (total population only)
	Total	Urban	Rural	Total	Urban	Rural	Total	Urban	Rural	
Northwest	3.2	3.4	2.8	2.3	2.4	2.2	0.9	1.0	0.6	5.5
West	1.7	2.2	1.0	1.3	1.7	0.6	0.4	0.5	0.4	3.0
Center	2.2	2.4	1.7	1.6	1.5	1.6	0.6	0.9	0.1	3.8
Volgo-Vyatsk	2.0	2.6	1.2	2.7	2.7	2.8	-0.7	-0.1	-1.6	4.7
Central Chernozem	1.7	2.8	1.0	2.5	2.9	2.3	-0.8	-0.1	-1.3	4.2
Volga	2.4	3.2	1.4	2.2	2.4	1.9	0.2	0.8	-0.5	4.6
Belorussia	1.5	2.4	0.9	1.5	2.0	1.1	0.0	0.4	-0.2	3.0
Moldavia	1.4	3.3	0.6	1.7	2.7	1.2	-0.3	0.6	-0.6	3.1
Southwest	1.1	2.1	0.5	1.7	2.1	1.5	-0.6	0.0	-1.0	2.8
South	4.2	4.5	3.9	2.6	2.8	2.3	1.6	1.7	1.6	6.8
Donetsk-Dnepr	2.1	2.5	1.3	1.8	2.0	1.5	0.3	0.5	-0.2	3.9
North Caucasus	2.8	3.2	2.3	2.5	3.2	1.8	0.3	0.0	0.5	5.3
Transcaucasus	0.4	0.7	0.2	0.9	1.4	0.4	-0.5	-0.7	-0.2	1.3
Urals	2.5	2.9	1.8	3.2	3.4	2.9	-0.7	-0.5	-1.1	5.7
West Siberia	2.7	3.1	2.2	3.5	3.6	3.4	-0.8	-0.5	-1.2	6.2
East Siberia	3.8	4.4	2.6	3.4	3.9	2.7	0.4	0.5	-0.1	7.2
Far East	6.0	5.7	6.9	4.1	4.1	4.1	1.9	1.6	2.8	10.1
Kazakhstan	3.2	4.6	1.8	3.4	3.9	2.9	-0.2	0.7	-1.1	6.6
Central Asia	1.0	2.2	0.3	1.7	3.0	0.9	-0.7	-0.8	-0.6	2.7
USSR total	2.2	2.9	1.4	2.2	2.6	1.8	0.0	0.3	-0.4	4.4

*Based on official urban definitions.

Source: 1970 Soviet census (see Chapter 1, n. 104).

MAP 2.40

Total In-Migration: 1968-70

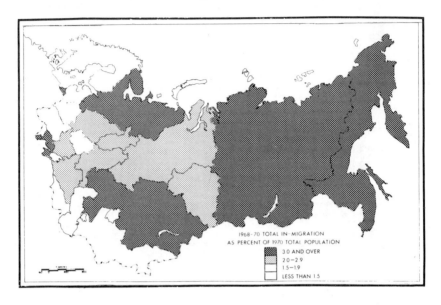

1968-70 TOTAL IN-MIGRATION
AS PERCENT OF 1970 TOTAL POPULATION

- 3.0 AND OVER
- 2.0—2.9
- 1.5—1.9
- LESS THAN 1.5

MAP 2.41

Total Out-Migration: 1968-70

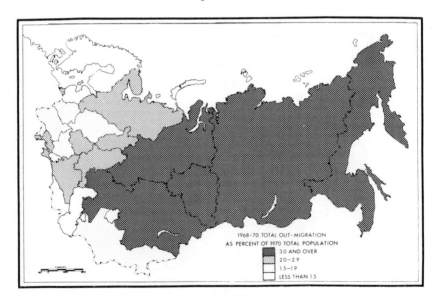

1968-70 TOTAL OUT-MIGRATION
AS PERCENT OF 1970 TOTAL POPULATION

- 3.0 AND OVER
- 2.0—2.9
- 1.5—1.9
- LESS THAN 1.5

MAP 2.42

Total Net Migration: 1968-70

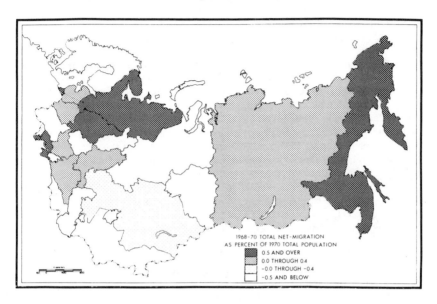

1968-70 TOTAL NET-MIGRATION
AS PERCENT OF 1970 TOTAL POPULATION
- 0.5 AND OVER
- 0.0 THROUGH 0.4
- -0.0 THROUGH -0.4
- -0.5 AND BELOW

MAP 2.43

Total Migration Turnover: 1968-70

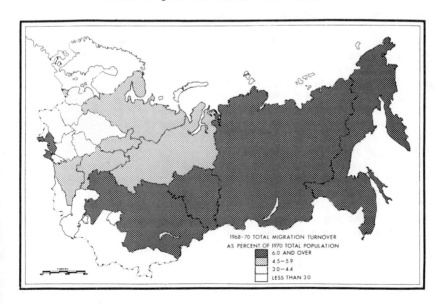

1968-70 TOTAL MIGRATION TURNOVER
AS PERCENT OF 1970 TOTAL POPULATION
- 6.0 AND OVER
- 4.5—5.9
- 3.0—4.4
- LESS THAN 3.0

Based upon available data on rural and urban natural increase, net rural-to-urban migration and net interregional migration by republic and economic regions of the RSFSR and the Ukraine, Theodore Shabad has classified migration trends for the 1959-70 period into four categories. The first category, those units with net in-migration and rural depopulation, includes the Baltic republics, the Ukraine, the Northwest, the Center, and Volga. The second category, those units having net in-migration and rural population growth, includes Kazakhstan, the Central Asian republics, Moldavia, the South, the North Caucasus, Armenia, and the Far East. Georgia and Azerbaydzhan comprise the third category, which is characterized by net out-migration and rural population growth. The fourth category, combining net out-migration with rural depopulation, includes the Central Chernozem, Volgo-Vyatsk, Urals, West Siberia, East Siberia, Belorussia, and the Southwest.[70] This classification is useful in interpreting the migratory processes that have occurred during this period. For example, the fourth category includes all of the economic regions in Table 2.17 that experienced net out-migration, and the first category includes many, but not all, of the regions characterized by net in-migration.

Interregional migration rates as measured by change of residence in the two years previous to the 1970 census are shown in Table 2.18 and Maps 2.40-2.43. In-migration refers only to migrants who moved into the region from beyond the region, and out-migration includes only those who moved beyond the region. Thus, only the migration that adds to or subtracts from the total population of the region is being considered, so that it can be related to the total population distribution. The urban and rural definitions are those of the 1970 census rather than referring to centers of 15,000 or more. The migration data from the 1970 census were ordered into the current official Soviet economic regions, which differ somewhat from the 1961 economic regions used in this study; it was not possible to reorder the data into the 1961 economic regions. The changes involved the transfer of an entire political-administrative unit from one region to another. Orlovskaya Oblast was transferred from the Central Chernozem to the Center; Bashkirskaya ASSR, from the Urals to the Volga; Kalmytskaya ASSR, from the North Caucasus to the Volga; Tyumenskaya Oblast, from the Urals to West Siberia; Yakutskaya ASSR, from East Siberia to the Far East; and Kirovogradskaya Oblast, from the Southwest to the Donetsk-Dnepr. Kaliningradskaya Oblast was transferred from the Northwest to the West, but in the 1970 census Kaliningradskaya Oblast is included in the data for the RSFSR but is not included in any of the economic regions. With respect to the total populations of the regions, these changes were relatively minor, and therefore general comparisons can be made between the two sets of regions, particularly since the comparisons are based primarily on rates.

In general, the migration patterns derived from the 1970 census data by economic region are fairly close to those for the 1959-70 period. The major differences are that Kazakhstan and Central Asia are regions of net in-migration in the 1959-70 period but are regions of net out-migration in the 1968-70 period. Net migration estimates based on vital statistics for the 1968-70 period indicate that Kazakhstan and Turkmeniya had net out-migration, Tadzhikistan and Kirgizia had a small amount of net in-migration, and Uzbekistan had a moderate amount of net in-migration.[71] It should be recalled, however, that these are different measures of migration, and thus different results might be expected. Other differences between the two periods include the following: the Transcaucasus changed from a very small rate of net in-migration in the 1959-70 period to net out-migration in the 1968-70 period; East Siberia changed from a relatively low rate of net out-migration to a relatively low rate of net in-migration; Moldavia went from net in-migration to net out-migration; and Belorussia changed from net out-migration to a rate of zero. Judging from estimates of net migration from vital statistics, many of these changes reflect changing patterns of migration in the latter part of the period. On the basis of comparing oblast and equivalent units between the 1959-70 and 1968-70 periods in terms of net in- or out-migration, there is close correspondence. The major divergences occur in East Siberia, Central Asia, and Kazakhstan, although data by oblast are not available for Kazakhstan, Central Asia, and Belorussia for the 1959-70 period.

With respect to total net in-migration in the 1968-70 period, the Far East and the South had the highest rates, and West Siberia, the Central Chernozem, Volgo-Vyatsk, Urals, and Central Asia experienced the greatest total net out-migration and also lost population through migration in both the urban and rural categories. All regions had more urban in-migration than rural, except the Far East. The Transcaucasus had the lowest rates of both in-migration and out-migration in all categories. Rank correlation coefficients indicate that the total net migration was associated more closely with total in-migration (0.566) than total out-migration (-0.011). More important, with regard to the contribution of net migration to the redistribution of the total population, total net migration for the 1968-70 period was not related closely to the growth (0.309) or the redistribution (0.210) of the total population between 1959 and 1970. The migration turnover of the total population was the greatest in the Russian East.

Whereas the previous discussion dealt with the contribution of migration to the redistribution and growth of the total population, Table 2.19 presents data designed to measure the migration that added to or subtracted from the urban and rural population between 1968 and 1970, so that the contribution of migration to the growth and redistribution of the urban and rural populations can be investigated. Urban in-migration includes migrants to the urban areas of a region, from urban centers beyond the region, and from rural areas within and beyond the region; rural in-migration includes those migrants from urban areas within and beyond the region and from rural areas beyond the region. Urban out-migrants include those migrants from the urban areas of the region to urban areas beyond the region and to rural areas within and beyond the region; rural out-migrants include those that moved out of rural areas within the region to urban areas within and beyond the region and to rural areas beyond the region.

As to urban migration, Moldavia, Belorussia, the South, and the Volga had the highest rates of urban in-migration (Table 2.19 and Maps 2.44-2.47). Passport data, which record movers to urban areas, substantiate the patterns

TABLE 2.19

Urban and Rural Migration Rates by Current Economic Region: 1968-70

Region	Percent of Urban Population Comprised of:			Percent of Rural Population Comprised of:			Migration Turnover	
	In-Migrants	Out-Migrants	Net Migrants	In-Migrants	Out-Migrants	Net Migrants	Urban	Rural
Northwest	5.1	3.1	2.0	4.9	7.0	-2.1	8.2	11.9
West	4.6	2.8	1.8	2.5	4.0	-1.5	7.4	6.5
Center	3.9	2.0	1.9	2.9	5.5	-2.6	5.9	8.4
Volgo-Vyatsk	5.7	3.4	2.3	2.0	6.3	-4.3	9.1	8.3
Central Chernozem	6.3	3.6	2.7	1.5	4.6	-3.1	9.9	6.1
Volga	6.1	3.1	3.0	2.3	5.8	-3.5	9.2	8.1
Belorussia	6.4	2.7	3.7	1.4	4.2	-2.8	9.1	5.6
Moldavia	7.5	3.4	4.1	0.9	3.2	-2.3	10.9	4.1
Southwest	5.4	2.5	2.9	0.8	3.6	-2.8	7.9	4.4
South	6.4	3.4	3.0	4.6	4.9	-0.3	9.8	9.5
Donetsk-Dnepr	3.8	2.4	1.4	2.2	4.8	-2.6	6.2	7.0
North Caucasus	5.7	4.2	1.5	3.3	4.3	-1.0	9.9	7.6
Transcaucasus	1.8	1.6	0.2	0.4	1.6	-1.2	3.4	2.0
Urals	5.2	4.3	0.9	3.6	7.9	-4.3	9.5	11.5
West Siberia	6.3	4.9	1.4	4.2	8.5	-4.3	11.2	12.7
East Siberia	8.1	5.4	2.7	5.1	8.6	-3.5	13.5	13.7
Far East	8.1	5.8	2.3	11.3	10.2	1.1	13.9	21.5
Kazakhstan	7.4	5.0	2.4	3.0	5.7	-2.7	12.4	8.7
Central Asia	3.9	3.6	0.3	0.7	2.0	-1.3	7.5	2.7
USSR total	5.2	3.3	1.9	2.4	4.8	-2.4	8.5	7.2

Note: Based on official urban definitions and origins and destinations influencing urban or rural change of the region. For a fuller explanation of these categories, see accompanying text and Appendix A.

Source: 1970 Soviet census (see Chapter 1, n. 104).

MAP 2.44

Urban In-Migration: 1968-70

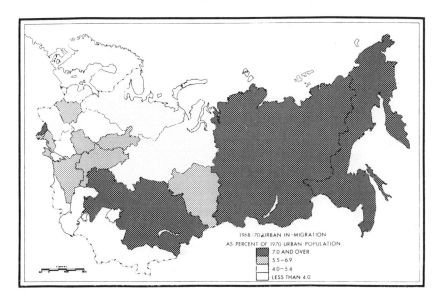

1968-70 URBAN IN-MIGRATION
AS PERCENT OF 1970 URBAN POPULATION
7.0 AND OVER
5.5 — 6.9
4.0 — 5.4
LESS THAN 4.0

MAP 2.45

Urban Out-Migration: 1968-70

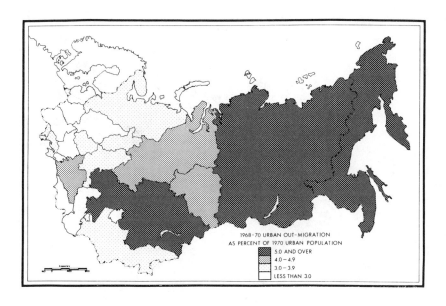

1968-70 URBAN OUT-MIGRATION
AS PERCENT OF 1970 URBAN POPULATION
5.0 AND OVER
4.0 — 4.9
3.0 — 3.9
LESS THAN 3.0

MAP 2.46

Urban Net Migration: 1968-70

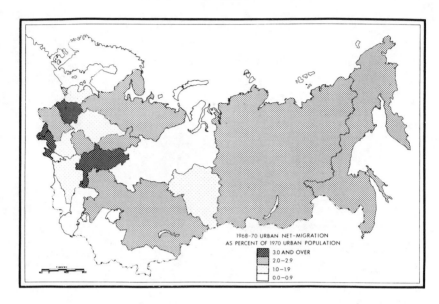

1968-70 URBAN NET-MIGRATION
AS PERCENT OF 1970 URBAN POPULATION

3.0 AND OVER
2.0 — 2.9
1.0 — 1.9
0.0 — 0.9

MAP 2.47

Urban Migration Turnover: 1968-70

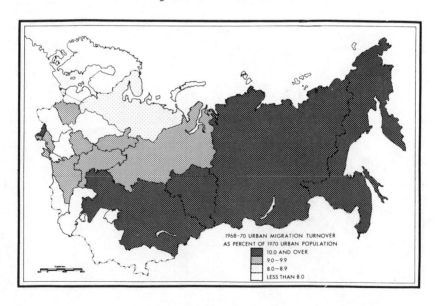

1968-70 URBAN MIGRATION TURNOVER
AS PERCENT OF 1970 URBAN POPULATION

10.0 AND OVER
9.0 — 9.9
8.0 — 8.9
LESS THAN 8.0

TABLE 2.20

Urban Migration Rates by Current Economic Region: Circa 1970

Region	1970 Census Data, Percent of 1970 Urban Population Comprised by 1968-70			Passport Data, Percent of 1970 Urban Population Comprised by 1969			Migration Turnover	
	In-Migrants	Out-Migrants	Net Migrants	In-Migrants	Out-Migrants	Net Migrants	Urban	Rural
Northwest[a]	7.0	5.0	2.0	7.2	6.2	1.0	12.0	13.4
West[b]	6.9	5.1	1.8	7.1	5.4	1.7	12.0	12.5
Center	5.3	3.4	1.9	4.9	3.7	1.2	8.7	8.6
Volgo-Vyatsk	7.1	4.8	2.3	6.6	5.6	1.0	11.9	12.2
Central Chernozem	7.2	4.5	2.7	7.3	5.3	2.0	11.7	12.6
Volga	7.9	4.8	3.1	7.4	5.6	1.8	12.7	13.0
Belorussia	8.6	5.0	3.6	8.3	5.7	2.6	13.6	14.0
Moldavia	8.9	4.8	4.1	8.1	5.4	2.7	13.7	13.5
Southwest	7.0	4.2	2.8	6.7	4.9	1.8	11.2	11.6
South	7.7	4.6	3.1	8.6	6.2	2.4	12.3	14.8
Donetsk-Dnepr	5.5	4.0	1.5	6.6	5.7	0.9	9.5	12.3
North Caucasus	7.5	5.9	1.6	8.3	6.7	1.6	13.4	15.0
Transcaucasus	2.7	2.5	0.2	2.9	2.2	0.7	5.2	5.1
Urals	7.5	6.6	0.9	7.5	7.1	0.4	14.1	14.6
West Siberia	8.7	7.2	1.5	8.7	7.7	1.0	15.9	16.4
East Siberia	11.4	8.7	2.7	10.1	9.3	0.8	20.1	19.4
Far East	12.4	10.1	2.3	11.4	9.8	1.6	22.5	21.2
Kazakhstan	10.0	7.6	2.4	8.8	7.5	1.3	17.6	16.3
Central Asia	5.7	5.4	0.3	5.8	4.9	0.9	11.1	10.7

aExcluding Kaliningradskaya Oblast.
bIncluding Kaliningradskaya Oblast.

Note: Based on official urban definitions and all origins and destinations of the migrants. Net migration and migration turnover rates are based on the subtraction or addition of out-migration rates from or to in-migration rates, respectively.

Sources: 1970 Soviet census (see Chapter 1, n. 104); and Vestnik Statistiki, no. 3 (1971), p. 74.

MAP 2.48

Rural In-Migration: 1968-70

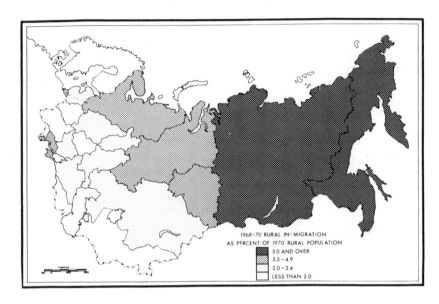

MAP 2.49

Rural Out-Migration: 1968-70

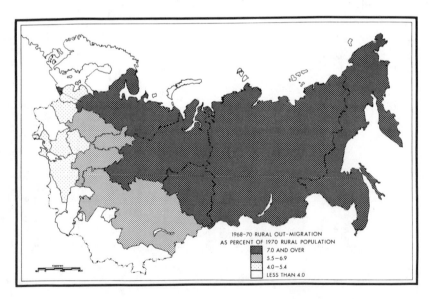

MAP 2.50

Rural Net Migration: 1968-70

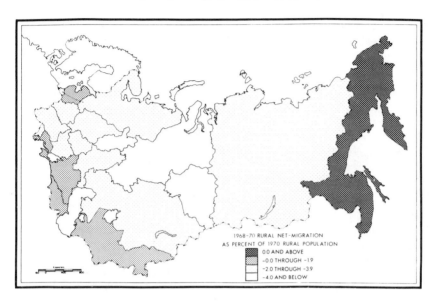

1968-70 RURAL NET-MIGRATION
AS PERCENT OF 1970 RURAL POPULATION
- 0.0 AND ABOVE
- -0.0 THROUGH -1.9
- -2.0 THROUGH -3.9
- -4.0 AND BELOW

MAP 2.51

Rural Migration Turnover: 1968-70

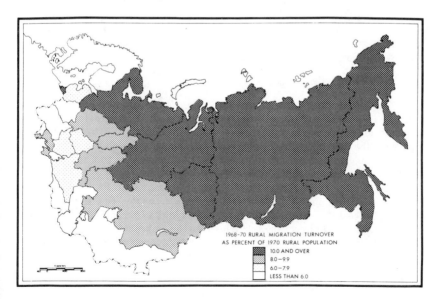

1968-70 RURAL MIGRATION TURNOVER
AS PERCENT OF 1970 RURAL POPULATION
- 10.0 AND OVER
- 8.0—9.9
- 6.0—7.9
- LESS THAN 6.0

derived from change of residence data in the 1970 census. In Table 2.20, the migration data from the census include migrants from urban areas within the region in addition to the sources of migration in Table 2.19, so that comparisons can be made with the passport data. There was close correspondence in terms of the net urban migration rates between the two sets of data. The rank correlation coefficient was 0.801. In 1969, Moldavia, Belorussia, and the South also were leading regions of net urban in-migration, according to the passport data, and the Volga was not far behind. The lowest rates of net urban migration were in the Transcaucasus, Central Asia, and the Urals, and the passport data also substantiate this pattern. In the regions of the Russian East, there were both high urban in-migration and out-migration rates, and thus high rates of migration turnover, which reflects the problem of labor turnover in these regions. Rank correlation coefficients indicate that there was a fairly close association (0.671) between urban in-migration and urban out-migration and urban in-migration and urban net migration (0.700), but urban out-migration was not related to urban net migration (0.026). With regard to the association between net urban migration in the 1968-70 period and growth of the urban population between 1959 and 1970, the relationship was moderate (0.485), and the association with urban distribution, total population growth, and distribution was low.

With respect to rural migration, all regions had negative net rates except the Far East, with the highest rates being in the Urals, West Siberia, Volgo-Vyatsk, Volga, and East Siberia (Table 2.19 and Maps 2.48-2.51). The South, North Caucasus, Transcaucasus, and Central Asia had the lowest rates of net rural out-migration. Once again the greatest migration turnover was in the Russian East, where both the in-migration and out-migration rates were the highest. The Transcaucasus and Central Asia had the least turnover and the lowest rates of rural in-migration and out-migration. Rank correlation coefficients indicate that there was a fairly high relationship between rural in-migration and rural out-migration (0.840). Rural out-migration was associated negatively with rural net migration (-0.384), and rural in-migration was related very weakly to rural net migration (0.039). Net rural migration was associated with total and rural growth between 1959 and 1970 (0.661 and 0.548) and total and rural redistribution (0.594 and 0.541).

Analysis of Total Migration

One of the chief purposes of this study is to attempt to ascertain the degree to which demographic processes in the USSR are universal. In this section, general patterns of total migration will be investigated from this perspective; the analysis of regional urbanization and urban migration and rural population change and rural migration will be investigated in subsequent chapters.

As to geographical mobility, there are no data as to the total number of movers each year in the USSR, but reasonable estimates can be made. According to the 1970 census, 13.9 million people changed their residence in the two years prior to the census. Urban-to-urban migrants constituted 38.1 percent of the total migrants; rural-to-urban, 31.6 percent; rural-to-rural

18.0 percent; and urban-to-rural, 12.2 percent. These data do not include changes of residence within urban settlements or rural rayony and do not take into account the possession of a propiska or whether it is permanent or temporary. Essentially, change of residence in the 1970 census is measured on the basis of urban settlements and rural rayony. Peter Grandstaff inflated the annual number of arrivals in urban centers in 1969 according to the passport data by a factor of 1.45, which takes into account rural-to-rural and urban-to-rural migration according to the 1970 census, and estimated total movers at 14 million. [72] The passport data do not include movers within cities. V. I. Perevedentsev has variously estimated current movers of from 13 to 15 million and from 15 to 16 million per year, without explaining how the estimates were made. [73] Perhaps he takes into account some error in reporting. A. V. Topilin estimates the number of average annual movers between 1959 and 1972 at 12 million. [74]

If we accept 14 to 16 million total movers around 1970, the mobility rate is 6 to 7 percent of the total population. This is less than might be expected, judging from other developed countries, especially considering the relatively rapid rate of economic growth and the relatively large rural population in the USSR. Excluding movers from abroad, 18.6 percent of the U.S. population, 15.7 percent of the Australian, 12.0 percent of the Japanese, and 11.1 percent of the British changed residence in one year around 1970. [75] The Soviet data do not include moves within urban settlements or rural rayony, so they are not comparable with the above data. Because of the severe housing shortages in Soviet cities, one would expect much less intraurban migration, and probably relatively few people move within rural rayony. If the maximum estimate is raised arbitrarily by 4 million to 20 million to take into account intraurban and intra-rayon movement, still the mobility rate is only about 8 percent, which is still relatively low.

Another approach would be to attempt to make the U.S. definition comparable to that of the USSR. Between March 1975 and March 1976, 17.1 percent of the U.S. population ages one year old and older changed their residence, excluding movers from abroad. It is not possible to isolate all movers within urban centers, but 3.4 percent of this U.S. population changed residence within central cities of Standard Metropolitan Statistical Areas (SMSAs), which roughly constitute cities of 50,000 or more. Another 4.5 percent moved between areas outside of SMSAs, which would include movers within towns, between towns, from rural to urban areas, and from urban to rural areas. [76] There are slightly more than 3,000 counties in the United States and slightly more than 3,000 rayony in the USSR, which is roughly 2.5 times the size of the United States. Therefore, if migration rates were the same for U.S. counties and Soviet rayony, there would be more migration in the USSR than the United States, because the units are larger and would require longer moves to be recorded as migrant. The problem in terms of comparability, which cannot be accurately resolved, is to isolate the intraurban moves in the area outside the SMSAs and to take into account the difference in size of the rayony as opposed to counties with respect to rural-to-rural migration. If we arbitrarily estimate that over 50 percent of the moves in

TABLE 2.21

Migration Rates by Nationality: 1968-70

Nationality	Migrants per Thousand Total Population of Nationality		
	Total	Male	Female
Russian	6.7	7.2	6.4
Ukrainian	5.0	5.5	4.5
Belorussian	5.4	5.7	5.1
Uzbek	1.4	1.7	1.1
Kazakh	4.6	4.7	4.5
Georgian	1.7	1.8	1.6
Azeri	1.3	1.7	1.0
Lithuanian	6.0	6.1	5.9
Moldavian	3.1	3.4	2.9
Latvian	5.1	5.4	4.8
Kirgiz	2.5	2.6	2.4
Tadzhik	2.2	2.7	1.7
Armenian	1.9	2.0	1.9
Turkmen	1.4	1.8	1.1
Estonian	5.8	6.2	5.5
USSR total	5.7	6.2	5.4

Source: 1970 Soviet census (see Chapter 1, n. 104).

the areas outside the SMSAs were within towns and due to the smaller size of the counties, one might estimate that 2.5 percentage points could be deducted from the percentage of the total U.S. movers, in addition to the 3.4 percent that moved within cities. Thus, roughly with respect to the Soviet definition about 11 percent of the U.S. population changed residence between March 1975 and March 1976. This is still considerably higher than the Soviet mobility rate of 6 to 7 percent. It is interesting to note that 6.4 percent of the U.S. population moved between counties during this period, although this figure cannot be compared with the Soviet rates. One might conclude, however, that if the British and Japanese rates were adjusted proportionately to that of the United States, their mobility rates would be close to that of the USSR.

One reason for the lower Soviet mobility rate relative to the United States and Australia might be that, as Perevedentsev has pointed out, there is not enough room in Soviet cities for all those that want to live there, and the migration data measure those that register in the cities and not those that desire to live there.[77] Another reason is that extensive suburbanization has not occurred in the USSR, and the boundaries of their cities are usually well beyond the built-up area. The immobility of many non-Slavic groups also contributes to this relatively low mobility rate (Table 2.21). Everett S. Lee suggests that the greater the uniformity with regard to race or ethnicity, the less migration might be expected.[78] Peter Grandstaff has tested this contention using Gini coefficients based on ethnic homogeneity by republic and correlated them with migration but obtained a slightly positive correlation rather than a strongly negative one.[79] Nevertheless, the migration rates for the "non-European" groups were lower, and one might expect ethnicity to impede migration, particularly at earlier stages of modernization and economic development, if economic conditions are not extremely bad. With respect to urban and rural migration rates, the rural mobility rate was 65 per thousand in the 1968-70 period and the urban was 53 per thousand, a pattern that might be expected in a country that is experiencing a rapid rate of economic development and still has a relatively large rural population.[80]

Migration normally occurs in well-defined streams and counterstreams develop. Grandstaff has established the major urban migratory streams of the USSR with more than 15,000 migrants and equal to or greater than 1.5 percent of the average population of the region of origin and destination (Table 2.22). His major conclusions were that 23 of the 29 streams (not all listed in the table) were contiguous and that there were major streams to the east. He also investigated migration and distance based upon the migratory zones of R. V. Tatevosov and concluded that elasticity of movement in terms of distance was close to -1, which approximated that of the United States. In short, a 1 percent increase in distance results in a 1 percent decrease in migration.[81] That migration normally decreases with distance is a well-established concept in the study of migration.

The chief economic function of migration is to equalize the supply of and demand for labor on a regional basis. Soviet authors claim that there is no relationship between the supply of and demand for labor and interregional migration and that people are moving out of labor-deficit into labor-surplus re-

TABLE 2.22

Streams of Interregional Migration, Urban Arrivals: 1969

Both Directions	Predominantly Single Direction
Volga and North Caucasus	Northwest to Center
Volga and Urals	Volgo-Vyatsk to Northwest
North Caucasus and Far East*	Volgo-Vyatsk to Volga
Urals and West Siberia	Volgo-Vyatsk to Urals
West Siberia and East Siberia	Central Chernozem to Donetsk-Dnepr
West Siberia and Far East*	North Caucasus to Donetsk-Dnepr
Donetsk-Dnepr and Southwest	
Donetsk-Dnepr and South	Urals to North Caucasus*
Southwest and South	Urals to East Siberia*
Kazakhstan and Central Asia	East Siberia to Far East

Note: Asterisks designate noncontiguous areas.

Source: Peter J. Grandstaff, "Recent Soviet Experience and Western 'Laws' of Population Migration," International Migration Review 9 (Winter 1975): 487.

gions.[82] If this is true, migration is not doing its job. However, it is difficult to find out precisely how they estimate labor supply and demand. Their national goal is full employment, which means that all able-bodied persons in the working ages (males, ages 16 to 59; females, ages 15 to 54) are to be employed in the social economy (state enterprises, collective farms, or educational institutions) on a full-time basis. About 92 percent of the labor resources were employed in the social economy in 1970. Thus, Soviet authors do not take into account voluntary and involuntary unemployment or work in the private sector. The Soviet citizen has the right and duty to work, and work in the social economy is preferred. Nor do they officially acknowledge the existence of unemployment or collect unemployment data, even though they admit to pockets of unemployment among youths and in smaller cities and a high rate of unplanned labor turnover. People are classified as either having a job or not having a job, and a person looking for a job (that is, unemployed) is not in the work force.[83] The supply of labor (that is, the able-bodied population) is estimated, therefore, mostly from demographic data on age and percentage of the able-bodied population in the work force and the present and future demand for labor, largely from planning balances. Because this calculation of labor supply would include those who do not want to work and those in the private sector, it overestimates the available supply of labor for the social economy.

According to Soviet estimates, the North Caucasus, Central Asia, and the Ukraine have a labor surplus and also net in-migration; and West Siberia and East Siberia have a labor deficit but net out-migration. However, some regions conform to expected patterns. Kazakhstan has a labor deficit and net in-migration; Belorussia, the Volgo-Vyatsk, and the Central Chernozem have labor surpluses and net out-migration. [84] The lack of correspondence between the supply of and demand for labor is related to variation in real wages. Prices are higher, and services, housing, and consumer goods are less adequate in the Russian East than in the western areas, and migrants are responding to these conditions. [85] The availability of jobs in most urban areas of regions with a labor surplus makes migration to these areas possible. (We will subsequently have more to say about Siberian migration and labor problems.)

For the period 1959-72, A. V. Topilin has made estimates as to the amount of economically irrational migration in the USSR by republic, based on the percentage of the labor resources not in the social economy and the level of fertility. He also somehow took into account the availability of natural resources. Out of 210 migratory streams, he estimates that 43.3 percent were irrational, 26.7 were rational, and the remaining 30 percent were neither rational nor irrational. Irrational migration streams contained more than 50 percent of all migrants. More than 1 million persons left the RSFSR in economically irrational streams, and if they had remained in the RSFSR the national income of the RSFSR would have been about R 2 billion greater, according to Topilin. [86] In the early 1970s, labor shortages in the RSFSR in the large cities, industrial centers, regions of new industrial development, and in many rural areas have been estimated at from 1 to 1.2 million workers. [87]

We have made an independent attempt to test how migratory patterns conform to the supply of and demand for labor in the USSR. People move primarily for jobs and economic improvement. The availability of economic opportunities depends on the rate of growth of the economy relative to the rate of growth of the native work force, although the rate of increase in labor productivity of the native workers can affect the demand for labor. If the native work force grows faster than the increase in job opportunities, out-migration or unemployment should occur. If job opportunities expand at a rate greater than the increase in the native work force, net in-migration should occur.

In order to determine whether expected and observed migration patterns coincided in the Soviet Union, a method used by A. J. Jaffe in a similar investigation of the United States was followed, with some modifications. [88] Essentially, the method involves computation of three variables: (1) net migration rates; (2) percentage increase in employment; and (3) percentage increase in the native work force, which is highly related to fertility and natural increase rates for the past generation. Because of the lack of regional employment data, increase in capital investment (including kolkozy) between 1960 and 1970 will be used as a substitute variable (Appendix A). Quite obviously, capital investment is associated highly with the expansion of job opportunities. The growth of the native work force during the 1959-70 period was estimated by calculating the ratio between the 10-19 age cohort in 1959 and the 20-59 age cohort in 1959 by economic region. The 10-19 cohort approximates the number of new native work force entrants in the 1959-70 period, while the 20-59 cohort is roughly indicative of the native work force size at the beginning of this period. In short, the ratio is an estimate of the probable percentage increase in the native work force during the 11-year period, excluding migration.

Analysis of these three variables reveals that expected migration patterns did not occur always.

1. Increase in jobs and native work force below national average (expect intermediate net migration rates):

Center, net in-migration, 0.9 percent
Volgo-Vyatsk, net out-migration, 9.6 percent
Central Chernozem, net out-migration, 5.7 percent
Donetsk-Dnepr, net in-migration, 2.6 percent
Urals, net out-migration, 4.6 percent

2. Increase in jobs and native work force above national average (expect intermediate net migration rates):

West, net in-migration, 4.5 percent
Volga, net in-migration, 1.9 percent
Belorussia, net out-migration, 3.1 percent
Moldavia, net in-migration, 2.3 percent
Southwest, net out-migration, 3.3 percent
Transcaucasus, net in-migration, 0.1 percent
Far East, net in-migration, 1.8 percent
Central Asia, net in-migration, 4.8 percent

3. Increase in jobs below and native work force above national average (expect highest net out-migration rates):

West Siberia, net out-migration, 7.3 percent
East Siberia, net out-migration, 0.8 percent
Kazakhstan, net in-migration, 6.6 percent

4. Increase in jobs above and native work force below national average (expect highest net in-migration rates):

Northwest, net in-migration, 2.1 percent
South, net in-migration, 12.1 percent
North Caucasus, net in-migration, 7.1 percent

Although some regions did have expected patterns (for example, the South, the North Caucasus, and West Siberia), a number did not (such as, the

Volgo-Vyatsk, the Central Chernozem, the Urals, and Kazakhstan). We also used increase in urban population between 1959 and 1970 as a substitute variable for the increase in jobs, and the results were roughly similar. However, we consider capital investment to be a better measure, because urban growth by region includes considerable intraregional migration, as well as interregional migration.

Nevertheless, our analyses should not be considered conclusive. All three variables were estimated, and there is no way to estimate the degree to which labor requirements were being met at the beginning of the period. Regional variation in the mix of capital investment could affect regional variations in labor productivity and thus the demand for labor. The amount of investment for social services and housing could also vary, and therefore a region's ability to attract or accommodate migrants could be affected. That migration into cities with severe housing shortages is restricted could affect the results. Our analysis suggests that migration to a significant degree is not meeting the needs of the economy. That large number of migrants are moving out of the labor-deficit Russian East and rural areas of the RSFSR further substantiates this contention, as we will discuss later.

As to migration selectivity, the universal experience indicates that those in the work force ages, younger people, the more educated, and those with professional and managerial occupations have the highest mobility. According to the 1970 census, 73 percent of the migrants were in the work force ages, although they comprised only 54 percent of the population. Migrants younger than the work force ages comprised 22 percent of the migrants and 31 percent of the total population, and those older than the work force ages, 6 and 15 percent. Thus, those in the work force ages had the highest propensity to migrate, well above their share of the total population, and the other age groups migrated at a rate well below their share of the total population. Passport data for 1964 indicate that over 60 percent of those arriving in or departing from urban centers were between the ages of 15 and 29, which conforms to expected patterns. [89]

Migration is normally not selective by sex. According to the 1970 census, 50.2 percent of the migrants were women, but it should be recalled that the migration data in the 1970 census did not include the military, those that moved outside the USSR, and those away from home for less than six months. According to passport data for 1969 and 1970, only about 45 percent of the arrivals in and 44 percent of the departures from urban centers were women. [90]

There are no data as to migration and education or occupation in the 1970 census, but educational data are available for the 15 nationalities with union republics, within their republics and for the total population of the nationality. If the more educated migrated beyond their republic, one might expect that the level of education of the total population of the nationality would be higher than the level within their republic. Completion of higher education is a reasonable surrogate for professional and managerial employment. The percentage of the Russians, Ukrainians, and Belorussians that have finished higher education or high school is higher for their total population than for their republic population, but the rates for the other nationalities are reversed or the same, with a few minor exceptions. If the educational rates of the urban populations are investigated, the same pattern generally prevails, except that the percentage of the Ukrainian and Belorussian urban populations that has finished high school is higher within their republics. One might infer that some of the more educated Russians, Ukrainians, and Belorussians are migrating beyond their republic, but this tendency appears not to be characteristic of the other nationalities. As will be discussed in a subsequent chapter, it has been reported widely that, upon completion of high school, most rural youths, particularly in the Slavic areas, migrate to the cities, which partially accounts for the considerably higher educational level in urban as opposed to rural areas.

The economic motive is generally very strong in migration. From a survey of the migration literature, one can conclude that people move primarily for jobs and economic improvement. Migration should be related to capital investment, because high rates of investment generally result in an expansion of job opportunities, which results in in-migration if surplus labor is not available. Table 2.23 presents rank correlation coefficients between total migration rates and various categories of state investment. The categories including kolkhozy also include investment in the population (social services), but the categories excluding kolkhozy do not. Because most of the migration and investment was to or in urban centers, an investigation of the relationship between investment and urbanization and urban in-migration constitutes a more refined analysis. Such an investigation will be undertaken in a subsequent chapter, as well as an analysis of rural migration.

The rank correlation coefficients between total net migration rates between 1959 and 1970 and investment are all rather weak, although they are generally positive. Investment for the 1950-60 period was included in order to test for a lag effect, but the sign is unexpected and the correlation is low. As has been previously pointed out, total migration estimates for the 1959-70 period are not particularly a good measure of migration in that they incorporate errors in vital registration and in the censuses. The correlation coefficients for the total net migration rates for the 1968-70 period are somewhat higher with respect to the per capita measures of investment. However, one might expect the correlation coefficient for per capita investment excluding kolkhozy between 1960 and 1970 to be lower than the one including kolkhozy, because the relationship with total migration is being investigated. Once again, investment in the 1950-60 period did not produce the expected correlation coefficient, although the other investment variables also include a lag effect.

Total in-migration rates (1968-70) are a more sensitive measure of investment attraction, because they exclude out-migration. Although some of the signs are unexpected, per capita investment in 1970 produced rather high correlation coefficients, and the other correlation coefficients with per capita investment were moderate to high. The correlation coefficients with total out-migration (1968-70) generally had an unexpected sign and do not support the contention that there should be less total out-migration if there is more investment. These correlation coefficients reflect the rather high association

TABLE 2.23

Rank Correlation Coefficients between Regional Total Migration Rates and Investment
by Economic Region: 1959–70

		Migration Variable			
Investment Variable	Net Migration 1959–70 (129)	Net Migration 1968–70 (105)	In-Migration 1968–70 (103)	Out-Migration 1968–70 (104)
Distribution, including kolkhozy, 1970 (22)	0.163	0.094	0.199	0.062
Distribution, excluding kolkhozy, 1970 (23)	0.072	0.143	0.302	0.129
Per capita, including kolkhozy, 1970 (115)	0.200	0.525	0.842	0.595
Per capita, excluding kolkhozy, 1970 (116)	0.128	0.512	0.798	0.547
Redistribution, including kolkhozy, 1960–70 (46)	0.332	0.111	-0.262	-0.340
Redistribution, excluding kolkhozy, 1960–70 (47)	0.349	0.044	-0.290	-0.340
Change per capita, including kolkhozy, 1960–70 (125)	0.081	0.402	0.444	0.225
Change per capita, excluding kolkhozy, 1960–70 (126)	0.179	0.470	0.572	0.314
Per capita, excluding kolkhozy, 1959–67 (127)	0.098	0.465	0.830	0.637
Percent increase, excluding kolkhozy, 1950–60 (128)	-0.253	-0.444	-0.056	0.262

Note: Numbers in parentheses indicate variable numbers.

Sources: 1959 and 1970 Soviet censuses (see Chapter 1, n. 104); and Appendix A, which also includes a listing and discussion of the variables.

of total in-migration with total out-migration (0.778), which probably in turn reflects the influence of counterstreams in migration.

One important factor that influences the correlation coefficients in Table 2.23 is the availability of labor within the economic regions, which, of course, affects the number of migrants that can be accommodated. If one could control for this factor, one might expect that the correlation coefficients would have been higher. Nevertheless, this analysis indicates a relationship between total migration and investment, although the correlation coefficients were not always as high as expected.

Peter Grandstaff did a regression analysis by republic and economic region using the number of net migrants (1959-70), total investment excluding kolkhozy, and an estimate of the net increase in the work force due to members of the 1959 population. The equations produced poor fits, and he concludes that the contention that migrants move according to investment cannot be supported. He also regressed migration rates (1959-70) on per capita trade levels, average wage levels, number of Russians per thousand population in 1959, employment growth (minus the growth of native work force), average annual temperature, and a dummy variable for government propaganda to migrate. His results indicate that the presence of Russian and employment growth variables were the most important and the economic variables were secondary.[91] This reflects the fact that Russians were the most mobile group, they are moving to Russian areas more, and the employment growth variable is a surrogate for migration.

Blaine Ball and George J. Demko grouped the economic regions, according to the relationship between net migration in thousands between 1968 and 1970 and the industrial wage index in 1968, into two groups: the western economically developed regions excluding the Central Chernozem, Volgo-Vyatsk, and the Southwest and the newly developed eastern regions including the above three regions. They regressed net migration on the industrial wage index and total population for the first group and found that wages accounted for 76 percent of the variation; they concluded that better living conditions were influential. In a further analysis, they demonstrated that there was a strong proximity effect in interregional migration with the regions of the less developed group losing migrants to regions of the more developed group.[92]

The relationship between modernization (and its driving force, industrialization) and population redistribution is of particular interest to our study. By necessity, surrogates must be used to measure this relationship. Rank correlation coefficients between the various measures of migration and industrial work force and urbanization variables are presented in Table 2.24. The industrial work force variable by economic region has been estimated, and the procedures are described in Appendix A. Obviously, the correlations between the measures of migration and the industrial work force and its change between 1959 and 1970 are not strong, and for the change variable the signs generally are unexpected; one would expect all signs to be positive, except the one for total out-migration.

Urbanization is a good surrogate for modernization and industrialization, and, as will be demonstrated later, during the period of planned development has been related rather strongly to measures of industrialization.

TABLE 2.24

Rank Correlation Coefficients between Regional Total Migration Rates and Industrial Work-Force and Urbanization Variables by Economic Region: 1959-70

Variable	Industrial Work Force 1970 (66)	Change in Industrial Work Force 1959-70 (90)	Level of Urbanization 1970 (55)	Change in the Level of Urbanization 1959-70 (79)
Net migration, 1959-70 (129)	-0.218	-0.300	0.026	-0.423
Net migration, 1968-70 (105)	0.324	-0.134	0.480	-0.115
In-migration, 1968-70 (103)	0.350	0.178	0.650	-0.192
Out-migration, 1968-70 (104)	0.116	-0.184	0.282	-0.214
Migration turnover, 1968-70 (106)	0.263	-0.151	0.472	-0.177

Note: Numbers in parentheses indicate variable numbers.

Sources: 1959 and 1970 Soviet censuses (see Chapter 1, n. 104); and Appendix A, which also includes a listing and discussion of the variables.

TABLE 2.25

Correlation Coefficients between Net Migration and
Socioeconomic Factors in Kazakhstan: 1968-71

Socioeconomic Factors	Men	Women
Rate of growth of industrial production	0.521	0.622
Index of employment in the social economy	0.351	0.531
Index of capital investment	0.750	0.797
Level of wages	0.185	0.168
Per capita housing fund	0.022	0.031
Per capita retail trade turnover	0.027	0.255
Availability of preschool facilities	-0.011	0.110
Level of social services	-0.190	0.256

Source: Akademiya Nauk Kazakhskoy SSR, Naseleniye Kazakhstana v 1959-1970 GG. (Alma-Ata: Izdatel'stvo "Nauka" Kazakhskoy SSR, 1975), p. 107.

With the exception of net migration between 1959 and 1970 and total out-migration, the correlations between the level of urbanization and migration have the expected signs and are moderately high. The turnover variable probably reflects the influence of counterstreams in migration. With respect to the change in the level of urbanization between 1959 and 1970, the signs are not expected, except for total out-migration. One problem that should be considered is that the variables depicting change in the work force and urbanization are for an 11-year period and most of the measures of migration are for a 2-year period. Another factor that should be taken into consideration is that total migration includes rural migration, and since most industry is located in cities, a higher correlation can be expected between urban in-migration and urbanization and industrial work force.

In recent years, there have been several attempts by Soviet authors to explain migration in the USSR based on mathematical statistics and data that frequently are not available in published sources. Much of this work has been motivated by the desire to regulate indirectly and rationalize migratory flows. G. D. Moskvina analyzed migration by oblast in Kazakhstan and the results are shown in Table 2.25. The dependent variable was the rate of net migration, 1968-71, estimated from vital statistics. The first three independent variables were considered to be general economic factors, and the remaining variables were considered as factors affecting living conditions. Her general conclusions were that the general economic factors were the most important, having a multiple correlation coefficient for men of 0.865 and for women, 0.701, and that the social factors were much less important with coefficients of 0.429 and 0.721. Although the level of wages was not correlated highly, she points out that survey data for 16 cities of Kazakhstan indicate that about 50 percent of the men and 9 percent of the women who left these cities were dissatisfied with their wages, and of those who changed jobs within the cities the respective percentages were 6.5 and 44.5. This survey further indicated that where the minimum wage for women was over R 120 per month migration began to decline, and the threshold wage for men was R 150.[93]

V. D. Zaytsev has conducted an elaborate statistical analysis of migration in the RSFSR by oblast or equivalent unit for the three years prior to 1970. He regressed net migration rates for a three-year period on the development and redistribution of productive forces (change in the number of jobs as a percentage of the growth of the native work force), level of industrial development (urbanization level), level of wages (corrected by an index of the cost of living), index of the increase in housing, level of medical services, level of higher and middle specialized education, quality of trade and household services, average January temperature, and the frost-free period. In short, he attempted to include factors relating to the economy, level of living, and natural environment. He concludes that three factors, the possibility of finding a job, the level of wages, and the possibility of acquiring an apartment, had about equal weight and were the most important in explaining net migration, with correlation coefficients of 0.534, 0.646, and 0.482, respectively. The equation explained about 67 percent of the variation in net migration.[94]

The above studies do not explain satisfactorily total migration in the USSR. V. I. Perevedentsev is correct when he claims that the modeling of and quantitative research on migration are impeded by the lack of statistics, in particular, on levels of living.[95] Yet, the existing studies to a significant degree support the contention that socioeconomic factors are influential in the exploration of total migration in the USSR, as they are elsewhere. In the Soviet literature there is a debate as to whether economic factors are more important than factors related to the level of living.[96] Both conditions are probably important in migration, but it could well be that where there are major labor shortages, such as in the RSFSR, conditions related to the level of living become more important, although there are insufficient data to demonstrate clearly this hypothesis. That Soviet writers are undertaking quantitative research on migration further supports the contention that migration is not controlled in the USSR, for their ultimate purpose is to explain migration so that it can be regulated indirectly. They repeatedly claim that migration proceeds according to individual volition and attempt to explain it on the basis of that assumption. If it were controlled centrally to an appreciable degree, it would not be logical to attempt to explain migration on the basis of socioeconomic determinants. Even though migration data in the USSR are not abundant, there appears to be a remarkable universality with respect to migratory processes, as the discussions on migration differentials and selectivity indicated, but more will be said on this subject later.

Population Redistribution: 1970-77

Trends of the 1970s

The patterns of total population redistribution between 1970 and 1977 are a continuation of the trends of the previous period (Table 2.1). The Eastern USSR continued to gain relative to the Western USSR, but the Non-Slavic South was the only quadrant to experience a positive shift. However, the average annual rates of redistribution declined for all quadrants, indicating a slowing of population redistribution, at least among the quadrants, even though the rate of the Eastern USSR increased slightly. Northern European USSR and the Russian East continued to decline relatively, and for the first time the European Steppe registered no gain.

There were also few significant changes in the redistribution of the total population by economic region since the 1959-70 period (Tables 2.2 and 2.3 and Maps 2.5, 2.9, and 2.12). Kazakhstan had the greatest decline in terms of average annual percentage point redistribution, and the shift to the North Caucasus and the Transcaucasus also diminished appreciably. The Northwest changed from negative to positive redistribution. The rates for the economic regions comprising the Russian East and the European Steppe all declined.

With respect to the average annual percentage change, the Soviet population grew 0.3 percentage points slower between 1970 and 1977 than it did in the 1959-70 period, but the difference in the rates between the Western USSR and the Eastern USSR increased to the extent that the Eastern USSR grew at more than twice the rate of the Western USSR (Table 2.10). The growth rate of all the quadrants declined, with the sharpest declines being registered in the Non-Slavic South and the European Steppe. All economic regions had a decline in their rate of growth relative to the 1959-70 period, except the Far East, which increased its growth rate appreciably relative to the previous period, and the Northwest, which maintained its rate of growth (Table 2.12 and Maps 2.26 and 2.29). The Volgo-Vyatsk and the Central Chernozem had negative rates of population change. Kazakhstan had the greatest decline, but significant declines also occurred in the North Caucasus, Moldavia, and the Transcaucasus. Thus, much of the decline in the growth of the Non-Slavic South was in Kazakhstan and the Transcaucasus. West Siberia and East Siberia had relatively slight declines in the growth of their populations since the 1959-70 period. The lowest rates of growth in the 1970-77 period were registered by the economic regions comprising Northern European USSR, although West Siberia and the Urals also had low rates of increase, and the highest rates were in those regions comprising the Non-Slavic South.

As to the sources of the total population redistribution, patterns of net migration between 1970 and 1974 differed somewhat from those of the 1959-70 period, as can be seen in Tables 2.17 and 2.26 (compare also Maps 2.38 and 2.52). When comparing these tables, however, one should bear in mind that the periods vary in length, the estimates are somewhat crude, and the economic regions vary somewhat from those used in this study. Because 1971 data on natural increase were not available for the economic regions within the RSFSR and the Ukraine, these data were estimated by averaging the data

TABLE 2.26

Net Migration and Natural Increase by Economic Region: 1970-74

Region	January 1, 1974 Population (thousands)	Population Growth (thousands)	Natural Increase (thousands)	Net Migration (thousands)	Net Migration as Percent of 1974 Population	Net Migration as Percent of Population Growth	Natural Increase as Percent of 1974 Population	Percent of Total Soviet Natural Increase
Northwest	12,611	454	244	210	1.7	46.3	1.9	2.7
West	7,905	325	161	164	2.1	50.6	2.0	1.8
Center	28,136	484	322	162	0.6	33.5	1.1	3.6
Volgo-Vyatsk	8,271	-77	153	-230	-2.8	0.0	1.9	1.7
Central Chernozem	7,823	-175	78	-253	-3.2	0.0	1.0	0.9
Volga	18,845	471	500	-29	-0.2	-6.2	2.7	5.5
Belorussia	9,268	266	305	-39	-0.4	-14.7	3.3	3.4
Moldavia	3,764	195	183	12	0.3	6.2	4.9	2.0
Southwest	21,158	469	558	-89	-0.4	-19.0	2.6	6.2
South	6,743	363	185	178	2.6	49.0	2.7	2.1
Donetsk-Dnepr	20,620	563	422	141	0.7	25.0	2.1	4.7
North Caucasus	14,899	618	457	161	1.1	26.1	3.1	5.1
Transcaucasus	13,120	825	828	-3	-0.0	-0.3	6.3	9.2
Urals	15,233	48	430	-382	-2.5	-795.8	2.8	4.8
West Siberia	12,291	182	386	-204	-1.7	-112.1	3.1	4.3
East Siberia	7,733	270	315	-45	-0.6	-16.7	4.1	3.5
Far East	6,300	520	266	254	4.0	48.9	4.2	3.0
Kazakhstan	13,928	919	930	-11	-0.1	-1.2	6.7	10.3
Central Asia	22,221	2,429	2,298	131	0.6	5.4	10.3	25.5
USSR total	250,869	9,149	9,021	128	0.1	1.4	98.6	100.3

Source: Calculated from data in Naseleniye SSSR, 1973 (Moscow: Izdatel'stvo "Statistika," 1975), pp. 10-25, 69-95.

MAP 2.52

Total Net Migration: 1970-74

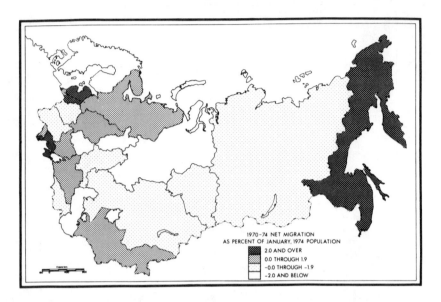

for 1970, 1972, and 1973. The difference between our estimated total natural increase and the reported total for the 1970-74 period was 85,000, or less than 1 percent. As in the previous period, the chief regions of net out-migration in the 1970-74 period in terms of rates were the Volgo-Vyatsk, Central Chernozem, Urals, and West Siberia, although there have been changes in their rankings. In the 1970-74 period, the Central Chernozem was the leading region of net out-migration, and there appears to be a decline in the rate for West Siberia and an increase for the Urals, although such inferences must be considered tentative, given the approximate nature of these estimates. It also would appear that the net out-migration rates for Belorussia and the Southwest also declined, and the Volga changed from a region of net in-migration to one with a low rate of net out-migration. The most significant change occurred in Kazakhstan, which previously was a major area of net in-migration, but in the 1970-74 period had a slight net out-migration rate; this change supports its decline with respect to rates of redistribution and growth.

As to regions of net in-migration, the rankings of the leading regions also changed. The Far East experienced an appreciable increase and displaced the South as the leading region of net in-migration, and the rates for the North Caucasus and Central Asia appear to have declined substantially, in addition to the sharp decline in the rate for Kazakhstan. The rate for the Northwest appears to have increased markedly, which probably accounts for the increase in its redistribution and growth rates.

The contribution of net in-migration to population growth appears to have increased substantially as natural increase has declined. Whereas in the 1959-70 period, there were only three regions where net in-migration accounted for more than 25 percent of the population growth. In the 1970-74 period, there were seven, four of which were close to 50 percent. Of course, in the regions of net out-migration all of the growth was due to natural increase. There was a sharp decline in the natural increase rates of the Slavic and Baltic areas and a moderate decline in Kazakhstan and the Transcaucasus, which greatly increased the contribution of Central Asia to the total growth and natural increase of the USSR. In the 1959-70 period, Central Asia accounted for about 19 percent of the Soviet population growth and 17 percent of the natural increase, but in the 1970-74 period the respective percentages were 27 and 26, even though Central Asia had only 9 percent of the Soviet population in 1974. The regions comprising the Non-Slavic South had 45 percent of the natural increase in the 1970-74 period. Consequently, although in some of the Slavic and Baltic areas migration has contributed substantially to population growth and redistribution, much of the redistribution of the total population to the Non-Slavic areas can be accounted for by differential natural increase, in that the total growth of these regions was due, virtually, to natural increase.

Siberian Labor Problems

One of the chief migration problems in the Soviet Union is that migration is not equalizing the supply of and demand for labor on a regional basis. In particular, Siberia has been a labor deficit area with high rates of net out-migration, even though it has had a high priority in terms of economic development. This situation supports our contention that Soviet migration policy has been largely ineffective in the USSR and that migration has been fundamentally uncontrolled, because people have been moving out of Siberia in large numbers primarily in response to differences in real income, as one would expect. However, the changes in migration trends since 1970 appear to indicate that net out-migration from Siberia has diminished, perhaps partially, in response to changes in policy.

There is a maldistribution of either people or resources in the USSR. Because of past agricultural technologies as related to the natural environment and other historical circumstances, most of the Soviet population is located in the European part of the USSR, whereas the bulk of the industrial resources are located in the Russian East. Even though the east has not been explored completely geologically, it is widely reported to have huge deposits of resources: about nine-tenths of the bituminous coal in the USSR, although much of it is inaccessible; four-fifths of the timber; most of the hydroelectric power potential; two-thirds of the iron ore; and vast reserves of oil and natural gas, as well as extensive reserves of a variety of other minerals. Clearly, if the Soviet population were to be redistributed solely in terms of industrial resources, its distribution would be vastly different.

In response to the availability of resources, as well as strategic considerations, the Soviet government began to develop the Russian East in the

1930s; the Urals-Kuznets Combine was a notable example. World War II provided a major impetus to the development of the Russian East, when over 1,300 major industrial enterprises were relocated to the Eastern USSR. Since the Sixth Five-Year Plan development of the Russian East has been emphasized. Even though investment plans have not always been fulfilled, per capita investment during the 1960s in Siberia and the Far East exceeded the all-union average.[97] The Tenth Five-Year Plan also emphasized the economic development of the eastern regions of the RSFSR.[98]

It is acknowledged widely, however, that a shortage of labor in Siberia and the Far East is and has been a major impediment to economic development.[99] A. Maykov estimates that between 1971 and 1980, Siberia and the Far East will require several million additional workers to fulfill developmental plans, and since only about 50 percent of these labor requirements can be met by increases in the native work force, still several million migrants in the work force ages will be required.[100] The Institute of Economics and the Organization of Industrial Production of the Academy of Sciences of the USSR estimate that between 1976 and 1980 planned development in Siberia will require an 18 percent increase in the work force in the social economy, even though the growth rate of the native work force will decline significantly.[101] If one adjusts for mortality, the 10-49 age group in 1970 will be the 20-59 age group in 1980 or roughly the working-age population, assuming no migration. Based on these procedures, the working-age population of Siberia will increase 23.5 percent between 1970 and 1980, which is well below the labor requirements on an average annual basis. Although in the past a relatively high percentage of the working-age population was not employed in the social economy,[102] currently only a very small percentage of the working-age population of Siberia is to be found in housework and private plots;[103] current plans, however, call for increasing employment for women.[104] Furthermore, there are no labor reserves for the labor deficits of urban areas in rural areas of Siberia; it has been estimated that between 1966 and 1967 available agricultural labor in West Siberia met only 70 percent of requirements, and labor shortages, relative to the level of mechanization, in agricultural areas have been a problem throughout the eastern regions for more than a decade.[105] Out-migration from rural areas continues at an intensified rate. Thus, a solution to the labor shortages of the eastern regions lies in migration from other parts of the country, even though labor shortages have arisen throughout the USSR, except for Central Asia and Moldavia.[106] Of course, one other major solution would be to increase labor productivity by means of capital investment, in particular to modernize existing enterprises and to emphasize capital-intensive production rather than labor-intensive. This has been recommended widely in the Soviet literature. However, low labor productivity has been a perennial problem in the USSR.

Yet, for the past decade or more, Siberia has been characterized by relatively high rates of net out-migration, and the Far East has been unable to meet its growing labor requirement through migration, even though it is a region of net in-migration. It would appear that unqualified workers move to the east and, after acquiring training and experience and making some money, return to the west or go elsewhere in the USSR.[107] It is reported widely and documented by surveys that the out-migrants have been the more qualified and younger workers, which further aggravates the labor problems, and that virtually all parts of Siberia have and are suffering labor shortages in both urban and rural areas.[108] Furthermore, the contribution of organized migration to the solution of Siberian labor problems has been insignificant;[109] in 1965, it was estimated that not more than 20 percent of the migrants to Western Siberia were from this source,[110] and the situation very probably has changed little since then, because organized migration in the USSR has been diminishing.

Between 1961 and 1973, net out-migration from Siberia has been estimated at about 1 million, 85 percent of which was attributed to West Siberia. Relative to the 1961-65 period, net out-migration from Siberia increased considerably during the 1966-70 period but declined to its lowest level in terms of the number of average annual net out-migrants in the 1971-73 period. Since 1969, the peak of out-migration, there has been a sharp decline in West Siberia, from an estimated 146,000 net out-migrants to 17,000 in 1973, and in East Siberia it fell to an even lower level. Between 1959 and 1973, net out-migration absorbed 50 percent of the natural increase in West Siberia and 11 percent in East Siberia; during this period, net out-migration from rural areas of Siberia resulted in a 15 percent decline in the rural population and a 45 percent decline in the rural population aged 20 to 29. The rate of rural out-migration increased during this period. The urban population of Siberia grew by about 1.8 million as a result of migration between 1961 and 1973, but the rate of increase of the urban population due to migration decreased, and the migration turnover increased, at least up to 1970. Between 1966 and 1970, intraregional migration accounted for the total growth of the urban population due to migration, because there were more urban out-migrants to other parts of the RSFSR and other republics than there were urban in-migrants from these sources (101 and 110 out-migrants per hundred in-migrants, respectively). Because of the relatively high migratory turnover of the urban population of Siberia, the solution to the labor problems does not lie necessarily in attracting more migrants, because each year about 500,000 migrants arrive in Siberian cities from other parts of the country. It has been estimated that if urban out-migration to other parts of the USSR were decreased by 25 percent, in 15 years the urban population of Siberia would increase by 2 million from this source.[111]

The world migration literature indicates that people move primarily for jobs and economic improvement, and thus regional differences in these factors are normally an impetus to interregional migration within a country. Because there are labor shortages in many parts of the USSR, especially in Siberia and the Far East, and there are regional differences in the standard of living within the USSR, one might expect that the regional differentials in the standard of living would take on particular significance with respect to interregional migration. In fact, V. I. Perevedentsev very rightly maintains that the standard of living in labor deficit areas should be higher than in labor surplus areas in order to attract and retain labor.[112]

It is widely acknowledged that in addition to a relatively less desirable natural environment and its relative isolation from the cultural centers of the USSR, the standard of living in Siberia is and has been significantly below that of the average for the RSFSR. Writing in the mid-1960s and drawing largely on 1959 data, V. I. Perevedentsev documents that urban housing, in terms of quantity and quality, wages, medical services, retail trade turnover, education, and life expectancy, in West Siberia was below that of the RSFSR and that, although average wages in East Siberia were slightly above the RSFSR average because of the structure of industry, indicators of the standard of living in East Siberia were similar to those of West Siberia.[113] A. Gladyshev also supports this contention and emphasizes the role of differential expenditures in social consumption funds in migration.[114]

By 1970, with respect to the chief indicators of the standard of living, West and East Siberia still generally ranked low among the economic regions of the RSFSR. In particular, per capita urban housing lagged in Siberia, even though the rate of increase of urban housing in West Siberia increased above the RSFSR average during the 1960s and the retail trade turnover increased since 1960, especially after 1970.[115] A case can be made that because of the nature and distribution of the population and natural conditions more services are required for an equivalent level of satisfaction; a younger population requires more school facilities, and the dispersed population of the east requires some 30 to 40 percent more medical facilities; the more severe natural environment requires more food, clothing, and better housing. In a recent survey among migrants in West and East Siberia, inadequate housing was cited as the chief reason for leaving in 17 of the 18 political units surveyed.[116] It has been estimated officially (around 1970?) that the cost of living for a family of four in the eastern regions of the RSFSR is 38 percent above that of the southern part of the country and 26 percent above the central part of the country. If one also takes into consideration the necessity to compensate for the less favorable conditions in addition to differences in the cost of living, it has been estimated roughly that wages in Siberia should be 30 to 40 percent higher and in the Far East, 50 to 60 percent. This would mean that, if real wages are not to be below those of European USSR, at a minimum equivalent workers in the east should have wages 20 percent, and in many cases 30 to 45 percent, above those of European USSR.[117]

Recently there have been increases in wages in the east, although it would appear that they have not reached or surpassed these levels, as Perevedentsev recommended. In conjunction with the wage reforms of 1956 to 1960, a set of regional wage coefficients (percentage additions to wages) and supplements according to length of service were instituted, although they were not applied to all workers or to all industries uniformly, or to all parts of a given region. Most frequently the service industries were not included, and rates for light industry, when included, were below that of heavy industry, which received the major emphasis. As of 1959, the coefficient for the Islands of the Arctic Ocean was 2.0; other regions of the Far North, 1.5-1.7; regions equivalent to the Far North, 1.3-1.4; certain regions of the European North, southern regions of East Siberia and the Far East, 1.2; and the Urals, southern West Siberia, Kazakhstan, and Central Asia, 1.15. Not all parts of Kazakhstan and Central Asia were included. Unspecified areas, such as the remaining regions of European USSR and the Transcaucasus had a coefficient of 1.0. [118]

Subsequently, the coefficients have been raised and gradually applied to all wage earners. By about 1972, the coefficient for the Islands of the Arctic Ocean and other regions of the Far North remained unchanged; for regions equivalent to the Far North (including Murmansk Oblast and central regions of Siberia) and to regions of the Far East it had been changed to 1.3-1.5; for certain regions of the European North, southern regions of East Siberia and the Far East, 1.2-1.3; for the Urals, southern regions of West Siberia, Kazakhstan, and Central Asia, 1.1-1.2. [119] Violet Conolly reports that the coefficients were abolished in the Far North in 1960, which led to an exodus of workers, but were restored in 1967. [120] We have been unable, however, to substantiate this assertion. In fact, Janet Chapman reports that in 1960 regional coefficients were applied to all workers in the Far North; in 1968 they were extended to all workers in the Far East, and in 1969 to all workers in East Siberia. [121] In 1972, they were applied to all workers in Western Siberia[122] and the appropriate areas of the Turkmen SSR. The Tenth Five-Year Plan calls for extending it to areas not covered. In addition, in the Islands in the Arctic Ocean and the Far North and roughly equivalent regions, workers receive graduated wage supplements according to length of service, based on their base salary, excluding the coefficient and other additions to pay. The maximum payment usually ranges from R 150 to R 300, based on a maximum monthly salary of R 300. There are also other benefits in these areas including additional leave time (12 to 18 days), pregnancy pay, certain additional pension benefits, a guarantee of housing in the former place of residence, and other benefits. [123] It would appear that in an attempt to solve the labor problems of the east, current plans call for additional investment in housing and services, although additional wage supplements are planned for the Far East. [124]

Our chief concern, however, is how these wage changes have affected migration trends since 1970. As has been pointed out (Tables 2.17 and 2.26), there appears to have been a rise in net in-migration in the Far East, and the volume and rate of net out-migration from West and East Siberia appear to have declined relative to the 1959-70 period, although the approximate nature of migration estimates based on natural increase and the estimated population for intercensal years do not permit definitive statements to be made. Exogenous factors also may play a role. Although a slight rise in the wage coefficient for southern West Siberia occurred around or before 1972, it was not applied to all workers in West Siberia until 1972. Yet, there was a sharp decline in net out-migration in West Siberia between 1969 and 1972, from 146,000 to 35,000 net out-migrants, according to the estimates of E. D. Malinin and A. K. Ushakov. [125] Nevertheless, the migration situation appears to have improved in the chief regions affected by the coefficients, and this includes the Northwest. However, all we can say with any certainty at this juncture is that these wage reforms may have affected these migration patterns and thus, to a degree, contributed to the solution of Siberian labor problems.

NOTES

1. Eugene M. Kulischer, Europe on the Move (New York: Columbia University Press, 1948), pp. 9-13.

2. The chief sources of information for this survey of early settlement were V. Z. Drobizhev, I. D. Koval'chenko, and A. V. Murav'yev, Istoricheskaya Geografiya SSSR (Moscow: Izdatel'stvo "Vysshaya Shkola," 1973) and V. V. Pokshishevskiy, "Ocherki po Zaseleniyu Lesostepnykh i Stepnykh Rayonov Russkoy Ravniny," Ekonomicheskaya Geografiya SSSR, vyp. 5 (1960), pp. 3-68. Other sources include George J. Demko, The Russian Colonization of Kazakhstan, 1896-1916 (The Hague: Mouton, 1969); Peter I. Lyashchenko, History of the National Economy of Russia to the 1917 Revolution (New York: Macmillan, 1949); W. H. Parker, An Historical Geography of the USSR (Chicago: Aldine, 1969); B. H. Sumner, A Short History of Russia (New York: Reynal and Hitchcock, 1947); and Donald Treadgold, The Great Siberian Migration (Princeton, N.J.: Princeton University Press, 1957).

3. Pokshishevskiy, "Ocherki po Zaseleniyu Lesostepnykh," p. 59.

4. Ibid.

5. Demko, Russian Colonization of Kazakhstan, pp. 51, 78.

6. Robert A. Lewis, Richard H. Rowland, and Ralph S. Clem, Nationality and Population Change in Russia and the USSR (New York: Praeger, 1976), p. 275.

7. B. S. Khorev and V. M. Moiseyenko, Sdvigi v Razmeshchenii Naseleniya SSSR (Moscow: "Statistika," 1976), p. 17.

8. J. William Leasure and Robert A. Lewis, "Internal Migration in Russia in the Late Nineteenth Century," Slavic Review 27 (September 1968): 375-94; and idem, "Internal Migration in the USSR: 1897-1926," Demography 4, no. 2 (1967): 479-96.

9. Frank Lorimer, The Population of the Soviet Union: History and Prospects (Geneva: League of Nations, 1946), pp. 45-49.

10. Ibid., pp. 35, 212.

11. Kulischer, Europe on the Move, p. 28.

12. Lorimer, Population of the Soviet Union, p. 35.

13. E. Z. Volkov, Dinamika Naseleniya SSSR za Vosem'desyat Let (Moscow: Gosudarstvennoye Izdatel'stvo, 1930), p. 209; and Lorimer, Population of the Soviet Union, pp. 37-41

14. Kulischer, Europe on the Move, pp. 56, 71.

15. B. Ts. Urlanis, Rozhdayemost' i Prodolzhitel'nost' Zhizni v SSSR (Moscow: Gosstatizdat, 1963), p. 23.

16. Volkov, Dinamika Naseleniya SSSR, p. 190.

17. L. I. Lubny-Gertsyk, Dvizheniye Naseleniya na Territorii SSSR (Rostov na Donu: Izdatel'stvo "Planovoye Khozyaystvo," 1926), pp. 23,27.

18. Ibid., p. 22.

19. Volkov, Dinamika Naseleniya SSSR.

20. Lubny-Gertsyk, Dvizheniye Naseleniya, pp. 27-29.

21. Kulischer, Europe on the Move, p. 70.

22. Ibid., pp. 31, 74.

23. Volkov, Dinamika Naseleniya SSSR, pp. 190-95.
24. Lubny-Gertsyk, Dvizheniye Naseleniya, pp. 59-62.
25. Kulischer, Europe on the Move, pp. 71-78.
26. Lorimer, Population of the Soviet Union, pp. 81-83.
27. Ibid., pp. 133-37.
28. Dana G. Dalrymple, "The Soviet Famine of 1932-34," Soviet Studies 15 (January 1964): 260.
29. Kulischer, Europe on the Move, p. 102.
30. V. M. Moiseyenko, "Rol' Migratsii v Formirovanii Gorodskogo Naseleniya SSSR v Sovremennykh Usloviyakh," Problemy Narodonaseleniya (Moscow: "Statistika," 1973), p. 50. There was a printing error in the table from which these data were derived. It was assumed that these data were for the 1926-39 territory of the USSR, because very similar data were published in 1940 and the urban growth conforms to that obtained from the two censuses. For the earlier data by category, see S. I. Sul'kevich, Terrotoriya i Naseleniya SSSR (Moscow: Politizdat, 1940), p. 30.
31. Kulischer, Europe on the Move, p. 81.
32. Ibid., pp. 93-94.
33. Ibid., pp. 82-84.
34. V. A. Shpilyuk, Mezhrespublikanskaya Migratsiya i Sblizheniye Natsii v SSSR (L'vov: Izdatel'stvo pri L'vovskom Gosudarstvennom Universitete, 1975), p. 42.
35. M. K. Karakhanov, ed., Problemy Narodonaseleniya (Moscow: Izdatel'stvo Moskovskogo Universiteta, 1970), pp. 21, 334.
36. V. A. Borisov, Perspektivy Rozhdayemosti (Moscow: "Statistika," 1976), p. 78.
37. USSR, Narodnoye Khozyaystvo SSSR v 1964 G (Moscow: "Statistika," 1965), p. 38.
38. V. V. Pokshishevskiy, Geografiya Naseleniya SSSR (Moscow: Izdatel'stvo "Prosveshcheniye," 1971), p. 87; Kulischer, Europe on the Move, p. 116.
39. A. L. Odud, Moldavskaya SSR (Moscow: Gosudarstvennoye Izdatel'stvo Geograficheskoy Literatury, 1955), pp. 62, 78.
40. M. Sonin, "Voprosy Pereleniya v Tret'yey Pyatiletke," Problemy Ekonomiki, no. 3 (1940), pp. 80-91.
41. Vestnik Statistiki, no. 1 (1965), pp. 87-91.
42. Pokshishevskiy, Geografiya Naseleniya SSSR, p. 34.
43. USSR, Naseleniye SSSR, 1973 (Moscow: Izdatel'stvo "Statistika," 1975), pp. 14-24.
44. Pokshishevskiy, Geografiya Naseleniya SSSR, p. 88.
45. Kulischer, Europe on the Move, pp. 274, 287, 292, 299.
46. Lorimer, Population of the Soviet Union, p. 194.
47. Pokshishevskiy, Geografiya Naseleniya SSSR, p. 87, and Sh. M. Munchayev, "Evakuatsiya Naseleniya v Gody Velikoy Otechestvennoy Voyny," Istoriya SSSR, no. 3 (1975), p. 138.
48. Kulischer, Europe on the Move, pp. 294-96.
49. Lewis, Rowland, and Clem, Nationality and Population Change, pp. 230-35.

50. Kulischer, Europe on the Move, p. 299.

51. Pokshishevskiy, Geografiya Naseleniya SSSR, p. 88.

52. Ibid., p. 88.

53. J. William Leasure and Robert A. Lewis, Population Changes in Russia and the USSR: A Set of Comparable Territorial Units (San Diego, Calif.: San Diego State College Press, 1966), pp. x-xi; O. A. Konstantinov, "Sovremennoye Sostoyaniye Deleniya Naselennykh Punktov SSSR na Gorodskiye i Sel'skiye," Izvestiya Akademii Nauk SSSR, Seriya Geograficheskaya, no. 6 (1958), pp. 69-78; B. S. Khorev, Problemy Gorodov, 2d ed. (Moscow: Izdatel'stvo "Mysl'," 1975), p. 57.

54. Naseleniye SSSR, 1973, p. 7.

55. Moiseyenko, "Rol' Migratsii," p. 50.

56. Robert J. Osborn, Soviet Social Policies: Welfare, Equality and Community (Homewood, Ill.: Dorsey Press, 1970), p. 143.

57. Narodnoye Khozyaystvo SSSR v 1964 G, p. 38.

58. Naseleniye SSSR, 1973, pp. 42-51.

59. Tsentral'noye Statisticheskoye Upravleniye, SSSR, Itogi Vsesoyuznoy Perepisi Naseleniya 1959 Goda, Svodnyy Tom (Moscow: Gosstatizdat, 1962), p. 8; and idem, Itogi Vsesoyuznoy Perepisi Naseleniya 1970 Goda, vol. 7 (Moscow: Izdatel'stvo "Statistika," 1974), p. 3.

60. U.S., Department of Commerce, Foreign Demographic Analysis Division, Estimates and Projections of the Population of the USSR by Age and Sex: 1950 to 2000, International Population Reports, Series P-91, no. 23 (Washington, D.C.: U.S. Government Printing Office, 1973), p. 6; and Peter J. Grandstaff, "Economic Aspects of Interregional Migration in the USSR, 1959-70," unpub. manuscript, pp. 22-35.

61. V. I. Perevedentsev, Metody Izucheniya Migratsii Naseleniya (Moscow: Izdatel'stvo "Nauka," 1975), pp. 42-51.

62. P. G. Pod'yachikh, "Sostoyaniye Statistiki Migratsii Naseleniya v SSSR i Mery po Eye Uluchsheniyu," Problemy Migratsii Naseleniya i Trudovykh Resursov (Moscow: Izdatel'stvo "Statistika," 1970), p. 122.

63. Perevedentsev, Metody Izucheniya Migratsii Naseleniya, p. 47; and A. V. Topilin, Territorial'noye Pereraspredeleniye Trudovykh Resursov v SSSR (Moscow: Izdatel'stvo "Ekonomika," 1975), p. 25.

64. Perevedentsev, Metody Izucheniya Migratsii, p. 49.

65. B. S. Khorev and V. M. Moiseyenko, eds., Migratsionnaya Podvizhnost' Naseleniye v SSSR (Moscow: Izdatel'stvo "Statistika," 1974), p. 45.

66. Peter J. Grandstaff, "A Note on Preliminary 1970 USSR Census Results Concerning Migration," The Association for Comparative Economic Studies Bulletin 16 (Fall 1974): 33-39.

67. Grandstaff, "Economic Aspects of Interregional Migration," p. 282.

68. Borisov, Perspektivy Rozhdayemosti, pp. 68, 78.

69. USSR, Narodnoye Khozyaystvo SSSR v 1967 G (Moscow: "Statistika," 1968), p. 625.

70. Theodore Shabad, "Soviet Migration Patterns Based on 1970 Census Data," in Demographic Developments in Eastern Europe, ed. Leszek A. Kosinski (New York: Praeger, 1977), pp. 175-82.

71. Grandstaff, "Economic Aspects of Interregional Migration," p. 152.

72. Peter J. Grandstaff, "Recent Soviet Experience and Western 'Laws' of Population Migration," International Migration Review 9 (Winter 1975): 481.

73. Perevedentsev, Metody Izucheniya Migratsii Naseleniya, p. 103; and B. Ts. Urlanis, ed., Narodonaseleniye Stran Mira (Moscow: "Statistika," 1974), p. 403.

74. Topilin, Territorial'noye Pereraspredeleniye Trudovykh Resursov v SSSR, p. 35.

75. Larry H. Long and Celia G. Boertlein, The Geographical Mobility of Americans, Current Population Reports, ser. P-23, no. 64 (Washington, D.C.: U.S. Government Printing Office), p. 3.

76. U.S. Bureau of the Census, Geographical Mobility: March 1975 to March 1976, Current Population Reports, ser. P-20, no. 305 (Washington, D.C.: Government Printing Office, 1977), pp. 1-7.

77. Perevedentsev, Metody Izucheniya Migratsii Naseleniya, p. 44.

78. Everett S. Lee, "A Theory of Migration," Demography 3, no. 1 (1966): 52-53.

79. Grandstaff, "Economic Aspects of Interregional Migration," pp. 485-86.

80. B. S. Khorev and V. M. Moiseyenko, eds., Migratsionnaya Podvizhnost' Naseleniya v SSSR (Moscow: "Statistika," 1974), p. 33.

81. Ibid., pp. 482, 486-87; and R. V. Tatevosov, "Isslendovaniye Prostranstvennykh Zakonomernostey Migratsii Naseleniya," in Statistika Migratsii Naseleniya, ed. T. V. Ryabushkin (Moscow: "Statistika," 1973), pp. 35-48.

82. V. I. Perevedentsev, "Sovremennaya Migratsiya Naseleniya v SSSR," Narodonaseleniye i Ekonomika (Moscow: Izdatel'stvo "Ekonomika," 1967), p. 104.

83. E. C. Brown, "Continuity and Change in the Soviet Labor Market," Industrial and Labor Relations Review 23 (1970): 171-90; and E. Manevich, "The Management of Soviet Manpower," Foreign Affairs 47 (October 1968): 176-84.

84. Perevedentsev, "Sovremennaya Migratsiya Naseleniya v SSSR," p. 104; and idem, "Nekotoryye Voprosy Mezhrayonnogo Pereraspredeleniye Trudovykh Resursov," Izvestiya Sibirskogo Otdeleniya Akademii Nauk SSSR: Seriya Obshchestvennykh Nauk, no. 9 (1964), p. 77.

85. V. I. Perevedentsev, "Territorial'noye Razmeshcheniye Naseleniya po Strane i ego Migratsiya," in Teoriya i Politika Narodonaseleniya, ed. D. I. Valentey (Moscow, 1967), pp. 126-43.

86. Topilin, Territorial'noye Pereraspredeleniye Trudovykh Resursov v SSSR, pp. 46-47.

87. A. Maykov, "Osnovnyye Napravleniya Migratsii i Sovershenstvovaniye Territorial'noye Pereraspredeleniye Trudovykh Resursov," Narodonaseleniye (Moscow: "Statistika," 1973), pp. 28-29.

88. A. J. Jaffe, "Manpower and Other Economic Contributions by Migrants: The United States Experience" (Paper presented at the Conference on Labor and Migration, Brooklyn College Center for Migration Studies, Brooklyn College, New York, March 13-14, 1970, pp. 13-17.

89. L. Denisova and T. Fadeyeva, "Nekotoryye Dannyye o Migratsii Naseleniya v SSSR," Vestnik Statistiki, no. 7 (1965), p. 20.

90. Khorev and Moiseyenko, Migratsionnaya Podvizhnost' Naseleniya v SSSR, p. 45.

91. Peter J. Grandstaff, "Interregional Migration Determinants in the U.S.S.R.: An Empirical Examination" (Paper presented at the Annual Meeting of the Population Association of America, April 21, 1977), pp. 18-22.

92. Blaine Ball and George J. Demko, "Internal Migration in the Soviet Union," Economic Geography 54 (April 1978): 95-114.

93. Akademiya Nauk Kazakhskoy SSR, Naseleniye Kazakhstana v 1959-70 GG (Alma-Ata: Izdatel'stvo "Nauka" Kazakhskoy SSR, 1975), pp. 100-7.

94. V. D. Zaytsev, "Problemy Modelironvaniya Migratsii Naseleniya," in Migratsiya Naseleniya RSFSR, ed. A. Z. Maykov (Moscow: "Statistika," 1973), pp. 3-31.

95. Perevedentsev, Metody Izucheniya Migratsii Naseleniya, pp. 100, 117.

96. Zaytsev, "Problemy Modelirovaniya Migratsii Naseleniya," p. 5.

97. Violet Conolly, Siberia Today and Tomorrow (New York: Toplinger, 1975), p. 57. This source includes an interesting summary discussion of Soviet regional investment policy and eastern investment.

98. V. G. Kostakov, Trudovyye Resursy Pyatiletki (Moscow: Izdatel'stvo Politicheskoy Literatury, 1976), p. 58.

99. For example, see ibid.; V. I. Perevedentsev, Migratsiya Naseleniya i Trudovyye Problemy Sibiri (Novosibirsk: Izdatel'stvo "Nauka" Sibirskoye Otdeleniye, 1966), p. 51; idem, Sovremennaya Migratsiya Naseleniya Zapadnoy Sibiri (Novosibirsk: Zapadno-Sibirskoye Knizhnoye Izdatel'stvo, 1965), p. 15; and B. V. Korniyenko and E. D. Malinin, "Migratsiya Naseleniya v Zapadnoy Sibiri," Izvestiya Sibirskogo Otdeleniya Akademii Nauk SSSR, Seriya Obshchestvennykh Nauk, no. 6 (1972), p. 93.

100. Maykov, "Osnovnyye Napravleniya Migratsii," pp. 34-35.

101. E. D. Malinin and A. K. Ushakov, Naseleniye Sibiri (Moscow: "Statistika," 1976), pp. 40-41.

102. Perevedentsev, Migratsiya Naseleniye i Trudovyye Problemy Sibiri, pp. 62-65.

103. Malinin and Ushakov, Naseleniye Sibiri, p. 41.

104. Kostakov, Trudovyye Resursy Pyatiletki, p. 59.

105. Malinin and Ushakov, Naseleniye Sibiri, p. 78; and Perevedentsev, Migratsiya Naseleniya i Trudovyye Problemy Sibiri, pp. 52-61.

106. R. Ivanova, "O Razvitii Vostochnykh Rayonov i Obespechenii ikh Rabochey Siloy," Voprosy Ekonomiki, no. 1 (1973), p. 42.

107. P. P. Litvyakov, ed., Demograficheskiye Problemy Zanyatosti (Moscow: Izdatel'stvo "Ekonomika," 1969), p. 165.

108. Maykov, "Osnovnyye Napravleniya Migratsii," p. 38; Perevedentsev, Migratsiya Naseleniya i Trudovyye Problemy Sibiri, pp. 51-109; and Malinin and Ushakov, Naseleniye Sibiri, pp. 42, 78-81.

109. Perevedentsev, Migratsiya Naseleniya i Trudovyye Problemy Sibiri, p. 81.

110. Perevedentsev, Sovremennaya Migratsiya Naseleniya Zapadnoy Sibiri, p. 63.

111. Malinin and Ushakov, Naseleniye Sibiri, pp. 40-83.

112. Cited in D. I. Valentey and I. F. Sorokina, eds., Naseleniye, Trudovyye Resursy SSSR (Moscow: Izdatel'stvo "Mysl'," 1971), p. 166.

113. Perevedentsev, Migratsiya Naseleniya i Trudovyye Problemy Sibiri, pp. 159-74.

114. A. Gladyshev, "Obshchestvennyye Fondy Potrebleniya i Migratsiya Naseleniya," Planovoye Khozyaystvo, no. 10 (1966), pp. 17-22.

115. Malinin and Ushakov, Naseleniye Sibiri, pp. 89-91.

116. Topilin, Territorial'noye Pereraspredeleniye Trudovykh Resursov v SSSR, pp. 102-9.

117. Ivanova, "O Razviti Vostochnykh Rayonov," p. 44.

118. Sbornik Zakonodatel'nykh Aktov o Trude (Moscow: "Yuridicheskaya Literatura," 1974), pp. 417-19, 650-55, 889-931; and E. Manevich, Problemy Obshchestvennogo Truda (Moscow: Izdatel'stvo "Ekonomika," 1966), p. 129.

119. E. F. Mizhenskaya, Lichnyye Potrebnosti pri Sotsializme (Moscow: Izdatel'stvo "Nauka," 1973), p. 94, as cited in Janet Chapman, "Recent Trends in the Soviet Industrial Wage Structure" (Paper presented at the Conference on Problems of Industrial Labor in the USSR, Kennan Institute for Advanced Russian Studies, Washington, D. C., September 27-29, 1977), p. 24.

120. Conolly, Siberia Today and Tomorrow, pp. 179-80.

121. Chapman, "Recent Trends," p. 25.

122. Ivanova, "O Razvitii Vostochnykh Rayonov," p. 44.

123. Sbornik Zakonodatel'nykh Aktov o Trude, pp. 891, 906-20.

124. Kostakov, Trudovyye Resursy Pyatiletki, p. 59.

125. Malinin and Ushakov, Naseleniye Sibiri, p. 43.

3

AGGREGATE PATTERNS OF
URBANIZATION AND URBAN GROWTH

Probably the greatest part of the population redistribution and migration in Russia and the USSR has involved a shift to urban centers. The process of urbanization deserves attention not only because it is a major aspect of population redistribution but because it is highly related to the process of social change and modernization and, indeed, is one of the best indicators of this process. The subject of Soviet urbanization and urban growth takes on even greater importance, because, as will be demonstrated in this chapter, the rate of urbanization in the USSR has probably been the most rapid in the history of mankind.

The purpose of this chapter is to examine the aggregate or national trends of urbanization and urban growth of Russia and the USSR since the turn of the century. The urban process will be analyzed in terms of urban natural increase, rural-to-urban migration, and reclassification of settlements from rural to urban status. A correlation analysis of urbanization and urban growth (for example, with industrialization) will be discussed in the following chapter dealing with regional aspects of urbanization and urban growth, because the correlations are based on regional variations. Subsequent chapters will focus upon other aspects of the urban process, specifically, the size of cities and urban regions or agglomerations. Nationality urbanization and the nationality composition of Soviet cities, also important facets of the Soviet urban process, have been discussed already in great detail in the first book of this series. Although a discussion of aggregate urban trends since the turn of the century is the prime purpose of this chapter, it will be preceded by background material concerning our approach, measures, and definitions.

SUMMARY DISCUSSION

The Soviet Union has experienced very rapid urbanization since the turn of the century. Only about 10 percent of the total population resided in urban centers in 1897, but by the 1970s roughly a majority lived in such centers. The overall rate of urbanization in Russia and the USSR has exceeded not only the world rate but also the rate of every major world region in the 1920-70 period.

The rate of urbanization has been particularly rapid in the Soviet period (post-1926), reflecting the era of planned economic development emphasizing rapid industrialization. The highest urbanization rate was experienced during the 1930s, a rate that was higher than that attained by any major world region in any decade between 1920 and 1970 and by the United States in any decade of its history. It was probably the highest rate ever experienced by any major country in the history of mankind. The rate of urbanization slowed during the World War II-stricken 1939-59 period but accelerated again after 1959 and has remained quite rapid through the 1970s.

The rapid urbanization of the USSR has been related to a very rapid rate of urban growth and slow rate of rural population change. Since the turn of the century, the urban population has increased roughly tenfold or by approximately 100 million people. The Russian and Soviet rate of urban growth also has exceeded the world rate and the rate of a number of other major world regions.

The greatest rate of urban growth and the vast majority of the urban population increase have occurred in the Soviet period. The 1930s was the outstanding period of urban growth, as the urban population roughly doubled during this decade—a situation not even approached by any other world region in any decade of the 1920-70 period, not even by any of the developing regions, which have had rapid urban growth in the recent decades. The rate of urban growth declined during the 1939-59 period, reflecting the presence of World War II. Given the tremendous loss of life during World War II and the chaos of other periods earlier in the twentieth century, one can postulate that the increase in the urban population of Russia and the USSR would have been well in excess of the astounding 100 million increase that actually occurred. The rate of urban growth increased again between 1959 and 1970, although during this period the population of more than 100 towns declined, a number unprecedented in any intercensal period in Russia and the USSR. Since 1970 the urban growth rate has tended to slow down in association with an overall decline in population growth and fertility in the USSR.

The very rapid urbanization and urban growth processes have, in turn, been due principally to a high degree of net rural-to-urban migration. This migration probably has accounted for the majority of the urban growth of Russia and the USSR since the turn of the century, although the overall importance of net rural-to-urban migration has declined, a decline that is inevitable with an increase in the level of urbanization. Rapid urbanization also has been caused by an increase in the relative importance of urban natural increase, which has been enhanced by an overall decline in urban mortality and the absence of war in recent years; like the world as a whole, a situation of urban natural decrease, which prevailed up to a century ago, no longer exists. The urbanization process also has been enhanced by a near closing of the gap between urban and rural natural increase rates, which has essentially eliminated the previous advantage of rural population change.

In summary, then, the rates of urbanization and urban growth in Russia and the USSR have been high by world standards. The underlying mechanisms and changes therein, however, generally have been similar to the world experience. The urbanization process has been brought about by a rate of urban growth that has exceeded that of the rural population, a situation enhanced primarily by net rural-to-urban migration; the relative importance of this migration generally has declined, primarily due to the increased importance of urban natural increase.

DETAILED DISCUSSION

Approach

Urbanization is defined normally as the process of population concentration involving the percentage of the total population of a region residing in urban centers (level of urbanization) and the change in this percentage. It is different from urban growth, which involves a change only in the urban population itself, irrespective of a change in the total or rural populations. Thus, urbanization involves the change in a relative number, whereas urban growth involves the change in an absolute number.

Because urbanization involves the change in the urban population compared with the change in total and rural populations, the first level of analysis will investigate urban growth vis-à-vis total and rural population changes.[1] Although urbanization and urban growth are not synonymous, urban growth usually has accompanied the process of urbanization. It should be pointed out, however, that there can be urbanization without urban growth and, conversely, urban growth without urbanization. If the urban population is declining but the total or rural populations are declining even more rapidly, then an increase, not a decrease, in the level of urbanization will occur. For example, the level of urbanization apparently increased in Ireland during the mid-nineteenth century, even though the urban population declined.[2] Moreover, the Jewish level of urbanization in the USSR increased despite the fact that the Jewish urban population declined.[3] The explanation for such developments is that, although the urban population was declining, the total and rural populations were declining at an even faster rate, and the result was an increase in the percentage of the population residing in urban centers (that is, urbanization).

In addition, urban growth can occur without urbanization. If the urban population is increasing, but the total and rural populations are increasing even more rapidly, then a decrease, not an increase, in the level of urbanization will occur despite urban growth. For example, in recent years the urban population of England and Wales has increased but the level of urbanization has declined according to the official definitions of urban and rural.[4] The explanation for this development is that although the urban population has increased, the total and rural populations have increased even more rapidly, and thus the percentage of the population residing in urban centers has declined. Another example is that many developing countries are currently experiencing very rapid urban growth, but they are not experiencing very high rates of urbanization, because the total and rural rates of growth are still very high in these areas. As we shall see in a later chapter, a similar situation exists in parts of the USSR (for instance, in Soviet Central Asia). However, in most cases urbanization and urban growth usually accompany each other, and urban growth is usually a necessary though not sufficient condition for urbanization, but the distinction between the two terms always should be kept in mind.

The next level of analysis assesses the relative importance of the three immediate hypothethical conditions that promote a more rapid growth of the urban population as compared to the total and rural populations. These three conditions are: (1) when urban natural increase exceeds rural natural increase; (2) when there is net rural-to-urban migration—that is, when the number of people migrating from rural to urban areas exceeds the number of people migrating from urban to rural areas; and (3) when settlements are reclassified from rural to urban status, due to either a sufficient size and/or economical change in a previously rural settlement (operationally, including the creation of a literally "new town") or the annexation of a rural settlement by an urban settlement. Kingsley Davis refers to the former as "reclassification by graduation" and to the latter as "reclassification by absorption." Each of these three mechanisms directly enhances the process of urbanization, because each promotes relatively rapid urban growth vis-à-vis total or rural population change. Net rural-to-urban migration and reclassification can be especially potent in this regard, since they have a "double-barreled" effect, in that they both not only add to the urban population but simultaneously deplete the rural population. Of course, variables comprising these three mechanisms also can be used to explain urban growth, which itself is the direct result of some combination of urban natural change, net rural-to-urban migration, and reclassification.

The actual and theoretical relative importance of these immediate factors in the urbanization and urban growth processes is not unchanging. Migration was of virtually sole importance in the past, primarily because high urban mortality resulted in very low urban natural increase and, very frequently, urban natural decrease. Thus, net rural-to-urban migration was about the only way cities could grow, especially since reclassification also has been of minor importance, although (as will be discussed below) the subject of reclassification itself requires clarification and elaboration.

Along with declining mortality in general, urban mortality has declined substantially throughout the world. As a result, whereas rural natural increase formerly was appreciably higher than urban natural increase, now the gap has been closed considerably. The increased importance of urban natural increase is reflected in the fact that it is now roughly equal in importance to net rural-to-urban migration as a factor in urban growth and urbanization. This represents a profound change in the historical demography of cities within the period of only about one century. It is no wonder that cities in developing countries today are growing so much more rapidly than did cities in present-day developed countries in the nineteenth century. Whereas the older cities had essentially one mechanism of growth (net rural-to-urban migration), cities of present-day developing countries have two mechanisms, net rural-to-urban migration and substantial natural increase.

Another situation can be cited in which the role of net rural-to-urban migration is of lesser and ultimately no importance. As the level of urbanization increases, the rural population becomes less important always in relative terms, since the ratio between the rural and urban populations necessarily decreases, and usually in absolute terms in that the rural population may actually decline. Therefore, the potential number of rural-to-urban migrants becomes progressively less, as the source for such migrants, the rural population, is reduced. Urbanization is a finite process in that a level of urbanization of 100 percent is the upper limit, and when that level is reached net rural-to-urban migration is impossible, since there is no rural population.

Finally, reclassification is regarded generally as having little significance in the process of urbanization and urban growth. This is apparently because a settlement changing from rural to urban status is normally of such a small size that its addition to the total urban population has little effect on that population.

The final level of analysis investigates the various factors, mainly socioeconomic, that in turn affect the immediate factors of urbanization and urban growth and, thus, urbanization and urban growth themselves. Industrialization is one such factor that will be assessed. However, as mentioned earlier, this investigation will be undertaken in the following chapter.

Measures and Definitions

The measures of urbanization employed in this study are in accord with our definition of urbanization. The measure of urbanization is the percentage of the total population residing in urban centers (level of urbanization). The measures of the change in the level of urbanization are both percentage point change and average annual percentage point change for each intercensal period. Average annual percentage point change is used because the intercensal periods vary in length and comparisons from period to period require a comparable measure.[5] The former is the absolute difference in two levels of urbanization and the latter is the absolute difference divided by the number of years in the period involved. For example, if an area is 10 percent urban in 1960 and 15 percent urban in 1970, the percentage point change is 5 (15 percent minus 10 percent) and the average annual percentage point change is 0.5 (5 percentage points divided by 10 years). A host of other measures exists for measuring both urbanization at one point in time and a change in urbanization. No one is necessarily better or worse than the other. Each simply measures the urbanization process from a somewhat different perspective. We use the "level of urbanization" because it is simple, conventional, and easy to understand. As for percentage point change (both overall and average annual), we employ this as a measure of change for a number of reasons. First, it is, perhaps, not as biased by the base level of urbanization as is the percentage change in the level of urbanization.[6] Also, we earlier found that, at least for the 1897-1959 period, this measure of change was a relatively good surrogate measure of the overall urbanization and urban growth processes in Russia and the USSR.[7] It should be acknowledged, however, that the measures used in this study do not cover completely all aspects of the urbanization and urban growth processes in Russia and the USSR, although they capture the essential aspects of urbanization and urban growth.

The topic of urban definitions also can be quite complex, given the great diversity of definitions that have been employed throughout the world and Russia and the USSR. The definition of <u>urban</u> used in this study is that of settlements with 15,000 or more people according to the Russian and Soviet censuses of 1897, 1926, 1939, 1959, and 1970 and appropriate sources for areas previously outside but now within the USSR. Reasons for using this definition have been discussed elsewhere and need only be summarized briefly here.[8] Urban definitions in Russia and the USSR have differed generally from one census to another and even by region within a given census and are thus not necessarily comparable either over time or space.[9] Consequently, it was necessary to derive a comparable definition, that is, settlements of 15,000 and over.

In general terms, the following urban definitions have been employed in the Russian and Soviet censuses, which will hereafter be referred to as "official urban definitions." In the 1897 census, urban centers consisted primarily of administrative centers (in particular <u>guberniya</u> and <u>uyezd</u> centers), as well as a number of other legal cities (<u>zashtatnyy</u> and <u>bezuyezdnyy</u>). The main deficiency of this definition is that it excluded a number of large settlements, many of which were manufacturing centers, and included a number of small, agricultural villages.[10] In particular, 35 centers of the Russian Empire with 15,000–41,000 people in 1897 were not defined officially as urban, while a number of small settlements, sometimes with less than 1,000 people, were defined as urban simply because they were <u>uyezd</u> centers. Thus, if one accepts the idea that an urban center is theoretically a relatively large settlement that is predominantly nonagricultural in function, the 1897 definition is somewhat deficient.

Fortunately, the 1926, 1939, 1959, and 1970 census urban definitions conform more closely to the theoretical definition of an urban center in that they are based for the most part on some combination of minimum population sizes and percentages of the work force in nonagricultural occupations. Unfortunately, the actual minimum size and percentage are not necessarily the same in all of the censuses, nor are they necessarily the same in one census year from one area of the country to the next.

Because of these shortcomings in comparability we have adopted one urban definition (centers of 15,000 or more people) to be employed for all census years and to serve as the basis for our urbanization study. This lower limit was selected primarily on the basis of practical considerations, in that among the lists of individual settlements and their population sizes in all of the censuses, the 15,000 population size was the lowest common denominator. Although the 1897 and 1926 censuses included settlements much smaller than this for all areas of the country, the 1939, 1959, and 1970 censuses did not. The 1939 census, which is included in the 1959 census, and the 1959 census did include a listing of some settlements with less than 15,000 people, but, most important, the list for the RSFSR, by far the largest union republic, included only official urban centers with 15,000 or more people. Moreover, in the 1970 census, for all union republics, only official urban centers with 15,000 or more people were listed. Thus, the 15,000 and over definition was adopted, because this was the smallest center for which data were available by individual settlements in all census years for all parts of the country.

Additional comments on the adopted urban definition are necessary. First, although it excludes many smaller centers that might be regarded also as urban, it undoubtedly contains the vast majority of the population that would be defined as urban on the basis of most, if not all, reasonable urban definitions. For example, in 1970, over 80 percent of the urban population based on the official urban definitions resided in centers of 15,000 and over. Indeed, roughly the same definition has been adopted by the major studies of world urbanization. For example, the United Nations has adopted a definition of 20,000 and over for its studies of world urbanization in the twentieth century, as will be seen in greater detail later. Second, the urban populations (15,000 and over) in 1897 and 1926 include a few settlements that were not defined officially as urban, whereas the 1939, 1959, and 1970 populations include only official urban centers with 15,000 or more people. This difference is due to the fact that the 1897 and 1926 censuses list most settlements separately, regardless of whether they are defined as urban or rural officially, while the post-1926 censuses do not. These differences are minor in terms of comparing the urban populations of each year. Also, the list of 1939 settlements does not necessarily include all urban centers with 15,000 or more people in 1939. The 1939 list is included in the 1959 census and is based upon the 1959 listing. Thus, an indeterminable number of centers with 15,000 or more people in the RSFSR in 1939 are not listed in the 1959 census because they dropped to less than 15,000 by 1959. Once again, the impact of this problem is minimal. Finally, the rural population in each year is defined simply as the total population minus the population residing in centers with 15,000 or more people.

Although the forthcoming discussion of Soviet urbanization, urban growth, and rural change is based essentially on an urban definition of settlements with 15,000 or more people, we also will employ data based upon other urban definitions whenever appropriate. A great number of relevant studies are based on the official urban definitions and will be used in our study, despite being based on a different urban definition. However, the 1897-1970 urban data for Russia and the USSR to be presented are based on the 15,000 and over definition, unless otherwise indicated.

This study is concerned also with urbanization, urban growth, and rural change after 1970. Unfortunately, other censuses and comprehensive listings of all centers of 15,000 and over after 1970 did not exist at the time this research was being conducted. Therefore, other post-1970 sources and urban definitions were used, each of which only involved Soviet estimates of the populations of urban centers. A highly comprehensive listing of urban centers and populations is available for 1974.[11] This list includes all official cities with 15,000 or more people in 1974, but this does not include all official urban centers with 15,000 or more people. Official urban centers of the USSR in recent years consist of two types: cities (goroda) and urban-type settlements (poselki gorodskogo tipa). Hence, the 1974 listing does not include urban-type settlements with 15,000 or more people. This is only a minor problem, however, since the vast majority (for example, well over 90 percent in 1970) of the population residing in all urban centers of 15,000 and over is located in official cities with 15,000 or more people.

Urban data based on official urban definitions are also available for 1977 and are the most recent available data at the time this research was being conducted. [12] These data along with similar data for 1959, 1970, and other recent years, will be incorporated into this study. Although they are based on official urban definitions rather than our comparable definition of 15,000 and over, these data can be used fairly safely, because the vast majority of the official urban population resides in centers of 15,000 and over and the official urban definitions have remained unchanged apparently since the late 1950s. [13]

It should be noted that there appears to be some deviation between the official urban definitions of the urban republics and those employed in the census. According to O. P. Litovka, "due to historical conditions, there exists in the majority of union republics some urban settlements with a population which is less than that stipulated by the corresponding legislation of the republic." [14] For example, official "cities" of the RSFSR are supposed to be no smaller than 12,000 in population, but, according to the 1970 census, more than 100 "cities" of the RSFSR had less than 12,000 people. [15] This does not appear to be much of a problem. A brief comparison of the official minimum size requirements with actual listings in the 1970 census reveals that in general only a very small percentage of the urban population as defined in the census resided in settlements that were smaller than the legal minimum size established in their respective republics. For example, from the census it can be determined that there were 129 "cities" in the RSFSR in 1970 that had a population of less than 10,000. However, the total population residing in such centers was only about 850,000, which represented only about 1 percent of the total population (roughly 70 million) of the RSFSR residing in "cities" according to the census. Thus, although there are discrepancies between the "official" or "legal" urban population as specified by official urban definitions and as indicated in the censuses and other sources, such discrepancies are slight. Hence, we will continue to refer to the urban population as presented in the censuses and other sources as the "official" or "legal" definitions of urban.

Use will be made also of the list of cities with 50,000 or more people in 1977 in the source containing the 1977 data. Of course, the "annual" Narodnoye Khozyaystvo series also provides a list of cities of 50,000 and over, as well as urban data based on official urban definitions. This source will be used when appropriate.

Aggregate Urbanization Trends since 1897

Overall Trends

Although city life within the contemporary borders of the USSR emerged before the birth of Christ in Central Asia, the Transcaucasus, and the Black

TABLE 3.1

Level of Urbanization of Russia and the USSR: 1897-1970

Year	Percent of Total Population Residing in Urban Centers
1897	9.9
1926	13.3
1939	25.3
1959	38.2
1970	46.6*

*The 1970 level presented here differs slightly from the 1970 level (45.7) we presented in an earlier study: Robert A. Lewis and Richard H. Rowland, "Urbanization in Russia and the USSR: 1897-1970," in The City in Russian History, ed. Michael F. Hamm (Lexington, Ky.: University Press of Kentucky, 1976), p. 207. The difference is due to the fact that the 45.7 figure is based upon provisional census data as presented in a noncensus source (the final 1970 census data were not available at the time of the writing of that article), and this source does not list urban-type settlements with a population of 15,000 or more.

Sources: See Chapter 1, nn. 104 and 105.

Sea region and around the turn of the first millennium A.D. in the Slavic areas, the overall urban process prior to the twentieth century was quite slow.[16] As a result, by the turn of the century only about 10 percent of the population of Russia and the USSR resided in urban centers. Nonetheless, the rate of urbanization and urban growth within the last several decades of the nineteenth century appears to have been fairly appreciable. One author estimated that, between 1885 and 1897, the level of urbanization increased from 8.3 percent to 9.9 percent, or by 0.13 percentage points per year, while the urban population increased by 2.9 percent per year, figures that were apparently about the same and perhaps above world standards at that time.[17]

Trends in the level of urbanization of Russia and the USSR for the 1897-1970 period and other intercensal periods within this period are shown in Tables 3.1 and 3.2. During the overall period 1897-1970 the level of urbanization increased from 9.9 percent to 46.6 percent—that is, by 36.7 percentage points or 0.50 percentage points per year. There were significant variations in the rate of urbanization among individual intercensal periods within

TABLE 3.2

Change in Level of Urbanization of Russia and the USSR:
1897-1970

Period	Percentage Point Change in Level	Average Annual Percentage Point Change in Level*
1897-1926	3.4	0.11
1926-39	12.0	0.99
1939-59	12.9	0.65
1959-70	8.4	0.76
1926-70	33.3	0.77
1897-1970	36.7	0.50

*Given the specific month of each census, the following lengths of periods were used to calculate the average annual percentage point changes: 1897-1926 (29.9 years); 1926-39 (12.1 years); 1939-59 (20.0 years); 1959-70 (11.0 years); 1926-70 (43.1 years); and 1897-1970 (73.0 years).

Sources: See Chapter 1, nn. 104 and 105.

the overall 1897-1970 period. By far the greatest share of the increase in the level of urbanization occurred in the Soviet era (1926-70). Between 1897 and 1926, the level of urbanization increased only from 9.9 percent to 13.3 percent, or by 0.11 percentage points per year. This partly reflects the disruptive effect of World War I, the Revolution, and the Civil War on the economy. However, between 1926 and 1970, a period not considerably longer than the 1897-1926 period, the level of urbanization increased from 13.3 percent to 46.6 percent, or by 0.77 percentage points a year, a rate that was seven times that of the 1897-1926 period.

Within the 1926-70 period, additional variations existed. Each intercensal period of the 1926-70 period had a fairly high rate of urbanization, but the 1926-39 period was especially outstanding. During this period, which included the first five-year plans with their emphasis on rapid industrialization, the level of urbanization increased by virtually one percentage point a year. In fact, within the relatively short period of about a dozen years (the 1926 census was in December and the 1939 in January), the level of urbanization of the territory of the contemporary USSR increased almost as much as it had in the entire history of the same territory prior to early twentieth century. Note that

TABLE 3.3

Level of Urbanization of the USSR: 1959-77

Year	Percent of Total Population Residing in Urban Centers	Change in Level from Preceding Listed Year	
		Percentage Point Change	Average Annual Percentage Point Change
Official urban defini- tions			
1959	47.9	—	—
1970	56.3	8.4	0.76
1977	61.9	5.6	0.80
Official cities of 15,000 and over			
1959	37.5	—	—
1970	.45.7	8.2	0.75
1974	49.0	3.3	0.83

Sources: 1959 and 1970 Soviet censuses and 1977 and 1974 estimates (see Chapter 1, nn. 104 and 113).

it took thousands of years for the level to increase 13 percentage points from 0.0 percent to 13.3 percent in 1926, but it took only somewhat more than one decade for the next approximate increase of 13 percentage points to occur. The forthcoming comparison with worldwide trends will further dramatize the truly astounding rate of urbanization in the USSR between 1926 and 1939.

The two other intercensal periods of the 1926-70 period experienced somewhat lower rates of urbanization, although both rates were quite high. The 1959-70 period was the higher of these two, partly due to the fact that this period was one of peacetime, whereas the 1939-59 period was subject to great turmoil because of World War II.

In order to investigate post-1970 aggregate urbanization trends, urban data based on official urban definitions for 1977 and data concerning official cities with 15,000 or more people in 1974 will be used. As Table 3.3 suggests, the pace of the urbanization process has not slackened to any great degree. Indeed, based upon both 1977 and 1974 data, the average annual percentage point change for both these years in the level of urbanization was slightly greater than that for the 1959-70 period.

In general, it can be concluded that as of the mid-to-late 1970s roughly 50 percent of the Soviet population resides in urban centers based on the 15,000 and over definition, and roughly 60 percent resides in urban centers based on official urban definitions. In either case, it is very apparent that a majority of Soviet citizens now reside in urban centers. Thus, within the period of a half century the USSR has been transformed from a predominantly rural country to an urban one. Indeed, there is still much latitude for the level of urbanization to increase, although it should be kept in mind that the rate will inevitably slow down as the maximum possible level of 100 percent is approached.

Comparison with World Trends

In order to evaluate the relative magnitude of the urbanization process in Russia and the USSR, a comparison with world urbanization patterns will be undertaken. Other studies have provided estimates of world urbanization since the turn of the century, especially those by the United Nations, Kingsley Davis, and Hilda Hertz Golden, and pertinent data from these studies have been incorporated in the following tables and discussion. Estimates of urbanization in these other studies are made on the basis of a 20,000-and-over size criterion, as well as other criteria (for example, 100,000 and over). Soviet trends based upon the 15,000-and-over definition can be compared with world trends based upon the 20,000-and-over definition, because there is very little difference in the definitions, as most people who reside in centers of 20,000 and over reside in centers of 15,000 and over (for example, in the USSR in 1970, 95.1 percent of the 20,000-and-over population resided in centers of 15,000 and over).

Table 3.4 shows the levels of urbanization for the world and for Russia and the USSR in 1897, 1900, and 1970. It is very clear that the rate of urbanization in Russia and the USSR has exceeded substantially the corresponding world rate since the turn of the century. Around the turn of the century, the levels for the world and for Russia and the USSR were both low and similar with only about 10 percent of the population of each residing in urban centers. However, by 1970 the USSR level approached 50 percent and was more than 15 percentage points above the world average. In other words, although the world and Russia and the USSR were both predominantly rural around the turn of the century, by 1970 the USSR was on the brink of being an urbanized nation (and was an urbanized nation according to official urban definitions), while the world as a whole was still predominantly rural. Overall, between the beginning of the century and 1970 the level of urbanization for the world increased by about 20 percentage points and approximately doubled, while the level for Russia and the USSR increased by more than 35 percentage points and more than quadrupled.

Data published by the United Nations afford a comparison of Soviet urbanization with urbanization in other major world regions. In particular, the United Nations has presented estimates of levels of urbanization for major world regions in 1920, 1930, 1940, 1950, 1960, and 1970, based upon the

TABLE 3.4

Level of Urbanization of the World and Russia and the USSR:
Circa 1900 and 1970
(percent)

	1897	1900	1970
Russia and the USSR (15,000-and-over definition)	9.9	—	46.6
World (20,000-and-over definition)	—	9.2	28.2-32.2

Sources: The world level for 1900 is from: Kingsley Davis and Hilda Hertz, "Patterns of World Urbanization for 1800-1950," United Nations, Bureau of Social Affairs, Report on the World Social Situation including Studies of Urbanization in Underdeveloped Areas (ST/SOA/33), 1957, p. 114. The world level for 1970 is based on estimates from United Nations, Department of Economic and Social Affairs, Growth of the World's Urban and Rural Population, 1920-2000 (ST/SOA/Series A/44), 1969, pp. 31, 58; and Kingsley Davis, Analysis of Trends, Relationships, and Development, World Urbanization, 1950-1970, vol. 2 (Berkeley: University of California, Institute of International Studies, 1972), p. 51. It should be noted that both the UN and Davis figures for 1970 are based on estimates made in the late 1960s before the publication of many censuses actually taken in 1970. The validity of these estimates is supported at least in the case of the USSR. For example, data from the 1970 census indicated that 44 percent of the USSR population resided in urban centers of 20,000 and over, while estimates from the United Nations for the USSR in 1970 indicated a corresponding USSR level of 43 percent (p. 58). Also, data from the 1970 census indicated that 31.7 percent of the USSR population resided in cities of 100,000 and over (including suburbs of Moscow, Leningrad, Minsk, and Baku), while Davis (p. 170) estimated a corresponding percentage of 31.4. However, Davis (pp. vii-viii) does note that his estimates of the level of urbanization based on the official urban population did deviate somewhat from the corresponding 1970 level according to the 1970 Soviet census. Because the UN and Davis urbanization estimates for the world in 1970 differed (28.2 and 32.2, respectively), both figures are presented in the table. Data for Russia and the USSR come from the 1897 Russian census and 1970 Soviet census and appropriate sources for other areas in 1897 (see Chapter 1, nn. 104 and 105).

TABLE 3.5

Level of Urbanization by Major World Region: 1920-70
(percent)

Region	1920	1930	1940	1950	1960	1970
Europe	35	37	40	41	44	47
Northern America	41	46	46	51	58	63
Soviet Union	10	13	24	28	36	43
Oceania	37	38	41	46	53	58
East Asia	7	9	12	14	19	22
South Asia	6	7	8	11	14	16
Latin America	14	17	20	25	33	38
Africa	5	6	7	10	13	17
World total	14	16	19	21	25	28

Note: Based on an urban definition of 20,000 and over.

Source: United Nations, Department of Economic and Social Affairs, Growth of the World's Urban and Rural Population, 1920-2000 (ST/SOA/Series A/44), 1969, pp. 31, 58.

TABLE 3.6

Percentage Point Change in Level of Urbanization
by Major World Region: 1920-70

Region	1920-30	1930-40	1940-50	1950-60	1960-70	1920-70	1930-70
Europe	2	3	1	3	3	12	10
Northern America	5	0	5	7	5	22	17
Soviet Union	3	11	4	8	7	33	30
Oceania	1	3	5	7	5	21	20
East Asia	2	3	2	5	3	15	13
South Asia	1	1	3	3	2	10	9
Latin America	3	3	5	8	5	24	21
Africa	1	1	3	3	4	12	11
World total	2	3	2	4	3	14	12

Note: Based on an urban definition of 20,000 and over.

Source: United Nations, Department of Economic and Social Affairs,
Growth of the World's Urban and Rural Population, 1920-2000 (ST/SOA/Series
A/44), 1969, pp. 31, 58.

20,000-and-over criterion. These levels of urbanization and percentage point changes therein, which are shown in Tables 3.5 and 3.6, further dramatize the astounding rate of urbanization that has taken place in the USSR. The USSR rate of urbanization not only exceeded the world average in every period but also exceeded the rate for all other major world regions during the 1929-70 period in general and a number of decades in particular.

The outstanding period of urbanization was the 1930-40 period, and, indeed, the Soviet rate of urbanization during this period may have surpassed any other country or region at any time in human history. The increase of 11 percentage points during this decade was by far the greatest increase experienced by any region of the world for any decade between 1920 and 1970, and it greatly exceeded the increases of all other regions during the 1930-40 period. In particular, Northern America had no increase at all, the lowest rate of change for any region in any decade of the 1920-70 period. A similar pattern was discovered by the authors in a comparison of the USSR and the United States in a previous study based on the 15,000-and-over criterion.[18] The extremely high rate of urbanization in the USSR during the 1930s as compared with other world regions reflects, of course, the Great Depression in the "capitalist" world during the 1930s.

It is also interesting to compare the USSR in the 1930s with the United States around the turn of the century during its period of most rapid urbanization. Data are available for the United States, which allow an assessment of urbanization trends for each decade of the period from 1790 to 1970, based on the population residing in urban centers of various size classes.[19] Given the data available, we will utilize an urban definition of 10,000 and over for the United States, since it roughly approximates the 15,000-and-over definition. Based on the percentage of the total population residing in urban centers of 10,000 and over, the most rapidly urbanizing decade in the history of the United States was the 1880-90 period, when the level of urbanization increased by 0.62 percentage points per year. Such an increase is well below the rate for the USSR during the 1930s and, for that matter, is somewhat lower than that for the USSR during the 1959-70 and post-1970 periods.

The extreme rapidity of the rates of urbanization in the USSR during the 1930s can be seen also by making some rough comparisons with individual countries in the 1950s and 1960s. Unfortunately, comparisons are impeded due to the lack of comprehensive urban data for individual countries based on the 15,000-and-over, or even the more conventional 20,000-and-over, definition for both the 1950-60 and 1960-70 periods. Instead, we will rely primarily on urban population estimates presented by Kingsley Davis based upon the official definition of urban for those countries.[20] These comparisons are thus fairly rough. In general, roughly two dozen countries of the world had an average annual percentage point change in the level of urbanization of 1.00 or more during the 1950-60 or 1960-70 period—that is, roughly equal to or above the Soviet increase of the 1930s. However, most were very small countries and none were as populous as the USSR in the 1930s. The only highly populated country included in the roughly two dozen rapidly urbanizing countries was Japan, but it appears that its rapid increase was due in part to urban definitional changes.[21]

Also notable is the fact that the USSR experienced the greatest urbanization increase of any world region between 1960 and 1970 and tied for this position between 1950 and 1960. Such a situation may be surprising in light of the publicity given to the burgeoning urban population of developing countries in recent years. It should be remembered, however, that we are concerned here with urbanization and not urban growth, which will be investigated in the next section.

The only periods when the Soviet urbanization increase was not the highest in the world were the 1920–30 and 1940–50 periods; both these decades were characterized by considerable turmoil and disruption, especially the World War II-stricken 1940–50 period. In addition, much of the 1920–30 period preceded the policy of rapid industrialization.

In conclusion, it is very doubtful that any region or country has ever experienced such a continuous and sustained high rate of urbanization as has the USSR in the last 40 years or so, with the exception of the World War II period. However, by 1970 the Soviet Union was still not as highly urbanized as some other advanced areas, especially North America; nevertheless, it was now nearly as urbanized as Europe. It is certainly an indication of the magnitude of the Soviet urbanization process that within a period of about 50 years the USSR has gone from the ranks of East Asia, South Asia, and Africa to approximately that of Europe.

Urban and Rural Population Change

Overall Trends

As discussed before, the most immediate explanation for an increase in the level of urbanization is that urban population change (usually urban growth) exceeds total and rural population change (frequently a decrease with respect to the rural population). In this section factors in the urbanization process will be discussed.

Major trends in the total, urban, and rural populations of Russia and the USSR are shown in Tables 3.7 and 3.8. It is quite clear from these tables that the rapid urbanization of Russia and the USSR has been due to an urban growth rate that has exceeded by far the rates of change for the total and rural populations. Between 1897 and 1970, the urban population increased from 12.3 million to 112.6 million or by virtually 100 million people. This entailed an overall increase in excess of nine times, or 3.0 percent per year. A population growing at this annual rate will double every 23 years. Enormous as the urban increase may appear, it should be remembered that it would have been even greater had not there been tremendous population losses in association with periods of turmoil, especially World War II.

The total population increased much less rapidly and the rural population even less so. The total population almost doubled between 1897 and 1970, which amounted to an annual rate of increase of about 1 percent. The rural population increased at only a very slight rate of 0.2 percent per year. However, once again, significant differences existed between the 1897–1926 and

TABLE 3.7

Total, Urban, and Rural Populations of Russia
and the USSR: 1897-1970

Year	Total	Urban	Rural
1897	125,042,841	12,321,040	112,721,801
1926	167,655,835	22,357,097	145,298,738
1939	193,077,145	48,862,449	144,214,696
1959	208,826,650	79,760,892	129,065,758
1970	241,720,134	112,623,584	129,096,550

Sources: See Chapter 1, nn. 104 and 105.

1926-70 periods. As discussed earlier, the 1897-1926 period was one of comparatively slow urbanization. As Tables 3.7 and 3.8 reveal, this slow urbanization resulted from an urban growth rate that was comparatively low (only 2 percent per year) and was not appreciably higher than the total and rural rates (about 1 percent per year). In fact, virtually all of the rural population increase between 1897 and 1970 occurred between 1897 and 1926, and after 1926 the rural population experienced an overall decline. The slow rate of urban growth during the 1897-1926 period reflects the chaos associated with World War I, the Revolution, and the Civil War. So tumultuous were these times that the populations of many cities declined precipitously, particularly between 1917 and 1920. [22]

After 1926, the gap between the urban growth rate, on the one hand, and the total and rural rates of change, on the other hand, widened considerably, accounting for the accelerated urbanization of this period. During the 1926-70 period, the urban population increased by 3.8 percent per year, which resulted in a doubling in about 18 years. In contrast, the total population increased by only about 1 percent per year and the rural population declined by -0.3 percent per year. Indeed, between 1926 and 1970, the urban population increased by more than 90 million people. Thus, of the total increase in the urban population in the 73-year period between 1897 and 1970, roughly 90 percent occurred in the 43.1-year period between the 1926 and 1970 censuses.

The three intercensal periods in the 1926-70 period experienced variations in their urban growth rates that were similar to variations in their rates of urbanization. Namely, the most rapid urban growth occurred in the 1926-39 period, and the slowest occurred in the 1939-59 period. Between 1926 and 1939, the urban population increased by more than 26 million people, more than doubling. This entailed an average annual increase of more than 6 percent. Thus, the size of the urban population of Russia and the USSR increased

TABLE 3.8

Average Annual Percentage Change of the Total, Urban,
and Rural Populations of Russia and the USSR: 1897-1970

Period	Total	Urban	Rural
1897-1926	1.0	2.0	0.9
1926-39	1.2	6.5	-0.1
1939-59	0.4	2.5	-0.6
1959-70	1.3	3.1	0.0
1926-70	0.8	3.8	-0.3
1897-1970	0.9	3.0	0.2

Sources: See Chapter 1, nn. 104 and 105.

more in the relatively short period of a dozen years than it did in the entire
period before 1926, which, of course, amounted to hundreds of years. In
contrast, during the 1926-39 period, the total population increased by slightly
more than 1 percent per annum, and the rural population declined by -0.1 percent per year. Thus, whereas the average annual urban growth rate was only
about one percentage point higher than the rural rate of change between 1897
and 1926, the gap had widened tremendously to more than six percentage
points between 1926 and 1939.

Between 1939 and 1959, the urban growth rate declined to 2.5 percent
per year, largely due to World War II. Although available data are not plentiful, other studies have provided figures that reveal a population decline
in Leningrad and certain Ukrainian cities during the war years.[23] Data for
the official urban population of the USSR as a whole in 1951 also reflect the
more immediate urban slowdown brought on by World War II.[24] They indicate that between 1939 and 1951, the urban population of the USSR increased
by slightly less than 2 percent per year, whereas it increased by roughly 7
and 4 percent per year in the immediately preceding (1926-39) and following
(1951-59) periods, respectively.

Between 1959 and 1970, the rates of urbanization and urban growth again
increased. The urban population increased by more than 30 million people
and exceeded 100 million in 1970. This increase was even greater than the
increase of more than 26 million between 1926 and 1939, a period of roughly
comparable length, which, of course, reflects the larger base population in
the more recent of these two periods. Between 1959 and 1970, the urban population increased by slightly more than 3 percent per year. In contrast, the
total population increased annually by 1.3 percent and the rural population

TABLE 3.9

Total, Urban, and Rural Populations of the USSR: 1959-77

Year	Total	Urban	Rural
Official urban definitions			
1959	208,826,650	99,977,695	108,848,955
1970	241,720,134	135,991,514	105,728,620
1977	257,824,000	159,593,000	98,231,000
Official cities of 15,000 and over			
1959	208,826,650	78,213,197	130,613,453
1970	241,720,134	110,391,425	131,328,709
1974	250,869,000	122,856,000	128,013,000

Sources: 1959 and 1970 Soviet censuses and 1977 and 1974 estimates (see Chapter 1, nn. 104 and 113).

increased by 30,000 people, which resulted in an annual rate of increase of 0.0 percent. However, that the rural population increased at all and did not continue to decline sharply is quite surprising in itself, because advanced urbanization often is accompanied by rural population decline. That the rural population for the USSR as a whole did not decline is primarily attributable to the rapid rural growth in such non-European areas as Central Asia, Kazakhstan, and the Transcaucasus. In most of the European regions the rural population did, in fact, decline between 1959 and 1970, and the total rural population of the USSR declined based upon official urban definitions (Tables 3.9 and 3.10). A more detailed discussion of these regional variations and the problems associated with rural depopulation will be presented in Chapter 7.

It is interesting to note, however, that, despite the existence of rapid urbanization and urban growth, the 1959-70 period was marked by a great number of cities experiencing population decline; approximately 130 cities with a population of 15,000 and over in 1959 suffered population declines. This was the first intercensal period in which such a large number of towns lost population between the beginning and end of the period. Many cities lost population between 1939 and 1959, but this was largely because of World War II. No such event could account for the decline between 1959 and 1970. A more detailed discussion of these declining towns and reasons for their decline will be presented in the next chapter. Suffice it to say here that they were principally coal mining and railroad towns in the Eastern USSR.

TABLE 3.10

Average Annual Percentage Change of the Total, Urban,
and Rural Populations of the USSR: 1959-77

Period	Total	Urban	Rural
Official urban definitions			
1959–70	1.3	2.8	−0.3
1970–77*	1.0	2.2	−1.0
Official cities of 15,000 and over			
1959–70	1.3	3.1	0.1
1970–74*	1.0	2.6	−0.8

*Since 1974 and 1977 data are available only for populations rounded to the nearest 1,000 people, the more accurate 1970 populations have also been rounded to the nearest 1,000 people in order to compute these rates.

Sources: 1959 and 1970 Soviet censuses and 1974 and 1977 estimates (see Chapter 1, nn. 104 and 113).

Another manifestation of the magnitude of the rapid process of urbanization and urban growth in Russia and the USSR has been the great increase in the number of urban centers (Tables 3.11 and 3.12). Table 3.11 shows the number of urban centers for Russia and the USSR for the 1897-1970 period. It should be remembered that "urban centers" here are those settlements with a population of 15,000 or more that constitute the urban population for each year as generally utilized in this study. There are a number of problems associated with the calculation of the number of urban centers. For example, some urban centers have been annexed subsequently to a larger city and are no longer considered an urban center in this study. For example, Kronstadt was an individual urban center in 1897 and 1926 but has been annexed since then to the city of Leningrad as defined in this study and is, consequently, not regarded as an individual urban center in 1939, 1959, or 1970. Also, it should be pointed out that the number of urban centers added from one year to another does not constitute necessarily all "new" urban centers, because some urban centers "disappeared" if their population changed from 15,000 or more to less than 15,000. Thus, the increase in the number of urban centers shown in Table 3.12 is essentially a net increase.

TABLE 3.11

Number of Urban Centers of Russia and the USSR: 1897-1970

Year	Number of Urban Centers
1897	250*
1926	384
1939	638
1959	1,019
1970	1,296

*The total of 249 presented in Table 1 of a previous article by the authors left out Bukhara. See Robert A. Lewis and Richard H. Rowland, "Urbanization in Russia and the USSR: 1897-1966," Annals of the Association of American Geographers 59 (December 1969): 780.

Sources: See Chapter 1, nn. 104 and 105.

Overall, the number of urban centers in Russia and the USSR increased by more than 1,000 between 1897 and 1970, from 250 to almost 1,300. This represented an average yearly addition of about 14 urban centers. As with urbanization and urban growth, the bulk of the increase (roughly 90 percent in this case) in the number of urban centers occurred after 1926. Between 1897 and 1926 only about 130 cities were added; that represented an increase of only about five urban centers per year. More than 900 urban centers were added between 1926 and 1970, representing an increase of about 21 urban centers per year. The greatest share of this increase occurred between 1939 and 1959 when nearly 400 urban centers were added. However, 1939-59 was the longest of the three intercensal periods of the 1926-70 period. When the increase per year is calculated, the other two periods register greater increases, reflecting the comparatively greater urbanization and urban growth of these periods. In particular, about 25 urban centers were added per year in the 1959-70 period and 21 per year were added in the 1926-39 period.

In order to examine post-1970 trends in rates of urban growth, previously mentioned data for 1974 and 1977 will again be used. Although rapid urbanization continued to occur after 1970, Tables 3.9 and 3.10 indicate that the rate of urban growth in the USSR actually slowed somewhat after 1970. However, the rate of rural population also continued to decline, enhancing an urbanization increase despite a slowing of urban growth. The rate of rural decline based on official urban definitions deepened between 1970 and 1977, and it now appears that the rural population based on the 15,000-and-over

TABLE 3.12

Change in Number of Urban Centers for Russia
and the USSR: 1897–1970

Period	Increase in Number of Urban Centers	Increase in Number of Urban Centers per Year
1897–1926	134	4.5
1926–39	254	21.0
1939–59	381	19.1
1959–70	277	25.2
1926–70	912	21.2
1897–1970	1,046	14.3

Sources: See Chapter 1, nn. 104 and 105.

urban definition has declined since 1970 after a period of stability between 1959 and 1970. The rural population based on the official urban definitions has, in fact, now fallen below 100 million. In contrast, the urban population (official urban definitions) increased by more than 20 million people between 1970 and 1977, while that based on the 15,000-and-over definition increased by 10 million between 1970 and 1974. Indeed, the urban population based on the 15,000-and-over definition now has increased apparently by more than 100 million people during the Soviet period.

Comparison with World Trends

To enhance further an understanding of the change in the Soviet total, urban, and rural populations, international comparisons will be undertaken once again. Table 3.13 allows a comparison of Soviet and world trends from around the turn of the century to 1970. Although exact comparisons are not possible, it is evident that the higher rate of urbanization in Russia and the USSR as compared with the world as a whole since the turn of the century has been due to the more rapid urban growth and less rapid total and rural growth in Russia and the USSR. The Soviet urban population increased by about nine times, while its rural population increased only very slightly (less than 20 percent), and its total population did not quite double. In contrast, the world urban population increased by "only" roughly seven or eight times, depending on the 1970 estimate used, while its rural population increased by about 60 percent and its total population more than doubled.

As before, comparisons can be made also with other major world regions for the 1920-70 period. Tables 3.14 and 3.15 show average annual rates

TABLE 3.13

Total, Urban, and Rural Populations of the World and
Russia and the USSR: Circa 1900 and 1970
(millions)

| | Population | | |
	Total	Urban	Rural
Russia and the USSR (15,000-and-over definition)			
1897	125.0	12.3	112.7
1970	241.7	112.6	129.1
World (20,000-and-over definition)			
1900	1,650.0	151.8	1,498.2
1970 United Nations	3,584.0	1,010.0	2,574.0
1970 Davis	3,628.0	1,169.5	2,458.5

Sources: World data for 1900 and the Davis estimates
for 1970 are from Kingsley Davis, Analysis of Trends, Relationships, and Development, World Urbanization, 1950-
1970, vol. 2 (Berkeley: University of California, Institute of International Studies, 1972), p. 56. The Davis
estimates for 1900 differ slightly from those previously
presented by Davis and Hertz, although the level of urbanization was the same in both studies—9.2 percent. See
Kingsley Davis and Hilda Hertz, "Patterns of World Urbanization for 1800-1950," United Nations, Bureau of Social
Affairs, Report on the World Social Situation including
Studies of Urbanization in Underdeveloped Areas (ST/SOA/
33), 1957, p. 114. World data based upon UN estimates are
from United Nations, Department of Economic and Social Affairs, Growth of the World's Urban and Rural Population,
1920-2000 (ST/SOA/Series A/44), 1969, p. 58. Data for
Russia and the USSR come from the 1897 Russian census and
1970 Soviet census and appropriate sources for other areas
in 1897 (see Chapter 1, nn. 104 and 105).

TABLE 3.14

Average Annual Percentage Change of the Urban Population by Major World Region: 1920-70

Region	1920-30	1930-40	1940-50	1950-60	1960-70	1920-70	1930-70
Europe	1.6	1.3	0.6	1.7	1.3	1.3	1.2
Northern America	2.7	0.7	2.4	3.2	2.1	2.2	2.1
Soviet Union	4.1	7.0	0.6	4.5	3.0	3.8	3.7
Oceania	2.0	1.8	2.6	3.5	3.2	2.6	2.5
East Asia	3.1	3.2	2.5	4.6	3.0	3.2	3.3
South Asia	2.5	3.9	4.3	4.3	4.0	3.7	4.0
Latin America	3.4	3.5	4.8	5.5	4.4	4.2	4.5
Africa	3.6	3.6	4.5	5.4	4.3	4.2	4.4
World total	2.4	2.5	2.1	3.6	2.9	2.7	2.7

Note: Based on an urban definition of 20,000 and over.

Source: United Nations, Department of Economic and Social Affairs, Growth of the World's Urban and Rural Population, 1920-2000 (ST/SOA/Series A/44), 1969, pp. 24, 27, 58. The first four columns were calculated by the United Nations (p. 27), while we calculated the last three columns based upon population figures rounded to the nearest million (pp. 24, 58).

TABLE 3.15

Average Annual Percentage Change of the Rural Population by Major World Region: 1920-70

Region	1920-30	1930-40	1940-50	1950-60	1960-70	1920-70	1930-70
Europe	0.5	0.3	0.1	0.2	0.1	0.2	0.2
Northern America	0.6	0.8	0.5	0.2	0.1	0.4	0.4
Soviet Union	1.1	-0.5	-1.3	0.5	0.4	0.0	-0.2
Oceania	1.5	0.4	0.4	0.9	0.0	0.9	0.7
East Asia	0.5	0.4	0.6	0.9	1.0	0.7	0.7
South Asia	1.1	1.2	1.0	1.8	2.2	1.5	1.6
Latin America	1.5	1.6	1.5	1.6	2.1	1.7	1.7
Africa	1.3	1.4	1.2	1.7	2.0	1.5	1.6
World total	0.8	0.7	0.6	1.2	1.4	1.0	1.0

Note: Based on the population not residing in centers of 20,000 and over.

Source: United Nations, Department of Economic and Social Affairs, Growth of the World's Urban and Rural Population, 1920-2000 (ST/SOA/Series A/44), 1969, pp. 24, 27, 58. The first four columns were calculated by the United Nations (p. 27), while we calculated the last three columns based upon population figures rounded to the nearest million (pp. 24, 58).

of change for the urban and rural populations of the major world regions, based upon the criteria of settlements 20,000 and over for urban and settlements of less than 20,000 for rural. Rapid urbanization in the USSR in the overall 1920-70 period was the result of rapid urban growth and a very low rate, in fact an absence, of rural growth. Between 1920 and 1970, only two other regions (Latin America and Africa) had a higher rate of urban growth than the Soviet Union. All three regions had average annual rates of urban growth approximating 4 percent. That the Soviet urban growth rate almost has approached that of these two regions and surpassed that of South Asia and East Asia is truly remarkable, given the devastating war in the USSR and the population explosions in these other regions. During the same period, the Soviet rural population essentially did not change at all, and, in fact, the USSR had the lowest rate of rural population change over the entire 50-year period. In contrast, such developing regions as Latin America, South Asia, and Africa experienced fairly rapid rural growth. This is the principal immediate reason why they have not experienced very rapid urbanization despite having very rapid rates of urban growth.

Regional rates of urban and rural population change in the 1939-70 period were virtually identical with those of the 1920-70 period. One difference was that the Soviet rural population of the USSR declined during the 1930-70 period, the only region to do so. In fact, the USSR was the only region to experience rural population decline in any specific decade, doing so in the 1939-40 and 1950-60 periods.

Although the 1930-70 regional urban and rural rates generally approximated those of 1920-70, considerable variations existed with respect to individual decades. Most noteworthy is the fact that between 1930 and 1940 the USSR rate of urban growth was by far the highest rate of growth for any region in any period. During this decade, the Soviet urban population increased by 7 percent per year, which indicates that the urban population roughly doubled. In contrast, no other region experienced an annual rate of greater than 5.5 percent. It is incredible that no other region had such a rapid rate of urban growth in any period, especially in light of the very rapid urban growth in the world and in developing regions in recent years.

It might be worthwhile to compare again the USSR of the 1930s with individual countries of the world between 1950 and 1970. Data compiled by Kingsley Davis based on official urban definitions will be utilized once again for the comparison.[25] During the 1950-60 and/or 1960-70 periods roughly 50 countries had an urban growth rate of about 7 percent per year or more, that is, equal to or greater than the Soviet rate of the 1930s. However, as with the analogous discussion concerning urbanization, some qualifying points have to be made. First, most of the countries involved were quite small, with only Japan being roughly 100 million in population, and as mentioned before, the Japanese rate appears to be too high due to urban definitional changes in the 1950s; furthermore, between 1950 and 1960, Japan's urban growth based on the 20,000-and-over definition was only about 3 percent per annum.[26]

As with urbanization, it is interesting to compare the rate of urban growth of the USSR in the 1930s with the U.S. rates in the same period and around the turn of the century. During the 1930s the U.S. urban growth rate was extremely low, reflecting the Great Depression. For example, Table 3.14 indicates that Northern America, which is basically the United States, had the lowest rate (0.7 percent per year) of urban growth of any major world region between 1930 and 1940. Indeed, except for war-torn Europe and the Soviet Union between 1940 and 1950, no region had a lower rate of urban growth in any decade of the 1920-70 period. In addition, in a previous study, we determined that the rate of urban growth based on the 15,000-and-over definition for the United States between 1930 and 1940 was also only 0.7 percent per year.[27]

The rate of urban growth of the United States around the turn of the century apparently also did not equal the rate of the USSR during the 1930s. It will be recalled that during the 1930s the Soviet urban population grew by roughly 7 percent per year or virtually doubled. Based again on urban centers with 10,000 or more people, in no decade around the turn of the century did the rate of urban growth of the United States approach the Soviet rate of the 1930s.[28] The highest rate during this time in the United States was roughly 5 percent per year in the 1860-70 and 1880-90 periods. It is true that rates of urban growth of the United States did exceed these rates in earlier decades and between 1840 and 1850 the U.S. urban population, like the Soviet urban population during the 1930s, virtually doubled, being the most rapid rate of urban growth in any decade of the history of the United States. However, the U.S. urban population was very small in the earlier periods and was in fact much smaller than the Soviet urban population of the 1930s. Hence, these earlier rapid rates of the United States are biased somewhat by low base populations. Thus, the rate of urban growth of the USSR in the 1930s greatly exceeded the rate of the United States during the 1930s; in fact, in no decade of the history of the United States did the U.S. rate of urban growth exceed the Soviet rate of the 1930s.

The extraordinary rate of urbanization in the USSR during the 1930s also was enhanced by rural population decrease. Indeed, the USSR had the lowest rate of rural population change of any of the eight regions during this period, and except for the USSR again between 1940 and 1950, no region in any period had a lower rate of rural population change than did the USSR between 1930 and 1940. The rural population in the USSR actually declined in both of these periods, a situation also never experienced by any other region in any decade of the 1920-70 period.

Between 1940 and 1950, the rates of urbanization and urban growth in the USSR slowed down, largely because of World War II. Nevertheless, the Soviet level of urbanization still increased at a rate above the world average during this period, primarily because, as touched upon above, the rural population underwent a very sharp decline, although the Soviet rate of urbanization was exceeded by most world regions.

During the 1950-60 and 1960-70 periods, the Soviet rate of urbanization was again the highest in the world, largely due to a rapid increase in the rate of urban growth. Although a number of other regions now had higher urban growth rates, the rate of rural growth in the USSR was still not very high, thus enhancing the acceleration of Soviet urbanization during these periods.

Urban Natural Increase, Urban In-Migration,
and Reclassification

The next level of analysis of urbanization and urban growth involves an
assessment of the relative importance of urban natural increase, urban in-
migration, and reclassification of settlements from rural to urban status.
Such an assessment is not easy because of the lack of a systematic set of data
for the entire 1897-1970 period.

Urban Natural Increase

Available data suggest that the importance of natural increase has increased as a factor in urbanization and urban growth in Russia and the USSR.
A. G. Rashin has assembled much data for the earlier period, and some of
these data are presented in Table 3.16. As can be seen, the urban crude natural increase rates were only about 50 percent of the natural increase rates
for the rural population. Such a situation was clearly not favorable to the urbanization process. The relatively high rates of rural natural increase were

TABLE 3.16

Crude Birth, Death, and Natural Increase Rates by Urban
and Rural Populations of the 50 Gubernii of European
Russia: 1859-63 and 1909-13
(per thousand)

	1859-63	1909-13
Urban		
Crude birth rate	45.9	33.9
Crude death rate	38.6	25.4
Crude rate of natural increase	7.3	8.5
Rural		
Crude birth rate	50.9	44.3
Crude death rate	35.8	28.0
Crude rate of natural increase	15.1	16.3

Note: Based on official urban definitions.

Source: A. G. Rashin, Naseleniye Rossii za 100 Let
(Moscow: Gosudarstvennoye Statisticheskoye Izdatel'stvo,
1956), p. 245.

TABLE 3.17

Crude Birth, Death, and Natural Change Rates for
St. Petersburg: 1764-1915
(per thousand)

Period	Crude Birth Rate	Crude Death Rate	Crude Rate of Natural Change
1764-1860	28.4	31.8	-3.4
1861-65	38.1	41.4	-3.3
1866-70	30.2	38.8	-8.6
1871-75	31.2	32.3	-1.1
1876-80	30.2	33.3	-3.1
1881-85	30.8	33.1	-2.3
1886-90	31.6	27.9	3.7
1891-95	30.8	26.3	4.5
1896-1900	30.3	25.6	4.7
1901-1905	30.5	24.7	5.8
1906-10	30.9	26.3	4.6
1911-15	26.1	21.9	4.2

Source: A. G. Rashin, Naseleniye Rossii za 100 Let
(Moscow: Gosudarstvennoye Statisticheskoye Izdatel'stvo,
1956), pp. 233-34.

the result of higher rural crude births rates and, in the earlier of the two periods indicated in Table 3.16, a lower rural crude death rate.

However, although urban natural increase was of minor importance during this earlier period, there is evidence to indicate that it was beginning to
increase in importance. For example, the urban crude natural increase rate
increased from 7.3 to 8.5 per thousand between the periods 1859-63 and 1909-
13 (Table 3.16). This increase occurred despite the fact that the urban crude
birth rate declined sharply (by 12.0 points per thousand), because the urban
crude death rate declined even more sharply (by 13.2 points). Additional data
indicate that St. Petersburg experienced natural decrease prior to the mid-
1880s but natural increase from the mid-1880s to 1915 (Table 3.17).

According to data presented by Frank Lorimer these trends were apparently still prevalent in 1926. He presents urban and rural vital statistics
for European USSR and other parts of the USSR at this time, although he notes
that "all of these statistics must be used with some caution."[29] Data for the

TABLE 3.18

Crude Birth, Death, and Natural Increase Rates by Urban
and Rural Populations of the European Part of USSR: 1926
(per thousand)

	Urban	Rural
Crude birth rate	33.9	45.6
Crude death rate	16.7	20.7
Crude rate of natural increase	17.2	24.9

Note: These data are based on official urban definitions and are for the USSR as it actually was constituted
in 1926.

Source: Frank Lorimer, The Population of the Soviet
Union: History and Prospects (Geneva: League of Nations,
1946), p. 81.

European USSR suggest that the urban crude natural increase rate was still
appreciably lower than that of the rural crude natural increase rate (Table
3.18). This was due primarily to the fact that the rural crude birth rate was
much higher than the urban crude death rates, although the urban crude death
rate was somewhat lower than the rural crude death rate, continuing the trend
that began roughly around the turn of the century.

The relative importance of urban natural increase after 1926 is possible
to assess, based upon data presented elsewhere, which indicate the amount of
urban growth (official urban definitions) due to natural increase, net rural-to-
urban migration, and reclassification. These data and calculations based upon
them are shown in Table 3.19. Average annual rates of urban natural increase
appear to have fluctuated. The rate declined between the 1926-39 and 1939-
59 periods and then increased in the 1959-70 period to its highest level in any
of the three periods. The lower rates in the 1926-39 and 1939-59 periods reflect the chaos and subsequent low fertility and high mortality rates throughout portions of these periods. The very low rate for 1939-59 reflects the effects of World War II; the comparatively high rate in the 1959-70 period, in
turn, mirrors the fact that this was a period of peacetime.

Reflecting these changes, the share of the urban growth accounted for
by natural increase rose considerably. It accounted for only about 20 percent of the urban growth between 1926 and 1959 but for more than 40 percent
of the urban growth between 1959 and 1970, although net rural-to-urban migration was still of slightly greater importance in this latest period. Further-

TABLE 3.19

Components of Urban Growth of the USSR: 1926-70

	1926-39	1939-59	1959-70	1926-70
Absolute Growth (in millions)				
Urban natural increase	5.6	8.0	14.6	28.2
Net rural-to-urban migration	18.8	24.6	16.4	59.8
Reclassification	5.9	7.0	5.0	17.9
Total urban growth	30.3	39.6	36.0	105.9
Absolute Growth as Percent of Total Urban Growth				
Urban natural increase	18.4	20.2	40.6	26.6
Net rural-to-urban migration	62.2	62.2	45.6	56.5
Reclassification	19.4	17.7	13.9	16.9
Total urban growth	100.0	100.1	100.1	100.0
Average Annual Absolute Growth per Thousand Midpoint Urban Population				
Urban natural increase	10.2	5.0	11.2	7.9
Net rural-to-urban migration	34.3	15.3	12.6	16.7
Reclassification	10.8	4.4	3.9	5.0
Total urban growth	55.3	24.7	27.7	29.6

Note: All data are based on official urban definitions. Because data for the 1926-39 period were based on
the reduced Soviet boundaries of those years, minor adjustments were made in order to provide data for the cur-

(continued)

TABLE 3.19 (continued)

rent boundaries of the USSR. Since appropriate data are
available for 1939 in the 1939 and current boundaries, adjustments were necessary only for 1926. According to the
1959 census, 18 percent of the 1926 USSR population resided in urban centers, based upon the official urban definitions. According to our estimates, the population of
the USSR in 1926 in current boundaries was 167,655,835.
Therefore, multiplication of this population times 18 percent resulted in an estimated "official" urban population
of 30.2 million for the USSR in 1926 in current boundaries. The 1939 urban population in current boundaries was
60.4 million, and, thus, the increase in the urban population between 1926 and 1939 was 30.2 million. According to
the figures presented by Urlanis for the 1926 and 1939
boundaries, 18.4 percent of the urban growth was due to
natural increase, 62.2 percent to net rural-to-urban migration, and 19.4 percent to reclassification. Application of these percentages to the increase of 30.2 million
resulted in estimates of the absolute amount for each of
the three components for the 1926-39 period in current
boundaries, and these are the figures that are included in
the table (due to rounding, the sum of the three totals
30.3 million, not 30.2 million). Actually, these adjustments made little difference, since the increase in the
urban population based upon the 1926 and 1939 boundaries
(29.8 million) was virtually the same as the corresponding
estimated 1926-39 increase based upon current boundaries
(30.2 million). Also, the original 1959-70 figures for
the three components summed to only 35.6 million, instead
of the actual increase of 36.0 million. Urlanis (p. 247)
adjusted this difference by adding 0.4 million to net
rural-to-urban migration, and the figures in this table
incorporate this adjustment. Rates per thousand urban
population were derived by dividing the total change (for
example, natural increase) by the length of the period involved, and then dividing this quotient by the midpoint
urban population of the period (that is, the summation of
the urban populations at the beginning and end of the period divided by two). Resulting rates are rough estimates
of the average annual rates of urban natural increase, net
rural-to-urban migration, and reclassification.

Source: B. Ts. Urlanis, Problemy Dinamiki Naseleniya
SSSR (Moscow: Izdatel'stvo "Nauka," 1974), pp. 245-49.

TABLE 3.20

Crude Birth, Death, and Natural Increase Rates by Urban
and Rural Populations of the USSR: 1965-73

	1965	1970	1973
Urban			
Crude birth rate	16.3	16.4	16.6
Crude death rate	6.8	7.5	7.8
Crude rate of natural increase	9.5	8.9	8.8
Rural			
Crude birth rate	20.8	18.7	19.0
Crude death rate	7.9	9.1	9.9
Crude rate of natural increase	12.9	9.6	9.1

Note: These rates are based on the official urban
definitions. They were calculated by dividing the absolute number of births and deaths by the midyear urban and
rural populations of 1965, 1970, and 1973. The midyear
populations were estimated by summing the January populations of 1965 and 1966, of 1970 and 1971, and of 1973 and
1974, respectively, and dividing the sums by two. The
crude rate of natural increase is simply the crude birth
rate minus the crude death rate.

Source: USSR, Tsentral'noye Statisticheskoye Upravleniye pri Sovete Ministrov SSSR, Naseleniye SSSR, 1973
(Moscow: Izdatel'stvo "Statistika," 1975), pp. 7, 99.

more, more than 50 percent of the absolute urban natural increase between
1926 and 1970 occurred in the 1959-70 period, while considerably less than
50 percent of the increase due to migration and reclassification occurred during this latter period.

Data are also available that allow a determination of rates of urban and
rural natural increase at the end of the overall 1897-1970 period. Rates for
1965, 1970, and 1973 are presented in Table 3.20 and are based on official
urban definitions. It appears that the gap between the urban and rural crude
natural increase rates now nearly has been closed. It will be recalled that
for European Russia the rural rate was about twice as high as the urban rate
(and about 8 per thousand higher) around the turn of the century and about 50

percent higher (and also about 8 per thousand higher) in 1926. Therefore, although it cannot be said that urbanization in the USSR has been promoted by the urban crude natural increase rate exceeding the rural crude natural increase rate, because this situation generally never has occurred, it can be concluded that the urbanization process has been promoted by the change between the urban and rural natural increase rates. Whereas in the past the urban and rural crude natural increase rates taken in themselves would have greatly impeded the process of urbanization, today this great disadvantage experienced by cities has been largely eliminated. Although this disadvantage has not yet been changed to an advantage, it certainly has been neutralized.

Two immediate reasons underlie the near closing of the gap between the urban and rural crude natural increase rates. Foremost is the fact that the rural crude birth rate is now nearly as low as the urban, after being decidedly higher in the past, although the urban and rural crude birth rates have both declined sharply. Also, from a longer perspective, the situation existing roughly a century ago in the mid-nineteenth century of urban mortality exceeding rural mortality now has been reversed, although the difference between the urban and rural crude death rates has remained slight. As with the crude birth rate, urban and rural mortality rates have both plummeted during the last century.

A more in-depth analysis of total, urban, and rural fertility, mortality, and natural increase trends will be undertaken in the next volume of this series. Suffice it to say here that these changes are in general related to the factors associated with modernization and economic development, which have brought about the "demographic transition" in urban and rural areas in many parts of the world.

Urban In-Migration

As the above discussions have suggested, net rural-to-urban migration has overall been the most important of the three immediate factors in urbanization and urban growth in Russia and the USSR. First, one author has estimated previously that nearly four-fifths of the population growth of 74 cities between 1885 and 1897 was due to net urban in-migration.[30] Although this variable was not exactly identical to net rural-to-urban migration, since it included an unknown number of migrants who originated in urban centers, it was concluded from place-of-birth and social class data in the 1897 census that most of this migration originated in rural areas and that this rural-to-urban migration exceeded urban-to-rural migration, thus, leading to net rural-to-urban migration.[31]

The 1926 census also provides place-of-birth data, including explicit data on the urban or rural origin of migrants. According to the official definitions of urban and rural, nearly one-half of the urban population was comprised of in-migrants, and of these in-migrants, roughly two-thirds originated in rural areas. The number of rural-to-urban migrants exceeded the number of urban-to-rural migrants, resulting in net rural-to-urban migration.

Data portraying net rural-to-urban migration for the 1926-70 period have been presented already in Table 3.19. They suggest that net rural-to-urban migration was the prime factor in urban growth and urbanization during this period, accounting for more than 50 percent of the urban growth from 1926 to 1970. The relative importance of net rural-to-urban migration, however, has been declining. Whereas it accounted for well over half of the urban growth between 1926 and 1939 and between 1939 and 1959, it accounted for less than half between 1959 and 1970 (Table 3.19). This decline has been due both to the increased importance of natural increase, as discussed above, and the general tendency for net rural-to-urban migration to decline in importance as a country becomes more urbanized.

The reduced degree of net rural-to-urban migration also is reflected in the declining rate of net rural-to-urban migration (Table 3.19). Net rural-to-urban migration annually amounted to a rate of 34.3 per thousand urban residents between 1926 and 1939, but in the following two periods this rate had declined to 15.3 and 12.6 per thousand, respectively. The much higher rate of net rural-to-urban migration during the 1926-39 period was a prime contributor to the extraordinarily high rates of urbanization and urban growth during this period.

The declining importance of net rural-to-urban migration is reflected in data from the 1970 census, which are based upon the previous place-of-residence definition. According to these data, less than half (45.2 percent) of the urban in-migrants came from rural areas (official definitions of urban and rural). Thus, the USSR now has reached the stage where urban-to-urban migration is more important than rural-to-urban migration, a situation that inevitably is realized with increasing urbanization. However, net rural-to-urban migration still existed as the number of rural-to-urban migrants exceeded the number of urban-to-rural migrants according to the 1970 census.

It should not be forgotten that, although net rural-to-urban migration is declining in relative importance, it is still of appreciable importance in the USSR. Furthermore, since the USSR is not yet an extremely highly urbanized nation (like the United States or England, for instance) and still contains a very large rural population, net rural-to-urban migration will continue to be an important factor in urbanization and urban growth at least in the near future.

Reclassification

The final immediate factor in urbanization and urban growth is reclassification. According to the data in Table 3.19 reclassification has been relatively unimportant as a factor in urban growth and urbanization, as it accounted for only about 17 percent of the total Soviet urban growth between 1926 and 1970. Furthermore, the reclassification share declined progressively in each of the three periods of the overall 1926-70 period. As with net rural-to-urban migration, this declining importance is understandable, since the source for such a mechanism, the rural population, decreases in relative and, usually, eventually in absolute importance with increased urbanization.

A specific aspect of reclassification involves annexation; that is "reclassification-annexation." The terms reclassification and annexation are not synonymous. There can be reclassification by means other than annexation, that is, the previously mentioned reclassification by graduation. There can also be annexation without reclassification in that, if a larger town annexes a smaller but already existing urban center, this will have no influence at all on the urban population of the region or nation, because the smaller town would have been defined as urban in any event. The annexation by Moscow in 1960 of an area including nearly 1 million people is a major example of this situation, because most of the areas annexed were previously defined as urban. In addition, one also must acknowledge that there can also exist what might be termed deannexation—that is, the situation where part of a city is removed to form an independent settlement.

It is difficult to estimate the importance of reclassification-annexation in the urban growth and urbanization of the USSR. Nevertheless, some conclusions can be made, based upon 1926 and 1939 data provided by Lorimer and data from the 1926, 1959, and 1970 censuses. Lorimer lists 174 cities with a population of 50,000 and over in 1939, apparently in their 1939 boundaries, and the population of the same cities in 1926, also apparently in the 1939 boundaries.[32] Comparison of the 1926 city populations in 1939 boundaries presented by Lorimer with the populations for the same cities as presented in the 1926 census itself, which we assume are in the 1926 city boundaries, suggests the extent of annexation. For example, the 1926 population of Irkutsk in East Siberia was 98,764 in 1926 boundaries and 108,129 in 1939 boundaries; thus, we can assume that Irkutsk annexed an area with 9,365 people in 1926.

The comparison procedure, in general, leads one to conclude that reclassification-annexation had very little effect on overall urban growth between 1926 and 1939. Indeed, the vast majority of the 174 towns had 1926 populations that were essentially the same in the 1939 boundaries as they were in the 1926 boundaries. It is true that annexation was important for some individual cities, especially in the Donets Coal Basin, where small mining centers frequently have been amalgamated or annexed to larger towns. It should be added, however, that the 1939 city populations actually used in our study are not based upon the 1939 city boundaries but, instead, generally are based upon the 1959 city boundaries. Therefore, it is even more difficult to estimate the extent of annexations between 1926 and 1939 based on urban data used in this study.

It also appears that annexations were not of great overall importance between 1939 and 1959. The extent of annexation for the same 174 cities between 1939 and 1959 can be assessed by comparing their 1939 populations in 1939 boundaries with their 1939 populations as listed in the 1959 census, generally in 1959 boundaries—namely, by using the same comparative procedure as for 1926-39. Although not to quite the extent as between 1926 and 1939, the majority of the 174 cities had no apparent boundary changes between 1939 and 1959. As before, some Donets Basin cities had significant annexations. However, the most significant annexation in terms of absolute numbers involved Moscow, which, in 1960, annexed areas with 1939 and 1959 populations approximating 400,000 and 950,000 people, respectively. Nevertheless, because the bulk of the areas annexed would have been considered as urban in the first place, it may have been annexation, but for the most part it was not reclassification-annexation.

Between 1959 and 1970, the importance of annexations can be determined more precisely. The 1959 populations in 1970 city boundaries are presented in the 1970 census for all urban centers with a population of 15,000 or more in 1970; the 1959 census provides data for centers with 1959 populations of 15,000 or more in January 1959 boundaries or, in a few cases, boundaries of roughly a year or two later. Thus, the population added by annexation can be approximated by comparing the 1959 population of an urban center in the 1959 census with its 1959 population in the 1970 census; this can be done for every urban center constituting the 1970 urban population as defined in this study. Investigation reveals that for cities apparently having annexations, their combined 1959 population in 1970 boundaries exceeded their 1959 population in 1959 boundaries by a figure approaching about 900,000 people. This figure is not very large when it is recalled that the urban population of the USSR increased by more than 30 million people between 1959 and 1970. In addition, of the roughly 1,300 urban centers of 15,000 and over in 1970, less than 100 had an apparent annexation during this period. Furthermore, as before, in many cases the annexation involved a center with a population of 15,000 and over in 1959, which would have been considered as urban anyway, and thus, its annexation added nothing to the total urban population. It appears that roughly a dozen cities with a population of 15,000 and over and a combined population of roughly 300,000 in 1959 were annexed to larger cities. Thus, out of the nearly 900,000 annexed population, roughly one-third of this population contributed nothing to the growth of the total or regional urban population of the USSR.

In conclusion, although city boundary changes have occurred in the USSR, their overall contribution to urban growth and urbanization apparently has not been great. Only a relatively small proportion of the total number of urban centers and of the urban population growth was involved with annexations, and most annexed areas, being on the urban fringe, would be classified as urban anyway.

Regarding the subject of urban annexation in the USSR, we would like to comment also on a recent statement by W. A. Douglas Jackson, who cites a previous conclusion of ours and confuses the terms reclassification and annexation.[33] Jackson states that 14 percent of the urban growth of the USSR between 1960 and 1970 was due to "administrative annexation." He then notes in a footnote "that the Soviet figure ascribing 14 percent of urban growth to administrative annexation is contradicted [italics ours] by information in Lewis and Rowland."[34] He is referring to a statement we made in an earlier article.[35] In footnote 10 of that article, we concluded that annexation has not been of much importance; specifically, we stated that "there has been comparatively little . . . annexation in the USSR. . . . For both of these periods [1926-39 and 1939-59] the number of annexations were remarkably few."[36] The information we have presented above supports this contention. It appears that the 14 percent figure was for reclassification and not only annexation (see also Table 3.19). Thus, our conclusion that annexation was of minor importance is not contradicted by Soviet figures as Jackson indicated.

Comparison with World

In summary, it appears that net rural-to-urban migration has been the main immediate factor in the rapid urbanization and urban growth of Russia and the USSR. However, its relative importance has declined overall and that of urban natural increase has increased in relative importance. The importance of reclassification has been relatively minor throughout the entire period under investigation.

As implied by the preceding discussion the relative importance of these three factors and changes therein are roughly similar to the experience of the world in general.[37] Like the world urban population experience in the past, net rural-to-urban migration was of paramount importance, because urban mortality rates were so high that urban natural increase was either very low or even nonexistent with a situation of natural decrease occurring. In addition, net rural-to-urban migration loomed large in the past, because given the very high percentage of the total population still in rural areas, the potential source for rural-to-urban migration was relatively high.

However, like the world situation as a whole, the relative importance of net rural-to-urban migration has declined. As elsewhere in the world, major factors contributing to this decline have been: (1) a sharp decline in urban mortality, which in turn has enhanced an increase in the importance of urban natural increase; (2) an approximate equality between urban and rural natural increase rates, which increases the ability of the urban population to "compete" with the rural population in the realm of relative natural increase rates; and (3) the decline in the percentage of the population residing in rural areas, which has progressively depleted the potential sources for rural-to-urban migration.

The next level of analysis of the urbanization and urban growth processes will assess the factors that in turn have contributed to urbanization, urban growth, urban in-migration, and urban natural increase. In particular, such potential factors as industrialization and those affecting fertility and mortality will be examined in greater depth. Because an investigation of some of these factors involves a correlation analysis based on regional variations (for example, the relationship between regional urbanization and regional industrialization), a discussion of these factors will be undertaken in the next chapter. Factors affecting fertility and mortality will be discussed in greater depth in the third volume of this series.

NOTES

1. This section is based primarily on Kingsley Davis, "The Urbanization of the Human Population," Cities (New York: Knopf, 1970); and idem, Analysis of Trends, Relationships, and Development, World Urbanization 1950-1970, vol. 2 (Berkeley: University of California, Institute of International Studies, 1972), pp. 47-73, 308-19.

2. Adna Ferrin Weber, The Growth of Cities in the Nineteenth Century (New York: Macmillan, 1899), pp. 64-65.

3. Robert A. Lewis, Richard H. Rowland, and Ralph S. Clem, Nationality and Population Change in Russia and the USSR (New York: Praeger, 1976), pp. 173-77.

4. Great Britain, Office of Population Censuses and Surveys, Census 1971, England and Wales: Preliminary Report, p. 5.

5. For a good discussion of general urbanization measures see Eduardo Arriaga, "Selected Measures of Urbanization," in The Measurement of Urbanization and Projection of Urban Population, ed. Sidney Goldstein and David F. Sly (Dolhain, Belgium: Ordina Editions, 1975), pp. 19-88; and Davis, Analysis of Trends, Relationships, and Development. Percentage point change is discussed or used specifically by Arriaga, "Selected Measures," pp. 36-45; and Davis, Analysis of Trends, Relationships, and Development, p. 174.

6. For an elaboration on this point, see Lewis, Rowland, and Clem, Nationality and Population Change, pp. 135-36.

7. Robert A. Lewis and Richard H. Rowland, "Urbanization in Russia and the USSR: 1897-1966," Annals of the Association of American Geographers 59 (December 1969): 779-80.

8. J. William Leasure and Robert A. Lewis, Population Changes in Russia and the USSR: A Set of Comparable Territorial Units (San Diego, Calif.: San Diego State College Press, 1966), pp. v-xiii; and Lewis and Rowland, "Urbanization in Russia," pp. 778-79.

9. For a more detailed discussion of these definitions, see, Leasure and Lewis, Population Changes, pp. x-xi.

10. B. S. Khorev and V. M. Moiseenko, "Urbanization and Redistribution of the Population of the U.S.S.R.," in Patterns of Urbanization: Comparative Country Studies, ed. Sidney Goldstein and David F. Sly, vol. 2 (Dolhain, Belgium: Ordina Editions, 1977), pp. 648-49, 653.

11. USSR, Prezidium Verkhovnogo Soveta Soyuza Sovetskikh Sotsialisticheskikh Respublik, SSSR: Administrativno-Territorial'noye Deleniye Soyuznykh Respublik na 1 Yanvarya 1974 Goda (Moscow, 1974), pp. 636-50.

12. USSR, Prezidium Verkhovnogo Soveta Soyuza Sovetskikh Sotsialisticheskikh Respublik, SSSR: Administrativno-Territorial'noye Deleniye Soyuznykh Respublik na 1 Yanvarya 1977 Goda (Moscow, 1977), pp. 5-502, 651-56.

13. See, for example, Khorev and Moiseenko, "Urbanization and Redistribution," pp. 649-53. These authors also include a list of specific official urban definitions by union republic.

14. O. P. Litovka, Problemy Prostranstvennogo Razvitiya Urbanizatsii (Leningrad: Izdatel'stvo "Nauka," Leningradskoye Otdeleniye, 1976), p. 12.

15. Khorev and Moiseenko, "Urbanization and Redistribution," p. 652.

16. For a discussion of historical urbanization in Russia prior to the twentieth century, see Chauncy D. Harris, Cities of the Soviet Union (Chicago: Rand McNally, 1970); W. H. Parker, An Historical Geography of Russia (Chicago: Aldine, 1968), p. 34; and M. Tikhomirov, The Towns of Ancient Rus (Moscow: Foreign Languages Publishing House, 1959).

17. Richard H. Rowland, "Urban In-Migration in Late Nineteenth Century Russia," (Ph.D. diss., Columbia University, 1971), pp. 112-15.

18. Lewis and Rowland, "Urbanization in Russia," pp. 780-83.

19. U.S., Department of Commerce, Bureau of the Census, Historical Statistics of the United States, Colonial Times to 1970, pt. 1, pp. 11-12.

20. Kingsley Davis, Basic Data for Cities, Countries and Regions, World Urbanization 1950-1970, vol. 1 (Berkeley: University of California, Institute of International Studies, 1969), pp. 54-82, 112-60.

21. Toshio Kuroda, "Urbanization and Population Redistribution in Japan," in Patterns of Urbanization: Comparative Studies, ed. Sidney Goldstein and David F. Sly, vol. 2 (Dolhain, Belgium: Ordina Editions, 1977), p. 438.

22. Harris, Cities of the Soviet Union, p. 238.

23. Harrison Salisbury, The 900 Days (New York: Harper & Row, 1969), pp. 513-17; and Frank Lorimer, The Population of the Soviet Union: History and Prospects (Geneva: League of Nations, 1946), pp. 196-97.

24. USSR, Naseleniye SSSR, 1973, (Moscow: Izdatel'stvo "Statistika," 1975), pp. 10-11.

25. Davis, Basic Data for Cities, Countries and Regions, pp. 54-82, 112-60.

26. United Nations, Department of Economic and Social Affairs, Growth of the World's Urban and Rural Population, 1920-2000 (ST/SOA/Series A/44), 1969, pp. 121-24.

27. Lewis and Rowland, "Urbanization in Russia," p. 781.

28. Historical Statistics of the United States, pp. 11-12.

29. Lorimer, Population of the Soviet Union, p. 80.

30. Rowland, "Urban In-Migration," pp. 116-17.

31. Ibid., pp. 86-88.

32. Lorimer, Population of the Soviet Union, pp. 250-53.

33. W. A. Douglas Jackson, "Urban Expansion," Problems of Communism 23 (November-December 1974): 15.

34. Ibid.

35. Lewis and Rowland, "Urbanization in Russia," p. 781.

36. Ibid.

37. World patterns once again are based primarily on Davis, "Urbanization of the Human Population"; and idem, Analysis of Trends, Relationships, and Development.

4

REGIONAL PATTERNS OF
URBANIZATION AND URBAN GROWTH

Although aggregate urbanization and urban growth trends in Russia and the USSR were very rapid, they masked an even more rapid urban process in certain regions of the country. This chapter will, thus, focus upon regional variations in urbanization and urban growth trends since the turn of the century. An investigation of regional variations is especially necessary in the case of the USSR, because the country is so large that many individual regions are larger than most individual countries in the world. A regional investigation will also allow a more detailed assessment of the relationships between urbanization and urban growth, on the one hand, and economic development (industrialization, capital investment, and so forth), on the other.

In addition, in order to investigate the urban process in even greater detail, this chapter will include a discussion of rapidly growing towns and towns with population decline during the most recent intercensal period of 1959-70. Regional patterns and functional characteristics of these towns will be focused upon. Attention will be given also to rates of population change by urban functional types.

SUMMARY DISCUSSION

Since the turn of the century the Eastern USSR has experienced more rapid urbanization and urban growth than the Western USSR, although urban processes have been quite rapid in both areas. Particularly rapid urbanization and urban growth were characteristic of the Russian East, which changed from being the least urbanized quadrant in 1897 to the most urbanized in 1970, the Urals, and West Siberia. Although rapid urbanization also occurred in such western regions as the Center and Donetsk-Dnepr, most western regions experienced relatively slow urbanization and urban growth. The planned shift of industry to the east and the existence of World War II and other periods of chaos, which were confined primarily to the Western USSR, contributed to these regional variations. Slow urbanization has been characteristic of the Non-Slavic South, especially Central Asia. This area did, however, have fairly rapid urban growth, but such growth was greatly offset by a rapidly

199

growing rural population. This situation in the Non-Slavic South is typical of developing countries in the world in recent years.

The regional trends existing for the overall period since 1897 were confined primarily to the pre-1959 period. During the 1926-39 period, a period in which the urban process was especially rapid, very high rates of urbanization and urban growth occurred in certain regions, particularly in the eastern regions. These regional rates were never attained either before or since in the USSR. Indeed, it is doubtful if any country in the history of mankind ever had rates of urbanization and urban growth that equaled or exceeded those of many Soviet regions during this extraordinary period. The somewhat slower urban process in the Western USSR at this time was especially noticeable in the extreme western areas then outside but now within the USSR, as these areas were not benefiting from the major push toward industrialization occurring within the USSR as it was constituted during this period. Also, the slower urban processes in the Western USSR between 1939 and 1959 reflected the disproportionately great impact of World War II on this zone, as exemplified by the fact that most of the towns that declined in population between these dates were located in the combat zone.

Since 1959, however, a major reversal of the regional variations in urbanization and urban growth has occurred. Between 1959 and 1970, the Western USSR had higher rates of urbanization and urban growth than did the Eastern USSR. There was a general tendency for the regions with the most rapid rates of urbanization and urban growth prior to 1959 to have the slowest rates between 1959 and 1970, and for those with the slowest rates to have now the most rapid rates. Between 1959 and 1970, the urbanization process was particularly rapid in Northern European USSR, especially in Belorussia, the Volgo-Vyatsk, the West, and the Central Chernozem, and the Russian East, the Urals, and West Siberia were no longer among the most rapidly urbanizing regions.

The 1959-70 period also was characterized by substantial differences in regional variations in rates of urbanization and urban growth. Most notable, the Non-Slavic South, had the slowest urbanization but the most rapid urban growth of any quadrant, a situation roughly approximated by each of its three component regions of Central Asia, Kazakhstan, and the Transcaucasus, as well as by Moldavia. However, a number of rapidly urbanizing regions also had rapid urban growth, especially Belorussia, the Central Chernozem, and the West. Reflecting the relative decline in the urban process in the Eastern USSR, the Urals and West Siberia had the lowest rates of urban growth of any region.

Since 1970 the new regional patterns of urbanization and urban growth emerging in the 1959-70 period generally have continued. However, it appears that the Eastern USSR and Russian East have experienced a slight relative resurgence in certain aspects of the urban process, although this has by no means marked a return to their outstanding positions prior to 1959.

Although data were lacking in many cases, a correlation analysis suggested that regional variations in urbanization and urban growth were related to a great extent to each other and to regional variations in urban migration, urban natural increase, industrialization, tertiary activities, and capital investment. In certain instances such relationships did not exist. The association between changes in urbanization and urban growth became greatly weakened after 1959, due to an increasingly strong relationship between urbanization and rural change. After 1959 a low relationship also existed between urbanization change and urban natural increase, and correlations involving urban migration were not especially high. The relationship between the urban process and industrialization was relatively weak prior to 1926 but greatly strengthened after 1926 with rapid industrialization, urbanization, and urban growth. Between 1926 and 1959 the urban and industrialization processes were especially rapid in the Eastern USSR, while after 1959 they were both quite rapid in many of the western areas of the country. Indeed, the relatively rapid urban process in the western areas in recent years has been due to a great extent to increased industrial investment in many of these areas.

The east-to-west shift in the urban process between 1959 and 1970 was reflected in an investigation of rapidly growing towns (at least doubling in population) and towns with population decline, which, as defined in this study, numbered approximately 130 each. Unlike the preceding period, the decided majority of the rapidly growing towns were located in the Western USSR. Of particular interest was the fact that a number of old, somewhat stagnant towns of the Western USSR were rejuvenated and experienced fairly rapid growth. The most rapidly growing towns in the USSR tended to be mining towns (especially oil towns), towns based on electric power production, and small industrial towns (particularly chemical towns), although relatively rapid growth also tended to be characteristic of major administrative centers throughout the country.

Perhaps of greater interest was both the existence of a large number of declining towns and the locational patterns of such towns. The presence of more than 100 declining towns is unprecedented in any other Soviet intercensal period. Furthermore, the vast majority of these declining towns were located in the Eastern USSR, especially the Urals, West Siberia, and East Siberia. A large number were located along the Trans-Siberian Railroad, and, in fact, about 40 percent of all the towns on this famous railroad, which helped spur the growth of the east, actually declined in population. The declining towns of the USSR tended to be primarily small, narrowly specialized mining towns, especially coal mining towns, and railroad service centers. The decline of these types of towns is not unusual in that declining coal towns, for example, are characteristic of Western Europe and the United States. In addition, the declining Soviet towns consisted to a great extent of relatively new eastern towns, which experienced rapid growth prior to 1959, rather than primarily of older towns in the Western USSR. Thus, unlike the United States, the declining towns of the USSR generally did not include large cities in the older areas of settlement. The largest cities of the USSR, in fact, all increased in population between 1959 and 1970.

In summary, regional variations in the urban process in the USSR were, as might be expected, related to a great extent to regional variations in various indicators of economic development. Industrial location policies and changes therein contributed in particular to a relatively rapid urban process in the Eastern USSR and more recently in the Western USSR.

DETAILED DISCUSSION

Regional urbanization and urban growth trends for the 1897-1977 period are shown in Tables 4.1-4.8, 4.11-4.14, and B.1-B.10 and Maps 4.1-4.21. The following discussion will be based to a great extent on average annual changes in urbanization and urban growth in order to enhance comparisons between one period and another. Average annual percentage point change will be used to assess urbanization changes, while average annual percentage change will be utilized for a discussion of urban growth. The maps for each period also are based on these average annual figures. In addition, in order to enhance a comparison of maps between one period and another, comparable class intervals also will be used.

Regional Urbanization and Urban Growth Trends:
1897-1970 and 1926-70

In 1897 the Western USSR was somewhat more highly urbanized than the Eastern USSR, although neither area was highly urbanized (10.7 percent and 6.3 percent, respectively). Of the four quadrants, the European Steppe was the most urbanized and the Russian East was the least urbanized, but once again none of the four was highly urbanized (Table 4.1). Only 13.0 percent of the European Steppe resided in urban centers.

The relatively high level of urbanization of the European Steppe is reflected in the urbanization levels by economic region (Table 4.2). The highest level of urbanization of any of the 19 regions occurred in the South, where nearly one-fourth (22.7 percent) of the population resided in urban centers. This level was more than twice the national average and was approached only by the Northwest Region (21.7 percent). Neither level, however, was very high. Aside from Volgo-Vyatsk and Kazakhstan, the lowest levels occurred in three of the four regions comprising the Russian East (the Urals, West Siberia, and East Siberia).

Between 1897 and 1970, the Eastern USSR urbanized somewhat more rapidly than the Western USSR (Tables 4.3 and 4.5). Although the Western USSR was still slightly more urbanized than the Eastern USSR in 1970, the difference in the level of urbanization between the two areas had been narrowed (47.1 percent as compared with 45.5 percent), as shown in Table 4.1. The relatively rapid urbanization of the Eastern USSR was reflected in the fact that its rate of urban growth was higher than that of the Western USSR (Table 4.7). Whereas the urban population of the Western USSR increased by "only" roughly seven times (10.8 million to 77.6 million), that of the Eastern USSR increased by more than 20-fold (1.5 million to 35.1 million). As a result, whereas nearly 90 percent of the urban population of the USSR was in

TABLE 4.1

Level of Urbanization by Gross Region: 1897-1970
(percent)

Region	1897	1926	1939	1959	1970
Western USSR	10.7	14.3	25.5	37.5	47.1
Eastern USSR	6.3	9.9	24.6	39.8	45.5
Northern European USSR	10.1	13.1	23.7	36.1	46.8
European Steppe	13.0	17.7	31.6	41.6	49.4
Russian East	5.7	9.9	27.7	45.6	53.2
Non-Slavic South	8.5	12.3	20.9	31.9	36.8
USSR total	9.9	13.3	25.3	38.2	46.6

Sources: See Chapter 1, nn. 104 and 105.

the western portion in 1897, by 1970 only about 70 percent of the urban population was contained in this area. The rapid urban growth of the Eastern
USSR was, however, biased by its lower base population. Roughly two-thirds
of the increase of the urban population of the USSR between 1897 and 1970 actually occurred in the western portion. In short, the process of urbanization
and urban growth in the USSR since the turn of the century has been outstanding in both the western and eastern areas, although somewhat greater in the
east.

The relatively rapid urbanization and urban growth of the Eastern USSR
is reflected dramatically in the extremely rapid urbanization of the Russian
East. Between 1897 and 1970, the level of urbanization of the Russian East
increased by 43.3 percentage points from 5.7 percent in 1897 to 53.2 percent
in 1970, and this quadrant changed from the least urbanized of the quadrants
in 1897 to the most urbanized of the quadrants in 1970 (Table 4.1). Its percentage point increase was well above that of any of the other three quadrants,
being more than 10 points above the increases for the Northern European
USSR and European Steppe and nearly 20 points more than the increase for the
Non-Slavic South (Table 4.3).

To a certain extent, similar patterns existed with respect to rates of
urban growth. The Russian East had the most rapid urban growth of any
quadrant as its urban population increased by roughly 30 times from about
800,000 in 1897 to more than 23 million in 1970 (Table 4.7). Whereas the
Russian East had the smallest urban population of any of the four quadrants

TABLE 4.2

Level of Urbanization by Economic Region: 1897-1970

Region	1897	1926	1939	1959	1970
Northwest	21.7	23.9	41.4	52.4	61.7
West	14.6	18.7	21.1	32.2	44.0
Center	12.1	17.6	36.0	53.0	63.8
Volgo-Vyatsk	1.9	5.2	15.6	29.2	41.4
Central Chernozem	7.4	7.3	10.9	21.4	33.4
Volga	8.6	11.3	23.7	41.6	52.6
Belorussia	6.9	8.8	13.7	21.1	34.2
Moldavia	13.4	11.5	8.6	15.2	22.9
Southwest	7.6	10.3	13.6	18.9	27.3
South	22.7	23.1	31.7	38.7	45.4
Donetsk-Dnepr	10.6	15.0	38.8	49.7	59.6
North Caucasus	10.1	19.8	26.8	37.9	44.4
Transcaucasus	11.5	18.0	25.1	36.6	41.7
Urals	5.6	9.6	27.3	47.4	54.9
West Siberia	6.5	9.8	26.5	47.0	56.1
East Siberia	3.7	8.8	23.4	37.4	44.9
Far East	14.6	16.3	40.5	47.4	53.9
Kazakhstan	2.5	5.5	21.8	34.3	41.1
Central Asia	11.4	13.5	17.2	26.9	30.9
USSR total	9.9	13.3	25.3	38.2	46.6

Sources: See Chapter 1, nn. 104 and 105.

TABLE 4.3

Percentage Point Change of the Level of Urbanization by Gross Region: 1897-1970

Region	1897-1926	1926-39	1939-59	1959-70	1926-70	1897-1970
Western USSR	3.6	11.2	12.0	9.6	32.8	36.4
Eastern USSR	3.6	14.7	15.2	5.7	35.6	39.2
Northern European USSR	3.0	10.6	12.4	10.7	33.7	36.7
European Steppe	4.7	13.9	10.0	7.8	31.7	36.4
Russian East	4.2	17.8	17.9	7.6	43.3	47.5
Non-Slavic South	3.8	8.6	11.0	4.9	24.5	28.3
USSR total	3.4	12.0	12.9	8.4	33.3	36.7

Sources: See Chapter 1, nn. 104 and 105.

in 1897, by 1970 its urban population was surpassed only by the Northern European USSR. In 1897 the urban population of the Russian East was only about one-tenth of that of Northern European USSR (776,000 as compared with 7,761,000), but by 1970 it was nearly one-half that of this western quadrant (23.6 million versus 51.0 million). However, the Non-Slavic South had the second highest rate of urban growth, despite having the slowest rate of urbanization.

Although the Russian East had the most rapid urbanization and urban growth of any of the four quadrants between 1897 and 1970, the other three quadrants still had appreciable rates of urbanization and urban growth. In fact, since the turn of the century all four quadrants had rates of urbanization and urban growth above the world average (Tables 3.4, 3.13, 4.1, 4.3, and 4.5).

That rapid urbanization between 1897 and 1970 was not confined to the Russian East is mirrored in regional variations in urbanization based upon the 19 economic regions (Table 4.2 and Map 4.11). It is true that the Russian East contained three of the six regions with the greatest increases in the level of urbanization (West Siberia, the Urals, and East Siberia). West Siberia and the Urals had the second and third greatest increases of any of the 19 regions and changed from being 2 of the 5 least urbanized regions in 1897 to 2 of the 7 regions in 1970 that had a majority of their population in urban centers. In both regions, the level of urbanization increased by just less than 50 percentage points each, roughly twice the world increase.

The greatest regional urbanization increase occurred in the western portion of the country. In particular, the level of urbanization of the Center increased by 51.7 percentage points, slightly higher than the increases for West Siberia and the Urals; the Donetsk-Dnepr, also of the Western USSR, had an urbanization increase (49.0 percentage points) virtually equal to the increases of West Siberia and the Urals.

Moderate increases (that is, roughly 30 to 45 percentage points) also occurred in a wide variety of areas (Table 4.4 and Map 4.11). Western regions included the Volga, Northwest, Volgo-Vyatsk, North Caucasus, and Transcaucasus, while eastern regions included East Siberia, the Far East, and Kazakhstan.

Regions experiencing the lowest urbanization increases were, except for one region, located exclusively along the borders of the USSR (Table 4.4 and Map 4.11). These regions included the West or Baltic, Belorussia, the Central Chernozem (which is not on the border), the South, the Southwest, Central Asia, and Moldavia. Except for Central Asia, all of these regions suffered considerably in World War II. Also, portions of many of these regions were outside the USSR during the 1930s and did not benefit from the very rapid industrialization occurring within the USSR as it was constituted during the interwar period.

Although substantial regional variations in rates of urbanization existed between 1897 and 1970, it should not be forgotten that nearly every region experienced very rapid urbanization by world standards. As noted before, the level of urbanization for the world as a whole increased by roughly 20 per-

TABLE 4.4

Percentage Point Change of the Level of Urbanization by Economic
Region: 1897-1970

Region	1897– 1926	1926– 39	1939– 59	1959– 70	1926– 70	1897– 1970
Northwest	2.2	17.5	11.0	9.3	37.8	40.0
West	4.1	2.4	11.1	11.8	25.3	29.4
Center	5.5	18.4	17.0	10.8	46.2	51.7
Volgo-Vyatsk	3.3	10.4	13.6	12.2	36.2	39.5
Central Chernozem	-0.1	3.6	10.5	12.0	26.1	26.0
Volga	2.7	12.4	17.9	11.0	41.3	44.0
Belorussia	1.9	4.9	7.4	13.1	25.4	27.3
Moldavia	-1.9	-2.9	6.6	7.7	11.4	9.5
Southwest	2.7	3.3	5.3	8.4	17.0	19.7
South	0.4	8.6	7.0	6.7	22.3	22.7
Donetsk-Dnepr	4.4	23.8	10.9	9.9	44.6	49.0
North Caucasus	9.7	7.0	11.1	6.5	24.6	34.3
Transcaucasus	6.5	7.1	11.5	5.1	23.7	30.2
Urals	4.0	17.7	20.1	7.5	45.3	49.3
West Siberia	3.3	16.7	20.5	9.1	46.3	49.6
East Siberia	5.1	14.6	14.0	7.5	36.1	41.2
Far East	1.7	24.2	6.9	6.5	37.6	39.3
Kazakhstan	3.0	16.3	12.5	6.8	35.6	38.6
Central Asia	2.1	3.7	9.7	4.0	17.4	19.5
USSR total	3.4	12.0	12.9	8.4	33.3	36.7

Sources: See Chapter 1, nn. 104 and 105.

centage points (Table 3.4). However, except for Moldavia, the level of urbanization of every region of the USSR increased by at least roughly 20 percentage points. In fact, ten, or a majority, of the regions had an increase at
least roughly twice that of the world—that is, by roughly 40 percentage points
or more (Table 4.4).

Regional changes in urbanization reflect regional rates of urban and
rural population change (Tables 4.4, 4.8, and 7.2). Of the four regions with
the greatest increases in urbanization (the Center, West Siberia, the Urals,
and the Donetsk-Dnepr), only one (West Siberia) was among the four leading
regions of urban growth. The other three regions experienced more moderate
rates of urban growth. Interestingly, the Center, the region which had the
greatest urbanization, had an urban growth rate below the national average.
The great increase in urbanization in these three regions in the absence of
extremely high rates of urban growth was due to their lack of substantial rural
population increases. The rate of rural population growth in both the Urals
and Donetsk-Dnepr was only 0.1 percent per year and below the national average. Furthermore, the rural population of the Center, the most rapidly
urbanizing region, not only declined but also suffered the greatest rate of
rural population loss (0.5 percent per year) of any of the 19 regions. Thus,
it could be argued that the region that experienced the greatest urbanization
between 1897 and 1970 actually owed such a position more to rural population
decline than to rapid urban growth.

Similarly, regions with moderate increases in urbanization had varying
rates of urban growth. For example, the Far East and Kazakhstan had moderate urbanization increases but extremely rapid urban growth rates. This
disparity reflected the relatively rapid rates of rural increase of each region,
especially the Far East, which had by far the most rapid rate of rural increase
of any of the four regions (Tables 4.4, 4.8, and 7.2). In contrast, the Northwest had a moderate-to-high urbanization increase but relatively slow urban
growth. Fairly rapid urbanization occurred here partly because of substantial rural population decline (Table 7.2).

Regions having a relatively low increase in urbanization, such as the
West, Belorussia, the Central Chernozem, the Southwest, the South, and
Moldavia, all had relatively low rates of urban growth, contributing to an
overall low urbanization increase. One slowly urbanizing region, Central
Asia, however, had a moderate rate of urban growth; the urbanization pro-
cess here was impeded by a rapidly growing rural population (Table 7.2).

The absolute increase in the urban population was highly concentrated
in a relatively few regions. In particular, over one-half (54.9 percent) of the
roughly 100 million urban increase between 1897 and 1970 was concentrated
in six of the nineteen regions: the Center, Urals, Donetsk-Dnepr, Volga,
Northwest, and West Siberia. These six regions also ranked among the top
seven regions in terms of level of urbanization in 1970 and in terms of urbanization increase between 1897 and 1970. Two of these regions, West Siberia and the Urals, were also outstanding in terms of urban growth rates,
ranking first (tied with East Siberia) and sixth, respectively, and of these
six regions, only the Northwest had an urban growth rate below the national
average.

TABLE 4.5

Average Annual Percentage Point Change of the Level of Urbanization by Gross Region:
1897-1970

Region	1897-1926	1926-39	1939-59	1959-70	1926-70	1897-1970
Western USSR	0.12	0.93	0.60	0.87	0.76	0.50
Eastern USSR	0.12	1.21	0.76	0.52	0.83	0.54
Northern European USSR	0.10	0.88	0.62	0.97	0.78	0.50
European Steppe	0.16	1.15	0.50	0.71	0.74	0.50
Russian East	0.14	1.47	0.90	0.69	1.00	0.65
Non-Slavic South	0.13	0.71	0.55	0.45	0.57	0.39
USSR total	0.11	0.99	0.65	0.76	0.77	0.50

Sources: See Chapter 1, nn. 104 and 105.

TABLE 4.6

Average Annual Percentage Point Change of the Level of Urbanization
by Economic Region: 1897–1970

Region	1897–1926	1926–39	1939–59	1959–70	1926–70	1897–1970
Northwest	0.07	1.45	0.55	0.85	0.88	0.55
West	0.14	0.20	0.56	1.07	0.59	0.40
Center	0.18	1.52	0.85	0.98	1.07	0.71
Volgo-Vyatsk	0.11	0.86	0.68	1.11	0.84	0.54
Central Chernozem	0.00	0.30	0.53	1.09	0.61	0.36
Volga	0.09	1.02	0.90	1.00	0.96	0.60
Belorussia	0.06	0.40	0.37	1.19	0.59	0.37
Moldavia	-0.06	-0.24	0.33	0.70	0.26	0.13
Southwest	0.09	0.27	0.27	0.76	0.39	0.27
South	0.01	0.71	0.35	0.61	0.52	0.31
Donetsk-Dnepr	0.15	1.97	0.55	0.90	1.03	0.67
North Caucasus	0.32	0.58	0.56	0.59	0.57	0.47
Transcaucasus	0.22	0.59	0.58	0.46	0.55	0.41
Urals	0.13	1.46	1.01	0.68	1.05	0.68
West Siberia	0.11	1.38	1.03	0.83	1.07	0.68
East Siberia	0.17	1.21	0.70	0.68	0.84	0.56
Far East	0.06	2.00	0.35	0.59	0.87	0.54
Kazakhstan	0.10	1.35	0.63	0.62	0.83	0.53
Central Asia	0.07	0.31	0.49	0.36	0.40	0.27
USSR total	0.11	0.99	0.65	0.76	0.77	0.50

Sources: See Chapter 1, nn. 104 and 105.

TABLE 4.7

Average Annual Percentage Change of the Urban Population by Gross Region: 1897–1970

Region	1897–1926	1926–39	1939–59	1959–70	1926–70	1897–1970
Western USSR	1.8	5.7	1.9	3.2	3.3	2.7
Eastern USSR	3.0	9.5	3.9	3.1	5.2	4.3
Northern European USSR	1.7	5.6	1.8	3.2	3.2	2.6
European Steppe	2.3	6.1	1.9	3.2	3.4	2.9
Russian East	3.7	10.7	3.9	2.3	5.4	4.7
Non-Slavic South	2.2	6.2	3.5	4.3	4.5	3.5
USSR total	2.0	6.5	2.5	3.1	3.8	3.0

Sources: See Chapter 1, nn. 104 and 105.

TABLE 4.8

Average Annual Percentage Change of the Urban Population
by Economic Region: 1897-1970

Region	1897–1926	1926–39	1939–59	1959–70	1926–70	1897–1970
Northwest	1.2	6.0	0.8	2.5	2.7	2.1
West	0.8	1.3	2.3	4.0	2.4	1.8
Center	2.3	7.4	1.8	2.4	3.5	3.0
Volgo-Vyatsk	4.0	10.6	2.9	3.3	5.1	4.7
Central Chernozem	0.9	2.8	2.5	4.3	3.0	2.2
Volga	1.7	5.9	3.0	3.4	3.9	3.0
Belorussia	1.4	4.9	1.7	5.4	3.5	2.7
Moldavia	0.4	-0.9	3.7	5.6	2.9	1.9
Southwest	1.7	2.4	1.3	4.1	2.3	2.1
South	0.7	3.1	1.2	3.6	2.3	1.7
Donetsk-Dnepr	2.6	9.6	1.8	2.8	4.2	3.6
North Caucasus	3.6	3.6	2.3	3.4	2.9	3.2
Transcaucasus	2.3	5.4	2.7	3.5	3.7	3.1
Urals	2.7	10.3	4.0	2.2	5.3	4.2
West Siberia	5.2	10.2	4.1	2.1	5.3	5.3
East Siberia	4.7	11.2	3.7	3.1	5.6	5.3
Far East	4.7	12.4	3.0	2.7	5.5	5.2
Kazakhstan	3.5	11.3	4.4	4.7	6.4	5.2
Central Asia	1.7	4.7	3.6	4.6	4.1	3.1
USSR total	2.0	6.5	2.5	3.1	3.8	3.0

Sources: See Chapter 1, nn. 104 and 105.

It will be recalled from Chapter 2 that these six regions were generally outstanding in terms of the regional distribution and redistribution of the urban population. In 1970 they constituted six of the leading eight regions in terms of each region's percentage of the urban population of the USSR and in terms of absolute urban population size (Table 2.6). In 1970 they contained a majority (54.1 percent) of the urban population of the USSR as a whole. In addition, these six regions combined had an increase in their share of the urban population of the USSR (roughly six percentage points from 48 percent in 1897 to 54 percent in 1970). Two of the regions, in particular, the Urals and West Siberia, were the two outstanding regions of the USSR in terms of increased share of the urban population, and the Donetsk-Dnepr ranked fourth in this respect. Only the Northwest had a sharply declining share, in fact, the greatest decline of any region.

Thus, it can be concluded generally that between 1897 and 1970 the urban process from all major perspectives was dominated by six regions: the Center, the Urals, the Donetsk-Dnepr, the Volga, the Northwest, and West Siberia. Regional variations in rates of urbanization and urban growth between 1926 and 1970 roughly duplicate those between 1897 and 1970 (Tables 4.1-4.8 and Maps 4.10, 4.11, 4.16, and 4.17). However, although regional variations may have been similar, the magnitudes of the regional rates were substantially higher in the 1926-70 period than in the 1897-1970 period, except for the North Caucasus in the case of urban growth rates. The vast majority of the increase in urbanization and the urban population for each region between 1897 and 1970 occurred between 1926 and 1970. These differences reflect the fact that the urban process had been especially great in the post-1926 period of planned rapid industrialization.

Regional Urbanization Trends
by Specific Intercensal Periods

Trends for the overall 1897-1970 and 1926-70 periods mask more specific temporal and regional trends in the urban process in Russia and the USSR. Therefore, these more specific trends will be discussed in this section.

1897-1926

Of the specific intercensal periods, the 1897-1926 period had the slowest rates of urbanization and urban growth, and regional rates of urbanization were not markedly different from this overall slow pace. Indeed, the urbanization changes in the Western USSR and Eastern USSR were exactly the same (Tables 4.1, 4.3, and 4.5). In addition, there was little variation among the four quadrants, with the European Steppe having the highest change (0.16 points per year) and Northern European USSR, the lowest (0.10 points per year).

The lack of substantial regional variations and presence of overall comparative slowness is reflected in Map 4.6, which shows regional variations in the average annual percentage point change in the level of urbanization for the 1897-1926 period. The almost complete blankness of the map reflects the slow urbanization of virtually all regions, especially in comparison with subsequent periods (Maps 4.6-4.9). Only the North Caucasus had an average annual change of more than 0.25 percentage points and it was just barely above this level (0.32).

The most rapid rates of urban growth between 1897 and 1926 occurred in the Eastern USSR, especially in regions of the Russian East: West Siberia, the Far East, and East Siberia. This reflects the significant migration to these regions and the very low base urban population of these regions in 1897 (Tables 4.7 and 4.8). Their urbanization rates were dampened, however, because they also had the most rapid rates of rural population growth (Table 7.2).

Interestingly, two regions (the Central Chernozem and Moldavia) actually had a decline in the level of urbanization (Tables 4.4 and 4.6). Aside from Moldavia again in the 1926-39 period, no other region ever had an urbanization decline in any period under investigation.

Given the generally slow rate of urbanization between 1897 and 1926 for all regions, it is not surprising that in 1926, regional variations in the level of urbanization differed little from those in 1897. As will be seen, greater regional changes occurred in the much shorter 1926-39 period.

1926-39

During the 1926-39 period the USSR experienced probably the most rapid urbanization of any major world region in the history of the world. This great overall increase was accompanied by significant regional variations in the rate of the urbanization process. Whereas the percentage point change in the level of urbanization for the Western and Eastern USSR was identical for the 1897-1926 period, between 1926 and 1939, the Eastern USSR urbanized at an appreciably greater rate (Table 4.7), reflecting the planned eastward shift of industry, although both areas urbanized much more rapidly in the 1926-39 period than between 1897 and 1926 (Table 4.5). The rate of urban growth was also higher in the Eastern USSR, although both regions experienced rates of urban growth never approached in any other period (Table 4.7). The urban population of the Eastern USSR more than tripled, from 3.7 million in 1926 to 11.6 million in 1939, increasing at an average annual rate of almost 10 percent, which would entail a doubling of the population every seven years. Although it increased more slowly, the urban population of the Western USSR almost doubled, from 18.7 million in 1926 to 37.3 million in 1939, for an annual rate of almost 6 percent.

These newly emergent patterns were also evident at the quadrant level. Between 1926 and 1939 the greatest urbanization increase was attained by the Russian East. Its level increased from 9.9 percent in 1926 to 27.7 percent in 1939, or by 17.8 percentage points or 1.47 percentage points per year, the most rapid increase of any quadrant in any period. The European Steppe had the next highest rate of increase, followed by Northern European USSR and the Non-Slavic South (Tables 4.3 and 4.5). Except for Northern European USSR, which had a slightly higher annual urbanization change in the 1959-70 period, the changes for the other three quadrants in the 1926-39 period were the greatest they attained in any intercensal period (Table 4.5).

All four quadrants also experienced rates of urban growth never approached in any other intercensal period. The Russian East, which was the most rapidly urbanizing region, also had the most rapid rate of urban growth. Its urban population more than tripled, from 2.3 million in 1926 to 8.4 million in 1939. The average annual rate of increase of 10.7 percent was by far the greatest of any quadrant in any intercensal period (Table 4.7). The urban population of the three remaining quadrants roughly doubled in each case, with each having urban growth rates approximating the 6 percent per year, rates that they never attained in any other intercensal period (Table 4.7).

Substantial regional variations in the change in the level of urbanization were also evident at the economic region level (Tables 4.4 and 4.6 and Map 4.7). The greatest rates were experienced by interior and eastern regions, with the slowest rates being confined to regions along the western and southern borders of the USSR. Although the greatest average annual percentage point change was experienced by the Far East (2.00 per year, the highest of any region in any period), the next greatest increases were basically in the most important industrial regions of the USSR: the Donetsk-Dnepr, Center, Urals, and Northwest. They were followed by West Siberia, Kazakhstan, and East Siberia, all in the Eastern USSR.

Most of the rapidly urbanizing regions also had extremely high rates of urban growth (Table 4.8 and Map 4.13). Average annual rates of increase of roughly 10 to 12 percent were achieved by the Far East, Kazakhstan, East Siberia, the Urals, West Siberia, and the Donetsk-Dnepr, as well as the Volgo-Vyatsk. These rates were the highest for any regions in any period and were perhaps the greatest rates of urban growth ever experienced in the world. The Center and Northwest had slower rates of urban growth (7.4 and 6.0 percent per year, respectively), but even here the urban populations more than doubled between 1926 and 1939. The slower rates of urban growth of these two regions reflect in part their larger base populations in that they had the largest urban populations in 1926 and the two largest cities of the USSR: Moscow and Leningrad.

Although considerable regional variations in rates of urbanization and urban growth did occur between 1926 and 1939, it should be kept in mind that rates for most regions were exceptionally high. A comparison of the largely "black" maps of the 1926-39 period with corresponding much "whiter" ones for other periods demonstrates the extraordinary rapidity of the urban process during this period (Maps 4.6-4.17).

The extreme rapidity of these rates of urbanization and urban growth also can be seen by making some rough international comparisons. As mentioned previously, the rate of urbanization and urban growth in the USSR as a whole during this period was unsurpassed by any world region in any decade of the 1920-70 period. Although the USSR is one country, the size of many of its individual regions are greater than many, if not most, of the world's countries. Therefore, it might be worthwhile to compare regional urbanization and urban growth in the USSR during the 1926-39 period with individual countries, especially developing countries during the 1950-60 and 1960-70 periods. As in the previous chapter, for other countries we will have to rely primarily on urban populations based upon their official definitions of urban.[1] The comparisons are thus, fairly rough.

With respect to rates of urbanization only two countries (Spanish Sahara and Japan) approached or exceeded the average annual rate of about two percentage points attained by the Donetsk-Dnepr and the Far East. However, Spanish Sahara is very small in population, and, as we discussed in the previous chapter, it appears that the Japanese rates are somewhat inflated due to definitional considerations.

In terms of urban growth many more countries compare with the regions of most rapid urban growth in the USSR between 1926 and 1939. This, of course, reflects the very rapid urban growth in developing countries in recent years, due to unprecedented rates of overall natural increase and population growth, although the urbanization rates are not as high as might be expected in such countries, because the rural population is still growing comparatively rapidly. The most rapid rates of urban growth in the USSR between 1926 and 1939 were roughly 9 to 12 percent per year, a range of rates being attained by seven regions, with the Far East having the highest, 12.4 percent (Table 4.8). Roughly a dozen countries had urban growth rates of at least 9 percent per year in the 1950-60 and/or 1960-70 periods. However, these countries were not very large, with only three having more than 5 million people in 1970 (Uganda, Congo Democratic Republic, and North Vietnam).

It is also interesting to compare regions of the USSR with California, the largest state of the United States (having between 10 and 20 million people in 1950, 1960, and 1970) and one that has experienced rapid urbanization and urban growth in recent years. Based on centers (both incorporated and unincorporated) of 15,000 and over, the levels of urbanization for California in 1950, 1960, and 1970 were 57.0, 66.1, and 74.5 percent, respectively. This entails average annual percentage point changes of 0.91 between 1950 and 1960 and 0.84 between 1960 and 1970, rates that are substantially below those of Soviet regions between 1926 and 1939.[2] In addition, based again on an urban definition of 15,000 or more people, the average annual urban growth rate for California was 5.4 percent between 1950 and 1960, and 3.6 percent between 1960 and 1970. Both rates were not only below the rates for some of the largest Soviet regions with extremely rapid urban growth between 1926 and 1939, but also were below the total Soviet urban growth rate between 1926 and 1939.

In summary, it appears that rates of urbanization and urban growth experienced by a number of Soviet regions between 1926 and 1939 were unsurpassed by any country in the world between 1950 and 1960 or 1960 and 1970, even by those developing countries experiencing very rapid rates recently.

In order to describe further regional aspects of rapid urban growth within the USSR during the 1926-39 period, we will refer briefly to the work of Chauncy Harris. Based upon the 174 cities with 50,000 or more people in 1939, he notes that there were "3 major and 2 minor districts where most of the cities trebled in population during this 12-year period": the Dnepr-Donbas Industrial District in the Ukraine, the Ural Industrial District, the Kuzbas Industrial District in West Siberia, the suburbs of Moscow, and a string of cities along the Turk-Sib (Turkestan-Siberia) Railroad, respectively.[3] Harris also notes that a few cities outside these districts increased their population by at least ten times, and in the Central Industrial District and the area extending eastward to the Urals, the larger cities generally more than doubled in population.[4] Reflecting the strong impact of this first period of planned rapid industrialization, these regions were, as a rule, the major industrial areas of the USSR. These regions correspond roughly to the Donetsk-Dnepr, Urals, West Siberia, and Center, which we have seen were four of the outstanding economic regions of urbanization and urban growth. In fact, so tremendous was the urban process in these four regions that slightly more than one-half (51.4 percent) of the total urban growth of the USSR between 1926 and 1939 occurred in these regions combined; individually they were the four leading regions with respect to absolute urban population increase.

Although extremely high rates of urbanization and urban growth were characteristic of some regions of the USSR between 1926 and 1939, other regions had fairly slow rates and one even had declining rates. The regional range in both the average annual percentage point change in the level of urbanization and average annual percentage change in the urban population during the 1926-39 period was unsurpassed in any other intercensal period (Tables 4.6 and 4.8). The range for urbanization change was 2.24 percentage points (2.00 for the Far East to -0.24 for Moldavia), while that for urban population change was 13.3 (12.4 for the Far East to -0.9 for Moldavia).

Regions where the urban process was fairly slow were concentrated along the western and southern borders of the USSR (Tables 4.4, 4.6, and 4.8 and Maps 4.7 and 4.13). Regions along the western border generally had the lowest rates. Moldavia had not only a declining level of urbanization, continuing a pattern that it shared along with the Central Chernozem in the 1897-1926 period but also a declining urban population, the only case where this occurred in any region in any intercensal period. Paradoxically, this urban decline in Moldavia occurred in what was in general the period of most rapid urbanization and urban growth in the USSR. A prime explanation for this decline was that Moldavia continued to be primarily part of Romania during this period and thus continued to be subjected to a policy of withdrawal of industry from this area (see Chapter 2).

The relatively slow urban process in all of the extreme western regions (Moldavia, the South, the Southwest, Belorussia, and the West) was due to a great extent to the fact that substantial parts of these regions and, in fact, the entire West Region, were outside the official boundaries of the USSR as it was constituted during this period. Being outside the USSR at this time, these areas did not receive the benefits of the emphasis on rapid industrialization that was occurring with the first five-year plans being carried out in the USSR. In order to investigate this situation more thoroughly, we have calculated rates of urban population change for two types of areas of each of the five western regions in question: (1) the area that was outside the USSR as it ac-

TABLE 4.9

Average Annual Percentage Change of the Urban Population
by Areas outside and inside the USSR of the Five Western
Border Regions with Slow Urban Growth: 1926-39

	Rate of Urban Change for	
Region	Area of Region outside USSR	Area of Region inside USSR
West	1.2	—*
Belorussia	3.9	5.2
Moldavia	-1.6	4.5
Southwest	1.8	2.7
South	-3.1	3.5
Total of five regions	1.3	3.5
Areas in Romania	-1.8	n.a.

n.a.:   data not available

*All of the West Region was outside the USSR between
1926 and 1939.

Sources: See Chapter 1, nn. 104 and 105.

tually existed in the 1926-39 period and (2) the area that was inside the USSR
as it actually existed in this same period (Table 4.9). The urban growth rate
collectively of the area outside the USSR was much slower than that for the
area inside: 1.3 percent per year for the area outside as compared with 3.5
percent per year for the area inside. This pattern was also in evidence for
each of the regions, except for the West Region, which is not applicable to
this part of the discussion since it was completely outside the USSR at this
time. The areas of Moldavia and the South, which were outside the USSR,
actually had fairly substantial rates of urban population decrease. The impact
on those areas within Romania at this time is also again noticeable. Not only
was most of Moldavia within Romania at this time but also were parts of the
South and Southwest. Altogether, the urban population of those areas then in
Romania and now in the USSR declined by nearly -2.0 percent per annum during this period.

　　Given the very rapid urbanization and sharp regional differences in urbanization rates between 1926 and 1939, regional variations in levels of urbanization in 1939 were somewhat different from those in 1926. First, the

MAP 4.1

Level of Urbanization: 1897

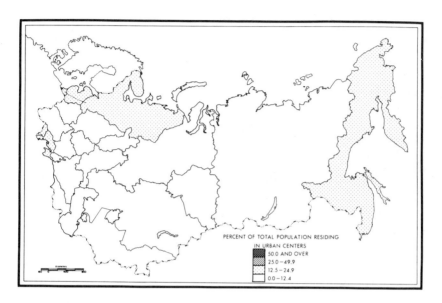

MAP 4.2

Level of Urbanization: 1926

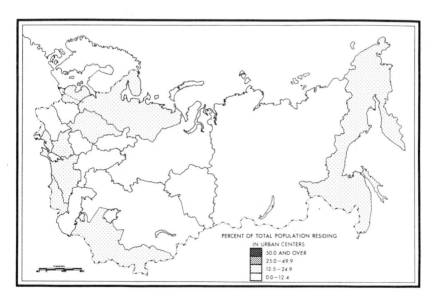

MAP 4.3

Level of Urbanization: 1939

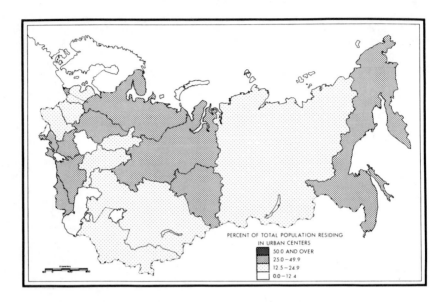

PERCENT OF TOTAL POPULATION RESIDING
IN URBAN CENTERS

50.0 AND OVER
25.0 – 49.9
12.5 – 24.9
0.0 – 12.4

4.4 percentage point gap between the urbanization level of the Western and Eastern USSR nearly had been closed, with the Western level now only 0.9 percentage points higher (Table 4.1). Changes also occurred among the four quadrants. The European Steppe was still the most urbanized quadrant in 1939, but the Russian East now had changed from being the least urbanized quadrant in both 1897 and 1926 to the second most urbanized quadrant in 1939. Northern European USSR and the Non-Slavic South were now the least urbanized quadrants, although the levels of both of these quadrants nearly doubled, and slightly more than 20 percent of their populations were urbanized by 1939.

Changes in ranks involving the 19 regions were also quite appreciable. Although the Northwest was still the most urbanized region in 1939, the next three highest ranking regions were all regions that experienced a substantial increase in rank: the Far East, the Donetsk-Dnepr, and the Center. The greatest increases in ranks were attained by the Urals and Kazakhstan, and West Siberia also experienced a substantial increase.

Substantial regional declines in ranks also occurred, especially by Moldavia, the West, the Southwest, and Central Asia (Table 4.2). In 1939, these regions along with the Central Chernozem, Belorussia, and the Volgo-Vyatsk comprised the least urbanized regions in the USSR.

The regional changes discussed above are also evident when comparing the maps for 1897, 1926, and 1939 (Maps 4.1-4.3). In 1897 and 1926, the most urbanized regions were located to an appreciable extent along the western or southern borderlands of the European part of the USSR, with the least urbanized regions being more in the interior. However, by 1939, some of the most highly urbanized regions were now located in the interior, while an appreciable number of the least urbanized regions were now located on the western or southern periphery. In addition, the most highly urbanized regions were now concentrated more than before in the RSFSR. Six of the eight most urbanized regions in 1939 were in the RSFSR, while in contrast, in 1897 and 1926, only three and four, respectively, of the eight most urbanized regions were located in this union republic. These patterns reflect the fact that the increased emphasis on industrial investment of this period was especially directed toward the RSFSR.

1939-59

Although the urban process of the USSR as a whole and most of its regions slowed down during the 1939-59 period, due in great part to the impact of World War II, many of the regional trends under way in the 1926-39 period continued. Although both areas urbanized more slowly than between 1926 and 1939, the Eastern USSR continued to urbanize more rapidly than did the Western USSR (Tables 4.3 and 4.5). This reflects the fact that the urban growth rate of the Eastern USSR was about twice that of the Western USSR and entailed more than a doubling of the Eastern USSR's urban population, although for both areas the urban growth rate was slower than between 1926 and 1939.

The relatively greater rapidity of the urban process in the Eastern USSR is reflected also in data presented by Harris.[5] According to his calculations, there were 381 "growth cities" in the USSR between 1939 and 1959. Growth cities are defined generally as those urban centers of 1959 whose population either more than doubled between 1939 and 1959 or who presumably emerged as a new city between 1939 and 1959.[6] It appears that 174 or 45.7 percent of the growth cities were located in the Eastern USSR as we define it in our study. Thus, although the Eastern USSR contained only about one-third of the total and urban populations of the USSR, in 1959 it had nearly one-half of the growth cities or rapidly growing towns between 1939 and 1959. Focusing only on those cities with 15,000 or more people in 1959 (297 in number), much the same pattern emerges but with even slightly more emphasis toward the east, as 50.8 percent of these growth cities were located in the Eastern USSR.

At the other end of the spectrum, the vast majority of towns that declined in population between 1939 and 1959 were located in the Western USSR, especially in the combat zone of World War II. In 1959 there were 54 cities with a population of 15,000 or more whose population declined between 1939 and 1959.[7] Of these 42 or 77.8 percent were located in the Western USSR and, apparently except for only two towns, all of the western towns were located within the combat zone.[8] Thus, 40 or nearly three-fourths (74.1 percent) of the 54 declining towns were located in the combat zone of the west.

With respect to the quadrants, the Russian East still had the highest rate of urbanization and urban growth, although it had, like all of the quadrants, lower rates in both cases as compared with the 1926-39 period (Tables

4.3, 4.5, and 4.7). The relatively rapid urban process of the Russian East was favored by its being beyond the major area of fighting during World War II and by the considerable shift of industry to this area during the war. The biggest turnabout was experienced by the European Steppe. Of the four quadrants, it ranked first and second with respect to rate of urbanization in the 1897-1926 and 1926-39 periods, respectively, but, between 1939 and 1959, it ranked last among the four quadrants. Its urban growth rate was also low, being only very slightly above that of Northern European USSR, the region with the slowest urban growth between 1939 and 1959. The slow urban process of the European Steppe greatly reflects the impact of World War II on such regions as the South and Donetsk-Dnepr of the Ukraine. Northern European USSR and the Non-Slavic South urbanized at roughly equal rates. However, in terms of urban growth rates they were substantially different, with Northern European USSR having an average annual rate that was the slowest of all the quadrants and only about 50 percent that of the Non-Slavic South. The rate for the Non-Slavic South was nearly equal to the highest rate attained by the Russian East. These differentials reflect in part, once again, regional differences in the impact of the war, with Northern European USSR being heavily hit and the Non-Slavic South being generally beyond the main combat zone. That these two quadrants urbanized at roughly the same rate despite having substantially different rates of urban growth reflects their rates of rural population change (Table 7.1). The Non-Slavic South had the most rapid rate of rural increase of any region, thus offsetting much of the rapid urban growth and impeding a more rapid rate of urbanization. In contrast, Northern European USSR had the greatest rate of rural population decline of any quadrant in any period, thus enhancing the urbanization process.

Greater insights emerge with an investigation of the 19 economic regions. Map 4.8 reveals that the greatest rates of urbanization occurred in the interior regions of the USSR, or as Harris terms it "the Interior Core."[9] The most rapid urbanization occurred in West Siberia, the Urals, the Volga, the Center, East Siberia, the Volgo-Vyatsk, and Kazakhstan, while the most rapid urban growth occurred in Kazakhstan, West Siberia, the Urals, East Siberia, Moldavia, Central Asia, and the Volga (Table 4.8 and Map 4.14). Thus, such interior regions as the Urals, West Siberia, the Volga, East Siberia, and Kazakhstan were among the top seven regions with respect to both rates of urbanization and urban growth. All five of these regions benefited greatly from the shift of industry to behind the front line into the interior of the USSR during World War II. However, it will be recalled that, with the exception of the Volga, these regions already had been urbanizing relatively rapidly between 1926 and 1939 in association with the eastward shift of industry during that period.

The rapidity of the urban process in the interior regions of the USSR also is reflected in the number of rapidly growing towns in these regions. Based upon towns with only 15,000 or more people in 1959 and upon Harris's study, we can assess by economic region the number of towns that at least doubled in population between 1939 and 1959, including new towns. As mentioned before, there were 297 of these towns in the USSR. Of them, the greatest number were in the Urals (52), the Center (34), Kazakhstan (26), West Siberia (24), and Central Asia (23), all of which can be considered "interior regions."

Regions with the slowest urbanization and urban growth were located primarily in the western and southern portions of the USSR (Tables 4.4, 4.6, and 4.8 and Maps 4.8 and 4.14). The slowest rates of urbanization were experienced by the Southwest, Moldavia, the South, and Belorussia, as well as the Far East. The regions with the slowest urban growth often coincided with these regions: the Northwest, South, Southwest, Belorussia, the Center, and the Donetsk-Dnepr. All of these regions are in the western part of the USSR and were devastated during World War II.

Towns with population decline between 1939 and 1959 were, to a great extent, located in these war-torn regions of slow urbanization and/or urban growth. Of the 54 previously mentioned declining towns with 15,000 or more people in 1959, the Southwest, Northwest, and Center had the greatest numbers (11, 9, and 8, respectively) and together contained slightly more than one-half of the declining towns between 1939 and 1959.

Although it is apparent that most of the declining towns were located in the war zone, it appears that the sharpest declines occurred in those areas that were acquired by the USSR and from which native peoples (Germans, Poles, and so forth) were evacuated. The population of a number of towns was cut by a fifth to nearly a half between circa 1939 and 1959, and most of these "sharply" declining towns were located in the acquired "evacuated" areas;[10] whereas only about one-third (16 or 29.6 percent) of all 54 declining towns were located in acquired areas, roughly two-thirds (12 of 17) of the sharply declining towns were found in acquired areas. In addition, whereas only about one-third (17 of 54) of the declining towns were sharply declining towns, three-fourths (12 of 16) of all declining towns in acquired areas were sharply declining towns. Although these towns eventually received migrants, especially Russians, to replace the evacuees, by 1959 their populations had not yet reached their circa 1939 populations.

Unfortunately, it is not possible to assess comprehensively the more immediate impact of the war on urban population change for the economic regions. However, data available for the 15 union republics reveal how hard hit were the Ukrainian and Belorussian republics, both of which were completely in the combat zone. Based on the official urban definitions, the Ukraine and Belorussia were the only two republics to experience urban population decline between 1939 and 1951: -0.9 and -7.0 percent, respectively.[11] In comparison, the urban population of the USSR still managed to increase by 20.9 percent during the same period.[12] It did not take long, though, for the Ukraine and Belorussia to offset this decline; between 1951 and 1959 their urban populations increased by more than 40 percent each (42.4 and 43.7, respectively), rates that exceeded the national average of 36.9 percent.[13] Undoubtedly, some western portions of the RSFSR also experienced urban population decline between 1939 and 1951, but there are no data by economic regions or major administrative units to document this.

As a result of the continued relatively rapid urbanization in the eastern areas of the USSR between 1939 and 1959, by 1959 these areas for the first

MAP 4.4

Level of Urbanization: 1959

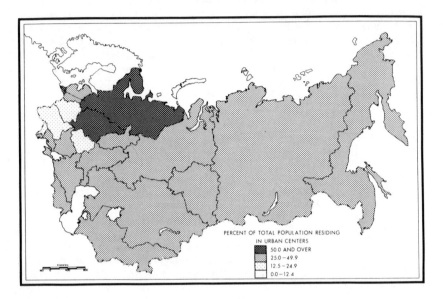

PERCENT OF TOTAL POPULATION RESIDING
IN URBAN CENTERS

50.0 AND OVER
25.0 — 49.9
12.5 — 24.9
0.0 — 12.4

time at any census date became the most urbanized areas of the USSR (Table
4.1). In 1959, the Eastern USSR had become slightly more urbanized than the
Western USSR, and the Russian East had now become the most urbanized of
the four quadrants, a remarkable change from its being the least urbanized
of the quadrants in 1897 and 1926. The European Steppe, the most urbanized
quadrant in the three preceding census years, was now the second most urbanized quadrant, followed by Northern European USSR and the Non-Slavic
South.

There were only relatively small changes in ranks among the 19 economic
regions (Table 4.2 and Maps 4.3 and 4.4). Relatively highly urbanized regions
experiencing the greatest increases in ranks were those either partly or wholly
outside the combat zone of World War II: the Center, the Volga, West Siberia,
and the Urals. The high rankings of the latter two regions, along with the
continued high ranking of the Far East, further reflects the emergence of the
Russian East as the most highly urbanized quadrant of the USSR. The three
most highly urbanized regions were still in the Western USSR: the Center,
the Northwest, and the Donetsk-Dnepr. Indeed, in 1959, the Center and the
Northwest became the first economic regions to have a majority of their population in urban centers, and the Donetsk-Dnepr was also virtually at the 50
percent level.

1959-70

Between 1959 and 1970 major changes occurred in the regional variations in rates of urbanization and urban growth in comparison with the preceding 1897-1959 period. Most notably, the long-term shift to the eastern areas of the USSR was reversed (see Map 4.5). First, whereas the Eastern USSR urbanized more rapidly than the Western USSR between 1897 and 1959, between 1959 and 1970, the Western USSR urbanized more rapidly than the Eastern USSR (Tables 4.3 and 4.5). This regional change reflected changes in urban growth rates (Table 4.7). Whereas the urban growth rate of the Eastern USSR exceeded that of the Western USSR between 1897 and 1959, between 1959 and 1970, the Western USSR's rate was slightly higher, although both were essentially equal in this regard. The urban growth rate of the Eastern USSR between 1959 and 1970 was slower than that for the 1897-1959 (3.1 percent per year as compared with 4.5 percent per year), while the rate for the Western USSR was faster (3.2 percent per year as compared with 2.6 percent per year).

Similar changes occurred at the level of the four quadrants (Tables 4.3 and 4.5). The Russian East, which had the highest rate of urbanization between 1897 and 1959, especially from 1926 to 1959, now had a rate of urbanization that surpassed only that of the Non-Slavic South. Between 1959 and 1970 the greatest rate of urbanization by far was experienced by Northern Eu-

MAP 4.5

Level of Urbanization: 1970

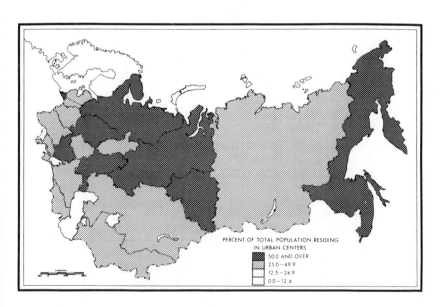

ropean USSR, and that of the European Steppe also exceeded the urbanization rate of the Russian East, although just barely.

With respect to urban growth rates the reversal was even greater (Table 4.7). The Russian East plummeted from a position of having the most rapid rate of urban growth in all of the intercensal periods between 1897 and 1959 to having the slowest rate of urban growth between 1959 and 1970. Indeed, its rate of 2.3 percent per year was less than one-half of its annual rate of 5.1 percent between 1897 and 1959. In contrast, the rate for each of the other three quadrants was higher than its corresponding rate between 1897 and 1959.

The most rapid rate of urban growth of any of the quadrants between 1959 and 1970 was experienced not by the most rapidly urbanizing quadrants but by the slowest urbanizing quadrant, the Non-Slavic South. The urbanization rate in the Non-Slavic South was dampened by its very rapid rate of rural growth, a rate unsurpassed by any quadrant in any period (Tables 4.7 and 7.1). The Non-Slavic South pattern is similar to that of developing countries in recent decades: high fertility, low mortality, high natural increase, rapid total population growth, and rapid urban growth but also fairly rapid rural growth, which leads to slower rates of urbanization than might be expected based upon urban growth rates alone.

These substantial changes in regional patterns of urbanization and urban growth between the pre-1959 and post-1959 periods are also evident at the economic region level (Tables 4.4, 4.6, and 4.8 and Maps 4.6-4.9 and 4.12-4.15). Between 1959 and 1970 the most rapidly urbanizing regions were all in the Western USSR and Northern European USSR: Belorussia, the Volgo-Vyatsk, the Central Chernozem, the West, the Volga, and the Center. In contrast, except for the North Caucasus and the South, the most slowly urbanizing regions were all in the Eastern USSR, the Russian East, and the Non-Slavic South: Central Asia, the Transcaucasus, the Far East, Kazakhstan, the Urals, and East Siberia.

To a great extent, a similar situation existed with regard to regional patterns of urban growth. Except for Central Asia and Kazakhstan, regions with the most rapid urban growth were all located in the Western USSR, Northern European USSR, and the European Steppe: Moldavia, Belorussia, the Central Chernozem, the Southwest, the West, and the South. The rapid urban growth but relatively slow urbanization of Central Asia and Kazakhstan was related to the very rapid rural population growth of these two regions. Regions with the slowest urban growth included all regions of the Russian East (West Siberia, the Urals, the Far East, and East Siberia) as well as three western regions (the Center, Northwest, and Donetsk-Dnepr).

Table 4.10 shows regional ranks in urbanization and urban growth rates in the 1897-1959 and 1959-70 periods and changes in those ranks. From this table it is very evident that the 1959-70 period marked a sharp reversal of preexisting trends. The rank correlation coefficient between rates of urbanization for 1897-1959 and for 1959-70 was -0.039, while that between urban growth rates of the same two periods was -0.602. The existence of negative correlations in each case indicates that regional variations in urbanization and urban growth rates for 1959-70 were quite dissimilar to those of 1897-1959.

MAP 4.6

Change in Level of Urbanization: 1897-1926

MAP 4.7

Change in Level of Urbanization: 1926-39

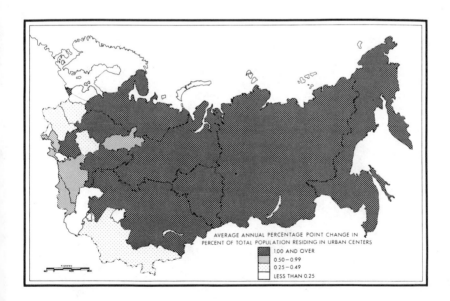

MAP 4.8

Change in Level of Urbanization: 1939-59

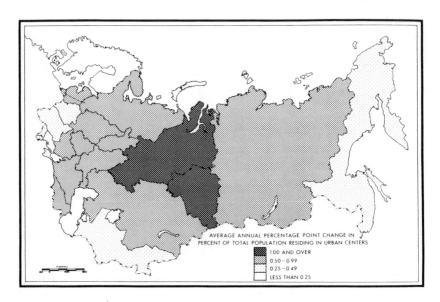

MAP 4.9

Change in Level of Urbanization: 1959-70

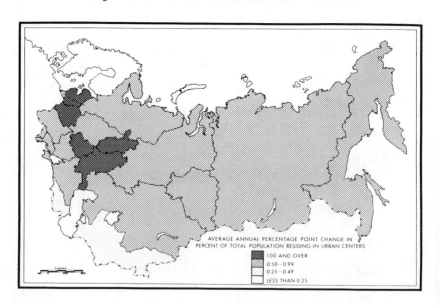

MAP 4.10

Change in Level of Urbanization: 1926-70

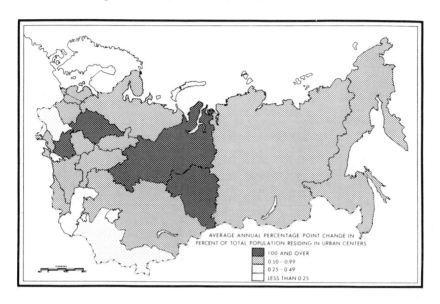

MAP 4.11

Change in Level of Urbanization: 1897-1970

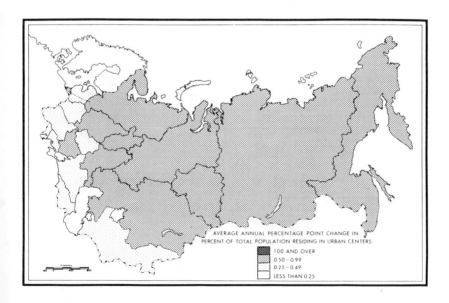

MAP 4.12

Change in Urban Population: 1897-1926

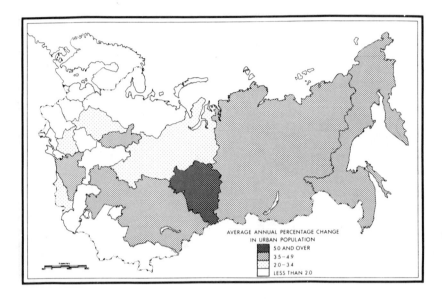

MAP 4.13

Change in Urban Population: 1926-39

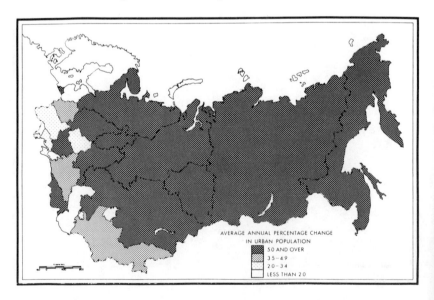

MAP 4.14

Change in Urban Population: 1939-59

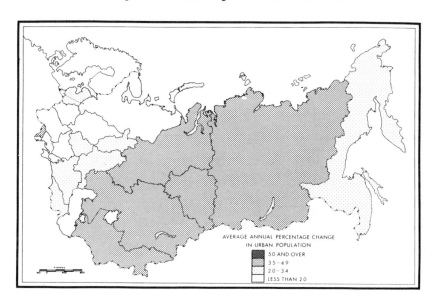

MAP 4.15

Change in Urban Population: 1959-70

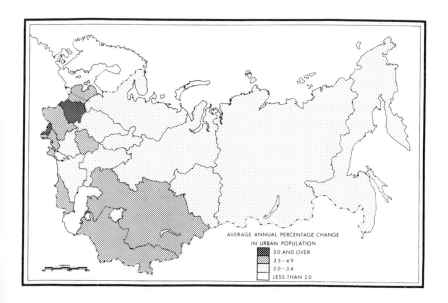

MAP 4.16

Change in Urban Population: 1926-70

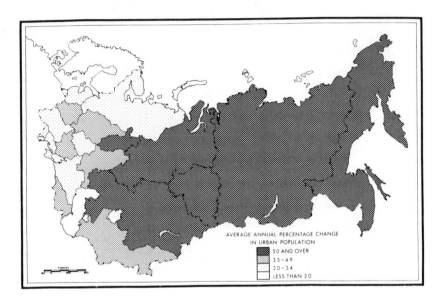

MAP 4.17

Change in Urban Population: 1897-1970

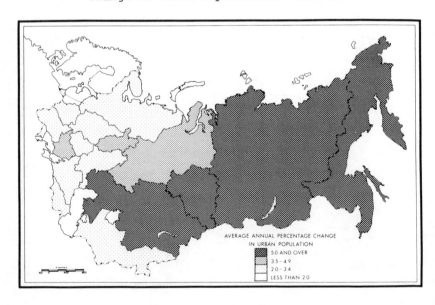

TABLE 4.10

Change in Ranks of Urbanization and Urban Growth Rates
by Economic Region: 1897-1959 as Compared with 1959-70

Region	Urbanization: Rank, 1897-1959, to Rank, 1959-70, and Change in Rank		Urban Growth: Rank, 1897-1959, to Rank, 1959-70, and Change in Rank
Belorussia	16 to 1: + 15	Moldavia	19 to 1: + 18
Central Chernozem	17 to 3: + 14	Belorussia	13 to 2: + 11
West	13 to 4: + 9	West	17 to 7: + 10
Volgo-Vyatsk	11 to 2: + 9	Central Chernozem	15 to 5: + 10
Moldavia	19 to 11: + 8	Southwest	16 to 6: + 10
Southwest	18 to 10: + 8	South	18 to 8: + 10
Northwest	9 to 8: + 1	Central Asia	12 to 4: + 8
Volga	6 to 5: + 1	Transcaucasus	10 to 9: + 1
South	14 to 15: - 1	Kazakhstan	4 to 3: + 1
Donetsk-Dnepr	4 to 7: - 3	Volga	11 to 10.5: + 0.5
Center	2 to 6: - 4	Northwest	14 to 16: - 2
Central Asia	15 to 19: - 4	North Caucasus	8.5 to 10.5: - 2
Transcaucasus	12 to 18: - 6	Volgo-Vyatsk	5 to 12: - 7
West Siberia	3 to 9: - 6	Donetsk-Dnepr	7 to 14: - 7
Kazakhstan	8 to 14: - 6	Center	8.5 to 17: - 8.5
North Caucasus	10 to 16.5: - 6.5	East Siberia	3 to 13: - 10
East Siberia	5 to 12.5: - 7.5	Urals	6 to 18: - 12
Far East	7 to 16.5: - 9.5	Far East	2 to 15: - 13
Urals	1 to 12.5: - 11.5	West Siberia	1 to 19: - 18

Sources: See Chapter 1, nn. 104 and 105.

With respect to changes in the level of urbanization, the greatest increases in rank were achieved by six regions of the Western USSR (Belorussia, the Central Chernozem, the West, the Volgo-Vyatsk, Moldavia, and the Southwest).

Conversely, regions undergoing the greatest decline in ranks were, with the exception of the North Caucasus, all located in the Eastern USSR, Russian East, and Non-Slavic South (the Urals, the Far East, East Siberia, Kazakhstan, West Siberia, the Transcaucasus, and Central Asia).

Regional reversals in urban growth rates followed much the same pattern (Table 4.10). The greatest gains in ranks occurred primarily in the Western USSR and the greatest declines primarily in the Eastern USSR, with the four regions of the Russian East having the four greatest declines. However, these reversals were even greater than those with regard to urbanization. Most notably, Moldavia changed from being the region with the slowest rate of urban growth between 1897 and 1959 to that with the fastest rate between 1959 and 1970, while West Siberia changed from being the region with the most rapid urban growth between 1897 and 1959 to that with the slowest rate between 1959 and 1970.

Regional Urbanization and Urban Growth since 1970

In order to investigate regional trends in urbanization and urban growth since 1970, we will once again utilize urban data for 1974 and 1977. To repeat, the 1977 data are for all urban centers according to the official definitions of urban, while the 1974 data are for official cities with 15,000 or more people. Regional urbanization and urban growth patterns based on these data are presented in Tables 4.11-4.14 and Maps 4.18-4.21. Corresponding 1959 data are included in the tables in order to enhance an assessment of the post-1970 regional urban trends. Regional patterns based on these post-1970 data probably reflect regional trends that would emerge on the basis of our comparable urban definition (all urban centers with 15,000 or more people), if such data were available. A comparison of 1959-70 regional trends based on each of the two types of urban definitions used for the post-1970 trends in Tables 4.11-4.14 with those based on the 15,000-and-over definition in Tables 4.1-4.8 reveals strong similarities. Such similarities are not surprising, because the vast majority of the urban population based on the official definitions of urban resides in centers of 15,000 and over, and nearly all of the population in urban centers of 15,000 and over resides in official cities of 15,000 and over.

In general, it appears that regional urban trends occurring between 1959 and 1970 continued during the 1970s. The Western USSR continued to urbanize more rapidly than the Eastern USSR, and Northern European USSR and the Non-Slavic South continued to have the highest and lowest rates of urbanization of the four quadrants. The Non-Slavic South was the only quadrant that did not have a higher rate of urbanization than during the 1959-70 period, again reflecting the fact that it continued to have the highest rate of rural population

TABLE 4.11

Urbanization and Urban Growth by Gross Region: 1959-77

Region	Level of Urbanization			Average Annual Percentage Point Change of Level of Urbanization		Average Annual Percentage Change of Urban Population	
	1959	1970	1977	1959-70	1970-77	1959-70	1970-77
Western USSR	47.1	56.8	63.3	0.88	0.93	2.8	2.2
Eastern USSR	49.8	55.1	59.1	0.48	0.57	2.7	2.5
Northern European USSR	45.3	56.6	64.2	1.03	1.09	2.8	2.2
European Steppe	52.3	59.0	63.8	0.61	0.69	2.7	2.0
Russian East	56.3	64.1	70.6	0.71	0.93	2.1	2.1
Non-Slavic South	40.6	45.1	47.6	0.41	0.36	3.9	2.8
USSR total	47.9	56.3	61.9	0.76	0.80	2.8	2.2

Note: Based on official urban definitions.

Sources: 1959 and 1970 Soviet censuses and 1977 estimates (see Chapter 1, nn. 104 and 113).

TABLE 4.12

Urbanization and Urban Growth by Economic Region: 1959-77

Region	Level of Urbanization			Average Annual Percentage Point Change of Level of Urbanization		Average Annual Percentage Change of Urban Population	
	1959	1970	1977	1959-70	1970-77	1959-70	1970-77
Northwest	64.6	73.3	78.8	0.79	0.79	2.2	2.0
West	48.2	57.4	63.3	0.84	0.84	2.8	2.4
Center	60.8	72.4	78.4	1.05	0.86	2.2	1.6
Volgo-Vyatsk	38.9	52.9	61.5	1.27	1.23	2.9	2.1
Central Chernozem	26.9	40.1	51.6	1.20	1.64	3.9	3.1
Volga	48.4	59.8	68.1	1.04	1.19	3.2	2.6
Belorussia	30.8	43.4	53.2	1.15	1.40	4.2	3.5
Moldavia	22.3	31.7	37.9	0.85	0.89	5.1	3.7
Southwest	28.7	38.7	45.9	0.91	1.03	3.4	2.8
South	48.7	57.1	62.9	0.76	0.83	3.6	2.7
Donetsk-Dnepr	65.7	72.1	76.6	0.58	0.64	2.0	1.5
North Caucasus	42.4	49.5	54.5	0.65	0.71	3.3	2.2
Transcaucasus	45.9	51.1	54.2	0.47	0.44	3.3	2.4
Urals	56.4	63.5	70.3	0.65	0.97	2.0	1.9
West Siberia	52.9	63.0	69.4	0.92	0.91	2.0	1.7
East Siberia	52.5	61.4	68.1	0.81	0.96	2.9	2.7
Far East	69.6	73.4	77.3	0.35	0.56	2.0	2.8
Kazakhstan	43.7	50.3	54.4	0.60	0.59	4.3	2.7
Central Asia	34.9	38.0	39.9	0.28	0.27	4.2	3.5
USSR total	47.9	56.3	61.9	0.76	0.80	2.8	2.2

Note: Based on official urban definitions.

Sources: 1959 and 1970 Soviet censuses and 1977 estimates (see Chapter 1, nn. 104 and 113).

TABLE 4.13

Urbanization and Urban Growth by Gross Region: 1959-74

Region	Level of Urbanization			Average Annual Percentage Point Change of Level of Urbanization		Average Annual Percentage Change of Urban Population	
	1959	1970	1974	1959-70	1970-74	1959-70	1970-74
Western USSR	36.9	46.4	50.2	0.86	0.95	3.2	2.6
Eastern USSR	38.8	44.1	46.5	0.48	0.60	3.0	2.8
Northern European USSR	35.6	46.2	50.4	0.96	1.05	3.1	2.6
European Steppe	40.5	48.4	51.5	0.72	0.78	3.2	2.6
Russian East	44.6	52.0	55.8	0.67	0.95	2.3	2.4
Non-Slavic South	31.0	35.6	37.2	0.42	0.40	4.3	3.3
USSR total	37.5	45.7	49.0	0.75	0.83	3.1	2.6

Note: Based on official cities of 15,000 and over.

Sources: 1959 and 1970 Soviet censuses and 1974 estimates (see Chapter 1, nn. 104 and 113).

TABLE 4.14

Urbanization and Urban Growth by Economic Region: 1959-74

Region	Level of Urbanization			Average Annual Percentage Point Change in Level of Urbanization		Average Annual Percentage Change of Urban Population	
	1959	1970	1974	1959-70	1970-74	1959-70	1970-74
Northwest	50.7	60.5	64.0	0.89	0.88	2.7	2.4
West	32.2	44.0	47.9	1.07	0.98	4.0	3.1
Center	52.3	62.5	66.0	0.93	0.88	2.3	1.9
Volgo-Vyatsk	28.7	41.1	45.3	1.13	1.05	3.4	2.2
Central Chernozem	21.2	32.9	38.4	1.06	1.38	4.2	3.3
Volga	41.1	51.8	56.4	0.97	1.15	3.4	3.1
Belorussia	21.1	34.2	39.4	1.19	1.30	5.4	4.3
Moldavia	15.2	22.9	26.3	0.70	0.85	5.6	4.8
Southwest	18.9	27.1	31.1	0.75	1.00	4.0	3.9
South	38.4	45.0	49.0	0.60	1.00	3.6	3.5
Donetsk-Dnepr	48.5	58.5	61.6	0.91	0.78	2.9	1.9
North Caucasus	36.4	43.0	46.1	0.60	0.78	3.4	2.8
Transcaucasus	36.6	41.7	43.4	0.46	0.43	3.5	2.6
Urals	46.6	54.1	58.2	0.68	1.03	2.2	2.2
West Siberia	45.9	54.6	58.4	0.79	0.95	2.0	1.9
East Siberia	36.0	44.1	48.2	0.74	1.03	3.3	3.3
Far East	47.0	51.0	53.2	0.36	0.55	2.2	3.1
Kazakhstan	32.0	39.0	41.9	0.64	0.73	4.8	3.5
Central Asia	26.3	29.7	30.6	0.31	0.23	4.4	3.7
USSR total	37.5	45.7	49.0	0.75	0.83	3.1	2.6

Note: Based on official cities of 15,000 and over.

Sources: 1959 and 1970 Soviet censuses and 1974 estimates (Chapter 1, nn. 104 and 113).

238

MAP 4.18

Change in Level of Urbanization: 1970-77

MAP 4.19

Change in Level of Urbanization: 1970-74

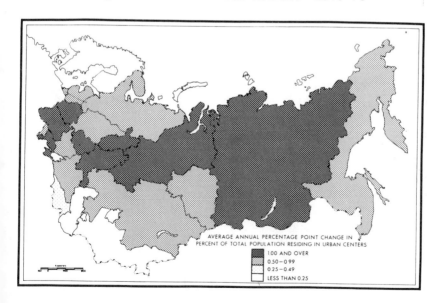

MAP 4.20

Change in Urban Population: 1970-77

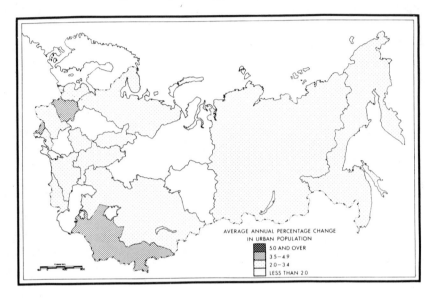

MAP 4.21

Change in Urban Population: 1970-74

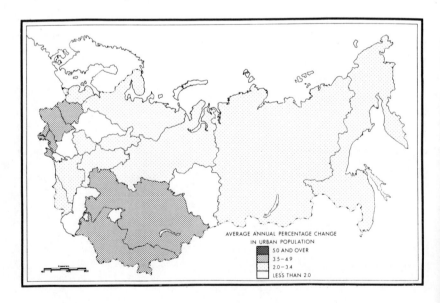

change of any quadrant, although it also continued to have the most rapid rate of urban growth of any quadrant (Tables 4.11, 4.13, and 7.3). By the late 1970s, the Western USSR continued to be slightly more urbanized than the Eastern USSR, while the Russian East and the Non-Slavic South maintained their positions as the most and least urbanized quadrants.

The great similarity between the 1959-70 and post-1970 regional urban trends was also evident at the economic region level (Tables 4.12 and 4.14 and Maps 4.18-4.21). This similarity is indicated by the fact that the rank correlation coefficient between regional urbanization rates of 1959-70 and 1970-77 was 0.886, while that between regional rates of urban growth for each period was 0.775. Such western regions as Belorussia, the Central Chernozem, the Volgo-Vyatsk, the Volga, and the West continued to have among the highest rates of urbanization, while Central Asia and the Transcaucasus again had among the lowest rates of urbanization. In general, the most urbanized regions continued to be the Center, the Northwest, the Donetsk-Dnepr, the Urals, West Siberia, the Volga, and the Far East, while Moldavia, Central Asia, and the Southwest continued to be the least urbanized. Also, similar to 1959-70, such western regions as Moldavia, Belorussia, the Southwest, the Central Chernozem, and the West, along with Central Asia and Kazakhstan, generally had the most rapid rates of urban growth, while the Center, West Siberia, the Urals, the Donetsk-Dnepr, and the Northwest tended to have the lowest rates of urban growth.

Although a general continuation of regional urban trends existed, the post-1970 period differed from the 1959-70 period in certain respects. First, virtually every region had a lower rate of urban growth after 1970, although many had higher rates of urbanization. This disparity between urban growth and urbanization patterns reflects a deepening of rates of rural population decline in the post-1970 period (Tables 7.3 and 7.4).

Another difference was the occurrence of a slight relative resurgence of the urban process in the Eastern USSR, especially the Russian East (Tables 4.11 and 4.13). Unlike the 1959-70 period, the Eastern USSR had a slightly higher rate of urban growth than the Western USSR and the Russian East urbanized more rapidly than the national average. The Russian East was also the only quadrant not to have a lower rate of urban growth in the post-1970 period.

Within the Russian East, the major regions of urban resurgence were the Far East and East Siberia (Tables 4.12 and 4.14). The Far East was the only economic region to have a higher rate of urban growth in the post-1970 period as compared to the 1959-70 period. East Siberia also had an urban growth rate that was decidedly above the national average after 1970.

The relative increase in the urban process in the Far East and East Siberia partly reflects the fact that this region includes a number of rapidly growing towns in the zone of the Baykal-Amur Mainline (BAM), the railroad currently being constructed through East Siberia and the Far East much to the north of the Trans-Siberian railroad zone. We have calculated a combined rate of growth for towns in the immediate service zone of the BAM as defined by Viktor B. Sochava.[14] In particular, there were 13 towns in this zone that had both a population of 15,000 and over in 1970 and were "cities" with 15,000 and over in 1974. In addition, we have included the rapidly growing city of Tynda. Although Tynda did not have a population of at least 15,000 in 1970, it is reported to have had a population of 30,000 in 1976.[15] Operationally assuming a population of slightly less than 15,000 in 1970, we have calculated its average annual rate of growth between 1970 and 1976 and projected its assumed 1970 population to 1974 on the basis of this rate. It was determined ultimately that the rate of growth for the 14 BAM towns (including Tynda) was 3.5 percent per year between 1970 and 1974. This was somewhat higher than the rates of urban growth for both the Far East and East Siberia as a whole and the USSR between 1970 and 1974 (Table 4.14).

Despite the slight urban resurgence of the east, it should be emphasized that the 1959-70 east-to-west shift in the urban process generally continued after 1970. The Eastern USSR and the Russian East have not returned to their pre-1959 position of strong superiority in terms of urbanization and urban growth rates. In addition, the two most dynamic eastern regions prior to 1959, the Urals and West Siberia, continued to have relatively slow rates of urban growth. Also, but despite its relative upsurge, the rate of urbanization for the Far East continued to be one of the very slowest in the USSR, due to a relatively high rate of rural population change (Tables 4.12 and 7.4).

Analysis

This section is devoted to an analysis of regional trends in Soviet urbanization and urban growth from 1897 to 1970. It will involve in part a summary of many points that have been discussed previously. The most fundamental relationships to be tested are those between regional urbanization and urban growth, and between these two variables and urban in-migration, natural increase, industrialization, and capital investment.

Relationships among Regional Urbanization, Urban Growth, and Rural Change

As frequently mentioned, urbanization and urban growth are not synonymous, although urban growth is usually a necessary immediate condition for an increase in the level of urbanization. Table 4.15 shows rank correlation coefficients for the intercensal periods between the average annual percentage point change in the level of urbanization and the average annual percentage change in the urban population. There was a fairly high positive relationship between regional rates of urbanization and urban growth between 1897 and 1959, but a very low relationship existed between 1959 and 1970.

Within the 1897-1959 period an especially high correlation existed during the 1926-39 period, while the 1897-1926 and 1939-59 periods were characterized by moderate relationships.

The existence of a very low relationship in the 1959-70 period was mainly due to Central Asia, Kazakhstan, the Center, the Volgo-Vyatsk, Moldavia, the Transcaucasus, the Northwest, and West Siberia (Tables 4.4, 4.6,

TABLE 4.15

Rank Correlation Coefficients between Regional Rates of
Urbanization and of Urban and Rural Change: 1897-1970

Period	Urbanization versus Urban Change	Urbanization versus Rural Change
1897-1926	0.531	-0.068
1926-39	0.842	-0.266
1939-59	0.471	-0.209
1959-70	0.000	-0.812
1926-70	0.526	-0.524
1897-1970	0.588	-0.167
1897-1959	0.753	0.112
1926-59	0.734	-0.158

Sources: See Chapter 1, nn. 104 and 105.

and 4. 8). Central Asia, had the lowest rate of urbanization and one of the
highest rates of urban growth, and, to a somewhat lesser degree, a similar
situation existed with Kazakhstan, Moldavia, and the Transcaucasus. The
great disparities in the ranks of these regions were due to their relatively high
rates of rural population change (Table 7.2).

The opposite situation occurred in the Center, the Volgo-Vyatsk, West
Siberia, and the Northwest. These regions ranked fairly high with regard to
urbanization increase but low with respect to urban growth. These disparities
were due to the low rates of rural population change of these regions (Table
7.2).

Between 1959 and 1970, the only regions that conformed to a pattern of
a high linkage between urbanization and urban growth were Belorussia, the
Central Chernozem, the West, East Siberia, and the Far East. The first
three regions ranked high with respect to both urbanization and urban growth,
while the last two had fairly low ranks.

As is apparent, regional rates of urbanization can be highly influenced
by rates of rural population change. Table 4.15 also shows rank correlation
coefficients between the average annual percentage point change in the level
of urbanization and the average annual percentage change in the rural population. In interpreting these correlations, it should be kept in mind that a high
negative correlation is hypothesized, because high rates of rural population

change should lead to low rates of urbanization. Indeed, in every period, a negative correlation existed, although not necessarily a high negative correlation in each case. In addition, while the regional linkages between urbanization and urban population change generally weakened over time, those between urbanization and rural population change increased. A relatively weak negative relationship existed for the 1897-1970 and 1897-1926 periods, but between 1926 and 1970 it strengthened. In fact, during the 1959-70 period a very high negative relationship existed. This high negative relationship in recent years was, of course, due to a very great extent to regions with relatively slow urbanization and relatively high rates of rural change (for example, Central Asia), as well as regions with relatively rapid urbanization and relatively low rates of rural change (for example, the Center).

It appears that the weak relationship between regional urbanization change and urban growth and the strong relationship between regional urbanization change and rural change continued after 1970. In particular, based on official urban definitions and the 19 regions, a rank correlation coefficient of only 0.101 existed between the two urban variables, while a coefficient of -0.761 occurred between urbanization change and rural change.

In summary, since the turn of the century there has been a fairly strong tie between regional variations in urbanization and urban growth. In recent years, this association has weakened greatly, and a fairly high association now exists between urbanization change and rural population change.

Relationships among Regional Urbanization, Urban Growth, Fertility, Mortality, Natural Increase, and Migration

The next level of analysis of regional urbanization and urban growth involves an investigation of their relationships with regional natural increase and migration. Unfortunately, given the lack of appropriate data, it is not possible to investigate these relationships in a rigorous fashion throughout the entire 1897-1970 period, although data are more abundant for the 1959-70 period.

With respect to the influence of fertility, mortality, and natural increase in the 1897-1959 period, it is obvious that the turmoil during this period influenced regional rates of urbanization and urban growth as a result of its effects on regional fertility, mortality, and natural increase patterns. It was noted earlier that the rates of urbanization and urban growth were higher in the Eastern USSR than the Western USSR during this period. It seems reasonable to conclude that the lesser rates of the Western USSR were due partly to protracted periods of war and resulting low fertility, high mortality, and low natural increase.

In the 1959-70 period, it is possible to assess more precisely the relationships between regional variations in urbanization and urban growth, on the one hand, and regional variations in crude birth, death, and natural increase rates, on the other. Rank correlation coefficients involving these variables are shown in Table 4.16. Regional urbanization rates were associated negatively with crude birth rates and natural increase rates and positively with crude death rates, and in each instance the association was fairly

TABLE 4.16

Rank Correlation Coefficients between Regional Rates of Urbanization, Urban Growth, and Rural Change and Crude Birth, Death, and Natural Increase Rates by Economic Region: 1959–70

Variable	Change in Level of Urbanization (79)	Rate of Urban Growth (141)	Rate of Rural Change (142)
Crude birth rate, 1970 (112)	−0.697	0.506	0.902
Crude death rate, 1970 (113)	0.638	−0.273	−0.703
Crude rate of natural increase, 1970 (114)	−0.702	0.432	0.852
Change in crude birth rate, 1960–70 (122)	−0.000	0.104	0.027
Change in crude death rate, 1960–70 (123)	0.432	−0.319	−0.630
Change in crude rate of natural increase, 1960–70 (124)	−0.139	0.158	0.172
Natural increase rate, 1959–70 (130)	−0.685	0.339	0.794

Note: Numbers in parentheses indicate variable numbers.

Sources: 1959 and 1970 Soviet censuses (see Chapter 1, n. 104); and Appendix A, which includes a listing and discussion of the variables.

strong. The high negative relationship reflects, once again, the fact that regions with slow urbanization have relatively high natural increase, which promotes not only rapid urban growth but also rapid rural growth, which in turn impedes a more rapid rate of urbanization. As might be expected, Central Asia was the outstanding region in this regard in that it had the slowest rate of urbanization but also the highest crude birth rate, lowest crude death rate, and highest crude natural increase rate. Given this situation, it is not surprising that there was a moderate, positive relationship between urban growth rates on the one hand and crude birth and natural increase rates on the other.

Data are not available, unfortunately, by economic region for urban and rural fertility, mortality, and natural increase rates. However, other data suggest that regional variations and relationships would conform roughly to those of the total population. Support for this contention comes from a set of graphs provided by B. S. Khorev.[16] These graphs show total, urban, and rural annual crude birth, death, and natural increase rates by union republic for 1940 and the 1950-70 period. A visual investigation of the graphs reveals that republic variations in crude birth, death, and natural increase rates for the urban and rural population roughly conform to those of the total population. It is difficult to present these patterns more precisely, because Khorev does not provide tabulated statistical data nor cite sources for the statistical data. Therefore, we have had to estimate the rates by making measurements from the graphs, not an ideal procedure, but, nonetheless, one that does have some merit, given the limitations involved. We have estimated the urban and rural rates for 1964 and 1970 from the graph and, along with total rates available elsewhere, have presented these in Tables 4.17 and 4.18. The year 1964 was selected, because it is the midpoint for the 1959-70 period. As Tables 4.17 and 4.18 reveal there was a very strong similarity between republic variations in the crude birth and natural increase rates of the total population, on the one hand, and the urban and rural populations, on the other. Therefore, it is possible to conclude that correlations between regional urbanization and urban growth and the regional crude birth and natural increase rates of the urban population would be similar to those between regional urbanization and urban growth and regional crude birth and natural increase rates of the total population. Thus, there apparently was a high negative relationship between regional rates of urbanization and urban crude birth and natural increase rates and a fairly strong positive relationship between regional rates of urban growth and urban crude birth and natural increase rates.

Furthermore, such relationships existed, based on republic variations. Table 4.19 shows levels of urbanization and rates of urbanization and urban growth for the 15 union republics between 1959 and 1970, based on the official definitions of urban. Rank correlation coefficients were calculated between these rates of urbanization and urban growth and crude rates of urban natural increase for 1964, assuming that regional variations for this midpoint year in the 1959-70 period were roughly indicative of crude birth and natural increase rate variations for the entire period. Results revealed that there was a high negative correlation (-0.596) between rates of urbanization and urban natural increase and a fairly high positive correlation (0.529) between rates

TABLE 4.17

Crude Birth, Death, and Natural Increase Rates for the Total, Urban,
and Rural Populations by Union Republic: 1964
(per thousand)

Union Republic	Crude Birth Rate			Crude Death Rate			Crude Rate of Natural Increase		
	Total*	Urban	Rural	Total*	Urban	Rural	Total*	Urban	Rural
RSFSR	17	15	19	7	7	9	10	8	10
Ukraine	17	16	17	7	7	9	10	9	8
Belorussia	19	20	20	6	5	8	13	15	12
Uzbek	35	29	39	5	7	5	30	22	34
Kazakh	28	23	33	6	6	6	23	17	27
Georgia	22	20	23	7	6	7	15	14	16
Azerbaydzhan	40	32	46	7	7	8	33	25	38
Lithuania	19	19	20	7	6	10	12	13	10
Moldavia	23	18	24	6	6	7	16	12	17
Latvia	15	15	15	9	9	11	5	6	4
Kirgiz	32	24	36	6	6	7	26	18	29
Tadzhik	35	31	38	5	6	6	29	25	32
Armenia	30	27	37	6	6	7	24	21	30
Turkmen	38	35	42	6	7	6	32	28	36
Estonia	15	16	15	10	8	13	5	8	2
USSR total	20	17	22	7	7	8	13	10	14

*There may be slight discrepancies between the total birth, death, and
natural increase rates, because of the rounding of the original data, which
included a figure to one decimal place.

Note: Based on official urban definitions.

Sources: Total population data come from USSR, Naseleniye SSSR, 1973
(Moscow: Izdatel'stvo "Statistika," 1975), pp. 69-83. Urban and rural data
come from B. S. Khorev, Problemy Gorodov, 2d ed. (Moscow: Izdatel'stvo
"Mysl'," 1975), Figure 11 inserted between pp. 248 and 249.

TABLE 4.18

Crude Birth, Death, and Natural Increase Rates for the Total, Urban,
and Rural Populations by Union Republic: 1970
(per thousand)

Union Republic	Crude Birth Rate			Crude Death Rate			Crude Rate of Natural Increase		
	Total*	Urban	Rural	Total*	Urban	Rural	Total*	Urban	Rural
RSFSR	15	15	15	9	9	10	6	6	5
Ukraine	15	15	15	9	8	11	6	7	4
Belorussia	16	19	15	8	6	10	9	13	5
Uzbek	34	27	38	6	7	5	28	20	33
Kazakh	23	20	27	6	7	6	17	13	21
Georgia	19	18	20	7	7	8	12	11	12
Azerbaydzhan	29	24	34	7	6	7	23	18	27
Lithuania	18	19	16	9	7	11	9	12	5
Moldavia	19	19	20	7	7	8	12	12	12
Latvia	15	15	15	11	10	15	3	5	0
Kirgiz	31	25	35	7	8	9	23	17	26
Tadzhik	35	30	39	6	6	7	28	24	32
Armenia	22	20	23	5	5	5	17	15	18
Turkmen	35	36	40	7	12	7	29	24	33
Estonia	16	17	15	11	10	16	5	7	-1
USSR total	17	16	19	8	8	9	9	8	10

*There may be slight discrepancies between the total birth, death, and
natural increase rates, because of the rounding of the original data, which
included a figure to one decimal place.

Note: Based on official urban definitions.

Sources: Total population data come from USSR, Naseleniye SSSR, 1973
(Moscow: Izdatel'stvo "Statistika," 1975), pp. 69-83. Urban and rural
data come from B. S. Khorev, Problemy Gorodov, 2d ed. (Moscow: Izdatel'stvo "Mysl'," 1975), Figure 11 inserted between pp. 248 and 249.

TABLE 4.19

Urbanization and Urban Growth by Union Republic: 1959-70

Union Republic	Level of Urbanization 1959	Level of Urbanization 1970	Percentage Point Change of Level of Urbanization	Percentage Change of Urban Population
RSFSR	52.4	62.3	9.9	31.4
Ukraine	45.7	54.5	8.8	34.2
Belorussia	30.8	43.4	12.6	57.5
Uzbek	33.6	36.6	3.0	58.4
Kazakh	43.8	50.3	6.5	60.8
Georgia	42.4	47.8	5.4	30.8
Azerbaydzhan	47.8	50.1	2.3	45.1
Lithuania	38.6	50.2	11.6	50.3
Moldavia	22.3	31.7	9.4	76.0
Latvia	56.1	62.5	6.4	25.8
Kirgiz	33.7	37.4	3.7	57.6
Tadzhik	32.6	37.1	4.5	66.6
Armenia	50.0	59.5	9.5	68.0
Turkmen	46.2	47.9	1.7	47.6
Estonia	56.4	65.0	8.6	30.4
USSR total	47.9	56.3	8.4	36.0

Note: Based on official urban definitions.

Sources: 1959 and 1970 Soviet censuses (see Chapter 1, n. 104).

of urban growth and urban natural increase. As with the economic regions, the republics influencing the high negative relationship were the republics in Central Asia and the Transcaucasus, as well as the RSFSR as a whole.

In summary, it appears that during the 1959-70 period regional variations in rates of urbanization were not strongly and positively related to those of urban fertility and natural increase but instead were fairly highly negatively related. On the other hand, regional variations in rates of urban growth did tend to be fairly strongly and positively related to those of urban fertility and natural increase.

The other major immediate factor influencing regional variations in rates of urbanization and urban growth are variations in urban migration rates. As with fertility, mortality, and natural increase, it is difficult to assess rigorously the extent of these influences due to the lack of data. In the pre-1959 period, the only appreciable data concerning migration to urban centers are found in the 1897 and 1926 censuses. The authors previously have undertaken studies utilizing these data; Richard H. Rowland investigated 223 urban centers of the Russian Empire from the 1897 census with a population of 15,000 or more and for which place-of-birth data were provided. [17] As part of a factor analysis it was discovered that there was a fairly moderate positive rank correlation coefficient (0.345) between the growth rates of these cities from 1885 to 1897 and the percentage of their 1897 populations comprised of in-migrants.

Previous studies carried out by J. William Leasure and Robert A. Lewis also lend pertinent insights. [18] They show rates of urban in-migration for some large regions of the Russian Empire in 1897 and the USSR in 1926. These regions can be compared roughly with the four quadrants used in the present study. It will be recalled that between 1897 and 1926 rates of urbanization and urban growth were relatively high in the Russian East and European Steppe and relatively low in the Non-Slavic South and Northern European USSR (Tables 4.3, 4.5, and 4.7). Regions roughly comparable to the Russian East and European Steppe generally had relatively high urban in-migration rates (urban in-migrants as a percentage of the urban population) in both 1897 and 1926. Similarly, regions roughly comparable to the Non-Slavic South and Northern European USSR had relatively low rates of urban in-migration in both years. Thus, although the regions are rather gross and not strictly comparable, it appears that areas with relatively rapid urbanization and urban growth between 1897 and 1926 tended to have comparatively high rates of urban in-migration, while those with relatively slow rates of urbanization and urban growth tended to have comparatively low rates of urban in-migration.

Between 1926 and 1959, there are virtually no regional data concerning migration to urban centers. One might assume, however, that, given the continued substantial migration from the Western USSR to the Eastern USSR, the rapidly urbanizing regions of the east had higher rates of urban in-migration than did regions of the west.

During the 1959-70 period, appreciable urban migration data are available for the late 1960s. Because regional patterns of urban migration based on these data have been presented and discussed in Chapter 2 (Tables 2.23 and

TABLE 4.20

Rank Correlation Coefficients among Regional Rates of Urbanization and Urban Growth, and Urban Migration by Economic Region: 1959-70

Variable	Percent of 1970 Urban Population Comprised by 1968-70			
	In-Migrants (132)	Out-Migrants (133)	Net Migrants (134)	Migration Turnover (135)
Change in level of urbanization, 1959-70 (79)	-0.027	-0.372	0.368	-0.210
Rate of urban growth, 1959-70 (141)	0.224	-0.129	0.485	0.005
Percent urban in-migrants (132)	—	0.671	0.700	0.906
Percent urban out-migrants (133)	—	—	0.026	0.884
Percent urban net migrants (134)	—	—	—	0.398
Percent urban migration turnover (135)	—	—	—	—

Note: Numbers in parentheses indicate variable numbers.

Sources: 1959 and 1970 Soviet censuses (see Chapter 1, n. 104); and Appendix A, which includes a listing and discussion of the variables.

2.24 and Maps 2.44-2.47), we will focus here only upon the relationships among urbanization, urban growth, and urban migration.

Table 4.20 shows rank correlation coefficients between regional variations in rates of urbanization and urban growth between 1959 and 1970 and rates of urban migration based on migration data from the 1970 census. It appears that there was a moderate and positive relationship between urban net in-migration and urbanization and a moderate and, as might be expected, negative relationship between urban out-migration and urbanization. However, a very weak relationship existed between urban in-migration and urbanization.

Similar to the correlations between rates of urbanization and rates of urban migration, correlations between rates of urban growth and urban migration were, generally speaking, not very high. A moderate positive relationship did exist between rates of urban growth and urban net in-migration, one that was somewhat higher than that between urbanization and urban net migration and one that was the highest of any migration variable with urbanization or urban growth. However, the correlation was not a very high one, partly because Central Asia and the Transcaucasus, which had fairly rapid urban growth, also had the two lowest rates of net urban in-migration. The rapid urban growth of these regions was due to a great extent to the relatively high fertility and natural increase rates of these two regions.

Specific attention should be given to the Russian East, the quadrant that had a relative slowdown in the urbanization and urban growth processes after 1959. It appears that this slowdown was related to a relatively low rate of urban net in-migration. For the Russian East as a whole, the rate of urban net in-migration, according to the 1970 census, was only 1.6 percent as compared with a national urban average of 1.9 percent. The Urals and West Siberia, the two most populated regions of this quadrant, had very low rates of urban net in-migration, and, in fact, only Central Asia and the Transcaucasus had lower rates. The regions of the Russian East generally did have relatively high rates of urban in-migration, but they were greatly offset by very high rates of urban out-migration (Tables 2.23 and 2.24).

Rates of urban in-migration, out-migration, and net in-migration generally were highly and positively related to one another, except for net and out-migration (Table 4.20). Of greatest interest, perhaps, is the fact that rates of urban in-migration and out-migration were highly and positively related to each other. This implies that regions of high urban in-migration also tended to be regions of high urban out-migration, and thus regions of high migration turnover. Migration turnover rates are, in fact, highly and positively correlated with in-migration and out-migration rates. The prime examples of this situation are the regions of the Russian East or "Siberia."

Relationships among Regional Urbanization,
Urban Growth, and Economic Development Indicators

In order to analyze regional variations in urbanization and urban growth in greater depth, it is necessary to examine their relationships with regional variations in aspects of economic development, especially industrialization, tertiary activities, and capital investment. Table 4.21 shows correlations between regional urbanization and urban growth and regional industrialization.

TABLE 4.21

Rank Correlation Coefficients between Regional
Urbanization and Urban Growth, and Industrialization
by Economic Region: 1897-1970

Years	Level of Urbanization versus Percent of Total Population in Industrial Work Force	Distribution of Urban Population versus Distribution of Industrial Work Force
1897	0.416	0.755
1926	0.705	0.916
1959[a]	0.828	0.903
1970	0.804	0.903
1897-1926	0.361	0.418[b]
1926-59[a]	0.794	0.763[b]
1897-59[a]	0.803	0.772[b]
1959-70	0.846	0.882[b]
1926-70	0.899	0.821[b]
1897-70	0.841	0.778[b]

[a]1959 industrial data are actually for 1961.
[b]These correlations are between the redistribution of
the urban population and industrial work force and are
used, for convenience' sake, as surrogates for the rate of
increase of the urban population and industrial work
force, respectively.

Sources: See Chapter 1, nn. 104 and 105; and Appendix A and Robert A. Lewis, Richard H. Rowland, and Ralph
S. Clem, Nationality and Population Change in Russia and
the USSR (New York: Praeger, 1976), pp. 32-53, 393-94,
which include a listing and discussion of the variables.

With regard to the relationship between urbanization and industrialization, there was a strong positive relationship in the overall 1897-1970 and 1926-70 periods between regional variations in the percentage point change of the percentage of the total population residing in urban centers and comprised by the industrial work force. This indicates that the most rapidly urbanizing regions, such as the Center, Donetsk-Dnepr, Urals, West Siberia, Volga, and Northwest, also generally had the greatest increases in the percentage of the total population comprised of the industrial work force. In addition, there was generally also a high positive correlation in each census year between the level of urbanization and the percentage of the total population in the industrial work force.

A high positive relationship did not exist in 1897 or between 1897 and 1926 (Table 4.21). The existence of a low correlation in late nineteenth century Russia has been discussed previously by ourselves and others. In our earliest study we discovered that there tended to be a relatively weak relationship between urbanization and industrialization in late nineteenth century Russia, especially in comparison with subsequent periods.[19] Roger L. Thiede subsequently contended, however, that there was a strong relationship between urbanization and industrialization.[20] In response to Thiede, we provided additional data supporting our original and still present-day conclusion that there was not a strong relationship, and in addition, we noted that Thiede's computations were based only on the 50 gubernii of western Russia and on somewhat questionable pre-1897 urban data.[21] More recently, we further discussed this topic and a study by Thomas Stanley Fedor generally has supported our conclusions.[22] Reasons for the lack of a strong relationship between urbanization and industrialization also have been discussed extensively in these previous studies by ourselves and Fedor.[23] They include a relatively high rural orientation of industry, the considerable importance of nonindustrial activities in cities (for example, personal services), and unfavorable aspects of industrial work at this time. Some of these patterns are exemplified by the results of a previous study by one of the authors, based on 223 cities in 1897, which revealed in particular a relatively strong relationship between urban in-migration and personal services and a relatively weak relationship between urban in-migration and industrialization (Table 4.22).

In and after 1926, a very strong positive relationship emerged between regional variations in urbanization and industrialization (Table 4.21). This is not surprising in light of the governmental policy of emphasizing rapid industrialization beginning in the late 1920s. The existence of such a relationship between 1959 and 1970 in particular indicates that the reversal in regional rates of urbanization after 1959 was accompanied by roughly similar changes in industrialization. Rapid urbanization and industrialization during this period was especially characteristic of such western regions as Belorussia, the West, the Volgo-Vyatsk, the Donetsk-Dnepr, the Volga, and the Center. The strong relationship between regional urbanization and industrialization in 1970 was promoted by the fact that the six most urbanized regions (Center, Northwest, Donetsk-Dnepr, West Siberia, the Urals, and Volga) ranked among the eight leading regions with respect to the percentage of the

TABLE 4.22

Rank Correlation Coefficients between Urban In-Migration and Various Work Force Sectors by 223 Urban Centers: 1897

Work Force Sector	Percent of Population Comprised of In-Migrants versus Percent of Population Comprised of Work Force Sector
Personal services	0.671
Tertiary occupations in general	0.654
Total trade	0.555
Institutions and free professions	0.502
Transportation	0.490
Construction	0.453
Armed forces	0.269
Industry	0.104
Agriculture	-0.388

Sources: 1897 Russian census (see Chapter 1, n. 104); and Richard H. Rowland, "Urban In-Migration in Late Nineteenth Century Russia" (Ph.D. diss., Columbia University, 1971), pp. 91-106.

total population comprised of the industrial work force, and the Center, Northwest, and Donetsk-Dnepr comprised the top three regions in both cases, with the Center ranking first in each case. Furthermore, in 1970 five of the most urbanized regions (Center, Northwest, Donetsk-Dnepr, Urals, and Volga) were the five leading regions with respect to the percentage of the total industrial work force in the USSR (that is, distribution of the industrial work force), and, in fact, these five regions combined alone contained the majority (53 percent) of all industrial workers in the USSR.

In order to investigate the relationships between industrialization and urban growth, the already available correlations for the distribution and redistribution of the urban population and industrial work force are used as surrogates. Although regional variations in rates of urban growth and the percentage point redistribution of the urban population do differ, they are so highly similar and interrelated that it is possible to use urban redistribution as a surrogate for urban growth. For example, between 1897 and 1959, the rank correlation coefficient between the two variables was 0.880, while between 1959 and 1970 it was 0.879. Thus, correlations between the redistribution of the urban population and industrial work force can be interpreted as rough surrogates for those correlations between the rates of change of the urban population and industrial work force. Table 4.21 indicates that a high positive correlation existed during the 1897-1970 and 1926-1970 periods and all periods within, except for the 1897-1926 period, between urban growth and industrial growth.

Table 4.21 also shows correlations between the distribution and redistribution of the urban population and the industrial work force. In all years, a very high, positive correlation existed between the regional distribution of the two variables, although it was somewhat lower in 1897 as compared with 1926, 1959, and 1970.

In summary, regional variations in the urban process have been strongly and positively related to those of industrialization. Only in 1897 and between 1897 and 1926 did a relatively weak positive relationship exist.

The other main portion of the nonagricultural work force is the tertiary or service sector. Data for this sector by economic region are available only for the 1897-1959 period, and even these data consist only of a residual category, with the tertiary work force being operationally defined as the total work force minus the agricultural and industrial work forces. For 1959 and 1970, regional data are available, however, for the population in the sluz-hashchiye or "white-collar" social group. These data will be used here as a surrogate for the tertiary work force during the 1959-70 period. The tertiary work force encompasses a wide variety of specific sectors, but, unfortunately, these sectors cannot be investigated on a systematic and comprehensive economic regional basis. Table 4.23 suggests that, generally speaking, in all years and periods there was a high positive relationship between regional variations in urbanization and urban growth, on the one hand, and the degree of tertiary activities on the other. Table 4.22 also suggests that urban in-migration in the late nineteenth century was associated strongly with tertiary activities, especially with personal services.

In order to investigate further the regional relationships between urbanization and economic development, it is possible to examine relationships involving regional variations in capital investment in recent years. Table 4.24 shows rank correlation coefficients between urbanization and urban growth (urban population distribution and redistribution) and relevant investment indicators for the 1959-70 period. It appears that regional variations in the level of urbanization in 1970 were strongly and positively related to those in per capita levels of capital investment for 1970 and for 1959-67. As suggested, there was a very high rank correlation coefficient (0.960) between these two per capita investment indicators. In addition, a very high correlation (0.949) existed between per capita investment excluding kolkhozy in 1959 and in 1970. Thus, regional variations in 1970 in per capita investment are roughly indicative of these throughout the 1959-70 period. Also, in 1959, the rank correlation coefficient (0.752) between the level of urbanization and per capita investment excluding kolkhozy was almost the same as that men-

TABLE 4.23

Rank Correlation Coefficients between Regional Rates of
Urbanization and Urban Growth, and the Tertiary
Work Force by Economic Region: 1897-1970

Years	Level of Urbanization versus Percent of Total Population in Tertiary Work Force	Distribution of Urban Population versus Distribution of Tertiary Work Force
1897	0.738	0.845
1926	0.802	0.958
1959[a]	0.792	0.937
1970[b]	0.688	0.946
1897-1926	0.716	0.693[c]
1926-59[a]	0.798	0.888[c]
1897-59[a]	0.793	0.857[c]
1959-70[b]	0.569	0.739[c]

[a]1959 tertiary work force data are actually for 1961.

[b]These correlations involve the sluzhashchiye "social group" of the population, which is used as a surrogate for the tertiary work force.

[c]These correlations are between the redistribution of the urban population and tertiary work force and are used, for convenience' sake, as surrogates for the rate of increase of the urban population and tertiary work force, respectively.

Sources: See Chapter 1, nn. 104 and 105; and Appendix A and Robert A. Lewis, Richard H. Rowland, and Ralph S. Clem, Nationality and Population Change in Russia and the USSR (New York: Praeger, 1976), pp. 32-53, 393-94, which include a listing and discussion of the variables.

TABLE 4.24

Rank Correlation Coefficients between Regional Urbanization and Urban Growth, and Investment Indexes by Economic Region: 1959-70

| | Urban Variable | | | |
Investment Variable	Level of Urbanization (55)	Change of Level of Urbanization (79)	Distribution of Urban Population (2)	Redistribution of Urban Population[a] (26)
Per capita, excluding kolkhozy, 1970 (116)	0.732	-0.133	0.200	-0.504
Change in per capita, excluding kolkhozy, 1959-70 (126)	0.425	-0.097	-0.120	-0.171
Distribution, excluding kolkhozy, 1970 (23)	0.649	-0.117	0.878	-0.405
Redistribution, excluding kolkhozy, 1959-70 (47)[b]	-0.461	-0.299	-0.409	0.676
Per capita, excluding kolkhozy, 1959-67 (127)	0.756	-0.196	0.277	-0.554
Percent increase, excluding kolkhozy, 1950-60 (128)	-0.465	0.252	-0.309	0.319

[a]This variable is also used, for convenience' sake, as a surrogate for the rate of urban growth.
[b]This variable is also used, for convenience' sake, as a surrogate for the rate of investment growth.

Note: Numbers in parentheses indicate variable numbers.

Sources: 1959 and 1970 Soviet censuses (see Chapter 1, n. 104); and Appendix A, which includes a listing and discussion of the variables.

tioned above for the same two variables in 1970. In short, it appears that a fairly high positive relationship existed between urbanization and investment throughout the entire 1959-70 period. Although regional variations of urbanization and per capita investment were fairly highly related during the 1959-70 period, Table 4.24 indicates that changes in these variables were only weakly, and in fact negatively, related. However, it appears that a fairly high, positive correlation existed between regional rates of urban growth and investment growth (Table 4.24, redistribution variables).

Brief attention should be given also to the regional rates of investment increase from 1950 to 1960. This variable was included in order to examine the lag effect of investment on urbanization and industrialization. Table 4.24 shows that there was only a fairly weak positive correlation between this variable and rates of urban growth between 1959 and 1970.

In summary, it is apparent that the interrelations between regional variations in the urban process and regional variations in measures of economic development were generally fairly strong. Regional levels of urbanization, on the one hand, and levels of industrialization, tertiary activities, and per capita investment, on the other, tended to be fairly highly and positively correlated. In addition, regional growth rates of the urban population and those of industrialization, tertiary activities, and investment also tended to be fairly highly and positively related. Regional variations in the changes in levels of urbanization, industrialization, and tertiary activities were highly related, but changes in urbanization were only weakly related to changes in per capita investment.

Rapidly Growing Towns, Declining Towns, and Population Change by Urban Functions: 1959-70

The east-to-west shift in the urban process in the post-1959 period is reflected further by regional variations of the most rapidly growing towns and towns with population decline. This section will focus specifically upon regional and functional aspects of rapidly growing towns and towns with population decline in the most recent intercensal period of 1959-70, as well as upon population changes by urban functions in general. [24] Such an investigation will lend more specific insights into the recent urban process in the USSR. The following investigation of these towns is based upon the tabulation of urban centers in the 1970 census, and thus both the 1959 and 1970 populations are based on 1970 urban territories, although there are some exceptions from this general procedure. Only the general results will be presented here.

Rapidly Growing Towns: 1959-70

"Rapidly growing towns" are operationally defined as those 129 towns of 15,000 and over whose population at least doubled between 1959 and 1970. They include a number of "new towns" or towns with no listed population in 1959. Some of these towns (25 out of 51) were not included, because further investigation suggested that they probably did not have rapid growth. For ex-

TABLE 4.25

Number of Rapidly Growing and Declining Towns by
Gross Region: 1959-70

	Rapidly Growing	Declining
Western USSR	79	44
Eastern USSR	50	89
Northern European USSR	51	18
European Steppe	19	25
Russian East	22	79
Non-Slavic South	37	11
USSR total	129	133

Sources: 1959 and 1970 Soviet censuses (see Chapter
1, n. 104).

ample, many were large villages of the North Caucasus, which simply were
reclassified as urban centers.[25]

Regional patterns of the 129 rapidly growing towns are shown in Tables
4.25 and 4.26 and Map 4.22. Of these towns 79, or 61.2 percent, were located in the Western USSR, while only 50, or 38.8 percent, were in the Eastern USSR. This marks a considerable departure from the preceding 1939-59
period, when it will be recalled that the Eastern USSR had roughly 50 percent
of the rapidly growing towns, based on the Harris study.

Although economic regions with the greatest number of rapidly growing
towns were located in the Eastern USSR (Kazakhstan and Central Asia), most
of the regions with the next highest numbers of towns were located in the
Western USSR. Especially noticeable clusters existed in the Donetsk-Dnepr
and Center, mainly in the Moscow area.

The 129 rapidly growing towns were associated with a variety of growth-
stimulating functions. Although it is difficult to designate specifically only
one function for each city due to either a lack of information or the presence
of a number of growth-stimulating activities, it appears that most of the towns
had a manufacturing, mining, and/or electric power function.

More than 30 towns were industrial towns without any significant local
mining activities. In roughly 20 of these towns, the chemical industry was of
great importance, reflecting the recent increased Soviet attention to this
branch of industry. Towns of this type comprised a large share of the rapidly

TABLE 4.26

Number of Rapidly Growing and Declining Towns by Economic
Region: 1959-70

Region	Rapidly Growing	Declining
Northwest	8	8
West	3	0
Center	11	5
Volgo-Vyatsk	4	2
Central Chernozem	5	0
Volga	8	3
Belorussia	4	0
Moldavia	0	0
Southwest	8	0
South	1	1
Donetsk-Dnepr	12	19
North Caucasus	6	5
Transcaucasus	9	1
Urals	11	35
West Siberia	1	21
East Siberia	7	15
Far East	3	8
Kazakhstan	14	7
Central Asia	14	3
USSR total	129	133

Sources: 1959 and 1970 Soviet censuses (see Chapter
1, n. 104).

MAP 4.22

Rapidly Growing Towns: 1959-70

• URBAN CENTER WHOSE POPULATION AT LEAST
DOUBLED BETWEEN 1959 AND 1970

growing towns along the western borderlands of the USSR, in particular, the Northwest, Belorussia, and the Southwest. Perhaps the most interesting and illuminating example of a rapidly growing town of this type is provided by Novgorod of the Northwest. Despite its name, which literally means "new town," Novgorod is one of the oldest and most famous of the Russian cities. With an estimated population of 10,000 to 15,000 in the early eleventh century and 20,000 to 30,000 in the early thirteenth century, it was one of the two largest cities of "Ancient Rus," the other being Kiev.[26] By 1897 Novgorod's population was only 26,000 and by 1969 only 61,000. However, between 1959 and 1970 its population more than doubled to 128,000. The rapid growth of Novgorod in recent years has been associated with a new major chemical complex based on natural gas pipelines from the North Caucasus to Leningrad. Novgorod is not a unique case, however. It is but one of a number of fairly old and previously stagnating towns in the western portion of the USSR that has experienced rapid growth in association with new chemical complexes based on oil or natural gas pipelines from the interior portions of the USSR.

More than 30 of the rapidly growing towns were primarily mining towns. Of these the greatest number (more than 20) were associated with various nonfuel minerals. Notable examples include towns in Kazakhstan, East Siberia, and the Central Chernozem. Of the fuel towns, seven were based on oil and were perhaps the most rapidly growing specific functional type. Of

...e seven oil towns, six were new towns with no recorded population in 1959, and the remaining one, Surgut, more than quintupled its population. These oil towns were located mostly in the Urals, which, based on the 1961 economic regions, included the West Siberian Lowland. The other fuel towns, also seven in number, were based on coal. These were located chiefly in the Donetsk-Dnepr. As will be seen later, coal mining was associated more with towns having population decline than with those having rapid population growth.

Roughly two dozen rapidly growing towns between 1959 and 1970 appeared to be based primarily on new electric power stations. Of these towns, roughly two-thirds were based on hydroelectricity and about one-third on thermal electricity. Hydroelectric towns were found chiefly in the Volga, Transcaucasus, and East Siberia.

The Volga included two of the most highly publicized of the recently rapidly growing towns based partly on hydroelectric power projects: Naberezhnyye Chelny and Tol'yatti. Naberezhnyye Chelny experienced the most rapid growth of any sizable Soviet city in the post-1970 period, with its population increasing from 38,000 in 1970 to 253,000 in 1977. Tol'yatti has been perhaps the most spectacular of all of the recently rapidly growing towns in the USSR. With a population of well under 100,000 in 1959, its population increased to 251,000 in 1970, making it the largest of all of the rapidly growing towns in 1970, and to 479,000 in 1977. Although these two cities are based on hydroelectric power projects, they are perhaps better known as the sites of two new major motor vehicle producing plants: the Kama Truck Plant and a new large automobile plant built with the assistance of Fiat of Italy, respectively.

Altogether, roughly 100 of the rapidly growing towns were mining, manufacturing, and/or electric power towns. Of the remaining two dozen towns, roughly half were suburbs of Moscow and Kiev. These towns, of course, may have had manufacturing or other types of functions also. Probably no more than four towns each were either centers of expanding agricultural areas or resort towns. Two towns (Lensk in East Siberia and Ordzhonikidzebad in Central Asia) were apparently base towns or gateway towns for areas with new activities (Mirnyy, diamond mining and Nurek, hydroelectric power, respectively). Reflecting the relatively low importance of foreign trade in the Soviet economy, only one town (Il'chevsk) was a port town.

It should be noted that nine of the towns were major administrative centers (that is, centers of an SSR [union republic], ASSR [autonomous republic], oblast, or kray), reflecting the fact that major administrative centers of the USSR continue to grow quite rapidly. The rates of growth of the 150 major administrative centers are shown collectively in Table 4.27. In nearly one-half of these towns (67, or 44.7 percent) the population increased by more than 50 percent, and in nine of these the population more than doubled, qualifying them, as mentioned above, as "rapidly growing towns." The population of 50 percent (75) of the major administrative centers increased by 25 to 49 percent. Indeed, when it is recalled that the urban population of the USSR as a whole increased by 41.2 percent between 1959 and 1970, this indicates that a sizable majority (91, or 60.7 percent) of the major administrative centers grew at a rate faster than the rate of increase for the entire urban population.

TABLE 4.27

Number of Major Administrative Centers of the USSR by Rate
of Population Change: 1959-70

Percentage Change of Population*	Number of Administrative Centers
100 and over	9
75-99	14
50-74	44
25-49	75
0-24	8
Decline	0
USSR total	150

*These rates are based solely on the listing in the 1970 census. Thus, 1959 and 1970 populations in 1970 city boundaries are used. The listed rates of growth, which are rounded to the nearest whole percent, are also used. Only urban centers with 15,000 or more people in 1970 are included.

Note: The political units used as the basis here include all oblasts, krays, and ASSRs. In addition, an SSR is counted as a unit if it is not subdivided into an oblast, kray, and/or ASSR—namely, Lithuania, Moldavia, Latvia, Armenia, and Estonia. For the five republics that have "regions of republic subordination" (Georgia, Azerbaydzhan, Kirgiz, Tadzhik, and Turkmen), the capital of the republic is considered as the capital of the administrative unit called "region of republic subordination." Moscow, Leningrad, Kiev, Minsk, Tashkent, and Alma-Ata are regarded as the administrative center of the oblast bearing their name, although they are officially separate from these oblasts. An administrative center is considered an administrative center only once, even though it may be an administrative center at two or more levels, such as Moscow, which is the capital of the USSR, the RSFSR, and Moscow Oblast. In these cases, the city is regarded as the administrative center of the smallest of the major political units. For example, Moscow is considered here to be the center of Moscow Oblast and not the USSR or RSFSR.

Sources: 1959 and 1970 Soviet censuses (see Chapter 1, n. 104).

Of the 150 capitals, only eight failed to achieve an increase of at least 25 percent. However, none of these eight towns came close to losing population. The slowest growing of such centers was Moscow, whose population still managed to increase by 17 percent, while Leningrad had the next slowest rate of growth (19 percent). The slow rates of growth of these two largest cities of the USSR were related in part to their large base populations, low fertility, and restrictions on their growth. Nevertheless, the absolute population increase in each city was unsurpassed by any other Soviet city. Moscow's population increased by slightly more than 1 million people and Leningrad's by more than 600,000.

The rapid growth of the major administrative centers is also evident in terms of their status within their own political units. Based on centers of 15,000 and over in 1970, nearly one-third (44, or 29.3 percent) of these 150 centers were the most rapidly growing urban centers in their respective political unit, although ten of these towns were the only urban centers of 15,000 or more in their respective units. Roughly one-fourth (35, or 23.3 percent) of the 150 centers were the second most rapidly growing towns of their particular unit, although two were tied for second and four were the slowest growing towns, because there were only two towns with 15,000 or more people in their unit. Thus, depending on whether one includes or excludes those units with only one or two urban centers with 15,000 or more people, slightly more than a majority or slightly less than a majority of the 150 major administrative centers were the most rapidly growing urban centers in their respective political units. In either case, the proportion is quite high, especially when it is recalled that a major administrative center in the USSR is almost without exception the largest city of its political unit and thus should possibly have a slower rate of growth if only because it has a larger base population. Indeed, unlike the United States, the largest cities of the USSR are major administrative centers. In 1970 the 29 largest cities were major administrative centers, with Krivoy Rog, the thirtieth largest city, being the largest city that was not a major administrative center. In the United States, none of the eight largest cities in 1970 were major adminstrative centers (Washington, D.C. and state capitals). The largest major administrative centers of the United States were Washington, D.C. and Indianapolis, the ninth and tenth largest cities of the United States.

The relatively rapid growth of major administrative centers in the USSR is also apparent in data presented by V. G. Davidovich. In an investigation of the major administrative units of the USSR, he reveals that in the majority (59.6 percent) of these units the administrative center of the unit grew more rapidly than the remaining urban centers (apparently official urban definitions) of the corresponding units. [27]

The relatively rapid rate of growth of major administrative centers appears to be part and parcel of the phenomenon of a relatively high concentration of Soviet industry in large administrative centers. This topic will be discussed in greater detail in the next chapter.

In order to examine further rates of population change by urban function, we will refer to some of the few available functional classification

TABLE 4.28

Rate of Population Change by Functional Type of USSR Cities: 1959-70

Functional Type	Number of Cities	Population		Percentage Change of Population, 1959-70
		1959	1970	
I. Diversified administrative centers	134	44,808,933	61,475,735	37.2
A. Capitals of union republics	16	16,462,774	21,475,388	30.4
B. Centers of oblasts or similar units	118	28,346,159	40,000,347	41.1
II. Local centers	15	1,152,770	1,620,936	40.6
III. Industrial cities	136	13,943,358	17,791,729	27.6
A. Manufacturing	82	7,341,000	10,143,208	38.2
B. Manufacturing and mining	44	6,005,418	6,971,280	16.1
C. Mining, primary processing, and energy	10	596,940	677,241	13.5
IV. Transport centers	5	279,904	382,184	36.5
V. Resorts	4	331,594	486,131	46.6
VI. Education and research cities	2	197,355	252,824	28.1
VII. Naval bases	2	169,529	257,359	51.8
Total of included cities	298	60,883,443	82,266,898	35.1

Note: Unlike the original scheme, Table 4.28 excludes an eighth type, "suburbs," since five of the six "suburbs" listed were annexed subsequently by Moscow and thus have no 1970 data presented for them.

Sources: 1959 and 1970 Soviet censuses (see Chapter 1, n. 104); Chauncy D. Harris, Cities of the Soviet Union (Chicago: Rand McNally, 1970), pp. 68-78; B. S. Khorev, Gorodskiye Poseleniya SSSR (Moscow: Izdatel'stvo "Mysl'," 1968), pp. 39-80; and idem, "Issledovaniye Funktsial'noy Struktury Gorodskikh Poseleniy SSSR v Svyazi s Zadachami ikh Ekonomiko-Geograficheskoy Tipologii," Goroda Mira (Moscow: Izdatel'stvo "Mysl'," 1965), pp. 34-58.

schemes. The most extensive scheme for the USSR as a whole is that developed by Khorev and later elaborated on by Harris. This scheme provides a functional classification of the roughly 300 cities with 50,000 or more people in 1959. We have calculated the population sizes for each functional type in 1959 and 1970, based on the populations for both years as listed in the 1970 census and have calculated the growth rates for each type (Table 4.28). At this point we will focus only on the types with relatively rapid growth. The most rapid growth was experienced by resorts, naval bases, local centers, and diversified administrative centers. The first two categories, although of interest, are relatively unimportant, because they consist of very few cities (four and two, respectively). "Local centers" are cities that generally (1) had a low level of industrialization, (2) had a relatively small size (between 50,000 and 100,000) in 1959, (3) were scattered throughout the settled areas of the USSR, (4) functioned as central places, (5) were all old cities, and (6) were former centers of oblasts or similar units that no longer exist. [28] These towns included a number of old cities in the Western USSR, which have been rejuvenated in recent years. However, local centers, like resort towns and naval bases, include only a very few cities.

In terms of types with a comparatively large number of cities, the most rapid growth was experienced by the diversified administrative centers. Within this category, centers of oblasts or similar units grew faster than capitals of union republics. However, if the relatively slow growing cities of Moscow and Leningrad, the latter of which also has the status of a union republic capital here, are excluded, the growth rate of the 14 remaining union republic capitals (47.4 percent) exceeds that of centers of oblasts or similar units. The relatively rapid growth of diversified administrative centers reflects the rapid growth of major administrative centers, which we have discussed already in some detail.

Only two other types of cities grew faster than the average for the roughly 300 cities included in the functional classification: manufacturing cities and transport centers. "Manufacturing" cities are a specific segment of "industrial" cities and are defined implicitly as manufacturing cities that do not also have significant mining activities (for example, Tol'yatti). It should be kept in mind that a great share of the rapidly growing diversified administrative centers could be regarded also as rapidly growing manufacturing cities, because they include many major industrial centers.

It is surprising that transport centers grew fairly rapidly, because, as will be seen, one of the predominant types of towns with a declining population were railroad towns. That the "transport centers" category did not experience slower growth is probably due to the fact that declining railroad towns were mainly small in size, generally having populations of less than 50,000, and, thus, were not included in the Khorev-Harris scheme presented in Table 4.28.

A study by A. Grishanova and O. Sergeyev allows an investigation of growth rates between 1959 and 1970 of various functional types for urban centers with both more than and less than 50,000 people, although it only includes centers of the RSFSR. Specifically, this study is based on 518 of the 969 official cities of the RSFSR in 1970 and the functional typology developed by

TABLE 4.29

Rate of Population Change by Functional Type of RSFSR Cities: 1959-70

Functional Type	Number of Cities	Decline	No Change	Percent of Cities with Percentage Change of:						
				0-6.1	6.1-10	10.1-20	20.1-30	30.1-40	40.1-50	Over 50
Multifunctional cities (oblast and republic centers)	76	0.0	0.0	0.0	0.0	3.9	17.1	26.3	23.7	29.0
Industrial centers	198	23.2	0.5	8.1	4.0	22.2	17.6	9.6	5.2	9.6
Transport centers	36	36.0	0.0	8.2	8.2	19.4	11.3	2.8	2.8	11.3
Cities of transitional type (between industrial and local organizing centers)	78	20.5	1.3	6.4	6.4	26.0	19.1	5.1	3.8	11.4
Nonindustrial unprofited cities	110	30.0	2.7	16.7	9.0	19.1	15.4	2.7	2.7	1.7
Newly constructed industrial cities	15	0.0	0.0	0.0	13.4	6.6	6.6	0.0	13.4	60.0
Health centers	5	0.0	0.0	0.0	0.0	20.0	20.0	20.0	20.0	20.0
RSFSR total	518	20.8	1.0	8.1	5.4	18.7	16.6	9.3	7.3	12.7

Source: A. Grishanova and O. Sergeyev, "Nekotoryye Cherty Demograficheskoy Situatsii v Gorodakh Razlichnykh Funktsional'nykh Tipov," Narodonaseleniye, Prikladnaya Demografiya (Moscow: "Statistika," 1973), pp. 50-51.

TABLE 4.30

Rate of Population Change by Industrial Type
of RSFSR Cities: 1959-70

Industrial Type	Number of Cities	Percentage Change of Population: 1959-70
Machine building and metal processing	40	37.2
Ferrous and nonferrous metallurgy	9	31.3
Fuel industry	9	4.0
Chemical and petrochemical industry	8	51.7
Light industry	4	22.4
Machine building in combination with other branches	20	41.2

Source: B. S. Khorev and V. M. Moiseyenko, Sdvigi v Razmeshchenii Naseleniya SSSR (Moscow: "Statistika," 1976), p. 75.

Khorev. The results of this study support some of the points made earlier (Table 4.29). First, the relatively rapid growth of major administrative centers (multifunctional cities), "newly constructed industrial cities," and "health centers" is evident. All of the cities in each of the three groups experienced a rate of growth of at least 6.1 percent, and no cities in each group declined in population, a feature not characteristic of any other functional types. Also, unlike any other functional type, over half of the cities in each of these groups grew by 30.1 percent or more. The four other types of cities grew more slowly and included large shares (20 percent or more) of cities with population decline. Hence, they will be discussed in the next section concerned with declining towns.

It should be noted that "industrial cities," the most predominant functional type in terms of number of representative cities, presented somewhat of a mixed picture in that a moderate share (roughly one-fourth, or 24.4 percent) of the cities of this group increased by at least 30.1 percent. The relative rates of growth of various types of large industrial cities in the RSFSR have been investigated by B. S. Khorev and V. M. Moiseyenko. They indicate that out of the 124 large cities (100,000 or more people) in the RSFSR,

96 were "cities with mainly developed industrial functions." They have calculated rates of growth for six different types of industrial towns and these are presented in Table 4.30. Given the previous discussion, it is not surprising that the greatest rate of growth was attained by cities where chemical industries were outstanding. The exceptionally low rate of growth of fuel-industry cities will be commented on in the next section, which deals with declining towns.

Declining Towns: 1959-70

The recent reversal in regional rates of urbanization and urban growth is reflected also in the regional distribution of towns that had a declining population between 1959 and 1970. A determination of the declining towns, like that of the rapidly growing towns, is based on 1959 and 1970 populations, according to the listing in the 1970 census. Also included in the declining towns are "disappearing" urban centers of 15,000 and over, according to the 1959 census, which are not listed in the 1970 census. As these towns are not listed in the 1970 census, it is assumed that they declined below 15,000 in 1970, because the 1970 census only lists those urban centers with 15,000 or more people. However, if there is evidence that such a town simply was annexed to another town (for example, Yudino to Kazan'), it is not regarded as a "disappearing" declining town.

Altogether, 133 urban centers (including the 28 "disappearing" towns) had a population decline between 1959 and 1970. Such a large number of declining towns between two successive census dates is unprecedented in any of the intercensal periods.

Reflecting the reversal in regional urbanization and urban growth, roughly two-thirds or the vast majority (89, or 66.9 percent) of the 133 declining towns were located in the Eastern USSR (Table 4.25 and Map 4.23). In contrast, it will be recalled that between 1939 and 1959 the vast majority of the 54 declining towns during this period were located in the Western USSR.

By far the greatest number of declining towns between 1959 and 1970 were located in the Urals. In fact, 35 or roughly one-fourth (26.3 percent) of all 133 declining towns in the USSR were located in this region alone. Most were concentrated in two north-south extending strings of settlements in the western half of the region and were principally mining centers (Map 4.23).

Second only to the Urals in terms of number of declining towns was West Siberia with 21. The proportion of its towns that declined in population was quite extraordinary; roughly 40 percent of the total number of towns in West Siberia with 15,000 or more people in 1959 declined in population between 1959 and 1970, while the corresponding figure for all Soviet urban centers was only about 10 percent.

The declining towns of West Siberia were basically of two types, both geographically and functionally. As Map 4.23 shows there were two strings of declining towns, one east-west and another north-south. The east-west string consisted primarily of a number of towns on the Trans-Siberian Railroad. These towns were principally railroad towns, that is, towns specializing in the servicing of the railways. The north-south string consisted

MAP 4.23

Declining Towns: 1959-70

• URBAN CENTER WHOSE POPULATION
DECLINED BETWEEN 1959 AND 1970

mainly of coal mining towns in the Kuznets Basin. Foremost was Prokop'-yevsk, which was the largest Soviet town to decline in population from 1959 to 1970 (281,958 to 274,485).

The patterns of West Siberia were repeated to a certain extent in East Siberia, which with 15 declining towns had the third greatest number of declining towns in the Eastern USSR and the fourth greatest number in the USSR. Like West Siberia, a very high proportion (more than one-third) of the towns of East Siberia declined in population. As Map 4.23 suggests, most of the declining towns of East Siberia were essentially on the Trans-Siberian Railroad, and five of these were principally railroad towns.

The Far East had eight declining towns, the next greatest number of any region of the Eastern USSR. Like the preceding regions, a large proportion of the declining towns of the Far East were on the Trans-Siberian Railroad.

It is apparent by now that a great number of towns on the Trans-Siberian Railroad in the Eastern USSR declined in population between 1959 and 1970. In fact, investigation shows that <u>nearly one-half</u> (40 percent, or 24 of 60) of all urban centers on the Trans-Siberian Railroad from Chelyabinsk in the Urals to the Pacific Coast declined in population between 1959 and 1970.

In summary, the four regions of the Russian East contained the sizable majority (59.4 percent, or 79 of 133) of all of the declining towns of the USSR. Furthermore, aside from the Donetsk-Dnepr, no other region in the USSR had more declining towns than any individual region of the Russian East, and roughly one of every three urban centers of the Russian East with 15,000 or more people in 1959 declined in population between 1959 and 1970, a proportion that was more than twice the proportion for the entire USSR.

Only about one-third (44 of 133) of all of the declining towns were located in the Western USSR and nearly one-half of these (19) were found in the Donetsk-Dnepr. As Map 4.23 reveals, they formed the most distinct cluster of declining towns in the USSR. As might be expected, virtually all of the declining towns of the Donetsk-Dnepr were coal mining towns of the Donets Coal Basin in the eastern part of the region.

Interestingly, five western regions did not have even one declining town between 1959 and 1970: the West, the Central Chernozem, Belorussia, Moldavia, and the Southwest. Four of the five regions are along the western border of the USSR, resulting in a substantial void of declining towns here (Map 4.23). Each was, as mentioned before, a region of relatively rapid urban growth between 1959 and 1970.

The functions of the declining towns were basically of two types: mining towns, especially coal mining towns, and railroad towns. As with the rapidly growing towns, it is often difficult to assess precisely the functions of the towns and, of course, many have more than one major function. Nevertheless, it can be stated with some certainty that roughly 100 or approximately four-fifths of the 133 declining towns were mining or railroad towns, with the remainder being chiefly narrowly specialized manufacturing towns.

Roughly 75, or more than one-half, of the declining towns were mining towns, and of these around 50, or more than one-third, of all declining towns were coal mining towns. The decline of a large number of mining towns reflects the fact that according to the 1959 and 1970 censuses, the number of miners in the USSR declined between 1959 and 1970 from 1,187,129 to 1,003,718, or by about 15 percent. Similarly, the decline of a great number of coal mining towns, in particular, reflects a decline in the average annual number of workers and employees in the fuel industry in the USSR between 1960 and 1970.[29] The decline of towns based almost solely on mining activities is related to such developments as the depletion of the mineral deposits or increased labor productivity. It will be recalled, however, that a great share of the rapidly growing towns were also mining towns. The rapid rise or fall of mining towns is, of course, a situation that is not unique to the USSR.

The other major type of declining towns was those referred to as railroad towns. Altogether, roughly 25 or nearly one-fifth of the declining towns could be regarded as being primarily railroad towns. The decline of railroad towns in the USSR is related to technological improvements and increased labor productivity; since the 1950s there has been a major switch from steam to electric and diesel-electric motive power. Electric and diesel-electric locomotives require fewer stops and much less servicing, and consequently, fewer railway workers are now required.[30] Indeed, as with the mining industry, the 1959 and 1970 censuses indicate that the number of railroad workers declined fairly sharply between 1959 and 1970 (from 1,664,116 to 1,379,679, or by roughly 17 percent).

It should not be concluded from this situation that it is more advantageous for a city not to be located on a railway rather than to be on one. Obviously, it is more advantageous for a city's economic base to be on a railway line rather than not to be on one at all, especially in the USSR where the transportation system, both freight and passenger traffic, is still highly railroad-oriented. A number of declining towns, in fact, apparently suffered because they were quite distant from railway lines.[31] The point with respect to declining railroad towns is that such towns are so narrowly specialized in railway activities that when the demand for workers required for such activities subsides their population also may decline.

Another major characteristic of the declining towns is that they were primarily small in size. In particular, 126 of the 133 declining towns had a population below 100,000 in 1959, and 114 had a population of less than 50,000. Furthermore, 51 or nearly two-fifths of all the declining towns had a population of only 15,000-19,999, while only about one-fifth of all towns had a population within this range. Only 7 or about 5 percent of the 133 declining towns had 100,000 or more people, whereas more than 10 percent of all urban centers with 15,000 or more people in 1959 in the USSR had a population of 100,000 or more. Prokop'yevsk, the largest declining town, had a population of 281,958 in 1959 and was only the forty-ninth largest city of the USSR, based upon the listing of urban centers in the 1959 census. Put differently, virtually all of the largest cities of the USSR increased in population between 1959 and 1970. This situation contrasts greatly with the United States, where most of the largest cities have been declining in population. For example, of the 21 U.S. cities with more than 500,000 people in 1960, 15 or roughly three-fourths declined in population by 1970.

Thus, there emerges a picture of the declining towns consisting primarily of small, narrowly specialized towns. The decline of such towns without a diversified economic base is not unusual.

At this point, we would like to refer once again to the studies and tables concerning rates of growth by functional types of cities of the USSR and the RSFSR (Tables 4.28-4.30). Table 4.28, which shows rates of growth for cities of 50,000 and over in 1959 for the USSR as a whole reveals that, not unexpectedly, by far the slowest rates of growth were in cities with mining activities: "manufacturing and mining" cities and "mining, primary processing, and energy" cities. Each of the two types included some of the declining towns. As with transport centers, the lack of even slower growth or decline on the part of these types is related partly to the fact that they exclude small mining and/or manufacturing towns with less than 50,000 people.

To investigate growth rates by different functional types for cities with both more than and less than 50,000 people, we will refer to the Grishanova and Sergeyev study for the RSFSR (Table 4.29). Four of the functional types had large proportions (20 percent or more) of their cities comprised of declining cities. Supporting much of the above discussion, the "transport centers" type, which basically consisted of railroad towns, had the largest proportions, as more than one-third of the cities (13 of 36) of this functional type declined in population between 1959 and 1970. Not surprisingly, all of the declining "transport centers" were relatively small in population, with none exceeding 50,000 in population.

"Nonindustrial unprofiled cities" also had a relatively high proportion of declining cities, as nearly one-third of the cities of this functional type had a declining population between 1959 and 1970 (Table 4.29). Generally speaking these towns: (1) had a weakly developed industrial sector; (2) lacked a strikingly dominant function; (3) were typically local organizing or service centers for agricultural regions; (4) were quite small in size, with none exceeding 50,000 in population; and (5) were far from railroad lines and large industrial centers and on the periphery of oblasts. Thus, they typically had a poorly developed and narrow economic base. In response, there was substantial out-migration of young people from these towns, resulting in a declining or slowly growing population.

The remaining two types of cities were industrial cities and cities that were transitional between industrial centers and local organizing centers. The proportion of declining towns here was not as high as the previous two types, but nonetheless, fairly substantial, with roughly 20 to 25 percent of the towns in each type being comprised of cities with population decline between 1959 and 1970. Of the 46 declining industrial towns, the majority were mining centers of the Urals (for example, Kizel). The majority of these 46 towns were small in size, with roughly two-thirds (31, or 67.4 percent) having a population of less than 50,000. Once again, the problems of small mining and/or manufacturing towns are manifested. The "transitional" towns represent a similar situation. Of the 16 declining towns in this group, all had a population of less than 50,000.

The study by Grishanova and Sergeyev for towns of the RSFSR once again brings forth the point that the declining towns were primarily small, narrowly specialized towns. Indeed, the vast majority (93, or 86.1 percent) of the 108 RSFSR towns that declined in population between 1959 and 1970 had a population of less than 50,000.

Finally, reference again to Table 4.30 reveals that among large industrial cities of the RSFSR those termed "fuel cities" had by far the slowest rate of growth between 1959 and 1970. In fact, the nine cities constituting this group barely increased in population overall, increasing by only 4 percent. Furthermore, six of nine were declining cities.

Another interesting aspect of the declining towns between 1959 and 1970 was that they consisted to a great extent of previously rapidly growing newer towns in the east rather than primarily of older stagnant towns in the west. In fact, based on a modification of Harris's definition of a rapidly growing town between 1939 and 1959 (basically all towns with 15,000 or more people in 1959 at least doubling in population plus those towns with more than 15,000 people in 1959 without a recorded 1939 population that are believed to have had legitimate rapid growth), nearly 50, or roughly 40 percent, of the declining towns between 1959 and 1970 were rapidly growing towns between 1939 and 1959.[32] In contrast, only about 30 percent of all towns with 15,000 or more people in 1959 were rapidly growing towns between 1939 and 1959. Cheremkhovo is a classic example of a town whose population more than doubled between 1939 and 1959 but declined between 1959 and 1970. Also, the population of Prokop'yevsk, the largest declining town between 1959 and 1970, more than doubled between 1939 and 1959 and increased by roughly ten times between 1926 and 1939. Furthermore, only 9 of the declining towns between 1959 and 1970 were among the 54 declining towns between 1939 and 1959.

Although post-1970 data are not plentiful and consist only of population estimates, it is possible to assess in a general manner the subsequent fate of the 133 declining towns. This assessment is based on the previously mentioned 1974 data for official cities of 15,000 and over and specifically upon population figures rounded to the nearest thousand people for both 1970 and 1974. It appears that virtually none of the 133 towns experienced a resurgence in growth between 1970 and 1974. Nearly one-fourth had a recorded decline and about another one-fourth had no increase. The change of roughly another one-fourth of the towns could not be assessed specifically, because their population had declined to less than 15,000 by 1970 ("disappearing towns") or because they were "urban-type settlements." Thus, they were not included in the 1974 data, which included official "cities" of 15,000 and over only. It is probable that many if not most of these towns continued to decline or at least did not grow significantly between 1970 and 1974, because if they had experienced substantial growth they very probably would have been included in the 1974 list. Finally, roughly one-fourth of the towns had a recorded increase between 1970 and 1974, but virtually none experienced substantial or rapid increase. It should be added that 65 towns that were official "cities" of 15,000 and over in 1970 declined in population between 1970 and 1974. Of these 65 towns, 30 were not declining towns of the 1959-70 period. However, like the 1959-70 period the vast majority of the 65 declining towns were located in the Eastern USSR, especially the Urals and West Siberia.

In summary, the substantial turnabout in regional rates of urbanization and urban growth from the pre-1959 to the post-1959 period was reflected in changes in the regional distribution of rapidly growing towns and declining towns. Between 1939 and 1959, roughly half of the rapidly growing towns were in the Eastern USSR and the vast majority of the declining towns were in the Western USSR. However, between 1959 and 1970, a sizable majority of the rapidly growing towns were in the Western USSR, while the vast majority of declining towns were in the Eastern USSR. Particularly great turnabouts transpired in the Russian East, especially the Urals and West Siberia, which changed from principal areas of rapidly growing towns to principal areas of declining towns.

NOTES

1. Kingsley Davis, Basic Data for Cities, Countries and Regions, World Urbanization 1950-1970, vol. 1 (Berkeley: University of California, Institute of International Studies, 1969), pp. 54-82, 154-60.

2. The 1970 World Almanac and Book of Facts (New York: Newspaper Enterprise Association, 1969), pp. 254, 265-67; and U.S., Department of

Commerce, Social and Economic Statistics Administration, Bureau of the Census, County and City Data Book, 1972, pp. 54, 842-48.

3. Chauncy D. Harris, Cities of the Soviet Union (Chicago: Rand Mc-Nally, 1970), pp. 303-4.

4. Ibid.

5. Ibid., pp. 305-68.

6. Ibid., pp. 315, 318.

7. For some areas, data are not for 1939 per se; for example, 1940 is the data year for those areas previously in Finland. In addition, there were 12 towns outside the RSFSR whose population declined from 15,000 or more in 1939 to less than 15,000 in 1959, and seven of these were located in the Western USSR. Since the RSFSR volume in the 1959 census listed only towns with 15,000 or more people as of 1959, it was impossible to detect those RSFSR towns that declined from more than 15,000 in 1939 to less than 15,000 in 1959. Therefore, for consistency, these 12 towns outside the RSFSR also are excluded from this discussion. This investigation is based upon circa 1939 and 1959 data presented in Chauncy D. Harris, "Population of Cities of the Soviet Union, 1897, 1926, 1939, 1959, and 1967. Tables, Maps, and Gazetteer." Soviet Geography: Review and Translation 11 (May 1970): 307-43.

8. Determination of the combat zone is based upon Harris, Cities of the Soviet Union, pp. 306-7; and B. H. Liddell Hart, History of the Second World War (New York: G. P. Putnam's Sons, 1971), pp. 156, 240, 250, 262, 476, 568.

9. Harris, Cities of the Soviet Union, p. 292.

10. Determination of the towns in acquired areas is based on National Geographic Atlas of the World, rev. 3d ed. (Washington, D.C.: National Geographic Society, 1970, pp. 130-33.

11. USSR, Naseleniye SSSR, 1973 (Moscow: Izdatel'stvo "Statistika," 1975), pp. 10-13.

12. Ibid., pp. 10-11.

13. Ibid., pp. 10-11.

14. Viktor B. Sochava, "The BAM: Problems in Applied Geography," in Gateway to Siberian Resources (The BAM), ed. Theodore Shabad and Victor L. Mote (Washington, D.C.: Scripta, 1977), p. 165.

15. Victor L. Mote, "The Baykal-Amur Mainline: Catalyst for the Development of Pacific Siberia," in Gateway to Siberian Resources (The BAM), ed. Theodore Shabad and Victor L. Mote (Washington, D.C.: Scripta, 1977), pp. 86, 182.

16. B. S. Khorev, Problemy Gorodov, 2d ed. (Moscow: Izdatel'stvo "Mysl'," 1975), fig. 11 inserted between pp. 248 and 249.

17. Richard H. Rowland, "Urban In-Migration in Late Nineteenth Century Russia" (Ph.D. diss., Columbia University, 1971).

18. J. William Leasure and Robert A. Lewis, "Internal Migration in Russia in the Late Nineteenth Century," Slavic Review 27 (September 1968): 385; and idem, "Internal Migration in the USSR: 1897-1926," Demography 4, no. 2 (1967): 488.

19. Robert A. Lewis and Richard H. Rowland, "Urbanization in Russia and the USSR: 1897-1966," Annals of the Association of American Geographers 59 (December 1969): 790-92.

20. Roger L. Thiede, "Urbanization and Industrialization in Pre-Revolutionary Russia," The Professional Geographer 25 (February 1973): 16-21.

21. Robert A. Lewis and Richard H. Rowland, "A Further Investigation of Urbanization and Industrialization in Pre-Revolutionary Russia," The Professional Geographer 26 (May 1974): 177-82.

22. Robert A. Lewis and Richard H. Rowland, "Urbanization in Russia and the USSR, 1897-1970," in The City in Russian History, ed. Michael F. Hamm (Lexington: University Press of Kentucky, 1976), pp. 211-14; and Thomas Stanley Fedor, Patterns of Urban Growth in Russian Empire during the Nineteenth Century (Chicago: University of Chicago, Department of Geography, 1975), pp. 138-78.

23. Lewis and Rowland, "Urbanization in Russia"; idem, "A Further Investigation of Urbanization"; idem, "Urbanization in Russia and the USSR: 1897-1970"; and Fedor, Patterns of Urban Growth.

24. A determination of the functions of these towns and the following discussion is based primarily on Harris, Cities of the Soviet Union, pp. 315-82; Theodore Shabad, Basic Industrial Resources of the U.S.S.R. (New York: Columbia University Press, 1969), esp. pp. 93-393; and Kratkaya Geograficheskaya Entsiklopediya, 5 vol. (Moscow: Gosudarstvennoye Nauchnoye Izdatel'-stvo "Sovetskaya Entsiklopediya," 1960-66); and Bol'shaya Sovetskaya Entsiklopediya, 26 vol. (Moscow: Izdatel'stvo "Sovetskaya Entsiklopediya," 1970-76). The last two sources include most individual urban centers and descriptions thereof. Unfortunately, at the time this research was being conducted, the Bol'shaya Sovetskaya Entsiklopediya was incomplete, only extending through volume 26 with Ul'yanovo being the last entry.

25. Elimination of each of these 25 "new towns" was based on one or more of the following considerations; in particular, if it was a: (1) town that Chauncy Harris suggests was actually a large village and implicitly did not experience rapid growth (Harris, Cities of the Soviet Union, pp. 392-93; and idem, "Population of Cities of the Soviet Union," pp. 344-47); (2) town that was a rural settlement based on an atlas of the USSR in the early 1960s and/or was in an agricultural area (USSR, Glavnoye Upravleniye Geodezii i Kartografii Ministerstva Geologii i Okhrany Nedr SSSR, Atlas SSSR [Moscow, 1962]); (3) town that did not evince rapid growth based on 1967-70 and/or 1970-74 data (Harris, "Population of Cities of the Soviet Union," pp. 344-47; and USSR, Prezidium Verkhovnogo Soveta Soyuza Sovetskikh Sotsialisticheskikh Respublik, SSSR: Administrativno Territorial'noye Deleniye Soyuznykh Respublik na 1 Yanvarya 1974 Goda [Moscow, 1974], pp. 636-50); (4) town that was not indicated as a new town from 1959 to 1970 in an article by G. M. Lappo (G. M. Lappo, Rasskazy o Gorodakh [Moscow: Izdatel'stvo "Mysl'," 1972], pp. 166-91); and (5) a town that apparently did not have any major development that might lead to rapid growth, for example, new mining activities, construction of a hydroelectric plant, significant new industry, and so forth (this consideration is based primarily on: (a) ibid.; (b) Harris, Cities of the

Soviet Union; (c) Shabad, Basic Industrial Resources; (d) Kratkaya Geografi-cheskaya Entsiklopediya; and (e) Bol'shaya Sovetskaya Entsiklopediya. In ad-dition, three suburbs of Moscow were eliminated, because investigation of an additional source indicated that they actually had populations in 1959 or there-abouts, which suggested that they did not have at least a doubling of their pop-ulation between 1959 and 1970 (Moskovskoy Filial Geograficheskogo Obshche-stva SSSR, Vsë Podmoskov'ye [Moscow: Izdatel'stvo "Mysl'," 1967], pp. 53, 169, 303). In conclusion the elimination procedure is to a certain extent ar-bitrary and admittedly arguable in some cases. Nevertheless, we believe these eliminations are generally valid and are certainly more valid than an approach of blindly accepting the fact that all urban centers in the 1970 census without a listed 1959 population were new towns and thus rapidly growing towns.

26. M. Tikhomirov, The Towns of Ancient Rus (Moscow: Foreign Lan-guages Publishing House, 1959), pp. 145-48.

27. V. G. Davidovich, "Rasseleniye v Prigorodnykh Zonakh," Rasse-leniye v Prigorodnykh Zonakh (Moscow: Izdatel'stvo "Mysl'," 1971), p. 16.

28. Harris, Cities of the Soviet Union, pp. 88-89.

29. USSR, Narodnoye Khozyaystvo SSSR 1922-1972 GG, p. 147.

30. See, for example, Holland Hunter, The Soviet Transport Experience (Washington, D.C.: Brookings Institution, 1968), pp. 61-64.

31. For example, in the mid-1960s, the declining towns of Velikiy Ustyug, Krasnovishersk, Sysert', Tara, Bodaybo, Baley, Nikolayevsk-na-Amure, Aleksandrovsk-Sakhalinskiy, and Mayli-Say were all 50 kilometers (about 30 miles) or more from the nearest railroad station. See USSR, Prezidium Verkhovnogo Soveta Soyuza Sovetskikh Sotsialisticheskikh Respublik, SSSR: Administrativno-Territorial'noye Deleniye Soyuznykh Respublik, Yanvar' 1965 Goda (Moscow, 1965), pp. 40, 65, 78, 140, 152, 168, 172, 199, 456.

32. Harris, Cities of the Soviet Union, pp. 315, 318.

CITY SIZE

5

The rapid shift of the population of Russia and the USSR to urban centers has involved a substantial shift to large urban centers. In previous chapters we have touched upon various aspects of the size of Soviet cities. In this chapter, we will discuss this subject in greater depth. Emphasis will be placed upon growth patterns by urban size classes and testing of Soviet policies regarding city sizes. The former topic is important, because it involves a major aspect of the urban structure of the USSR and the distribution and re- distribution of the Soviet population. The latter is of particular interest be- cause of official Soviet attempts to limit the growth of large cities. This chapter is concerned only with the sizes of individual official cities. An in- vestigation of urban agglomerations or regions will be undertaken in the next chapter.

SUMMARY DISCUSSION

The urban process of Russia and the USSR has involved an overall in- crease in the proportion of both the total and urban populations residing in large cities, that is, cities with 100,000 or more people. Around the turn of the century (1897) and at the beginning of the Soviet era (1926) well under one-tenth of the total population and about two-fifths of the urban population resided in large cities. However, by 1970, roughly one-third of the total population and two-thirds of the urban population resided in such cities. The number of large cities has increased by more than 200, or more than tenfold, since the turn of the century. Within recent years there has been an explo- sion of the number of cities with 1 million or more people. Whereas only 3 cities were "millionaire" cities as recently as 1959, the number of cities attaining such a status increased to 11 by 1970 and 16 by 1977, and probably will be at least 20 by 1980.

The increased concentration in the USSR of the total and urban popula- tions in large cities is similar to a general worldwide process. It appears that with well over 200 large cities, the Soviet Union probably has the great- est number of such cities of any country in the world.

However, the fact that the population residing in large cities has been growing more rapidly than that of the population residing in small cities or rural areas, thus leading to an increased concentration of the total and urban populations in such cities, does not mean necessarily that large cities have been growing more rapidly than small cities. In order to assess the latter situation, we computed subsequent rates of growth for all urban centers, roughly 1,000 in number, based on their population of 1959. Results revealed that large cities and small cities grew at about the same rates after 1959, and a similar investigation based on 1970 size classes for the 1970-74 period indicated that large cities actually grew somewhat more rapidly.

Investigation of more specific size classes indicated that the most rapid rates of growth were experienced by cities of intermediate size (roughly 50,000-500,000), while the slowest rates of growth were experienced by the very largest (especially 1 million and over) and smallest (less than 50,000) cities. The rapid growth of intermediate size cities appears to have been brought about by relatively high crude birth and natural increase rates and net in-migration, as compared with the more slowly growing largest and smallest cities. The growth of the largest cities, such as Moscow and Leningrad, was impeded by relatively low crude birth and natural increase rates and relatively high crude death rates, all of which reflect a rather old population, as well as by low rates of in-migration, due in part to restrictions on migration to these cities. The slow growth of small cities was due, in particular, to high out-migration rates, which was prompted by their limited economic and social bases, and, to a certain extent, to reduced crude birth rates, which was partly the result of the high out-migration of young adults.

Large cities of the USSR have continued to grow fairly rapidly, despite official policy favoring the limitation of their growth and an increased growth of small cities. Several additional indicators further demonstrate the lack of success of this policy. First, we discovered that certain large cities where new industrial expansion was to be either "prohibited" or "limited" according to a decree of the late 1950s continued to grow about as rapidly or even more rapidly than the urban population as a whole, and none came close to declining in population. Second, a number of examples indicate that projected limited maximum size of many large cities already has been easily surpassed. Also, the number of cities of the USSR that have exceeded an approximate "optimum" size of about 250,000 has proliferated; between 1959 and the late 1970s, the number of cities with more than 250,000 people nearly doubled and came to exceed 100.

A number of reasons for the continued rapid growth of large cities can be cited. Such cities continue to receive a great share of industrial investment, and industrial production tends to remain highly concentrated in such cities. Apparent reasons for the continued industrial investment in large cities include advantages of productivity, market size, labor quantity and quality, transportation accessibility, social overhead capital, and desire to increase production as quickly as possible. Thus, similar to many other areas of the world, the forces of industrial inertia are also quite important in the USSR. The dominance of large cities in the USSR is promoted also by the fact that, unlike the United States, governmental and educational functions are highly concentrated in large cities, adding to their base and attractiveness. Large cities also tend to have a more available consumer goods. Small towns suffer from a relative lack of these many advantages of large cities.

Although the growth of small cities has not been perhaps as rapid over-all as envisaged in the policies concerning city size, there are instances where some smaller cities have received increased investment and grown rapidly. Furthermore, if there were no policy, large cities would grow even more rapidly.

Nonetheless, despite a policy to limit city size, large cities of the USSR continue to grow quite rapidly. The contradictions between policy and reality are reflected in the ongoing debate in the USSR between antilarge and prolarge city advocates. It may be too soon to test the full repercussions of this policy.

DETAILED DISCUSSION

Definitions

In broadest terms, we will subdivide the urban population of Russia and the USSR into two classes: (1) "large cities," which we define as cities with 100,000 or more people, and (2) "small cities," which we define as cities with 15,000-99,999 people. In addition, we will often subdivide each of these two broad categories into more specific size classes, although we will not necessarily assign any verbal names to these classes.

Soviet urban literature is replete with more refined size categories and corresponding names. For example, according to B. S. Khorev, the follow-ing classification of cities has been used considerably in the USSR in recent years: small cities (malyye goroda) are those with less than 50,000 inhabi-tants; medium (sredniye), 50,000-100,000 inhabitants; large (bol'shiye), 100,000-250,000; large-scale (krupnyye), 250,000-500,000; and the largest scale (krupneyshiye), more than 500,000.[1] Khorev believes it is necessary to subdivide further cities of less than 50,000 in population, which he terms "not large" (nebol'shiye), into two groups: small (malyye), less than 20,000, and semimedium (polusredniye), 20,000-50,000.[2] Other classifications exist and will be referred to whenever appropriate; we will often make use of data for such classes. But, to repeat, the prime divisions of the urban centers of 15,000 and over in our study fall into two size classes: large (100,000 and over) and small (15,000-99,999).

Major Trends

Table 5.1 shows major trends in the share of the Russian and Soviet population residing in various urban size classes. Although there was an in-crease in the percentage of the total population residing in all size classes between 1897 and 1970, the biggest shift was to large cities, that is, cities

TABLE 5.1

Percent of Total and Urban Populations of Russia and the USSR Residing
in Various Urban Size Classes: 1897-1970

Size Class	Percent of Total Population					Percent of Urban Population				
	1897	1926	1939	1959	1970	1897	1926	1939	1959	1970
15,000-49,999	3.8	4.1	6.1	9.0	9.6	39.0	31.0	24.3	23.6	20.7
50,000-99,999	1.9	2.7	3.6	5.2	5.3	19.1	19.9	14.1	13.7	11.4
100,000-249,999	1.7	2.2	4.7	6.5	9.0	17.6	16.5	18.5	17.0	19.2
250,000-499,999	0.5	1.9	3.8	5.1	6.9	5.6	14.0	15.0	13.2	14.7
500,000-999,999	0.0	0.3	3.0	7.4	7.2	0.0	2.3	11.9	19.3	15.4
1,000,000 and over	1.8	2.2	4.1	5.0	8.7	18.7	16.3	16.2	13.1	18.6
15,000-99,999	5.7	6.8	9.7	14.2	14.9	58.2	50.9	38.4	37.3	32.1
100,000 and over	4.1	6.5	15.6	24.0	31.7	41.8	49.1	61.6	62.7	67.9
250,000 and over	2.4	4.3	10.9	17.4	22.7	24.3	32.6	43.1	45.7	48.7
500,000 and over	1.8	2.5	7.1	12.4	15.8	18.7	18.6	28.1	32.4	34.0

Sources: See Chapter 1, nn. 104 and 105.

TABLE 5.2

Population of Urban Centers of Russia and the USSR by Size Class: 1897-1970

Size Class	Population				
	1897	1926	1939	1959	1970
15,000-49,999	4,809,479	6,922,465	11,851,890	18,834,887	23,284,990
50,000-99,999	2,355,971	4,456,155	6,913,805	10,894,106	12,832,959
100,000-249,999	2,166,034	3,696,426	9,031,593	13,598,742	21,638,569
250,000-499,999	686,045	3,128,459	7,332,165	10,551,833	16,601,082
500,000-999,999	0	513,637	5,806,073	15,416,839	17,349,701
1,000,000 and over	2,303,511	3,639,955	7,926,923	10,464,485	20,916,283
15,000-99,999	7,165,450	11,378,620	18,765,695	29,728,993	36,117,949
100,000 and over	5,155,590	10,978,477	30,096,754	50,031,899	76,505,635
250,000 and over	2,989,556	7,282,051	21,065,161	36,433,157	54,867,066
500,000 and over	2,303,511	4,153,592	13,732,996	25,881,324	38,265,984

Sources: See Chapter 1, nn. 104 and 105.

283

TABLE 5.3

Number of Urban Centers of Russia and the USSR
by Size Class: 1897-1970

Size Class	Number				
	1897	1926	1939	1959	1970
15,000-49,999	195	281	450	718	889
50,000-99,999	36	65	97	155	186
100,000-249,999	15	26	58	89	141
250,000-499,999	2	9	22	32	47
500,000-999,999	0	1	9	22	23
1,000,000 and over	2	2	2	3	10
15,000-99,999	231*	346	547	873	1,075
100,000 and over	19	38	91	146	221
250,000 and over	4	12	33	57	81
500,000 and over	2	3	11	25	33
USSR total	250*	384	638	1,019	1,296

*The total of 249 presented in Table 1 of a previous article by the authors left out Bukhara. See Robert A. Lewis and Richard H. Rowland, "Urbanization in Russia and the USSR: 1897-1966," Annals of the Association of American Geographers 59 (December 1969): 780.

Sources: See Chapter 1, nn. 104 and 105.

with 100,000 or more people. In 1897 and 1926, only about 4 to 7 percent of the total population resided in such cities, but by 1970 nearly one-third of the Soviet citizenry was located in a city of 100,000 or more people. Substantial shifts of the total population have occurred also to the 250,000-and-over, 500,000-and-over, and 1,000,000-and-over classes. Comparatively little shift has occurred to the 15,000-49,999 and 50,000-99,999 categories. The shift to large cities is also noticeable within the urban population. Whereas only about two-fifths of the urban population resided in large cities in 1897, by 1970 roughl two-thirds of the urban population resided in cities with 100,000 or more people. Thus, today, about one-third of the Soviet total population and about two-thirds of the Soviet urban population now reside in large cities. The shift to large cities reflects, of course, the fact that between 1897 and 1970 the pop-

ulation residing in large urban centers increased more rapidly than that in
small urban centers. Although the population of small cities roughly quintupled, that of large cities increased by roughly 15 times (Table 5.2).

Within the large-city class there has been a particularly substantial
shift to cities of 250,000-999,999. Interestingly, between 1897 and 1970, the
share of the urban population residing in "millionaire" cities (that is, cities
with 1,000,000-or-more people) did not increase. However, this decline was
confined to the 1897-1959 period, and between 1959 and 1970 the "millionaire"
share increased.

The shift to large cities also is reflected in the number of urban centers
within various size classes (Table 5.3). Although there has been a marked
rate of increase in the number of urban centers of all size classes, there has
been an especially substantial rate of increase in the number of large cities.
The number of cities with 100,000-or-more people increased more than tenfold, from 19 in 1897 to 221 in 1970, and within the relatively short 1959-70
period it increased by 75. In addition, between 1897 and 1970, the number of
cities of 250,000-499,999 increased from only 2 to 47 and those of 500,000-
999,999 increased from 0 to 23. Finally, although there were only three
"millionaire" cities as recently as 1959 (Moscow, Leningrad, and Kiev), by
1970 the number of cities of 1 million and over increased to ten, with the addition of seven cities—Tashkent, Baku, Gor'kiy, Khar'kov, Novosibirsk,
Kuybyshev, and Sverdlovsk (Table 5.4). Furthermore, a number of cities
with 800,000-999,999 people in 1970 subsequently have entered the millionaire category based on estimates for 1977, the most recent estimates available at the time this research was being conducted (Minsk, Tbilisi, Odessa,
Omsk, Chelyabinsk). Thus, according to the most recent estimates, 15 cities
of the USSR have 1 million or more people. As Table 5.4 also shows, eight
other Soviet cities had between 900,000 and 999,999 people in 1977 and are
apparently on the verge of entering the millionaire status (Dnepropetrovsk,
Donetsk, Perm', Kazan', Yerevan, Ufa, Volgograd, and Rostov-na-Donu).
By 1980, it is probable that the USSR will have roughly 20 cities with 1 million or more people.

Among the largest cities of the USSR, the most spectacular growth has
been experienced by Minsk. In 1959, Minsk was only the twenty-fourth largest
city of the USSR, but by 1970 it ranked eleventh and by 1977, ninth; an increase
of 15 positions since 1959 has been the greatest increase in rank of any of the
largest Soviet cities. Furthermore, the population of Minsk more than doubled
between 1959 and 1977, from about 500,000 to well over 1 million. The recent
rapid growth of Minsk reflects the current rapid urbanization and urban growth
of Belorussia. Although none of the other largest Soviet cities experienced
a doubling between 1959 and 1977, some came fairly close (Kiev, Tashkent,
Omsk, and Yerevan).

However, it should be made clear that the relatively rapid growth of
the population residing in large cities as compared with that residing in small
cities does not necessarily mean that large cities were growing faster than
small ones. For example, the large-city population increased partly because many smaller cities increased and crossed the 100,000 population total.

TABLE 5.4

Population of Cities with 900,000 or More People in 1977:   1959-77

City	Population (thousands)			Rank of Population among Soviet Cities		
	1959	1970	1977	1959	1970	1977
Moscow	6,009	7,061	7,819	1	1	1
Leningrad	3,321	3,950	4,425	2	2	2
Kiev	1,104	1,632	2,079	3	3	3
Tashkent	912	1,385	1,689	7	4	4
Baku	971	1,266	1,435	4	5	5
Khar'kov	934	1,223	1,405	6	6	6
Gor'kiy	942	1,170	1,319	5	7	7
Novosibirsk	886	1,161	1,304	8	8	8
Minsk	509	917	1,231	24	11	9
Kuybyshev	806	1,045	1,204	9	9	10
Sverdlovsk	779	1,025	1,187	10	10	11
Tbilisi	695	889	1,042	12	13	12
Odessa	667	892	1,039	14	12	13
Omsk	581	821	1,026	20	19	14
Chelyabinsk	689	875	1,007	13	15	15
Dnepropetrovsk	660	862	995	15	17	16
Donetsk	699	879	984	11	14	17
Perm'	629	850	972	17	18	18
Kazan'	647	869	970	16	16	19
Yerevan	509	767	956	25	23	20
Ufa	547	771	942	23	22	21
Volgograd	592	818	931	19	20	22
Rostov-na-Donu	600	789	921	18	21	23

Note: Data are for city boundaries of the corresponding year, except that Moscow data in 1959 are for 1961 boundaries.

Sources: 1959 and 1970 Soviet censuses and 1977 estimates (see Chapter 1, nn. 104 and 113).

TABLE 5.5

Rate of Population Change by Urban Size Class of 1959: 1959-70

Size Class in 1959	Number of Urban Centers	Population		Percentage Increase
		1959	1970	
15,000-19,999[a]	247	4,271,371	5,364,924	25.6
20,000-24,999[b]	135	3,001,497	3,686,883	22.8
25,999-49,999	320	11,152,455	14,435,024	29.4
50,000-74,999	109	6,654,360	9,424,929	41.6
75,000-99,999	54	4,795,597	6,741,580	40.6
100,000-249,999	90	13,733,242	19,275,755	40.4
250,000-499,999	33	11,147,295	15,104,411	35.5
500,000-749,999	14	8,708,622	11,719,967	34.6
750,000-999,999	7	6,257,683	8,273,866	32.2
1,000,000 and over	3	10,475,180	12,642,417	20.7
15,000-99,999	865	29,875,280	39,653,340	32.7
100,000 and over	147	50,322,022	67,016,416	33.2
USSR total	1,012	80,197,302	106,669,756	33.0

[a]Includes 25 towns with a population of 15,000-19,999 in 1959, according to the 1959 census, which were not listed in the 1970 census and apparently not annexed to some other town, and thus are assumed to have declined to less than 15,000 in 1970. It is operationally assumed that their 1970 population was 14,000 each, or 350,000 for the 25 towns altogether.

[b]Includes three towns similar to those in note a but with a population of 20,000-24,999 in 1959. The population of such towns also is assumed to be 14,000 in 1970, or 42,000 for the three towns altogether.

Sources: 1959 and 1970 Soviet censuses (see Chapter 1, n. 104).

Thus, their entire population is included ultimately in the large city population total, although they were small cities at the beginning of the period of investigation.

Consequently, to examine the rates of growth of urban centers of various sizes between 1959 and 1970 we have calculated the rates of growth of towns of various sizes according to their 1959 sizes. These calculations were extremely time-consuming, because it was necessary to investigate each and every urban center of a given size class in 1959 and sum not only the 1959 populations of the centers of this class but also their corresponding 1970 populations. Unfortunately, centers of a given class were not listed conveniently together but instead were scattered throughout the listing of all urban centers by political units in the 1970 census. Also, roughly 1,000 urban centers were involved. The results of this investigation are presented in Table 5.5. The data presented in this table are based upon the 1959 and 1970 populations in 1970 city boundaries for each urban center with a population of 15,000 or more in 1959 as presented in the 1970 census. In addition, we have included the 28 declining towns ("disappearing" towns) that had a population of 15,000 or more in 1959 according to the 1959 census but that apparently declined to below 15,000 in population in 1970, because they are not listed in the 1970 census. They are assumed operationally to have had a population of 14,000 each in 1970 (totaling 392,000 for the 28 towns). To the best of our knowledge no one has made similar calculations for towns below 100,000 in population for the 1959-70 period, very probably because of the great number of towns with a population of less than 100,000 in population.

From Table 5.5 it is apparent that the growth rates for large cities (100,000 and over) and small cities (15,000-99,999) were nearly identical. Two implications of this are: (1) although the population residing in large cities has been growing more rapidly than that of small cities (for example, 52.9 and 21.5 percent, respectively between 1959 and 1970), this has not necessarily meant that large cities have been growing faster than small cities and (2) although the government has tried to restrict the growth of large cities, they have, nonetheless, been growing as rapidly as small cities, a subject that will be discussed in more detail later. Furthermore, the absolute population increase of large cities was much higher than that of small cities and accounted for over 60 percent of the growth of all urban centers, despite the fact that there were nearly six times as many small cities as there were large cities.

With regard to rates of growth by more specific size classes, Table 5.5 shows that an inverted U-shaped curve existed. Namely, the slowest growth was experienced by the smallest and largest size classes, particularly the 15,000-24,999 and 1 million-and-over classes, while the greatest rates of growth were experienced by intermediate size classes, especially each of the three classes of 50,000-249,999 size class. The slow rate of growth of the smallest cities partly reflects the fact that, as discussed before, the declining towns of the USSR consisted primarily of small towns. The slowest rate of growth, however, was experienced by the 1 million-and-over class, which consisted in this case of Moscow, Leningrad, and Kiev. The slow growth of this class primarily reflects the slow growth of Moscow and Leningrad (17 and 19 percent, respectively), while Kiev grew relatively rapidly (47 percent).

TABLE 5.6

Rate of Population Change for Various Large City Size
Classes by Urban Size Class of 1959: 1959-70

Size Class in 1959 (thousands)	Number of Cities	Population (thousands)		Percentage Increase
		1959	1970	
100-199	75	10,518	14,263	35.7
200-299	27	6,593	9,440	43.2
300-399	13	4,389	5,575	27.0
400-499	8	3,476	5,106	46.9
500-599	6	3,387	4,819	42.3
600-699	6	3,910	5,137	31.4
700-899	5	3,881	5,002	28.9
900-1,200	5	4,899	6,671	36.2
More than 3,000	2	9,365	11,011	17.6
USSR total	147	50,418	67,029	32.9

Source: V. I. Perevedentsev, Metody Izucheniya Migratsii Naseleniya (Moscow: Izdatel'stvo "Nauka," 1975),
p. 97.

In a similar manner, V. I. Perevedentsev has calculated 1959-70 rates
of growth for more-detailed size classes of 1959 within the large city category (Table 5.6). The most rapid growth was attained by the 400,000-499,999,
200,000-299,999, and 500,000-599,999 categories. The slowest growth occurred in the 3 million-and-over class, which consisted solely of Moscow and
Leningrad. Fairly slow growth was characteristic also of the 300,000-399,999
and 700,000-899,999 categories. This is a reflection of the inclusion of a number of slow-growing major industrial cities in these classes, particularly three
of the largest cities of the Donbas Coalfield (Donetsk, Makeyevka, and Gorlovka) and two steel cities of the Urals (Magnitogorsk and Nizhniy Tagil). The
Donbas and Urals were, as mentioned in the last chapter, major areas of declining towns.

Thus, Tables 5.5 and 5.6 suggest that, in general, the highest rates of
city growth were experienced by cities with 50,000 to 600,000 people. Policy
implications of rates of growth by urban size classes and post-1970 trends will
be discussed in a later section.

Comparison with World

The increased concentration of the total and urban populations of the USSR in large cities is not a unique phenomenon but instead is a characteristic of the world in general. As can be seen in Table 5.7, the percentage of the world's total and urban populations residing in cities with 100,000 or more people also has increased since the turn of the century. Comparisons between the USSR and the world, in this regard, involve some problems. First, whereas Soviet cities of 100,000 and over are legal cities, those for the world include, whenever possible, agglomerations of 100,000-or-more people.[3] (This problem will be discussed in greater detail in a later section.) Second, the Soviet urban population is based on centers of 15,000 and over, while the world urban population is based on centers of 20,000 or more people. This is not a major problem, because the overwhelming majority of the 15,000-and-over population resides in centers of 20,000 and over; for example, in the USSR in 1970, roughly 95 percent of the 15,000-and-over population resided in towns with 20,000 or more people. Despite these problems, rough comparisons still can be made. In general, it appears that the shares of the Soviet total and urban populations residing in large cities approximate those of the world. For example, in 1970, about one-fourth to one-third of the total populations and roughly two-thirds to three-fourths of the urban populations resided in large cities. However, the share of the total Soviet population residing in large cities was somewhat above the world average (31.7 versus 23.8 percent), reflecting the fact that the USSR is more urbanized than the world.

With respect to the number of large cities, the USSR is perhaps now the world leader. As mentioned before, 221 Soviet cities had a population of 100,000 or more people in 1970. In the same year, the United States had 156 official cities with 100,000 or more people.[4] A problem in comparing Soviet with U.S. cities is that Soviet cities are apparently overbounded to a great extent; that is, the official area is larger than the built-up area. In the United States, of course, the opposite is often true in that many cities are "under-bounded," with the legal city area being smaller than the built-up area of the metropolis, although some U.S. cities are also somewhat overbounded (for example, Jacksonville, Florida). Due to the absence of more information on Soviet cities, it is virtually impossible to assess this difference more precisely. It may be worthwhile to use broader definitions of U.S. cities, namely, Standard Metropolitan Statistical Areas (SMSAs) and Urbanized Areas, keeping in mind, however, that these definitions also may be broader than the definition of a Soviet city. Unfortunately, the Soviet censuses do not employ any broader metropolitan concept. In 1970 there were 217 SMSAs and 172 Urbanized Areas with 100,000 or more people in the United States.[5] Thus, if these broader U.S. concepts are used, it is apparent that the U.S. number of "large cities" comes closer to that of the USSR. Even utilizing these broader U.S. concepts, the number of large cities in the United States still does not exceed the Soviet total. The problem of the delineation of metropolitan areas in the USSR will be discussed in greater detail in Chapter 6.

TABLE 5.7

Percentage of World and Russian and Soviet Populations
Residing in Large Cities: Circa 1900-70

| | Population Residing in Cities with 100,000 or More People as a Percent of: | | | | | |
| | Total Population | | | Urban Population* | | |
	Circa 1900	Circa 1960	1970	Circa 1900	Circa 1960	1970
World	5.5	19.7	23.8	59.8	73.1	73.9
Russia and the USSR	4.1	24.0	31.7	41.8	62.7	67.9

*The urban definition for the world is centers with 20,000 or more people, while the definition for the USSR is centers with 15,000 or more people.

Note: World data are for 1900, 1960, and 1970, while Soviet data are for 1897, 1959, and 1970.

Sources: 1897 Russian census and various foreign sources and 1959 and 1970 Soviet censuses (see Chapter 1, nn. 104 and 105); and Kingsley Davis, Analysis of Trends, Relationships, and Development, World Urbanization, 1950-70, vol. 2 (Berkeley: University of California, Institute of International Studies, 1972), p. 56.

As for other countries, none comes very close to either the Soviet Union or the United States in terms of the number of large cities. According to recent data presented in the Demographic Yearbook, Japan and India each had roughly 150 cities with 100,000 or more people in circa 1970.[6] A substantial number of large cities apparently also exists in China. Unfortunately, no census has been taken there since the 1950s, and the United Nations does not present a comprehensive list of all Chinese cities with 100,000 or more people as of circa 1970. However, Kingsley Davis has provided 1970 population estimates for Chinese cities, which indicate that about 140 cities of China had 100,000 or more people in 1970.[7] Although these are only estimates, it is probably safe to conclude that the number of large cities in China is also considerably less than that of the USSR or the United States.

In terms of the number of cities with 1 million or more people, the Soviet position in the world is apparently not as outstanding. The USSR did have ten millionaire cities in 1970, while the United States had only six official cities of 1 million and over in the same year (New York, Chicago, Los Angeles,

Philadelphia, Detroit, and Houston). However, in terms of broader urban definitions, the United States had 33 SMSAs and 25 Urbanized Areas with 1 million or more people in 1970.[8] In comparison, the USSR had approximately 20 urban regions or metropolitan areas of 1 million and over in 1970. It also appears that the Soviet and U.S. totals might have been matched or even surpassed by China, which had roughly 30 millionaire cities in 1970 according to Davis's estimates.[9] Japan and India had only eight millionaire cities each in 1970.[10]

Analysis: Factors Related to Growth Rates

Variations in growth rates by city size are influenced by fertility, mortality, natural increase, and migration variations. There are little comprehensive data available on these factors. The most extensive data available are fertility, mortality, natural increase, and migration patterns by urban size classes of the RSFSR for the 1959-67 period, which are presented in studies undertaken by Khorev.[11] These data are based on size classes as of January 1, 1967, and the composition of each category of cities is unchanging during the entire 1959-67 period.[12] Some problems exist with these data. First, they are for the RSFSR and not the USSR as a whole. Nevertheless, because roughly 60 percent of the urban population (official urban definitions) of the USSR in 1970 was located in the RSFSR, these data can be considered as somewhat representative of the USSR. Also, they are based on size classes of 1967 and not of 1959, and thus are not strictly comparable to our growth rates by size classes as of 1959. However, this problem is probably not that great, because it appears that the vast majority of cities within a given size class were in the same size class in 1959. Using Khorev's size classes (1 million and over; 500,000-999,999; 100,000-499,999; 50,000-99,999; 20,000-49,999; 10,000-19,999; and less than 10,000) and a list of all cities with 15,000 or more people in 1967, we have determined that, of the nearly 600 cities with 15,000 or more people in 1967, nearly four-fifths (77.7 percent) were in the same size class in 1959 as they were in 1967.[13] Thus, cities constituting a certain size class in 1959 generally constituted the same size class in 1967. In addition, as Table 5.8 suggests, relative rates of growth for various size classes of the RSFSR between 1959 and 1967 were somewhat similar to those of the USSR between 1959 and 1970 (Table 5.5). It should be pointed out that rates of growth for the RSFSR in Table 5.8 are presented in relation to a base figure of 100 for the urban population of the RSFSR as a whole. A comparison of these two tables reveals that the most rapid growth in both cases occurred in the 50,000-999,999 range and the slowest growth in both cases occurred in urban centers of less than 50,000 and 1 million and over. Data provided by Khorev, therefore, can be regarded probably as roughly indicative of fertility, mortality, natural increase, and migration patterns of cities of different sizes for the USSR as a whole.

According to these data for the RSFSR, it appears that growth rate variations were related in part to fertility, mortality, and natural increase vari-

TABLE 5.8

Rate of Population Change by Urban Size Class of 1967
for the RSFSR: 1959-67

Size Class in 1967	Index of Percentage Change of Population of Size Class*
Less than 10,000	42.7
10,000-19,999	76.5
20,000-49,999	77.7
50,000-99,999	97.7
100,000-499,999	113.8
500,000-999,999	110.8
1,000,000 and over	56.9

*Base percent for urban population of the RSRSF is 100.

Source: B. S. Khorev, ed., Malyy Gorod (Moscow: Iz-datel'stvo Moskovskogo Universiteta, 1972), p. 64.

ations, as measured by crude birth rates and crude death rates. Crude birth and natural increase rates were apparently relatively low and crude death rates relatively high in the largest and smallest cities, the most slowly growing cities (Table 5.9). Conversely, crude birth rates were highest and crude death rates lowest in cities of 50,000-499,999, which was the most rapidly growing size class of cities for the USSR as a whole. Crude natural increase rates for 1967 were highest for the 50,000-999,999 class. It is interesting to note that, although the smaller centers of 20,000-49,999 had the highest fertility and natural increase rates in 1959, by 1967 this situation no longer existed. Between 1959 and 1967 the 20,000-49,999 class had the sharpest decline in crude birth rate of any size class listed in Table 5.9, thus, contributing to the slow growth of cities below 50,000 in population.

Table 5.9 also includes data for urban-type settlements. Such settlements are quite small, being primarily less than 10,000 in population; in 1970 no urban-type settlement of the USSR exceeded 50,000 in population. They had the highest crude birth rate in 1959, but only an average crude birth rate by 1967. In addition, in both years their crude natural increase rates were high and their crude death rates were low. However, these settlements are of limited importance to our discussion, because they comprise only a small share of the population of settlements of 15,000-49,999; for example, in 1970, less than one-tenth (9.6 percent) of the total population of the USSR residing in urban centers of 15,000-49,999 was located in urban-type settlements.

TABLE 5.9

Crude Birth, Death, and Natural Increase Rates by Urban Size Class of 1967 for the RSFSR:
1959 and 1967
(per thousand)

Size Class	Crude Birth Rate		Crude Death Rate*		Crude Rate of Natural Increase	
	1959	1967	1959	1967	1959	1967
Urban-type settlements	24.0	13.8	6.4	6.7	17.6	7.1
Less than 10,000	19.4	14.1	7.8	8.7	11.6	5.4
10,000–19,999	21.4	14.2	7.6	7.9	13.8	6.3
20,000–49,999	22.9	14.1	7.3	7.6	15.6	6.5
50,000–99,999	22.3	14.5	7.0	7.3	15.3	7.2
100,000–499,999	21.0	14.5	6.7	6.7	14.3	7.8
500,000–999,999	19.8	14.1	6.6	6.6	13.2	7.5
1,000,000 and over	14.6	11.3	7.3	8.5	7.3	2.8
RSFSR total	20.6	13.8	6.9	7.2	13.7	6.6

*Calculated by subtracting available natural increase rates from available birth rates.

Source: B. S. Khorev, Problemy Gorodov (Moscow: Izdatel'stvo "Mysl'," 1971), pp. 245–46.

The very lowest crude birth and natural increase rates were experienced by cities of 1 million or more, which also had relatively high crude death rates. With the exception of Riga in certain years, Moscow and Leningrad, in particular, have had the lowest crude birth and natural increase rates and highest crude death rates of any of the largest cities in the USSR in recent years.[14] For example, in 1965, the crude birth, death, and natural increase rates for Moscow were 10.8, 8.5, and 2.3 per thousand, respectively; in 1970, corresponding rates were 11.8, 9.5, and 2.3 per thousand, respectively.[15] For Leningrad, crude birth, death, and natural increase rates were 11.2, 7.8, and 3.4 per thousand for 1965, and 12.7, 9.2, and 3.5 per thousand for 1970.[16] The crude birth and natural increase rates for Moscow and Leningrad were undoubtedly among the lowest in the world. For example, in comparison, the crude birth rate for New York City in 1968 was 17.3 per thousand.[17] However, it should be remembered that retirement towns such as Miami Beach tend to have even lower rates due to their extremely old populations.

The relatively low crude birth and natural increase rates and relatively high crude death rates of the largest cities of the USSR are indicated also by data for Soviet cities with 500,000 or more people. These data reveal that the crude birth and natural increase rates for cities of 500,000 and over were lower than those for all urban centers (official urban definitions) of the USSR, while their crude death rates were higher. In 1968, there were 33 cities with 500,000 or more people and the crude birth, death, and natural increase rates for such cities combined in 1967 were 13.8, 7.3, and 6.5 per thousand, respectively. In comparison, corresponding rates for all urban centers were 15.5, 7.0, and 8.5 percent, respectively.[18] Not surprisingly, crude birth and natural increase rates for Moscow and Leningrad in 1967 were below the average rates for all urban centers and for all cities of 500,000 and over, while the death rates for these two largest cities were relatively high. In particular, the crude birth, death, and natural increase rates for Moscow were 10.9, 9.2, and 1.7 percent, respectively, while the corresponding rates for Leningrad were 11.2, 8.4, and 2.8 percent.[19]

Rates of growth by cities of various size classes also were apparently related to migration rates. The 1970 census provides appropriate data in this regard. These data are for cities according to their 1970 and not their 1959 populations. Two sets of migration rates are presented in Table 5.10. The first set of rates (first three columns) is based on all origins or destinations of migrants to or from urban centers of a given size class. Thus, for example, the number of in-migrants to urban centers of 20,000-49,999 includes migrants from all origins, including centers of 20,000-49,999. The problem with these figures is that they include people who moved from cities of a given size class to cities of that same size class. Hence, this migration does not really add or subtract from the population of that size class. Therefore, we also have computed rates (last three columns) for migration excluding the same size class. For example, in these figures, the number of in-migrants to urban centers of 20,000-49,999 includes all migrants to such centers, except those from centers of 20,000-49,999.

TABLE 5.10

Migration Rates by Urban Size Class: 1970

Size Class	Percent of Population of Size Class Comprised of:			In-Migrants to Size Class (excluding those from same class)	Out-Migrants from Size Class (excluding those to same class)	Net Migrants (excluding those from same class)
	In-Migrants to Size Class (all origins)	Out-Migrants from Size Class (all destinations)	Out-Migrants from Size Class (all destinations)			
Less than 20,000	8.7	7.4	1.3	7.1	5.8	1.3
20,000–49,999	8.2	6.2	2.1	7.5	5.4	2.1
50,000–99,999	7.7	5.8	1.9	7.2	5.3	1.9
100,000–499,999	7.5	5.0	2.6	6.4	3.9	2.6
500,000 and over	4.6	3.0	1.6	4.2	2.6	1.6
Less than 100,000	8.3	6.7	1.7	5.8	4.1	1.7
100,000 and over	6.1	4.0	2.1	4.6	2.5	2.1

Source: 1970 Soviet census (see Chapter 1, n. 104).

The significance of the difference between these two sets of rates is evident in Table 5.10. According to rates of in-migration from all origins, the highest rate of in-migration was for centers of less than 20,000. However, such centers had a relatively large share of their in-migrants coming from centers of their own size class, here centers of less than 20,000. In particular, 17.9 percent of all the in-migrants to centers of less than 20,000 came from the same size class. Corresponding percentages for other size classes were 9.2 percent for centers of 20,000-49,999 (that is, 9.2 percent of all the in-migrants came from other centers of 20,000-49,999); 6.9 percent for centers of 50,000-99,999; 14.8 percent for centers of 100,000-499,999; and 9.1 percent for centers of 500,000 and over. When migration excluding that to and from centers of the same size class was eliminated, somewhat different patterns emerged. Centers of less than 20,000 no longer had the highest rate of in-migration but instead were surpassed by the 20,000-49,999 and 50,000-99,999 size classes. The lowest rates of in-migration were experienced by the two largest size classes. Especially low rates were characteristic of Moscow and Leningrad. According to the 1970 census, in-migrants comprised only 2.9 and 4.0 percent of the populations of these two premier cities, with both percentages being below the average for all cities with 500,000 and more people (Table 5.10). It should be pointed out, however, that Moscow and Leningrad still received larger absolute numbers of in-migrants than any of the other Soviet cities. For example, according to passport data for 1973, 237,000 people migrated to Moscow and 196,000 to Leningrad; among the remaining cities of 500,000 or more people in that same year, only Kiev had a figure exceeding 100,000 (114,000), and no other city came close to having 100,000 in-migrants, with Minsk being the closest at 81,000.[20] In addition, 1970 passport data and data from the 1970 census also indicate that Moscow and Leningrad again had by far more in-migrants than any of the other cities for which data were available, namely, the 14 SSR capitals outside the RSFSR.[21] Thus, although comparable and comprehensive data are not available for smaller cities, it seems safe to conclude that Moscow and Leningrad have had by far the greatest number of in-migrants of any of the Soviet cities.

The change of the population is also dependent on the extent of out-migration. Out-migration rates tended to decline progressively with an increase in size class (Table 5.10). The highest rates of out-migration were experienced by the smallest towns, again reflecting their narrow and limited economic base and opportunities. The lowest rates of out-migration were from the largest cities, reflecting their better opportunities. (Social and economic differences between large and small cities will be discussed in greater detail later.) The low rate of out-migration from the largest cities also may reflect the impact of restrictions upon residence in many of these cities, especially Moscow. Moscow is quite difficult to get into or to return to. Consequently, once people are there, they are apparently somewhat reluctant to leave. It has been suggested, for example, that old people and graduates of Moscow tend to want to stay in the city, because of the difficulties of returning to the city once they leave.[22] Passport data indicate that Moscow has the

TABLE 5.11

Rates of Migration and Natural Increase by Urban Size Class of 1967 for the RSFSR: 1959-67

Size Class	Index of Percent of Population of Size Class Comprised of:[a]		Percent of Growth due to:	
	Migration-Reclassification[b]	Natural Increase	Migration-Reclassification[b]	Natural Increase
Less than 10,000	15.1	86.1	21.2	78.8
10,000-19,999	61.0	101.0	48.6	51.4
20,000-49,999	59.1	106.9	46.6	53.4
50,000-99,999	90.6	109.9	56.5	43.5
100,000-499,999	117.0	108.9	62.6	37.4
500,000-999,999	115.1	104.0	63.7	36.3
1,000,000 and over	59.1	53.5	62.9	37.1
RSFSR total	100.0	100.0	61.2	38.8

[a]Base percent for urban population of the RSFSR is 100.
[b]Migration plus growth due to reclassification of rural areas to urban areas.

Source: B. S. Khorev, ed., Malyy Gorod (Moscow: Izdatel'stvo Moskovskogo Universiteta, 1972), p. 64.

lowest rate of out-migration for any of the largest cities of the USSR. For example, in 1973, the number of out-migrants from Moscow per thousand people was 18.6 (or 1.86 percent). [23] Among other cities of 500,000 and over only Tbilisi and Yerevan, cities that typically have low rates of in-migration and out-migration, had lower rates of out-migration in 1973. [24]

Ultimately, the rates of population change are influenced by net migration rates. It appears that variations in net migration rates by urban size class based on 1970 census data roughly corresponded to variations in total rates of growth (Table 5.10). The lowest net migration rates were experienced by the smallest and largest size classes, while the highest rates were attained by the 100,000-499,999 size class.

Rates of migration for cities of various sizes in the RSFSR between 1959 and 1967 roughly correspond to the patterns revealed by the 1970 census. In particular, Khorev has presented data for various urban size classes, which show the amount of growth due to migration-reclassification as a percentage of the total population of a size class (Table 5.11). Although the data for migration include growth due to reclassification, reclassification was a relatively minor contributor to urban growth in the USSR, and migration accounted for the majority of the growth because of migration-reclassification (Table 3.19). The reclassification share for the urban population of the RSFSR was probably similar to that of the USSR as a whole, because a sizable majority of the urban population of the USSR is located in the RSFSR. Furthermore, it is interesting to note that the percentage of the urban growth comprised by natural increase, on the one hand, and migration-reclassification, on the other hand, is apparently quite similar for the USSR and RSFSR. As mentioned before, between 1959 and 1970, roughly 40 percent of the urban growth of the USSR was due to natural increase, with the remaining 60 percent being due to migration-reclassification (Table 3.19). As Table 5.11 reveals, approximately the same corresponding percentages were characteristic of the RSFSR between 1959 and 1967. The reader should be aware also that the rates of migration-reclassification and natural increase in Table 5.11 are presented in relation to a base figure of 100 for the urban population of the RSFSR as a whole. From Table 5.11, it can be seen that the highest rates of migration-reclassification were experienced by cities in the 100,000-499,999 and 500,000-999,999 size classes. All other size classes had rates below the RSFSR urban average. The lowest rates were again experienced by the smallest (less than 50,000) and very largest (1 million and over) size classes.

Other data also tend to suggest that the rate of net migration for cities of 500,000-999,999 was moderately high and that for cities of 1 million and over was relatively low. Based upon 1967 birth, death, and natural increase data for the 33 cities of 500,000 and over in 1968, it is possible to compute the amount of net migration for the 500,000-999,999 and 1 million-and-over size classes by means of the residual or vital statistics method: namely, by computing the total absolute population growth of these cities between January 1967 and January 1968 and subtracting the absolute natural increase from this total growth. [25] Results revealed that net migration to cities of 500,000-999,999 represented 1.5 percent of the January 1968 population of such cities.

In comparison, the corresponding net migration rates were lower for cities of 1 million and over and urban centers (official definitions) of less than 500,000 people (1.1 and 1.4 percent, respectively).

It might be useful to summarize the preceding discussion in terms of growth rate variations by size class and underlying factors (crude birth, death, and natural increase rates and migration rates), which contributed to these variations. First, the most rapidly growing cities (50,000-74,999, 75,000-99,999, 100,000-249,999, and 250,000-499,999) generally had relatively high crude birth and natural increase rates, high migration rates, and moderate-to-low crude death rates. Most outstanding in this regard was the 100,000-499,999 size class. It had: (1) the highest crude birth rate (tied with 50,000-99,999) and natural increase rate and next-to-lowest crude death rate in the RSFSR in 1967, (2) the highest rate of migration-reclassification for the RSFSR between 1959 and 1967, and (3) the highest rate of net migration for the USSR according to the 1970 census. The rapidly growing 50,000-99,999 size class had: (1) the highest crude birth rate (tied with 100,000-499,999), a moderate crude death rate, and an above-average natural increase rate for the RSFSR in 1967 and (2) rates of migration-reclassification for the RSFSR between 1959 and 1967 and net migration in 1970 that, although surpassed by larger size classes, were not among the lowest for the size classes.

Average rates of growth were characteristic of cities of 500,000-999,999, although there were considerable variations in growth rates within this overall class. The 500,000-999,999 class in the RSFSR had a moderate crude birth rate, the lowest crude death rate, and a relatively high natural increase rate in 1959 and 1967, and a relatively high rate of migration-reclassification between 1959 and 1967. This class in the USSR as a whole also had a moderately high rate of net migration in 1967/68. Unfortunately, this specific size class is not presented in 1970 census tables dealing with migration but instead is included in the 500,000-and-over category.

The most slowly growing size classes (15,000-19,000, 20,000-24,999, 25,000-49,999, and 1,000,000 and over) generally had relatively high crude death rates and low crude natural increase and migration rates. In particular, the 1,000,000-and-over class had relatively high crude death rates and by far the lowest crude birth and natural increase rates in the RSFSR in 1959 and 1967. The sub-50,000 classes (except for urban-type settlements) had moderate-to-low crude birth and natural increase rates in 1967, and the 20,000-49,999 class experienced sharp crude birth and natural increase rate declines between 1959 and 1967. They also had relatively high crude death rates in 1959 and 1967, with the less than 10,000 class having the highest crude death rate of any size class in both years. These smallest and largest classes also experienced by far the lowest rates of migration-reclassification in the RSFSR between 1959 and 1967, and cities of 1 million or more in the USSR as a whole had a relatively low net migration rate in 1967/68. Finally, according to the 1970 census, urban centers of less than 20,000 and of 500,000 and over experienced the lowest net migration rates. Cities of 500,000 and over had the lowest in-migration rates and urban centers of less than 50,000 had the highest out-migration rates.

Thus, although information on fertility, mortality, natural increase, and migration is somewhat fragmentary, it appears that the relatively slow growth of the smallest and largest cities, as compared with intermediate-size cities, was due in part to the relatively high rates of mortality and relatively low rates of fertility, natural increase, and net in-migration of the smallest and largest cities. It is interesting that the smallest and largest cities were demographically quite similar in many respects, a point also mentioned by Khorev.[26] The lower fertility and natural increase and higher mortality of such towns reflect their relatively "old" age structure.

Another aspect of migration variations by urban size class concerns the patterns of migration between cities of different sizes. A specific question is whether there has been a typical "stepping-stone" migration from smaller cities to larger cities. Data from the 1970 census tend to support the existence of a small-city-to-large-city migration in the USSR. Data from the 1970 census show that the net in-migration rate for large cities was somewhat higher than that for smaller ones (Table 5.10).

The information in Table 5.10, although somewhat illuminating, is not completely satisfactory, because it includes migration to and from rural areas. Therefore, we have deleted rural migration from the investigation to determine the direction of migration between urban centers of various sizes. Results indicate that there is a more pronounced movement from smaller cities to larger ones than vice versa. In particular, 1,450,759 people moved from urban centers of less than 100,000 to centers of 100,000 and over, while only 1,150,815 people moved from centers of 100,000 and over to those of less than 100,000. Hence, the net migration between large and small cities was +299,944 for large cities and, of course, -299,944 for small ones. In short, the number of people moving from small to large cities exceeded the number of people moving from large to small cities by nearly 300,000.

This net migration shift from smaller to larger cities is reflected also on the basis of more specific size classes. Table 5.12 shows the amount of net migration between the five size classes, for which migration data are presented in the 1970 census. For example, the figure of 82,915 indicates that the number of people moving from centers of less than 20,000 to centers of 500,000 and over exceeded the number of people moving from centers of 500,000 and over to those of less than 20,000 by 82,915. From this table it is apparent that each size class has net out-migration with respect to every size class larger than itself, and net in-migration with respect to every size class smaller than itself. In particular, the 500,000-and-over class had net in-migration with respect to all other size classes, which were, of course, all smaller size classes; the 100,000-499,999 had net in-migration with all smaller size classes but net out-migration with the 500,000-and-over class; and so forth down to the less than 20,000 class, which had net out-migration with respect to all other size classes, which were all larger size classes.

It is also interesting to note that larger cities depended more upon migration for their growth than did smaller cities. In the RSFSR between 1959 and 1967, generally speaking, the larger the size class, the greater was the percentage of growth that could be attributed to migration-reclassification and the lower was the percentage comprised by natural increase (Table 5.11).

TABLE 5.12

Net Migration between Urban Size Classes: 1970

To:	From:				
	Less than 20,000	20,000–49,999	50,000–99,999	100,000–499,999	500,000 and over
Less than 20,000	0	-38,706	-29,527	-99,187	-82,915
20,000–49,999	38,706	0	-5,383	-47,346	-33,211
50,000–99,999	29,527	5,383	0	-20,399	-16,886
100,000–499,999	99,187	47,346	20,399	0	-4,980
500,000 and over	82,915	33,211	16,886	4,980	0

Source: 1970 Soviet census (see Chapter 1, n. 104).

Crude birth, death, and natural increase rate variations and migration patterns are not unrelated. For example, because migration is age-selective, low in-migration and net migration, characteristic of the smallest and largest cities, foster lower crude birth rates, higher crude death rates, and consequently lower crude natural increase rates. In addition, the high rate of out-migration from small cities also contributes to lower crude birth rates, because the substantial out-migration of young adults leads to lower fertility, higher mortality, and lower natural increase. [27]

Fertility, mortality, natural increase, and migration differences by size classes were intertwined somewhat with differences in the age-sex structure of towns of various sizes. [28] The relatively high net in-migration to the rapidly growing cities of 50,000-499,999 contributed to the fairly high share of the population being comprised of persons in the able-bodied ages—(males 16 to 59, females 16 to 54) and a relatively low share of young people (despite a comparatively high birth rate) and old people, especially females. The low percentage of old people, in turn, promoted a relatively low crude death rate, a high crude birth rate, and a relatively high percentage of males and persons of able-bodied years comprising the population of such cities. On the other hand, the relatively low net in-migration of the slowly growing, smallest and largest cities led to comparatively high percentages of old people and, accordingly, females in the populations of both size classes. The "old" age structure, in turn, led to very low crude birth and natural increase rates in the largest cities and sharply declining crude birth and natural increase rates in the smallest ones, as well as relatively high crude death rates in both types of cities. A more detailed discussion of these topics will be undertaken in the third volume of this series.

Policy Implications

As we discussed in the introduction of this book, a major Soviet policy regarding the size of cities has been to limit the growth of large cities and promote the growth of smaller ones. Generally speaking, there are a number of indications that this policy has not been very successful, although it should be kept in mind that without such a policy large cities might have proliferated even more than they have. Many points we have mentioned previously support this contention. First, the total and urban populations have become increasingly concentrated in large cities, indicating that the population residing in such cities has been growing more rapidly than the population residing in small urban centers. Second, there also has been a great explosion of the number of large cities and, more recently, of millionaire cities in the USSR. In fact, one can assume that if there had not been the millions of lives lost in various periods of turmoil, the number of and population residing in large cities in the USSR would be even greater than it is today. Third, based upon 1959 size classes, our investigation revealed that large cities grew as rapidly as small cities between 1959 and 1970.

However, because the policy to limit the growth of large cities and promote the growth of small cities is fairly recent, it is possible that its full effect may not have been realized as early as 1970. As D. G. Khodzhayev notes, referring to plans to emphasize industrial investment in small- and medium-sized towns in the 1967-70 period, "no noticeable turning point in plant location can be expected before 1970 since most of the projects under construction during this period were designed before the new emphasis on industrialization of small cities. But such a turning point may be reached about 1970 since most of the present designs are for plants in small and medium-size cities."[29]

Therefore, it seems highly appropriate to investigate the growth of urban centers after 1970 in a manner similar to that of Table 5.5 for the 1959-70 period. This will be undertaken from two perspectives: growth by size class as of 1959 and growth by size class as of 1970. At the time this research was being conducted, the most plentiful post-1970 urban population data were the previously mentioned data for official "cities" of 15,000 or more in 1974. The 1974 data, unfortunately, do not include urban-type settlements with 15,000 or more people in 1974, but this is not a major problem, because the vast majority of the urban population resides in official "cities."

Nevertheless, the exclusion of urban-type settlements from these 1974 data did entail some problems. In particular we wanted to trace the subsequent growth of all urban centers with a population of 15,000 or more in 1959 and of all urban centers with a population of 15,000 or more in 1970, but this was impossible, because most urban-type settlements of 15,000 or more in 1959 or in 1970 were still urban-type settlements in 1974. Thus, their population change to 1974 could not be ascertained and, consequently, we had to exclude such settlements from the post-1970 investigation. However, a few urban-type settlements in 1959 or in 1970 are included in the investigation, because by 1974 their status had been changed to "city" and, thus, they are included in the list of cities of 15,000 or more in 1974.

Another problem concerned changes in city boundaries between 1959 and 1970 on the one hand and 1974 on the other. Although we did not make adjustments for minor changes, we did adjust for major changes (see notes for Tables 5.13 and 5.14).

An additional problem concerned the fate of urban centers of 15,000 or more in one year that apparently declined to below 15,000 in population at a later date. This problem was discussed before in association with Table 5.5. In 1959, there were 28 centers of 15,000 or more that apparently declined to less than 15,000 in 1970. As with Table 5.5, we have assumed operationally their populations to be 14,000 each in 1970. In addition, we have assumed the population of 26 of these 28 urban centers to have been 13,500 each in 1974. For the remaining 2 of the 28 cities (Novyy Bug and Krasnovishersk) this 1974 assumption was unnecessary, because by 1974 their populations had rebounded to 15,000 or more and, thus, they are listed in the 1974 data. For cities as of 1970, this type of problem was not as great, because only one city of 15,000 and over in 1970 (Menzelinsk) apparently declined to less than 15,000 by 1974. Its 1974 population is operationally assumed to have been 14,500.

In summary, we have computed growth rates to 1974 for the population of urban size classes of 1959 and 1970. In general, we have included only those urban centers of either 1959 or 1970 for which 1974 population data were available or could be reasonably estimated, although it should be kept in mind that the included urban centers contained the overwhelming majority of the urban population. To the best of our knowledge, the data we will present have not been presented elsewhere, most probably because the computations for the hundreds of urban centers below 100,000 in population is so time-consuming. This situation is similar to that involving the data previously discussed in Table 5.5. The results of this post-1970 investigation are presented in Tables 5.13 and 5.14. The 1959 and 1970 populations have been rounded to the nearest thousands, because the available 1974 populations are rounded in this manner.

We will first discuss post-1970 trends for size classes of 1959 (Table 5.13). For the most part, the post-1970 trends were similar to those of the 1959-70 period. In particular, large and small cities grew at almost identical rates between 1970 and 1974, as they did between 1959 and 1970. In addition, growth rates between 1970 and 1974 were highest among intermediate-size cities, especially 50,000-249,999, and were generally lowest among the smallest and largest cities, patterns that were once again similar to those of the 1959-70 period.

Although Table 5.13 indicates that the growth rate of the 15,000-19,999 size class, the smallest of the size classes, was actually slightly above the national average between 1970 and 1974, this pattern was somewhat misleading. The relatively rapid rate of growth of this class between 1970 and 1974 was to a great extent due to its inclusion of one of the most rapidly growing cities of the USSR, Naberezhnyye Chelny. The population of this city was roughly 16,000 and 38,000 in 1959 and 1970, respectively, but then skyrocketed to 163,000 in 1974, and, subsequently, to 253,000 in 1977. In fact, between 1970 and 1974, the absolute increase of this city (125,000) accounted for over one-fourth (25.7 percent) of the absolute increase (486,000) of the increase of the 15,000-19,999 size class as of 1959, even though it was only 1 of 216 urban centers in this class. If Naberezhnyye Chelny is excluded from the 15,000-19,999 size class as of 1959, the growth rate of this class would again be considerably below the national average (instead of 10.3 percent, only 7.7 percent, as compared with an average of 9.8 percent).

Another perspective is to investigate growth rates by size class of 1970 (Table 5.14). Whereas large and small cities, based on 1959 size classes, grew at almost identical rates during the 1959-70, 1970-74, and 1959-74 periods, large cities grew at a somewhat higher rate than small cities between 1970 and 1974, based on 1970 size classes (Tables 5.13 and 5.14), although, as before, the lowest rates generally were experienced by the very largest and smallest towns. In addition, between 1970 and 1974, the most rapid rates of growth were experienced by cities in the size range of 100,000-499,999, while all size classes below 100,000 in population grew more slowly than the national average. Therefore, the 50,000-99,999 size class, which was one of the most rapidly growing classes based on 1959 size classes, actually grew slower than the national average between 1970 and 1974 based on 1970 size classes. This, of course, is partly due to the fact that many of the

TABLE 5.13

Rate of Population Change by Urban Size Class of 1959: 1959-74

Size Class in 1959	Number of Urban Centers	Population (thousands)			Percentage Increase		
		1959	1970	1974	1959-70	1970-74	1959-74
15,000-19,999[a,b,c]	216	3,751	4,700	5,186	25.3	10.3	38.3
20,000-24,999[c,d]	132	2,941	3,617	3,851	23.0	6.5	30.9
25,000-49,999[c,e]	314	10,960	14,263	15,411	30.1	8.0	40.6
50,000-74,999[f]	110	6,706	9,477	10,643[g]	41.3	12.3	58.7
75,000-99,999	54	4,796	6,742	7,560	40.6	12.1	57.6
100,000-249,999[h]	89	13,498	18,945	21,097	40.4	11.4	56.3
250,000-499,999[i]	34	11,398	15,467	16,906	35.7	9.3	48.3
500,000-749,999	14	8,709	11,720	12,887	34.6	10.0	48.0
750,000-999,999	7	6,258	8,274	9,006	32.2	8.8	43.9
1,000,000 and over[j]	3	10,491	12,670	13,658	20.8	7.8	30.2
15,000-99,999	826	29,154	38,799	42,651	33.1	9.9	46.3

100,000 and over	147	50,354	67,076	73,554	33.2	9.7	46.1
USSR total	973	79,508	105,875	116,205	33.2	9.8	46.2

aExcludes Krasnoye Selo, Zhovtevnoye, and Dimitrov (old boundaries), which were individual urban centers in 1959 with a population of 15,000–19,999. By 1974 Krasnoye Selo had been annexed to Leningrad and Zhovtevnoye to Nikolayev, while Dimitrov and Novoekonomicheskoye were combined into one larger city called Dimitrov.

bIncludes 25 towns with a population of 15,000–19,999 in 1959, according to the 1959 census, which were not listed in the 1970 census and apparently not annexed to some other town and are thus assumed to have declined to less than 15,000 in 1970. It is operationally assumed that their 1970 population was 14,000 each, or 350,000 for the 25 towns. By 1974, two towns had "rebounded" to 15,000 or more in population (Novvy Bug, 17,000, and Krasnovishersk, 16,000). It was operationally assumed that the 1974 population of each of the 23 other towns was 13,500, or 310,500 for the 23 towns.

cExcludes all appropriate urban centers of 15,000 and over in 1959, according to the 1970 census, that were not cities with 15,000 or more people in 1974.

dIncludes three towns similar to those in note b, but with a population of 20,000–24,999 in 1959. Accordingly, the combined population of such towns is operationally assumed to be 42,000 in 1970 and 40,500 in 1974.

eExcludes Novoekonomicheskoye, which had a population of 25,000–49,999 in 1959 but which by 1974 was combined with Dimitrov.

fIncludes the "new" larger city of Dimitrov, which was formed by 1974 by combining the "old" Dimitrov with Novoekonomicheskoye. The 1959 and 1970 populations of these two towns totaled between 50,000 and 74,999, and thus the "new" city of Dimitrov is included in this size class.

gIncludes the combination of Krasnodon (46,000 in 1974) and Sukhodol'sk (26,000 in 1974), which consisted of one city (Krasnodon) of 50,000–74,999 in 1959 and 1970.

hExcludes Nikolayev, which had a population of 100,000–249,999 in 1959 (old boundaries), for reasons discussed in note i.

iIncludes Nikolayev, which had a population of 100,000–249,999 (old boundaries) but had annexed Zhovtevnoye by 1974. The combined population of Nikolayev and Zhovtevnoye in 1959 and 1970 was between 250,000 and 499,999.

jLeningrad includes Krasnoye Selo, which it had annexed by 1974.

Sources: 1959 and 1970 Soviet censuses and 1974 estimates (see Chapter 1, nn. 104 and 113).

307

TABLE 5.14

Rate of Population Change by Urban Size Class of 1970:   1970-74

Size Class in 1970	Number of Urban Centers	Population (thousands) 1970	1974	Percentage Increase
15,000-19,999[a]	234	4,050	4,406[b]	8.8
20,000-24,999[a,c]	173	3,816	4,069	6.6
25,000-49,999[a,d]	378	13,340	14,605	9.5
50,000-74,999[e]	132	8,062	8,771[f]	8.8
75,000-99,999	55	4,823	5,271	9.3
100,000-249,999	141	21,639	24,338	12.5
250,000-499,999[g]	47	16,632	18,533	11.4
500,000-749,999	9	5,595	6,117	9.3
750,000-999,999	14	11,755	12,981	10.4
1,000,000 and over[h]	10	20,943	22,664	8.2
15,000-99,999	972	34,091	37,122	8.9
100,000 and over	221	76,564	84,633	10.5
USSR total	1,193	110,655	121,755	10.0

[a]Excludes all appropriate urban centers of 15,000 and over in 1970 that were not cities with 15,000 or more people in 1974.
[b]Includes Menzelinsk, a city with a population of 15,000-19,999 in 1970 but with no listed 1974 population, whose 1974 population is thus operationally assumed to be 14,500.
[c]Excludes Dimitrov (old boundaries), which had a population of 20,000-24,999 in 1970. By 1974, Dimitrov and Novoekonomicheskoye had been combined into one larger city called Dimitrov.
[d]Excludes Krasnoye Selo, Zhovtevnoye, and Novoekonomicheskoye, all which were individual urban centers in 1970 with a population of 25,000-49,999. By 1974 Krasnoye Selo was annexed to Leningrad and Zhovtevnoye to Nikolayev, while Novoekonomicheskoye and Dimitrov were combined into one larger city called Dimitrov.
[e]Includes the "new" larger city of Dimitrov, which was formed by 1974 by combining the "old" Dimitrov with Novoekonomicheskoye. The 1970 population of these two towns totaled between 50,000 and 74,999, and thus the "new" city of Dimitrov is included in this size class.
[f]Includes the combination of Krasnodon (46,000 in 1974) and Sukhodol'sk (26,000 in 1974), which consisted of one city (Krasnodon) of 50,000-74,999 in 1970.
[g]Nikolayev includes Zhovtevnoye, which it annexed by 1974.
[h]Leningrad includes Krasnoye Selo, which it annexed by 1974.

Sources: 1970 Soviet census and 1974 estimates (see Chapter 1, nn. 104 and 113).

rapidly growing towns of the 50,000-99,999 size class in 1959 were cities of over 100,000 in population in 1970. Hence, the continuing rapid growth of such smaller towns in 1959 was now credited to the 100,000-and-over class.

In conclusion, post-1970 data tend to indicate the continuation of 1959-70 patterns of growth by urban size classes. Large cities continued to grow at least as rapidly as smaller cities, thus suggesting that the policy to limit the growth of large cities and promote that of smaller cities has not been too successful.

In order to examine further the effectiveness of the policies concerning city sizes, we will refer to the list of large cities in which industrial investment was to be either "prohibited" or "limited" according to a decree of the Soviet government in 1956, a list we provided in the introduction of this volume. In particular, one way to test the degree of success or implementation of this policy is to assess the subsequent rates of population growth of cities on this list. We have calculated growth rates for these cities for the periods of 1959-70, 1970-77, and 1959-77 (Table 5.15). Data for cities of 50,000 or more people in 1977 were the most recently available data at the time this research was being conducted.

The main conclusion emerging from this investigation is that the cities subject to restrictions on their growth have essentially grown about as rapidly as all urban centers of the USSR. In particular, between 1959 and 1970, the 47 prohibited cities grew at a rate (2.4 percent per year) only slightly below that for all centers of 15,000 and over in 1959 (2.6 percent per year or 33.0 percent for the entire 11-year period according to Table 5.5). Moreover, the 23 limited cities grew at a rate (3.3 percent per year) in excess of all centers of 15,000 and over in 1959. Altogether, the 70 prohibited or limited cities grew at a combined rate (2.6 percent per year) that was equal to that of all centers of 15,000 and over in 1959. In addition, six cities added to the limited list in unspecified recent years grew even more rapidly (4.4 percent per year between 1959 and 1970). In short, the policy to limit the growth of these prohibited or limited large cities apparently has not been too successful.

As mentioned earlier, the 1956 decree also included "cities of Moscow Oblast" in the prohibited cities category. However, they have not been included in Table 5.15, because it is not clear which cities actually constitute the "cities of Moscow Oblast" according to the 1956 decree and because most of the cities of the oblast have not had a population of 100,000 or more.

Although the 70 prohibited and limited cities of 1956 did not grow faster than the urban population of the USSR based on either the 15,000-and-over or official urban definitions, it should be remembered that the total urban population does not consist of the same number of cities in both years. Hence, its growth rate is somewhat higher, simply because new settlements are included in the category of all urban centers by 1970. For example, Table 5.15 indicates that between 1959 and 1970 the urban population (15,000-and-over definition) grew slightly faster than the population of centers of 15,000 and over in 1959, which includes only the same cities in both 1959 and 1970 (3.1 percent per year versus 2.6 percent per year). Even with this qualification, the limited cities still grew faster than the entire urban population, regardless

TABLE 5.15

Rate of Population Change by Group of Large Cities
Designated for Prohibited or Limited Industrial Investment:
1959-77

Group of Cities	Number of Cities	Average Annual Percentage Change of Population		
		1959-70	1970-77[a]	1959-77[a]
Prohibited cities, 1956	47[b]	2.4	2.1	2.3
Limited cities, 1956	23[c]	3.3	2.2	2.8
Limited cities, recent years	6	4.4	4.6	4.5
Limited cities, 1956 and recent years	29[c]	3.4	2.7	3.1
Prohibited and limited cities, 1956	70[c]	2.6	2.1	2.4
Urban centers of 15,000 or more people in 1959	1,012	2.6	—	—
Urban population (15,000 and over definition)	—	3.1	—	—
Urban population (official urban definitions)	—	2.8	2.2	2.6

[a]Since 1977 data are available only for populations
rounded to the nearest thousand people, the more exact
1959 and 1970 populations also have been rounded to the
nearest thousand people in order to compute these rates.

[b]Although the Khorev list says 48 cities, he specifically lists only 47.

[c]Includes three "limited" cities in which certain
types of industries were not subject to limitations (Omsk,
Novokuznetsk, Astrakhan').

Sources: 1959 and 1970 Soviet censuses and 1977 estimates (see Chapter 1, nn. 104 and 113). The list of
cities comes from B. S. Khorev, Problemy Gorodov, 2d ed.
(Moscow: Izdatel'stvo "Mysl'," 1975), p. 86.

of the urban definition used, between 1959 and 1970. The prohibited cities grew at a rate not significantly below that of the entire urban population, and the combined list of 70 prohibited and limited cities grew at a rate only slightly below that of the entire urban population, particularly the urban population based on the official definitions of urban (2.6 percent per year versus 2.8 percent per year).

In order to trace the recent growth of the prohibited and limited cities, we have calculated their growth rates between 1970 and 1977 and between 1959 and 1977. Because 1977 data are available only for cities with 50,000 or more people in 1977, it is not possible to make comparisons with the growth of all urban centers with 15,000 or more people during these periods. Nonetheless, fairly meaningful comparisons can be made with the growth of the entire urban population based on the official definitions of urban, because, as mentioned in Chapter 3, an estimate is provided of the total urban population based on these definitions in 1977. As Table 5.15 reveals, the patterns discussed for the 1959-70 period generally occurred in the 1970-77 and 1959-77 periods. Between 1970 and 1977, the limited cities grew at the same rate as the entire urban population, and if the six very rapidly growing limited cities of recent years are included, the limited group grew faster than the entire urban population. The prohibited group alone and the prohibited and limited groups combined grew at almost the same rates as the entire urban population. Thus, the growth rates of the restricted cities were virtually the same as the rate of the urban population as a whole. The growth rates of the prohibited and limited cities did slow in the 1970-77 period as compared with the 1959-70 period, but the growth rate of the entire urban population also slowed.

Between 1959 and 1977, the same general patterns existed. The limited cities grew slightly faster than the urban population as a whole, and even faster if the six recent limited cities are included. The prohibited group and the combined prohibited and limited groups grew at almost the same rate as the entire urban population.

It is interesting to investigate some of the prohibited and limited cities on an individual city basis. First, every one of these cities grew in population in each of the periods examined, and none came close to losing population between 1959 and 1977. The ones that grew the slowest, Nizhniy Tagil and Makeyevka, still managed to have populations that increased by nearly one-fifth. Even the populations of Moscow and Leningrad increased by roughly one-third between 1959 and 1977. In fact, these restricted cities actually included some very rapidly growing towns, with two, Tol'yatti (recently limited) and Sumgait (prohibited) being "rapidly growing towns," as defined earlier, in that their populations at least doubled between 1959 and 1970. Also included in the prohibited list was Minsk, which has been perhaps the most rapidly growing very large city in the USSR in recent years. In fact, Minsk, along with nine other prohibited or limited cities, more than doubled in population between 1959 and 1977. As mentioned before, these restricted cities consisted mainly of cities with 200,000 or more people in 1959. Of the 72 cities with 200,000 or more people in 1959, only four (Tbilisi, Gorlovka, Kaliningrad, and Prokop'yevsk) were not included on the prohibited or limited lists. Paradoxically, however, these four cities, which apparently were not subject to growth restrictions, actually grew more slowly than those subject to such restrictions. The four cities combined grew at average annual rates of 1.7 percent in the 1959-70 period and 1.6 percent in the 1970-77 and 1959-77 periods. One of the four, Prokop'yevsk, declined in population in each of the periods and was the only city in the USSR with more than 200,000 people in 1959 to experience a decline.

Given the fact that the growth rate of the entire urban population was inflated relatively in comparison to growth rates of the various groups of restricted cities, which consisted of a constant number of cities, it seems reasonable to conclude that during the 1959-70, 1970-77, and 1959-77 periods the populations of the prohibited and limited groups increased at least as rapidly, and in some instances more rapidly, than those of urban centers that were not on the restricted list. Thus, it appears that the policy of sharply limiting the growth of these essentially large cities has not been achieved, although they probably would have grown even faster if there had been no policy in this regard.

Another indication that the policy to limit the growth of large cities has not been very successful is that the projected maximum size limits for some of the very largest cities have been surpassed. According to Robert J. Osborn, it was decreed in 1935 that Moscow's population was not to exceed 5 million.[30] Another source indicates that, more specifically, according to the 1935 plan, the population of Moscow was to be 5 million in 1960.[31] A population of 5 million was reached in 1959, and Moscow subsequently annexed areas, which increased its 1959 population to roughly 6 million. By 1970 a population of 7 million had been attained. In 1971 the second general plan for Moscow was approved, and it established a projected population limit for Moscow of 7.5 million by the 1990s.[32] However, by 1977, the population of Moscow already had exceeded that figure (7.8 million). In recent years the population of Moscow has increased consistently by roughly 100,000 people every year (Table 5.16). Osborn and Perevedentsev also provide a number of examples of cities, whose population at a particular date has exceeded a previously designated population target for that date.[33] For example, after World War II, a target of 850,000 in 1970 was set for Novosibirsk, but by 1959 the population already exceeded this limit, as Novosibirsk's population reached 886,000, and by 1970 the population of the city exceeded 1 million (1,160,963).

Another perspective on the lack of success of policies aimed at limiting the growth of large cities involves the idea of "optimum city size." As mentioned in Chapter 1, the Soviets have often regarded cities with a population of roughly 50,000-250,000 as being optimum in size. However, reference again to Tables 5.1-5.3 shows that, instead of stopping cities from growing beyond the optimal limit of 250,000, the opposite has occurred. The number of cities in the USSR with a population larger than this optimum has ballooned from 12 or less, in 1897 and 1926, to 33 in 1939, 57 in 1959, and 81 in 1970; by 1977 the number of cities in the USSR with 250,000 or more people had increased to 105. Thus, by the late 1970s, the number of cities of 250,000 or more had nearly doubled since 1959 and more than tripled since 1939. The

TABLE 5.16

Annual Population of Moscow: 1970-77
(thousands)

Year	Population	Absolute Increase in Population from Previous Year
1970	7,077*	—
1971	7,188	111
1972	7,299	111
1973	7,410	111
1974	7,528	118
1975	7,632	104
1976	7,734	102
1977	7,819	85

*This figure is slightly larger than the population of Moscow (7,061,008), as reported in the 1970 census.

Sources: The 1970-76 populations come from RSFSR, Tsentral'noye Statisticheskoye Upravleniye pri Sovete Ministrov RSFSR, RSFSR v Tsifrakh v 1975 Godu (Moscow: "Statistika," 1976), p. 7. The 1977 population comes from the 1977 estimates (see Chapter 1, n. 113).

population residing in such cities has grown more rapidly than the total and urban populations, and, consequently, the share of the total and urban populations residing in these cities has increased in every intercensal period (Tables 5.1 and 5.2). In 1970 nearly one-fourth of the total population and nearly one-half of the urban population of the USSR resided in cities of 250,000 or more (Table 5.1).

Another goal mentioned earlier was the limitation of cities in the 100,000-250,000 range to populations of no more than 200,000 or 250,000, according to planning guidelines published in 1958. Investigation reveals that this aspect of limiting the growth of large cities also has not met with much success. In 1959 there were 89 cities with a population of 100,000-249,999 according to the 1959 census (Table 5.3). By 1977 the vast majority had populations in excess of 200,000 or 250,000. Virtually one-half (45 or 50.6 percent) of these cities, in fact, had a population of more than 250,000 in 1977. Thus, by 1977, only about one-half of the cities (44 or 49.4 percent) had a population conforming to the 1958 guidelines, that is, below either 200,000 or 250,000, and a good share (18 of 44) of these exceeded 200,000 in population. The rapid growth of cities in the 100,000-250,000 size class range is also evident from Table 5.5, which shows, as discussed before, that the 100,000-249,999 size class experienced one of the most rapid rates of growth between 1959 and 1970 of any of the 1959 size classes.

Reasons for the Continued Rapid Growth of Large Cities

Why have large cities continued to grow rapidly in the face of governmental policies aimed at limiting their growth? First and foremost, perhaps, is the fact that large cities have received a disproportionately high share of the total industrial investment in the USSR. The allocation of industrial funds is quite crucial for city growth in the USSR, because Soviet cities continue to be rather highly manufacturing-oriented, especially as compared with their counterparts in the United States or Japan, for example.[34] A number of studies have discussed in considerable detail the concentration of Soviet industry in large cities and the reasons for such a continued concentration.[35] In general, industry in the USSR tends to be attracted to large cities due to their characteristic high productivity, skilled labor, high degree of transportation accessibility, economies of scale, benefits of agglomeration, good social infrastructure, and large market, as well as their desire to increase production as quickly as possible. The attraction of industry to large cities elsewhere in the world is, of course, also related to these forces of industrial inertia. On the other hand, the comparative absence of these characteristics in smaller towns tends to impede industrial investment in such places.[36]

It even appears that one of the supposed attractive characteristics of small towns for industry now has been reduced greatly. As touched upon in the introduction, it has been somewhat implicit that increased investment in small- and medium-size towns is necessary to help absorb the excess labor in such towns, particularly of female labor.[37] A major basis for the contention of the existence of a labor surplus in smaller cities is provided by age, sex, and occupation patterns for cities of various size classes. Data for 1959 have indicated that the smaller the city, the higher is the percentage of the able-bodied population comprised of those not occupied in social production, although for all size classes most of those not so occupied are females (Table 5.17). In short, smaller cities have been regarded as having unused labor reserves, because a relatively high percentage of their able-bodied population has not been occupied in the social economy. Those not occupied in the social economy include housewives, people working on private plots, and unemployed persons, including both persons seeking work and persons not seeking work. According to Khorev, by the late 1960s, so many of these people had been attracted into social production that this reserve of labor in cities had already "dried up," and, in fact, many small- and medium-size cities, like large cities, now had a deficit of laborers.[38] In a similar vein, in the mid-1970s O. P. Litovka concluded that "the long-standing existing opinion about the availability of a significant number of free labor resources in small cities at the present time does not correspond to reality."[39]

Industrial concentration in large cities of the USSR also means, to a great extent, industrial concentration in major administrative centers.

TABLE 5.17

Degree of Utilization of Labor Resources in Social Production by Urban Size Class: 1959

| Size Class | Percent of Able-Bodied Population Comprised of Those Not Occupied in Social Production* | | | | |
	Total	Females	Females with Children Younger than 14	Females without Children	Males
Less than 20,000	19.8	18.8	9.8	9.0	1.0
20,000-99,999	17.6	16.7	9.9	6.8	0.9
100,000-999,999	14.1	13.4	8.1	5.3	0.7
1,000,000 and over	8.5	8.2	4.7	3.5	0.3
USSR urban total	15.8	15.0	8.6	6.4	0.8

*The able-bodied population consists of males, 16 to 59, and females, 16 to 54.

Source: B. S. Khorev, ed., Malyy Gorod (Moscow: Izdatel'stvo Moskovskogo Univer-siteta, 1972), p. 94.

William Taubman has noted, for instance, that "half the industrial output of the RSFSR is produced in seventy-one province capitals."[40] As we have mentioned previously, nearly all of the largest cities of the USSR are both major administrative centers and industrial centers. Many large cities, therefore, not only have a significant industrial base but added to this are administrative functions, which also contribute to the base and, consequently, to the size and importance of these cities. In almost every SSR, ASSR, oblast, or kray, the largest city is also the "capital" of that political unit. A different type of situation, of course, exists in the United States, where a great proportion of the largest cities of the country are not capitals; for example, New York City is neither the capital of the United States nor of New York State.

Computations undertaken by Chauncy Harris also can be used to summarize and support some of the advantages of large cities that have been noted already.[41] Based on the more than 1,000 urban centers in 1959 and 30 variables, he conducted a principal components analysis, which is highly similar to a factor analysis. The leading component or factor to emerge from the analysis in terms of percent of matrix variance explained was a "Size Factor." Among the most highly loaded variables were city size, manufacturing output, number of branches of manufacturing, number of administrative functions, and measures of transportation accessibility. This further demonstrates the industrial, administrative, and transportational advantages of larger cities in comparison to smaller ones.

The comparative attractiveness of larger cities is reflected also in migration patterns. We have indicated previously that there apparently has been a step migration from smaller to larger cities in the USSR and that, except for the very largest cities such as Moscow and Leningrad, the net migration rates for larger cities have been greater than those for smaller cities. Reasons for the relatively greater migration attractiveness of large cities are numerous. First, it appears that job opportunities are greater in large cities than in small ones; labor deficits exist in large cities, and although deficits also occur in small cities, it appears that those who have a choice will opt for the large city for a number of additional reasons. As Osborn notes:

> Among those migrants who are able to choose between big-city jobs and jobs elsewhere, doubtless the greatest single lure offered by the big cities is choice and variety. Among the types of choice that large cities offer, the most important would be likely to be job choices and advancement possibilities within one's specialty, jobs suitable for wives, choices involving further education and training and choices of human association.[42]

People seeking educational opportunities tend to be attracted especially to large cities, because there is a high concentration of higher educational institutions or universities (vuzy) in such cities. Khorev again provides considerable data on this subject for the late 1960s.[43]

Also attracting people to large cities is their advantageous position with regard to the availability of consumer goods and services. Osborn notes that "consumers' goods are decidedly more plentiful in the larger cities than else-where."[44] In addition, Taubman indicates that "small and medium-sized cities provide consumer services at a per capita volume as low as one-twelfth that of large cities."[45]

A discussion of the repellent or "push" factors stimulating out-migration from smaller towns to larger ones to a great extent, therefore, involves the opposing conditions of large and small cities. To reiterate, smaller cities have lesser job opportunities, poorer educational facilities, and less-available consumer goods and services, differences that are also applicable to an understanding of rural-to-urban migration. Small towns also suffer from other problems, such as budgetary problems, poor transportation, an "old" age structure, and so forth.[46] Although small cities have a number of dis-advantages, one should not lose sight of the fact that large cities also have a number of problems. These include pollution, labor shortages, low fertility, traffic congestion, and housing shortages.[47]

The presence of advantages and disadvantages in both large and small towns is reflected in the existence of a debate in the USSR concerning the relative merits of large and small cities. As we have seen, the Party and the government, in terms of policy statements, tend to be antilarge town and pro-small town. A number of prominent urban scholars also adhere to this view, the prime example, perhaps, being Khorev.[48] On the other hand, many de-cision makers in industrial ministries and Perevedentsev are examples of those tending to be more prolarge city.[49] Generally speaking, the prosmall city arguments seem to center around the diseconomies of large cities, the retardedness of small towns, the idea of a unified system of settlement, and the ideologically inspired desire to eliminate the differences between town and country, while the prolarge city arguments seem to be based on the eco-nomic advantages of large cities.[50]

Given the existing differences of opinion and the resulting ambiguities, it is little wonder that the policy of limiting the growth of large cities and promoting the growth of small cities has not met with much success. This does not mean, however, that the policy has had no effect whatsoever. In the absence of any such policy it is possible that large cities might have grown even more rapidly and that small cities would have been even more neglected and slower growing. As Osborn comments, "one wonders whether Moscow today would be the same size as London or New York had there been no cen-tral control over the location of new industries."[51] In addition, we have noted a number of examples of small- or medium-size cities that have grown rapidly as a result of recent increased industrial investment (for example, Novgorod, Balakovo, Saransk, and Belgorod), although, ironically, they have been transformed now into rapidly growing large cities. It is, perhaps, still too early to assess the full impact of the policy. However, as we have dem-onstrated, the policy to date has not been very successful.

Regional Variations

Unlike previous topics, little attention will be given here to a discus-sion of regional aspects of city sizes for a number of underlying reasons.

First, regional variations and changes therein in the percentage of the total population residing in large cities and small cities (that is, "large-city urbanization" and "small-city urbanization") were correlated highly with—and, thus, greatly similar to—variations in the percentage of the total population residing in all urban centers (that is, "total urbanization"). In particular, based on the 19 economic regions, between 1897 and 1959 the rank correlation coefficient between the percentage point change in large-city urbanization and total urbanization was 0.956, while that between the change in small-city urbanization and total urbanization was 0.809. Between 1959 and 1970, corresponding correlations were 0.619 and 0.503. Also, in 1970 the rank correlation coefficient between large-city urbanization and total urbanization was 0.956, while that between small-city urbanization and total urbanization was 0.721. Correlations between the growth rates of large cities and small cities, on the one hand, and the total urban population, on the other, were also quite high as based on the regional redistribution of each characteristic: for 1897-1959, 0.841 and 0.793; and for 1959-70, 0.765 and 0.576.

Regional variations in the percentage of the urban population residing in large cities, and, obversely, in small cities, and changes therein were also either not that great or not that difficult to explain. In 1970, there was very little regional variation in the percentage of the urban population residing in large cities. The range was only 21.3 percentage points, from 78.5 percent for West Siberia to 57.2 percent for the North Caucasus. In comparison, the range in regional levels of urbanization in 1970 was nearly twice as great (40.9 percentage points from 63.8 to 22.9 percent) (Table 4.2).

On the other hand, it is true that there were great regional variations in the percentage point change in the percentage of the urban population residing in large and small cities. However, these variations can be explained primarily by the size-class structure of the earliest census years. Between 1897 and 1970 regions having either a relatively low increase in the percentage of their urban population residing in urban centers (the Center, West, Moldavia, and Transcaucasus) or even having a decrease (the Northwest) also had the highest percentages in 1897 of the urban population residing in large urban centers (at least 50 percent or more). Therefore, the lack of a great increase in these regions was due mainly to the fact that the share of the urban population in large cities was so high in the first place that it could not increase greatly, there being, of course, a limit of 100 percent. Indeed, in 1897, the Northwest already had more than four-fifths (83.4 percent) of its population in large cities, reflecting its inclusion of the city of St. Petersburg (now Leningrad), which had more than 1 million people and was the largest city of the Russian Empire at this time.

Conversely, regions with a great increase in the percentage of their urban population residing in large cities between 1897 and 1970 generally had very low percentages residing in these cities in 1897. In fact, the eight regions with the greatest increases (West Siberia, Belorussia, the Volgo-Vyatsk, Kazakhstan, the Central Chernozem, the Urals, the Far East, and East Siberia), each of which had a percentage point increase of roughly 60 to 80 percent, were the only regions to have no large cities at all in 1897.

NOTES

1. B. S. Khorev, ed., Malyy Gorod (Moscow: Izdatel'stvo Moskovskogo Universiteta, 1972), p. 9.

2. Ibid., pp. 10-12.

3. Kingsley Davis, Basic Data for Cities, Countries, and Regions, World Urbanization, 1950-1970, vol. 1 (Berkeley: University of California, Institute of National Studies, 1969), p. 24.

4. U.S., Department of Commerce, Bureau of the Census, Statistical Abstract of the United States, 1976, p. 18. This total includes three unincorporated places with 100,000 or more people in 1970: apparently East Los Angeles, California; Metairie, Louisiana; and Arlington, Virginia.

5. Ibid., p. 18; and U.S., Department of Commerce, Social and Economic Statistics Administration, Bureau of the Census, County and City Data Book, 1972, pp. 590-613.

6. According to the 1971 and 1974 Demographic Yearbooks, Japan had 150 and India had 147 cities with 100,000 or more people in 1970 and 1971, respectively. See United Nations, Department of Economic and Social Affairs, Demographic Yearbook—1971 (New York, 1972), p. 386; and idem, Demographic Yearbook—1974 (New York, 1975), p. 390.

7. Davis, Basic Data for Cities, Countries, and Regions, pp. 183-89.

8. U.S., Department of Commerce, Bureau of the Census, Statistical Abstract of the United States, 1976, p. 18; and U.S., Department of Commerce, Social and Economic Statistics Administration, Bureau of the Census, County and City Data Book, 1972, pp. 590-613.

9. Davis, Basic Data for Cities, Countries, and Regions.

10. United Nations, Demographic Yearbook—1971, pp. 362-65; and idem, Demographic Yearbook—1974, pp. 201-3.

11. Khorev, Malyy Gorod; and idem, Problemy Gorodov (Moscow: Izdatel'stvo, "Mysl'," 1971).

12. Khorev, Malyy Gorod, p. 28; and B. S. Khorev and V. M. Moiseenko, "Urbanization and Redistribution of the Population of the U.S.S.R.," in Patterns of Urbanization: Comparative Country Studies, ed. Sidney Goldstein and David S. Sly, vol. 2 (Dolhain, Belgium: Ordina Editions, 1977), p. 672.

13. The 1867 city population data can be found in Chauncy D. Harris, "Population of Cities of the Soviet Union, 1897, 1926, 1939, 1959, and 1967, Tables, Maps, and Gazetteer," Soviet Geography: Review and Translation 11 (May 1970): 308-23.

14. USSR, Naseleniye SSSR, 1973 (Moscow: Izdatel'stvo "Statistika," 1975), pp. 96-99.

15. Ibid., p. 97.

16. Ibid.

17. U.S., Department of Commerce, Social and Economic Statistics Administration, Bureau of the Census, County and City Data Book, 1972, p. 739.

18. Vestnik Statistiki, no. 12 (1968), p. 79.

19. Ibid.

20. USSR, Naseleniye SSSR, 1973, pp. 186-87.

21. Passport data for 1970 come from Vestnik Statistiki, no. 11 (1971), p. 78. This was the first year for which passport data were separately available for an appreciable number of cities.

22. B. Khorev et al., "Osobennosti Demograficheskoy Sitsuatsii v Moskve," Narodonaseleniye Prikladnaya Demografiya (Moscow: "Statistika," 1973), p. 67.

23. USSR, Naseleniye SSSR, 1973, pp. 186-87.

24. Ibid.

25. Vestnik Statistiki, no. 12 (1968), pp. 78-80; USSR, Narodnoye Khozyaystvo SSSR v 1967 G., p. 7; and Chauncy D. Harris, Cities of the Soviet Union (Chicago: Rand McNally, 1970), pp. 256-57.

26. Khorev, Problemy Gorodov (1971), p. 190.

27. Khorev, Malyy Gorod, p. 89.

28. For a discussion of age and sex variations by city size, see Khorev, Problemy Gorodov (1971), pp. 254-55; idem, Problemy Gorodov, 2d ed. (Moscow: Izdatel'stvo "Mysl'," 1975), p. 282; idem, Malyy Gorod, pp. 92-93; Khorev et al., "Osobennosti Demograficheskoy Sitsuatsii v Moskve," p. 61; and M. Ya. Vydro, Naseleniye Moskvy (Moscow: "Statistika," 1976), p. 24.

29. D. G. Khodzhayev, "The Planning of the Distribution of Production in Population Centers and Some Problems in Population Geography," Soviet Geography: Review and Translation 8 (October 1967): 627.

30. Robert J. Osborn, Soviet Social Policies: Welfare, Equality and Community (Homewood, Ill.: Dorsey Press, 1970), p. 202.

31. F. E. Ian Hamilton, The Moscow City Region (London: Oxford University Press, 1976), p. 39.

32. Ibid., p. 43.

33. Osborn, Soviet Social Policies, pp. 206-7; and V. I. Perevedentsev, Goroda i Vremya (Moscow: "Statistika," 1975), p. 41.

34. Harris, Cities of the Soviet Union, pp. 58-59.

35. For example, see Khodzhayev, "Planning of the Distribution," p. 621; Khorev, Problemy Gorodov (1971), p. 356; idem, Problemy Gorodov, 2d ed., p. 182; A. S. Akhiyezer and A. V. Nochetkov, "Urbanizatsiya i Intensifikatsiya Proizvodstva v SSSR," Problemy Sovremennoy Urbanizatsii (Moscow: "Statistika," 1972), pp. 84-87; Richard E. Lonsdale, "Regional Inequity and Soviet Concern for Rural and Small-Town Industrialization," Soviet Geography: Review and Translation 18 (October 1977): 599; and George A. Huzinec, "The Impact of Industrial Decision Making upon the Soviet Urban Hierarchy," Urban Studies 15 (June 1978): 139-48.

36. Huzinec, "Impact of Industrial Decision Making."

37. Harris, Cities of the Soviet Union, p. 47.

38. Khorev, Malyy Gorod, pp. 95, 97; and idem, Problemy Gorodov (1971), pp. 266-68.

39. O. P. Litovka, Problemy Prostranstvennogo Razvitiya Urbanizatsii (Leningrad: Izdatel'stvo "Nauka," Leningradskoye Otdeleniye, 1976), p. 19.

40. William Taubman, Governing Soviet Cities (New York: Praeger, 1973), p. 73.

41. Harris, Cities of the Soviet Union, pp. 166-85.

42. Osborn, Soviet Social Policies, p. 221.

43. Khorev, Problemy Gorodov (1971), pp. 160-66. In a later study, Khorev also presents similar but less extensive data for the early 1970s, which generally portray results similar to those based on the data for the late 1960s whenever comparable data are presented. See Khorev, Problemy Gorodov, 2d ed., pp. 196-200.

44. Osborn, Soviet Social Policies, p. 221.

45. Taubman, Governing Soviet Cities, p. 73.

46. For good summary discussions of the problem of small towns in the USSR, see Khorev, Malyy Gorod, p. 15; Litovka, Problemy Prostranstvennogo, pp. 15-16; and Osborn, Soviet Social Policies, pp. 227-30.

47. For example, see Litovka, Problemy Prostranstvennogo, pp. 14-15; and W. A. Douglas Jackson, "Urban Expansion," Problems of Communism 23 (November-December 1974): 14-24.

48. For example, see Khorev, Problemy Gorodov (1971), p. 393.

49. For example, see V. I. Perevedentsev, "Kontsentratsiya Gorodskogo Naseleniya i Kriterii Optimal'nosti Goroda," Urbanizatsiya i Rabochiy Klass v Usloviyakh Nauchno-Tekhnicheskoy Revolyutsii (Moscow: Izdano Sovetskim Fondom Mira, 1970), p. 221.

50. For example, see Osborn, Soviet Social Policies, pp. 201-2.

51. Ibid., p. 193.

6

URBAN REGIONS

Our investigation of city size, has been, by necessity, based only on individual cities and does not take into consideration the development of large urban regions or agglomerations. Major trends in the distribution and redistribution of the world's population include an increase in the number of large urban agglomerations, an increasing concentration of the total population of the world in these agglomerations, and a deconcentration of population within such agglomerations. [1] In this chapter we will attempt to delineate the development of urban regions in Russia and the USSR between 1897 and 1970, in order to investigate further the distribution of the urban population and to facilitate comparisons with other areas.

SUMMARY DISCUSSION

The USSR has experienced, like the world in general, an increased concentration of its population in large urban regions or agglomerations and a deconcentration of the population within such regions, although some differences with other industrialized countries also can be noted. These conclusions are based on 22 urban regions or agglomerations with 1 million or more people in 1970 and a radius of 50 miles. In 1897 and 1926, only about 4 to 5 percent of the total population of Russia and the USSR resided in these regions, but by 1970 a proportion of nearly 20 percent had been reached. More than 40 million Soviet citizens now reside in the 22 regions.

A concurrent trend of deconcentration was indicated by a subdivision of the 50 mile zone into two zones, 0-25 and 25-50 mile zones. The proportion of the population of these regions residing in the zone 25-50 miles from the center of the agglomeration (the "outer suburbs") increased from 5 percent in 1897 to 16 percent in 1970 or by roughly 11 percentage points; conversely, the share residing in the 0-25 mile zone declined from 95 to 84 percent.

However, the principal shift within the urban regions was not from the 0-25 mile zone to the 25-50 mile zone but within the 0-25 mile zone from the central cities of the regions to the remainder of the 0-25 mile zone or the "inner suburbs." The share of the population of the urban regions residing in the inner suburbs increased by 14 percentage points while that of the central cities declined by 24 points.

Although these shifts correctly imply that the greatest rates of urban growth were experienced by the inner suburbs and outer suburbs, all zones have increased in population, including the central cities. Indeed, in contrast to the central cities in many other industrialized countries in recent years, every central city of the 22 regions increased in population, even in the most recent intercensal period of 1959 and 1970. However, more specific data indicate that the central parts of some central cities are declining in population, especially those of Moscow and Leningrad.

Generally speaking, the greatest number of the individual urban regions conformed to these overall patterns in recent years. However, some regions had a low but increasing share of the population of their region in the central city. These regions were primarily in mining areas, especially coal mining areas.

These emergent general patterns suggest that although the USSR has, like other countries, experienced a process of increased concentration in large urban agglomerations and a decreased concentration within these agglomerations, the extent of deconcentration (or "suburbanization" or "urban sprawl") has not been as pronounced as many areas elsewhere in the world. This conclusion received support from a number of additional perspectives. First, based on comparable procedures, it appears that during the 1960s the Moscow region both had a higher concentration of its population in the central city and the 0-25 mile zone and experienced a lesser shift to the outer suburbs than did the other major world urban regions of New York, Tokyo, London, and Los Angeles. In addition, it appears that although the official areas of Soviet cities are quite large in some cases, the actual populated or built-up areas are comparatively not great.

The increased concentration of the Soviet population in large urban agglomerations is related apparently to forces contributing to a similar trend elsewhere in the world. Most important would be the agglomerating forces of industrialization.

Reasons for the apparent lesser degree of urban deconcentration in the USSR are, perhaps, of greater interest. These include relative recency of the growth of Soviet urban regions, comparative lack of sprawl-enhancing automobiles and single-family houses, green belt policy, lack of a racially motivated white flight to the suburbs, and continued attractions of large central cities.

DETAILED DISCUSSION

Data Problems and Procedures

The Russian and Soviet censuses, unfortunately, do not provide explicit data on the extent of development of urban regions or agglomerations. For example, unlike the U.S. census, there is no attempt to distinguish anything

TABLE 6.1

Population of the 22 Urban Regions of Russia and the USSR: 1897-1970

Urban Region	Population in Settlements with 15,000 or More People				
	1897	1926	1939	1959	1970
Moscow	1,053,746	2,158,102	5,195,941	7,483,853	9,555,318
Leningrad	1,346,925	1,705,641	3,444,241	3,461,119	4,161,150
Donetsk	47,392	267,865	1,537,143	2,467,859	3,039,195
Dnepropetrovsk	185,412	356,752	1,056,501	1,456,852	1,992,498
Kiev	283,101	593,399	929,994	1,298,312	1,991,145
Gor'kiy	90,053	241,654	867,806	1,390,907	1,772,233
Tashkent	155,673	323,613	583,443	1,078,294	1,762,446
Voroshilovgrad	20,404	122,144	779,918	1,363,045	1,747,520
Rostov-na-Donu	284,806	530,150	1,064,447	1,403,048	1,740,763
Kuybyshev	89,999	175,662	465,572	1,120,108	1,640,303
Khar'kov	200,553	485,208	989,137	1,161,395	1,627,699
Sverdlovsk	43,239	136,421	648,501	1,213,536	1,566,652
Baku	111,904	453,333	774,811	1,023,244	1,390,005
Novosibirsk	0	120,128	404,444	949,811	1,299,409
Tula	145,304	208,626	496,214	938,913	1,193,000
Chelyabinsk	19,998	59,226	333,269	1,001,403	1,172,767
Novokuznetsk	0	0	342,254	986,126	1,108,130
Tbilisi	159,590	294,044	538,848	824,161	1,093,730
Minsk	105,975	157,645	286,603	595,044	1,073,557
Yerevan	29,006	64,613	221,821	578,462	1,028,760
Perm'	61,542	138,508	372,175	783,329	1,015,725
Kazan'	129,959	179,207	447,730	761,048	1,006,807
Total population in all 22 regions	4,564,581	8,771,941	21,780,813	33,339,869	43,978,812
Total population in 1 million and over only	2,400,671	3,863,743	12,298,273	26,922,975	43,978,812

Sources: See Chapter 1, nn. 104 and 105.

like an "Urbanized Area" or "Standard Metropolitan Statistical Area." Recently, however, there have been attempts by Soviet scholars to define the major urban agglomerations of the USSR, but these are only for the more recent period and not for the overall 1897-1970 period.[2]

In order to examine the extent of the concentration of the Soviet population in large urban regions and the deconcentration of the urban population within these regions since the turn of the century, it was necessary to devise a number of procedures. First, the major urban regions of 1970 were determined by drawing a circle with a radius of 50 miles around the major Soviet cities and summing the population residing in centers with 15,000 or more people in such regions.[3] A radius of 50 miles was selected, because it is or may be eventually the approximate maximum limit of many individual agglomerations. For example, V. G. Davidovich has noted that the limits of some Soviet agglomerations in 1959, based mainly on commuting linkages, extended up to 70 to 80 kilometers or approximately 44 to 50 miles. Undoubtedly, the limits of the agglomerations in 1959 had been expanded by 1970.[4] There are limitations to the definition of urban regions being employed. Such regions, for example, are not necessarily functional regions in all years. Nonetheless, the definition employed probably captures the major trends in urban agglomeration.

On the basis of these procedures, 22 "major urban regions" with an urban population of 1 million or more were distinguished for 1970 (Table 6.1). Namely, in 1970, within a radius of 50 miles of 22 major Soviet cities, the total population residing in urban centers of 15,000 and over in population exceeded 1 million. The subsequent discussion will focus on these 22 urban regions. In only one case did the regions overlap to such an extent that an individual urban center fell within the boundaries of two urban regions. Not unexpectedly, this situation occurred in the Donbas, where the Donetsk and Voroshilovgrad urban regions overlapped to such an extent that roughly a half dozen towns were located in both urban regions. In order to avoid double-counting, each town was allocated to either the Donetsk or Voroshilovgrad region, depending upon which of the two major cities it was closer to. The population totals presented in Table 6.1 for these two urban regions reflect this minor adjustment.

The general validity of the 22 urban regions is supported by regional schemes developed by F. M. Listengurt, Yu. L. Pivovarov, and Davidovich.[5] These schemes also distinguish roughly 20 agglomerations or regions with 1 million or more people in 1970, and the specific regions are also generally the same as ours. According to Listengurt, there were 19 urban agglomerations in the USSR in 1970 with more than 1 million people each.[6] The agglomerations in this scheme are determined by a host of criteria. Each agglomeration has: (1) a minimum central-city population of 100,000, (2) at least 10 percent of its population residing outside the central city, (3) at least three urban places outside the central city, (4) a minimum population of 110,000 for the entire agglomeration, (5) a maximum of two hours travel time from the outer zone to the central city, and (6) a spatial structural index of at least 0.1 (representing the ratio of the density of urban places to the mean nearest neighbor distance).[7] Unlike our set of regions, Listengurt's excludes Yerevan, Perm', Voroshilovgrad, and Minsk and includes Volgograd. According to Listengurt, Yerevan, Perm', and Voroshilovgrad were agglomerations but did not have 1 million people. Minsk was excluded apparently because it has so few suburbs that it did not meet the first criterion. In our scheme, the Volgograd area fell just slightly short of being at least 1 million in population.

According to Pivovarov, there were 20 agglomerations with over a million people in 1970.[8] His scheme, like ours, is based on a simple radius criterion, although the distance differs somewhat, being 60 kilometers (roughly 37 miles), except for Moscow and Leningrad, which were accorded a greater radius of 100 kilometers (roughly 62 miles).[9] Unlike our scheme but also like Listengurt's, Pivovarov's excludes Yerevan, Voroshilovgrad, and Minsk and includes Volgograd.

Finally, Davidovich also distinguished 20 agglomerations with more than 1 million people in 1970.[10] His scheme is based on areas that are up to three hours from the center of the main city along lines of suburban passenger transport.[11] Unlike our scheme, Davidovich's, like Listengurt's and Pivovarov's, includes Volgograd and excludes Voroshilovgrad and Yerevan. In addition, it excludes Tula. Yerevan and Tula are, however, agglomerations with 500,000 to 1 million people in the Davidovich scheme.

After determining the 22 major urban regions for 1970 in the USSR, the urban populations for the same 22 regions were calculated for 1897, 1926, 1939, and 1959 (Table 6.1). This allowed an assessment of changes in the degree of concentration of the Soviet population in these regions.

We were, however, also interested in the extent of the deconcentration of population within these regions. In order to investigate this process, we subdivided the urban population of each region into two zones, one with a 0-25 mile radius and the other with a 25-50 mile radius. In addition, the population in the main central city alone was separated out in order to investigate the amount of deconcentration from a more narrowly defined center of the agglomeration to the periphery. * Subtraction of the central city population from the population of the 0-25 mile zone resulted in a residual category—namely, the

---

*Whenever appropriate, the "central city" included those centers with 15,000 or more people, which were separate cities in the past but eventually were annexed to the larger central city by 1970. For example, in 1897, the central city of St. Petersburg (Leningrad) included not only St. Petersburg itself (1,264,920) but also Kronstadt (59,525) and Tsarskoye Selo, now Pushkin (22,480), since the latter towns are included in the city of Leningrad today. Other cases where such a situation existed were: (1) Kronstadt, Detskoye Selo (now Pushkin), and Kolpino to Leningrad in 1926; (2) Losinoostrovskaya (now Babushkin, part of Moscow) to Moscow in 1926; (3) Motovilikha to Perm' in 1897 and 1926; (4) Sormovo to Gor'kiy in 1926; (5) Nakhichevan' to Rostov-na-Donu in 1897; (6) Novotul'skiy to Tula in 1959; and (7) Yudino to Kazan' in 1959.

population in the 0-25 mile zone outside the central city. For convenience, this area will be referred to frequently as the "inner suburbs," although the 25-mile limit is probably somewhat greater than the limit for "inner suburbs" as conventionally defined in the United States. Similarly, the 25-50 mile zone often will be referred to as the "outer suburbs."

Major Patterns of the Urban Regions

Table 6.1 indicates that there has been a great increase in the number of urban regions with a million or more people. In 1897 and 1926, there were only two urban regions of Russia and the USSR with a population in excess of 1 million: Leningrad (St. Petersburg) and Moscow. However, by 1939, after the period of the most rapid urbanization in the history of Russia and the USSR, the number of urban regions with a population of 1 million or more had increased to five, with the addition of Donetsk, Dnepropetrovsk, and Rostov-na-Donu. The emergence of these three regions reflects the rapid development of heavy industry in the USSR in general, and in the coal-rich Eastern Ukraine and adjacent areas thereof in the RSFSR in particular. By 1959, the number of urban regions with more than a million people had increased by nine, nearly tripling as the total increased to 14. The nine additional regions were Kiev, Gor'kiy, Tashkent, Voroshilovgrad, Kuybyshev, Khar'kov, Sverdlovsk, Baku, and Chelyabinsk. By 1970, eight more had been added, raising the total to 22. Regions added during this short 11-year period were Novosibirsk, Tula, Novokuznetsk, Tbilisi, Minsk, Yerevan, Perm', and Kazan'. Thus, since the turn of the century (1897) and the eve of the planned economic era in the USSR (1926), the number of urban regions with a population of 1 million or more has increased 11-fold, truly a tremendous increase.

The share of the Russian and Soviet population residing in these 22 urban regions and the population of the same regions increased sharply also (Tables 6.1 and 6.3). In 1897 and 1926 less than 10 million people resided in these 22 urban regions, accounting for a mere 4 or 5 percent of the total population of the country. But by 1939 the same regions contained over 20 million people or more than 10 percent of the Soviet population. By 1959 corresponding figures had increased to more than 30 million or roughly one-sixth of the Soviet population, and by 1970, to over 40 million or nearly one-fifth. In short, nearly one out of every five Soviet citizens is now a resident of an urban center in 1 of the 22 urban regions. The preceding involves a computation of all 22 urban regions in all census years regardless of whether their population exceeded 1 million in any particular year prior to 1970. If only those regions with more than 1 million in population in each census year are considered, the same general trend of increased concentration in such regions is still evident—namely, from roughly 2 percent of the total population in 1897 and 1926 to 6 percent in 1939, to 13 percent in 1959, and to 18 percent in 1970. Either way you look at it, there has been a great increase in the share of the population of Russia and the USSR residing in these urban agglomerations.

TABLE 6.2

Population by Zone of the 22 Urban Regions of Russia and the USSR: 1897–1970

Year	0–25 Mile Radius	25–50 Mile Radius	Population in Settlements with 15,000 or More People	
			Central City	Inner Suburbs
1897	4,319,994	244,587	4,213,058	106,936
1926	8,120,565	651,376	7,812,458	308,107
1939	19,077,291	2,703,522	16,881,932	2,195,359
1959	28,166,700	5,173,169	23,325,117	4,841,583
1970	36,914,478	7,064,334	29,956,467	6,958,011

Sources: See Chapter 1, nn. 104 and 105.

TABLE 6.3

Distribution Aspects of the Population of the 22 Urban Regions of Russia and the USSR: 1897–1970

Year	Percent of USSR Total Population Residing in Urban Regions	Percent of Population of Urban Regions of Russia and the USSR Residing in:			
		0–25 Mile Radius	25–50 Mile Radius	Central City	Inner Suburbs
1897	3.7	94.6	5.4	92.3	2.3
1926	5.2	92.6	7.4	89.1	3.5
1939	11.3	87.6	12.4	77.5	10.1
1959	16.0	84.5	15.5	70.0	14.5
1970	18.2	83.9	16.1	68.1	15.8

Sources: See Chapter 1, nn. 104 and 105.

In addition, within these 22 urban regions, a concurrent process of de-concentration was noticeable. As Tables 6.2-6.4 reveal, the percentage of the population of the 22 regions residing in the 0-25 mile zone has declined steadily since 1897. In 1897, well over 90 percent of the population of the ur-ban regions was found in the 0-25 mile zone. By 1926, the percentage had declined slightly to just over 90 percent. But by 1939, this zone contained slightly less than 90 percent of the urban regions' population and by 1959 and 1970, roughly 84 percent. In short, the share of the population of the urban regions residing in the 0-25 mile zone declined by roughly ten percentage points between 1897 and 1970. However, it should be kept in mind that de-spite a decline in relative importance, the absolute population of this zone in-creased greatly from 4 million in 1897 to nearly 37 million in 1970. Indeed, the increase in this zone accounted for over 80 percent of the increase in the total population of these regions between 1897 and 1970. This zone also still accounted for the vast majority of the urban regions' population in 1970 and of their growth between 1959 and 1970. Despite the substantial population in-crease of the 0-25 mile zone, even more rapid growth occurred in the 25-50 mile zone (from less than 300,000 in 1897 to over 7 million in 1970), and the share of the urban regions' population residing here, of course, increased by roughly ten percentage points between 1897 and 1970.

Subdivision of the 0-25 mile zone into two subzones (central cities and inner suburbs) reveals that the greatest shift within the urban regions was not from the 0-25 mile zone to the 25-50 mile zone or outer suburbs but from the central cities to the inner suburbs. Whereas the 0-25 mile zone share of the population of the urban regions declined by roughly ten percentage points be-tween 1897 and 1970, the share residing in the central cities declined by more than 30 percentage points during the same period (Tables 6.3 and 6.4). In 1897 the central cities contained over 90 percent of the population of the urban regions and in 1926, just slightly under 90 percent. However, by 1939 the central city share had declined to slightly under 80 percent, by 1959 to 70 per-cent, and by 1970 to slightly below 70 percent. In short, whereas the central cities contained roughly nine-tenths of the urban regions' population in 1897 and 1926, they contained only roughly two-thirds of this population in 1970, although they still contained a sizable majority of the urban regions' popula-tion in this most recent census year.

It should be noted, however, that unlike many central cities of urban agglomerations elsewhere in the world, which are declining in both absolute and relative terms, the declining relative importance of the central city in the USSR has yet to be accompanied by a decline in the absolute population re-siding in such cities. Indeed, even in the most recent 1959-70 period the pop-ulation of the central cities increased by over 2 percent annually (Table 6.5). Moreover, in the same period all of the 22 central cities increased in popu-lation. As mentioned before, the largest Soviet city to decline in population between 1959 and 1970 was not an exceptionally large city—namely, Prokop'-yevsk, a city of the Novokuznetsk urban region, which declined from 282,000 to 274,000 during this period. Furthermore, although the share of the urban regions' population residing in the central cities declined sharply, the greatest

TABLE 6.4

Redistribution Aspects of the Population of the 22 Urban
Regions of Russia and the USSR: 1897-1970

	Percent of USSR Total Population Residing in Urban Regions	Percentage Point Change of:			
		Percent of Population of Urban Regions Residing in:			
Period		0-25 Mile Radius	25-50 Mile Radius	Central City	Inner Suburbs
1897-1926	1.5	-2.0	2.0	-3.2	1.2
1926-39	6.1	-5.0	5.0	-11.6	6.6
1939-59	4.7	-3.1	3.1	-7.5	4.4
1959-70	2.2	-0.6	0.6	-1.9	1.3
1897-1970	14.5	-10.7	10.7	-24.2	13.5
1926-70	13.0	-8.7	8.7	-21.0	12.3

Sources: See Chapter 1, nn. 104 and 105.

TABLE 6.5

Rates of Population Change by Zone of the 22 Urban
Regions of Russia and the USSR: 1897-1970

	Total Population of the Urban Regions	Average Annual Percentage Change of:			
		Population Residing in:			
Period		0-25 Mile Radius	25-50 Mile Radius	Central City	Inner Suburbs
1897-1926	2.2	2.1	3.3	2.1	3.5
1926-39	7.5	7.1	11.8	6.4	16.2
1939-59	2.1	2.0	3.2	1.6	4.0
1959-70	2.5	2.5	2.9	2.2	3.3
1897-1970	3.1	2.9	4.6	2.7	5.7
1926-70	3.7	3.5	5.5	3.1	7.2

Sources: See Chapter 1, nn. 104 and 105.

share of the increase in population of the urban regions actually occurred in these cities. Between 1897 and 1970 the total population of the urban regions increased by 39,414,231, and of this increase, 25,743,409 or 65.3 percent was accounted for by central cities. Even in the most recent 1959-70 period, central cities accounted for a sizable majority (62.3 percent) of the growth of the urban regions' population. The lack of a declining central city population may be due in part to annexations and the overbounded nature of some Soviet cities, although it is difficult to assess this influence in depth because of a lack of data.

As is typical of Western cities, however, it does appear that the very central portions of some Soviet cities are declining in population. This conclusion is based to a great extent on data available for Moscow and Leningrad, because there are very little data available for the internal sections of most other Soviet cities. According to data presented by F. E. Ian Hamilton, the central portion of Moscow experienced a very precipitous decline in population between 1959 and 1970.[12] The population of the very central area of Central Moscow (extending from the Kremlin to the Sadovoye Kol'tso or Garden Ring) declined in population between 1959 to 1970 from 930,000 to 420,000 or by 55 percent. The population of the Inner Ring, the next major zone beyond the central area (roughly the Garden Ring to the Okruzhnaya Zheleznaya Doroga or Circle Railway), also declined fairly sharply in population during the same period from 4,116,000 to 3,300,000 or by 20 percent. The final zone or Outer Ring (roughly the outer portion of the Inner Ring to the Circumferential or Ring Motorway, which marks the city limits of Moscow), increased extremely rapidly in population from 998,000 in 1959 to 3,341,000 in 1970 or by 335 percent.

Reflecting the effects annexation can have on central city population totals, it is interesting to note that the Outer Ring of Moscow roughly coincides with the area of approximately 200 square miles annexed by Moscow in 1960 and that the city of Moscow as it existed prior to this huge annexation roughly coincides with Central Moscow and the Inner Ring. This means that the population of Moscow as it was constituted just prior to 1960 annexation actually declined extremely sharply between 1959 and 1970. In short, it is possible to conclude that without the 1960 annexation, Moscow's population would have declined by more than 1.3 million people or by 26 percent (from roughly 5 million to 3.7 million) instead of actually increasing in population, based upon the new boundaries, by slightly over 1 million (from roughly 6 million to 7 million).

Lest anyone thinks that this indicates that the Soviets have succeeded in limiting the growth of large cities, excluding annexations, a few additional comments should be made. Although the Moscow plan of 1935 stated that Moscow's population was to be limited eventually to a maximum of 5 million, this population was not to be within the boundaries of 1935 but in a greatly enlarged territory. Specifically it was to be in a territory that was slightly more than twice the territorial size of 1935 (roughly 240 square miles as opposed to about 110 square miles in 1935).[13] By 1959 the actual area of Moscow was about 140 square miles, and the annexation of 1960 increased it to approximately 350 square miles.[14] Thus, by 1959 and in 1959 boundaries, a population of roughly 5 million had been reached in an area much smaller than the planned maximum size of 240 square miles. The eventual total Moscow territory after the 1960 territorial expansion, as is obvious, greatly exceeded that envisaged by the 1935 plan (a total area of 350 square miles as opposed to the 240 square mile limit of the 1935 plan). However, a great share of these 350 square miles, especially much of the peripheral zone, is not built-up but, instead, is fairly sparsely populated. Therefore, although it is difficult to make a more precise assessment due to the lack of more specific data, the present population of Moscow resides in an area that perhaps more approaches that of the 240 square mile limit of the 1935 plan.[15] However, instead of 5 million people residing in the land area envisaged by the 1935 plan, considerably more people apparently reside in that same area.

Data for Leningrad, though less plentiful, also suggest a central-area population decline somewhat similar to that of Moscow. Between 1959 and 1967, the combined population of the most central rayony of Vasileostrov, Dzerzhinsk, Kuybyshev, Lenin, Oktyabr', Petrograd, Smol'nyy, and Frunze declined from 1,818,000 to 1,473,000 or by almost 20 percent.[16]

As mentioned previously, the greatest shift within the urban regions has been toward the inner suburbs. The share of the urban regions' population residing in this zone increased substantially, from only 2 to 3 percent in 1897 and 1926 to 10 percent in 1939, and to roughly 15 percent in 1959 and 1970 (Table 6.3). The shift to this zone of 13.5 percentage points between 1897 and 1970 exceeded that to the outer suburbs by over two percentage points (Table 6.4). Indeed, except during the 1897-1926 period, the shift to the inner suburbs exceeded that to the outer suburbs in all of the intercensal periods under investigation, even in the most recent 1959-70 period (Table 6.4). This shift reflects the fact that the inner suburbs grew more rapidly in every intercensal period under investigation than both the central cities and the outer suburbs (Table 6.5).

Although differential zonal growth and zonal shifts have occurred, appreciable growth has been characteristic of all zones, including the central cities (Table 6.5). The slowest rate of growth, of any zone in any period, was experienced by the central city zone between 1939 and 1959, when its population increased by 1.6 percent per year. However, this rate of growth still entails a doubling of the population roughly every 40 years and, furthermore, undoubtedly would have been considerably higher had it not been for the population losses of Leningrad during World War II.

It should be added that other calculations also reveal that the patterns just discussed for the various zones of the urban regions generally hold true when only those urban regions with a million or more people in each respective year are investigated.

Although there are few studies for comparison, it is interesting to note that at least for the 1959-70 period, some of the trends discussed above also were discovered in studies by G. M. Lappo and Pivovarov.[17] Lappo distinguished 75 agglomerations in 1970 with a central city population of 250,000 or more, which were, in turn, subdivided into core and satellite zones. According to Lappo, there was a slight dispersal of the agglomerations' population from the core zones to the satellite zones between 1959 and 1970, as the core's share declined from 76 to 75.7 percent, although the vast majority (74.8 percent) of the growth of the agglomerations occurred within the core zones. Similarly, according to Pivovarov, the overall share of the population residing in the center or centers of the agglomerations based on his scheme declined slightly from 72.9 percent in 1959 to 71.7 percent in 1970, and the majority (67.6 percent) of the growth of the agglomerations was accounted for by the centers of the agglomerations. Our calculations, of course, also revealed that there was a slight shift away from the central cities and that the majority of the growth of the urban regions between 1959 and 1970 occurred within the central cities.

In summary, the USSR has experienced an increased concentration of its population in large urban regions, and within those regions there has been a deconcentration of population. However, although in the deconcentration process there has been a shift from the 0-25 mile zone to the 25-50 mile zone, the greatest shift has been actually within the 0-25 mile zone—namely, from the central city to the remainder of the 0-25 mile zone or inner suburbs, where the rate of growth has exceeded that even of the 25-50 mile zone or outer suburbs. Furthermore, although the central cities have declined in relative terms, they, like the other zones, have, nevertheless, increased in population and have accounted for the majority of the population size and population growth of the urban regions, even in recent years.

Individual Urban Regions

Although the urban regions generally have had a high concentration of their population in the central cities and inner suburbs along with a decentralizing trend, many urban regions deviated considerably from these patterns. First, it will be recalled that 83.9 percent of the population of all urban regions was concentrated in 1970 in the 0-25 mile zone and roughly 68.1 percent was located within the central city. In both cases, the majority of the 22 urban regions (13 and 15 regions, respectively) exceeded these averages. In each instance, the two leading urban regions were Baku and Leningrad, which had more than 90 percent of their populations in both the 0-25 mile zone and the central city.

However, a number of urban regions had a relatively low percentage of their population in the 0-25 mile zone and the central city; for the most part, these regions included mining districts. In both cases, the very lowest percentages (31.1 and 21.9, respectively) were experienced by the Voroshilovgrad (formerly Lugansk) region of the extreme eastern part of the Donets Coal Basin of the Ukraine. Actually, Voroshilovgrad is located more toward the periphery of its region in that the greatest number of towns are located in the western portion of the region and not in and around the city of Voroshilovgrad itself. The largest of these towns is Kadiyevka and, indeed, Kadiyevka is sometimes acknowledged (for example, Listengurt) as the center of a major agglomeration here.[18] Admittedly, the Voroshilovgrad region is included among the urban regions primarily because of the specific operational procedures used in this investigation. Nevertheless, irrespective of what the actual center of the eastern Donbas complex is, the same pattern would probably emerge, because a low percentage residing in the central city tends to be characteristic of mining districts in general, as they typically consist of numerous relatively small mining centers. That this is the case is reflected by the urban region located immediately to the west of the Voroshilovgrad region: the Donetsk urban region, which essentially comprises the western portion of the Donbas Coalfield. Here, roughly 66 percent of the population was located in the 0-25 mile zone, and only 28.9 percent was located within the central city of Donetsk itself. Excluding Voroshilovgrad, only three other regions had a lower percentage for the 0-25 mile zone and no other region had a lower percentage for the central city. Even if the large, nearby city of Makeyevka (392,250 in 1970) was added to Donetsk to form a "twin" central city, as it often is, the Donetsk-Makeyevka central city still would have contained only 41.8 percent of the population of this urban region. This percentage still would be well below the national average of 68 percent and only Voroshilovgrad and Tula would have lower percentages.

The Donetsk and Voroshilovgrad regions combined form the most decentralized major zone of urban settlement in the USSR, and, indeed, it is probably more realistic to consider this as one large urban region. The combined population of both urban regions in 1970 was nearly 5 million, which would make it the second largest urban region in the USSR, exceeding even Leningrad. In addition, according to our procedures, a 50-mile urban region centered on the small city of Debal'tsevo (35,366 in 1970), which lies roughly halfway between the cities of Donetsk and Voroshilovgrad, would have a population of more than 4 million in 1970, a total that is roughly the same as that for Leningrad. However, it should be remembered that this urban complex of the Eastern Ukraine has not been developed along the normal lines of suburbanization but instead is, to a great extent, a large complex of mining and/or manufacturing towns.

Other urban regions with comparatively low percentages of their population found in the 0-25 mile and central city zones also contained mining districts. In addition to Voroshilovgrad and Donetsk, three other urban regions had both less than 70 percent of their population in the 0-25 mile zone and less than 50 percent of their population in the central city in 1970. These included the Tula region of the Moscow Coal Basin and Rostov-na-Donu, which contains some coal mining towns in the portion of the Donets Basin lying in the RSFSR. The third region was the Dnepropetrovsk region. Although it includes a portion of the extreme western part of the Donbas, the primary explanation for the low percentages here is the fact that the peripheral part of the region contains the large city of Zaporozh'ye. This city had a population of 657,890 in 1970, and although the population of the city of Dnepropetrovsk exceeded this figure by 200,000, the presence of such a large outer suburb tended to reduce the 0-25 mile zone and central city shares of the population of the Dnepropetrovsk region. In fact, in no other urban region did the population of the second largest city of the region even approach that of Zaporozh'ye. Zaporozh'ye was also larger than the largest or central cities of three other regions (Novokuznetsk, Tula, and Voroshilovgrad).

The other major pattern of the urban regions was a trend toward decentralization, particularly to the inner suburbs. Between 1959 and 1970, a number of urban regions deviated from this overall pattern. In seven urban regions (Donetsk, Rostov-na-Donu, Sverdlovsk, Tula, Chelyabinsk, Novokuznetsk, and Perm') a concentrating trend actually occurred in that the greatest shift of population within the region was toward the central city! Deeper investigation reveals that this shift was not due so much to an extremely rapidly growing central city as to slowly growing and even declining populations of cities outside the central city. Generally speaking, the central cities of these seven regions increased about 25 to 35 percent (2.0 to 2.7 percent per year) between 1959 and 1970, but the central cities of all 22 urban regions grew at a rate generally within this range or higher, except for Moscow and Leningrad (17.5 and 18.9 percent or 1.5 and 1.6 percent per annum, respectively). Indeed, the regions with the most rapidly growing central cities (Minsk, Tashkent, Yerevan, and Kiev) paradoxically are not among these regions where the most pronounced shift was toward the central city. In the case of two of these seven urban regions (Chelyabinsk and Novokuznetsk), the inner suburbs actually declined in population. For the most part, these seven regions included coal mining districts, which contained many mining towns that either declined in population or increased only very slowly.

In six regions, the greatest shift between 1959 and 1970 was to the outer suburbs (Dnepropetrovsk, Kiev, Tashkent, Kuybyshev, Khar'kov, and Minsk). Unlike the previous regions where the principal shift was toward the central city, the shift in these six regions was accompanied by genuine rapid growth of the outer suburbs. In all six of these regions, the outer suburbs grew by at least 80 percent (4.8 percent per year) between 1959 and 1970, and in three cases by more than 150 percent or 8.3 percent annually (the outer suburbs of Tashkent, Yerevan, and Kuybyshev, the latter of which includes the extremely rapidly growing city of Tol'yatti). Indeed, no other urban region had a growth rate in the outer suburbs that even approached that of any of these six regions.

Finally, the most common situation was that which conformed to the general trend of a shift to the inner suburbs. In particular, in nine of the urban regions, the greatest shift in population was toward this zone (Moscow, Leningrad, Gor'kiy, Voroshilovgrad, Baku, Novosibirsk, Tbilisi, Yerevan, and Kazan'). Except for Gor'kiy, the inner suburbs of each region experienced very rapid growth in that the rate of increase exceeded 50 percent (3.7 percent per year) in these eight urban regions. The most rapid growth occurred in Yerevan, where the inner suburbs increased by more than 500 percent (16.3 percent annually) between 1959 and 1970. This was by far the most rapid increase for any of the three zones for any of the 22 urban regions between 1959 and 1970.

Comparison of Moscow with Tokyo,
New York, London, and Los Angeles

In order to provide greater insights into the development of urban regions in the USSR, comparisons with other countries would be most useful.
Unfortunately, an investigation of the United States, for example, following
the procedures we have applied to the USSR (that is, radii of 25 and 50 miles
and settlements of 15,000 and over in population in a number of census years),
is well beyond the scope of this study. Derivation of the data for the USSR
alone was a very time-consuming venture in itself.

However, we have decided to undertake a more limited comparative
study, which itself turned out to be fairly time-consuming. In particular, we
have decided to compare the Moscow urban region with other great urban regions of the world: Tokyo, New York, London, and Los Angeles. We have
estimated the urban population of these four urban regions based on censuses
of or around 1960 and 1970 following the same procedures as applied to Moscow and the 21 other major urban regions of the USSR (namely, 25- and 50-
mile radii and urban centers of 15,000 and over).[19] The central points for
each region were the Ginza District, Times Square, Trafalgar Square, and
the Civic Center, respectively.

Settlements with a population of 15,000 and over were determined by
using census data from each country.[20] For Tokyo all settlements considered
to be a <u>shi</u> (city) with a population of 15,000 and over originally were included.
However, because the <u>shi</u> contains a considerable amount of rural areas, we
also extracted data for "Densely Inhabited Districts" (DIDs) with 15,000 or
more people (excluding <u>machi</u>) in order to provide a more precise accounting
of individual urban agglomerations. The discussion of Tokyo will, thus, be
based on the DIDs. For New York and Los Angeles, we included all cities,
townships, and unincorporated places with a population of 15,000 and over.
Finally, the urban population for London was based upon the 32 boroughs of
Greater London as defined in the 1971 census plus all county boroughs, urban
districts, and separately listed "new towns" with a population of 15,000 and
over. Obviously, the definitions of the urban settlements of these agglomerations are not the same as those in the USSR, nor are they necessarily comparable with each other. Nevertheless, it still seems that comparisons between the five urban regions can be undertaken reasonably well.

Based upon these procedures, it is possible to compare the Moscow urban region with the other four major world urban regions (Tables 6.6-6.9).
Except for Los Angeles, Moscow was the smallest of the five urban regions
(Table 6.6). The Tokyo urban region was by far the largest of the five;
around 1970 it was about twice as populous as the Moscow urban region and
exceeded the Moscow region by almost 9 million people. Indeed, in 1970, the
Tokyo region, with more than 18 million people, was much larger than either
the New York or London agglomerations and exceeded each by roughly 5 and 7
million people, respectively. However, in both 1960 and 1970, New York and
London substantially surpassed Moscow in size (by roughly 4 and 2 million
people, respectively, in 1970).

TABLE 6.6

Population by Zone of the Urban Regions of Moscow, New York, London, Tokyo, and Los Angeles: Circa 1960 and 1970

Urban Region (year)	Urban Region	Population in Settlements with 15,000 or More People in:			
		0-25 Mile Radius	25-50 Mile Radius	Central City	Inner Suburbs
Circa 1960					
Moscow (1959)	7,483,853	6,961,101	522,752	6,008,827	952,274
New York (1960)	12,716,209	11,673,447	1,042,762	7,781,984	3,891,463
London (1961)	11,705,320	9,585,016	2,120,304	7,992,443	1,592,573
Tokyo—DID (1960)	12,430,659	11,419,204	1,011,455	8,108,157	3,311,047
Los Angeles (1960)	5,777,475	5,327,964	449,511	2,479,015	2,848,949
Circa 1970					
Moscow (1970)	9,555,318	8,827,431	727,887	7,061,008	1,766,423
New York (1970)	13,927,854	12,187,594	1,740,260	7,895,563	4,292,031
London (1971)	11,783,690	9,176,144	2,607,546	7,379,014	1,797,130
Tokyo—DID (1970)	18,485,577	16,775,786	1,709,791	8,793,123	7,982,663
Los Angeles (1970)	8,107,378	6,926,076	1,181,302	2,809,813	4,116,263

Sources: 1959 and 1970 Soviet censuses (see Chapter 1, n. 104); and sources cited in Chapter 6, n. 19.

TABLE 6.7

Distribution of Population by Zone of the Urban Regions of
Moscow, New York, London, Tokyo, and Los Angeles:
Circa 1960 and 1970

	Percent of Population of Urban Region Residing in:			
Urban Region (year)	0-25 Mile Radius	25-50 Mile Radius	Central City	Inner Suburbs
Circa 1960				
Moscow (1959)	93.0	7.0	80.3	12.7
New York (1960)	91.8	8.2	61.2	30.6
London (1961)	81.9	18.1	68.3	13.6
Tokyo—DID (1960)	91.9	8.1	65.2	26.6
Los Angeles (1960)	92.2	7.8	42.9	49.3
Circa 1970				
Moscow (1970)	92.4	7.6	73.9	18.5
New York (1970)	87.5	12.5	56.7	30.8
London (1971)	77.9	22.1	62.6	15.3
Tokyo—DID (1970)	90.8	9.2	47.6	43.2
Los Angeles (1970)	85.4	14.6	34.7	50.8

Sources: 1959 and 1970 Soviet censuses (see Chapter
1, n. 104); and sources cited in Chapter 6, n. 19.

The Moscow region also had the highest percentage of its population
within the 0-25 mile zone and the central city (Table 6.7). In both 1959 and
1970, more than 92 percent resided within the 0-25 mile zone and more than
70 percent resided in the central city. The four non-Soviet regions generally
had between 80 and 92 percent of their populations within the 0-25 mile zone.
The lowest percentages in this regard were experienced by London, which
had approximately 80 percent of its population in the 0-25 mile zone in both
years.

Even greater differences are noticeable when Moscow is compared with
the other regions on the basis of the central city share of the population.
Whereas well over 70 percent of the Moscow region's population was concentrated in the city of Moscow per se in both years, the corresponding percent-

TABLE 6.8

Redistribution of Population by Zone of the Urban Regions
of Moscow, New York, London, Tokyo, and Los Angeles:
Circa 1960-70

| Urban Region (period) | Percentage Point Change of Percent of Population of Urban Region Residing in: | | | |
	0-25 Mile Radius	25-50 Mile Radius	Central City	Inner Suburbs
Moscow (1959-70)	-0.6	0.6	-6.4	5.8
New York (1960-70)	-4.3	4.3	-4.5	0.2
London (1961-71)	-4.0	4.0	-5.7	1.7
Tokyo—DID (1960-70)	-1.1	1.1	-17.6	16.6
Los Angeles (1960-70)	-6.8	6.8	-8.2	1.5

Sources: 1959 and 1970 Soviet censuses (see Chapter
1, n. 104); and sources cited in Chapter 6, n. 19.

ages for the other regions were under 70 percent and usually considerably so.
The lowest percentages were experienced by the Los Angeles region, which
had only around 35 to 40 percent of its population in the central city.

Considerable variations also existed with regard to the share residing
in the inner suburbs (Table 6.7). Moscow generally had a low percentage residing in this zone as compared with the other urban regions, except London.
In both years, less than 20 percent of the Moscow region's population resided
in the inner suburbs. In contrast, roughly 30 to 40 percent of New York's and
Tokyo's population was located in this zone, and roughly 50 percent of Los
Angeles's population was located here.

Of course, Moscow had a comparatively low percentage in the 25-50
mile zone, or outer suburbs. Whereas in both years only about 7 to 8 percent
of the population of the Moscow region resided in the 25-50 mile zone, corresponding figures were roughly 8 to 13 percent for Tokyo, New York, and Los
Angeles and roughly 20 percent for London.

The lesser suburban development of the Moscow urban region also is
reflected in the fact that the Moscow region contained the fewest number of
individual urban centers of any region in circa 1970. The New York region
contained by far the greatest number. In 1970, the New York region had 160
urban centers (with more than one-half being in New Jersey), while Los Angeles had roughly 100 and London and Tokyo roughly 90 urban centers each.

TABLE 6.9

Rate of Population Change by Zone of the Urban Regions of Moscow, New York, London, Tokyo, and Los Angeles: Circa 1960-70

	Average Annual Percentage Change of Population Residing in:				
Urban Region (period)	Urban Region	0-25 Mile Radius	25-50 Mile Radius	Central City	Inner Suburbs
Moscow (1959-70)	2.2	2.2	3.0	1.5	5.6
New York (1960-70)	1.0	0.4	5.1	0.1	1.0
London (1961-71)	0.1	-0.4	2.1	-0.8	1.2
Tokyo—DID (1960-70)	4.0	3.9	5.2	0.8	8.8
Los Angeles (1960-70)	3.4	2.6	9.7	1.2	3.6

Sources: 1959 and 1970 Soviet censuses (see Chapter 1, n. 104); and sources cited in Chapter 6, n. 19.

Moscow, in comparison, had only 51 urban centers. Furthermore, in the 25-50 mile zone of Moscow there were only 14 urban centers in 1970. In contrast, the 25-50 mile zones of London and New York had about four times that number, while for Tokyo and Los Angeles there were roughly twice that number.

The much smaller number of urban centers in the Moscow urban region partly results from the fact that, as mentioned before, Moscow annexed a number of would-be individual urban centers in 1960. Nevertheless, even if these towns were still separate urban centers, the Moscow region would still have the fewest number of urban centers of any of the regions. Moreover, London also underwent a similar territorial change in the 1960s when a number of towns (for example, Wimbledon) were amalgamated to form the new unit, "Greater London," which is counted as one urban center there.[21] Thus, although London, like Moscow, also essentially annexed a number of individual urban centers, the London region still had nearly twice as many urban centers as Moscow in 1970. The great differences between Moscow and the other four regions in terms of number of individual urban centers, therefore, is to a great extent a further indication of the lesser size and extent of the Moscow region as compared with the other four.

Equally, if not more, interesting is a comparison of changes in the Moscow urban region with those of Tokyo, New York, London, and Los Angeles between circa 1960 and circa 1970 (Tables 6.6-6.9). In terms of overall growth, Moscow was surpassed only by Tokyo and Los Angeles in the period under consideration. The Tokyo region increased by more than 6 million people and by 4 percent per year, or 1.5 times between 1960 and 1970. Los Angeles increased by well over 2 million people and by over 3 percent per year. Moscow increased by slightly more than 2 million people or by more than 2 percent annually. The population of the New York urban region, however, increased by only slightly more than 1 million people and by only 1 percent per annum, and that of the London urban region virtually did not increase at all (only by 78,000 people and by less than 1 percent over the entire decade).

Although all five urban regions experienced deconcentration between circa 1960 and circa 1970, the Moscow region, generally speaking, had the least overall deconcentration (Tables 6.7 and 6.8). In all five regions the share of the population residing within the 0-25 mile zone declined and, of course, the share within the 25-50 mile radius increased. Nevertheless, whereas the change was roughly seven percentage points for Los Angeles, roughly four percentage points for New York and London, and slightly more than one percentage point for Tokyo, the change was only 0.6 percentage points for Moscow. The slight relative decline in the 0-25 mile zone of Moscow reflects the fact that population growth in absolute terms was still fairly considerable here (nearly 2 million or more than 2 percent per year) (Tables 6.6 and 6.9). Only the 0-25 mile zone of Tokyo exceeded both of these figures (over 5 million or nearly 4 percent per year). The 0-25 mile zone of Los Angeles increased at a slightly higher rate than that of Moscow (2.6 percent per year), but increased somewhat less in absolute population size. Only in New York and London was the declining relative share of the 0-25 mile zone not accompanied by fairly appreciable population growth in this zone. The population of the 0-25 mile zone of New York increased by only about 0.5 million or 0.4 percent per year, and in London it declined by nearly 0.5 million or -0.4 percent annually.

In addition, the Moscow region had the highest percentage of its growth in the 0-25 mile zone of any of the five urban regions. Between 1959 and 1970, 90 percent of its growth occurred within the 0-25 mile zone. The corresponding figure for Tokyo was slightly less than this (88.5 percent), but for Los Angeles and New York corresponding figures were only 68.6 percent and 42.4 percent, and in London the 0-25 mile zone declined in population.

The shift away from the 0-25 mile zone obviously entailed a shift toward the 25-50 mile zone. Moscow, of course, experienced the least shift in this direction, while Los Angeles, New York, and London experienced the greatest shifts toward this zone (Table 6.8). Moreover, all four non-Soviet regions had a greater absolute population increase in this zone and, except for London, a greater rate of increase (Tables 6.6 and 6.9). The population increase in the 25-50 mile zone was roughly in the range of 500,000 to 750,000 for the four non-Soviet regions, with Los Angeles having the greatest increase (731,791). However, the 25-50 mile zone of Moscow increased by only about 200,000 people. The rate of population increase in the 25-50 mile zone was very high for Los Angeles (nearly 10 percent per year) and moderately high for New York and Tokyo (roughly 5 percent per year in both cases). In comparison, the rate of increase for the outer suburbs of Moscow was but 3 percent per year, a figure that only London failed to attain (roughly 2 percent annually). In short, similar to the patterns previously discussed for all 22 urban regions of the USSR, the population of the Moscow region experienced only a relatively slight shift toward the 25-50 mile zone, and the 0-25 mile zone is still growing appreciably in both absolute and relative terms.

Also like the general Soviet pattern, the greatest shift in the Moscow region's population has not been from the 0-25 mile zone but instead within the 0-25 mile zone from the central city to the inner suburbs. As Table 6.8 reveals, the share of the population of the Moscow region residing in the central city declined by roughly six percentage points, while the share for the inner suburbs increased by nearly six percentage points. As mentioned before, the shift between the 0-25 mile zone and 25-50 mile zone involved only 0.6 percentage points. In the four non-Soviet urban regions the central city also underwent a declining share of the population of the urban region as a whole. The greatest percentage point declines in the central city share occurred in Tokyo (-17.6 percentage points) and Los Angeles (-8.2 percentage points). Paradoxically, the absolute population of these central cities increased more rapidly than the central city populations of the other three regions, except for the city of Moscow, which had the most rapid increase of all five central cities (Table 6.9). This reflects the fact that growth was so rapid in the suburban zones of Tokyo and Los Angeles that it entailed a decline in the share of the population residing in the central cities. The central city of New York barely increased at all in population, and that of London declined considerably.

However, although the central city share of all five urban regions declined appreciably, only in Moscow and Tokyo was the decline accompanied by a sharp shift to the inner suburbs, a shift that exceeded that to the outer suburbs. The great shift to the inner suburbs of Moscow and Tokyo was accompanied by very rapid population growth in these zones. In Moscow the population of the inner suburbs nearly doubled between 1959 and 1970 and increased at an annual rate of 5.6 percent. Indeed, some of the most rapidly growing suburbs of Moscow were truly inner suburbs in that they consisted of cities lying just beyond the Circumferential Highway, which functions as the city boundary of Moscow. The most prominent examples include Odintsovo (20,337 to 67,202), Dolgoprodnyy (25,267 to 53,095), Reutov (24,268 to 50,150), Vidnoye (14,191 to 35,446), Khimki (47,800 to 86,645), and Krasnogorsk (35,183 to 62,690). Even more astounding was the growth of the inner suburbs of Tokyo, which increased in population from 3.3 million to nearly 8 million or by nearly 9 percent per annum. The greatest share of this growth was concentrated in the two suburbs of Yokohama and Kawasaki. Based upon the "Densely Inhabited Districts" concept, between 1960 and 1970 the population of Yokohama increased from 1.1 to 1.9 million and that of Kawasaki increased from 566,000 to 907,000. Needless to say, these two cities were by far the largest suburbs of any of the five urban regions. Furthermore, seven other inner suburbs of Tokyo grew from within the range of 34,000 to 167,000 in 1960 to the range of 203,000 to 365,000 in 1970.

In New York, London, and Los Angeles, however, there was relatively little shift toward the inner suburbs (Table 6.9). Although the share of the populations of these urban regions residing in the inner suburbs increased, in no case did the increase attain even two percentage points. In all these regions, the shift to the outer suburbs greatly exceeded these figures. In fact, in New York there was virtually no shift at all toward the inner suburbs (0.2 percentage points) (Table 6.8). Not unexpectedly, the rate of population increase of the inner suburbs of these three regions was relatively slow as compared with Moscow and Tokyo (Table 6.9). In Los Angeles, the population of the inner suburbs increased by 3.6 percent per year, but in New York and London it increased by only about 1 percent per year. New York, of course, contains a number of large inner suburbs that are declining in population, such as Newark (405,220 in 1960 to 381,930 in 1970) and Jersey City (276,101 to 260,350).

In summary, a comparison of the Moscow urban region with four other major urban regions of the world reveals that, in general, the Moscow region has experienced a lesser amount of deconcentration or suburbanization. In particular, the Moscow region has had a relatively high share of its population in the 0-25 mile zone and central city and a relatively small shift to the outer suburbs. The patterns of the Moscow region exemplify those of the 22 Soviet urban regions combined.

Populations, Areas, and Population
Densities of Major Soviet Cities

In addition to the data already presented and discussed (Tables 6.2-6.9),
data concerning the populations, areas, and population densities of some major
Soviet cities also testify to the relative lack of urban deconcentration or sprawl
in the USSR. For instance, the city of Moscow in 1970 had an official area of
about 340 square miles and a population of roughly 7 million, while the city of
Los Angeles had an area of about 460 square miles in 1970 but a population of
only about 2.8 million.[22] Thus, Moscow's population, which was nearly three
times as large as Los Angeles's, resided on an area only about three-fourths
the size of Los Angeles. In addition, in 1970, the population of the Los Angeles-Long Beach Urbanized Area, an area essentially consisting of the built-up
area, was somewhat more than 8.4 million people, or about 1.4 million and
20 percent more than the population of the city of Moscow in the same year.[23]
However, the area of the Los Angeles-Long Beach Urbanized Area was roughly
1,600 square miles or about 4.5 times the size of the city of Moscow. In
short, the population of the city of Moscow, which was only slightly less than
that of the Los Angeles-Long Beach Urbanized Area, resided in an area that
was only about one-fifth the size of the Los Angeles-Long Beach area.

Moscow's lesser degree of sprawl can be seen also in a comparison
with London. The official cities of Moscow and London (here "Greater London"
as constituted in 1965 and not the very small "city of London") had roughly the
same population in 1970 (1971 in the case of London)—Moscow, 7 million and
London 7.8 million.[24] However, the area of London was about 620 square
miles, nearly twice the area of the city of Moscow.[25] Thus, the population
of the city of Moscow, which was only slightly less than that of London resided
on an area that was only about one-half the area of London.

These data may be somewhat surprising because they contradict a possible visually based conclusion that Moscow is quite spread out, because it
lies on a plain and has a relatively low skyline, especially as compared with
skyscraper-dominated New York. It must be remembered, however, that in
Moscow and most Soviet cities the major share of the population is housed in
multistory dwellings and not in single-family houses, a situation promoting
high densities and a lesser degree of sprawl. Indeed, the population density
of New York City and the city of Moscow are not appreciably different. In
1970 New York City had a population of 7.9 million and an area of 300 square
miles, resulting in a very high density of about 26,000 people per square
mile.[26] As mentioned earlier, Moscow in 1970 had a population of 7 million
and an area of 350 square miles, which results in a density of about 20,000
people per square mile. The density of Moscow in 1970 was in fact closer to
that of New York City than to that of the city of Los Angeles (6,000 people per
square mile) and of London or Greater London (13,000 people per square
mile).

Densities in sections of Moscow often reach very high levels. Although
data are not available for parts of Moscow comparable to the census tracts in
U.S. cities, population and area data are available in 1970 for the 29 official

(rayony) regions of Moscow (excluding the outlying city of Zelenograd).[27] These data indicate that two rayony (Bauman and Sverdlovsk, both of which extend outward from just beyond the Kremlin), each had densities of nearly 60,000 people per square mile. In addition, three rayony had densities of 40,000 to 50,000, eight had 30,000 to 40,000, and only two had less than 10,000. The lowest density was 6,400 (Krasnogvardeysk), which was still slightly higher than the density for the entire city of Los Angeles.

It would be desirable to investigate populations, areas, and densities for other Soviet cities to assess further their degree of sprawl. This information can be obtained for some major cities of the USSR.[28] Given the apparent overbounded nature of some Soviet cities, however, it is probable that density figures based on these data may be underestimates, because they include much peripheral open space. Unfortunately, there are few appropriate maps of Soviet cities that enable one to determine the extent of the overboundedness. Maps are available for Moscow and they suggest that even some portions of the city of Moscow, particularly the periphery, consist of open space. Hence, the density figures presented above for Moscow are probably underestimates, thus further buttressing the points we made, although, obviously, portions of the official cities of New York, London, and Los Angeles also include some open space.

Not unexpectedly, of the remaining major Soviet cities, a comparatively great amount of appropriate information is available for the second largest city of the country, Leningrad. The population of Leningrad is presented generally in two ways: (1) Leningrad city and settlements subordinated to the city soviet and (2) Leningrad city by itself. In 1970 the Leningrad and subordinated settlements had a population of nearly 4 million and an area of 525 square miles, resulting in a very low density of only about 7,000 people per square mile.[29] In comparison, in 1970 the city of Chicago, its U.S. counterpart, had a population of 3.4 million and an area of 223 square miles, or a density of roughly 15,000 people per square mile.[30] It appears then that Leningrad's density was comparatively quite low. Reflecting the overbounded nature of Soviet cities, a great share of the area of the city of Leningrad and subordinated settlements had very low densities. In 1970 the subordinated zone by itself had a population of 440,000 and an area of roughly 300 square miles, resulting in a density of only about 1,500 people per square mile. The city of Leningrad per se had a population of 3.5 million and an area of 222 square miles, nearly the same as Chicago in both cases, thus resulting in a density of about 16,000 people per square mile. Thus, Leningrad including subordinated settlements was a relatively sparsely settled urban area, but Leningrad per se is more than twice as densely populated as Los Angeles and about as densely populated as Chicago. Appreciable urban settlement virtually ends at the official boundary of the central city of Leningrad, and, except for strips along the Gulf of Finland and Neva River, the built-up area of Leningrad drops off sharply at a distance of approximately 5 to 7 miles from downtown Leningrad. In the Chicago area, however, substantial suburban settlement extends well beyond the official boundary of the central city, and, except for the Lake Michigan side obviously, the built-up area of Chicago does not begin to drop off sharply until at least roughly 12 to 20 miles from downtown Chicago.[31] This Leningrad-Chicago comparison again demonstrates the relative lack of urban sprawl in the USSR.

A comparison of Leningrad with other U.S. cities further supports this conclusion. For example, the Philadelphia and Detroit Urbanized Areas in 1970 both had a population of about 4 million and an area of about 800 to 900 square miles (750 and 870, respectively), resulting in a density of about 5,000 people per square mile in each case.[32] As mentioned before, Leningrad including subordinated settlements had a population of 4 million but an area of only 525 square miles, resulting in a higher density of 7,500 people per square mile. Although this density was described as low in the above discussion, it is somewhat higher than that of the Philadelphia and Detroit Urbanized Areas. In short, the population of Leningrad and subordinated settlements, which is virtually identical to that of these two U.S. Urbanized Areas, resides on an area that is only about two-thirds the size of the Philadelphia or Detroit Urbanized Areas. Furthermore, as indicated above, the inclusion of Leningrad's subordinated settlement zone in the total population of the city results in a much lower density as compared with that for the city per se. The city of Leningrad excluding subordinated settlements has a population only slightly smaller than that of the Philadelphia and Detroit areas—more specifically, a population that is equal to about 90 percent of these two U.S. areas. However, the area of Leningrad city per se is only about 200 square miles, resulting in a density that is three times that of the Philadelphia and Detroit areas. Thus, the population of Leningrad city per se, which is nearly the same as the Philadelphia and Detroit Urbanized Areas, resides on a territory that is only about one-fourth the size of the territories of these two U.S. urban areas.

Data from our study of the urban regions of the USSR further demonstrate the lack of deconcentration and sprawl of the Leningrad area. It will be recalled that of the 22 urban regions in 1970, Leningrad, along with Baku, had the highest percentage of its total population residing in the 0-25 mile zone and central city. In particular, of the total population of the Leningrad region, 97.6 percent resided in the 0-25 mile zone and 94.9 percent resided in the central city. The latter figure included subordinated settlements, which were, for the most part, within the 0-25 mile zone. In addition, the percentage point shift to the 25-50 mile zone of the Leningrad urban region between 1959 and 1970 was only 0.4, slightly below the average of 0.6 for all 22 regions combined. The relatively meager settlement in the outer portions of the Leningrad region is partly due to the fact that the city was somewhat of an artificial creation in that it, or more appropriately, St. Petersburg, was a newly built capital city in a fairly sparsely settled area.

The problems brought forth by the overbounded nature of Soviet cities are evident also in the case of the third largest city of the country, Kiev. In 1970 Kiev had a population of 1.6 million and an area of about 300 square miles, resulting in a seemingly low density of only about 5,000 people per square mile, or about one-fourth the density of Moscow.[33] It appears, however, that a great share of the Kiev city region consists of open land. Maps showing Kiev's built-up area lead one to believe that the size of this area is only about 100 square miles.[34] Robert J. Osborn notes that Kiev, apparently in the early 1960s, annexed an entire forest and open-space belt up to 22 miles from the city center.[35] If the 1.6 million people of Kiev are regarded as residing on about 100 square miles instead of 300, then the density of the city increases to about 16,000 people per square mile, more in line with the densities of Moscow and Leningrad.

It is difficult, unfortunately, to assess the density patterns of Soviet cities in greater detail due to a general lack of data and maps on the official and built-up areas. Fragmentary information for other smaller towns can be gathered and probably would support the general conclusion that the built-up areas of Soviet cities are relatively small in areal extent, especially in comparison to the built-up areas of U.S. cities. The travel experience of both authors in the USSR also tends to support this conclusion.

Analysis

The preceding discussion has brought forth a number of major patterns that deserve further explanation. These patterns include an increased concentration of the Soviet population in the urban regions, a deconcentration of population within these regions, and, perhaps most interesting, the lack of an even more appreciable deconcentration.

Forces underlying an increased concentration are generally similar to those elsewhere in the world. Economic development usually entails (up to a certain point) an agglomeration of many activities and the Soviet experience is apparently no exception in this regard.[36] For example, it appears that the so-called "benefits of agglomeration" factor in industrial location is also present in the USSR—that is, subcontracting interlinkages and by-product interlinkages, to which could be added other characteristics of large agglomerations that attract industry (large market, large labor supply, developed transportation system, and so forth).[37]

Forces underlying the deconcentration of settlement within large urban agglomerations or regions in the USSR are also similar to a certain extent to those operating elsewhere. Urban deconcentration elsewhere has, of course, been related to improved transportation and increased commuting over longer distances. In the USSR urban commuting, often long-distance in nature, is apparently now a feature of Soviet urban life. For example, V. G. Gluchkova and N. P. Shepelev indicate that more than 500,000 people now commute daily from places outside the city in Moscow Oblast to the city of Moscow itself.[38] These commuters come from roughly 30 to 40 miles beyond the city limits of Moscow, which means that they come from as far out as 45 to 50 miles from the center of Moscow, although 90 percent of these commuters originate from places within 40 to 45 miles of the center of Moscow.[39] And, as B. S. Khorev notes, "the development of suburban transportation favors the drawing in of newer and newer settlements. Today suburbanites travel to their place of work over distances of 10-70 kilometers [6-44 miles], spending from a half hour to four hours per day."[40]

Industrialization also has been involved in the urban deconcentration process in the USSR, as it has elsewhere. For example, in the Moscow region, factories in the inner portions of the city are being closed, while new industries are being built in the suburbs outside the city and others are being relocated there. [41]

Of greatest interest, perhaps, is an analysis of the apparent phenomenon in the USSR of somewhat lesser urban deconcentration or sprawl than elsewhere, especially in the United States. In attempting to explain the lesser deconcentration or sprawl of Soviet cities, a combination of universal factors and factors fairly unique to the USSR emerges. First, the historical stage of urbanization and urban growth in the USSR has contributed perhaps the lesser degree of deconcentration. It would seem obvious that the greater the length of time involved, the greater is the chance of an outward spread of agglomerations. Although many Soviet cities are very old (for example, Moscow and Kiev were founded around the turn of the first millennium A.D.), most Soviet cities, old and new, have experienced appreciable growth only in the last half century or so. Data for all urban centers with 15,000 or more people indicate, in fact, that the vast majority (80.1 percent) of the urban growth (from 0 to 112,623,584) occurred between 1926 and 1970. In contrast, according to data for urban centers of 10,000 and over, which have been used in previous sections, slightly less than half (48.1 percent) of the urban growth of the United States (from 0 to 112,451,000) occurred in the roughly comparable 1930-70 period. The relative recency of the urban process in the USSR also is exemplified by another comparison between Moscow and New York City. It is generally accepted that Moscow was founded in 1147 A.D., about 4.5 centuries before the founding of New York City. However, whereas only about 12 percent of the growth of New York City (from a population of 0 to 7,895,563 in 1970) occurred in the 1930-70 period, 70.8 percent of the growth of Moscow (from 0 to 7,061,008 in 1970) occurred in the 1926-70 period. Although it was only slightly larger than Moscow in population in 1970, New York City had achieved Moscow's 1970 population of about 7 million people by 1930. Thus, it appears that one reason for the lesser deconcentration of Soviet cities is the relative recency of their growth.

On the other hand, one could argue that an opposite situation should occur. If a city is relatively new, one might expect greater sprawl in that such a city would have essentially evolved during the era of the widespread use of the automobile, which, of course, has been a major contributor to urban sprawl or deconcentration. The Los Angeles area is probably the prime example of this situation. Given the fact that most of the growth of Soviet cities has occurred only fairly recently, one actually might expect them also to be very spread out like Los Angeles and other newer, automobile-oriented U.S. cities.

The Soviet situation is actually quite the opposite in that there is a relative lack of both urban sprawl and the automobile. In fact, one of the major factors, if not the major factor, for the relative lack of greater urban deconcentration in the USSR is the fact that the automobile is a comparatively unimportant means of transportation in the USSR. The USSR is probably the least automobile-oriented major industrial country in the world. It has the fewest automobiles per capita of any major industrial power and a very poor highway system, one that has been described as being roughly equivalent to the U.S. highway system in the 1920s in size and structure.[42] Essentially absent from the Soviet urban picture are such automobile-related phenomena as suburban shopping centers and malls and extensive and blatant commercial development along major arterial roads. Gas stations are also few and far between. Soviet urbanites, instead, depend primarily on streetcars, trolley-buses, buses, subways, and their own feet for urban commuting and shopping. The relative lack of the automobile and an associated good road system in the USSR is due primarily to the governmental policy promoting heavy industry and generally neglecting agriculture, consumer goods, transportation, and housing. There have been recent efforts to give more attention to these items. For example, automobile production and the housing supply has increased rapidly in recent years. However, both are still in short supply.

Regarding the housing situation of the USSR, it bears repeating that the lesser degree of urban sprawl in the USSR also has been due to a predominance of apartment buildings rather than single-family houses. The main emphasis in the recent Soviet housing "boom" has been on the construction of multi-storied apartment houses. Unlike the United States, virtually absent from the Soviet urban scene are single-family houses on half-acre or more plots. Population densities in Soviet cities are heightened not only due to an emphasis on multistoried dwellings but also perhaps to the shortage of these dwellings, which leads to very high densities in terms of housing space per capita. In fact, the amount of useful housing space per capita in the USSR is only about one-half that of the United States.[43]

Another factor to be considered is the "green belt" policy of the USSR. This consists of efforts to limit urban sprawl by preserving much of the remaining open land around cities. For example, in the Moscow area, a green belt or forest belt extends for some 10 to 20 miles from the edge of the Circumferential Highway, which serves as the city limits of Moscow.[44] However, pressures exist in the USSR to develop these areas for urban uses.[45] The green belt zone of Moscow, for instance, contains many large cities (for example, Mytishchi, with a population of 119,000 in 1970), and, indeed, as mentioned before, some of the most rapidly growing suburbs of Moscow are just beyond the Circumferential Highway and, thus, within the general area of the green belt. It is interesting to note that the London region also has had a green belt policy, but, as we have seen, it has experienced relatively great deconcentration. This reflects the fact that green belt policies, although restricting the sprawl of the older interior built-up area, can actually contribute to overall deconcentration, because suburbs now must be located beyond the green belt and, thus, quite distant from the central city, as exemplified by the "new towns" of Britain and the "satellite cities" of the USSR.[46]

The previously discussed policy of the Soviet government to limit the growth of large cities perhaps also has had a retarding impact on the development of large urban regions. On the other hand, it could be argued that this policy, which specifically tries to limit the growth of such large central cities as Moscow and Leningrad, actually has contributed to urban deconcentration. For example, this limitation has led to increased investment in urban centers beyond the major central cities. [47] In addition, limitations on residence in the central city often lead to residence in the suburbs and commuting to the central city. [48]

Another reason that might be cited for the relative lack of urban deconcentration in the USSR is the general absence of a racial problem like that of the United States, at least during the past and for the present. Unlike U.S. cities and some European cities, Soviet cities generally do not have large minority populations concentrated in the central cities. Thus, there has not been a "white flight to the suburbs," although the Soviet situation might be changed somewhat with an increased flow of non-Slavic peoples (especially Turkic-Muslims) into Slavic cities (particularly Russian cities), a topic we have discussed at length in the first volume of this series.

Another factor possibly influencing the extent of urban deconcentration is the physical layout of the area. However, given the fact that Soviet cities are basically inland and on a vast plain, one might expect great sprawl rather than the little sprawl that has actually occurred. The lesser deconcentration of Soviet agglomerations also has been due to the continued fairly rapid growth of the large, central cities. The attractions of large cities were discussed in the previous chapter.

In summary, the apparent lesser deconcentration or sprawl of the urban regions of the USSR evidently has been related to a number of factors. These included: (1) the more recent stage of urbanization and relative newness of Soviet cities and urban regions; (2) the comparative absence in the USSR of automobiles, roads, single-family houses, and housing space in general; (3) a green belt policy; (4) lack of a racially motivated flight to the suburbs; and (5) the attractions of large, central cities and the continued growth of such cities.

Comments on Other Recent Studies

Before we depart from the subject of Soviet urban regions or metropolitan areas, it would seem appropriate to comment on recent articles by Richard Pipes and Russell B. Adams, which assume individual Soviet cities to be representative of metropolitan areas, an assumption that we, of course, consider as being somewhat questionable. [49] According to Pipes:

> The Soviet Union is inherently less vulnerable than the United States to a counter-value attack. According to the 1970 Soviet census, the U.S.S.R. had only nine cities with a population of 1 million or more; the aggregate population of these cities was 20.5 million or 8.5 percent of the country's total. The U.S. 1970 census showed 35 metropolitan centers with over 1 million inhabitants, totaling 84.5 million people, or 41.5 percent of the country's aggregate. It takes no professional strategist to visu-

alize what these figures mean. In World War II, the Soviet Union lost 20 million—i.e., 12 percent; yet the country not only survived but emerged stronger politically and militarily than it had ever been. Allowing for the population growth which has occurred since then, this experience suggests that as of today the U.S.S.R. could absorb the loss of 30 million of its people and be no worse off, in terms of human casualties than it had been at the conclusion of World War II. In other words, all of the U.S.S.R.'s multimillion cities could be destroyed without trace or survivors, and, provided that its essential cadres had been saved, it would emerge less hurt in terms of casualties than it was in 1945.

Such figures are beyond the comprehension of most Americans. But clearly a country that since 1914 has lost, as a result of two world wars, a civil war, famine and various "purges," perhaps up to 60 million citizens, must define "unacceptable damage" differently from the United States. . . . Such a country tends also to assess the rewards of defense in much more realistic terms.[50]

Previous data presented by ourselves and others suggest that Pipes has understated the urban population in metropolitan areas of over a million people. First he compares Soviet cities with U.S. metropolitan areas (apparently SMSAs), although they are not comparable. It could be argued that individual Soviet cities are similar to metropolitan areas, because they are somewhat overbounded and, thus, contain a number of suburbs. However, data for urban regions compiled by ourselves and others suggested that data for individual cities underestimate the metropolitan population of the USSR, because they exclude a number of suburbs, which are outside the boundaries of the official central city. Indeed, the existence of these exclusions was the prime reason for the derivation of these urban region schemes. Based on our urban regions, it appears that in 1970 more than 40 million people rather than 20 million people resided in Soviet metropolitan areas with 1 million or more people (Table 6.1). Other urban agglomeration schemes previously referred to also tend to suggest a figure of roughly 40 million people residing in Soviet metropolitan areas with more than 1 million people in 1970. According to Listengurt, 37.4 million people resided in the 19 agglomerations with more than 1 million people in 1970 that he distinguished.[51] Similarly, Pivovarov's 20 urban agglomerations with more than 1 million people in 1970 contained 40.4 million people.[52] Therefore, it appears from the available evidence that the figure presented by Pipes for the Soviet population residing in metropolitan areas with more than 1 million people underestimates such a population by about one-half or by about 20 million people.[53]

One can imply from Pipes's statements that he believes that the Soviet government would consider tolerable wartime population losses of 20 to 30 million people, beyond which lies an area of "unacceptable damage." We do not want to enter the argument as to whether there are tolerable limits. If such limits exist, the figure presented by Pipes falls short of the actual tolerable population losses. Since the population residing in metropolitan areas actually approximates 40 million, the Soviet Union would not "emerge less hurt in terms of casualties than it was in 1945" in the event of a war. If the Soviets actually would be willing to give up the population in their metropolitan areas with more than a million people, this means that they actually would have losses of roughly 40 million people plus much of the industrial plant.

We do not mean to imply that the Soviet population is as concentrated in metropolitan areas as is the U.S. population. Even a figure of 40 million signifies that only about 16 percent of the Soviet population resides in the metropolitan areas with 1 million or more people as compared with a U.S. (SMSA-based) percentage of slightly more than 40 percent. Of course, it still remains to be seen in further research if U.S. metropolitan data can be compared with Soviet metropolitan data calculated by ourselves or others. Although such data are not perfect and are not strictly comparable with metropolitan data for the United States or other countries, the use of such data is probably preferable to equating city data with metropolitan data as done by Pipes.

In the Adams's study, the author undertakes a comparison of Soviet and U.S. metropolitan change. A principal shortcoming of this study is that Adams, like Pipes, considers individual Soviet cities to be surrogates for metropolitan areas. His reasoning is that "Soviet cities . . . normally include suburban development" and that "most Soviet municipal limits are set far enough out to encompass most of the built-up area around a city."[54] We have discussed this point concerning the overbounded nature of Soviet cities before, and Adams's rationale does have some merit. As we have seen, nonetheless, the official Soviet city does not necessarily include all suburban development, prompting various Soviet scholars and ourselves to devise broader metropolitan definitions. Adams, in fact, admits that there is a "bias" that "usually favors a larger American SMSA figure over a comparable Soviet city value."[55] Thus, comparisons made by Adams between the Soviet and U.S. "metropolitan" hierarchies are somewhat questionable due to the different metropolitan concepts utilized. Unfortunately, Adams (and for that matter no one else) has derived and applied a comparable concept that would allow a comparison of the major Soviet and U.S. metropolitan areas. To perform such a comparison would involve an enormous amount of work. The comparable data we derived for only New York and Los Angeles took a great deal of time to calculate.

NOTES

1. For example, see Joseph Spengler, Population Change, Modernization, and Welfare (Englewood Cliffs, N.J.: Prentice-Hall, 1974), pp. 30-33.
2. For example, see V. G. Davidovich, "Goroda i Poselki-Sputniki v SSSR," Goroda-Sputniki (Moscow: Gosudarstvennoye Izdatel'stvo Geograficheskoy Literatury, 1961), pp. 5-39; G. M. Lappo, "Problems in the Evolution of Urban Agglomerations," Soviet Geography: Review and Translation 15 (November 1974): 531-42; F. M. Listengurt, "Criteria for Delineating

Large Urban Agglomerations in the USSR," Soviet Geography: Review and Translation 16 (November 1975): 559-68; V. G. Davidovich, "Rasseleniye v Prigorodnykh Zonakh," Rasseleniye v Prigorodnykh Zonakh (Moscow: Izdatel'stvo "Mysl'," 1971), pp. 5-43; and Yu. L. Pivovarov, Sovremennaya Urbanizatsiya (Moscow: "Statistika," 1976), pp. 87, 133-38.

3. Maps utilized to draw circles in this study come from USSR, Glavnoye Upravleniye Geodezii i Kartografii Ministerstva Geologii i Okhrany Nedr SSSR, Atlas SSSR (Moscow, 1962).

4. Davidovich, "Gorod i Poselki-Sputniki v SSSR," p. 30.

5. Listengurt, "Criteria for Delineating"; Pivovarov, Sovremennaya Urbanizatsiya; and Davidovich, "Rasseleniye v Prigorodnykh Zonakh."

6. Listengurt, "Criteria for Delineating," p. 567.

7. Ibid., p. 563.

8. Pivovarov, Sovremennaya Urbanizatsiya, pp. 135-37.

9. Ibid., pp. 136-37.

10. Davidovich, "Rasseleniye v Prigorodnykh Zonakh," p. 8.

11. Ibid.

12. F. E. Ian Hamilton, The Moscow City Region (London: Oxford University Press, 1976), p. 20.

13. Ibid., p. 39.

14. Ibid., p. 36.

15. This conclusion is based in part on a map of the Moscow area in A. A. Grigor'yev, ed., Kratkaya Geograficheskaya Entsiklopediya, 5 vols. (Moscow: Gosudarstvennoye Nauchnoye Izdatel'stvo "Sovetskaya Entsiklopediya," 1962), 3: 45. This map shows boundaries for both before and after the 1960 annexation plus boundaries as envisaged in the 1935 plan.

16. Leningrad, Statisticheskoye Upravleniye Goroda Leningrada, Planovaya Komissiya Ispolkoma Lengorsoveta, Leningrad za 50 Let (Leningrad: Lenizdat, 1967), p. 23.

17. Lappo, "Problems in the Evolution"; and Pivovarov, Sovremenneya Urbanizatsiya.

18. Listengurt, "Criteria for Delineating," p. 567.

19. Tokyo data for 1960 come from Japan, Bureau of Statistics, Office of the Prime Minister, 1960 Population Census of Japan, vol. 1 (1961); and idem, 1960 Population Census, Densely Inhabited District: Its Population, Area, and Map, December 1961. Tokyo data for 1970 come from idem, 1970 Population Census of Japan, vol. 3 (1971), pts. 8-14, 19, and 22. New York and Los Angeles data for 1960 and 1970 come from: The World Almanac & Book of Facts, 1975 (New York: Newspaper Enterprise Associates, 1974), pp. 160-63, 172-75. This source was used instead of directly using the U.S. censuses, because it conveniently provides the 1960 and 1970 census population of all cities, townships, and unincorporated places with more than 5,000 people. London data for 1961 and 1971 come from Great Britain, Office of Population Censuses and Surveys, Census, 1971: England and Wales, Preliminary Report (1972). Conveniently available atlases were used to make the necessary map radius measurements; for example, The Odyssey World Atlas (New York: Golden Press, 1967).

20. Ibid.

21. Donald L. Foley, Governing the London Region (Berkeley: University of California Press, 1972), pp. 5, 32-38.

22. Areas for major Soviet cities (all republic capitals and/or cities with 1 million or more people) can be estimated from population and population density data in Vestnik Statistiki, no. 3 (1971), p. 84. Los Angeles data come from U.S., Department of Commerce, Social and Economic Statistics Administration, Bureau of the Census, County and City Data Book, 1972 (Washington, D.C.: U.S. Government Printing Office, 1973), p. 642 (hereafter cited as County and City Data Book, 1972).

23. County and City Data Book, 1972, p. 596.

24. Data for London come from Foley, Governing the London Region, p. 4.

25. Ibid.

26. County and City Data Book, 1972, p. 738.

27. Moscow, Statisticheskoye Upravleniye Goroda Moskvy, Moskva v Tsifrafkh (1966-1970 GG.) (Moscow: Izdatel'stvo "Statistika," 1972), p. 153. For a map showing these density variations (though in terms of population per square kilometer), see G. M. Lappo, A. Chikishev, and A. Bekker, Moscow —Capital of the Soviet Union (Moscow: Progress, 1976), p. 93.

28. Vestnik Statistiki.

29. Area data come from Leningrad, Statisticheskoye Upravleniye Goroda Leningrada, Planovaya Komissiya Ispolkoma Lengorsoveta, Leningrad za 50 Let, p. 19.

30. County and City Data Book, 1972, p. 678.

31. This comparison of Leningrad's and Chicago's built-up area is based upon Oxford World Atlas (New York: Oxford University Press, 1973), pp. 71, 76.

32. County and City Data Book, 1972, pp. 590, 602.

33. The area estimate comes from Vestnik Statistiki.

34. For example, see USSR, Glavnoye Upravleniye Goedezii i Kartografii pri Sovete Ministrov SSSR, Malyy Atlas SSSR (Moscow: 1973), p. 81.

35. Robert J. Osborn, Soviet Social Policies: Welfare, Equality, and Community (Homewood, Ill.: Dorsey Press, 1970), p. 212.

36. Lappo, "Problems in the Evolution," pp. 532-36.

37. Ibid.

38. V. G. Gluchkova and N. P. Shepelev, "Definition of the Boundary of Moscow's Active Zone of Influence," Soviet Geography: Review and Translation 17 (April 1976): 271.

39. Ibid.

40. B. S. Khorev, Problemy Gorodov, 2d ed. (Moscow: Izdatel'stvo "Mysl'," 1975), p. 350.

41. William A. Dando, "The Moscow City Region: Land Development in an Expanding Socialist City," The Middle Atlantic 6 (July 1975): 21, 23; and G. M. Lappo, "Trends in the Evolution of Settlement Patterns in the Moscow Region," Soviet Geography: Review and Translation 14 (January 1973): 16, 20.

42. For example, see Imogene U. Edwards, "Automotive Trends in the USSR," Soviet Economic Prospects for the Seventies, U.S. Congress, Joint

Economic Committee Print (Washington, D.C.: Government Printing Office, 1973), pp. 291-314.

43. For example, see Willard S. Smith, "Housing in the Soviet Union—Big Plans, Little Action," Soviet Economic Prospects for the Seventies, U.S. Congress, Joint Economic Committee Print (Washington, D.C.: Government Printing Office, 1973), p. 406.

44. Osborn, Soviet Social Policies, pp. 209-11.

45. Ibid., pp. 209-14.

46. Ibid., pp. 214-20.

47. Ibid.

48. Ibid., p. 205.

49. Richard Pipes, "The Soviet Strategy for Nuclear Victory," Washington Post July 3, 1977, pp. C1, C4; and Russell B. Adams, "The Soviet Metropolitan Hierarchy: Regionalization and Comparison with the United States," Soviet Geography: Review and Translation 18 (May 1977): 313-28.

50. Pipes, "Soviet Strategy for Nuclear Victory," p. C4.

51. Listengurt, "Criteria for Delineating," p. 565.

52. Pivovarov, Sovremennaya Urbanizatsiya, p. 137.

53. Unfortunately, the other scheme developed by Davidovich ("Rasseleniye v Prigorodnykh Zonakh") does not contain an estimate of the population residing in his 20 agglomerations with more than 1 million people in 1970.

54. Adams, "Soviet Metropolitan Hierarchy," pp. 315, 317.

55. Ibid., p. 317.

RURAL POPULATION CHANGE

7

A major facet of the redistribution of population in Russia and the USSR has been a shift from rural areas to urban areas. However, because rural population change has been discussed to a considerable extent already and it is not the primary emphasis of this study, our discussion of this subject will be comparatively brief. In particular, brief attention will be devoted to the subjects of aggregate and regional patterns of rural population change, the size of rural settlements, rural migration and natural increase, and appropriate policies.

SUMMARY DISCUSSION

Since 1897 the level of ruralization in the USSR has declined sharply, reflecting a corresponding sharp increase in the level of urbanization. Whereas roughly 90 percent of the total population resided in rural settlements in 1897, by the late 1970s less than one-half of the Soviet population was rural.

The decline in the level of ruralization has been related partly to the fact that the rural population has grown very slowly since the turn of the century and actually has declined in the Soviet period. A sharp rural decline occurred prior to 1959, reflecting the losses of World War II, but between 1959 and 1970, such a decline did not occur, largely because of the rapid rural growth of the Non-Slavic South. However, since 1970, the rural population again has declined sharply and for the first time in the twentieth century, it has dropped below the 100 million level.

Sharp regional variations in rates of rural population change have occurred also. Most notably, the regions of Northern European USSR and, more recently, the Russian East, have experienced considerable rural population decline, while the regions of the Non-Slavic South have had a considerable rural population increase. Since 1970 the rates of rural change for nearly all regions has declined in comparison to 1959-70, nearly every region has had rural decline, and the rates of rural decline have been unprecedented apparently in any of the preceding periods.

356

Concurrent with these trends has been a shift of the rural population from smaller to larger rural settlements. Between 1959 and 1970, the number of and absolute population within small rural settlements declined.

The components of rural population change are rural natural increase and rural net migration. The slowing down of rural population growth and eventual rural population decline have been related to declining rural crude birth and natural increase rates and very substantial rural-to-urban migration. Just as the USSR can be dichotomized generally in the 1959-70 period with respect to rural population change into the Slavic and Baltic areas and the areas of the southern tier, so it is with respect to rural natural increase. Largely as a result of rural out-migration, rural natural increase rates in the Slavic and Baltic areas declined in the 1960s to very low levels, whereas in Central Asia, Kazakhstan, and Azerbaydzhan rural natural increase rates remained high, and in Georgia, Armenia, and Moldavia they declined from high to moderate levels. The same geographic dichotomy prevails with respect to net rural out-migration. The Slavic and Baltic areas were characterized generally by relatively high rates of net rural out-migration and a decline in the rural population of working age, whereas low rates of net rural out-migration and a stationary or increasing rural population of working age were characteristic of the republics in the non-Slavic southern tier. According to available data on rural labor shortages and surpluses, the amount of time worked on kolkhozy, and agricultural income, it would appear that a similar dichotomy prevails with respect to these variables. The rural population of the southern tier appears generally to have labor surpluses, higher kolkhoz family incomes, and work less time than in the Slavic and Baltic areas.

It would appear that migrant characteristics and the processes that are related to rural out-migration in the USSR are similar to those that have occurred in other developed countries. The young and the more educated have the highest propensities to migrate, and there is no significant selectivity according to sex. Appreciable differences in the standard of living between rural and urban areas exist in the USSR, although these differences may be significantly less in the southern tier than in the Slavic and Baltic areas. Rural out-migration appears to be the greatest where the rural-urban wage differential is the greatest. The rural population of the southern tier is less mobile than might be expected, but this can be attributed, in the most general sense, to higher incomes, smaller urban-rural differences in the standard of living, less economic development in the local urban areas, and ethnic and linguistic factors.

Intensive investigations of certain labor-deficit areas within the RSFSR indicate that, in addition to considerable out-migration to urban areas, there was a considerable redistribution within rural areas from poorer farms to more prosperous ones, thus contributing to a concentration of the rural population. Surveys in these areas indicate a general dissatisfaction with the material conditions of rural life.

Only very general statements can be made concerning the effectiveness of policies directed toward rural population change. That there is an exodus out of labor-deficit rural areas and that the rural population in areas having a labor surplus is relatively immobile indicate that migration is not meeting the economic needs of the USSR. The long-term policy of eliminating economic and cultural differences between urban and rural areas has not been implemented to a significant degree, judging from the rather great differences in living standards between rural and urban areas, which has been the impetus for considerable rural out-migration. It is difficult to appraise the effectiveness of the current program initiated in the mid-1960s to increase investment, mechanization, and wages and to raise rural living standards in order to diminish rural out-migration. Over much of the USSR, however, rural population decline has intensified since 1970, although it is not known what would have happened in the absence of this program. It would appear that the Soviet government is in the process of adjusting to a declining rural population, which in the not-too-distant future should, at least in the Slavic and Baltic areas, approach the levels characteristic of other developed countries. Finally, it should be noted that only a fragmentary picture of conditions in rural areas of the USSR can be derived, because of a general lack of data.

DETAILED DISCUSSION

The following discussion of rural population change is based largely on our comparable set of data. The rural population is defined as that population not residing in settlements of 15,000 and over. As before, data based on official urban definitions also will be utilized whenever appropriate. The rural population in this case is defined as that population not residing in an urban center based on official urban definitions and will be referred to as that based on the "official rural definitions." In addition, the term level of ruralization will be employed to denote the percentage of the total population residing in rural areas. As a point of information, it should be noted that the rural population of the USSR lives principally in villages rather than on individual farmsteads as in the United States. Villages are called by a variety of names, such as selos, derevnyas, slobodas, stanitsas, auls, kishlaks, and so forth. Individual farmsteads do exist, however, in certain areas, mainly in the Baltic and adjacent areas, and are called khutors. Collective farms (kolkhozy) and state farms (sovkhozy), the main types of Soviet farms, generally consist of a number of rural settlements.

Aggregate Patterns

Because the level of ruralization and its change involve the obverse of the urbanization process, the following discussion will be based on tables in Chapters 3 and 4. For Russia and the USSR as a whole, the rapid urbanization process has entailed obviously a sharp decline in the level of ruralization. Whereas in 1897 roughly 90 percent of the total population resided in rural areas, by 1970 only a slight majority (53.4 percent) of the population was rural (Table 3.1). Post-1970 data suggest that by the late 1970s less than a majority of the population resided in rural areas, especially data based on the official rural definitions, which indicate that only 38.1 percent of the total population resided in rural areas in 1977 (Table 3.3). Although declining, the level of ruralization in the USSR is, however, still quite high in comparison to other industrialized regions (Table 3.5).

The decline in the level of ruralization has been related partly to the fact that the rural population of Russia and the USSR has grown very slowly since 1897 and has actually declined since 1926 (Tables 3.7-3.10). Although the rural population declined somewhat between 1926 and 1939 because of reactions to the collectivization of agriculture and rapid economic development, most of the decline in the rural population has occurred since 1939. A fairly sharp decline (more than 10 percent or roughly 15 million people overall) occurred during the 1939-59 period, reflecting the impact of World War II. Indeed, all of the rural population decline between 1939 and 1959 based on official rural definitions occurred between 1939 and 1951, while a very slight increase transpired between 1951 and 1959.[1] Between 1959 and 1970, the rural population just barely increased, based on the 15,000-and-over urban definition, but slightly declined, based on official rural definitions (Tables 3.7-3.10). The lack of a sharp rural decline between 1959 and 1970 was due primarily to the substantial rural population increase in the Non-Slavic South.

However, since 1970, the rural population has declined quite sharply according to both rural criteria (Tables 3.9 and 3.10). The average annual rate of decline of roughly 1 percent per year represents a greater rate of decline than ever experienced between any two successive census dates between 1897 and 1970 (Tables 3.8 and 3.10). In terms of absolute numbers, the rural population has been declining by roughly 1 million people annually since 1970, and by the late 1970s the rural population, based on official rural definitions, fell below the 100 million level for the first time in the twentieth century.[2] The emergence of rural population decline and a deepening of the rates of decline are, of course, expected occurrences with an intensification of the processes of economic development, modernization, and rural out-migration.

Nonetheless, the Soviet rural population is still quite large in both absolute and/or relative terms. Roughly 100 to 130 million people and roughly 40 to 50 percent of the Soviet population still reside in rural areas, depending on the rural definition used.

A number of factors contribute to the continued existence of a fairly large rural population in the USSR. First, given the fact that the urban-industrial process is relatively recent, there has, perhaps, not been enough time to deplete the rural population to a greater extent. In addition, despite a considerable decline in the number of agricultural workers in recent years, the Soviet agricultural sector still requires a substantial number of farm workers due to its relatively low degree of mechanization in comparison to other industrialized countries. Furthermore, an appreciable share of the rural population is nonagricultural (roughly one-third in 1968, based on official rural definitions) and thus is not affected by a decline in agricultural workers.[3] Also, as mentioned many times, the USSR contains significant areas, most notably the Non-Slavic South, with continued substantial rural population increase. Regional aspects of rural population change will now be discussed in more detail.

Regional Patterns

Regional levels of ruralization and changes therein, of course, are the obverse of the regional urbanization patterns and, therefore, do not have to be discussed in the detail that the urbanization patterns were (Tables 4.1-4.6 and 4.11-4.14). The main point that should be stressed in this regard is that, whereas nearly every region had a level of ruralization of 90 percent or more in 1897, by 1970 the highest regional level was less than 80 percent and most were less than 60 percent.

Regional variations in levels of ruralization in 1970, which can be inferred from Tables 4.1 and 4.2, are shown in Map 7.1. All gross regions, except for the Russian East, still had a majority of their population residing in rural areas, with the Non-Slavic South having the highest level. Economic regions having especially high levels of ruralization included Moldavia, the Southwest, and Central Asia, each of which had more than two-thirds of their population residing in rural areas. Other regions having a majority of their population in rural areas included Belorussia, Kazakhstan, the Volgo-Vyatsk, the West, the North Caucasus, East Siberia, and the South. These rural populations are based on the urban definition of 15,000 and over, which tends to inflate the size of the rural population, because all settlements up to 15,000 in population are considered to be rural.

MAP 7.1

Level of Ruralization: 1970

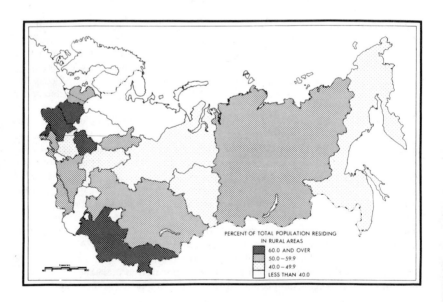

PERCENT OF TOTAL POPULATION RESIDING
IN RURAL AREAS

60.0 AND OVER
50.0 – 59.9
40.0 – 49.9
LESS THAN 40.0

TABLE 7.1

Average Annual Percentage Change of the Rural Population by Gross Region: 1897-1970

Region	1897-1926	1926-39	1939-59	1959-70	1926-70	1897-1970
Western USSR	0.7	-0.2	-0.9	-0.5	-0.6	-0.1
Eastern USSR	1.3	0.5	0.3	0.9	0.5	0.9
Northern European USSR	0.6	-0.3	-1.1	-0.9	-0.9	-0.3
European Steppe	1.0	-0.2	-0.3	0.3	-0.1	0.4
Russian East	1.7	0.4	-0.1	-0.5	-0.0	0.7
Non-Slavic South	0.8	1.0	0.7	2.3	1.2	1.0
USSR total	0.9	-0.1	-0.6	0.0	-0.3	0.2

Sources: See Chapter 1, nn. 104, 105, and 113.

TABLE 7.2

Average Annual Percentage Change of the Rural Population
by Economic Region: 1897–1970

Region	1897–1926	1926–39	1939–59	1959–70	1926–70	1897–1970
Northwest	0.8	-0.7	-1.4	-1.0	-1.1	-0.3
West	-0.2	0.0	-0.6	-0.6	-0.4	-0.3
Center	0.9	-0.6	-1.6	-1.7	-1.3	-0.5
Volgo–Vyatsk	0.4	0.6	-1.1	-1.6	-0.8	-0.3
Central Chernozem	1.0	-0.8	-1.6	-1.3	-1.3	-0.4
Volga	0.7	-1.4	-1.2	-0.7	-1.1	-0.4
Belorussia	0.5	0.8	-0.9	-0.7	-0.4	0.0
Moldavia	1.0	1.8	0.4	1.0	1.0	1.0
Southwest	0.6	-0.2	-0.6	-0.3	-0.4	0.0
South	0.7	-0.5	-0.3	1.0	0.0	0.2
Donetsk–Dnepr	1.2	-1.0	-0.4	-0.9	-0.7	0.1
North Caucasus	1.0	0.2	-0.3	0.9	0.2	0.5
Transcaucasus	0.6	1.8	0.0	1.6	0.9	0.8
Urals	0.7	-0.2	-0.4	-0.6	-0.4	0.1
West Siberia	3.7	0.2	-0.4	-1.3	-0.4	1.3
East Siberia	1.7	1.6	0.4	0.3	0.7	1.1
Far East	4.3	2.1	1.5	0.3	1.4	2.6
Kazakhstan	0.7	-1.6	1.3	2.0	0.6	0.7
Central Asia	1.0	2.4	0.7	2.9	1.7	1.4
USSR total	0.9	-0.1	-0.6	+0.0	-0.3	0.2

Sources: See Chapter 1, nn. 104, 105, and 113.

TABLE 7.3

Average Annual Percentage Change of the Rural Population
by Gross Region: 1959-77

Region	Official Rural Definitions		Population Not Residing in Official Cities of 15,000 and over	
	1959-70	1970-77	1959-70	1970-74
Western USSR	-0.8	-1.7	-0.4	-1.0
Eastern USSR	0.8	0.1	1.0	0.2
Northern European USSR	-1.4	-2.3	-0.9	-1.6
European Steppe	0.3	-0.9	0.4	-0.5
Russian East	-0.9	-2.2	-0.4	-1.6
Non-Slavic South	2.2	1.5	2.3	1.7
USSR total	-0.3	-1.0	0.1	-0.8

Sources: 1959 and 1970 Soviet censuses and 1977 and
1974 estimates (see Chapter 1, nn. 104 and 113).

An investigation of levels of ruralization based on official rural definitions reveals that in 1970 and/or 1977, very few gross regions or economic
regions continued to have a majority of their population in rural areas, as inferred from Tables 4.11 and 4.12. These included the Non-Slavic South,
Moldavia, the Southwest, and Central Asia, which had a rural majority in both
1970 and 1977, and the Central Chernozem, Belorussia, and the North Caucasus, which had a majority only in 1970, but not by 1977.

Regional variations in rates of rural population change since the turn of
the century have been quite substantial (Tables 7.1-7.4 and Maps 7.2-7.9).
Between 1897 and 1970, the rural population increased in all gross regions
except for the Western USSR and Northern European USSR, with the Non-
Slavic South and the Eastern USSR having the greatest rates of increase.

In terms of economic regions, the highest rates of rural increase were
experienced by the Far East, Central Asia, and East Siberia, all regions of
either the Non-Slavic South and/or the Eastern USSR. Rural population decline was confined exclusively to the regions of Northern European USSR and
the Western USSR. All of the regions of Northern European USSR, in fact,
had a decline, as did all of the regions of the Western USSR, except for the

TABLE 7.4

Average Annual Percentage Change of the Rural Population
by Economic Region: 1959–77

Region	Official Rural Definitions		Population Not Residing in Official Cities of 15,000 and over	
	1959–70	1970–77	1959–70	1970–74
Northwest	−1.5	−2.3	−1.0	−1.3
West	−0.6	−1.2	−0.6	−0.8
Center	−2.5	−3.0	−1.5	−2.1
Volgo-Vyatsk	−2.3	−3.0	−1.6	−2.1
Central Chernozem	−1.6	−3.5	−1.3	−2.6
Volga	−1.1	−2.5	−0.6	−1.8
Belorussia	−0.9	−2.2	−0.7	−1.3
Moldavia	0.8	−0.1	1.0	0.2
Southwest	−0.7	−1.3	−0.3	−0.8
South	0.4	−0.7	1.0	−0.5
Donetsk–Dnepr	−0.8	−1.8	−0.8	−1.3
North Caucasus	0.7	−0.6	0.9	−0.3
Transcaucasus	1.4	0.6	1.6	1.0
Urals	−0.8	−2.5	−0.6	−2.1
West Siberia	−1.7	−2.3	−1.2	−2.1
East Siberia	−0.5	−1.5	0.2	−0.8
Far East	0.3	−0.1	0.8	1.0
Kazakhstan	1.9	0.3	2.0	0.5
Central Asia	2.9	2.4	2.9	2.6
USSR total	−0.3	−1.0	0.1	−0.8

Sources: 1959 and 1970 Soviet censuses and 1977 and
1974 estimates (see Chapter 1, nn. 104 and 113).

MAP 7.2

Change in Rural Population: 1897-1926

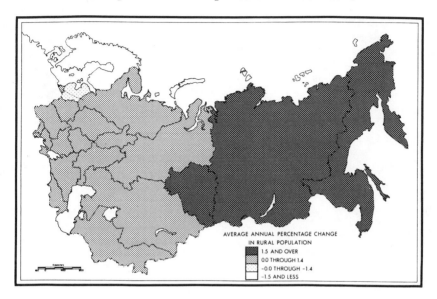

MAP 7.3

Change in Rural Population: 1926-39

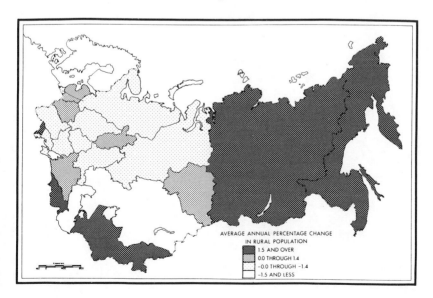

MAP 7.4

Change in Rural Population: 1939-59

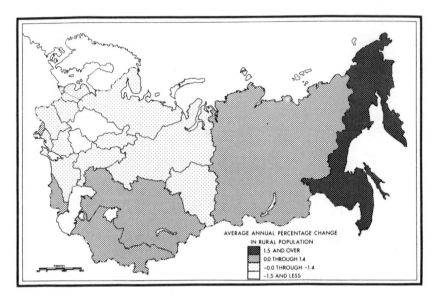

MAP 7.5

Change in Rural Population: 1959-70

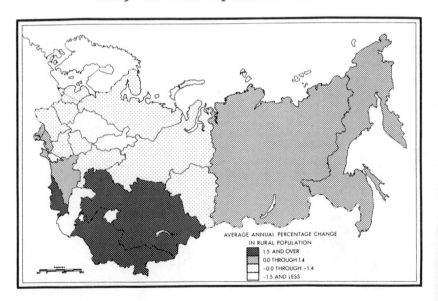

MAP 7.6

Change in Rural Population: 1926-70

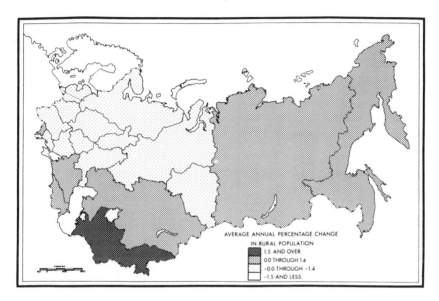

MAP 7.7

Change in Rural Population: 1897-1970

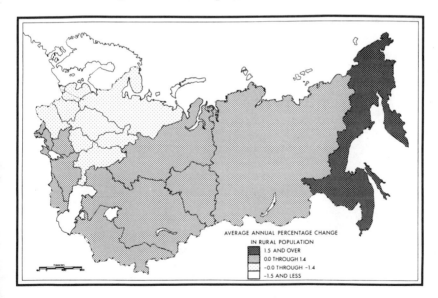

MAP 7.8

Change in Rural Population: 1970-77

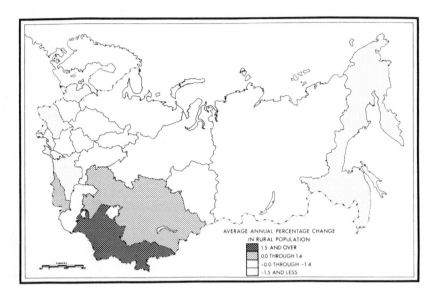

MAP 7.9

Change in Rural Population: 1970-74

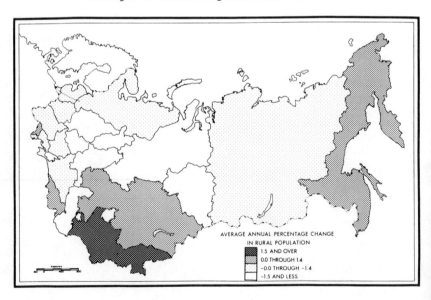

regions of the European Steppe (Moldavia, the South, Donetsk-Dnepr, and North Caucasus), and the Transcaucasus. The greatest rates of decline were experienced by the Center, Central Chernozem, and Volga.

Although regional variations during the 1926–70 period were roughly similar to those of the 1897–1970 period, some noteworthy differences also occurred (Tables 7.1 and 7.2 and Maps 7.2–7.9). First, virtually every gross and economic region had a slower rate of growth during the 1926–70 period as compared with the 1897–1970 period, the only exceptions being the Non-Slavic South and two of its three component regions, Central Asia and the Transcaucasus. In addition, whereas rural population decline was confined solely to Northern European USSR and each of its component regions during the 1897–1970 period, between 1926 and 1970 not only did this quadrant and all of its regions again have rural decline but so did two of the other three quadrants, the European Steppe and Russian East, and a number of regions therein (the South, Donetsk-Dnepr, Urals, and West Siberia). Also, in the 1926–70 period, Central Asia surpassed the Far East as the leading region of rates of rural population increase. The greater importance of the Non-Slavic South and Central Asia in the post-1926 period reflects the more recent mortality decline of this area.

Interesting patterns occurred with respect to regional rural population change by specific intercensal periods (Tables 7.1 and 7.2 and Maps 7.2–7.5, 7.8, and 7.9). During the 1897–1926 period, except for the West, every region, both gross and economic, had rural population increase. Unlike all other periods, when the most rapid rural growth occurred in the Non-Slavic South and Central Asia, the most rapid rural growth during the 1897–1926 period occurred in the Russian East and three of its four component regions, the Far East, West Siberia, and East Siberia. In fact, the rates of rural growth for the Far East and West Siberia were the highest experienced by any region in any period (Tables 7.1–7.4), reflecting the low base populations of these regions and the existence of the rural-oriented phase of the "Great Siberian Migration."

The 1926–39 period marked the beginning of the ascendance of the Non-Slavic South and Central Asia in terms of rates of rural population growth (Tables 7.1 and 7.2 and Map 7.3). The Transcaucasus, another component region of the Non-Slavic South, also had fairly rapid rural growth during this period, but the other component region, Kazakhstan, had the greatest rate of rural population decline of any region of the USSR during this period due to losses of the nomadic Kazakh population, which resulted from their resistance to the collectivization and settlement processes.

The 1926–39 period also marked the beginning of the trend of a substantial number of regions with rural population decline (Tables 7.1 and 7.2 and Map 7.3). Indeed, nine or nearly one-half of the economic regions experienced rural population decline, regions that were located primarily in Northern European USSR and the European Steppe.

However, the next period, 1939–59, had the greatest number of regions (13 of 19) with rural population decline of any intercensal period, greatly due to World War II (Tables 7.1 and 7.2 and Maps 7.2–7.5). Northern European

USSR again had the greatest rate of rural decline of all gross regions, and the rural population of each of its component economic regions also declined, with the Center, Central Chernozem, and Northwest having the sharpest rural declines of any economic regions in the USSR. The European Steppe and Russian East also experienced rural population decline. Within the Russian East, the rural population of West Siberia declined for the first time. The most rapid rural growth of any economic region, however, was experienced by another region of the Russian East, the Far East (Table 7.2).

The most rapid rural growth in general occurred in the Non-Slavic South, but, unlike the preceding period, Kazakhstan was the principal area of rural population increase. Kazakhstan rebounded from having the sharpest rate of rural decline between 1926 and 1939 to having the second highest rate of rural increase of any of the 19 regions between 1939 and 1959, a rate that, in fact, exceeded that of Central Asia. Furthermore, Kazakhstan had the greatest absolute rural population growth of any of the 19 economic regions, as its rural population increased by nearly 1.4 million people (Table B.6). The significant rural population increase of Kazakhstan between 1939 and 1959 was due, to a great extent, to the considerable rural in-migration to the region, especially into Tselinnyy Kray, during the mid-to-late 1950s in association with the New Lands Program. Indeed, between 1951 and 1959, the rural population of Kazakhstan (official rural definitions) increased more rapidly (26.3 percent) than that of any of the 15 union republics. [4]

During the 1959-70 period, very great regional differences in rates of rural population occurred (Tables 7.1 and 7.2 and Map 7.5). The average annual rate of the Eastern USSR exceeded that of the Western USSR by 1.4 percentage points, a difference not equaled in any previous intercensal period. The rate of increase of the Non-Slavic South was the greatest of any quadrant in any period and exceeded the rate of Northern European USSR, the quadrant with the greatest rate of decline, by 3.2 percentage points, a range that was also greater than that of any intercensal period prior to 1959. Similarly, the difference between the greatest rates of rural increase and decline for the economic regions was 4.6 percentage points, the largest range for economic regions in any period. Furthermore, the economic region difference based on official rural definitions was 5.4 percentage points (Table 7.4).

In general, the 1959-70 period was characterized by fairly rapid rural growth in the Non-Slavic South and fairly sharp rural decline in most other areas, especially Northern European USSR and, to a lesser extent, the Russian East. The rapid rural increase in the Non-Slavic South was, as commented on before, one of the main reasons the rural population of the USSR as a whole did not decline sharply between 1959 and 1970. It is interesting to note that, if the Non-Slavic South would be excluded from the USSR, the rural population of the country would have declined by more than 6 million or by 0.6 percent per year rather than increasing barely by about 30,000 or 0.0 percent annually. Similarly, if one views the rural population based on official rural definitions, the exclusion of the Non-Slavic South would have resulted in a rural population decline of nearly 9 million or -1.0 percent per year rather than 1 of about 3 million or by -0.3 percent per year.

Outside the Non-Slavic South, the only other regions to experience rural population increase between 1959 and 1970 were three of the four regions of the European Steppe, namely, Moldavia, the South, and the North Caucasus, as well as the Far East and East Siberia (Table 7.2 and Map 7.5). Except for East Siberia, these regions were also the only regions beyond the Non-Slavic South to experience rural growth based on official rural definitions (Table 7.4).

Although rural growth in both the Non-Slavic South and the European Steppe is associated principally with agriculture, that of the Far East and East Siberia is not. Political units with rural increase (official rural definitions) in these two regions included many that are located in the Far North and, thus, have little agricultural basis. This is exemplified best by Magadan Oblast of the Far East, which had the most rapid rural growth (official rural definitions) of any unit of the Far East or East Siberia between 1959 and 1970, as its rural population nearly doubled, and which is located almost exclusively north of the sixtieth parallel north latitude. It appears that the relatively high rate of rural population change in the Far East and East Siberia is due to the growth of many small mining, forestry, and animal-raising or -hunting settlements, which are classified as rural.[5] However, in the European Steppe some of the rural growth also is associated with nonagricultural activities, particularly in the Crimea of the South, where many resorts are classified as rural; indeed, based on official rural definitions, the rural population of Crimean Oblast increased by more than 50 percent between 1959 and 1970.

Since 1970 there have been three especially outstanding aspects of regional rural population change in the USSR: (1) nearly every region has had rural decline; (2) the rates of rural decline evidently have been unprecedented in any of the preceding intercensal periods, especially for a peacetime era; and (3) virtually every region has had a lower rate of change as compared with the 1959-70 period (Tables 7.1-7.4 and Maps 7.8 and 7.9). First, the only gross regions with rural population increase since 1970 have been the Eastern USSR and the Non-Slavic South, and, furthermore, the only economic regions to have rural growth based on both types of rural definitions have been the three component regions of the Non-Slavic South (Central Asia, the Transcaucasus, and Kazakhstan). Thus, in the post-1970 period rural population increase in the USSR has been confined even more exclusively to the Non-Slavic South than between 1959 and 1970. The only region outside the Non-Slavic South to have rural growth was the Far East, but that was only for the less than 15,000 definition and not for the official rural definitions. Put differently, 14 or 16, depending on the rural definition used, of the 19 economic regions have had rural population decline after 1970, a number unprecedented in any previous period.

Also unprecedented were the regional rates of rural population decline, especially for a peacetime period. Depending on the rural definition being employed, the greatest regional rates of decline after 1970 were in the range of roughly 2.0 to 3.5 percent per year (Table 7.4). In no period between two successive census dates did the rate of rural decline of any region ever reach 2 percent per year, although, obviously, rates of decline were probably greater during periods of turmoil within some of these periods. The greatest rates of rural decline after 1970 were found in Northern European USSR, particularly in the Central Chernozem, Center, Volgo-Vyatsk, and Volga, with that of the Central Chernozem being the greatest of any region in any period. Sharp rural decline was also characteristic of the Russian East, in particular, the Urals and West Siberia.

Finally, every region except for one had a lower rate of change after 1970 than between 1959 and 1970 (Tables 7.3 and 7.4). Particularly sharp declines in average annual rates were experienced by the Central Chernozem and the Urals, regions with rural decline, and Kazakhstan, a region still with rural increase, with the rate for each of these regions declining by at least 1.5 percentage points per year. The only exception was the Far East, which had a slightly higher rate between 1970 and 1974, based on the less than 15,000 criterion. Like all regions, it had a lower rate based on official rural definitions between 1970 and 1977, although only a slightly lower rate of change.

Generally speaking, it can be seen that a north-south dichotomy exists in the USSR with respect to rural population patterns. Specifically, the northern areas are characterized generally by lower levels of ruralization and rural population decline, while the southern areas are notable for higher levels of ruralization and continued rural population increase.

These regional patterns also have ethnic implications. As was discussed in greater detail in the first volume of this series, the Slavic peoples (especially the Russians) of the north are the more dominant group in Soviet society, are more modernized and urbanized, and, thus, also are characterized by rural population decline and a low level of ruralization. In contrast, the Central Asians of the south are the last major group to be integrated into modern Soviet society and are, as to be expected, characterized by a low level of ruralization and continued rural population increase.

Rural Settlement Size

The rural population, like the urban population, has become concentrated increasingly in larger settlements. The following discussion will be based principally on settlement size data for the official rural population.

S. A. Kovalev, one of the foremost Soviet authorities on rural settlement, recognizes three broad classes of settlement sizes: small (less than 101 inhabitants), middle-sized (101-1,000 inhabitants), and large (over 1,000 inhabitants). [6] The share of the Soviet rural population residing in each class in 1926, 1959, and 1970 can be seen in Table 7.5, although it should be pointed out that the 1926 data are only for the USSR as it was constituted then. From this table, it is apparent that the USSR rural population has become increasingly concentrated in large rural settlements, especially since 1959, and, accordingly, less concentrated in small settlements. The share residing in small settlements probably has declined even more since 1926 than is shown in Table 7.5, because the 1926 share would have been higher had not the 1926 data excluded the Baltic area, an area of individual farmsteads (khutors), and, thus, very small settlements. However, the greatest share of the rural pop-

TABLE 7.5

Rural Settlement Size: 1926-70

Size Class	Number of Settlements (thousands)			Population (millions)			Percent of Rural Population		
	1926[a]	1959[b]	1970	1926[a]	1959[b]	1970	1926[a]	1959[b]	1970
Less than 101	379.2	501.7	292.6	12.9	10.8	7.5	10.7	10.1	7.1
101-1,000	206.8	182.9	153.2	59.4	56.8	51.9	49.3	53.0	49.1
More than 1,000	22.9	20.2	23.5	48.1	39.4	46.3	40.0	36.9	43.8
USSR total	608.9	704.8	469.3	120.4	107.0	105.7	100.0	100.0	100.0

[a]Data for 1926 are for the USSR as it was constituted in 1926 and for size classes of less than 100, 100-1,000, and more than 1,000.
[b]Data for 1959 are for the status of settlements as of January 1961.

Note: Based on official rural definitions.

Source: S. A. Kovalev, "Transformation of Rural Settlements in the Soviet Union," Geoforum 9 (September 1972): 35, 40.

TABLE 7.6

Rural Settlement Size: 1959-70

Size Class	Number of Settlements		Population (thousands)		Percent of Rural Population Residing in Each Class	
	1959	1970	1959	1970	1959	1970*
Less than 6	212,076	94,296	644.0	277.7	0.6	0.3
6-10	71,617	39,206	541.2	299.2	0.5	0.3
11-25	69,675	51,607	1,191.4	887.3	1.1	0.8
26-50	67,410	50,709	2,517.5	1,877.7	2.4	1.8
51-100	80,924	56,781	5,897.7	4,121.4	5.5	3.9
101-200	76,402	55,373	10,983.8	7,989.0	10.3	7.6
201-500	74,762	64,753	23,688.4	20,815.8	22.1	19.7
501-1,000	31,763	33,032	22,105.9	23,116.8	20.7	21.9
1,001-2,000	14,218	16,677	19,337.0	22,785.4	18.1	21.6
2,001-3,000	3,482	3,911	8,398.1	9,424.2	7.8	8.9
3,001-5,000	1,807	2,040	6,732.2	7,656.4	6.3	7.2
More than 5,000	675	868	4,973.2	6,446.7	4.6	6.1
USSR total	704,811	469,253	107,010.4	105,697.6	100.0	100.1

*Based on original complete absolute figures not rounded to nearest thousand.

Note: Based on official rural definitions.

Sources: 1959 and 1970 Soviet censuses (see Chapter 1, n. 104).

ulation has resided not in the largest or smallest settlements but in the middle-sized settlements, which have housed roughly one-half of the rural population. Nonetheless, since 1959, the share residing in middle-sized settlements has declined along with that of small settlements, while that residing in large settlements has increased to more than 40 percent. Furthermore, between 1959 and 1970, both the absolute number and population of small- and middle-sized settlements declined, while the number and population of large settlements increased.

Rural settlement size patterns for the 1959-70 period for more specific size classes (in fact, the most detailed classes presented in published census materials) are shown in Table 7.6. It can be seen that the most noteworthy differentiating settlement size was 500. All size classes below 500, without exception, had a decline in the absolute number of settlements as well as in both the absolute population and the share of the rural population residing in these settlements, while all size classes of more than 500, also without exception, had an increase in each instance. The most precipitous decline in the number of settlements and population therein occurred in the very smallest settlements of ten people or less, both of which were more than cut in half. The number of settlements of ten people or less declined by roughly 150,000, from approximately 280,000 to about 130,000, with the bulk of the decline (more than 100,000) being experienced by the very smallest size class of less than six people. The great decline in the number of settlements of ten people or less accounted for the majority of the decline of more than 200,000 rural settlements for the USSR as a whole. The sharp decline in the number of rural settlements in the USSR overall has led to the fact that, although the rural population (official rural definitions) also declined between 1959 and 1970, the average size of a rural settlement actually increased from about 150 to 225 people.

The shift of the rural population from smaller to larger settlements has been due partly to the policy of Party and government to bring forth such a result. It is interesting to juxtapose this against the policy regarding city sizes, which, as we have discussed before, is just the opposite in that it has been antilarge urban settlements. The rural policy specifically involves the amalgamation of rural settlements. Kovalev notes that "as is well-known, the Programme of the Communist Party of the Soviet Union adopted by [the] XXII Party Congress in 1961 set the liquidation of socioeconomic and cultural differences between town and country as one of the most important tasks of the Soviet society. This task, which is being gradually and steadily carried out, calls for the transformation of the kolkhoz villages and selo's [sic] into amalgamated settlements featuring high living standards and a high degree of public services development."[7] The amalgamation process even has gone so far as to involve the dismantling, moving, and reassembling of houses, although in many instances new dwellings are being built, both individual houses and apartment houses.[8] The apparent underlying reason for the amalgamation policy is that it is easier to provide public services and facilities in larger rural settlements.[9] The shift from smaller to larger settlements is, obviously, partly a result of the voluntary migration of people from smaller to larger

TABLE 7.7

Rural Settlement Size by Economic Region: 1970

Region	Population Residing in Settlements of:				Percent of Rural Population Residing in Settlements of:		
	Less Than 101	101-1,000	1,001 and over	Total	Less Than 101	101-1,000	1,001 and over
Northwest	1,041,506	1,740,956	657,127	3,439,589	30.3	50.6	19.1
West	1,512,906	1,311,159	94,870	2,918,935	51.8	44.9	3.3
Center	1,800,292	4,101,614	1,477,988	7,379,894	24.4	55.6	20.0
Volgo-Vyatsk	518,807	2,323,413	1,093,523	3,935,743	13.2	59.0	27.8
Central Chernozem	288,892	2,855,887	2,208,087	5,352,866	5.4	53.4	41.3
Volga	186,651	3,336,099	2,213,776	5,736,526	3.3	58.2	38.6
Belorussia	615,993	3,719,775	758,787	5,094,555	12.1	73.0	14.9
Moldavia	4,574	364,009	2,070,242	2,438,825	0.2	14.9	84.9
Southwest	64,316	4,997,939	8,393,184	13,455,439	0.5	37.1	62.4
South	34,653	1,127,401	1,577,586	2,739,640	1.3	41.2	57.6
Donetsk-Dnepr	115,151	2,626,782	2,500,945	5,242,878	2.2	50.1	47.7
North Caucasus	89,858	2,172,131	5,077,115	7,339,104	1.2	29.6	69.2
Transcaucasus	84,105	2,712,813	3,193,152	5,990,070	1.4	45.3	53.3
Urals	434,306	4,788,823	2,217,936	7,441,065	5.8	64.4	29.8
West Siberia	103,269	2,269,805	1,588,533	3,961,607	2.6	57.3	40.1
East Siberia	104,550	1,697,122	1,339,301	3,140,973	3.3	54.0	42.6
Far East	27,090	697,981	634,022	1,359,093	2.0	51.4	46.7
Kazakhstan	237,707	2,674,941	3,557,426	6,470,074	3.7	41.3	55.0
Central Asia	198,701	6,402,898	5,659,117	12,260,716	1.6	52.2	46.2
USSR total	7,463,327	51,921,548	46,312,717	105,697,592	7.1	49.1	43.8

Note: Based on official rural definitions.

Source: 1970 Soviet census (see Chapter 1, n. 104).

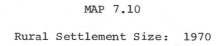

MAP 7.10

Rural Settlement Size: 1970

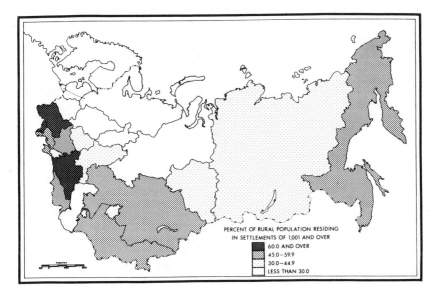

PERCENT OF RURAL POPULATION RESIDING
IN SETTLEMENTS OF 1,001 AND OVER

60.0 AND OVER
45.0—59.9
30.0—44.9
LESS THAN 30.0

settlements because of the advantages of the latter settlements. This migration is but another example of the general step-migration apparently occurring
in the USSR from smaller to larger settlements, both urban and rural.

There is reluctance on the part of some to move to larger rural settlements from smaller ones (including individual farmsteads), and inducements
to move sometimes are offered.[10] Although larger rural settlements have
advantages as compared with smaller rural settlements, they also have disadvantages, particularly the greater average distance of travel from residence
to the fields.[11] It should not be forgotten, in addition, that there is still a
considerable exodus from such settlements to the more favorable urban settlements. It is hoped evidently that the larger settlements with their generally
greater amenities as compared with smaller rural settlements will be attractive to young adults and, thus, impede the exodus of young people from rural
areas.

Unlike the corresponding situation with respect to city sizes, it appears
that there are considerable regional differences in the size class structure of
the rural settlements. Regional patterns for large rural settlements (over
1,000 people) for 1970 can be seen in Table 7.7 and Map 7.10. Large centers
predominate particularly in the southern portion of the country in the regions
of the European Steppe (Moldavia, North Caucasus, South, Donetsk-Dnepr) and

the Non-Slavic South (Kazakhstan, Transcaucasus, and Central Asia), as well as the Southwest, which actually is located partly in the steppe, and the Far East, probably reflecting the greater nonagricultural nature of rural settlements here. In contrast, smaller rural settlements are of relatively greater importance in the northern regions of the USSR. Very small rural settlements are of particularly great importance in the extreme northwestern portion of the USSR, especially the West, Northwest, and Center. Most notable is the West or Baltic Region, which was the only region where more than one-half of the rural population still resided in settlements of 100 people or less in 1970 (Table 7.7). This reflects the fact that the Baltic area, as mentioned earlier, has been the outstanding region of individual farmstead or khutor settlement in the USSR, especially Latvia. The relatively outstanding position of the West with respect to small rural settlement still existed in 1970 despite the fact that the extent of such settlements in this region declined quite sharply between 1959 and 1970.

Analysis

Rural population change in this study has been considered largely with respect to other patterns of population redistribution. Limitations of data, resources, and space preclude a detailed analysis of rural population change since 1897. Our purpose here is to investigate briefly processes related to rural population change since 1959, in an attempt to distinguish the chief interrelationships and to determine roughly the extent to which these processes can be considered universal. This investigation will be based largely on recent Soviet studies.

Rural population change is, of course, related primarily to rural natural increase and net rural-to-urban migration. It should be kept in mind that these components are closely interrelated. Rural out-migrants are primarily young adults, and the result is an aging rural population. This, in turn, dampens crude birth and natural increase rates and enhances rural crude death rates. Reclassification of settlements from rural to urban status also influences rural population change, but due to the relatively minor importance of this factor, no attention will be devoted to it in this chapter.

Rural Natural Increase

Previously presented data suggest that the slowing of rural population growth and eventual decline of the rural population of the USSR has been due partly to declining rural crude birth and natural increase rates. Indeed, by the 1970s it appears that each rate was only roughly half of its level in the early twentieth century (Tables 3.16, 3.18, and 3.20).

Although rural vital statistics by economic region are, unfortunately, not available, a rough approximation of broad regional trends can be made on the basis of rural crude birth and death rates by union republic, which have been graphed by B. S. Khorev. Previously we have presented estimates for 1964 and 1970 in Tables 4.17 and 4.18, although it is possible to estimate

corresponding rates from the graphs for all years in the 1950-70 period, as
well as for 1940. Reference to these tables suggests that regional variations
in rural rates of population are related strongly to variations in rural crude
birth and natural increase rates but only weakly related to rural crude death
rates, which were roughly uniform throughout the country. In particular, the
Slavic and Baltic republics, which generally experienced rural depopulation
or very slow growth between 1959 and 1970, had relatively low rural crude
birth and natural increase rates. Indeed, by 1970 the rural natural increase
rate had declined to 4 to 5 per thousand in the RSFSR, Ukraine, Belorussia,
and Lithuania, to 0 in Latvia, and to -1 (that is, natural decrease) in Estonia.
Areas that had experienced particularly intense rural out-migration were
characterized by natural decrease. Writing in 1972, Yu. Evsyukov reported
that the rural areas of Estonia and Latvia had natural decrease; that the rural
areas of many oblasts in the RSFSR, including Pskov, Novgorod, Kalinin, Kos-
troma, Smolensk, Yaroslavl', Tula, and others, also were experiencing natural decrease; and that the out-migration of the working-age population to a
significant degree had exceeded its natural increase in the Slavic and Baltic
republics. [12] For example, in 1970, the rural population of working age in the
RSFSR, Belorussia and the Ukraine ranged from 79 to 84 percent of the 1959
population. Rural out-migration has been and continues to be particularly intense in the Non-Chernozem Zone of European USSR, where the cultivated
acreage has decreased, and West Siberia. Rural natural decrease probably
will be characteristic of these areas in the near future, if not at present, assuming the present trends continue. The decline in natural increase has not
been solely the result of out-migration, because rural fertility also has declined in most Slavic and Baltic areas.

At the other end of the spectrum, republics of the Non-Slavic South and
Moldavia, the principal areas of rural population increase, had relatively high
crude birth and natural increase rates. Especially high rates were characteristic of the republics of Central Asia, Kazakhstan, and Azerbaydzhan. It
should be noted, however, that in the 1960s Kazakhstan and Azerbaydzhan experienced sharp declines, each upwards of 15 points per thousand, in reported
rural crude birth rates. Nevertheless, the rural population of working age
increased from 3 to 15 percent in these republics. Rural out-migration comprised not more than 25 to 50 percent of the natural increase of the working-
age population in Central Asia and the Transcaucasus. [13] In Georgia, Armenia,
and Moldavia, rural crude birth and natural increase rates were comparatively
moderate. Because of the relatively moderate rates of natural increase and
relatively low rates of mobility in these republics, the rural population of
working age has remained roughly stationary since 1959.

It should be added that a more precise statistical presentation of rural
crude birth rates by republic has been undertaken by V. A. Borisov for
1958/59 and 1969/70. [14] Conclusions about regional variations in rural crude
birth and natural increase rates based upon the Borisov data would generally
be the same as those based on the Khorev estimates, if we assume that there
was little regional variation in rural crude death rates, which would lead to a
general similarity between regional variations in rural crude birth and natural
increase rates.

Rural Migration

The slowdown and eventual decline of the rural population of the USSR also has been related to significant rural out-migration. Between 1926 and 1970 net rural-to-urban migration in the USSR totaled roughly 60 million people; the corresponding figure for the 1959-70 period was 16.4 million people or 1.5 million per year (Table 3.19).

With respect to both destination and origin, rural migrants comprise a relatively large percentage of the total migration in the USSR. According to data from the 1970 census, 17.8 percent of the migrants in the previous two years moved between rural settlements and 12.7 percent moved from urban areas to rural areas. Thus, some 30 percent of the migrants had a rural destination. Migrants from rural settlements to urban areas comprised 31.4 percent of the total migrants, so almost half of the migrants had a rural origin.

Regional variations in rural population change were apparently related somewhat to rural migration variations. Unfortunately, because rural natural increase data are lacking, regional variations in rural net migration cannot be estimated between 1959 and 1970. Estimates of net rural migration for 1970 have been made, however, although the original source of the estimates did not provide the natural increase data on which the estimates were made (Table 7.9).[15] According to these data, rural net out-migration rates were much higher in the Slavic and Baltic areas than in the non-Slavic southern tier. Similar patterns were revealed by 1970 census data (Table 2.19). The labor hours worked generally were well above the average in the areas of high out-migration and generally well below average in the southern areas, especially the Transcaucasus. Nationalities that reside in the non-Slavic southern tier, which is characterized by moderate-to-high rural natural increase and an increasing agricultural work force, had the lowest rates of rural out-migration and rural mobility (Table 7.8). These groups predominate in the rural areas of their ethnic units. The Slavic and Baltic nationalities also predominate in their ethnic units and are characterized by low natural increase rates and relatively high rates of rural out-migration and rural mobility.

In the aggregate, net rural out-migration in the USSR does not appear to be excessive. The chief problem, however, is that where there is a surplus of agricultural labor there is generally little rural out-migration, and where there are labor shortages in agriculture high rates of net rural out-migration generally prevail. In 1959 severe kolkhoz labor shortages, ranging from 70 to 83 percent of the requirements in the period of greatest need, were reported in West Siberia, Kazakhstan, the Northwest, Estonia, and East Siberia, whereas Kirgizia, the Ukraine, Moldavia, Belorussia, and Georgia were characterized by a considerable surplus of kolkhoz labor.[16] More recently severe labor shortages in agriculture have been reported in Siberia, the Center, and the Northwest, where out-migration is particularly high.[17] In West Siberia, available labor met only about 70 percent of the requirements in the 1966/67 period.[18] Labor surpluses in agriculture are reported throughout the non-Slavic southern tier.[19] Thus, intense rural out-migration is occurring in areas deficient in rural labor, but the rural population of areas with surplus and growing rural labor supply is relatively immobile.

TABLE 7.8

Urban and Rural Migration by Nationality of the USSR:
1968-70

| Nationality | Number of Migrants as a Percent of Population of Nationality | | |
	Rural-to-Urban	Urban-to-Rural	Rural-to-Rural
Russians	1.9	0.9	1.0
Ukrainians	1.8	0.6	0.9
Belorussians	2.2	0.6	1.0
Uzbeks	0.5	0.2	0.4
Kazakhs	1.4	0.5	1.8
Georgians	0.7	0.1	0.5
Azeri	0.6	0.1	0.2
Lithuanians	2.0	0.6	1.8
Moldavians	1.5	0.3	0.9
Latvians	1.4	0.9	1.6
Kirgiz	1.2	0.2	0.7
Tadzhiks	0.7	0.3	0.7
Armenians	0.7	0.2	0.3
Turkmen	0.6	0.1	0.2
Estonians	1.7	1.1	1.6
USSR total	1.8	0.7	1.0

Note: Based on official urban definitions.

Source: 1970 Soviet census (see Chapter 1, n. 104).

381

Central Intelligence Agency (CIA) analysts forecast a decline in the growth rate of the Soviet GNP in the 1980s, as a result of the need for increasing investment in agriculture, labor shortages related to a sharp decline in the growth of the work force, a slowdown in the growth of capital and labor productivity, and an impending energy crisis.[20] In the past two decades investment in agriculture has increased greatly; currently about a third of the total Soviet gross fixed investment and about 20 percent of the total productive investment are allocated to agriculture, including industries that serve it.[21] Agricultural labor shortages, however, are related to investment and mechanization. In 1974 average annual employment in agriculture comprised 22.5 percent of total socialized employment or some 26 million persons, which is very high by Western standards.[22] Continued rural out-migration from labor-deficit rural areas will alleviate labor shortages in the nonagricultural sector in the 1980s but will require even more investment in these rural areas if production is to be maintained. The surplus rural population in the southern tier is the last major source of surplus labor in the Soviet economy, and its utilization would seem crucial to Soviet planners. We will have more to say on this subject in Chapter 9 on implications.

As might be expected, the young and the more educated have the highest propensity to migrate from the rural areas. In the 1961-65 period relative to the 1966-70 period, the share of the migrants that were ages 16 to 19 increased from 20 to 45 percent and those ages 20 to 24 increased from 12 to 26 percent.[23] Surveys from various parts of the USSR indicate that the higher the educational attainment the greater the propensity to migrate.[24] As a whole the sex composition of the migrants is fairly balanced. According to the 1970 census, the sex ratio of the rural-urban migrants was 99; urban-rural migrants, 96; and rural-rural, 94. In the Slavic and Baltic areas, women outnumbered men among the migrants to urban areas, whereas elsewhere men tended to outnumber women. In 1970, the sex ratio of the rural population aged 20 to 29 of the RSFSR was 107.

The world over a major impetus to rural out-migration is differences in the standard of living between rural and urban areas, which is measured generally by rural-urban wage differentials. The subject of rural wages in the USSR is complex because of the many sources of income, and data are relatively limited.[25] However, at least in the aggregate, in the USSR there is a substantial rural-urban differential that is much greater than in most developed countries. Even though since 1965 there have been major increases in agricultural wages, agriculture remains the lowest paid major sector of the Soviet economy. In 1965 the average monthly income of collective farm workers was only a half and state farmers roughly three-fourths that of industrial workers. By 1969/70 the corresponding percentages had risen to 75 and 85, respectively. There also appears to be significant regional variations, with areas of intense out-migration having a greater differential. In 1969/70, the differential in the Urals and Siberia was two-thirds that of the industrial wage, and in the Northwest it was even greater.[26] Furthermore, transfer payments per family member to workers and employees were about twice that of the kolkhoz population.[27] Agricultural workers supplement their wages with income from their private plots, but this requires much labor and there are opportunity costs relative to the urban families. In 1972 income from private plots comprised 27.1 percent of kolkhoz family income, and in 1969 it accounted for 21 percent of state farm family income. Regional variations, however, appear to be great. In 1966, 59.1 percent of the family income in Georgia came from the private plot, but in Turkmeniya the corresponding proportion was only 27.3 percent.[28]

Moreover, agricultural workers work longer hours than urban workers and have less leisure time. Relative to their counterparts in industry, male kolkhoz workers have annually 1,000 fewer hours of free time and female kolkhoz workers have 400 fewer hours, which constitute 84.8 percent of the free time of the industrial workers for men and 63.4 percent for women. About a third of all agricultural workers in the USSR work the whole year without vacation or days off. Kolkhoz workers spent more time in housework and on their private plots during the 1960s than their counterparts in industry, 32 percent more time for men and 16 percent more time for women.[29]

From the limited data that are available, it would appear that rural migrants to urban areas receive a sizable wage increase. In a survey taken in Novosibirsk Oblast of those that migrated to urban centers between 1956 and 1965, 73.8 percent increased their wages by more than R 30 per month, 52.4 percent by more than R 50, and 32.0 percent by more than R 70. The wage increases between those that had increased their education and those that had not were very slight. Within the first three years almost 60 percent increased their wages more than R 30 per month.[30] In 1964 the average monthly wage in agriculture in the USSR was R 52.2—R 70.8 in sovkhozy and R 44.6 in kolkhozy. By 1973 the corresponding figures were R 98.4, R 117.5, and R 86.9.[31] Thus, migrants on a percentage basis greatly increased their income. In Perm' Oblast, in an unspecified period, rural migrants to urban areas increased their monthly wages from 50 to 130 percent.[32] Such increases probably are not representative of all regions. For example, the combined per capita income of kolkhozniki was 87.4 percent of that of urban workers and employees in Uzbekistan in 1968,[33] so a move to an urban area would not necessarily have resulted in appreciable wage gains.

Aside from lower wages, there is a general dissatisfaction with life in rural areas, at least in those areas experiencing intense rural out-migration. Major complaints include the nature and conditions of agricultural labor, inadequate educational facilities and services, poor housing, a shortage of consumer goods, a lack of recreational facilities, inferior medical facilities, and a relative lack of leisure time.[34] Most of the surveys investigating reasons for rural discontent were taken in West Siberia, more specifically, Novosibirsk Oblast, but they are probably characteristic of other areas experiencing intense rural out-migration, even though the surveys are not ideal in terms of design. In 1970 it was reported that 52.4 percent of the rural-urban migrants in the USSR moved for work and 24.7 percent for study; so education is a major stimulus to movement.[35] Based on a sample survey of sovkhozy in the RSFSR in 1967 and regression analysis, T. I. Zaslavskaya and E. Vinogradova conclude that the chief reasons for migration in the order of importance were wages, retail trade turnover, and the availability of services.[36] Thus, it might be concluded that the generally lower standard of living in rural areas is also a major stimulus for out-migration, at least in the areas of considerable rural out-migration. It is highly probable, however, that material conditions are not the only important ones. David E. Powell concludes that, "What is clear is that Soviet young people, like their counterparts in most countries, are strongly attracted to cities and will bend every effort to get there."[37]

From available census data, only gross patterns of rural population change and concentration by settlement size can be derived, and underlying processes often are obscured or not revealed. Based on 26 geographical units covering the USSR, a variety of surrogates for agricultural conditions for the 1959-70 period, and correlation and factor analysis, Nicholas Dima concludes that agricultural "push" factors were not important and that urban-industrial "pull" factors were more important.[38] Clearly, migratory factors are difficult to dichotomize into push and pull categories, but urbanization and industrialization are necessary conditions for the considerable rural-urban migration that generally is associated with economic development and usually more people move short distances than long distances. Viktor Perevedentsev reports that most rural migrants in the USSR move to the nearest city and that about three-fourths move within their economic region and about a half within their oblast.[39] The decision to migrate in the USSR is very probably the result of an evaluation of rural conditions relative to urban conditions, as it is elsewhere, so both sets of conditions are important.

Conditions in Labor-Deficit Rural Areas

A number of recent Soviet surveys provide insights into the processes that are occurring in local areas. It is interesting to note that these surveys were taken in labor-deficit rural areas experiencing considerable out-migration and that no comparable studies have been performed in rural areas with a labor surplus, even though this is their last major source of surplus labor. Two of the surveys were taken in the Non-Chernozem Zone in rayony north of Moscow. Total income per collective farm family (including wages from the socialized sector and income from private plots, state enterprises, and social consumption funds) in 1970 generally was estimated to be lower in Slavic areas than the USSR average. As a percentage of the USSR average, the RSFSR registered 102; Belorussia, 84; and the Ukraine, 80.[40] However, despite the rise in kolkhoz income since 1965, regional differences persist, and the lowest incomes continue to exist in most of the oblasts of the Volgo-Vyatsk, Northwest, and Center.[41]

A sample survey of about 1,500 people was taken in 1967 in Krasnokholmskiy Rayon of Kalininsk Oblast, covering the 1960-67 period.[42] Between 1960 and 1967, the rural population of the rayon decreased by 26.1 percent or 2.3 percent per year. Per hundred rural-urban migrants, there were only 14 urban-rural migrants. Of the out-migrants, 76.9 percent went to cities, 8.7 percent to rural settlements, and the destination of the remainder was unknown. Of the migrants to urban areas, 54.2 percent moved to study and 27.2 percent to work. Of the total out-migrants, 54.5 percent were ages 16 to 29, and the corresponding percentage for in-migrants was 34.6. In 1967, 3.8 percent of the population was 16 to 19 and 1.8 percent was 20 to 24, and the working-age population declined from 55 to 51 percent. The labor deficit in some farms reached 40 percent. Men comprised 52.8 percent of the out-migrants and 44.0 percent of the in-migrants. Of the out-migrants 81 percent had more than seven years of schooling and 61 percent had eight to ten years of schooling. Machine operators had the highest propensity to migrate, comprising about a fourth of all migrants that had been employed before migrating. Since 1963 the rayon has experienced natural decrease as a result of declining crude birth rates and rising crude death rates. Combined family income from the socialized sector and the private plot averaged about R 60 per month or about half that of an individual industrial worker. Furthermore, it was estimated that an acceptable standard of living would require a monthly income per kolkhoz worker of R 120 in addition to the income from the private plot.

As to the factors associated with migration, the farms were grouped into three economic categories (high, medium, and low) on the basis of income per hectare, cultivated acreage per worker, and wages. The highest category experienced net in-migration (0.5 percent) and the medium and low categories were characterized by increasing net out-migration (3,5 and 13.1 percent, respectively). The investigation of a number of variables relating to socioeconomic development generally revealed a similar pattern, a net in-migration to the more prosperous farms and increasing net out-migration in the other two categories. In the few instances where there was net out-migration in all categories, there was a decrease in net out-migration with socioeconomic development. Thus, the greater the investment per hectare, the greater the gross and net incomes per hectare, the greater the wages per labor day, the greater the family income, the greater the availability of industrial enterprises on farms, the larger the settlement, the closer the settlement to the rayon center, the greater the transportation accessibility, and the greater the services, the less the out-migration. Rank correlation coefficients supported this analysis; specifically, the highest correlated variables with out-migration were net income per annual worker (-0.8) and wages per labor day (-0.4). Thus, in general, the more prosperous farms are increasing in population and the poorer ones are declining, which would seem to indicate the importance of economic push factors.

An intensive study of Starorusskiy Rayon of Novgorod Oblast for the period 1963 to 1967, based on sample surveys of migrants and nonmigrants, interviews, and register dates, revealed similar migratory patterns.[43] This rayon was considered characteristic of the southern part of the Northwest Region. Between 1963 and 1967, the rural population of the rayon decreased by 8 percent and the population loss as a result of migration was 10.5 percent, because the rayon was experiencing natural increase. For every 100 rural out-migrants there were 55.5 rural in-migrants. Of the out-migrants, 88.6 percent went to cities, and 31.3 percent of the in-migrants came from cities. Available labor during the harvest season comprised only 41 percent of the labor requirements. Average income per family member including private plot income was R 668 per year or only slightly above the minimum monthly norm per urban family member of R 51.5. Despite a rise in wages during the period, out-migration intensified during the period, comprising in the aggregate 24.7 percent of the initial rural population. However, within the rayon there were considerable regional variations. Net in-migration or only slight out-migration was characteristic of sel'sovets having sovkhozy, more economically prosperous kolkhozy, or relatively large industrial enterprises. Within the rayon, there were migratory flows to sovkhozy and state and industrial enterprises. Only 13 percent of the migrants moved to kolkhozy, whereas 42 percent moved to sovkhozy and 45 percent to state and industrial enterprises.

As to the characteristics of the migrants, 69.4 percent of the out-migrants and 27.6 percent of the in-migrants were aged 16 to 29. Men comprised 41.4 percent of the out-migrants and 34.5 percent of the in-migrants. Single adults comprised 62.0 percent of the out-migrants and 69.6 percent of the in-migrants. Of the out-migrants, 79.3 percent had seven or more years of schooling and 27.1 percent had ten or more years. Corresponding percentages for in-migrants were 29.8 and 24.1 percent. As to the reasons for migrating, material need, the desire to acquire a profession, dissatisfaction with the conditions of labor, the desire to continue one's education, and dissatisfaction with services were cited by 76.4 percent of the migrants. Of the out-migrants, 27.9 percent moved to study.

Kolkhozy were grouped according to their level of economic development into three categories (high, medium, and low), according to capital per 100 hectares, gross and net income, and wages per labor day. All kolkhozy had net out-migration, but the lowest was in the high category (-12.2 percent), the next lowest was in the medium category (-16.3 percent), and the highest out-migration was in the lowest category (-23.0 percent). Thus, the higher the capital, income, and wages, the lower was the net out-migration. Where the days worked per year were less than 300, net out-migration was higher. Generally, the lower the income per family member, the higher the out-migration, except for the highest category (over R 1,000 per year). The more developed the private plot, the less the out-migration. The larger the settlement, the less the net out-migration. The settlements that contained industrial enterprises had less net out-migration. The greater the availability of services (schools, library, house of culture, movie theater, general store, and so forth), the less the net out-migration. The highest category had net in-migration. The closer the settlement was to the rayon center, the less the out-migration. Those within three kilometers had significant net in-migration. Generally, the greater the transportation accessibility in terms of quality of roads, the less the net out-migration, but the settlements along the railroad had greater net out-migration than the next category, settlements connected by asphalt roads. Those without roads had by far the greatest net out-migration.

Migratory processes in these two rayony are probably more or less representative of the Non-Chernozem Zone, at least the northern part, which has experienced considerable rural depopulation. Between 1959 and 1970, the rural population of the Non-Chernozem Zone declined from about 19 to 15 million. Whereas in the USSR the rural working-age population declined 15 percent, in such oblasts as Kalininsk, Novgorod, Smolensk, Kirov, and Ivanovo, the decline ranged between 34 and 42 percent. In oblasts that experienced considerable out-migration, the population aged 20 to 29 was only about a third of the 1959 level in 1970.[44] Around 1970 annual kolkhoz wages in this zone were only 89 to 93 percent of the RSFSR average, but they worked 11 to 12 percent more days.[45] There are labor shortages throughout the zone, in particular, among machine operators and technicians. Only about 10 to 15 percent of the newly trained machine operators in the USSR remain in agriculture.[46]

Novosibirsk Oblast also has been studied intensively with respect to rural migration and can be considered roughly representative of the rural migratory processes occurring in West Siberia.[47] These studies are based upon local sources of data and sample surveys taken in 1967 (about 8,000 rural workers) and 1972 (about 2,000 rural workers). Between 1959 and 1970, the rural population of the oblast declined by 15.4 percent and the rural population of working age declined by 23.3 percent. Rural population loss intensified during this period. In the 1961/62 period, the rural population increased, but between 1963 and 1969 there was an average annual decrease of 2.3 percent and between 1970 and 1972, 2.8 percent. Natural increase declined, and in 1970 only 14 percent of the loss of population through migration was replaced by natural increase. Between 1959 and 1970, the crude birth rate declined more than 50 percent and the crude death rate increased by 20 percent, largely as a result of the changing age composition, although there was a decline in rural fertility. More than 70 percent of the migratory loss was accounted for by persons younger than 25 years of age. Between 1964 and 1966, migrants aged 15 to 29 comprised about 59 percent of all out-migrants. The out-migration of the young has intensified. Of those 19 years old born between 1940 and 1944, 52 to 58 percent remained in the village, whereas of those born between 1953 and 1954 only 33 to 35 percent remained. The higher the education the greater the propensity to out-migrate. In the 1964-66 period, 29.7 percent of those completing high school (ten years) worked in rural areas, but by 1969-71 only 25.1 percent remained, although since 1969 there has been a reversal in this trend.

Sample villages (170) in 1967 and 1970 were classified into seven categories, according to the availability of services, distance from service centers, the quality of construction, and the degree of development of nonagricultural production. The seven categories were: (1) those on the remote agricultural periphery, (2) those close to the agricultural periphery, (3) those close to the urbanization periphery, (4) remote rural local centers, (5) those close to the agricultural local centers, (6) urbanized agrarian centers, and (7) urbanized agrarian-industrial centers. With respect to population losses between 1962 and 1971, there was a population decline with socioeconomic development from -36.5 to -9.0 percent in the first five categories, and the sixth and seventh categories had increases of 15.6 and 20.5 percent, respectively. With respect to net migration, there was a decline in net out-migration in the first five categories from -46.7 to -16.2 percent, but the last two categories were characterized by net in-migration of 3.6 and 8.7 percent. Only 24 percent of the workers in the highest category had been born in their village and only 12.8 percent had lived there all their lives. The corresponding percentages for the first category were 47.6 and 32.3 percent. There was no roughly linear pattern in the other categories. Results of the 1967 survey generally indicated that the greater the availability of housing, transportation, retail enterprises, educational facilities, and medical, cultural, and child-care facilities, the less the net out-migration.

The intensive studies undertaken in Krasnokholmskiy and Starorusskiy rayony and Novosibirsk Oblast provide insights into migratory processes occurring in labor-deficit areas that have experienced considerable rural depopulation. Much of the RSFSR, Belorussia, the Ukraine, and the Baltic republics have or probably soon will have analogous conditions with respect to rural depopulation and labor shortages. The picture that emerges is that most of the young and the more educated are leaving for the city to work and study, the working-age population is declining, and natural increase is declining. In 1970 the working-age population in the RSFSR, Ukraine, Belorussia, and the Baltic republics ranged from 79 to 86 percent of the 1959 level, and the population aged 20 to 24 in the RSFSR and Ukraine was only slightly over half that of 1959.

Limitations of space in this volume prevent us from analyzing the age and sex consequences of rural out-migration, but these consequences will be investigated in the next volume of this series. Within the rural areas, a concentration of the rural population is occurring; people are moving to the more prosperous kolkhozy and sovkhozy, which tend to be the larger ones with better services and higher incomes. Much of the amalgamation of kolkhozy and the transformation of kolkhozy into sovkhozy is very probably out of economic necessity, in that the depleted kolkhozy are no longer economically viable. The most important factor related to rural out-migration is probably rural-urban differentials in the standard of living, including differentials in wages and services, but the attraction of urban life is also probably very important. The migratory processes that are occurring in these rural areas are strikingly similar to those in other developed countries, where there has been a mass exodus of the young and a consolidation of land holdings, which have necessitated mechanization.

Conditions in Labor-Surplus Rural Areas

Migratory processes in the non-Slavic southern tier differ greatly from those in the Slavic and Baltic areas, but there are insufficient data to analyze these processes. It would appear that agricultural incomes are generally higher in the southern tier, even though they work less in terms of time. Gertrude Schroeder estimates total kolkhoz family income in 1970 as a percentage of the USSR average as follows: Turkmeniya, 153; Kazakhstan, 148; Uzbekistan, 118; Armenia, 117; Georgia, 105; Tadzhikistan, 95; Kirgizia, 93; Azerbaydzhan, 92; and Moldavia, 85.[48] Data for 1960 and 1965 also indicate generally higher kolkhoz incomes in the southern tier. Drawing from a different

TABLE 7.9

Rural Population Change and Kolkhoz Labor Participation by Economic Region or Republic: 1959-72

Units	Rural Population in 1970 as a Percent of 1959	Rural Net Migration in 1970 per Thousand People	Labor Hours per Able-Bodied Kolkoznik in 1972	Labor Hours as a Percent of USSR Average
RSFSR	87.8	-23.3	1,538	112
Northwest	84.4	-26.8	2,148	157
Central	76.2	-26.3	1,824	133
Volgo-Vyatsk	78.1	-25.4	1,332	97
Central Chernozem	84.6	-21.1	1,419	104
Volga	91.5	-21.5	1,449	106
North Caucasus	108.0	-9.8	1,497	109
Urals	89.2	-30.3	1,720	126
West Siberia	84.6	-34.9	1,617	118
East Siberia	93.2	-29.7	1,562	114
Far East	105.1	-17.1	1,565	114
Ukraine	94.4	-14.7	1,281	94
Baltic	93.7	-12.6	1,793	131
Transcaucasus	116.8	-9.9	903	66
Central Asia	137.6	-4.9	1,323	96
Kazakhstan	123.8	-16.7	1,461	107
Belorussia	91.4	-20.0	1,418	104
Moldavia	108.8	-9.0	1,111	81
USSR total	97.1	-17.5	1,368	100

Note: Based on official rural definitions.

Source: L. L. Rybakovskiy, ed., Territorial'nyye Osobennosti Narodonaseleniya RSFSR (Moscow: "Statistika," 1976), p. 191.

389

source, Karl-Eugen Wädekin presents data for total family income in 1970 that are considerably higher than those of Schroeder, with only Moldavia (97 percent) below the USSR average. These data indicate that the range by republic in Central Asia and Kazakhstan was from 105 to 140 percent, and in the Transcaucasus from 106 to 127 percent. Moldavia was below the USSR average, registering 97 percent. Payment per day worked on the kolkhoz was also higher in the southern tier, ranging from 104 to 153 percent, except for Georgia (98 percent) and Moldavia (92 percent).[49] In terms of labor hours worked on the kolkhoz in 1972, the Transcaucasus (66 percent) was well below the USSR average, Moldavia moderately below (81 percent), Central Asia (96 percent) slightly below, and Kazakhstan (107 percent) above the USSR average (Table 7.9). Kolkhoz income per family member, however, was considerably lower in the southern tier, primarily because of the larger families. Combined kolkhoz income as a percentage of the USSR average, taking into consideration the amount of time worked, has been calculated as 71.8 to 78.8 percent for Belorussia, the RSFSR, and the Ukraine; 87.9 to 105.3 percent for Latvia, Estonia, and Lithuania; 110.0 to 125.5 percent for the republics of Central Asia and Kazakhstan; and 112.1 to 156.7 percent for the republics of the Transcaucasus. For example, rural income (apparently kolkhoz) was 70 percent higher in Georgia than Estonia, even though Estonian rural workers expended more than twice as much time.[50] However, Georgia appears to be rather atypical, in that in 1966 only 28.8 percent of kolkhoz income was derived from the socialized sector and 59.1 percent from the private plot.[51] During the Eighth Five-Year Plan, 27.3 percent of the rural population of working age in Georgia was not employed in the socialized sector.[52]

Regardless of the problems involved in estimating rural income, it would appear that at least on the kolkhozy during the 1960s workers generally made more and worked less in the southern tier than in the areas to the north. Furthermore, although the rural population of the southern tier has been growing rapidly in the 1960s and 1970s, this growth has been accompanied by a rapid rise in rural wages, which appears generally to have offset the influence of increasing numbers on rural wages. Taking into account higher prices for industrial products used in agriculture, between 1965 and 1973 the income of kolkhozy and sovkhozy in the USSR increased by R 87 billion, as a result of higher prices paid by the government. About 40 percent of this increase went for wages and about 8 percent for social consumption.[53]

It would appear that rural-urban wage differentials in the southern tier are generally less than in many parts of the north, which would tend to impede rural-urban migration. Rural wages appear to be higher in the southern tier, and there are not great regional variations in the centrally established employee wages, which affect urban wage levels. Existing regional differences are the result of regional differences in the employment structure, regional coefficients, and differences in administration and labor productivity relating to piece-rate wage payments. However, urban wages appear to be generally somewhat lower than the USSR average in the southern tier. Leslie Dienes estimates industrial wages in the Transcaucasus at 93.5 percent and Central Asia at 95.0 percent of the USSR average in 1968.[54] Schroeder estimates that in 1970 average annual wages in the state sector (including sovkhozy) were at or slightly above the USSR average in Armenia, Kazakhstan, and Turkmeniya but below in the remaining republics of the southern tier, ranging from 84.3 percent of the USSR average in Moldavia to 96.4 percent in Tadzhikistan.[55] In 1969 average sovkhoz family income in the USSR was 93.6 percent that of industrial families.[56]

Furthermore, by all indicators of economic development (urbanization, industrial employment, industrial output, fuel consumption, and national income), the non-Slavic southern tier is by far the least developed part of the USSR, and current investment plans will not significantly change this situation. Moreover, with the exception of Armenia and Georgia, large numbers of "European" in-migrants to urban areas have taken many of the available jobs, as was demonstrated in our previous volume. Thus, it would appear that job opportunities for the indigenous population are much more limited in the local urban area than in the Slavic and Baltic areas, where labor shortages in urban areas are generally characteristic. This is an impediment to migration, because most people worldwide generally move short distances rather than long distances. Recall that in the USSR currently 50 percent of the rural-urban migrants moved within their administrative unit and 75 percent within their economic region.

Another important impediment to rural out-migration is ethnicity. Local rural-to-urban migration and migration out of most of the ethnic homelands to northern cities have been scant, partly due to the different ethnic environment of the destinations. Everything else being equal, it would seem reasonable to assume that most people would rather remain in familiar surroundings of family, language, and ethnic group than move to alien areas. Migration history indicates, however, that the world over when economic or political conditions so dictate people abandon their ethnic homelands, so ethnicity is not a complete deterrent to migration. Given the apparent relative prosperity of the rural areas of the non-Slavic southern tier, it is not surprising that there has been so little out-migration to alien areas. The central question, however, is, Will economic conditions deteriorate in these rural areas as the rural population continues to grow rapidly, or at least moderately rapidly, to the extent that such out-migration will occur? We will have more to say on this subject in the final chapter.

Governmental Policy

Limitations of space and resources preclude a detailed investigation of the effectiveness of direct governmental policies designed to affect rural population change. Although not a population policy, the emphasis of the Soviet government on economic development has resulted in rapid urbanization, the creation of job opportunities in urban areas, and considerable rural out-migration. The chief economic function of migration is to equalize the supply of and demand for labor on a regional basis, and judging from the frequent complaints of government officials with respect to irrational migration, it can be inferred that this is a primary concern of the Soviet government. With respect to rural migration, it is apparent that their policies to achieve this goal have not been very effective, because areas with rural labor shortages have high and intensifying rates of rural out-migration and areas with rural labor surpluses and rapid rural population growth have relatively little out-migration. In the Slavic and Baltic areas, rural out-migration undoubtedly has alleviated urban labor shortages but has resulted in increasing rural labor shortages and substantial declines in the working-age population. In the 1980s when the work force of these areas will be barely increasing, these problems will intensify greatly if current trends prevail.

In response to the problem of excessive rural out-migration, the Soviet government has initiated a massive program designed to overcome economic and social differences between urban and rural areas in the USSR. Beginning in the Eighth Five-Year Plan and continuing to the present, investment in agriculture has been increased greatly in order to raise wages; improve the conditions of labor; increase mechanization and electrification; provide more free time; improve housing, education, transportation, and all types of services; and build industrial plants in rural areas to provide auxiliary employment. In short, what is planned is a complete transformation of rural life in the USSR. Because this program is primarily in response to rural out-migration, it can be assumed that investment is being directed to labor-deficit areas in the Slavic and Baltic republics. Particular attention has been devoted to the Non-Chernozem Zone, where in the Tenth Five-Year Plan R 35 billion in capital investment, 120 million tons of mineral fertilizer, 380,000 tractors, 94,000 combines, 230,000 trucks, 25,000 roads, and other investments were planned. Long-term plans call for abandoning 100,000 of the 143,000 villages in the Non-Chernozem Zone.[57]

Because of a lack of data, it is not possible to appraise the effectiveness of this policy on rural out-migration. Since 1970, however, as we have noted before, rural population decline has intensified in most regions outside the Non-Slavic South, in particular, in the Non-Chernozem Zone. Nevertheless, one cannot judge the decline that would have occurred if there had been no change in agricultural investment nor the long-term effects of such investment. Undoubtedly, increased mechanization could release considerable labor for industry, because the level of mechanization of Soviet agriculture is low by Western standards. It has been estimated that, if the present-day agricultural technology were applied, the work force in agriculture could be reduced by 15 to 17 million, and only about 9 to 10 million workers would be required in agriculture.[58]

The location of industry in rural areas and small towns and the elimination of the cultural and economic distinction between town and country long has been a policy of Marxism and the Soviet government. It was first stated in the Communist Manifesto and incorporated in the locational guidelines of the Soviet government, although it received low priority until the early 1960s. In 1961 only 10.6 percent of the industrial-production personnel, 7.5 percent of the value of industrial production, and 9.9 percent of the fixed capital were located in rural settlements.[59] Since 1961 considerable emphasis has been placed on industrialization in rural areas and small towns, largely to stem the flow of out-migrants. After investigating this policy in some detail, Richard E. Lonsdale concludes that:

> It seems unlikely that the Soviet government will provide the capital required to develop small-town infrastructures to the level sufficient to support industry and retain young people. . . . Growth and investment efficiency often discourage small-town locations. . . . Regarding prospects for additional small-scale industrial productions in or near farm villages in connection with agro-industrial integration, the program seems to be making only modest progress.[60]

Furthermore, most of the subsidiary enterprises that are located in rural areas operate on a permanent basis and do not provide off-season employment, so they frequently attract labor away from agriculture.[61]

It is very difficult to forecast the results of the increased investment in agriculture. Clearly, increased mechanization could alleviate labor shortages, if there are sufficient machine operators. The rise in rural living standards could slow the redistribution of the rural population in labor-deficit areas to the more prosperous farms, if an equalization of income and services is achieved, but this would appear not to solve the problem of labor shortages and out-migration of the young. The world over cities have an attraction for the young above and beyond material incentives, and this also is reported widely in the USSR. Because the more educated have a higher propensity to migrate, improving educational facilities could well stimulate more out-migration. In the not too distant future, the Soviet government very probably will have to accommodate itself, at least in the Slavic and Baltic areas, to levels of rural population approaching those found in Western Europe and the United States, and this should require considerably more agricultural investment.

NOTES

1. USSR, Naseleniye SSSR, 1973 (Moscow: Izdatel'stvo "Statistika," 1975), pp. 10-11.

2. See ibid. and Table 3.9.

3. B. Ts. Urlanis, Problemy Dinamiki Naseleniya SSSR (Moscow: Izdatel'stvo "Nauka," 1974), pp. 251-52.

4. Naseleniye SSSR, 1973.

5. S. Kovalev, "Farewell to the Rural Scene," The Geographical Magazine, vol. 48 (April 1976).

6. S. A. Kovalev, "Transformation of Rural Settlements in the Soviet Union," Geoforum, 9 (September 1972): 38.

7. Ibid., p. 7.

8. Ibid., pp. 36-37.

9. U.S., Central Intelligence Agency, USSR Agricultural Atlas (Washington, D.C.: U.S. Government Printing Office, December 1974), p. 39 (hereafter cited as USSR Agricultural Atlas).

10. Hedrick Smith, "Lithuania Inducing Farmers to Quit Tiny Homesteads," New York Times, October 24, 1974, p. 18.

11. USSR Agricultural Atlas.

12. Yu. Evsyukov, "Migratsiya Naseleniya iz Sela v Gorod," Planovoye Khozyaystvo, no. 12 (1972), pp. 124, 128.

13. Ibid., p. 129.

14. V. A. Borisov, Perspektivy Rozhdayemosti (Moscow: "Statistika," 1976), p. 108; USSR, Narodnoye Khozyaystvo SSSR v 1965 G. (Moscow: "Statistika," 1966), p. 46.

15. B. Ts. Urlanis, ed., Narodonaseleniye Stran Mira (Moscow: "Statistika," 1974), p. 406.

16. V. Perevedentsev, "Migratsiya Naseleniya i Ispol'zovaniye Trudovykh Resursov," Voprosy Ekonomiki, no. 9 (1970), p. 35.

17. L. L. Rybakovskiy, ed., Territorial'nyye Osobennosti Narodonaseleniya RSFSR (Moscow: "Statistika," 1976), p. 192.

18. T. I. Zaslavskaya, ed., Migratsiya Sel'skogo Naseleniya (Moscow: Izdatel'stvo "Mysl'," 1970), p. 89.

19. Rybakovskiy, Territorial'nyye Osobennosti, pp. 192-93.

20. U.S., Joint Economic Committee, Western Perceptions of Soviet Economic Trends, 95th Cong. (Washington, D.C.: U.S. Government Printing Office, 1978).

21. James R. Millar, "The Prospects for Soviet Agriculture," Problems of Communism 26 (May-June 1977): 8-10.

22. Stephen Rapawy, Estimates and Projections of the Labor Force and Civilian Employment in the USSR, 1959 to 1990, U.S. Department of Commerce, Foreign Economic Report, no. 10 (September 1976), p. 36.

23. Evsyukov, "Migratsiya Naseleniya," p. 123.

24. E. S. Kutaf'yeva et al., Migratsiya Sel'skogo Naseleniya (Moscow: Izdatel'stvo Moskovskogo Universiteta, 1971), p. 43; T. I. Zaslavskaya and V. A. Kalmyk, eds., Sovremennaya Sibirskaya Derevnya, pt. 1 (Novosibirsk: S.O., A.N. SSSR, 1975), p. 51; and David E. Powell, "The Rural Exodus," Problems of Communism 23 (November-December 1974): 3-4.

25. For a discussion of this subject, see Karl-Eugen Wädekin, "Income Distribution in Soviet Agriculture," Soviet Studies 27 (January 1975): 3-26.

26. Powell, "Rural Exodus," p. 8.

27. Wädekin, "Income Distribution in Soviet Agriculture," pp. 6-7.

28. Ibid., pp. 6-13.

29. V. I. Staroverov, Sotsial'no-Demograficheskiye Problemy Derevni (Moscow: Izdatel'stvo "Nauka," 1975), pp. 144, 212.

30. Zaslavskaya, Migratsiya Sel'skogo Naseleniya, pp. 269-70.

31. Zaslavskaya and Kalmyk, Sovremennaya Sibirskaya Derevnya, p. 152

32. Rybakovskiy, Territorial'nyye Osobennosti, p. 191.

33. Grey Hodnett, "Technology and Social Change in Soviet Central Asia: The Politics of Cotton Growing," in Soviet Politics and Society in the

1970's, ed. Henry W. Morton and Rudolph L. Tokes (New York: Free Press, 1974), pp. 93-94.

34. Zaslavskaya, Migratsiya Sel'skogo Naseleniya, pp. 150-65; Zaslav-skaya and Kalmyk, Sovremennaya Sibirskaya Derevnya, pt. 2, pp. 3-105; Powell, "Rural Exodus," pp. 4-9; and V. I. Perevedentsev, Metody Izucheniya Migratsii Naseleniya (Moscow: Izdatel'stvo "Nauka," 1975), pp. 142-45.

35. B. S. Khorev and V. M. Moiseyenko, eds. Migratsionnaya Podvizh-nost' Naseleniya v SSSR (Moscow: "Statistika," 1974), p. 32.

36. T. I. Zaslavskaya, ed., Sotsial'nyye Problemy Trudovykh Resursov Sela (Novosibirsk: Izdatel'stvo "Nauka," 1968), pp. 87-140.

37. Powell, "Rural Exodus," p. 13.

38. Nicholas Dima, "Rural Population Change in the Soviet Union and Its Implications: 1959-1970," (Ph.D. diss., Department of Geography, Columbia University, 1976), pp. 135-210.

39. Viktor Perevedentsev, "Iz Derevni v Gorod," Nash Sovremennik, no. 11 (1972), p. 104.

40. Gertrude E. Schroeder, "Soviet Wage and Income Policies in Re-gional Perspective," Bulletin of the Association for Comparative Economic Studies, Fall 1974, p. 10.

41. Evsyukov, Migratsiya Naseleniya, p. 125.

42. Kutaf'yeva et al., Migratsiya Sel'skogo, pp. 3-83; and A. Gol'tsov, "Regional'nyye Problemy Sovremennoy Migratsii Sel'skogo Naseleniya," Voprosy Ekonomiki, no. 10 (1969), pp. 64-74.

43. Staroverov, Sotsial'no Demograficheskiye, pp. 3-261.

44. Ibid., pp. 247-48.

45. Ibid., pp. 249-50.

46. Evsyukov, Migratsiya Naseleniye, p. 125.

47. Zaslavskaya and Kalmyk, Sovremennaya Sibirskaya Derevnya, pp. 42-71; and Zaslavskaya, Migratsiya Sel'skogo Naseleniya, pp. 3-312.

48. Schroeder, "Soviet Wage and Income Policies," p. 10.

49. Wädekin, "Income Distribution in Soviet Agriculture," p. 13.

50. Staroverov, Sotsial'no Demograficheskiye, p. 208.

51. Wädekin, "Income Distribution in Soviet Agriculture," pp. 12-13.

52. Staroverov, Sotsial'no Demograficheskiye, p. 8.

53. Zaslavskaya and Kalmyk, Sovremennaya Sibirskaya Derevnya, p. 152.

54. Leslie Dienes, "Investment Priorities in Soviet Regions," Annals of the Association of American Geographers 62 (September 1972): 444.

55. Schroeder, "Soviet Wage and Income Policies," p. 7.

56. Zaslavskaya and Kalmyk, Sovremennaya Sibirskaya Derevnya, p. 153.

57. Staroverov, Sotsial'no Demograficheskiye, pp. 219-56.

58. Ibid., p. 178.

59. Richard E. Lonsdale, "Regional Inequality and Soviet Concern for Rural and Small-Town Industrialization," Soviet Geography: Review and Translation 18 (October 1977): 591.

60. Ibid., p. 599.

61. Staroverov, Sotsial'no Demograficheskiye, pp. 211-12.

SUMMARY AND CONCLUSIONS

8

Population redistribution is a major indicator of modernization because of its many linkages with economic development. In particular, urbanization is a surrogate for the economic, social, and cultural change that is associated with modernization and normally results in a drastic transformation in lifestyle. On the basis, largely, of our comparable array of data, we have attempted to delineate the major patterns of population redistribution in Russia and the USSR since 1897. Universal concepts were employed in an attempt to explain the redistributional processes. In general, the universality of these concepts was confirmed in the Soviet context, although the expected relationships did not always emerge, and these concepts proved to be useful in organizing and systematizing the data applied to them. There is no model or formula, of course, that can be used to interrelate modernization or economic development with population redistribution. Nor can, for example, levels of urbanization relative to economic development be specified, largely because of international differences in labor productivity and the structure of the economies. However, one generally can compare the universal patterns and their correlates with those that occurred in the USSR in an attempt to make a judgment as to the universality of these processes. We do not maintain that redistributional processes can be explained completely by universal concepts. The determining conditions of the modernization process vary from country to country, theory is not well formulated, and Soviet data are often lacking. It must also be acknowledged that there are historic and cultural conditions and, above all, catastrophic events unique to the Soviet Union that affect the processes under investigation. Nonetheless, the overall generality of the redistributional processes was much greater than was anticipated at the outset of the study.

Although the forces of modernization have been by far the most influential in Soviet population redistribution and change, wars, in particular, but also economic disorganization resulting from them, the formation of the Soviet state, famines, and other catastrophic events have affected greatly these processes. Because demographic processes are interrelated closely and are, in turn, closely and complexly interrelated with the socioeconomic environment, wars have had a major impact on population change in the USSR. As a result of wars, mortality, fertility, and migration were affected drastically, and because of the interrelated nature of demographic processes, virtually all aspects of population were affected, including sex ratios, age composition, urbanization, densities, the composition of the work force, and natural increase. In addition, the demographic consequences of the wars also contributed to the creation of a new set of socioeconomic conditions. For example, the altered sex ratios resulting from World War II affected marriage rates, which affected fertility, which in a couple of decades affected the work force. There was also a discernible impact on such interrelated social aspects as family life, divorce, sexual mores, and the participation of women in the work force. Wars tend to form major discontinuities with respect to demographic and socioeconomic trends and conditions, and after a war a new set of conditions frequently prevails. Therefore, in the analysis of demographic processes for a period after a war, one must differentiate between the effect of the war and the effect of the new set of socioeconomic conditions. In the Soviet context, this is particularly difficult because of a lack of data, and demographic trends between two Soviet censuses frequently are not representative of the period because of the intervening war.

If Soviet policy with respect to population redistribution were effective, universal formulations would not contribute substantially to the explanation of population redistribution in the USSR, because policy would explain practice. However, we have questioned the conventional wisdom as to the control that the Soviet government exercises over population movement. The rapid urbanization that has occurred in the USSR has been largely the result of migration from rural areas. Since 1926 upwards of 100 million people have migrated from rural to urban areas. Currently, about 15 million people annually move between settlements in the USSR. Tremendous effort would be required to control such a volume of migration. Soviet writers acknowledge the lack of an effective policy as to population redistribution and the economic irrationality of much of the migration in the USSR, in that there is considerable migration from labor-deficit to labor-surplus areas. In particular, the Russian East and rural Slavic areas, which are experiencing intense labor shortages, are characterized by net out-migration. Rural areas having labor surpluses, the Non-Slavic South, especially, are experiencing relatively little rural out-migration, while labor shortages continue and will intensify in the 1980s in the major regions of economic development. Thus, migration is not fulfilling its chief economic function, the redistribution of labor resources. Moreover, organized migration, which generally has been voluntary, has decreased in importance since the 1930s.

Despite a long-standing policy to limit the growth of large cities, they have grown fairly rapidly and greatly increased in number, which has resulted in a significant and increasing concentration of the total and urban population in large cities. Furthermore, cities that were specifically targeted for population control in the late 1950s have grown about as rapidly as the urban population as a whole, and the projected maximum size of many large cities already has been exceeded. Registration regulations and internal passport requirements appear to have impeded the growth of large cities but have not controlled it. Although Marxist ideology calls for the combination of agriculture and manufacturing, the elimination of the distinction between town and country, and a more even distribution of the population over the country, scant attention has been devoted to these policies. An increasing percentage of the population is found in large urban areas, the rural population is concentrating in the larger rural settlements, the emphasis on heavy industry has resulted in the development of regions that are well endowed with resources or have other locational advantages, and most non-Russian republics (in particular the non-Slavic southern tier) are considerably below the USSR average with respect to industrialization and urbanization.

Because each empirical chapter was preceded by a summary discussion, only the major redistributional trends will be summarized. As to the redistribution of the total population, trends have been remarkably stable for the past 400 years, which demonstrates the continuity of major migratory streams and the difficulty in controlling them. After the Russians were driven into the forests of Northern European USSR by the Mongols, major migratory streams flowed to the south and east, first to agricultural and later to urban frontiers. Recently, there have been two major changes in this long-term pattern of redistribution. Since 1959 the Russian East has experienced a declining share of the total population, and since 1970 the European Steppe has registered no relative gain. Thus, since 1970 the Non-Slavic South is the only quadrant to experience a relative gain with respect to population redistribution.

Despite major wars, revolution, and the attendant economic disorganization, the Soviet Union has experienced very rapid urbanization and urban growth since the turn of the century. Between 1920 and 1970, the rate of urbanization exceeded that of every major world region and was particularly rapid in the 1930s, when its rate was probably the highest ever experienced by any major country. Since 1897 the Eastern USSR has urbanized more rapidly than the Western USSR, and the Russian East was characterized by especially rapid urbanization and the Non-Slavic South by particularly slow urbanization. There has been a reversal since 1959 in the regional trends of urbanization and urban growth; Western USSR, especially Northern European USSR, experienced the highest rates. The urban process has involved an overall increase in proportion of both the total and urban population residing in large cities (over 100,000 population) and a great increase in the number of such cities. In particular, the USSR has experienced an increased concentration of its population in urban agglomerations and a deconcentration of the population within them, especially from the central city to the inner suburbs.

As might be expected, the level of ruralization in the USSR has declined sharply, because the rural population has grown very slowly since 1897 and has declined since 1926. The decline since 1970 has been sharp. Northern European USSR and the Russian East have experienced considerable rural population decline, whereas the Non-Slavic South has had a considerable rural population increase and since 1970 has been the only quadrant to have a rural population increase. Within rural areas, there has been a shift in population from smaller to larger rural settlements. The Slavic and Baltic areas are characterized by low rates of rural natural increase and relatively high rates of rural out-migration, whereas opposite conditions prevail in the Non-Slavic South.

There appears to be much universality in the redistributional processes that have occurred in the USSR. The general patterns of population redistribution, high rates of urbanization and migration and increasing rural depopulation, are in conformance with the universal experience in countries that have experienced considerable economic development. As to total migration, the expected relationships largely emerged with respect to mobility, distance, age, ethnicity, education, and the links to economic variables, although the relationships with economic variables were not always as strong as might be expected. With respect to the analysis of urbanization, regional variations in urbanization and urban growth were related to each other until fairly recently and to regional variations in urban migration, urban natural increase, industrialization, tertiary activities, and capital investment. In conformity with world patterns, the relative contribution of urban in-migration to urbanization has declined over time and that of urban natural increase has increased; there has been an increasing concentration of the total and urban population in large cities and in agglomerations and an increase in their number; small mining towns have decreased in population; and there has been a deconcentration of population within agglomerations, although the outer suburbs have not grown as much as elsewhere. Rural depopulation has been related to rural out-migration and the associated decline in rural natural increase, and rural out-migration appeared to be the greatest where the rural-urban wage differential was the greatest. As elsewhere, the young and the more educated have the highest propensity to migrate from rural areas, and the more economically developed regions generally have higher rates of rural out-migration. Within rural areas there was a considerable redistribution from poorer farms to more prosperous areas. Clearly, the economic motivation in migration is as strong in the USSR as elsewhere.

It is interesting to note that the Soviet experience also generally corresponds with the conceptual schemes developed by Jack P. Gibbs and Wilbur Zelinsky concerning urban and migration changes over time.[1] Gibbs maintains that there are five stages in the evolution of population concentration: (1) cities arise, (2) urban growth eventually exceeds rural growth, (3) the rural population declines, (4) the population of small towns declines, and (5) population deconcentration occurs. It is apparent from the preceding chapters that the USSR has, to a great extent, gone through these five stages. Cities obviously arose and urban growth has exceeded rural growth, leading, of course, to urbanization. Rural population decline also has occurred in most areas of the USSR, with the notable exception of the Non-Slavic South, and small-town population decline has occurred with the recent emergence of a large number of declining towns, most of which are relatively small in population, although most are not the rural service centers as indicated in Gibbs's scheme. Deconcentration within major urban areas also has occurred in the USSR, although to a comparatively limited extent.

Zelinsky also proposes a five-stage model. In particular, he attempts to formulate a migration model analogous to the demographic transition theory for fertility and mortality in that he hypothesizes temporal changes in mobility (migration and circulation) in association with the modernization process. In general terms, the five stages set forth by Zelinsky include: (1) little mobility in a premodern society; (2) increased frontier, international, and rural-to-urban migration; (3) a slackening or peaking of the movements of the second stage and an increase in urban-to-urban and intraurban migration, as well as circulation (for example, commuting); (4) a reduction in the types of migration of the second stage and a further increase in the types of mobility in the third stage, including a migration from underdeveloped areas to developed areas; and (5) a "future superadvanced society" with a decline in residential migration and a continuation though deceleration of urban-to-urban and intraurban migration and of some types of circulation with improvements in communications, as well as the imposition of strict political controls on internal and international movements. The USSR has progressed from the first through the second, third, and parts of the fourth stage. The second stage has been especially well expressed in the USSR. Three aspects of migration have been represented with the frontier migration to the steppe and Siberia, the emigration of Jews around the turn of the century, and the massive rural-to-urban migration, which occurred principally since the 1930s. The third and fourth stages are exemplified by the reversal of the Great Siberian Migration and the current dominance of urban-to-urban migration and increased commuting in the USSR, although Roland J. Fuchs and George J. Demko contend that the nature of and factors involved in Soviet commuting differ from the Zelinsky model and Western experience.[2] Another aspect of the fourth stage, migration from underdeveloped to developed areas, has yet to occur in the USSR to any great extent, but the projected future migration of Turkic-Muslims from the Non-Slavic South to the Slavic or European areas would certainly provide correspondence to this particular movement of the "Mobility Transition." The fifth stage, being more futuristic, has yet to be reached to any great extent in any area of the world, including the West or the USSR.

In conclusion, the USSR experience generally corresponds to the models proposed by Gibbs and Zelinsky and thus to the experience of Western areas, upon whose experience the models are based. However, neither the experience of the USSR nor of all developed countries correspond completely to the five stages of both of the models. It is beyond the scope of this book to test the Gibbs and Zelinsky models in greater depth in the USSR. This would seem to provide the basis for a number of future studies on urbanization and migration in the USSR. Nonetheless, at least in very general terms, it appears that the USSR experience is similar to that proposed by both models and thus demonstrates the universality of urbanization and migration processes in the USSR.

In collaboration with A. J. Jaffe, we have done some preliminary research on occupational mobility between 1960 and 1970 by sex and age, which further suggests a universality of redistributional processes. Our preliminary results are for males only, and the individual occupations have been grouped into three gross categories: agricultural workers, other manual

TABLE 8.1

Male Occupational Mobility in the USSR: 1960-70

	Agri- cultural Jobs	Manual Jobs excluding Agriculture	Intel- lectual Jobs
1960 work force	14,744,000	28,596,000	9,718,000
New entries	3,669,000	8,961,000	1,639,000
Net mobility	-7,442,000	2,682,000	4,760,000
Retirements	2,064,000	1,925,000	1,329,000
Deaths	1,623,000	2,305,000	882,000
1970 work force	7,284,000	36,009,000	13,906,000
Percent change in work force	-51	26	43

Sources: 1959 and 1970 Soviet censuses (see Chapter 1, n. 104).

workers, and intellectual workers. The last category is reasonably similar to white-collar workers in the United States. At this juncture, we will not describe our methodology in detail, aside from indicating that we used the model developed by Jaffe and R. O. Carleton to calculate occupational mobility, the Stephan inflation formula to estimate the 1970 occupational composition by age and sex, and the procedures used by Mary J. Powers and John J. Holmberg to calculate socioeconomic status scores so that comparisons can be made with the United States.[3]

In 1960 there were 53,058,000 men in the USSR work force (Table 8.1). Between 1960 and 1970, there were 14,268,000 new entries, 5,317,000 retirements, and 4,810,000 deaths, so the 1970 male work force was 57,199,000 or 8 percent greater than in 1960. During this decade about one-fourth of all young males who joined the work force entered agriculture, just short of two-thirds found their first job in manual work excluding agriculture, and a little over one-tenth entered "intellectual" or white-collar jobs. Subsequently there was a vast out-mobility from agriculture, almost 7.5 million, and the male agricultural work force declined by 51 percent. About one-third of this net moved into other manual jobs and two-thirds into intellectual work. New entries were youth up to about the age of 20. Net out-mobility was very heavy up to age 35, and in general, men who remained in agriculture into their thirties tended to remain in this field until death or retirement. Presumably, many of the rural youth first entered agriculture after leaving school and re-

TABLE 8.2

Male Age Pattern of Net Mobility for the USSR and the
United States: 1960-70

Age in 1960	Age in 1970	Net Mobility Index	
		USSR	United States
5-9	15-19	18	12
10-14	20-24	84	89
15-19	25-29	100	100
20-24	30-34	48	72
25-29	35-39	51	53
30-34	40-44	28	33
35-39	45-49	20	26
40-44	50-54	22	30
45-49	55-59	10	26

Sources: 1959 and 1970 Soviet censuses (see Chapter
1, n. 104).

mained there until they were drafted into the armed forces. Upon leaving the
armed forces the large majority entered nonagricultural occupations or returned to school and later went into nonagricultural occupations.

Net mobility into manual jobs excluding agriculture totaled more than
2.5 million, and the male work force in this category increased by 26 percent
between 1960 and 1970 (Table 8.1). Net in-mobility was heaviest to about age
35, and beyond this age there was very little in- or out-mobility. There were
more new entries than net in-mobility into these jobs, and there were over
twice as many new entries into these manual jobs than into agricultural jobs.

Clearly, the white-collar jobs are the fastest growing, and in this respect the USSR resembles the United States (Table 8.1). Young men continued
to enter this area as new entries into their thirties. Presumably, these are
the university-trained, who remain in school to a significantly older age than
those who enter manual or agricultural jobs. Net mobility into these white-
collar jobs continues only to about age 35 or so; any man who has not made it
by that age is not likely to do so. Generally, the number of white-collar jobs
increased much more through net in-mobility than via new entries. Presumably, this reflects one version of climbing the occupational ladder; while working at manual jobs, some youths continue their schooling until they can achieve
white-collar jobs.

The age pattern of net mobility in the USSR is very similar to that of the United States, which is another striking parallel with respect to universal processes in the USSR. The highest mobility rate is between the ages of 15 to 19 in 1960 and 25 to 29 in 1970, and this rate is set at 100 (Table 8.2). It is possible that net mobility continues to a somewhat older age in the United States, but because of the differences in the statistics we cannot be certain on the basis of this preliminary analysis. Rather, we are impressed by the similarities between the two countries. Thus, the patterns of shifting occupations may be much more similar than has been thought to be the case.

NOTES

1. Jack P. Gibbs, "The Evolution of Population Concentration," in Population Geography: A Reader, ed. George J. Demko, Harold M. Rose, and George A. Schnell (New York: McGraw-Hill, 1970), pp. 171-81; and Wilbur Zelinsky, "The Hypothesis of the Mobility Transition," Geographical Review 61 (April 1971): 219-49.

2. Roland J. Fuchs and George J. Demko, "The Postwar Mobility Transition in Eastern Europe," Geographical Review 68 (April 1978): 171-82.

3. A. J. Jaffe and R. O. Carleton, Occupational Mobility in the United States, 1930-1960 (New York: King's Crown Press, 1954); W. E. Deming, Statistical Adjustments of Data (New York: John Wiley and Sons, 1943); and Mary J. Powers and John J. Holmberg, "Occupational Status Scores: Changes Introduced by the Inclusion of Women," Demography 15 (May 1978): 183-205.

9

IMPLICATIONS

If, as we maintain, there is a considerable universality of processes related to population redistribution, migration, urbanization, and rural population change in the USSR, then guarded forecasts based on the universal experience in other developed countries can be made for the USSR in the coming decades. This does not, of course, mean that we can predict with precision the interaction of demographic, socioeconomic, and political processes in the USSR and their consequences for Soviet society; this would require a knowledge of these processes far in advance of current scholarship and there are catastrophic events in human affairs that defy prediction. If, however, it is assumed that the existing societal trends and conditions will more or less continue, say, to the end of the century and that socioeconomic and demographic trends normally are remarkably stable, then the broad outline of the impact of some of these processes can be sketched reasonably.

In the introduction, we pointed out the importance of demographic and geographic forces in shaping a society and the interrelated nature of demographic and socioeconomic processes. At this juncture, it would seem appropriate to repeat once again some of the demographic and geographic forces that will shape Soviet society in the coming decades, if for no other reason than to emphasize further their importance. As we stated before, many of these forces are related to population redistribution and include a low and generally declining rate of population growth, sharp regional differentials in rates of population growth related to low Slavic and generally moderate-to-high non-Slavic fertility, an aging "European" population, severe regional labor shortages resulting from the fact that migration is not meeting the needs of the economy, widespread rural depopulation in "European" areas, rapidly growing rural populations in many "non-European" areas, rapid urbanization, the maldistribution of population relative to industrial resources, the multinational character of the USSR and the differential geographical mixing and integration of the nationalities into the modern society, and very high and increasing female work force participation rates. (Some of these subjects will be discussed in the planned third volume of this series, which will be devoted primarily to such subjects as population growth, mortality, fertility, age and sex composition, occupational mobility, work force, and education.)

For example, that almost four-fifths of the women in the able-bodied years were in the work force in the USSR in 1970 has a tremendous effect on family and social life, and the USSR might well serve as a model as to what will happen in countries, such as the United States, where the work force participation of women is rapidly rising. Other trends as well will have societal consequences in the coming decades. Such trends as rising divorce and crime rates and the significant rise and convergence of educational levels among the younger cohorts of the various nationalities will have far-reaching effects. Once a majority of the young people in a society begin to complete high school, that society will never be the same, because aspirations grow and horizons broaden, which affect virtually all aspects of demographic and socioeconomic change. Above all, however, the decline in mortality and fertility and the rapid urbanization of Soviet society associated with modernization has drastically and irrevocably altered peoples' lives.

Limitations of space preclude a discussion of all the possible consequences of population redistribution in the USSR. For example, migration has resulted in regional variations in the age and sex structure, particularly between urban and rural areas, which affects dependency ratios, the proportion of the population of working age, and so forth. This subject will receive major consideration in our subsequent volume. Suffice it to say, as has been discussed, that rural areas experiencing considerable out-migration have a declining percentage of the population in the work force ages and an aging population, whereas the urban population is generally younger and has a higher proportion of its population in the work force ages. These trends, of course, affect the economy, in particular the regional supply of labor. Although a general discussion of urbanization and its consequences and migration and the work force is included, our major emphasis will be devoted to population redistribution and ethnicity, because we feel that in multinational modernizing states such as the USSR these interrelated processes will have the greatest impact.

URBANIZATION AND ITS CONSEQUENCES

The rapid urbanization of Soviet society has had and will continue to have a momentous impact on the lives of the Soviet people. It is beyond the scope of this study to investigate in detail these societal consequences, even if the necessary data were available.[1] Although the interaction between modernization and urbanization has not been worked out sufficiently, conceptually or empirically, it is obvious to even the casual observer that they are intimately interrelated. Louis Wirth has hypothesized how size, density, and heterogeneity of cities are associated with such factors as impersonal relationships; greater but secondary, segmental, and impersonal interaction; economic and occupational differentiation; separation of work and residence; segregation of peoples; erosion of traditional values; and secularization of thought.[2] In short, urbanization is related to a fundamental alteration of traditional ways of life and is a basis for social change. In the Soviet context, that the urban areas are centers of modernization and differ drastically from the rural areas is empirically obvious. Visually these differences are usually stark, especially in Slavic areas, and much greater than one usually finds in the Western world. Virtually all available indicators of social change for the urban areas of the USSR, such as fertility, education, divorce, and crime, support the contention that universal processes are in operation and that urban problems characteristic of more urbanized societies are developing in the USSR. For example, the crime rate in the USSR appears to be rising and is higher in urban than rural areas, although crime statistics are not readily available. This phenomenon appears to be related to the disintegration of family, kinship, and social relations, which magnifies peer group pressure and varies with educational and occupational levels.[3] Sexual mores and the status of women have changed drastically, in particular in the major cities, and about 10 percent of all births are currently illegitimate. About 28 percent of all marriages now end in divorce, and the highest rates are in the cities, particularly the larger ones.[4] In addition, wages and the standard of living are normally higher in Soviet urban areas, and cultural and educational facilities and consumer goods are much more abundant. All of these trends are indicative of Louis Wirth's characterization of urban life. In short, the urbanization that has occurred and will occur in the USSR has and will have a momentous impact on the lives of the Soviet people.

As was discussed in the introduction, urbanization is linked with other demographic trends associated with modernization. Because the young and more educated migrate to urban centers, the age composition and educational levels are affected in both urban and rural areas, in particular the percentage of the population in the work force ages are notably higher in urban areas as is the level of educational attainment. Fertility is notably lower in the urban areas of the USSR. In terms of gross reproduction rates, rural fertility in the USSR was almost twice that of urban fertility (0.94 as opposed to 1.70) in the 1974/75 period.[5] Thus, if this ratio were to remain roughly constant, further urbanization would result in even lower fertility in the USSR. In the 1973/74 period, the gross reproduction rate of the USSR was 1.18 and the net reproduction rate was 1.12, but in the Slavic and Baltic areas, the net reproduction rate in the aggregate was below one or below replacement if the age distribution is not taken into consideration, and these are, of course, the areas with highest urbanization rates. Thus, the impact of urbanization on fertility would be the greatest in the areas of lowest fertility, but we will have more to say on this subject in our subsequent volume.

WORK FORCE AND MIGRATION

Another demographic problem that is related to migration and will have major consequences for Soviet society is that in the 1980s there will be a sharp decline in the growth of the population of working age (here defined as the population aged 20 to 59), particularly in the Slavic areas. Between 1970 and 1980, this population increased by 1.7 percent per year, but in the 1980-90 period it will increase by only 0.7 percent per year. Moreover, the bulk of the increase in the population of working age will be in non-Slavic areas. Between 1980 and 1990, almost three-fourths of the net increase, not taking migration into consideration, will come from Central Asia, Kazakhstan, and the Transcaucasus, where the working-age population will be increasing by 2.5 percent per year. In the remainder of the USSR, it will be growing by 0.2 percent per year, and if Moldavia and the non-Russian ethnic units in the RSFSR are excluded, it would be very close to stationary. Highly industrialized economic regions such as the Northwest, Center, and Donetsk-Dnepr will experience absolute declines, and other economic regions outside the Non-Slavic South will increase barely. Central Asia will have by far the most rapid increase in the population of working age and the population aged 20 to 29, potential entrants to the work force. Between 1980 and 1990, 40.2 percent of the net increase in the population of working age will be accounted for by Central Asia, and whereas with respect to potential new entrants, there will be a decline of more than 2 million in the USSR as a whole, Central Asia will experience an increase of almost 2 million.[6]

The slow growth of the working-age population and the maldistribution of this growth should result in slower economic growth and other problems in the USSR in the 1980s. After investigating potential sources of employment growth in the USSR and finding them to be generally inadequate with respect to increasing the growth of the work force, CIA analysts conclude:

A slowdown in economic growth seems certain by the 1980s, however. Productivity is unlikely to increase sufficiently to offset the retardation in employment growth. A GNP growth rate of 5.0% per year would require an increase in output per manhour of 3.5% annually in 1976-80, compared with less than 2.0% in 1971-75. The required productivity increase would reach 4.5% per year in 1986-90 when increments in the labor force slow to a trickle. This acceleration in the growth of labor productivity would have to overcome the resistance posed by declining rates of growth in the amount of capital per worker.[7]

They further conclude that planners will attempt to accelerate migration from such labor-surplus areas as Central Asia, Kazakhstan, and the Transcaucasus, but such an effort would be formidable because if the population of working age in these labor-surplus regions were to grow at a rate equal to the rest of the country between 1976 and 1990, a shift of about 9 million persons of working age would be required.[8]

The slowdown in the growth of the potential supply of 18-year-old males and their ethnic composition also should have a major impact on military manpower. After analyzing the various estimates of the size and composition of the Soviet armed forces and the potential supply of recruits, Murray Feshbach and Stephen Rapawy conclude that "Unless changes are made in the term of military service, the length of the workweek, or some other aspect of manpower allocation, demographic, educational, and military factors oblige

the Soviet government and the Party to reduce the size of the armed forces."[9]
Their estimates further indicate that by the end of the century, 34.6 percent
of the potential draftees will be accounted for by Central Asia, Kazakhstan,
and the Transcaucasus.[10] The ramifications of this are rather obvious and
would bring to mind questions of loyalty and Russian language competence.

MIGRATION AND NATIONALITY PROBLEMS

Clearly, these developments are important in that they probably will affect modernization, economic development, Soviet foreign policy, and international relations. However, economic and military consequences may not
be the most important ones, at least in the longer run. If, say, by the end
of the century considerable numbers of "non-Europeans" migrate to the regions of economic development, which are located primarily in Slavic areas,
nationality problems could intensify greatly and become the dominant force
shaping Soviet society. We will have more to say subsequently about non-European migration. However, if such a migration should occur and contribute
to the solution of their economic problems, a whole new set of nationality
problems should arise, assuming that demographic and ethnic processes in the
USSR are more or less universal.

We have demonstrated in this study that there has been a considerable
universality in the processes related to population redistribution in the USSR.
In our previous work, we also demonstrated that universal processing had to
a significant degree occurred with respect to ethnic and demographic processes in the USSR, one of the most multinational states in the world. Specifically, we stated that:

> The theme of this study is the impact of modernization on the pop-
> ulation of the multinational Soviet state. The authors hypothesized
> that population trends among the various Soviet nationality group-
> ings would conform to the patterns found in other modernizing,
> multinational states. Universal experience indicates that modern-
> ization affects various ethnic groups in multinational states to dif-
> ferent degrees and at different times, and this differential modern-
> ization is reflected by demographic trends indicative of moderniza-
> tion. The more modernized groups would be characterized by
> higher levels of urbanization, geographic mobility, employment in
> the nonagricultural work force, higher education levels, and lower
> levels of fertility. On the other hand, those ethnic groups that
> were less modernized would retain many of the demographic
> characteristics of premodern societies, which include continued
> rural residence, mainly agricultural employment, lower levels
> of educational attainment, and higher fertility. These demo-
> graphic conditions, of course, reflect the degree to which a group
> is integrated into the modern sectors of society, and thus the degree
> to which a group benefits from the economic development that occurs

with modernization. Specifically, it was hypothesized that the dominant ethnic group, the Russians, and certain other ethnic groups with cultural traits that facilitate early modernization, the Tatars, Jews, and Mobilized Europeans, would be the more modernized groups in Soviet society. We cannot, of course, completely determine in an objective manner which groups would be expected to modernize, because there has been insufficient conceptual work on this subject. This deficiency does not, however, undermine our assertion that ethnic stratification along socioeconomic lines does occur in multinational modernizing states.[11]

We then assessed the implications of the impact of modernization upon the multinational Soviet state in terms of the establishment and realignment of systems of ethnic stratification, which occurs when two or more nationalities come into contact. In short, ethnicity is a common criterion from which status is inferred in multinational states, and nationality is reinforced when it corresponds with other categories such as occupation, class, or urban-rural residence. Modernization and economic development are the most important catalysts for change in ethnically stratified societies, because ultimately the integration of all or most ethnic groups into the modernized sectors is required. Consensus over the relative status of the groups breaks down and ethnic tensions inevitably result. However, systems of ethnic stratification do not break down completely during the period of change but realign, and ethnic inequities persist, which is a source of tension. The dominant group or groups tend to preempt the most favorable positions in society and benefit disproportionately from the economic development that is occurring. Demographic and socioeconomic change associated with modernization also leads to increased ethnic animosities. The influx of outsiders into national homelands and increased interethnic contact, urban-rural dichotomies among nationalities, rising levels of education, and discrimination in employment in the advanced sectors, all promote discontent among ethnic groups. We then demonstrated that the USSR conforms to these general patterns.[12]

Walker Connor takes a slightly different approach to the existence and rise of national consciousness, but the implications with respect to the influence of modernization, in general, and migration, in particular, are very similar. He stresses that the essence of nationality is the popularly held, intuitive sense of the vital uniqueness of one's own group, which is highly emotional in content. He maintains that both objective and subjective factors are important in the definition of ethnic identity, although subjective factors are the more important, and that its study has been overly dichotomized into either the subjective or the objective schools. He maintains that comparative research indicates that no particular set of objective attributes (language, homeland, religion, history, and so forth) adequately explains ethnic identity, but such factors are important as reinforcing elements. The basic subjective factor is the concept of the us-them dichotomy, which essentially maintains that it is the existence of another ethnic group that is the necessary precondition for ethnic identity.

According to Connor, ethnic groups are characterized by a prenational stage, when interaction among groups is limited and ethnic identity is either weakly developed or absent, but the processes of modernization intensify ethnicity through such forces as transportation, migration, communication, and political integration. As groups come into contact and competition with one another, ethnic differences are perceived, which heightens the feeling of ethnic identity of all the groups involved and generally results in animosities and tensions. These processes result in heightened national identity even after considerable cultural change has occurred (such as among the Scots and Welsh), so culture and ethnicity must be isolated in the study of national consciousness, because it is psychological and not cultural assimilation that affects the intuitive feeling of group identity. Connor contends that cultural, economic, and political deprivation have been overemphasized in the study of ethnonationalism, because ethnic conflicts tend to persist even after equality among various groups in a multinational state is achieved.

Another important precondition, according to Connor, is the spread of the notion of self-determination of peoples, which is the wedding of popular sovereignty to ethnicity and occurred at the time of the French Revolution. This precondition also has been affected by modernization, in particular, the associated advances in communications through the medium of the "demonstration effect. " On the basis of geographically broad comparative research, Connor has established a considerable universality of ethnic processes with respect to his conceptual framework. Specifically, he has established that ethnic consciousness in multinational states definitely has been on the rise and that this rise has not been related to the form of government, geography, or the level of economic development. However, the concomitants of economic development, social mobilization and communication, appear to have played an influential role. [13]

We are in total agreement with Connor's thinking. We would emphasize, however, more the effect of migration and urbanization on the rise of ethnic identity. We have pointed out that there are regional inequalities in economic development in the USSR, as is the case in other countries, and this ultimately requires a massive redistribution of a population, which in multinational states results in much geographical mixing of the various ethnic groups. Rural areas characterized by out-migration in multinational states tend to be ethnically homogeneous, whereas urban areas experiencing in-migration are ethnically heterogeneous. It is precisely in these ethnically heterogeneous urban areas that the national "us" comes into direct contact with the alien "them," which is the primary basis of ethnic conflict. Therefore, it is not surprising that virtually all of the reported ethnic conflict in the USSR has occurred in cities, for direct physical interaction among various ethnic groups is generally minimal in rural areas. Nevertheless, ethnic consciousness can be affected, although to a lesser degree, in rural areas by exposure to means of communication such as radio and television and occasional contacts with alien groups. As multinational modernizing states become more integrated, such contacts become more frequent even in rural areas. Thus, migration and urbanization are crucial elements in ethnic identity, and it is frequently in the urban areas in multinational states outside a group's national homeland that national consciousness reaches its peak.

As we have demonstrated, there has been a considerable redistribution and urbanization of the Soviet population largely as a result of economic development, and it can be expected that these processes will continue in conjunction with further economic development. As might be expected, the Russians, the dominant group, and a few other more modernized groups, such as the Jews and the Tatars, have been the most geographically mobile ethnic groups.[14] Historically, however, the dominant trend with respect to ethnic migration in the USSR has been the migration of Russians to non-Russian areas; in particular, for at least the last 100 years there has been a shift in the share of the Russian population to Siberia and the Far East. Between 1897 and 1970, the Russian population of these regions, which formerly were non-Russian areas, increased from about 3 million to 20 million and in 1970 accounted for almost 16 percent of the Russian population. In addition, nearly 10 million Russians resided in the non-Russian nationality units of the RSFSR in 1970, accounting for nearly half of their population. There was also a major shift of the Russian population to non-Russian areas outside the RSFSR. Between 1897 and 1970, the Russian population of these areas increased by more than 15 million and totaled more than 21 million in 1970 or about 16 percent of all Russians and about 20 percent of the population of these non-Russian areas. Thus, by 1970 some 30 million Russians, or 23 percent of the Russian population, lived in non-Russian administrative units.[15]

The Russians, moreover, have moved primarily to the cities in both Russian and non-Russian areas. Indeed, the Russians have urbanized at an unprecedented rate; between 1897 and 1970, the Russian urban population increased by more than 65 million people, and its level of urbanization increased from 13 to 56 percent or by 43 percentage points, a rate surpassed only by the Jews. Of the total Russian population outside the RSFSR, 64 percent were urban in 1970, and they comprised almost one-third of the urban population in these areas. In the non-Russian units of the RSFSR, the Russians accounted for 65 percent of the urban population in 1959 and 61 percent in 1970. Thus, the Russians have migrated to urban areas of non-Russian ethnic units to the extent that most urban areas in these areas are Russian cultural enclaves. The Russians, furthermore, have preempted the most desirable positions in these urban areas, which is characteristic of dominant ethnic groups in multinational states, and the urban economy of many of these regions has been unable to absorb the surplus indigenous labor.[16] With respect to the geographic mixing of ethnic groups, Russian rural areas and, to a considerable extent, urban areas generally have remained ethnically homogeneous, but the urban areas of the non-Russian units have become increasingly heterogeneous with respect to their ethnic composition.

However, these patterns can be expected to change in the next few decades, because a set of conditions is developing that should result in considerable out-migration from non-Russian, in particular Turkic-Muslim regions, to Russian and other Slavic regions. In short, the Slavic regions generally are characterized by low natural increase, a relatively low and declining growth rate of their work force, and labor shortages and contain the major regions of economic development. The Turkic-Muslim population is growing rapidly, their ethnic units are relatively underdeveloped, and there are labor surpluses. Barring any drastic changes in these trends, in the coming decades there should be considerable Turkic-Muslim migration into the Slavic areas, as migration regionally equalizes the supply of and demand for labor. Thus, it might be expected that Russian and other Slavic areas will become less ethnically homogeneous and ethnic tensions might be expected to increase. Clearly, a multinational country experiencing relatively rapid economic development and severe regional labor shortages cannot long expect its major areas of economic development to be ethnically pure.

CENTRAL ASIAN LABOR PROBLEMS

Central Asia provides the best example of an area where these processes are occurring, although to a lesser degree analogous processes are taking place in Kazakhstan, the Transcaucasus, and many of the ethnic units of the RSFSR. We have discussed Central Asian labor problems in some detail in the first volume of this series, but because a debate has arisen as to whether the Turkic-Muslim population of Central Asia will migrate to other parts of the USSR, we find it necessary to summarize our previous discussion in order to further this debate. However, for a more detailed discussion of this issue, we refer the reader to our previous discussion. [17]

The Turkic-Muslims of Central Asia are experiencing an extremely rapid rate of population growth, which of course affects the growth of the working-age population. The total Turkic-Muslim population of Central Asia increased at an average annual rate of 3.4 percent between 1959 and 1970, and the titular groups grew almost 4 percent per year. If the rate for the total Turkic-Muslims were to continue, the 15 million Turkic-Muslims, excluding Tatars, in 1970 would roughly double their population by 1990 and triple it by the turn of the century. Even if there were a decline in fertility, crude birth rates probably would not decline appreciably in the next couple of decades, because about 50 percent of the population of the titular nationalities was under age 15 in 1970. Most of this growth would occur in rural areas, because in 1970 only 21 percent of the Turkic-Muslim population of Central Asia lived in urban areas. The total working-age population (here defined as the population aged 20 to 59) in Central Asia also will double roughly and increase by about 7.5 million between 1970 and 1990 (excluding migration), and the number of new entrants to the work force (population aged 20 to 29) will almost triple. Between 1980 and 1990, Central Asia will account for about 40 percent of the increase of the total Soviet work force.

Of course, such a rapidly growing population by itself does not mean that there are population pressures. However, the rapidly growing rural population of Central Asia lives in irrigated oases with limited water and irrigable land, and the irrigated acreage has been expanded very slowly, well below the rate of population increase. Between 1959 and 1970, the number of rural inhabitants per sown hectare in Central Asia increased by roughly 25 percent, after remaining stable for at least the previous half century. In addition, there has been, and undoubtedly will continue to be, a concerted drive by the government to mechanize agriculture in order to produce more cotton and to lower the cost of producing it. These factors, in addition to the rapidly growing rural population, have resulted in labor surpluses throughout the rural areas of Central Asia.

Moreover, there has been relatively little migration of the indigenous population to local urban centers, largely because Russians and others have been moving into Central Asian cities. The estimated net migration to Central Asia between 1959 and 1970 was 450,000, and between 1970 and 1974, it was 131,000. Thus, the urban in-migration of the indigenous population has been impeded. Furthermore, even if there were no in-migration into Central Asia, the nonagricultural economy has not expanded rapidly enough to absorb the surplus labor, and current investment plans are not directed toward alleviating this problem. If these trends continue, labor surpluses in Central Asia will continue to grow, as they have for at least the last decade, and should provide the motivation for considerable rural out-migration.

Another factor that should promote out-migration is the rise in educational levels and the concomitant social and cultural change, because the world over the young and the more educated tend to have a high propensity to migrate. In 1970 the cohort aged 20 to 29 for the total Uzbek population of the USSR had completed ten or more years of education at the same rate as the Russian population of the USSR (54 percent). The urban rate for the Uzbeks was 66 percent and the rural rate was 48 percent. The rates for the other Central Asian titular groups were somewhat lower, with the Tadzhiks having the lowest rate, 45 percent completing more than ten years of school. Furthermore, in the rural areas of the Uzbek republic, the ratio between the percentages of men and women completing ten years of school is approaching parity, which of course affects the status of women. Similar trends are also evident elsewhere in Central Asia. There also has been a sharp decline in the percentage of females aged 16 to 19 who are married. Furthermore, a common pattern in most societies is that when individuals complete high school, regardless of the quality of education, there are many jobs, such as working on a farm, that are beneath their dignity or below their aspirations. Thus, the Central Asian rural population cannot be viewed as a static, traditional, uneducated Muslim population, because these gross indicators reflect important societal changes.

To date, there has been very little out-migration from the rural areas of Central Asia. In the two years preceding the 1970 census, rural-to-urban migrants comprised 1.8 percent of the total USSR population, whereas for the four Central Asian titular nationalities it ranged from 1.1 percent for the Kirgiz to 0.5 percent for the Uzbeks, by far the largest Turkic-Muslim nationality. Only about 2 percent of the urban Uzbeks and virtually none of the rural Uzbeks live in the RSFSR.

Probably the chief reason that there has been little rural out-migration in Central Asia is that agricultural wages have remained relatively high and the rural-urban wage differential is small (see Chapter 7). At least in the 1960s, the government raised cotton prices, and thus wage rates, faster than productivity increases in an effort to obtain more and cheaper cotton. Thus, it would appear that at least by 1970, economic conditions had not yet begun to deteriorate significantly in the rural areas of Central Asia.

Wage levels and rural-urban wage differentials are important mechanisms in rural out-migration, because when the economic crunch is sufficiently severe people move regardless of family, ethnicity, homelands, climate, or whatever. In 1974 there were over 600,000 legal Turkish workers in West Germany, 26 percent of which were women, which reflects a drastic change in a society that before structural changes in its economy had no continuing migratory tradition.[18] Moreover, more than a million applicants for jobs in West Germany were reportedly on a waiting list in Turkey, largely because Turkish workers can earn 20 times as much in West Germany than Turkey, assuming they can find jobs in Turkey.[19] Although on both sides this migration was considered temporary, much of the migration is becoming permanent because of the need of the German economy for workers in the more undesirable jobs, and because families are joining the workers either legally or illegally. More recently, those Turkish workers who have become unemployed are being forced to leave, as unemployment has increased in Germany.[20] This considerable migration of Turks to West Germany has occurred despite considerable discrimination and ethnic tension.

Clearly, if analogous economic conditions prevailed in Central Asia relative to other parts of the USSR, as exist between Turkey and West Germany, there would be Turks all over the USSR, particularly considering there are no restrictions such as are imposed in international migration. But, of course, such wage differentials currently do not exist in the USSR. The central question is, Will economic conditions in rural areas of Central Asia deteriorate to the extent that large numbers migrate to the cities of the region and beyond to other labor-deficit areas of the USSR? A 20-to-1 wage differential is not required, even though the exact threshold is unknown. As we have seen, in some Russian rural areas where there has been considerable rural out-migration, rural migrants to urban areas have at least doubled their wages after a few years in urban centers.

Considering the rapidly growing rural work force, the slow expansion of the irrigated areas, and the mechanization of agriculture, without migration labor productivity in agriculture and wages can be expected to decline appreciably if the young enter kolkhozy and sovkhozy, unless the government continues to raise cotton and other agricultural prices, which is in opposition to their goal of cheaper cotton. For example, V. I. Perevedentsev reports that in parts of the Fergana Valley kishlaks merge into one another and form one continuous village extending for tens of kilometers and that in Andizhan Oblast there is less than one hectare of agricultural land per worker, and it is difficult to find work for the kolkhoz members, whereas the norm for newly irrigated land in Uzbekistan is eight hectares per worker.[21] As this rural population grows, labor productivity should reach very low levels, which is the opposite that one might expect with the mechanization of agriculture.

Conditions such as these are building throughout Central Asia. Such population pressure cannot be alleviated by transferring workers to the small private plots, because there are limits to the number that these small plots can absorb. L. Bulochnikova, writing in 1969, reported that in Uzbekistan almost 90 percent of those released from agriculture continued to work their private plots and did not move and that this pattern was characteristic of the other republics of Central Asia.[22] In 1975 the total area of the private plots on kolkhozy in Central Asia comprised 0.2 percent of the total kolkhoz agricultural acreage, and the cultivated portion of the private plots comprised 3.5 percent of the total kolkhoz cultivated acreage.[23] As the rural population grows, the very small acreage in such plots should become crowded, and labor productivity and wages should decline to Asian levels.

Judging from similar situations elsewhere in the world, such a demographic caldron should provide the impetus for considerable out-migration, first to local urban areas and then to labor-deficit areas elsewhere in the USSR, if the current processes persist. However, it is difficult to ascertain when and how many will leave because of the difficulty in determining how rapidly the pressures are building and what policies the Soviet government might adopt. However, pressure for out-migration should be high in the 1980s and thereafter.

As to conceivable government policies, so far there has been no concerted effort to solve this problem, and inactivity or late or minimal response, which is generally characteristic of governments, cannot be ruled out. These alternatives would, of course, promote out-migration. Moreover, migration policies in the USSR have not been very effective, primarily because the government has not been willing to devote the necessary effort or expense. The Soviet government has been unable to induce people to move to and remain in Siberia, or to control the out-migration from rural Slavic areas, or to limit the growth of large cities. The government also has been unwilling to rely upon compulsory mobilization to solve its labor problems, and wage incentives, such as in eastern regions, appear to be inadequate.

The Soviet Union is a welfare society with considerable equalization of income and transfer payments. Wages could be maintained by raising the price paid for cotton in the rural areas of Central Asia, but this, in effect, would be supporting a large, unproductive welfare population on the land and would be very costly, not in their economic interest, and in conflict with their goal of cheaper cotton. If cotton prices are not raised, this would be an impetus for out-migration and probably the most inexpensive course of action, considering their labor requirements elsewhere. However, it should be acknowledged that welfare aspects of Soviet society could deter migration.

Although labor generally has been the mobile factor of production, the government could invest heavily in Central Asia to utilize the surplus labor. However, Central Asia generally has the lowest return to capital and combined factor productivity in the USSR, few economies of concentration, scant resources for heavy industry, a remote location from major markets, and a relatively poorly developed infrastructure, particularly with respect to transportation. Such a policy would be in conflict with their goal of maximizing the efficiency of the total economy, which at present is not highly efficient. One also might question if they want to invest heavily for a relatively long period of time in a peripheral, non-Russian, and potentially troublesome area. However, in terms of minimizing ethnic tensions in a multinational state, keeping the Central Asians in their homelands would be a wise policy, but governments most frequently opt for short-term economic benefits and overlook the more long-term social costs, such as the Western European governments have done with respect to immigrant labor.

Of some relevance in this respect is that current Soviet doctrine maintains that the problem of economic inequality by republic, the equalization principle in Soviet planning, has been "in effect" solved and that regional economic policy is now directed toward "the need to ensure the utmost efficiency of the whole economy."[24] Yet, despite some progress toward the goal of equalization, the Soviet economy continues to be characterized by significant spatial anomalies in development. Whether measured by indexes such as industrial employment, urbanization, fuel consumption, or per capita national income, certain regions are considerably more developed than others, and virtually all of the less developed regions (Central Asia, Belorussia, Moldavia, the Southwest, the Central Chernozem, and the Transcaucasus) are non-Russian ethnoterritories. Moreover, 1976-80 plans indicate few major changes in republic investment and development, so that gaps in regional development will remain appreciable. This probably reflects the fact that the non-Russian republics generally offer Soviet planners a less-than-optimum set of economic performance criteria, because at least through the 1960s gross return to capital was well below the USSR average in Central Asia, Kazakhstan, and the Transcaucasus, as was industrial labor productivity.[25]

It is virtually impossible to predict what policies the Soviet government might institute. The government, however, probably will be motivated primarily by economic considerations. Eventually, there probably will be more investment in Central Asia, but it is questionable whether it will be sufficient to absorb the surplus labor even if in-migration to the region is limited, given the economic costs of investing in Central Asia. They probably will attempt to encourage out-migration, because it would be in their economic interest. Either by choice or inaction, they could allow the standard of living in rural areas to decline, because this is also in their economic interest. Minimal measures probably will be undertaken, such as reserving jobs in the local urban centers for the indigenous population, and efforts may be made to facilitate the transition of the rural population to urban areas. For the most part, however, the processes involved very probably will be beyond the control of the government, and expected migratory patterns will prevail ultimately.

Our argument is based conceptually and is essentially that, if current demographic and socioeconomic trends in Central Asia and other parts of the USSR persist, this will create a set of determining conditions that elsewhere in the world has resulted in considerable out-migration; the same outcome can be expected in Central Asia, because the processes involved are largely universal and strong. The linchpin of this argument is that there will be deteriorating economic conditions in the region, but if for reasons of policy or the welfare nature of Soviet society, wages and employment are maintained in Central Asia, one reasonably cannot expect significant out-migration.

A number of scholars have disagreed with our conclusions, pointing to more particularistic aspects of Soviet and Central Asian society, in particular to Turkic-Muslim culture. For example, Alexandre Bennigsen concludes that the Moslem peoples of the Soviet Union will not willingly trade the intimacy of their cultural preserve for a higher living standard within an alien, urban, non-Moslem environment.[26] Admittedly, cultural factors can and do influence most facets of human behavior, including migration. The tug of family, locale, ethnic homeland, and the like does exert an important countervailing effect against those forces working for migration. Even in those cases in which economic forces have led large numbers of a people to migrate in search of greater economic opportunity (for example, migrants to the United States during the late nineteenth and early twentieth centuries or to Western Europe during the third quarter of the twentieth century), still much larger numbers customarily have chosen to remain at home, even though many of them experienced similar economic pressures. Furthermore, a close relationship between religion and culture also must be acknowledged. The religious map of the world does more than depict zones of theology. It designates culture zones that are readily identifiable with regard to such tangible areas of human endeavor as art, architecture, mode of dress, eating habits, and the like. Less discernible, but no less real, is the impact that the cultural milieu in turn exerts upon perceptions or ways of looking at things.

All religions and denominations have not, of course, exerted the same degree of influence upon the surrounding culture. One rough measure of a religion's general pervasiveness is the degree of cultural homogeneity exemplified by the people who, or whose ancestors, were its devotees. Judging by the heterogeneity of life-styles within the societies in which it predominates, Christianity is one of the least pervasive religions in terms of cultural impact, although the secularization relative to modernization has been influential. Islam, by contrast, is a particularly pervasive force, affecting the everyday mode of life of its followers much more thoroughly than does any of the major forms of Christianity. Its greater impact upon the general cultural milieu, as manifested in eating and drinking habits, dress, sex roles, mores, and architecture, is apparent to even the most inattentive tourist. Its impact upon thought patterns has been commented on by several authorities (for example, the fatalism manifest in such everyday expressions as "If Allah wills").

As noted, numerous characteristics of Islamic culture survive in the Soviet Union and have a discernible impact upon behavior. Intermarriage between Moslems and non-Moslems, for example, are rare, and, in the case of Moslem women, virtually non-existent. The sex variable reflects the traditional lowly and secluded status of women within Islamic culture, a factor also manifest in a study recording that 100 percent of all of the offspring of mixed marriages involving Turkmen males chose to adopt the national identity of their father rather than that of their mother.[27]

To recapitulate: (1) certain features of Islamic societies (for example, the fact that they are, by and large, substantially more homogeneous and tradition-bound than are Christian societies, that they place less emphasis upon individualism and more on adherence to prescribed behavior and norms, and that fatalism occupies an important place in their outlook, thereby lessening the urge to improve one's plight through the taking of corrective action) work against voluntary migration to non-Moslem areas; and (2) such societal features are far from extinct among Soviet Moslem peoples. But it is a jump of impressive dimensions from the acceptance of these propositions to the conclusion that the Moslem peoples will not migrate in response to economic inducements. While elements of Moslem culture may well exert a negative impact upon the tempo of migration and the proportion of the entire community who elect to migrate, comparative data establish that Moslem societies have not been immune to migratory pressures. During the nineteenth and early twentieth centuries, Islamic peoples from the Asian subcontinent migrated in substantial numbers to southeastern Asia, to eastern and southern Africa, and to the Caribbean region in search of greater economic opportunities. And in the post-World War II period, far greater numbers of Moslems, particularly from Pakistan, were desirous of entering the United Kingdom and Canada than those two states were prepared to accommodate. Moreover, Moslems have represented a substantial proportion of the postwar, so-called "guest workers" who migrated to northwestern Europe. In 1974, for example, France alone contained more than 1.4 million migrants from the Moslem states of Algeria, Morocco, and Tunisia,[28] a figure representing more than 3 percent of the aggregate population of those three states. As we have pointed out, large numbers of Turks have migrated to West Germany and more would have if they had had the opportunity. These migrations have been largely in response to wage differentials. The Tatars of the USSR have experienced a considerable redistribution. In 1926, 38.3 percent of the Tatars lived in Tatariya, but by 1970 only 25.9 percent lived in their homeland. The percentages for the Volga Region were 50.5 and 33.2, respectively.

It is important to note that most of the preceding illustrations of significant migration involved the crossing of state borders. In addition to posing severe institutional inhibitions to migration (for example, the need to obtain, in advance, such documents as passports, exit permits, visas, and health certificates), the crossing of a state border also poses psychological inhibitions. Trading the secure status of citizen for that of alien has more than legal connotations. Moreover, within relatively integrated states such as the Soviet Union, the inhabitants of quite diverse cultural areas (in this case, Moslems and non-Moslems) share a multitude of common learned experiences. Centralized state control of school curriculum and educational materials and of the content of electronic and written communications media produces a measure of uniform experience among people throughout the country. Though many aspects of life in Moscow would indeed be "strange" to one brought up in the Moslem region of the Soviet Union, the total environment would be much less strange than would that of Hamburg to a Moslem from Turkey. We conclude, therefore, that, particularly given the numerous illustrations of interstate migration by Moslem groups, there is nothing so unique in Islamic culture as to justify the assumption that Soviet Moslem peoples will not migrate within the USSR in response to economic forces and employment opportunities. Furthermore, that so far the Turkic-Muslims of Central Asia have been relatively immobile does not demonstrate that they always will be immobile. The working hypothesis of this study is that people throughout the world tend to react in a similar manner to the forces that affect their demographic behavior. When conditions change, demographic behavior can be expected to change.

When considering the effect of culture on migration, one must specify what aspects of culture influence migration, and this is difficult because culture is a very complex phenomenon and many of its attributes are difficult to measure. We have pointed out that a rise in ethnic identity or national consciousness does not mean necessarily an intensification of culture, because rising ethnicity has been associated frequently with considerable cultural change. Gross indicators (education, marriage, and so forth) seem to indicate that some cultural change is occurring in Central Asia. Alexandre Bennigsen has pointed out that in the prerevolutionary period national consciousness was developed very weakly among the Turkic-Muslim peoples of Russia.[29] Subsequently, there has been an appreciable rise in national identity in Central Asia, but it would seem doubtful that there has been a commensurate intensification of culture. In any event, we do not argue that cultural change must necessarily precede social change, such as migration. Clearly, a person does not need to be acculturated before he migrates; the migration history of the United States demonstrates this and it can be documented worldwide.

As to the more specific measurable aspects of culture, some writers stress the lack of Russian-language proficiency as a major barrier to the migration of Central Asians.[30] Between 14 and 19 percent of the population of the titular groups of Central Asia claimed fluency in Russian in 1970, but the accuracy of these data are not above question.[31] Comparative research in migration indicates that millions of people have migrated despite language differences and lack of language proficiency. Language differences, in particular, and cultural differences, in general, can impede, to an unknown degree (depending on demographic and socioeconomic conditions), but cannot stop it. Clearly, the Russian-language competence of the Central Asian Turks is much greater than the German-language proficiency of the Turks that migrated to Germany, and the exposure to the Russian language must be considerable in Soviet society.

Others have pointed to the large Central Asian families as a major impediment to migration.[32] The world over, including the USSR, the young and the more educated have the highest migration rates, and both of these categories have fewer children. That there was an appreciable decline between 1959 and 1970 in the percentage of the women married aged 16 to 19 in Central Asia also would be influential.

If these processes continue in Central Asia and other ethnic homelands in the USSR and there is a considerable redistribution of the population analogous to that which has occurred in other multinational, modernizing societies, an appreciable rise in ethnic conflict can be expected. It has been pointed out that conceptually one can expect heightened ethnicity and conflict with economic development and that, of the forces resulting in increased interaction and the reinforcement of the us-them dichotomy, interethnic migration is probably the most influential. Even though people migrate from ethnic home-lands when conditions dictate, the importance and emotionalism involved with ethnic homelands should not be underestimated, particularly in the Soviet con-text, where the territory of the state has been divided legally into ethnic home-lands. With respect to ethnic homelands and migration, Walker Connor has stated:

> The ethnic homeland is more than territory. In Bismarckian ter-minology, blood and soil become mixed in the popular imagination, and the national territory takes on an emotional value, as evident in such terms as the homeland, the ancestral land, the native land, land where my fathers died, the motherland, the fatherland, etc. An alien intrusion into this sanctuary becomes an act of desecra-tion and therefore something to be resented and resisted. [33]

Elsewhere, he has added:

> Nearly 90 percent of all states are multinational units whose pop-ulation consists of at least two ethnonational groups, each of whom live within an ethnic homeland considered by the group to be the cultural hearth and, very often, the cradle of the national group. The homeland is thereby infused with an emotional, almost rev-erential dimension. The group is convinced that it has a unique and exclusive title to this place of territory believed to be its peculiar ethnonational preserve, and intrusion by aliens, even though those aliens be compatriots, is apt to meet with deep resentment. [34]

The validity of such statements has been substantiated in a wide variety of geographical and cultural milieus. [35] But perhaps most instructive as a harbinger of developments within the Soviet Union has been the recent experi-ence of the millions of "guest workers" who migrated to the more industrial-ized states of northwestern Europe and Canada in the 1960s and early 1970s. The term guest workers was indeed appropriate, for the migrants had been "invited" by the authorities in response to the need for additional labor gen-erated by expanding economies. Moreover, once arrived, the migrants tended to fill the least desirable positions, those eschewed by the indigeneous popu-lation. Yet despite (1) the fact that they had been encouraged to come, (2) the general lack of economic competition between themselves and the host popu-lation, and (3) the essentiality of their role in the rising living standard of their hosts, the migrants were everywhere the object of resentment. In a posthumously published, detailed study of the migrants' experience in Bel-gium, France, West Germany, Luxembourg, the Netherlands, Sweden, Swit-zerland, and the United Kingdom, Arnold Rose recorded a high incidence of xenophobic responses throughout all eight states and nowhere found a wide-spread willingness to grant the migrants equality of status. [36]

In Switzerland the negative psychological response triggered by the alien intrusion led to the creation of a Nationale Aktion gegen die Überfremdung von Volk und Heimat (National Campaign against Foreign Domination of the People and Homeland). And in 1974 this organization demonstrated the breadth of antialien sentiment among the populace when more than one-third of the electorate supported a referendum drafted by the Nationale Aktion that would have deported summarily large numbers of the foreign workers, despite fervid opposition to the referendum by overwhelming majorities in both houses of Parliament (157 to 3 and 42 to 0), by political parties from left to right, as well as by labor, management, and church authorities, and despite the fact that proponents of the referendum did not deny that the proposed exodus would cause serious economic dislocation and a drop in living standards.[37]

These negative reactions to trespassers cannot be ascribed simply to the fact that the migrants came from outside the state. Postwar Europe also offers several illustrations of one ethnonational group railing against the presence of compatriots of a different national background. Belgium offers a striking case. There a militant Flanders-for-the-Flemish movement, replete with violence, ultimately led to a division of the state into ethnic zones and the purging of institutions within Flanders of French (Walloon) influence. Elsewhere, during the late 1960s and early 1970s, Corsicans resorted to violence to protest the influx of Frenchmen; Basque nationalism was fed by the growing number of Castilians entering Basqueland in search of employment; and Scottish nationalist newspapers regularly drew attention to the purchase of old Scottish homes by non-Scottish elements. Outside Europe, the separatist-minded Franco-Canadian Parti Québecois increasingly won converts by drumming incessantly upon the theme that "English" influence had been permitted to make serious inroads within the Quebec homeland and that the Franco-Canadians must become once again, in the words of a Party slogan, "masters in our home."

The people of the Soviet Union have not been immune to such impulses. Though data on the relations among national groups are closely monitored by authorities and though the official position is that those intergroup relations are characterized by socialist fraternity, there is a sufficient body of evidence to establish that the combination of distinct ethnic homelands and internal migration has produced results similar to those in Western Europe. Indeed, in some republics there has been resistance to new investment, on the grounds that increased industrialization brings with it more Russians.[38] Soviet statistics further show that willingness to enter into an interethnic marriage is influenced heavily by whether one lives within his ethnic homeland; intermarriages are much more common in the case of two Soviet citizens meeting on ethnically neutral territory than if they meet within one of the couple's homeland. Moreover, in the case of children resulting from interethnic marriage, the most influential variable determining the child's choice of national identity is the homeland within which the family resides.[39] Furthermore, the findings of a number of Soviet opinion studies concerning interethnic relations agree that the greatest hostility toward members of other national groups is harbored by those dwelling within their respective homeland.[40] Finally, in an understandably very few cases, "Russian, go home!" sentiments have been paraded overtly.[41]

We have seen that migrations are apt to trigger such sentiments within any state that is divided into ethnic homelands. The observer of ethnic homelands distinguishes immigrant societies such as the United States from other multinational states. However, the fact that the Soviet government confers official status upon the homeland unquestionably has lent the issue a cutting edge. Draping the homeland in a political form with explicit borders (a union republic, autonomous republic, autonomous oblast, or national area) and then regularly describing the unit as sovereign or, at the least, autonomous encourages the inhabitants in the belief that the territory should be free of the taint of an alien presence. Should not "Mother Ukraine," as politically and territorially manifested in the "sovereign" Ukrainian Soviet Socialist Republic, logically be purged of all alien (Russian) influences?[42] It is surprising that the slogan "Russians, get out of Uzbekistan!" (literally, "land of the Uzbeks") should have been raised among a people who have been granted their "sovereign" Uzbek SSR?[43] Thus, the idea of the homeland, given flesh by a definite territorial expanse and a governmental structure, has exerted its influence upon the perceptions of Soviet peoples.

We are, however, not interested principally here in how the notion of the ethnic homeland has influenced attitudes in the past, but how it is apt to influence attitudes in response to our projected out-migration of Moslem peoples into non-Moslem areas. We perceive no reason not to expect the customary negative response. The usual reaction may be intensified because of the unusually wide gulf separating Moslem and non-Moslem cultures. In Connor's words, "Do all aliens produce the same measure of ethnic reaction, or are some aliens more foreign than others? . . . If there is no such distinction among aliens, then slogans such as 'Asia for the Asiatics,' 'pan-African,' 'pan-Islam,' and 'the colored peoples of the world' would not be resurrected so often."[44]

Recent events in Western Europe support this thesis. Thus, the English did not perceive the same magnitude of threat in the large migrations of Irish and Scots into England that continued over many decades, as they did in the much smaller postwar immigration of people from Asia and the West Indies. Moreover, Western European experience also suggests, albeit less conclusively, that the Moslem-non-Moslem divide may have greater consequences than a racial division. Within the United Kingdom, for example, the Moslem "Paks," though of Indo-European heritage, became more of a target of resentment than did people of negroid background from the West Indies. In any case, it is likely that the cultural divide separating Moslem and non-Moslem will exacerbate further the customary negative reaction of homeland-dwelling people to intruders.

Presuming our prophecy of increased tension to be correct, the fact that the principal homeland within which this confrontation will occur is that of the state's predominant national group—the Great Russians—will have momentous implications for the officially propagated image of the USSR as a society within which tensions between national groups have been eradicated through the application of Leninist national policy. Non-Russians returning to their homelands with tales of being unwelcome in the cities of the RSFSR clearly would disprove the claim that the Soviet Union is "a state of all the people," in which "the friendship of the USSR's nations and nationalities has been consolidated" and throughout which "Soviet citizens of different nationalities and races have equal rights."[45]

Finally, we anticipate that the migration of Asians will encourage a rise of national consciousness and resentment among that segment of the Moslem peoples who elect to remain at home. As earlier noted, out-migration in search of better economic opportunities, though often substantial, usually has accounted for only a fraction of the entire population. Among that larger segment who remain at home, the loss of members of the national family (those who have migrated) is apt to be viewed as the result of exploitation by the state's central authorities. A sympathetic writer put it this way with regard to the Slovaks:

> The Slovak economists were certainly bitter about the migration of Slovak labour to the Czech lands. Tens of thousands of Slovaks were forced to settle there permanently because they could not find employment at home. It was felt that these Slovaks, or at least their children, would be lost to the nation. . . . No nation, and for that matter, no region welcomes a situation in which a large part of its population finds it necessary to emigrate, even if it is a case of inner-state migration.[46]

In a similar vein, a Ukrainian writer, after accusing the Soviet authorities of forcing Ukrainians to migrate by limiting investment, lamented that "emigration undermines the strength of a nation."[47] In the case of the Central Asian area, the potential for conflict is magnified by the fact that the urban and more modern sector of the economy is dominated currently by outsiders. Therefore, out-migration can be expected to raise not just the plaint that the loss to the family's membership is attributable to the unfair allocation of developmental investments but also the charge that the loss is aggravated because aliens hold the relatively few desirable positions that are available within the homeland. Thus the traditional negative reactions to both in-migration by aliens and out-migration by conationals here will reinforce one another. We conclude, therefore, that an out-migration of peoples from the Central Asian region and other ethnic homelands will lead to an escalation of ethnic tensions at either end of the migratory process.

Thus, the ethnic consequences of migration should be of paramount importance in the future and rising ethnic tensions can be anticipated, if the expected patterns of migration occur in the USSR, as they have in other modernizing multinational states. We maintain that there is great utility in applying universal formulations in the Soviet context. Our guarded forecasts on the prospect of Central Asian migration are based on this assumption. What we have done here and elsewhere, essentially, is to investigate those initial or determining conditions in Central Asia that universally have promoted migration, such as the growth of the native working-age population, labor surpluses, mechanization of agriculture, social and cultural change, investment, wage differentials, the ability of the nonagricultural sector to absorb the growing rural population, the expansion of irrigation, job availability elsewhere in the USSR, and so forth. We do not deny that there could be conditions specific to Central Asia that might impede migration, at least in the short run, but so far we can see no particularistic factors in Central Asia that are sufficiently strong and resistant to change related to modernization to counter the strong demographic, economic, and social forces that are intensifying in Central Asia and that elsewhere in the world generally have resulted in substantial out-migration. With respect to interethnic migration, other more modernized Turkic-Muslim groups, such as those along the Volga, might be expected to migrate in greater numbers and before the Central Asian groups, probably first to the cities in their ethnic territories and then beyond. We cannot determine precisely when significant out-migration will begin or the numbers involved, because we have insufficient information on a number of factors and future conditions, as usual, are impossible to assess. However, we can predict with some certainty that unless trends in the USSR change drastically one can expect considerable migration from one ethnic territory to another in the USSR and the universally associated ethnic problems. Our contention is that one cannot understand population change in the USSR solely by studying these processes in the USSR. A universal knowledge of how demographic processes interrelate with economic, social, cultural, and ethnic processes is required, because such processes in the USSR are not totally unique.

NOTES

1. For conceptual approaches to such an investigation, see Allan Schnaiberg, "The Modernizing Impact of Urbanization: A Causal Analysis," Economic Development and Cultural Change 20 (October 1971): 80-104; and Alex Inkeles, "Making Men Modern: On the Causes and Consequences of Individual Change in Six Developing Countries," American Journal of Sociology 75 (September 1969): 208-25.

2. Albert J. Reiss, Jr., ed., Louis Wirth on Cities and Social Life (Chicago: University of Chicago Press, 1969), pp. 60-83.

3. David K. Shipler, "Soviet Crime Problem Tied to City Life and Social Ills," New York Times, March 6, 1978, p. 1.

4. Christopher S. Wren, "Soviet Study Finds More Premarital Sex," New York Times, June 17, 1975, p. 2.

5. Vestnik Statistiki, no. 11 (1976), p. 86.

6. Robert A. Lewis, Richard H. Rowland, and Ralph S. Clem, Nationality and Population Change in Russia and the USSR (New York: Praeger, 1976), pp. 355, 371-75. Murray Feshbach and Stephen Rapawy present somewhat different figures, because they use different procedures and the official Soviet definition of work force (Murray Feshbach and Stephen Rapawy, "Soviet Manpower Trends and Policies," Soviet Economy in a New Perspective, U.S.

Congress, Joint Economic Committee Print [Washington, D.C.: Government Printing Office, 1976], pp. 128-29).

7. U.S., Central Intelligence Agency, USSR: Some Implications of Demographic Trends for Economic Policies, ER 77-10012, January 1977, p. 2.

8. Ibid., p. 16.

9. Feshbach and Rapawy, "Soviet Manpower Trends and Policies," p. 114.

10. Ibid., p. 148. Jeremy Azrael also has discussed the military consequences of these demographic processes in Emergent Nationality Problems in the USSR, Rand, R-2172-AF (September 1977), pp. 16-23.

11. Lewis, Rowland, and Clem, Nationality and Population Change, pp. 330-31.

12. Ibid., pp. 343-50.

13. Walker Connor, "Nation-Building or Nation-Destroying?" World Politics 24 (April 1972): 319-55; idem, "Ethnonationalism in the First World: The Present in Historical Perspective," in Ethnic Conflict in the Western World, ed. Milton J. Esman (Ithaca: Cornell University Press, 1977), pp. 19-46; idem, "Self-Determination: The New Phase," World Politics 20 (October 1967): 30-53; and conversations with Walker Connor.

14. For a detailed discussion of these groups, in particular, the Russians, see Lewis, Rowland, and Clem, Nationality and Population Change, chaps. 4-6; and Robert A. Lewis and Richard H. Rowland, "East is West and West is East . . . Population Redistribution in the USSR and Its Impact on Society," International Migration Review 11 (Spring 1977): 3-31.

15. Ralph S. Clem has ordered an array of census variables for 1926, 1959, and 1970 into oblast and equivalent ethnic administrative units (see Ralph S. Clem, "The Changing Geography of Soviet Nationalities and Its Socioeconomic Correlates: 1926-1970" [Ph.D. diss., Columbia University, 1975]).

16. Lewis, Rowland, and Clem, Nationality and Population Change, pp. 333-54.

17. Ibid., pp. 354-81

18. Nermin Abadan-Unat, "Implications of Migration on Emancipation and Pseudo-Emancipation of Turkish Women," International Migration Review 11 (Spring 1977): 31-33.

19. Kurt B. Mayer, "Intra-European Migration during the Past Twenty Years," International Migration Review 9 (Winter 1975): 441-47.

20. Craig R. Whitney, "Foreign Workers Quitting West Germany," New York Times, October 25, 1975, p. 4.

21. V. I. Perevedentsev, "Step Out of the Village," The Current Digest of the Soviet Press 28 (February 25, 1976): 1.

22. L. Bulochnikova, "Sel'skaya Migratsiya i Puti eye Regulirovaniya," Planovoye Khozyaystvo, no. 8 (July 1969), p. 71.

23. USSR, Narodnoye Khozyaystvo v 1975 G. (Moscow: "Statistika," 1976), pp. 344-45.

24. M. Khalmukhamedov, "Soviet Society: Complete Equality of Nations," International Affairs, no. 3 (1978), p. 29.

25. Leslie Dienes, "Investment Priorities in Soviet Regions," Annals of the Association of American Geographers 62 (September 1972): 437–39.

26. Comments made by Alexandre Bennigsen at the Conference on Potential Central Asian Migration in the Next Decade, January 10, 1977, Foreign Demographic Analysis Division, Department of Commerce, Washington, D. C.

27. L. N. Terent'eva, "Ethnic Self–Identification by Adolescents in Ethnically Mixed Families," Soviet Sociology 12 (Summer 1973): 54. The study, based on marriages in Ashkhabad, the capital of the Turkmen Republic, found the marriage rate between Moslem males and non–Moslem females to be "very low" and failed to uncover a single case of the reverse situation.

28. Le Monde, June 5, 1974. Cited in Keesing's Contemporary Archives (1975), p. 27361.

29. Alexandre Bennigsen, "Islamic or Local Consciousness among Soviet Nationalities?" in Soviet Nationality Problems, ed. Edward Allworth (New York: Columbia University Press, 1971), p. 175.

30. Murray Feshbach, "Prospects for Massive Out-Migration from Central Asia during the Next Decade," Foreign Demographic Analysis Division, Bureau of Economic Analysis, U.S. Department of Commerce, February 1977, p. 13.

31. Ibid.

32. Azrael, Emergent Nationality Problems, p. 12.

33. Walker Connor, "A World of Nations within a World of States," unpubl. manuscript, p. 39. Cited with the permission of the author.

34. Walker Connor, "America's Melting Pot: Myth and/or Reality," Byliner (U.S. Information Service) no. 33 (June 1977).

35. See, for example, Connor's "Self-Determination: The New Phase," pp. 30–53; idem, "Ethnology and the Peace of South Asia," World Politics 22 (October 1969): 51–86; idem, "Nation-Building or Nation-Destroying?" pp. 319–55; idem, "The Politics of Ethnonationalism," Journal of International Affairs 27 (January 1973): 1–21; idem, "An Overview of the Ethnic Composition and Problems of Non-Arab Asia," Journal of Asian Affairs 1 (Spring 1976): 9–25; idem, "Political Fusion and Ethnic Fission," Concilium 13, no. 1 (1977): 13–24; idem, "The Political Significance of Ethnonationalism within Western Europe" in Ethnicity in an International Context, ed. Abdul Said and Luiz Simmons (Edison, N. J.: Transaction Books, 1976), pp. 110–33; and idem, "Ethnonationalism in the First World," pp. 19–45.

36. Arnold Rose, Migrants in Europe (Minneapolis: University of Minnesota Press, 1969).

37. Connor, "Ethnonationalism in the First World," p. 37.

38. See, for example, the New York Times, March 8, 1970 and June 8, 1972 and the Christian Science Monitor, June 9, 1971 and June 30, 1972.

39. If the family resides outside the homeland of either parent, the child is apt to choose the national identity of the father over that of the mother and that of a Russian parent over the non-Russian one. However, if the family resides in the ethnic homeland of one of the parents, the child is most apt to select that parent's national identity as his or her own. See Terent'eva, "Ethnic Self-Identification," particularly table 2 on p. 41.

40. See, for example, A. I. Kholmogorov, International Traits of Soviet Nations (Based on Data of Concrete Sociological Research in the Baltic Area) (Moscow: "Mysl" Publishing House, 1970), as translated in Soviet Sociology 11 (Winter-Spring 1972-73): 294, 325; 12 (Summer 1973): 30; and 12 (Fall 1973): 49.

41. See, for example, Zev Katz, ed. Handbook of Major Soviet Nationalities (New York: Free Press, 1975), pp. 89, 90, 137.

42. This is the theme of an influential work by a Ukrainian scholar. The work was addressed to the leadership of the Ukrainian SSR, and its subsequent limited distribution to other officials of that SSR was a factor in the downfall of the first secretary of the Ukrainian Communist party. See Ivan Dzyuba, Internationalism or Russification? (New York: Monad Press, 1968).

43. Katz, Handbook, p. 103.

44. Connor, "Ethnology and the Peace of South Asia," p. 84.

45. Extracted from the preamble and Articles 1 and 36 of the 1977 Draft Constitution of the USSR.

46. Eugen Steiner, The Slovak Dilemma (Cambridge: At the University Press, 1973), p. 134. Similarly, the Scottish National party has made the Scottish diaspora a campaign issue for many years.

47. Dzyuba, Internationalism or Russification?, p. 109. As his tone makes clear, however, emigration may decrease the numerical strength of a nation, but it bolsters its sense of resentment.

APPENDIX A
VARIABLES FOR POPULATION MATRIX:
1970 and 1959-70

DISTRIBUTION AND REDISTRIBUTION VARIABLES
(variables 1-54)

For variables 1-48 the first number is for 1970 distribution (variables 1-30) and the second number in parentheses is for 1959-70 redistribution (variables 31-54).

1. (25) Total population
2. (26) Urban population
3. (27) Urban population in size class 15,000 to 99,999
4. (28) Urban population in size class 100,000 and over
5. (29) Rural population
6. (30) Kolkhozniki
7. (31) Industrial work force
8. (32) Rabochiye
9. (33) Sluzhashchiye
10. (34) Education (higher and secondary, complete and incomplete)
11. (35) Education (higher only, complete and incomplete)
12. (36) Russians
13. (37) Ukrainians
14. (38) Belorussians
15. (39) Tatars
16. (40) Turkic-Muslims (excluding Tatars)
17. (41) Jews
18. (42) Mobilized Europeans (excluding Jews)
19. (43) Finnic peoples (excluding Estonians)
20. (44) Lithuanians
21. (45) Moldavians and Romanians
22. (46) Investment including kolkhozy
23. (47) Investment excluding kolkhozy
24. (48) Ages 20 to 39
49. Total in-migrants, 1968-70
50. Total out-migrants, 1968-70
51. Urban in-migrants, 1968-70
52. Urban out-migrants, 1968-70
53. Rural in-migrants, 1968-70
54. Rural out-migrants, 1968-70

COMPOSITION AND CHANGE IN COMPOSITION
VARIABLES (variables 55-106)

For variables 55-102, the first number is for 1970 (variables 55-78 and
103-6), and the second number in parentheses is for 1959-70 change (variables
79-102).

55.	(79)	Urban population (level of urbanization)
56.	(80)	Urban population in size class 15,000 to 99,999
57.	(81)	Urban population in size class 100,000 and over
58.	(82)	Ages 0 to 9
59.	(83)	Ages 10 to 19
60.	(84)	Ages 0 to 19
61.	(85)	Ages 20 to 39
62.	(86)	Ages 40 to 59
63.	(87)	Ages 60 and over
64.	(88)	Ages 0 to 19 and 60 and over (the obverse is ages 20 to 59)
65.	(89)	Kolkhozniki
66.	(90)	Industrial work force
67.	(91)	<u>Rabochiye</u>
68.	(92)	<u>Sluzhashchiye</u>
69.	(93)	Russians
70.	(94)	Ukrainians
71.	(95)	Belorussians
72.	(96)	Tatars
73.	(97)	Turkic-Muslims (excluding Tatars)
74.	(98)	Jews
75.	(99)	Mobilized Europeans (excluding Jews)
76.	(100)	Finnic peoples (excluding Estonians)
77.	(101)	Lithuanians
78.	(102)	Moldavians and Romanians
103.		Total in-migrants, 1968-70
104.		Total out-migrants, 1968-70
105.		Total net migrants, 1968-70
106.		Total migration turnover, 1968-70

SPECIALIZED VARIABLES AND CHANGES IN
SPECIALIZED VARIABLES (variables 107-42)

For variables 107-26, the first number is for 1970 (variables 107-16),
and the second number in parentheses is for circa 1959-70 change (variables
117-26).

107. (117) Child-woman ratio ([population aged 0-9 ÷ females aged 20-49]
times 100)
108. (118) Sex ratio ([males ÷ females] times 100)
109. (119) Percent of population aged ten and over with higher and secondary
education, complete and incomplete
110. (120) Percent of population aged ten and over with higher education
only, complete and incomplete.

111. (121) Percent of urban population in size class 100,000 and over
112. (122) Crude birth rate
113. (123) Crude death rate
114. (124) Crude rate of natural increase
115. (125) Per capita investment including kolkhozy
116. (126) Per capita investment excluding kolkhozy
127. Per capita investment excluding kolkhozy, 1959-67, from Dienes
128. Percentage change of investment excluding kolkhozy, 1950-60
129. Net migration, 1959-70, as percent of July 1964 population
130. Natural increase, 1959-70, as percent of July 1964 population
131. Net migration, 1959-70, as percent of total population change, 1959-70
132. Urban in-migrants, 1968-70, as percent of 1970 urban population
133. Urban out-migrants, 1968-70, as percent of 1970 urban population
134. Urban net migrants, 1968-70, as percent of 1970 urban population
135. Urban migration turnover, 1968-70, as percent of 1970 urban population
136. Rural in-migrants, 1968-70, as percent of 1970 rural population
137. Rural out-migrants, 1968-70, as percent of 1970 rural population
138. Rural net migrants, 1968-70, as percent of 1970 rural population
139. Rural migration turnover, 1968-70, as percent of 1970 rural population
140. Average annual percentage change of total population
141. Average annual percentage change of urban population
142. Average annual percentage change of rural population

COMMENTS

For the post-1959 period factor analysis, the variables derived differ
to a certain extent from those of the 1897-1959 matrices both in terms of
quantity and quality. Foremost is the fact that the plethora of distribution-
redistribution and urbanization variables has been reduced. In particular,
those involving age and sex have been eliminated since the 1897-1959 factor
analyses revealed a great redundancy in that these variables were very highly
correlated with overall distribution, redistribution, and urbanization. A few
other variables of the 1897-1959 matrices have not been included, because
they could not be derived (for example, agricultural and tertiary work forces)
or were regarded as of minimal importance (for example, population density).
Also, the nationality variables have been derived in accordance with the main
format of the first book of the series—that is, ten mutually exclusive groupings. On the other hand, a great number of variables not included in the
1897-1959 matrices have been included because of data availability; these involve such variables as migration, fertility, mortality, education, and investment.

In all, 142 variables are included in the post-1959 matrix, roughly 50
more than in the 1897-1959 matrices. The variables for the combined 1970
and 1959-70 matrix have been divided into three types, types that were distinguished for the 1897-1959 matrices: (1) distribution and redistribution
variables or the regional distribution and redistribution of a characteristic,

(2) composition variables or the percentage of the total population of a region comprised by a characteristic and the changes therein, and (3) specialized variables or various types of perspectives on a number of characteristics. Unlike the 1897-1959 matrices, a category of level of urbanization variables is not included, because the redundant large number of urbanization variables was eliminated.

Of the 142 variables, 77 are so similar to those of the 1897-1959 matrices that their derivation requires no further explanation (variables 1-5, 12-21, 24-29, 36-45, 48, 55-64, 69-88, 93-102, 111, 121, and 140-42). Included in this list are the mutually exclusive nationality groupings. Although the post-1959 matrix, unlike the 1897-1959 matrices, includes eight education variables (10, 11, 34, 35, 109, 110, 119, 120), their derivation also requires no further explanation. The inclusion and/or derivation of the remaining 57 variables, however, require further comment, even some characteristics included in the previous matrices such as the industrial work force, child-woman ratio, and sex ratio.

Variables Involving Kolkhozniki, Rabochiye, and Sluzhashchiye (6, 8, 9, 30, 32, 33, 65, 67, 69, 89, 91, 92)

These variables, which are based on the de jure population, were used as rough surrogates for the agricultural, industrial, and tertiary work forces, respectively, because data for all three sectors were not available by economic region in 1970, although, as will be seen, it was possible to derive an industrial work force category. These variables do have some deficiencies as surrogates; for example, sovkhozniki are not included in the kolkhozniki or "agricultural" category. Nevertheless, additional checks suggest that these variables are fairly good surrogates. For example, in 1959, when data were available both for these surrogates and for the three work force categories, correlations between the two could be undertaken to test their degree of similarity. In particular, rank correlations were run on the basis of the 19 regions between the percentage of total population comprised of the given work force sector and the percentage of the total population comprised of the corresponding surrogate. Resulting rank correlations were 0.891 for agriculture—kolkhozniki, 0.600 for industry—rabochiye, and 0.811 for tertiary—sluzhashchiye.

Variables Involving Industrial Work Force
(7, 31, 66, 90)

Derivation of the industrial work force for circa 1959 (1961) has been discussed elsewhere (J. William Leasure and Robert A. Lewis, Population Changes in Russia and the USSR: A Set of Comparable Territorial Units [San Diego, Calif.: San Diego State College Press, 1966], pp. 38-40).

In 1970 the manufacturing work force for the six economic regions outside the RSFSR and Ukraine could be obtained directly from Narodnoye

Khozyaystvo SSSR 1922-1972 GG. (p. 148). This source lists the average annual number of industrial workers and employees by republic, thus enabling the derivation of totals for these six regions.

In order to estimate the number of industrial workers for the regions of the RSFSR and Ukraine, the industrial work forces in these regions in 1961 were projected to 1970 on the basis of average annual rates of industrial production growth for the regions between 1960 and 1970 (Narodnoye Khozyaystvo SSSR v 1970 G., p. 138), although the regions involved were the 1970 economic regions and not the 1961 regions. A further refinement was to multiply the average annual rate of production increase by the ratio between the average annual percentage increase in all industrial workers in the USSR from 1960 to 1970 and the average annual percentage increase in industrial production over the same period (Narodnoye Khozyaystvo SSSR v 1970 G., pp. 139, 158). The percentage regional distributions of the projected totals for the RSFSR and Ukraine were then applied to the number of industrial workers and employees for both republics in 1970 (Narodnoye Khozyaystvo SSSR 1922-1972 GG., p. 148). Thus, the number of industrial workers and employees was derived for all 19 regions in 1970 in conformance with the reported number of industrial workers and employees in 1970. One final minor refinement was to subtract from each regional total the estimated number of persons in "industry" who participated in logging activities in order to make this industry category comparable with that derived for earlier censuses. This number was derived by calculating the percentage of manufacturing workers involved in logging according to the 1970 census, multiplying this percentage times the number of industrial workers and employees in 1970 as reported in Narodnoye Khozyaystvo, and allocating this product to individual regions on the basis of the regional distribution of timber production in 1967 (Narodnoye Khozyaystvo SSSR v 1967 G., pp. 274-75), although regional timber production was based on the 1970 economic regions and not the 1961 regions.

Variables Involving Capital Investment
(22, 23, 46, 47, 115, 116, 125-28)

Derivation of regional capital investment changes between 1960 and 1970 was impeded by the manner in which the data were presented in various Narodnoye Khozyaystvo volumes. For example, sometimes the data included collective farms and other times collective farms were excluded. Also, data were not presented always by economic region in 1970, and when they were, often no totals for 1960 were given. Changes in prices from one year to another also impeded the investigation.

Two indicators of regional capital investment have been derived: (1) total investment including collective farms based on the current regions and (2) total investment excluding collective farms for the 1961, or our set of, regions, the kind of investment data available for 1961 regions in Narodnoye Khozyaystvo SSSR v 1961 G.

Derivation of regional investment data including collective farms for the current regions entailed a number of problems. Unfortunately, the Narodnoye

Kohzyaystvo SSSR v 1970 G. does not present capital investment data for economic regions. However, it does present such data for 1960 and 1970 in comparable prices by republic (p. 488), and thus investment for the six regions outside the RSFSR and the Ukraine could be derived easily, although a minor adjustment was necessary because of Kaliningradskaya Oblast, as discussed below. With respect to the RSFSR the Narodnoye Khozyaystvo RSFSR v 1970 G. does not present regional capital investment data including collective farms, but the Narodnoye Khozyaystvo RSFSR v 1971 G. does present regional capital investment for 1970 (pp. 296-97) on the basis of the same prices as the data for the 1970 Narodnoye Khozyaystvo. However, the Narodnoye Khozyaystvo RSFSR v 1971 G. does not present equivalent data for 1960 in 1970 prices by economic region. In order to estimate these 1960 data, regional investment data in Narodnoye Khozyaystvo SSSR v 1967 G. were used. This is the most recently available Narodnoye Khozyaystvo SSSR, which provides investment data by economic region, and it presents such data for 1960, 1967, and some years in between (p. 625). On the basis of these data, the percentage regional distribution of capital investment including collective farms for the RSFSR was calculated and applied to the total amount of capital investment for the RSFSR in 1960 as reported in 1970. Minor adjustments also were made for the RSFSR and West Region due to problems associated with the inclusion or exclusion of Kaliningradskaya Oblast, an oblast that is currently in the West Region but still in the RSFSR. The same procedures just discussed for the RSFSR in 1960 and 1970 were undertaken for the three regions of the Ukraine, which entailed the use of Narodnoye Gospodarstvo Ukrains'koy SSSR v 1970 Rotsi (p. 350). Thus, totals were derived for the amount of capital investment including collective farms in both 1960 and 1970 in comparable prices for the current 19 economic regions. It should be pointed out that variables 22 and 46 (regional distribution and redistribution) are based on these current regions and not the 19 regions of 1961 and that the per capita investment figure for 1960 utilizes the 1959 population total.

Derivation of regional investment data excluding kolkhozy for the 1961 regions also entailed a number of problems. For the six regions outside the RSFSR and the Ukraine, appropriate data are available for 1960 and 1970 in Narodnoye Khozyaystvo SSSR v 1970 G. (p. 488), although minor adjustments were necessary because of Kaliningradskaya Oblast. However, in order to provide estimates for 1960 and 1970 for regions of the RSFSR and the Ukraine other procedures were necessary. Estimates for 1960 for regions of both republics were made by applying the regional distribution (1961 regions) of capital investment in 1960 (Narodnoye Khozyaystvo SSSR v 1961 G., pp. 548-49) to the total amount of investment of each republic for 1960 in 1970 prices (Narodnoye Khozyaystvo SSSR v 1970 G., p. 488). These 1960 figures then were projected to 1970 on the basis of the percentage increase in capital investment excluding collective farms between 1960 and 1970 for the corresponding current economic regions. In order to derive these necessary figures for 1960 and 1970 by current regions, additional procedures had to be undertaken. Data by current region for the RSFSR and Ukraine for 1970 can be found in Narodnoye Khozyaystvo RSFSR v 1970 G. (p. 320) and Narodnoye

Gospodarstvo Ukrains'koy SSSR v 1970 Rotsi (p. 351). Data for 1960 were estimated by deriving regional distribution percentages for 1960 on the basis of data for current regions in Narodnoye Khozyaystvo SSSR v 1967 G. (p. 626) and applying these percentages to 1960 totals in 1970 prices found in Narodnoye Khozyaystvo SSSR v 1970 G. (p. 488), again adjusting for Kaliningradskaya Oblast. The derived percentage increases in investment for the current regions then were applied to investment figures derived above for the 1961 regions. Thus, estimates were made for capital investment excluding collective farms for 1960 and 1970 on the basis of comparable prices and the set of regions employed in this study. Per capita figures for 1960 are based on 1959 populations.

Two other investment variables (127 and 128) have been included. Variable 127 is an estimate of overall capital investment by current economic region for the period 1959-67, which was computed by Leslie Dienes in his article ("Investment Priorities in Soviet Regions," Annals of the Association of American Geographers 42 [September 1972]: 442) from data in Narodnoye Khozyaystvo SSSR v 1967 G. (pp. 12, 626) and Narodnoye Khozyaystvo SSSR v 1965 G. (p. 539). It apparently excludes collective farms. Variable 128 has been included in order to portray regional changes in capital investment between 1950 and 1960, changes that conceivably could have a lag effect on regional economic development and population redistribution between 1959 and 1970. This variable is calculated on the basis of data from Narodnoye Khozyaystvo SSSR v 1967 G. (p. 626). These data exclude collective farms and are for the current economic regions and not the 1961 regions.

Variables Involving Migration Data from the
1970 Census (49-54, 103-6, 132-39)

Migration data in the census are based upon previous place of residence and, generally speaking, a migrant is anyone who has changed his or her place of residence in the two years preceding the census (1968-70). The variables under consideration are based upon the current economic regions and not the 1961 regions. The underlying rationale for each characteristic is to consider as migrants only those persons who add to or deplete the population of the region under investigation, either total, urban, or rural:

1. Total in-migrants—persons residing in the region who originated from outside the region;
2. Total out-migrants—persons who originated from the region but who resided outside the region;
3. Urban in-migrants—persons residing in urban centers of the region who originated from either urban or rural areas outside the region or from rural areas within the region;
4. Urban out-migrants—persons who originated from urban areas within the region but who resided either in urban or rural areas outside the region or in rural areas within the region;

5. Rural in-migrants—persons residing in rural areas of the region who originated from either urban or rural areas outside the region or from urban areas within the region;

6. Rural out-migrants—persons who originated from rural areas within the region but who resided either in urban or rural areas outside the region or in urban areas within the region.

Net migration in each case is the number of in-migrants minus the number of out-migrants, while migration turnover is the number of in-migrants plus the number of out-migrants. Rates are calculated on the basis of the corresponding population, either total, urban, and rural, and urban and rural data are based on the official definitions of urban and rural. The distribution variables are based on the summation of the total number of total, urban, or rural in-migrants and out-migrants as defined above for the 19 regions. It should be kept in mind that the spatial unit serving as the reference point differs for total population on the one hand and the urban and rural categories on the other. Thus, the total number of in-migrants to a region will not be equal to the sum of the "urban in-migrants" and "rural in-migrants," because the urban and rural categories include some migrants who originated from rural and urban areas within the region, respectively, whereas the total category does not.

Variables Involving Net Migration and
Natural Increase for 1959 to 1970 (129-31)

Net migration data for the 1959-70 period are based upon the vital statistics or residual method; that is, population change due to natural increase (fertility and mortality) is derived first, and the difference or residual between total population change and population change due to natural increase is indicative of the amount of net migration.

The use of vital statistics entails additional problems. First of all, regional data are not available for all years in the 1959-70 period. Fortunately, data for the midpoint year, 1964, are available and will be used here to represent the entire period (Vestnik Statistiki, no. 12 [1966], pp. 83-85). However, these vital statistics are presented for the post-1961 regions and consequently do not necessarily conform to our set of regions. This problem was solved in the following manner. Regional natural increase rates were multiplied by the July 1964 population, which was estimated by computing the average of the January 1964 and January 1965 populations as presented in Narodnoye Khozyaystvo SSSR v 1963 G. (pp. 12-17) and Narodnoye Khozyaystvo SSSR v 1964 G. (pp. 13-17). Absolute natural increase for each region was the result. An identical procedure was followed for all component units that were shifted from one region to another after 1961. Absolute natural increase totals for these units were then added to or subtracted from regional values whenever appropriate. For example, in our set of regions, Orel Oblast is in the Central Chernozem Region, while in 1964 it was in the Center. Therefore, its absolute natural increase was subtracted from that of the Center and added to that of the Central Chernozem. After these changes were made, new 1964 natural increase rates were then computed for our set of regions (1964 absolute natural increase divided by estimated July 1964 population). To calculate net migration rates for each region the following steps were taken. The estimated July 1964 population was multiplied by the 1964 rate of natural increase, thus, giving an estimate of absolute natural increase for 1964. This product then was multiplied by 11 to derive an estimate for the entire 11-year period. One final refinement was to multiply the 11-year estimate by a correction factor of 1.03. This factor represents the ratio between (1) the 1959-70 absolute national population increase, which was assumed to be entirely due to natural increase since there was virtually no immigration or emigration to or from the Soviet Union during this period and (2) the absolute national natural increase derived on the basis of steps discussed above, prior to the discussion of this factor. Absolute natural increase for each region then was subtracted from its total 1959-70 population increase. The resulting differentials are thus estimates of the absolute net migration of each region over the entire 11-year period. Division of these estimates by July 1964 populations resulted in the net migration rates for the entire intercensal period (variable 129). Variable 130 (natural increase rate for the period) was derived by also dividing the absolute natural increase calculated above by the July 1964 population. Variable 131 (percentage of total population change due to net migration) was calculated by dividing absolute net migration, be it positive or negative, by the total population change between 1959 and 1970. It should be added that those migration and natural increase variables do not incorporate refinements in Table 2.17 for the West, Transcaucasus, Kazakhstan, and Central Asia. These refinements would have little effect on overall regional variations, correlations, and factors.

Variables Involving Crude Birth, Death, and
Natural Increase Rates (112-14, 122-24)

Rates for 1960 come from Vestnik Statistiki, no. 1 (1965), pp. 86-91; rates for 1970 are from Vestnik Statistiki, no. 2 (1971), pp. 76-79. In both cases rates are for the current economic regions and not the 1961 regions.

Variables Involving Child-Woman Ratios
(107, 117)

The derivation of child-woman ratios (population aged 0 to 9 per 100 females aged 20 to 49) by economic region in 1970 was impeded by the lack of age data by sex for appropriate political units of the RSFSR and Ukraine. For the regions of these two republics, the number of females aged 20 to 49 could not be extracted directly from the census. In order to estimate the number of females aged 20 to 49 by economic region, the total population aged 20 to 49 was multiplied by 0.52, the proportion that females comprised of the

total population aged 20 to 49 for the USSR as a whole. For the other 13 republics (and, thus, six regions) appropriate data are presented explicitly in
the census.

Variables Involving Sex Ratios (108, 118)

Quite astonishingly, the 1970 census does not provide data on the total
number of males and females for units below the republic level. For the six
regions outside the RSFSR and Ukraine, the total number of males and females
could be derived easily from these republic totals. For the regions in the
RSFSR and Ukraine, other procedures were again necessary. Fortunately,
the 1970 census does provide data for the number of males and females aged
ten and over by oblast or equivalent unit. Therefore, the problem became
one of estimating the number of males and females below the age of ten and
adding this estimate to the corresponding ten-and-over populations. The
total population under ten by economic region could be calculated easily. This
figure then was multiplied by the percentage that males comprised of the population under ten for the RSFSR and Ukraine as a whole, resulting in estimates
of the number of males and females less than ten by economic region. Although there were some slight complications resulting from different published
totals of the population not indicating any age at all, addition of these estimates
to the number of males and females ten and over resulted in an estimate of
the total number of males and females by economic region of the RSFSR and
Ukraine.

TOTAL, URBAN, AND RURAL POPULATIONS BY REGION: 1897-1977

TABLE B.1

Total Population by Gross Region: 1897-1970

Region	1897	1926	1939	1959	1970
Western USSR	101,141,876	130,586,628	145,972,632	145,768,985	164,563,977
Eastern USSR	23,900,965	37,069,207	47,104,513	63,057,665	77,156,157
Northern European USSR	77,181,176	96,843,664	105,369,081	99,979,555	108,973,267
European Steppe	19,365,604	27,881,436	32,576,040	36,284,620	43,295,398
Russian East	13,601,979	23,289,003	30,480,553	40,080,005	44,356,715
Non-Slavic South	14,894,082	19,641,732	24,651,471	32,482,470	45,094,754
USSR total	125,042,841	167,655,835	193,077,145	208,826,650	241,720,134

Note: The tables in Appendix B show absolute total, urban, and rural populations by region for the 1897-1977 period.

Sources: See Chapter 1, nn. 104 and 105.

TABLE B.2

Total Population by Economic Region: 1897-1970

Region	1897	1926	1939	1959	1970
Northwest	8,002,979	10,341,034	12,366,560	11,474,054	12,888,896
West	5,725,779	5,638,518	5,816,773	6,001,694	6,848,442
Center	15,245,585	21,049,713	25,308,098	24,789,349	26,720,545
Volgo-Vyatsk	6,181,344	7,255,893	8,698,149	8,253,038	8,347,817
Central Chernozem	8,285,760	11,035,835	10,439,270	8,697,909	8,929,242
Volga	9,712,792	12,433,500	12,124,989	12,454,354	14,287,358
Belorussia	6,468,422	7,640,980	8,909,994	8,054,648	9,002,338
Moldavia	1,534,261	2,035,581	2,452,023	2,884,477	3,568,873
Southwest	17,558,515	21,448,191	21,705,248	20,254,509	21,948,629
South	3,759,355	4,599,128	4,852,279	5,066,132	6,380,614
Donetsk-Dnepr	7,846,363	11,978,274	14,760,227	16,548,405	18,797,274
North Caucasus	6,225,625	9,268,453	10,511,511	11,785,606	14,548,637
Transcaucasus	4,595,096	5,861,528	8,027,511	9,504,810	12,295,312
Urals	9,105,907	11,847,333	14,443,875	18,613,230	20,409,372
West Siberia	1,975,600	6,257,867	7,936,870	10,159,437	10,703,400
East Siberia	2,097,908	3,624,449	5,279,392	6,960,535	8,127,557
Far East	422,564	1,559,354	2,820,416	4,346,803	5,116,386
Kazakhstan	4,825,013	6,179,050	6,093,507	9,309,847	13,008,726
Central Asia	5,473,973	7,601,154	10,530,453	13,667,813	19,790,716
USSR total	125,042,841	167,655,835	193,077,145	208,826,650	241,720,134

Sources: See Chapter 1, nn. 104 and 105.

442

TABLE B.3

Urban Population by Gross Region: 1897-1970

Region	1897	1926	1939	1959	1970
Western USSR	10,805,246	18,675,509	37,293,779	54,634,360	77,555,067
Eastern USSR	1,515,794	3,681,588	11,568,670	25,126,532	35,068,517
Northern European USSR	7,760,817	12,697,164	24,988,803	36,055,647	51,035,999
European Steppe	2,517,362	4,925,467	10,290,325	15,097,387	21,390,886
Russian East	776,244	2,316,902	8,428,755	18,258,663	23,618,250
Non-Slavic South	1,266,617	2,417,564	5,154,566	10,349,195	16,578,449
USSR total	12,321,040	22,357,097	48,862,449	79,760,892	112,623,584

Sources: See Chapter 1, nn. 104 and 105.

443

TABLE B.4

Urban Population by Economic Region: 1897-1970

Region	1897	1926	1939	1959	1970
Northwest	1,736,473	2,469,953	5,121,735	6,013,233	7,950,265
West	836,750	1,057,003	1,229,285	1,930,000	3,016,593
Center	1,846,177	3,699,813	9,102,896	13,131,619	17,043,796
Volgo-Vyatsk	115,061	375,964	1,354,616	2,410,329	3,454,095
Central Chernozem	609,060	804,484	1,134,755	1,862,925	2,985,379
Volga	835,750	1,402,387	2,873,286	5,184,212	7,508,654
Belorussia	444,088	673,415	1,219,141	1,698,213	3,077,590
Moldavia	205,725	233,796	210,872	438,971	817,979
Southwest	1,337,458	2,214,145	2,953,089	3,825,116	5,999,627
South	854,477	1,060,185	1,539,909	1,958,645	2,898,768
Donetsk-Dnepr	828,645	1,798,739	5,720,972	8,230,656	11,212,489
North Caucasus	628,515	1,832,747	2,818,572	4,469,115	6,461,650
Transcaucasus	527,067	1,052,878	2,014,651	3,481,326	5,128,182
Urals	508,433	1,131,841	3,946,618	8,821,227	11,200,409
West Siberia	127,872	610,859	2,102,596	4,775,992	6,008,902
East Siberia	78,172	319,969	1,236,319	2,600,304	3,651,661
Far East	61,767	254,233	1,143,222	2,061,140	2,757,278
Kazakhstan	121,238	340,388	1,330,570	3,189,383	5,343,052
Central Asia	618,312	1,024,298	1,809,345	3,678,486	6,107,215
USSR total	12,321,040	22,357,097	48,862,449	79,760,892	112,623,584

Sources: See Chapter 1, nn. 104 and 105.

444

TABLE B.5

Rural Population by Gross Region: 1897-1970

Region	1897	1926	1939	1959	1970
Western USSR	90,336,630	111,911,119	108,678,853	91,134,625	87,008,910
Eastern USSR	22,385,171	33,387,619	35,535,843	37,931,133	42,087,640
Northern European USSR	69,420,359	84,146,500	80,380,278	63,923,908	57,937,268
European Steppe	16,848,242	22,955,969	22,285,715	21,187,233	21,904,512
Russian East	12,825,735	20,972,101	22,051,798	21,821,342	20,738,465
Non-Slavic South	13,627,465	17,224,168	19,496,905	22,133,275	28,516,305
USSR total	112,721,801	145,298,738	144,214,696	129,065,758	129,096,550

Sources: See Chapter 1, nn. 104 and 105.

TABLE B.6

Rural Population by Economic Region: 1897-1970

Region	1897	1926	1939	1959	1970
Northwest	6,266,506	7,871,081	7,244,825	5,460,821	4,938,631
West	4,889,029	4,581,515	4,587,488	4,071,694	3,831,849
Center	13,399,408	17,349,900	16,205,202	11,657,730	9,676,749
Volgo-Vyatsk	6,066,283	6,879,929	7,343,533	5,842,709	4,893,722
Central Chernozem	7,676,700	10,231,351	9,304,515	6,834,984	5,943,863
Volga	8,877,042	11,031,113	9,251,703	7,270,142	6,778,704
Belorussia	6,024,334	6,967,565	7,690,853	6,356,435	5,924,748
Moldavia	1,328,536	1,801,785	2,241,151	2,445,506	2,750,894
Southwest	16,221,057	19,234,046	18,752,159	16,429,393	15,949,002
South	2,904,878	3,538,943	3,312,370	3,107,487	3,481,846
Donetsk-Dnepr	7,017,718	10,179,535	9,039,255	8,317,749	7,584,785
North Caucasus	5,597,110	7,435,706	7,692,939	7,316,491	8,086,987
Transcaucasus	4,068,029	4,808,650	6,012,860	6,023,484	7,167,130
Urals	8,597,474	10,715,492	10,497,257	9,792,003	9,208,963
West Siberia	1,847,728	5,647,008	5,834,274	5,383,445	4,694,498
East Siberia	2,019,736	3,304,480	4,043,073	4,360,231	4,475,896
Far East	360,797	1,305,121	1,677,194	2,285,663	2,359,108
Kazakhstan	4,703,775	5,838,662	4,762,937	6,120,464	7,665,674
Central Asia	4,855,661	6,576,856	8,721,108	9,989,327	13,683,501
USSR total	112,721,801	145,298,738	144,214,696	129,065,758	129,096,550

Sources: See Chapter 1, nn. 104 and 105.

446

Total, Urban, and Rural Populations by Gross Region: 1970 and 1977

Region	Total[a] 1977	Urban 1970	Urban 1977	Rural 1970	Rural 1977
Western USSR	172,481,000	93,468,885	109,150,000	71,095,092	63,331,000
Eastern USSR	85,343,000	42,522,629	50,459,000	34,633,528	34,884,000
Northern European USSR	112,743,000	61,659,720	72,345,000	47,313,547	40,398,000
European Steppe	46,070,000	25,523,344	29,398,000	17,772,054	16,672,000
Russian East	46,687,000	28,453,977	32,938,000	15,902,738	13,749,000
Non-Slavic South	52,324,000	20,354,473	24,928,000	24,740,281	27,396,000
USSR total	257,824,000	135,991,514	159,609,000[b]	105,728,620	98,215,000[b]

[a]See Table B.1 for 1970 data.

[b]These figures differ from published urban and rural populations of 159,593,000 and 98,231,000, respectively, due to Ukrainian urban and rural figures by oblast, which result in a 16,000 difference.

Note: Based on official urban definitions.

Sources: 1970 Soviet census and 1977 estimates (see Chapter 1, nn. 104 and 113).

Total, Urban, and Rural Populations by Economic Region: 1970 and 1977

Region	Total[a] 1977	Urban 1970	Urban 1977	Rural 1970	Rural 1977
Northwest	13,817,000	9,449,307	10,884,000	3,439,589	2,933,000
West	7,301,000	3,929,507	4,620,000	2,918,935	2,681,000
Center	27,599,000	19,340,651	21,638,000	7,379,894	5,961,000
Volgo-Vyatsk	8,291,000	4,412,074	5,101,000	3,935,743	3,190,000
Central Chernozem	8,617,000	3,576,376	4,446,000	5,352,866	4,171,000
Volga	15,070,000	8,550,832	10,256,000	5,736,526	4,814,000
Belorussia	9,414,000	3,907,783	5,012,000	5,094,555	4,402,000
Moldavia	3,885,000	1,130,048	1,474,000	2,438,825	2,411,000
Southwest	22,634,000	8,493,190	10,388,000	13,455,439	12,246,000
South	7,006,000	3,640,974	4,405,000	2,739,640	2,601,000
Donetsk-Dnepr	19,660,000	13,554,396	15,067,000	5,242,878	4,593,000
North Caucasus	15,519,000	7,197,926	8,452,000	7,350,711	7,067,000
Transcaucasus	13,668,000	6,285,821	7,407,000	6,009,491	6,261,000
Urals	20,984,000	12,968,307	14,748,000	7,441,065	6,236,000
West Siberia	10,952,000	6,741,793	7,599,000	3,961,607	3,353,000
East Siberia	8,827,000	4,986,584	6,014,000	3,140,973	2,813,000
Far East	5,924,000	3,757,293	4,577,000	1,359,093	1,347,000
Kazakhstan	14,498,000	6,538,652	7,880,000	6,470,074	6,618,000
Central Asia	24,158,000	7,530,000	9,641,000	12,260,716	14,517,000
USSR total	257,824,000	135,991,514	159,609,000[b]	105,728,620	98,215,000[b]

[a]See Table B.2 for 1970 data.
[b]These figures differ from published urban and rural populations of 159,593,000 and 98,231,000, respectively, due to Ukrainian urban and rural figures by oblast, which result in a 16,000 difference.

Note: Based on official urban definitions.

Sources: 1970 Soviet census and 1977 estimates (see Chapter 1, nn. 104 and 113).

448

TABLE B.9

Total, Urban, and Rural Populations by Gross Region: 1970 and 1974

Region	Total* 1974	Urban		Rural	
		1970	1974	1970	1974
Western USSR	169,338,000	76,380,679	84,930,000	88,183,298	84,408,000
Eastern USSR	81,531,000	34,010,746	37,926,000	43,145,411	43,605,000
Northern European USSR	111,189,000	50,312,050	56,022,000	58,661,217	55,167,000
European Steppe	45,029,000	20,940,447	23,211,000	22,354,951	21,818,000
Russian East	45,382,000	23,067,259	25,303,000	21,289,456	20,079,000
Non-Slavic South	49,269,000	16,071,669	18,320,000	29,023,085	30,949,000
USSR total	250,869,000	110,391,425	122,856,000	131,328,709	128,013,000

*See Table B.1 for 1970 data.

Note: Based on official cities of 15,000 and over.

Sources: 1970 Soviet census and 1974 estimates (see Chapter 1, nn. 104 and 113).

TABLE B.10

Total, Urban, and Rural Populations by Economic Region: 1970 and 1974

Region	Total* 1974	Urban 1970	Urban 1974	Rural 1970	Rural 1974
Northwest	13,382,000	7,794,557	8,564,000	5,094,339	4,818,000
West	7,134,000	3,016,593	3,418,000	3,831,849	3,716,000
Center	27,239,000	16,713,392	17,990,000	10,007,153	9,249,000
Volgo-Vyatsk	8,271,000	3,427,536	3,748,000	4,920,281	4,523,000
Central Chernozem	8,720,000	2,936,998	3,345,000	5,992,244	5,375,000
Volga	14,751,000	7,396,239	8,322,000	6,891,119	6,429,000
Belorussia	9,268,000	3,077,590	3,656,000	5,924,748	5,612,000
Moldavia	3,764,000	817,979	989,000	2,750,894	2,775,000
Southwest	22,424,000	5,949,145	6,979,000	15,999,484	15,445,000
South	6,743,000	2,868,428	3,307,000	3,512,186	3,436,000
Donetsk-Dnepr	19,354,000	10,994,235	11,923,000	7,803,039	7,431,000
North Caucasus	15,168,000	6,259,805	6,992,000	8,288,832	8,176,000
Transcaucasus	13,120,000	5,128,182	5,697,000	7,167,130	7,423,000
Urals	20,594,000	11,031,905	11,978,000	9,377,467	8,616,000
West Siberia	10,755,000	5,846,220	6,285,000	4,857,180	4,470,000
East Siberia	8,469,000	3,580,574	4,081,000	4,546,983	4,388,000
Far East	5,564,000	2,608,560	2,959,000	2,507,826	2,605,000
Kazakhstan	13,928,000	5,071,205	5,832,000	7,937,521	8,096,000
Central Asia	22,221,000	5,872,282	6,791,000	13,918,434	15,430,000
USSR total	250,869,000	110,391,425	122,856,000	131,328,709	128,013,000

*See Table B.2 for 1970 data.

Note: Based on official cities of 15,000 and over.

Sources: 1970 Soviet census and 1974 estimates (see Chapter 1, nn. 104 and 113).

BIBLIOGRAPHY

PUBLIC DOCUMENTS

Connor, Walker. "America's Melting Pot: Myth and/or Reality." Byliner
(U.S. Information Service), no. 33 (June 1977).

Davis, Kingsley, and Hilda Hertz, "Patterns of World Urbanization for 1800-
1950." Report on the World Social Situation Including Studies of Urbanization in Underdeveloped Areas. United Nations, Bureau of Social Affairs. (ST/SOA/33, 1957).

Edwards, Imogene U. "Automotive Trends in the USSR." Soviet Economic
Prospects for the Seventies. U.S. Congress. Joint Economic Committee
Print. Washington, D.C.: Government Printing Office, 1973.

Feshbach, Murray, and Stephen Rapawy, "Soviet Population and Manpower
Trends and Policies." Soviet Economy in a New Perspective. U.S.
Congress. Joint Economic Committee Print. Washington, D.C.:
Government Printing Office, 1976.

Great Britain. Office of Population Censuses and Surveys. Census 1971,
England and Wales: Preliminary Report. 1972.

Japan. Bureau of Statistics. Office of the Prime Minister. 1960 Population
Census, Densely Inhabited District: Its Population, Area, and Map.
December 1961.

_____. 1960 Population Census of Japan. 1961.

_____. 1970 Population Census of Japan. 1971.

Leningrad. Planovaya Komissiya Ispolkoma Lengorsoveta. Leningrad za 50
Let. Leningrad: Lenizdat, 1967.

Long, Larry H., and Celia G. Boertlein. The Geographical Mobility of Americans. Current Population Reports. Series P-23, no. 64. Washington,
D.C.: Government Printing Office, p. 3.

Moscow. Statisticheskoye Upravleniye Goroda Moskvy. Moskva v Tsifrakh
(1966-1970 GG.) Moscow: Izdatel'stvo "Statistika," 1972.

Rapawy, Stephen. Estimates and Projection of the Labor Force and Civilian Employment in the USSR, 1959 to 1990. U.S. Department of Commerce. Foreign Economic Report no. 10, p. 36. September 1976.

RSFSR. Tsentral'noye Statisticheskoye Upravleniye pri Sovete Ministrov RSFSR. Narodnoye Khozyaystvo RSFSR v 1970 G. Moscow: "Statistika," 1971.

_____. Narodnoye Khozyaystvo RSFSR v 1971 G. Moscow: "Statistika," 1972.

_____. RSFSR v Tsifrakh v 1975 Godu. Moscow: "Statistika," 1976.

Russian Empire. Tsentral'nyy Statisticheskiy Komitet Ministerstva Vnutrennikh Del. Pervaya Vseobshchaya Perepis' Naseleniya Rossiyskoy Imperii, 1897 G. 89 vols. St. Petersburg, 1899-1905.

_____. Sbornik Svedeniy po Rossii za 1884-1885 GG. Statistika Rossiyskoy Imperii, vol. 1. St. Petersburg, 1887.

Smith, Willard S. "Housing in the Soviet Union—Big Plans, Little Action." Soviet Economic Prospects for the Seventies. U.S. Congress. Joint Economic Committee Print. Washington, D.C.: Government Printing Office, 1973.

Ukrainian SSR. Tsentral'ne Statistichne Upravlinnya pri Radi Ministriv URSR. Narodne Gospodarstvo Ukrains'koy RSR u 1970 Rotsi. Kiev: Ordena Trudovogo Chervonogo Prapora Vidavnitsvo Politichnoi Literaturi Ukraini, 1971.

United Nations. Department of Economic and Social Affairs. Demographic Yearbook—1971. New York, 1972.

_____. Demographic Yearbook—1974. New York, 1975.

_____. Economic Survey of Europe in 1954. Geneva, 1955.

_____. Growth of the World's Urban and Rural Population, 1920-2000 (ST/SOA/Series A/44), New York, 1969.

U.S., Central Intelligence Agency. USSR Agricultural Atlas. Washington, D.C.: Government Printing Office, December 1974.

_____. USSR: Some Implications of Demographic Trends for Economic Policies. ER 77-10012. January 1977.

U.S., Congress. Joint Economic Committee. Soviet Economy in a New Perspective. 94th Cong. Washington, D.C.: U.S. Government Printing Office, 1976.

_____. Western Perception of Soviet Economic Trends. 95th Cong. Washington, D.C.: U.S. Government Printing Office, 1978.

U.S., Department of Commerce. Bureau of the Census. County and City Data Book, 1972.

_____. Geographical Mobility: March 1975 to March 1976. Current Population Reports. Series P-20, no. 305. Washington, D.C.: Government Printing Office, 1977.

_____. Historical Statistics of the United States, Colonial Times to 1970, Part 1.

_____. Projections of the Population of the U.S.S.R. and Eight Subdivisions, by Age, and Sex, 1973 to 2000. International Population Reports. Series P-91, no. 24, June 1975.

_____. Statistical Abstract of the United States, 1976.

USSR. Glavnoye Upravleniye Goedezii i Kartografii Ministerstva Geologii i Okhrany Nedr SSSR. Atlas SSSR. Moscow, 1962.

USSR. Glavnoye Upravleniye Goedezii i Kartografii pri Sovete Ministrov SSSR, Malyy Atlas SSSR. Moscow, 1973.

USSR. Prezidium Verkhovnogo Soveta SSSR. SSSR: Administrativno-Territorial'noye Deleniye Soyuznykh Respublik na 1 Yanvarya 1965 Goda. Moscow, 1965.

_____. SSSR: Administrativno-Territorial'noye Deleniye Soyuznykh Respublik na 1 Yanvarya 1974 Goda. Moscow, 1974.

_____. SSSR: Administrativno-Territorial'noye Deleniye Soyuznykh Respublik na 1 Yanvarya 1977 Goda. Moscow, 1977.

USSR. Tsentral'noye Statisticheskoye Upravleniye, SSSR. Itogi Vsesoyuznoy Perepisi Naseleniya 1959 Goda. 16 vols. Moscow, 1962-63.

_____. Tsentral'noye Statisticheskoye Upravleniye, SSSR. Itogi Vsesoyuznoy Perepisi Naseleniya 1970 Goda. 7 vols. Moscow.

_____. Narodnoye Khozyaystvo SSSR 1922-1972 GG. Moscow: "Statistika," 1973.

_____. Narodnoye Khozyaystvo SSSR v 1961 G. Moscow: Gosstatizdat, 1962.

_____. Narodnoye Khozyaystvo SSSR v 1963 G. Moscow: "Statistika," 1964.

_____. Narodnoye Khozyaystvo SSSR v 1964 G. Moscow: "Statistika," 1965.

_____. Narodnoye Khozyaystvo SSSR v 1965 G. Moscow: Gosstatizdat, 1966.

_____. Narodnoye Khozyaystvo SSSR v 1967 G. Moscow: "Statistika," 1968.

_____. Narodnoye Khozyaystvo SSSR v 1970 G. Moscow: "Statistika," 1971.

_____. Narodnoye Khozyaystvo SSSR v 1974 G. Moscow: "Statistika," 1975.

_____. Narodnoye Khozyaystvo SSSR v 1975 G. Moscow: "Statistika," 1976.

_____. Narodonaseleniye. Moscow: Izdatel'stvo "Statistika," 1973.

_____. Naseleniye SSSR, 1973. Moscow: Izdatel'stvo "Statistika," 1975.

USSR. Tsentral'noye Statisticheskoye Upravleniye SSSR. Vsesoyuznaya Perepis' Naseleniya 1926 Goda. 66 vols. Moscow.

BOOKS

Akademiya Nauk Kazakhskoy SSR. Naseleniye Kazakhstana v 1959-1970 GG. Alma-Ata: Izdatel'stvo "Nauka" Kazakhskoy SSR, 1975.

Aleksandrov, N. G. Soviet Labour Law. Dehli, India: University Book House, 1962.

Belolutskiy, F., ed. Kolkhozno Kooperativnoye Zakonodatel'stvo: Sbornik. Moscow: "Sovetskoye Zakonodatel'stvo," 1931.

Bol'shaya Sovetskaya Entsiklopediya. 26 vols. Moscow: Izdatel'stvo "Sovetskaya Entsiklopediya," 1970-76.

Borisov, V. A. Perspektivy Rozhdayemosti. Moscow: "Statistika," 1976.

Conolly, Violet. Siberia Today and Tomorrow. New York: Toplinger, 1975.

Davis, Kingsley. Basic Data for Cities, Countries and Regions. World Urbanization, 1950-1970, vol. 1. Berkeley: University of California, Institute of International Studies, 1969.

_____. Analysis of Trends, Relationships, and Development. World Urbanization, 1950-1970, vol. 2. Berkeley: University of California, Institute of International Studies, 1972.

Deming, W. E. Statistical Adjustments of Data. New York: John Wiley and Sons, 1943.

Demko, George J. The Russian Colonization of Kazakhstan: 1897-1916. The Hague: Mouton, 1969.

Drobizhev, V. Z., I. D. Koval'chenko, and A. V. Murav'yev. Istoricheskaya Geografiya SSSR. Moscow: Izdatel'stvo "Vysshaya Shkola," 1973.

Dzyuba, Ivan. Internationalism or Russification? New York: Monad Press, 1968.

Engels, Friedrich. Herr Eugen Duhring's Revolution in Science. Chicago: Charles H. Kerr, 1935.

Erlich, Alexander. The Soviet Industrialization Debate, 1924-1928. Cambridge, Mass.: Harvard University Press, 1960.

Fainsod, Merle. How Russia is Ruled. Cambridge, Mass.: Harvard University Press, 1965.

Fedor, Thomas Stanley. Patterns of Urban Growth in Russian Empire during the Nineteenth Century. Chicago: University of Chicago, Department of Geography, 1975.

Feldbrugge, F. J. M., ed. Encyclopedia of Soviet Law. Dobbs Ferry, N.Y.: Oceana, 1973.

Foley, Donald L. Governing the London Region. Berkeley: University of California Press, 1972.

Friedmann, John. Regional Development Policy: A Case Study of Venezuela. Cambridge: Massachusetts Institute of Technology Press, 1966.

Glass, D. V. Population Policies and Movements in Europe. London: Frank Cass, 1967.

Goldscheider, Calvin. Population, Modernization, and Social Structure. Boston: Little, Brown, 1971.

Gregory, James S. Russian Land, Soviet People. New York: Pegasus, 1968.

Hamilton, F. E. Ian. The Moscow City Region. London: Oxford University Press, 1976.

Harris, Chauncy D. Cities of the Soviet Union. Chicago: Rand McNally, 1970.

Hirschmann, Albert O. The Strategy of Economic Development. New Haven, Conn.: Yale University Press, 1958.

Holland, Stuart. Capital Versus the Regions. New York: St. Martin's Press, 1976.

Hunter, Holland. Soviet Transportation Policy. Cambridge: Harvard University Press, 1957.

_____. The Soviet Transport Experience. Washington, D. C.: Brookings Institution, 1968.

Jaffe, A. J. People, Jobs, and Economic Development. Glencoe, Ill.: Free Press, 1959.

Jaffe, A. J., and R. O. Carleton. Occupational Mobility in the United States, 1930-1960. New York: King's Crown Press, 1954.

Karakhanov, M. K., ed. Problemy Narodonaseleniya. Moscow: Izdatel'stvo Moskovskogo Universiteta, 1970.

Katz, Zev, ed. Handbook of Major Soviet Nationalities. New York: Free Press, 1975.

Katzman, Martin T. Cities and Frontiers in Brazil: Regional Dimensions of Economic Development. Cambridge: Harvard University Press, 1977.

Khodzhayev, D. G., ed. Puti Razvitiya Malykh i Srednikh Gorodov. Moscow: Izdatel'stvo "Nauka," 1967.

Kholmogorov, A. I. International Traits of Soviet Nations (Based on Data of Concrete Sociological Research in the Baltic Area). Moscow: "Mysl'," Publishing House, 1970.

Khorev, B. S. Gorodskiye Poseleniya SSSR. Moscow: Izdatel'stvo "Mysl'," 1968.

_____. Problemy Gorodov. Moscow: Izdatel'stvo "Mysl'," 1971.

_____. Problemy Gorodov. 2d ed. Moscow: Izdatel'stvo "Mysl'," 1975.

Khorev, B. S., ed. Malyy Gorod. Moscow: Izdatel'stvo Moskovskogo Universiteta, 1972.

_____. Sdvigi v Razmeshchenii Naseleniya SSSR. Moscow: "Statistika," 1976.

Khorev, B. S., and V. M. Moiseyenko, eds. Migratsionnaya Podvizhnest' Naseleniya v SSSR. Moscow: "Statistika," 1974.

Kolkhoznoye Pravo. Moscow: Yuridicheskaya Literatura, 1973.

Koropeckyj, I. S. Locational Problems in Soviet Industry before World War II. Chapel Hill: University of North Carolina Press, 1971.

Kostakov, V. G. Trudovyye Resursy Pyatiletki. Moscow: Izdatel'stvo Politicheskoy Literatury, 1976.

Kratkaya Geograficheskaya Entsiklopediya. 5 vols. Moscow: Gosudarstvennoye Nauchnoye Izdatel'stvo "Sovetskaya Entsiklopediya," 1960-66.

Kulischer, Eugene M. Europe on the Move. New York: Columbia University Press, 1948.

Kutaf'yeva, E. S., N. I. Moskaleva, K. V. Papenov, and M. G. Trudova. Migratsiya Sel'skogo Naseleniya. Moscow: Izdatel'stvo Moskovskogo Universiteta, 1971.

Lappo, G. M. Rasskazy o Gorodakh. Moscow: Izdatel'stvo "Mysl'," 1972.

Lappo, G. M., A. Chikishev, and A. Bekker. Moscow—Capital of the Soviet Union. Moscow: Progress, 1976.

Larmin, O. V. Metodologicheskiye Problemy Izucheniya Narodonaseleniya. Moscow: Izdatel'stvo "Statistika," 1974.

Leasure, J. William, and Robert A. Lewis. Population Changes in Russia and the USSR: A Set of Comparable Territorial Units. San Diego, Calif.: San Diego State College Press, 1966.

Lenin, V. I. The Development of Capitalism in Russia. Moscow: Foreign Languages Publishing House, 1956.

_____. Polnoye Sobraniye Sochineniy. Vol. 26. Moscow: Gosudarstvennoye Izdatel'stvo Politicheskoy Literatury, 1961.

Lewis, Robert A., Richard H. Rowland, and Ralph S. Clem. Nationality and Population Change in Russia and the USSR. New York: Praeger, 1976.

Liddell Hart, B. H. History of the Second World War. New York: G. P. Putnam's Sons, 1971.

Litovka, O. P. Problemy Prostranstvennogo Razvitiya Urbanizatsii. Leningrad: Izdatel'stvo "Nauka," Leningradskoye Otdeleniye, 1976.

Litvyakov, P. P., ed. Demograficheskiye Problemy Zanyatosti. Moscow: Izdatel'stvo "Ekonomika," 1969.

Lorimer, Frank. The Population of the Soviet Union: History and Prospects. Geneva: League of Nations, 1946.

Lubny-Gertsyk, L. I. Dvizheniye Naseleniya na Territorii SSSR. Rostov na Donu: Izdatel'stvo "Planovoye Khozyaystvo," 1926.

Lyashchenko, Peter I. History of the National Economy of Russia to the 1917 Revolution. New York: Macmillan, 1949.

Lydolph, Paul A. Geography of the U.S.S.R. 2d ed. New York: John Wiley, 1970.

Malinin, E. D., and A. K. Ushakov. Naseleniye Sibiri. Moscow: "Statistika," 1976.

Manevich, E. Problemy Obshchestvennogo Truda. Moscow: Izdatel'stvo "Ekonomika," 1966.

Marx, Karl, and Friedrich Engels. Collected Works. New York: International, 1975.

Mizhenskaya, E. F. Lichnyye Potrebnosti pri Sotsializme. Moscow: Izdatel'stvo "Nauka," 1973.

Moskovskoy Filial Geograficheskogo Obshchestva SSSR. Vsë Podmoskov'ye. Moscow: Izdatel'stvo "Mysl'," 1967.

Myrdal, Gunnar. Economic Theory and Under-Developed Regions. New Haven, Conn.: Yale University Press, 1958.

National Geographic Atlas of the World. Rev. 3d ed. Washington, D.C.: National Geographic Society, 1970.

The 1970 World Almanac and Book of Facts. New York: Newspaper Enterprise Association, 1969.

Nove, Alec. An Economic History of the USSR. Baltimore: Penguin, 1969.

Odud, A. L. Moldavskaya SSR. Moscow: Gosudarstvennoye Izdatel'stvo Geograficheskoy Literatury, 1955.

The Odyssey World Atlas. New York: Golden Press, 1967.

Osborn, Robert J. Soviet Social Policies: Welfare, Equality and Community. Homewood, Ill.: Dorsey Press, 1970.

Osnovnyye Napravleniya Razvitiya Narodnogo Khozyaystva SSSR na 1976-1980 Gody. Moscow: Izdatel'stvo Politicheskoy Literatury, 1975.

Oxford World Atlas. New York: Oxford University Press, 1973.

Ozertskovskiy, N., ed. Polozheniye o Sel'skokhozyaystvennoy Kooperatsii. Moscow: Knigosoyuz, 1928.

Parker, W. H. An Historical Geography of Russia. Chicago: Aldine, 1969.

Pashkov, A. S., ed. Sovetskoye Trudovoye Pravo. Moscow: "Yuridicheskaya Literatura," 1976.

Pavlovsky, George. Agricultural Russia on the Eve of the Revolution. New York: Howard Fertig, 1968.

Perevedentsev, V. I. Goroda i Vremya. Moscow: "Statistika," 1975.

_____. Metody Izucheniya Migratsii Naseleniya. Moscow: Izdatel'stvo "Nauka," 1975.

_____. Migratsiya Naseleniya i Trudovyye Problemy Sibiri. Novosibirsk: Izdatel'stvo "Nauka" Sibirskoye Otdeleniye, 1966.

_____. Sovremennaya Migratsiya Naseleniya Zapadnoy Sibiri. Novosibirsk: Zapadno-Sibirskoye Knizhnoye Izdatel'stvo, 1965.

Pivovarov, Yu. L. Sovremennaya Urbanizatsiya. Moscow: "Statistika," 1976.

Rashin, A. G. Naseleniye Rossii za 100 Let. Moscow: Gosudarstvennoye Statisticheskoye Izdatel'stvo, 1956.

Reiss, Albert J., Jr., ed. Louis Wirth on Cities and Social Life. Chicago: University of Chicago Press, 1969.

Robinson, Geroid Tanquary. Rural Russia Under the Old Régime. Rev. ed. Berkeley: University of California Press, 1972.

Rose, Arnold. Migrants in Europe. Minneapolis: University of Minnesota Press, 1969.

Rybakovskiy, L. L. Regional'nyy Analiz Migratsii. Moscow: Izdatel'stvo "Statistika," 1973.

Rybakovskiy, L. L., ed. Territorial'nyye Osobennosti Narodonaseleniya RSFSR. Moscow: "Statistika," 1976.

Salisbury, Harrison. The 900 Days. New York: Harper & Row, 1969.

Sbornik Zakonodatel'nykh Aktov o Trude. Moscow: "Yuridicheskaya Literatura," 1974.

Shabad, Theodore. Basic Industrial Resources of the U.S.S.R. New York: Columbia University Press, 1969.

Shaw, R. Paul. Migration Theory and Fact. Philadelphia: Regional Science Research Institute, 1975.

Shpilyuk, V. A. Mezhrespublikanskaya Migratsiya i Sblizheniye Natsii v SSSR. L'vov: Izdatel'stvo pri L'vovskom Gosudarstvennom Universitete, 1975.

Sklyarov, L. F. Pereseleniye i Zemleustroystvo v Sibiri v Gody Stolypinskoy Reformy. Leningrad, 1962.

Spengler, Joseph. Population Change, Modernization, and Welfare. Englewood Cliffs, N.J.: Prentice-Hall, 1974.

Spravochnik po Zakonodatel'stvu dlya Kolkhoznika. Moscow: Gosudarstvennoye Izdatel'stvo Yuridicheskoy Literatury, 1961.

Staroverov, V. I. Sotsial'no-Demograficheskiye Problemy Derevni. Moscow: Izdatel'stvo "Nauka," 1975.

Steiner, Eugen. The Slovak Dilemma. Cambridge: At the University Press, 1973.

Sul'kevich, S. I. Territoriya i Naseleniye SSSR. Moscow: Politizdat, 1940.

Sumner, B. H. A Short History of Russia. New York: Reynal and Hitchcock, 1947.

Sundquist, James L. Dispersing Population. Washington, D.C.: Brookings Institution, 1975.

Taubman, William. Governing Soviet Cities. New York: Praeger, 1973.

Tikhomirov, M. The Towns of Ancient Rus. Moscow: Foreign Languages Publishing House, 1959.

Topilin, A. V. Territorial'noye Pereraspredeleniye Trudovykh Resursov v SSSR. Moscow: Izdatel'stvo "Ekonomika," 1975.

Treadgold, Donald. The Great Siberian Migration. Princeton, N.J.: Princeton University Press, 1957.

Trudovoye Zakonodatel'stvo SSSR: Sbornik Zakonov, Ukazov, i Postanovleniy. Moscow: Yuridicheskoye Izdatel'stvo N. K. Yu. SSSR, 1941.

XXIV S'ezd Kommunisticheskoy Partii Sovetskogo Soyuza. Vol. 2. Moscow: Izdatel'stvo Politicheskoy Literatury, 1971.

Urlanis, B. Ts. Problemy Dinamiki Naseleniya SSSR. Moscow: Izdatel'stvo "Nauka," 1974.

_____. Rozhdayemost' i Prodolzhitel'nost' Zhizni v SSSR. Moscow: Gosstatizdat, 1963.

Urlanis, B. Ts., ed. Narodonaseleniye Stran Mira. Moscow: "Statistika," 1974.

Valentey, D. I., ed. Marksistsko-Leninskaya Teoriya Narodonaseleniya. Moscow: Izdatel'stvo "Mysl'," 1971.

Valentey, D. I., and I. F. Sorokina, eds. Naseleniye, Trudovyye Resursy SSSR. Moscow: Izdatel'stvo "Mysl'," 1971.

Volkov, E. Z. Dinamika Naseleniya SSSR za Vocem'desyat Let. Moscow: Gosudarstvennoye Izdatel'stvo, 1930.

Vydro, M. Ya. Naseleniye Moskvy. Moscow: Izdatel'stvo "Statistika," 1976.

Weber, Adna Ferrin. The Growth of Cities in the Nineteenth Century. Ithaca, N.Y.: Cornell University Press, 1963.

Wilsher, P., and R. Righter. The Exploding Cities. New York: Quadrangle/ New York Times Book Company, 1975.

The World Almanac & Book of Facts, 1975. New York: Newspaper Enterprise Associates, 1974.

Yamzin, I. L. Pereselencheskoye Dvizheniye v Rossii s Momenta Osvobozhdeniya Krest'yan. Kiev: 1912.

Yamzin, I. L., and V. P. Voshehinin. Ucheniye o Kolonizatsii i Pereseleniyakh. Moscow, 1926.

Zaslavskaya, T. I., ed. Migratsiya Sel'skogo Naseleniya. Moscow: Izdatel'stvo "Mysl'," 1970.

_____. Sotsial'nyye Problemy Trudovykh Resursov Sela. Novosibirsk: Izdatel'stvo "Nauka," 1968.

Zaslavskaya, T. I., and V. A. Kalmyk, eds. Sovremennaya Sibirskaya Derevnya. Novosibirsk: S. O., A. N. SSSR, 1975.

Zayonchkovskaya, Zh. A. Novosely v Gorodakh. Moscow: "Statistika,"
1972.

ARTICLES, JOURNALS, PROCEEDINGS,
MAGAZINES, AND NEWSPAPERS

Abu-Lughod, Janet. "Migration Adjustment to City Life: The Egyptian Case."
American Journal of Sociology 67 (July 1961): 22-32.

Adams, Russell B. "The Soviet Metropolitan Hierarchy: Regionalization and
Comparison with the United States." Soviet Geography: Review and
Translation 18 (May 1977): 313-28.

Akhiyezer, A. S., and A. V. Kochetkov. "Urbanizatsiya i Intensifikatsiya
Proizvodstva v SSSR." Problemy Sovremennoy Urbanizatsii. Moscow:
"Statistika," 1972.

Arriaga, Eduardo. "Selected Measures of Urbanization." In The Measurement of Urbanization and Projection of Urban Population, edited by
Sidney Goldstein and David F. Sly. Dolhain, Belgium: Ordina Editions,
1975.

Arutyunyan, Yu. V. "Izmeneniye Sotsial'noy Struktury Sovetskikh Natsiy."
Istoriya SSSR, no. 4 (July-August 1972), pp. 3-20.

Ball, Blaine, and George J. Demko. "Internal Migration in the Soviet Union."
Economic Geography 54 (April 1978): 95-114.

Bennigsen, Alexandre. "Islamic or Local Consciousness among Soviet Nationalities?" In Soviet Nationality Problems, edited by Edward Allworth.
New York: Columbia University Press, 1971.

Brown, E. C. "Continuity and Change in the Soviet Labor Market." Industrial and Labor Relations Review 23 (1970): 171-90.

Bulochnikova L. "Sel'skaya Migratsiya i Puti eye Regulirovaniya." Planovoye
Khozyaystvo, no. 8 (July 1969), p. 71.

Byulleten' Minvuza SSSR, no. 12 (1974), pp. 11-12.

Clem, Ralph S. "Economic Development of the Russian Homeland: Regional
Growth in the Soviet Federation." In Ethnic Russia Today: The Dilemma of the Dominant Group, edited by Edward Allworth. New York
and Oxford: Pergamon Press, 1978.

_____. "The Impact of Demographic and Socioeconimic Forces Upon the Nationality Question in Central Asia." In The Nationality Question in Soviet Central Asia, edited by Edward Allworth. New York: Praeger, 1973.

_____. "The Integration of Ukrainians Into Modernized Society in the Ukrainian SSR." In The Soviet West: Interplay Between Nationality and Social Organization, edited by Ralph S. Clem. New York: Praeger, 1975.

Connor, Walker. "Ethnonationalism in the First World: The Present in Historical Perspective." In Ethnic Pluralism and Conflict in the Western World, edited by Milton Esman. Ithaca: Cornell University Press, 1977.

_____. "Nation-Building or Nation-Destroying?" World Politics 24 (April 1972): 319-55.

_____. "An Overview of the Ethnic Composition and Problems of Non-Arab Asia." Journal of Asian Affairs 1 (Spring 1976): 9-25.

_____. "Political Fusion and Ethnic Fission." Concilium 13, no. 1 (January 1977): 13-24.

_____. "The Political Significance of Ethnonationalism within Western Europe." In Ethnicity in an International Context, edited by Abdul Said and Luiz Simmons. Edison, N.J.: Transaction Books, 1976.

_____. "The Politics of Ethnonationalism." Journal of International Affairs 27 (January 1973): 1-21.

_____. "Self-Determination: The New Phase." World Politics 20 (October 1967): 30-53.

Dalrymple, Dana G. "The Soviet Famine of 1932-1934." Soviet Studies 15 (January 1964): 250-84.

Dando, William A. "The Moscow City Region: Land Development in an Expanding Socialist City." The Middle Atlantic 6 (July 1975): 21, 23.

Davidovich, V. G. "Goroda i Poselki-Sputniki v SSSR." Goroda-Sputniki. Moscow: Gosudarstvennoye Izdatel'stvo Geograficheskoy Literatury, 1961.

_____. "Rasseleniye v Prigorodnykh Zonakh." Rasseleniye v Prigorodnykh Zonakh. Moscow: Izdatel'stvo "Mysl'," 1971.

Davis, Kingsley. "The Migration of Human Populations. The Human Population. San Francisco: W. H. Freeman, 1974.

_____. "Population Policy: Will Current Programs Succeed?" Science 158 (November 10, 1967): 730-39.

_____. "The Urbanization of the Human Population." Cities. New York: Knopf, 1970.

Denisova, L., and T. Fadeyeva. "Nekotoryye Dannyye o Migratsii Naseleniya v SSSR." Vestnik Statistiki, no. 7 (1965), p. 20.

Dienes, Leslie. "Investment Priorities in Soviet Regions." Annals of the Association of American Geographers 62 (September 1972): 437-54.

Evsyukov, Yu. "Migratsiya Naseleniya iz Sela v Gorod." Planovoye Khozyaystvo, no. 12 (1972), pp. 124, 128.

Field, Neil C. "Land Hunger and the Rural Depopulation Problem in the USSR." Annals of the Association of American Geographers 53 (December 1963): 465-78.

Fuchs, Roland J., and George J. Demko. "The Postwar Mobility Transition in Eastern Europe." Geographical Review 68 (April 1978): 171-82.

"Germans Join in $1-Billion Pact to Equip a Soviet Steel Plant." New York Times. March 23, 1974, p. 1.

Gibbs, Jack P. "The Evolution of Population Concentration." In Population Geography: A Reader, edited by George J. Demko, Harold M. Rose, and George A. Schnell. New York: McGraw-Hill, 1970.

Gibbs, Jack P., and Walter T. Martin. "Urbanization, Technology, and the Division of Labor: International Patterns." American Sociological Review 27 (October 1962): 667-77.

Gilbert, Alan G., and David E. Goodman. "Regional Income Disparities and Economic Development: A Critique." In Development Planning and Spatial Structure, edited by Alan Gilbert. London: Wiley, 1976.

Gladyshev, A. "Obshchestvennyye Fondy Potrebleniya i Migratsiya Naseleniya." Planovoye Khozyaystvo, no. 10 (1966), pp. 17-22.

Gluchkova, V. G., and N. P. Shepelev. "Definition of the Boundary of Moscow's Active Zone of Influence." Soviet Geography: Review and Translation 17 (April 1976): 271.

Gol'tsov, A. "Regional'nyye Problemy Sovremennoy Migratsii Sel'skogo Naseleniya." Voprosy Ekonomiki, no. 10 (1969), pp. 64-74.

Grandstaff, Peter J. "A Note on Preliminary 1970 USSR Census Results
Concerning Migration." The Association for Comparative Economic
Studies Bulletin 16 (Fall 1974): 33-39.

_____. "Recent Soviet Experience and Western 'Laws' of Population Migra-
tion." International Migration Review 9 (Winter 1975): 481, 487.

Green, Alan G. "Regional Inequality, Structural Change, and Economic
Growth in Canada, 1890-1956." Economic Development and Cultural
Change 17 (1969): 567-83.

Grishanova, A., and O. Sergeyev. "Nekotoryye Cherty Demograficheskoy
Situatsii v Gorodakh Raslichnykh Funktsional'nykh Tipov." Narodonaseleniye, Prikladnaya Demografiya. Moscow: "Statistika," 1973.

Harris, Chauncy D. "Population of Cities of the Soviet Union, 1897, 1926,
1939, 1959, and 1967. Tables, Maps, and Gazetteer." Soviet Geography: Review and Translation 11 (May 1970): 307-444.

Hauser, Philip M. "Observations on the Urban-Folk and Urban-Rural Dichotomies as Forms of Western Ethnocentrism." In The Study of Urbanization, edited by Philip M. Hauser and Leo F. Schnore. New York:
Wiley, 1967.

Hodnett, Grey. "Technology and Social Change in Soviet Central Asia: The
Politics of Cotton Growing." In Soviet Politics and Society in the 1970's,
edited by Henry W. Morton and Rudolph L. Tokes. New York: Free
Press, 1974.

Holubnychy, Vsevolod. "Some Aspects of Relations Among Soviet Republics."
In Ethnic Minorities in the Soviet Union, edited by Erich Goldhagen.
New York: Praeger, 1968.

Hoselitz, Bert F. "The Role of Cities in the Economic Growth of Underdeveloped Countries." Journal of Political Economy 61 (June 1953): 195-
208.

Huzinec, George A. "The Impact of Industrial Decision Making Upon the Soviet Urban Hierarchy." Urban Studies 15 (June 1978): 139-48.

Inkeles, Alex. "Making Men Modern: On the Causes and Consequences of
Individual Change in Six Developing Countries." American Journal of
Sociology 75 (September 1969): 208-25.

Ivanova, R. "O Razvitii Vostochnykh Rayonov i Obespechenii ikh Rabochey Siloy." Voprosy Ekonomiki, no. 1 (1973), p. 42.

Jackson, W. A. Douglas. "Urban Expansion." Problems of Communism 23 (November-December 1974): 15.

Jaffe, A. J. "Amount and Structure of International Migration: The Organizer's Report for Section 9.1." General Conference of the International Union for the Scientific Study of Population. London. September 1969, p. 9.17.

_____. "Urbanization and Fertility." American Journal of Sociology 48 (July 1942): 48-60.

Jaffe, A. J., and Seymour L. Wolfbein. "Internal Migration and Full Employment in the U.S." Journal of the American Statistical Association 40 (September 1945): 351-63.

Khalmukhamedov, M. "Soviet Society: Complete Equality of Nations." International Affairs, no. 3 (1978), p. 29.

Khodzhayev, D. G. "The Planning of the Distribution of Production in Population Centers and Some Problems in Population Geography." Soviet Geography: Review and Translation 8 (October 1967): 627.

Khorev, B. S. "Issledovaniye Funktsional'noy Struktury Gorodskikh Poseleniy SSSR v Svyazi s Zadachami ikh Ekonomiko-Geograficheskoy Tipologii." Goroda Mira. Moscow: Izdatel'stvo "Mysl'," 1965.

Khorev, B. S., and V. M. Moiseenko. "Urbanization and Redistribution of the Population of the U.S.S.R." In Patterns of Urbanization: Comparative Country Studies, edited by Sidney Goldstein and David F. Sly. Dolhain, Belgium: Ordina Editions, 1977.

Khorev, B. S., D. Zyugin, G. Kiseleva, and B. Romashkin. "Osobennosti Demograficheskoy Situatsii v Moskve." Narodonaseleniye Prikladnaya Demografiya. Moscow: "Statistika," 1973.

Konstantinov, O. A. "Nekotoryye Cherty Urbanizatsii v SSSR." Urbanizatsiya Mira. Moscow: Izdatel'stvo "Mysl'," 1974.

Korniyenko, B. V., and E. D. Malinin. "Migratsiya Naseleniya v Zapadnoy Sibiri." Izvestiya Sibirskogo Otdeleniya Akademii Nauk SSSR, Seriya Obshchestvennykh Nauk, no. 6 (1972), p. 93.

Koropeckyj, I. S. "Equalization of Regional Development in Socialist Countries." Economic Development and Cultural Change 21 (1972): 68-86.

Kovalev, S. "Farewell to the Rural Scene." The Geographical Magazine 48 (April 1976): 430, 432.

Kovalev, S. A. "Transformation of Rural Settlements in the Soviet Union." Geoforum 9 (September 1972): 38.

Kuznets, Simon. "Introduction: Population Redistribution, Migration and Economic Growth." Demographic Analyses and Interrelations, by Hope T. Eldridge and Dorothy Swaine Thomas. Population Redistribution and Economic Growth: United States, 1870-1950. Vol. 3. Philadelphia: American Philosophical Society, 1964.

Lappo, G. M. "Problems in the Evolution of Urban Agglomerations." Soviet Geography: Review and Translation 15 (November 1974): 531-42.

_____. "Trends in the Evolution of Settlement Patterns in the Moscow Region." Soviet Geography: Review and Translation 14 (January 1973): 16, 20.

Leasure, J. William, and Robert A. Lewis. "Internal Migration in Russia in the Late Nineteenth Century." Slavic Review 27 (September 1968): 375-94.

_____. "Internal Migration in the USSR: 1897-1926." Demography 4, no. 2 (1967): 479-96.

Lee, Everett S. "A Theory of Migration." Demography 3, no. 1 (1966): 47-57.

Lewis, Oscar. "Further Observations on the Folk-Urban Continuum and Urbanization with Special Reference to Mexico City." In The Study of Urbanization, edited by Philip M. Hauser and Leo F. Schnore. New York: Wiley, 1967.

Lewis, Robert A. "Early Irrigation in West Turkestan." Annals of the Association of American Geographers 56 (September 1966): 467-91.

Lewis, Robert A., and Richard H. Rowland. "East is West and West is East . . . Population Redistribution in the USSR and Its Impact on Society." International Migration Review 11 (Spring 1977): 3-29.

_____. "A Further Investigation of Urbanization and Industrialization in Pre-Revolutionary Russia." The Professional Geographer 26 (May 1974): 177-82.

_____. "Urbanization in Russia and the USSR: 1897-1966." Annals of the Association of American Geographers 59 (December 1969): 776-96.

_____. "Urbanization in Russia and the USSR: 1897-1970." In The City in Russian History, edited by Michael F. Hamm. Lexington: University Press of Kentucky, 1976.

Listengurt, F. M. "Criteria for Delineating Large Urban Agglomerations in the USSR." Soviet Geography: Review and Translation 16 (November 1975): 559-68.

Lonsdale, Richard E. "Regional Inequality and Soviet Concern for Rural and Small-Town Industrialization." Soviet Geography: Review and Translation 18 (October 1977): 599.

Manevich, E. "The Management of Soviet Manpower." Foreign Affairs 47 (October 1968): 176-84.

Matveyev, Yu. A. "Organizovannyy Nabor kak Odna iz Osnovnykh Form Planovogo Pereraspredeleniya Rabochey Sily." In Migratsiya Naseleniya RSFSR, edited by A. Z. Maykov. Moscow: Izdatel'stvo "Statistika," 1973.

Maykov, A. "Osnovnyye Napravleniya Migratsii i Sovershenstvovaniye Territorial'nogo Pereraspredeleniya Trudovykh Resursov." Narodonaseleniye. Moscow: "Statistika," 1973.

Millar, James R. "The Prospects for Soviet Agriculture." Problems of Communism 26 (May-June 1977): 8-10.

Moiseyenko, V. M. "Nekotoryye Voprosy Upravleniya Migratsionnymi Protsessami Naseleniya." In Voprosy Teorii i Politiki Narodonaseleniya, edited by D. I. Valentey and E. Yu. Burnashev. Moscow: Izdatel'stvo Moskovskogo Universiteta, 1970.

_____. "Rol' Migratsii v Formirovanii Gorodskogo Naseleniya SSSR v Sovremennykh Usloviyakh." Problemy Narodonaseleniya. Mosocw: "Statistika," 1973.

Mote, Victor L. "The Baykal-Amur Mainline: Catalyst for the Development of Pacific Siberia." In Gateway to Siberian Resources (The BAM), edited by Theodore Shabad and Victor L. Mote. Washington, D.C.: Scripta, 1977.

Munchayev, Sh. M. "Evakuatsiya Naseleniya v Gody Velikoy Otechestvennoy Voyny." Istoriya SSSR, no. 3 (1975), p. 138.

Ogburn, William Fielding. "Technology and Cities: The Dilemma of the Modern Metropolis." Sociological Quarterly 1 (July 1960): 139-53.

"Pasport." Bol'shaya Sovetskaya Entsiklopediya, 1939. Vol. 44, pp. 322-23.

"Pasport." Entsiklopedicheskiy Slovar'. Vol. 22. St. Petersburg: Type-Lithografiya I. A. Efrom, 1897, pp. 923-25.

Perevedentsev, V. I. "Goroda i Gody," Literaturnaya Gazeta. February 26, 1969, p. 2.

_____. "The Growth of Big Cities in the U.S.S.R." The Current Digest of the Soviet Press 27 (May 28, 1975): 3.

_____. "Kontsentratsiya Gorodskogo Naseleniya i Kriterii Optimal'nosti Goroda." Urbanizatsiya i Rabochiy Klass v Usloviyakh Nauchno-Tekh-nicheskoy Revolyutsii. Moscow: Izdano Sovetskim Fondom Mira, 1970.

_____. "Migratsiya Nascleniya i Ispol'zovaniye Trudovykh Resursov." Voprosy Ekonomiki, no. 9 (September 1970), pp. 34-43.

_____. "Nekotoryye Voprosy Mezhrayonnogo Pereraspredeleniya Trudovykh Resursov." Izvestiya Sibirskogo Otdeleniya Akademii Nauk SSSR: Seriya Obshchestvennykh Nauk, no. 9 (1964), p. 77.

_____. "Sovremennaya Migratsiya v SSSR." Narodonaseleniye i Ekonomika. Moscow: Izdatel'stvo "Ekonomika," 1967.

_____. "Territorial'noye Razmeshcheniye Naseleniya po Strane i ego Migratsiya." In Teoriya i Politika Narodonaseleniya, edited by D. I. Valentey. Moscow: Izdatel'stvo "Vysshaya Shkola," 1967.

Perevedentsev, Viktor. "Iz Derevni v Gorod." Nash Sovremennik, no. 11 (1972), p. 104.

Pipes, Richard. "The Soviet Strategy for Nuclear Victory." Washington Post. July 3, 1977, pp. C1, C4.

Pod'yachikh, P. G. "Sostoyaniye Statistiki Migratsii Naseleniya v SSSR i Mery po Eye Uluchsheniyu." Problemy Migratsii Naseleniya i Trudovykh Resursov. Moscow: Izdatel'stvo "Statistika," 1970.

Pokshishevskiy, V. V. "Migratsiya Naseleniya kak Obshchestvennoye Yavleniye i Zadachi Statisticheskogo ikh Izucheniya." In Statistika Migratsii Naseleniya, edited by A. G. Volkov. Moscow: "Statistika," 1973.

_____. "O Gipoteze Dinamiki Chislennosti Naseleniya za Dlitel'nyy Istoricheskiy Period." Istoriya Geograficheskikh Znaniy i Istoricheskaya Geografiya. Vol. 4. Materialy Moskovskogo Filiala Geograficheskogo Obshchestva SSSR. Moscow, 1974, p. 10.

_____. "Ocherki po Zaseleniyu Lesostepnykh i Stepnykh Rayonov Russkoy Ravniny." Ekonomicheskaya Geografiya SSSR 5 (1960): 3-68.

Powell, David E. "The Rural Exodus." Problems of Communism 23 (November-December 1974): 3-4.

Powers, Mary J., and John J. Holmberg. "Occupational Status Scores: Changes Introduced by the Inclusion of Women." Demography 15 (May 1978): 183-205.

Redfield, Robert. "The Folk Society." American Journal of Sociology 52 (January 1947): 243-308.

Rodgers, Allan. "The Locational Dynamics of Soviet Industry." Annals of the Association of American Geographers 64 (June 1974): 237-40.

Rowland, Richard H. "Urban In-Migration in Late Nineteenth Century Russia." In The City in Russian History, edited by Michael F. Hamm. Lexington: University Press of Kentucky, 1976.

Rutgayzer, V. "Torzhestvo Leninskoy Natsional'noy Politiki v Ekonomicheskom Stroitel'stve." Kommunist, no. 18 (December 1968), pp. 24-35.

Schnaiberg, Allan. "The Modernizing Impact of Urbanization: A Causal Analysis." Economic Development and Cultural Change 20 (October 1971): 80-104.

_____. "Soviet Migration Patterns Based on 1970 Data." In Demographic Developments in Eastern Europe, edited by Leszek A. Kosinski. New York: Praeger, 1977.

_____. "Soviet Starting Production in Largest Blast Furnace." New York Times. February 20, 1973, p. 43.

Schroeder, Gertrude E. "Soviet Wage and Income Policies in Regional Perspective." Bulletin of the Association for Comparative Economic Studies, Fall 1974, p. 10.

Shabad, Theodore. "Soviet Lists Plans to Expand Iron and Steel Industry." New York Times. April 3, 1971, p. 2.

Shipler, David K. "Soviet Crime Problem Tied to City Life and Social Ills." New York Times. March 6, 1978, p. 1.

Sochava, Viktor B. "The BAM: Problems in Applied Geography." In Gateway to Siberian Resources (The BAM), edited by Theodore Shabad and Victor L. Mote. Washington, D.C.: Scripta, 1977.

Tatevosov, R. V. "Issledovaniye Prostranstvennykh Zakonomernostey Migratsii Naseleniya." In Statistika Migratsii Naseleniya, edited by T. V. Ryabushkin. Moscow: "Statistika," 1973.

Terent'eva, L. N. "Ethnic Self-Identification by Adolescents in Ethnically Mixed Families." Soviet Sociology 12 (Summer 1973): 54.

Thiede, Roger L. "Urbanization and Industrialization in Pre-Revolutionary Russia." The Professional Geographer 25 (February 1973): 16-21.

Vedomosti Verkhovnogo Soveta SSSR, no. 20 (1940), p. 1.

Vestnik Statistiki, no. 1 (1965), pp. 87-91.

Vestnik Statistiki, no. 12 (1968), p. 79.

Vestnik Statistiki, no. 3 (1971), p. 84.

Vestnik Statistiki, no. 11 (1971), p. 78.

Vestnik Statistiki, no. 11 (1976), p. 86.

Wädekin, Karl-Eugen. "Income Distribution in Soviet Agriculture." Soviet Studies 27 (January 1975): 3-26.

Wagener, Hans-Jurgen. "Rules of Location and the Concept of Rationality: The Case of the USSR." In The Soviet Economy in Regional Perspective, edited by V. N. Bandera and Z. L. Melnyk. New York: Praeger, 1973.

Williamson, Jeffrey G. "Regional Inequality and the Process of National Development: A Description of the Patterns." Economic Development and Cultural Change 13, pt. 2 (1965): 3-45.

Wirth, Louis. "Urbanism as a Way of Life." American Journal of Sociology 44 (July 1938): 1-24.

Wren, Christopher S. "Soviet Study Finds More Premarital Sex." New York Times. June 17, 1975, p. 2.

Zaytsev, V. D. "Problemy Modelirovaniya Migratsii Naseleniya." In Migratsiya Naseleniya RSFSR, edited by A. Z. Maykov. Moscow: "Statistika," 1973.

Zelinsky, Wilbur. "The Hypothesis of the Mobility Transition." Geographical Review 61 (April 1971): 219-49.

UNPUBLISHED MATERIALS

Chapman, Janet. "Recent Trends in the Soviet Industrial Wage Structure." Paper presented at the Conference on Problems of Industrial Labor in the USSR, Kennan Institute for Advanced Russian Studies, Washington, D. C., September 27-29, 1977.

Clem, Ralph S. "The Changing Geography of Soviet Nationalities and Its Socioeconomic Correlates: 1926-1970." Ph. D. dissertation, Columbia University, 1975.

Demko, George J., and Roland J. Fuchs. "Demography and Urban and Regional Planning in Northeastern Europe." Paper presented at the Conference on Demography and Urbanization in Eastern Europe, University of California at Los Angeles, February 5-9, 1976.

Dima, Nicholas. "Rural Population Change in the Soviet Union and Its Implications: 1959-1970." Ph. D. dissertation, Columbia University, 1976.

Feshbach, Murray, "Prospects for Massive Out-Migration from Central Asia during the Next Decade." Foreign Demographic Analysis Division, Bureau of Economic Analysis, U. S. Department of Commerce, February 1977.

Grandstaff, Peter J. "Interregional Migration Determinants in the U. S. S. R.: An Empirical Examination." Paper presented at the Annual Meeting of the Population Association of America, April 21, 1977.

Jaffe, A. J. "Manpower and Other Economic Contributions by Migrants: The United States Experience." Paper presented at the Conference on Labor and Migration, Brooklyn College Center for Migration Studies, Brooklyn College, New York, March 13-14, 1970.

Rowland, Richard H. "Urban In-Migration in Late Nineteenth Century Russia." Ph. D. dissertation, Columbia University, 1971.

INDEX

ABOUT THE AUTHORS

ROBERT A. LEWIS is professor of geography and chairman of the Geography Department at Columbia University. His research has been concentrated on population change in Russia and the USSR since the end of the nineteenth century and its impact on society. He currently is studying, in collaboration with Richard Rowland, fertility, mortality, and age, sex, and work force composition in Russia and the USSR since 1897. Dr. Lewis holds a Ph. D. from the University of Washington.

RICHARD H. ROWLAND is associate professor of geography at California State College, San Bernardino. He was awarded the Ph. D. in geography from Columbia University. His research has focused upon population change in Russia and the USSR since the end of the nineteenth century. In particular, his publications have dealt with population redistribution, urbanization, migration, and the demography of Soviet nationalities. Dr. Rowland, in collaboration with Robert Lewis, is currently undertaking research on Soviet fertility, mortality, and age, sex, and work force composition.